ELEVENTH EDITION

Public Administration in America

ELEVENTH EDITION

Public Administration in America

Michael E. Milakovich
University of Miami, Florida

George J. Gordon
Illinois State University

WADSWORTH
CENGAGE Learning·

Australia • Brazil • Japan • Korea • Mexico • Singapore • Spain • United Kingdom • United States

WADSWORTH
CENGAGE Learning·

Public Administration in America, Eleventh Edition

Michael E. Milakovich and George J. Gordon

Publisher: Suzanne Jeans

Executive Editor: Carolyn Merrill

Acquisitions Editor: Anita Devine

Development Editor:
Lauren Athmer – LEAP Publishing Services

Assistant Editor: Laura Ross

Editorial Assistant: Nina Wasserman

Media Editor: Laura Hildebrand

Marketing Program Manager: Caitlin Green

Design and Production Services: PreMediaGlobal

Manufacturing Planner: Fola Orekoya

Rights Acquisitions Specialist: Jennifer Meyer Dare

Cover Designer: Lou Ann Thesing

Cover Image: trekandshoot/©istockphoto

Compositor: PreMediaGlobal

For product information and technology assistance, contact us at **Cengage Learning Customer & Sales Support, 1-800-354-9706**

For permission to use material from this text or product, submit all requests online at **www.engage.com/permissions.** Further permissions questions can be emailed to **permissionrequest@cengage.com.**

Library of Congress Control Number: 2011931172

ISBN-13: 978-1-111-82801-1

ISBN-10: 1-111-82801-6

Wadsworth
20 Channel Center Street
Boston, MA 02210
USA

Cengage Learning is a leading provider of customized learning solutions with office locations around the globe, including Singapore, the United Kingdom, Australia, Mexico, Brazil and Japan. Locate your local office at **international.cengage.com/region**

Cengage Learning products are represented in Canada by Nelson Education, Ltd.

For your course and learning solutions, visit **www.cengage.com.**

Purchase any of our products at your local college store or at our preferred online store **www.cengagebrain.com.**

Instructors: Please visit **login.cengage.com** and log in to access instructor-specific resources.

Printed in the United States of America
1 2 3 4 5 6 7 15 14 13 12 11

To Cindy, Nicole, Tiffany, Beth,
and
to the memory of Eli M. Milakovich

—M.E.M.

To the memory of my parents,
Theodore H. Gordon and Beryl B. Gordon;
Roscoe C. Martin; and Hibbert R. Roberts;
and to Myra, Dan, and Rachel

—G.J.G.

CONTENTS

LIST OF FIGURES AND TABLES

PREFACE

The close of the George W. Bush presidency and the election of Barack Obama as our 44th president and Joe Biden as our 47th vice president marked a significant transition in recent U.S. history. The period 2001–2008 saw dramatic changes in the collective life of the United States that in many respects were unprecedented—and largely unanticipated. When Bush assumed office in January of 2001, the twin towers of the World Trade Center stood tall on the skyline of New York City—who even thought twice about that? For that matter, how many of us, early in 2001, paid much attention to a foreign organization known as al-Qaeda? There was no Department of Homeland Security, no Office of the Director of National Intelligence, no Transportation Security Administration, and no long lines of passengers waiting to check in at airports. The price of gasoline was one-third to one-half of the levels reached during 2011. The phrase "faith-based initiatives" was hardly heard. The national debt—always a matter of some concern—stood at $5 trillion (but in the federal budget proposals for fiscal year 2010, the debt was estimated to increase to *$20* trillion by 2015!). The powers of the federal executive branch, while larger than in the past, had not yet expanded to their present scope. And the responsibilities of federal, state, and local administrators had not yet begun to grow at what has become the most rapid pace since the New Deal era of Franklin D. Roosevelt in the 1930s and 1940s. All these events have set the stage for new challenges—and perhaps new opportunities—for our governments generally, and for the Obama administration in particular.

The presidential election of 2008 brought to the Oval Office a young, mixed-race African-American with limited experience—Barack Obama was serving his first term as a U.S. Senator from Illinois, and had no prior experience as a government executive. Yet early on, the new president tackled an ambitious agenda in domestic policy making: a $787 billion "stimulus package" designed to reinvigorate the national economy, and major proposals that Congress enacted to protect consumers as well as reform healthcare and financial regulation in this country. President Obama also made a concerted effort to improve the global standing of the United States, with some notable success—at the same time that he faced (and still faces) foreign policy challenges such as pro-democracy popular revolts in the Middle East (with outcomes hard to predict, even in the short term), climate change (and what to do about it) around the globe, prevention of terrorist acts against American citizens, and disengagement from the war in Afghanistan. A widely-acclaimed foreign policy success of the Obama administration, of course, was the killing of Osama Bin Laden in 2011.

Politically, the Obama administration was beset by the "Great Recession," which cut deeply into his political support, and in large measure contributed to a Republican takeover of the U.S. House of Representatives in 2010. Thus, the president's ability to implement his ongoing policy agenda has been hampered by stronger congressional opposition on all matters relating to the federal budget, not to mention the continuing efforts being made to repeal—or at least sharply limit the impacts of—regulation and healthcare reforms (among other policy disputes). Because public administration, as an essential function of government, operates within both a formal institutional setting of government *and* a context of political support, the developments of the past decade are important to understand as we begin our study of the subject.

When the first edition of this book was published a generation ago, the role of government and public administration in America was even then rapidly changing in response to complex and often uncertain national and global political environments. Then as now, the United States faced difficult domestic and international challenges and relied on its appointed and elected officials, especially chief executives, for leadership. We have been led by six different presidents, three Democrats and three Republicans, each with vastly different challenges, ideologies and visions of the nation's current and future needs, each with sharply divergent policy priorities. President Jimmy Carter, a Democrat, became enmeshed in Middle East conflicts and tried unsuccessfully to use military force to free American citizens who were being held hostage in Iran. In 1980, Carter lost the White House to Ronald Reagan, a Republican, who negotiated freedom for the hostages and later received credit for ending the Cold War with the Soviet Union. The liberation of the hostages, however, was tainted during President Reagan's second term by the infamous Iran–Contra scandal in 1987, connecting officials of the Reagan administration to illegal arms shipments to anti-Communist *contra* rebels in El Salvador, and using profits from these illegal activities to bribe Iranian officials to release the hostages (detailed in Chapter 6). The Soviet Union collapsed soon after the fall of the Berlin Wall in 1989 and the United States entered a new phase of nuclear disarmament and (seeming) peaceful coexistence with Russia.

The federal government became more actively involved in enforcing civil rights and voting rights laws in southern U.S. states, where there was considerable resistance to federally mandated changes in prevailing cultural and social values (or, at least, behavior). Bolstered by Supreme Court rulings, Congress approved increased appropriations to accomplish these policy goals, as well as many others. Concurrently, presidential powers expanded with the need to respond to natural disasters, cope with economic downturns, reduce federal spending, and respond to military crises. Congressional cooperation with chief executives varied, and presidential policy initiatives were promoted or resisted by the mass media, organized lobbies, or various public interest groups; the image and prestige of individual chief executives such as Carter, Reagan, George H. W. Bush, Bill Clinton, and George W. Bush were damaged and enhanced by how well policies were implemented or crises averted. Then as now, presidential decision-making procedures and the advisory roles played by high-level appointed officials in the Obama administration were vital to success or failure of public policies.

The theme that ties all these actions, events, and policies together is the need to anticipate and effectively respond to change, with clear lines of command-and-control authority and with necessary resources. Our capacity to respond to unanticipated change is even more important today than it was in 1980, when the federal government spent less than one-fifth of the over $3 trillion now appropriated annually. The Soviet Union presented a unified and identifiable threat to our national security—as opposed to the diverse and fragmented dangers presented today by rogue states and terrorist groups. Yet, despite the heightened risk of international terrorism, the total percentage of revenue collected by all governments in America has not changed—it is still about one-third of all the goods and services produced by our economy, leaving two-thirds in the hands of the private sector (Chapter 8). Nonetheless, programs and regulatory actions funded by federal taxes, and similar policies supported by the ebb and flow of revenue collected by states and local governments, can have major consequences for individuals, institutions, and local communities. In recent years, all state and local governments have suffered from declining sales and property tax revenues because of the prolonged economic recession and the sharp drop in real estate values.

If anything, the challenges facing administrators accountable for implementing public programs today have become even more daunting—requiring more effective expenditures of scarcer public resources and increased commitment from all public servants. In addition to the World Trade Center and Pentagon terrorist strikes on September 11, 2001, similar attacks have been made against American businesses and its military and diplomatic posts aboard. Natural disasters such as tsunamis in Indonesia and Japan, the catastrophic earthquakes in Haiti, and numerous damaging hurricanes and tornadoes require massive mobilization of scarce global and national resources to assist victims in recovery efforts. Public administration provides most of the critical human resources—and the management capability—to try and prevent, respond to, and recover from the worst effects of both man-made and natural disasters.

This book is written for undergraduate and graduate students, interested citizens, government officials, and all others seeking to better understand how domestic and global changes are impacting the applied practice and the academic field of public administration. The subject reflects multiple perspectives and has complex roots in many different academic disciplines and "real world" fields of endeavor. That by itself should alert the reader to one of the essential features of public administration: There are many sides to it, with a wide variety of complex issues, questions, practices, and themes that have commanded attention (both in and out of the field) for well over a century. Public administration is both a subject for academic study and an increasingly challenging aspect of public service.

In the following pages, we discuss many themes and controversies of contemporary public policy and administration. One recurring focus is on the distinction between the political and managerial aspects of the field, and the need to understand the importance of each. We also describe the continuing efforts of federal, state, and local governments to realign, reorganize, and strengthen public-sector resources to maintain current services, combat continuing threats of domestic and international terrorism, respond to economic crises and natural disasters, secure our borders, and protect homeland security. We emphasize the need for more creative and innovative thinking; eliminating "unnecessary" internal regulations to enable public employees to do their best work; achieving results more effectively with fewer resources; linking citizens and government service providers with new Internet technologies; and serving government's "customers" efficiently and well. The need to sustain services and, at the same time, devote greater resources to protect Americans from serious economic downturns, natural disasters and terrorist acts has resulted in substantial changes in the ways governments operate, and the results of those changes are visible throughout all aspects of American society.

Another related theme is the increased concern with competence, ethics, and integrity in both the selection of appointed and elected public officials and in decisions made by governmental institutions and agencies. This concern has intensified recently in both the private and public sectors, focusing on various types of ethical considerations that enter into corporate, political, and administrative decisions, as well as examining ways to promote more responsiveness and accountability on the part of public administrators. Numerous challenges face leaders and managers in public, private, and nonprofit service organizations. These include dealing with complex and sensitive personnel issues, coping with budgetary and legal constraints, managing massive humanitarian relief efforts both here and abroad, applying the latest communication systems and information technologies, maintaining a professional and respected workforce, delivering quality education and health care services, and ensuring high levels of measurable performance in government programs.

A final and interconnected theme is the exponential growth of information and communication technologies, and performance management systems such as electronic government (e-gov), to enhance public knowledge, improve access, increase government transparency, and facilitate new forms of interaction among citizens, elected officials, and public administrators. Today, previously unavailable interactive network technologies are transforming the delivery of public services in ways not dreamt of just a few years ago. The Internet, Global Information Systems (GIS), social networking, and teleconferencing offer the potential for all citizens to participate in a much wider range of electoral and public-policy decision making. Relationships between citizens and governments are rapidly changing, making it more difficult for repressive regimes abroad to control access to information and manipulate public opinion. New technologies also are being applied worldwide to achieve greater access to decision makers, debate public issues, influence elections and voting, improve efficiency in government, and influence the outcomes of many important decisions.

We also devote considerable attention to more specific management-related topics in the field. These include, among others, continuity and change in complex relationships among national, state, and local governments (Chapter 3); management challenges, organizational design changes, and leadership responsibilities in public organizations (Chapters 4, 5, 6); both old and new personnel management concerns (Chapter 7); ongoing tensions in the budgetary process, including continuing attention to budget deficits and government spending (Chapter 8); implementation of various types of federal, state, and local government policies (Chapter 9); the emergence of government productivity, performance management, and customer service standards in the public sector (Chapter 10); and government regulation, privatization, and deregulation (Chapter 11). In the concluding chapter (Chapter 12), we look back at the field, and attempt to integrate the various themes and subject matters covered in this text, as well as look ahead to emerging issues and concerns.

Twenty-First-Century Public Administration

There have been significant changes in the academic field of public administration, as well as in the practical world of government service, since the first edition of this book was published in 1978. What characterizes public administration in the twenty-first century is the scope and rapidity of change affecting virtually all aspects of governmental activity. The rapid integration and increasing use of technology is but one element of this transformation. Other considerations include the need to devote greater resources to combat terrorism, secure our borders, and protect citizens from the devastation caused by natural disasters; reexamine basic social values and government's role in promoting them; reconsider social-insurance and entitlement programs; reassess government's responsibility to change social and economic environments; reemphasize serving citizens as "customers," measuring results, and encouraging job retraining to compete in global markets; counter the effects of outsourcing; and provide productive employment opportunities for all Americans. Also, very much with us are the need to develop new approaches to old budgetary dilemmas; engage in politically charged debates about how to curb massive budget deficits; promote freer trade; resolve the bloody and costly conflicts in Afghanistan, and Iraq; assure that federal agencies can effectively respond to emergencies, maintain border security, and reform traditional intelligence procedures; and protect the environment, combat crime, and reform health care delivery systems (among many other things). State and local government officials must find new sources of revenue, assist federal agencies in the war on terrorism, develop their own emergency management procedures, and experiment with new approaches for delivering services. All public administrators must cope with widespread frustration among many citizens about government's capacities to both manage and successfully reform a diverse range of public programs.

Thus public administration, which is always somewhat difficult to understand in the best of circumstances, is even more challenging for today's student because of the turbulence that characterizes so many administrative operations, political controversies, and social challenges. In this context, it is vital for all those seeking greater information about the field to better understand the way the public perceives the profession, the forces for change (such as the reorganized Department of Homeland Security and the Office of the Director of National Intelligence, and restrictions on civil liberties and public information seemingly designed to protect national security and actively pursue the war on terrorism), and the often larger forces resisting change or, alternatively, urging even more radical change (antiwar sentiment, bureaucratic inertia, and ideological opposition to government involvement in our economic and social lives). In addition, all students of the field must appreciate the ethical dilemmas inherent in the professional lives and commitments of public administrators—and in the challenges involved in their simply carrying out their day-to-day responsibilities.

Finally, four interrelated themes are very much at the heart of contemporary public administration and of our discussion in this book. First is increasing the internal accountability and efficiency of public agencies. Second is improving the performance and results of public programs—especially through the application of information technology, e-gov, and reliable measures of performance management. Third is strengthening ethical guidelines and practices shaping the decisions of public officials. Fourth is more effectively anticipating, planning for, and securing the resources necessary to respond to unexpected challenges in the complex real world of public management. To some extent, these concerns have been with us since the "administrative state" began to emerge in the late nineteenth century. But they have taken on greater urgency as we move forward to meet the increasing challenges facing governments in the twenty-first century.

Blending old and new concepts is an integral part of public administration. Old concerns never entirely disappear and new concerns usually have some roots in continuing issues. Nevertheless, what is new now—and what may emerge in the immediate future—may result in greater change, in a shorter time span, than in many previous periods of conflict, rapid change, and uncertainty.

What's New in the Eleventh Edition?

The changes made to *Public Administration in America* for the eleventh edition create a book that students may well wish to keep as a future reference in the context of their work lives.

This edition has been thoroughly revised in order to consolidate previous material, add important updates, and focus on current events and policies facing our nation and its citizens. Updated material includes analysis of President Obama's time in office up until this book's publication; discussion of current policy issues such as competitive sourcing, homeland security, intelligence reform, the war on terrorism, globalization, affirmative action, accountability, civil liberties, regulatory reform, performance management, and decision making in government; and the ongoing discussions of changing political and administrative values, federalism, information and communication technology (including e-gov), organizational development, human resources, budgeting, contracting, regulation, administrative law, and the international dimensions of the field.

Brand new to this edition, and included within each chapter, are two new boxed features: "Point/Counterpoint" and "How Would You Decide?" In keeping with reviewer and user feedback and comments, the previous boxed features have been streamlined, and these new features have been included with the aim of encouraging analysis, discussion, debate, and thought. "Point/Counterpoint" provides students with a timely issue and two opposing sides to each issue. The goal of this feature is to encourage students to engage in debate, as they are asked to rely upon the knowledge they have gained throughout each chapter and from independent study as they support one side or the other. "How Would You Decide?" uses popular culture and modern media outlets as examples to stimulate thought about current events and policy actions. Award-winning films and documentaries form the core of the examples found within each chapter, with a brief synopsis and summary included, before students are asked to consider how the given examples relate to real-life situations. The questions included within this particular feature are designed to encourage critical thinking and application, while serving as a connection between topics shown in different media outlets and everyday policy choices. (Viewer discretion is advised as some of the suggested learning aids use graphic language, depict sexually explicit situations and violent events.)

As in previous editions, the eleventh edition provides glossary terms in the margins for easier reference by students. Key terms are **boldfaced** and colored in blue in the text and then defined in the margins of each chapter. These key terms also appear in end-of-chapter material, and are cross-referenced in the glossary so that students can find a term easily and understand it in a variety of contexts.

New discussion questions have been added to each chapter in order to provoke critical thinking. Useful World Wide Web sites from a variety of government, private, and nonprofit organizations are provided throughout the chapters, to facilitate access to information on relevant issues as well as serving as a starting point for research. Students are encouraged to use available search engines such as Google, Microsoft Explorer, Mozilla Firefox, and Yahoo to conduct in-depth searches to find the most current information on specific topics. The eleventh edition uses updated chapter-opening epigraphs featuring quotes from presidents such as Harry S Truman, John F. Kennedy, Bill Clinton, George W. Bush, and Barack Obama to present students with a high-interest theme for each chapter. Finally, the appendix listing selected academic, professional, and public-interest organizations, job search links, and relevant journals for research in public administration has been revised for this edition to ensure that material provided is as up-to-date as possible. It is designed to help students with their post-graduation job search and to keep them abreast of the most current issues and legislation.

Acknowledgments

We are indebted to the many individuals who contributed in myriad ways to the preparation of this and earlier editions. Valuable research and feedback was provided by: Pam Anderson, Carlos Atienza, Joan Bortolon, Ellyn Broden, Jan Domlesky, Dawn Dress, Carrie Edmondson , Meghan Ewing, George A. Gonzalez, Sara Grossman, Jason Harr, Ailyn Hernandez, Bevin Horn, Alina Tejeda Houdak, Bettina Larsen, Mary Manzano, Larry Milov, Melanie Nathanson, Beto Negriel, Richard Newmark, Robert Ortiz, Shayna Owen, Terry Pearl, Leah Del Percio, Gamal Sabet, Ann Shaw, Miriam Singer, Bill Soloman, Leslie Swanson, Eileen Damaso Taube, and Dan Wall. Current and former faculty colleagues at our two universities and elsewhere who were especially helpful include George Beam, Bob Brantley, Ann Cohen, Lt. Col. Ramon DeArrigunaga (USAF-ret.), Gen. Robert L. Dilworth (USA-ret.), Thomas E. Eimermann, George Guess, Albert C. Hyde, Donald Klingner, Nancy S. Lind, Alan Rosenbaum, Frederick J. Roberts, Arthur Simon, Stuart Streichler, Richard J. Stillman II, James H. Svara, and Jonathan P. West.

Still others who were generous with time, energy, and information on our behalf include Jonathan Breul of the IBM Endowment for Business and Government; Cary R. Covington, University of Iowa; Rick Green, University of Utah; David Grinberg of the U.S. Office of Management and Budget; Paul Hershey and Jackie McCormick of the U.S. Office of Personnel Management; David McLaughlin, Northwest Missouri State; Steven M. Neuse, University of Arkansas; Laurence Putchinski, University of Central Florida; Nadia Rubaii-Barrett, Binghamton University; Alan V. Stevens of the U.S. Bureau of the Census (ret.); and John P. Stewart, Pennsylvania State University.

The reviewers commissioned by Cengage Learning were uniformly helpful in their critiques; we would like to thank Mary Bruce, Governors State University; Meena Chary, University of South Florida; James Howerton, North Carolina A&T State University; and Roy Kirby, Roanoke College, for their inputs. Also deserving of special recognition and sincere thanks are Cindy, Nicole, and Tiffany Milakovich and Myra, Dan, and Rachel Gordon, who were endlessly patient and supportive on this project, as on so many others before, and we are grateful. All of these individuals richly deserve much of the credit for whatever strengths are present in the book; ours alone is the responsibility for its weaknesses.

Michael E. Milakovich
Coral Gables, Florida

George J. Gordon
Normal, Illinois

To the Student

This text will help you expand your knowledge and understanding of what public administration is all about. A special feature of this edition is **boldfaced** key terms colored in blue and concepts noted in the text and defined in the margins of each chapter. This glossary of terms will help you review key concepts, techniques, laws, and institutions pertaining to public administration. A list of suggested readings at the end of each chapter notes important sources for further research and information. In addition, each chapter in this edition includes many uniform resource locators (URLs), hyperlinked Internet websites, and online resources to assist you in expanding your knowledge about the field, finding jobs, obtaining additional information, and preparing research papers for courses in political science, public policy, and public administration. All students, and especially those approaching this field for the first time, should be careful in their selection of source material from the Internet.

Not all websites are equally accurate or authoritative. The user should be wary of the source of the information provided in the website and always provide the web address (www.), title, author (if available), and date accessed, to permit verification.

Note to Instructors

Public Administration in America, Eleventh Edition, is accompanied by an instructor's manual containing chapter summaries, test questions, and PowerPoint slides for each chapter.

ABOUT THE AUTHORS

MICHAEL E. MILAKOVICH is professor of political science and international studies at the University of Miami, Coral Gables, Florida. A life member of the American Society for Public Administration, he serves as an expert witness in state and federal courts, and advises public and nonprofit organizations on policy analysis and quality improvement strategies. He is a member of editorial board of the *Journal of Global Business and Organizational Excellence* and the board of directors of the National Center for Public Productivity. His articles and reviews have appeared in referred journals such as the *American Political Science Review, American Review of Public Administration, Crime and Delinquency, eJournal of E-Democracy and Open Government, Health Care Management Review, International Public Management Review, Journal of Organizational Excellence, Journal of Politics, Public Administration, Public Productivity and Management Review, National Civic Review*, and *the Journal of Health and Human Resource Administration*. He is the author of *Digital Governance: New Technologies for Improving Performance and Participation* (2012), *Improving Service Quality in the Global Economy* (2006), *Florida State and Local Government* (1995), *and U.S. vs. Crime in the Streets*, with Tom and Tania Cronin (1981). He has consulted with numerous corporations, governments, and health care agencies both in the United States and abroad.

GEORGE J. GORDON is professor emeritus of political science at Illinois State University in Normal, Illinois. He is a member of the American Society for Public Administration and the American Political Science Association. His articles on federalism and intergovernmental relations have appeared in *Publius: The Journal of Federalism, Public Administration Quarterly*, and the *Journal of the American Planning Association*. He served as section head of the Public Administration Section at the 1997 Convention of the Midwest Political Science Association. He also served as a Democratic presidential elector from the state of Illinois in 1992 and has served on the McLean County, Illinois Board (county legislature) since 1996.

ELEVENTH EDITION

Public Administration in America

PART I

The Context, Nature, and Structure of Public Administration in America

THIS OPENING section explores essential facts and concepts in public administration in order to set the stage for further detailed discussion of the subject. The central themes are: (1) the roles and functions of public bureaucracies within the larger governmental and social systems, (2) the impacts of politics within that larger system, as well as the impacts of political and policy-making decisions on administrative actions and decisions, (3) the political implications of organizational and structural arrangements, and (4) the critical, and increasing, importance of information communication technologies, intergovernmental relations, and many other types of formal and informal exchanges among administrators at all levels of government. In Chapter 1, we first describe the most common structures of executive-branch agencies, stressing the growth of government generally and public administration in particular. We discuss the broader governmental system in which public administration and policy making operate, consider traditional conceptions of how public agencies ought to function, and then compare them with the current realities of American bureaucracy. We explore similarities and differences between public and private administration, taking note of some ways in which they overlap in practice. We then examine public administration as a field of study, especially its evolution from a relatively uncomplicated field in the late nineteenth century to the challenging and rapidly changing discipline impacting all societies in the twenty-first century. In addition, we analyze the impacts of domestic and international crises, the mass media (including social media), social change, and technology on our values.

In Chapter 2, we examine in more detail the underlying and sometimes conflicting values in American administrative practice. Of central importance are the tensions between *political values*—such as individual freedom to make a very wide range of choices in our personal lives, government accountability, fair representation, and popular control—and *administrative values*—such as efficiency, economy, responsiveness, and the ideal of "political" (usually meaning partisan) neutrality. We explore the need for political accountability, the extent of citizen participation, new ways to access information about public issues, and how definitions of representativeness have changed. We then focus on the nature and exercise of bureaucratic power and discuss various issues involved in the rise of the "bureaucratic state." The discussion centers on the dispersal of power throughout government and what that means for public administrators, the foundations of bureaucratic power, bureaucrats as political actors as well as public managers, and dilemmas of political and administrative accountability. Bureaucrats are seen as active participants in a broad range of political interactions that allow for considerable variety and complexity in the manner of their involvement.

Chapter 3 deals with the dynamic nature of federalism and intergovernmental (national-state-local) relations. A description of the formal federal setting is followed by an examination of intergovernmental relations within federalism. Particular attention is given to fiscal and administrative relations among the different levels and units of government, federal efforts to stimulate economic growth, the divisive issues of intergovernmental regulation and unfunded mandates (federal and state directives *without* funds to support them), and the devolution (transfer) of federal program authority to states and local governments. The evolution of American federalism has profoundly affected the management of government programs at all levels, and it is essential that we understand how the two are interrelated. Federalism is an important structural element in public administration that, in turn, creates a challenging organizational dynamic among local, state, and federal officials and other stakeholders.

Approaching the Study
of Public Administration

The governor of a large state publicly disagrees with the legislature on the condition of state government finances, taking issue especially over the question of which state employees and services are necessary to cut. A police officer is injured and requires emergency medical treatment following a traffic accident while pursuing a dangerous driver who has stolen a car. A teachers' union rejects an attempt by the school board to charge teachers higher fees for health insurance coverage. The Lieutenant Governor of California and the Governor of Kansas publicly assert that National Guard troops stationed in Iraq are needed at home to provide assistance after the wildfires and tornados that ravaged their states. The chairman of the powerful state legislative appropriations committee in a large Southern state bluntly announces that "We don't want any more government." To meet severe budget deficits, several states increase university fees and tuition for college students, cutting health care programs for the poor and elderly, closing state parks and recreation areas, and releasing prisoners before the end of their sentences. The city of Costa Mesa, in affluent Orange County, California, lays off nearly half of its employees. Record high oil prices contribute to an energy crisis that threatens major segments of the U.S. economy. Local government bargaining teams negotiate around-the-clock with a transportation workers' union in an effort to avert a threatened strike only days away. During the presidential campaign, a candidate promises to cut the size of the federal bureaucracy in half. The president and Congress fail to agree on federal budget priorities and, as a result, national parks must close, economic reports are delayed, and Social Security recipients fail to receive benefits.

What do these examples, all drawn from real-life situations, have in common? They represent critical aspects of public administration, one of the most important dimensions of the American governmental process and one with increasing influence both inside and outside of government.

Public administration in America today is a large and highly complex enterprise made up of thousands of smaller units that encompass the everyday activities of literally millions of citizens and government employees. The actions and decisions of public administrators touch the daily lives of virtually every American. The growth and reduction of government activity and public bureaucracy are among the most significant social phenomena of recent decades. The composition, mission, and size of bureaucracy have become the subject of heated debate among citizens, legislators, scholars, and practitioners. At the same time, politicians of every stripe have criticized bureaucracy at all levels of government.

Many politicians have run successfully "against" the bureaucracy: in 1976, Jimmy Carter promised to "clean up the bureaucratic mess in Washington"; in 1980, Ronald Reagan promised to "get the federal government off your backs"; in 1996, Bill Clinton declared prematurely that "the era of Big Government is over"; during the controversial 2000 presidential campaign, Republican candidate George W. Bush accused his opponent, former Vice President Al Gore, of representing "the government" while he (Bush) represented "the people." As president, however, George W. Bush led one of the largest expansions of the federal bureaucracy in history to maintain domestic security after September 11, 2001, respond to natural disasters, and implement U.S. foreign policy in Afghanistan and Iraq. As a result, President Bush was labeled by his political opponents as a "big government conservative." Typically, conservative chief executives such as Bush, Reagan, and George H. W. Bush gain public support and win elections by criticizing bureaucracy and by pledging to reduce government; once elected, however, they must inspire and lead the same government officials to achieve their own policy goals and respond to crises. The task for George W. Bush was even more challenging because he centralized government functions and expanded both presidential power and the role of the federal bureaucracy as no recent president has, primarily because of his administration's decisions to conduct protracted wars in Iraq and Afghanistan. Chief executives at all levels of government are elected by making similar promises and increasing bureaucracy to achieve them; ultimately, they are judged by the voters on their ability to fulfill those promises. The extent of Barack Obama's success as president depends almost entirely upon economic recovery and job growth, sectors of the economy that are only indirectly affected by presidential policies.

Our awareness of bureaucracy varies according to domestic and international conditions and situations in which we find ourselves. This awareness is usually higher before, during, and after a presidential election cycle; when we cast votes for other elected officials or fill out our income tax returns (especially when we have to pay additional taxes on April 15); apply for government loans to finance a college education; seek federal assistance after a natural

bureaucracy

(1) a formal organizational arrangement characterized by division of labor, job specialization with no functional overlap, exercise of authority through a vertical hierarchy (chain of command), and a system of internal rules, regulations, and record keeping; (2) in common usage, the administrative branch of government (national, state, or local) in the United States; also, individual administrative agencies of those governments.

disaster; or deal directly with the most visible street-level bureaucrats—"first responders" such as police officers, emergency service workers, and firefighters. We are less conscious of the role of **bureaucracy** under other more routine circumstances. (Throughout the book, key terms and concepts are highlighted in bold print, defined in the margins, and listed at the end of each chapter.) Much bureaucratic decision making is obscure or just not directly meaningful to most of us. Consider, for example, decisions by the U.S. State Department to change eligibility formulas for determining international student visas. Proposals such as these may be important to subsets of citizens (and noncitizens as well) and may even lend legitimacy to the final actions taken by public agencies, but they typically generate little media publicity or public attention by themselves. Some of the most important work of government agencies takes place away from public view. Yet everyone has a general opinion—usually negative—about bureaucracy and politics.

All Americans are far more aware of the role of bureaucracy in their daily lives as a result of tragic events such as September 11, 2001, the inept governmental response to Hurricane Katrina in 2005, and the assassination attempt on U.S. Congresswoman Gabrielle Giffords in Tucson, Arizona, in early 2011. All forms of security have become much tighter, more intrusive, and time-consuming; international students enrolled in American universities are subject to more thorough background checks; university graduations, public gatherings, and sports and entertainment events have faced increased security precautions and added extra expenses as a result. The era of inexpensive and secure air travel that spurred the development of the global economy is over. Airlines and travel-related rental car, cruise line, hotel, and restaurant businesses worldwide are struggling to regain customers who lost confidence in the ability of government to protect them. Scarce public resources are being diverted from much-needed domestic economic development and social programs to bolster security for Americans who are now more alert and aware of the protective and service responsibilities of public agencies.

Regardless of our level of awareness (or frustration) concerning particular bureaucratic activities or decisions, the institution of bureaucracy sparks strong emotions among millions of Americans. It has even been suggested that the language of bureaucracy (its jargon) has harmed the English language as a whole. In one way or another, most of us are familiar—if not always comfortable—with government bureaucracy. Mention of "the bureaucracy" usually evokes a strong response; bureaucrats are unpopular with many of those they serve. Bureaucracy has been blamed for many of society's current ills, for several reasons. Government agencies are clearly influential, and in all but a handful of cases, bureaucrats are not elected by the public; thus they are convenient and increasingly visible targets who in most instances cannot be removed from office by popular vote. We hear a great deal about the growing power of bureaucracy and bureaucrats, the arbitrary nature of many decisions, lack of accountability, questionable ethics, poor service quality, impersonal treatment, wasteful spending and cases of simple incompetence.

On the other hand, when natural and man-made disasters strike, citizens turn to government and its bureaucratic institutions for emergency relief and protection. Shifts in public opinion also reflect variations in confidence and trust in government, and are generally associated with government's ability to deliver services, maintain economic growth, protect citizens, and resolve basic social issues. Expressions of trust or mistrust in government largely reflect feelings about the condition of the economy and the incumbent national administration. Thus, as efforts to curb inflation bore fruit in the early 1980s, public confidence in government moved upward noticeably, but to a level still below that of the 1960s. Public trust in government reflects the national mood, which declined from the mid-1980s until the early 1990s. Trust moved up sharply in the mid-1990s as a result of strong economic growth and policies of the Clinton–Gore administration (1993–2001) (see Figure 1–1). As more citizens are affected by economic decline and job losses, their anger and frustration are focused on government and politicians.

Bureaucracy often becomes a focal point of discontent not only because of its obvious **discretionary authority** but also because of the widespread perception of its mismanagement of scarce resources, its relatively obscure and secretive decision-making processes, and the degree to which it is insulated from or vulnerable to direct (elective) political controls. Protests against the actions of local school boards, taxing authorities, and police departments; impatience with inefficiency and red tape; and negative public responses to

discretionary authority

power defined according to a legal and institutional framework and vested in a formal structure (a nation, organization, profession, or the like); power exercised through recognized, legitimate channels. The ability of individual administrators in a bureaucracy to make significant choices affecting management and operation of programs for which they are responsible; particularly evident in systems with separation of powers.

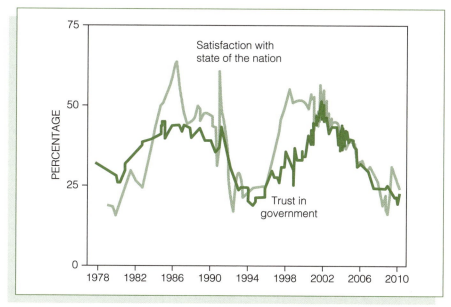

FIGURE 1-1

Trust in Government and Views of National Conditions (2011)

Source: "Distrust, Discontent, Anger and Partisan Rancor: The people and Their Government." Pew Research Center for the People & the Press: Washington, D.C., April 18, 2011. http://people-press.org/2010/04/18/distrust-discontent-anger-and-partisan-rancor/.

regulatory actions all testify to the intensity of feeling and, more generally, to growing frustration and a widening sense of distance between the people and their governing institutions. Our attitudes toward both public and private bureaucracies (that is, toward all large organizations) have been affected by the larger complex of feelings and reactions toward corporations, governments, and other major institutions in American society, such as business, labor, the mass media, the military, and especially education. Americans' confidence in our institutions has declined significantly since the 1960s, a decade of divisive social conflict, followed by the Watergate scandals and a decade of economic decline. The "taxpayers' revolt" that surfaced swiftly and intensely in the late 1970s was followed by decentralization, deregulation, and devolution of decision-making authority from the federal to state and local governments, in part as a reaction against perceived bureaucratic excesses. The 1980s brought a new Republican administration to Washington and optimism based on tax cuts, higher corporate profits, and less regulation of the economy. As economic conditions improved during the 1990s, public attitudes toward government also began to change for the better, notably in the form of rising support for government deregulation, tax relief, and reductions in government spending. Corporate scandals and the "downsizing" of many jobs resulting from globalization of the economy have significantly influenced people's feelings about their futures, leaders, and institutions in the early 2000s. President George W. Bush presided over a "Lost Decade" of unpopular wars, outsourcing jobs, tax breaks for the rich, and the loss of income for nearly 90 percent of the entire U.S. workforce. The election of Barack Obama in 2008 renewed optimism and hope for the future, but the nation has faced continued hardships and economic difficulty since.

To the extent that governmental activity is directed toward dealing with these problems but perceived by the public to be ineffective, public confidence is adversely affected. So, too, have been the electoral fortunes of incumbent presidents seeking second terms: Gerald Ford, a Republican, in 1976; Jimmy Carter, a Democrat, in 1980; and George H. W. Bush, a Republican, in 1992. Public trust in government is always a significant concern and, although the level of trust declined measurably during the late twentieth century, it increased in the mid-1990s and surged after October 2001. Since then, trust and confidence in both the Congress and the president have receded, related in part to a drop in public support for the war in Iraq. Public support for both Congress and President George W. Bush reached historic lows (38 percent and 28 percent respectively) in the months before the 2008 presidential election.[1]

By contrast, support for selected federal agencies, such as the U.S. Coast Guard, the Federal Reserve Board of Governors, the U.S. Department of Labor, the U.S. military services, the National Park Service, and the Social Security Administration, has improved dramatically. Fluctuations in public confidence, respect, and trust appear to be associated more closely with the strength or weakness of the national economy than the political party in power. For example, a worsening economy in the early 1990s was a major factor in Bill Clinton's victory over George H. W. Bush in the presidential election of 1992. The Clinton–Gore victory in 1996, the first time in thirty-two years that Democrats had been reelected for a second presidential term, reflected a positive national mood about the economy, lower federal budget deficits, job growth, and continued low rates of inflation. The election also reinforced a public preference for "divided government," with Republicans maintaining majorities in the U.S. House of Representatives and Senate as well as many statehouses. George W. Bush was first elected president in 2000 without strong support or a majority of popular votes in one of the closest elections in American history. President Bush was reelected in 2004 by wider electoral and popular vote margins. During his second term (2005–2009), federal budget deficits and public debt ballooned as more money was allocated for unpopular wars in Iraq and Afghanistan; ironically, the federal bureaucracy under Bush expanded more than at any other time since the New Deal (1932–1939). Public discontent with Republican policies contributed to Barack Obama's election to the presidency. It remains to be seen how voters will respond to the continued frustrations facing the nation currently.

Whether public attitudes toward government bureaucracy in general and bureaucrats in particular have followed broader opinion patterns exactly is unclear. What is certain, however, is that the public's regard for public administrators has fallen far below what it was seventy years ago, when the civil service was considered an esteemed profession. During the Great Depression of the 1930s, and throughout World War II, public administrators and their organizations enjoyed greater public confidence than they do today.[2] The general public, through its elected officials, looked to the administrative apparatus of government to take on increasing responsibility. Congress, state legislatures, and city councils, as well as presidents, governors, and mayors, all delegate certain amounts of discretionary authority to administrative officials, in effect directing them to make the day-to-day choices involved in applying laws and enforcing regulations. No national referendum was held on the question, "should bureaucrats be given more responsibility?" But public acceptance of greater governmental involvement in a wider range of societal activities outweighed any opposition to growth of government in general and government bureaucracy in particular. Indeed, once bureaucratic policy making began to increase, heightened public demand for government services ensured continuation of greater administrative activity; this pattern may have been interrupted by Republican election victories in 2010, reflecting voters' long-term concerns about federal spending, deficits, and debt.

Variations in bureaucracy's public standing have coincided with greater demands for a wider range of public services, the increasing complexity of the nation's problems, and much higher levels of competence and professionalism among government workers. Even as presidents such as Carter, George H. W. Bush, and Clinton tried to reduce the size and change the role of bureaucracies, they acknowledged the honesty, integrity, and demonstrated talents of the vast majority of administrative officials. George H. W. Bush, the forty-first president, was openly supportive of public administrators. President Bill Clinton placed considerable emphasis on "empowering" federal employees so that they might do their best work. Clinton went further than any other recent president in suggesting that it was "time to shift from top-down bureaucracy to **entrepreneurial government** that generates change from the bottom up. We must reward the people and ideas that work, and get rid of those that don't."[3]

entrepreneurial government

emphasizes productivity management, measurable performance, privatization, and change.

Public administration scholar Charles Goodsell, as well as others, has suggested that government bureaucracies and administrators do not deserve such harsh criticism.[4] The essence of his argument is that, despite shortcomings inevitably found in all complex organizations, America's government bureaucracies perform quite well. This is the case whether bureaucratic performance is measured by objective standards, in comparison with that in most of the other nations of the world, or (as noted earlier) in terms of citizens' satisfaction with their dealings with government administrators. Goodsell realistically summarizes his position this way:

> Our government agencies are riddled with examples of incompetence, negligence, inflexibility, and many other flaws. So, too, our government bureaucrats include men and women who should not be in their positions for reasons of sloth, bad manners, poor judgment, and other faults. My point, however, is that the flaws and the faults are far fewer on a proportional basis than is generally thought. And they are more than outweighed in frequency and importance by instances of dedicated service on behalf of public missions important to all citizens. Most governments of the world would be pleased to possess a public bureaucracy of the quality of our own.[5]

Goodsell focuses attention on the sometimes unthinking criticisms of bureaucracy that have characterized much of our national dialogue in the recent past. Scapegoating (that is, blaming bureaucracy as a whole, and individual bureaucrats, for societal ills) only makes it more difficult for the rest of us to acquire a clearer understanding of what it really is and how it really operates in our governmental system and our society at large.

At the same time, although people vent their frustrations on bureaucracy in general, there is strong evidence of favorable citizen reaction to direct dealings with individual bureaucrats and bureaucracies.[6] It has even been suggested by a reputable observer that public administrators "could not be engaged in more important or more honorable work . . . however they may be judged by the public they serve."[7] Why, then, has public respect for these officials varied so much?

Part of the answer is that they may appear to constitute something of a government "elite" in an era of economic scarcity when angry and cynical voices are heard more forcefully. Or, perhaps, the very complexity of the problems currently confronting government decreases the likelihood of complete solutions, despite the serious efforts of competent people. The more complex the problems, the greater the discretionary authority vested in bureaucracies to attempt to deal with them. Finally, perhaps, the public has come to expect too much from government (sometimes encouraged by the mass media and public officials themselves) and has made bureaucrats into scapegoats for not meeting public expectations. Whether bureaucrats are deserving of these harsh sentiments is another matter.

What Is Public Administration?

Public administration may be defined as all processes, organizations, and individuals (the latter acting in official positions and roles) associated with carrying out laws and other rules adopted or issued by legislatures, executives, and courts. This definition should be understood to include considerable administrative involvement in formulation as well as implementation of legislation and executive orders; we will discuss this more fully later. Public administration is simultaneously a field of academic study and of professional training, from which substantial numbers of government employees currently are drawn.

Note that this definition does not limit the participants in public administration to administrative personnel, or even to people in government. It can and does refer to a wide and varied assortment of **stakeholders**, that is, individuals and groups with a common interest in the consequences of administrative action. Among stakeholders, the foremost perhaps are the administrators themselves. Also included are members of the legislature, legislative committees, and their staffs; higher executives in the administrative apparatus of government; judges; political-party officials whose partisan interests overlap extensively with issues of public policy; lobbyists (that is, leaders and members of interest groups) seeking from the government various policies, regulations, and actions; private contractors who perform services or produce goods for public agencies; mass-media personnel (particularly in their "watchdog" role over the actions and decisions of public officials); and members of society at large who, even when they are not well organized, can have some impact on the directions of various public policies. Furthermore, public administration involves all those just mentioned in shifting patterns of reciprocal (mutual) relationships—in state, local, and federal governments as well as in national-state-local (that is, intergovernmental) relations. The politics of administration involves agency interactions with those outside the formal structure as well as interactions among those within administrative agencies; we are concerned with both.

public administration

(1) all processes, organizations, and individuals acting in official positions associated with carrying out laws and other rules adopted or issued by legislatures, executives, and courts (many activities are also concerned with formulation of these rules); (2) a field of academic study and professional training leading to public-service careers at all levels of government.

stakeholders

bureaucrats, elected officials, groups of citizens, and organized and unorganized interests affected by the decisions of federal, state, and local governments; those having a stake in the outcome of public policies.

The Managerial Role

Let us consider another dimension of public administration: the managerial, or management, side. Although the emphasis in this book is on the "politics of bureaucracy," as some have called it, managing government performance has always occupied a place of major importance in the discipline of public administration and is becoming increasingly important in making government more productive.[8] Managerial aspects of public administration have as their primary focus the internal workings of government agencies, that is, all the structures, dynamics, and processes connected with operating government programs. The terms public administration (as used in this text) and **public management** are both concerned with implementing policies and programs enacted through authoritative institutions of government. But, even though they may appear to be interchangeable terms, the latter emphasizes methods of organizing for internal control and direction for maximum effectiveness, whereas the former addresses a broader range of civic, electoral, and social concerns.

Despite these differences, there is general agreement that managerial skills and relevant experience are essential prerequisites to operate public agencies. Networking and organizing skills that can be performed with more or less competence are the indispensable foundation on which actual operations are built and sustained. An important point for the public manager is that action is expected, even if it is not necessarily advisable or convenient. Managers often take actions to move the organization in the face of strict deadlines within a range of choices that is far less than ideal. (One of the reasons the Bush administration suffered a "competence gap" following its delayed response to Hurricane Katrina was the absence of experienced leadership in key positions within agencies such as the Federal Emergency Management Agency [FEMA].)[9] These elements make up a large part of the public manager's existence in, and contribution to, the totality of public administration.

Another concern is the growing emphasis on individual character and leadership (stable personalities providing vision and direction for an organization) as opposed to simply managing established, routine operations (see Chapter 6). There is also a continuing interest in improving the quality and reliability of services provided in both public and private organizations and, with it, the possibility of a new conception of the relationship among managers, frontline service providers, and their "customers." Unlike the traditional top-down bureaucratic chain of command, this conception envisions a **reverse pyramid** with line workers responsive to the customers of public-service organizations, and managers at the base of the triangle, supporting the frontline employee (at the point or tip of the triangle). Another concern is the prospect of transforming organizational structures—given the many changes in **information communication technology (ICT)** and its enhanced uses regarding the changing roles of managers and leaders.[10] Still other concerns for managers

---

public management

a field of practice and study central to public administration that emphasizes internal operations of public agencies and focuses on managerial concerns related to control and direction, such as planning, organizational maintenance, information systems, budgeting, personnel management, performance evaluation, and productivity improvement.

reverse pyramid

a conception of organizational structure, especially in service organizations, whereby managerial duties focus on providing necessary support to frontline employees (particularly those whose work centers around information and information technology) who deal directly with individuals seeking the organization's services.

information communication technologies (ICT)

various forms of New Media technology connecting Internet users with service providers and websites. ICTs methods include communication protocols, transmission techniques, communications equipment as well as systems for computer storage and information retrieval.

include the challenge of providing career development and job enrichment for employees, encouraging participatory management, and applying emergent customer service management techniques to the tasks of running large, complex bureaucratic organizations. Public managerial responsibilities have become more complicated and, at the same time, more challenging and potentially beneficial to employees, citizens, managers, and their organizations.

Principal Structures of the National Executive Branch

Constitution of the United States

The U.S. Constitution is silent on the subjects of public administration and management, except to refer to Congress's legislative authorization and appropriation authority and the president's responsibility to "faithfully execute the laws." The structures that exist today are products of congressional action, as are many of the procedures followed within public administration. The national executive branch is organized primarily into five major types of agencies, four formal bases, or foundations, of organization, and four broad categories of administrative employees. These deserve consideration because they affect both the way administrative entities function and the content of policies they help to enact.

Cabinet-Level Executive Departments

Sometimes referred to simply as "departments," they are the most visible, though not necessarily the largest, national executive organizations; this is also true in most states and localities. There are fifteen departments in the national executive branch—examples include the Departments of State, Defense, Commerce, the Treasury, Justice, Labor, and the Interior (see Figure 1–2). Each department is headed by a secretary and a series of top-level subordinates, all of whom are appointed by the president with the approval of the Senate (such approval is rarely withheld). Their main function is to provide policy leadership to their respective departments on behalf of the president but, in practice, they also speak to the president for their departments (see Chapter 6). One of the newest cabinet-level divisions is the **Department of Homeland Security (DHS)**, the product of controversial reorganization of all or parts of twenty-two existing federal agencies with nearly a $50 billion budget (which more than tripled its available resources following Hurricane Katrina) and 180,000 employees, that centralizes functions as diverse as customs, immigration, transportation security, the Secret Service, and emergency management (see Figure 1–3).

Department of Homeland Security (DHS)

a U.S. federal "mega-agency" created in 2002 by merging twenty-two existing agencies. Its mission is to respond to natural and man-made disasters, secure our borders, and prevent domestic terrorism and violence.

FIGURE 1-2 The Government of the United States

THE GOVERNMENT OF THE UNITED STATES

THE CONSTITUTION

LEGISLATIVE BRANCH

THE CONGRESS

SENATE HOUSE

ARCHITECT OF THE CAPITOL
UNITED STATES BOTANIC GARDEN
GOVERNMENT ACCOUNTABILITY OFFICE
GOVERNMENT PRINTING OFFICE
LIBRARY OF CONGRESS
CONGRESSIONAL BUDGET OFFICE

EXECUTIVE BRANCH

THE PRESIDENT
THE VICE PRESIDENT

EXECUTIVE OFFICE OF THE PRESIDENT

WHITE HOUSE OFFICE
OFFICE OF THE VICE PRESIDENT
COUNCIL OF ECONOMIC ADVISERS
COUNCIL ON ENVIRONMENTAL QUALITY
NATIONAL SECURITY COUNCIL
OFFICE OF ADMINISTRATION

OFFICE OF MANAGEMENT AND BUDGET
OFFICE OF NATIONAL DRUG CONTROL POLICY
OFFICE OF POLICY DEVELOPMENT
OFFICE OF SCIENCE AND TECHNOLOGY POLICY
OFFICE OF THE UNITED STATES TRADE
REPRESENTATIVES

JUDICIAL BRANCH

THE SUPREME COURT OF THE UNITED STATES

UNITED STATES COURT OF APPEALS
UNITED STATES DISTRICT COURTS
TERRITORIAL COURTS
UNITED STATES COURT OF INTERNATIONAL TRADE
UNITED STATES COURT OF FEDERAL CLAIMS
UNITED STATES COURT OF APPEALS FOR THE
ARMED FORCES
UNITED STATES TAX COURT
UNITED STATES COURT OF APPEALS FOR VETERANS CLAIMS
ADMINISTRATIVE OFFICE OF THE
UNITED STATES COURTS
FEDERAL JUDICIAL CENTER
UNITED STATES SENTENCING COMMISSION

DEPARTMENT OF AGRICULTURE

DEPARTMENT OF COMMERCE

DEPARTMENT OF DEFENSE

DEPARTMENT OF EDUCATION

DEPARTMENT OF ENERGY

DEPARTMENT OF HEALTH AND HUMAN SERVICES

DEPARTMENT OF HOMELAND SECURITY

DEPARTMENT OF HOUSING AND URBAN DEVELOPMENT

DEPARTMENT OF THE INTERIOR

DEPARTMENT OF JUSTICE

DEPARTMENT OF LABOR

DEPARTMENT OF STATE

DEPARTMENT OF TRANSPORTATION

DEPARTMENT OF THE TREASURY

DEPARTMENT OF VETERANS AFFAIRS

INDEPENDENT ESTABLISHMENTS AND GOVERNMENT CORPORATIONS

AFRICAN DEVELOPMENT FOUNDATION
BROADCASTING BOARD OF GOVERNORS
CENTRAL INTELLIGENCE AGENCY
COMMODITY FUTURES TRADING COMMISSION
CONSUMER PRODUCT SAFETY COMMISSION
CORPORATION FOR NATIONAL AND COMMUNITY SERVICE
DEFENSE NUCLEAR FACILITIES SAFETY BOARD
ENVIRONMENTAL PROTECTION AGENCY
EQUAL EMPLOYMENT OPPORTUNITY COMMISSION
EXPORT-IMPORT BANK OF THE UNITED STATES
FARM CREDIT ADMINISTRATION
FEDERAL COMMUNICATIONS COMMISSION
FEDERAL DEPOSIT INSURANCE CORPORATION
FEDERAL ELECTION COMMISSION

FEDERAL HOUSING FINANCE BOARD
FEDERAL LABOR RELATIONS AUTHORITY
FEDERAL MARITIME COMMISSION
FEDERAL MEDIATION AND CONCILIATION SERVICE
FEDERAL MINE SAFETY AND HEALTH REVIEW COMMISSION
FEDERAL RESERVE SYSTEM
FEDERAL RETIREMENT THRIFT INVESTMENT BOARD
FEDERAL TRADE COMMISSION
GENERAL SERVICES ADMINISTRATION
INTER-AMERICAN FOUNDATION
MERIT SYSTEMS PROTECTION BOARD
NATIONAL AERONAUTICS AND SPACE ADMINISTRATION
NATIONAL ARCHIVES AND RECORDS ADMINISTRATION
NATIONAL CAPITAL PLANNING COMMISSION

NATIONAL CREDIT UNION ADMINISTRATION
NATIONAL FOUNDATION ON THE ARTS AND THE HUMANITIES
NATIONAL LABOR RELATIONS BOARD
NATIONAL MEDIATION BOARD
NATIONAL RAILROAD PASSENGER CORPORATION (AMTRAK)
NATIONAL SCIENCE FOUNDATION
NATIONAL TRANSPORTATION SAFETY BOARD
NUCLEAR REGULATORY COMMISSION
OCCUPATIONAL SAFETY AND HEALTH REVIEW COMMISSION
OFFICE OF THE DIRECTOR OF NATIONAL INTELLIGENCE
OFFICE OF GOVERNMENT ETHICS
OFFICE OF PERSONNEL MANAGEMENT
OFFICE OF SPECIAL COUNSEL
OVERSEAS PRIVATE INVESTMENT CORPORATION

PEACE CORPS
PENSION BENEFIT GUARANTY CORPORATION
POSTAL REGULATORY COMMISSION
NATIONAL RAILROAD RETIREMENT BOARD
SECURITIES AND EXCHANGE COMMISSION
SELECTIVE SERVICE SYSTEM
SMALL BUSINESS ADMINISTRATION
SOCIAL SECURITY ADMINISTRATION
TENNESSEE VALLEY AUTHORITY
TRADE AND DEVELOPMENT AGENCY
UNITED STATES AGENCY FOR INTERNATIONAL DEVELOPMENT
UNITED STATES COMMISSION ON CIVIL RIGHTS
UNITED STATES INTERNATIONAL TRADE COMMISSION
UNITED STATES POSTAL SERVICE

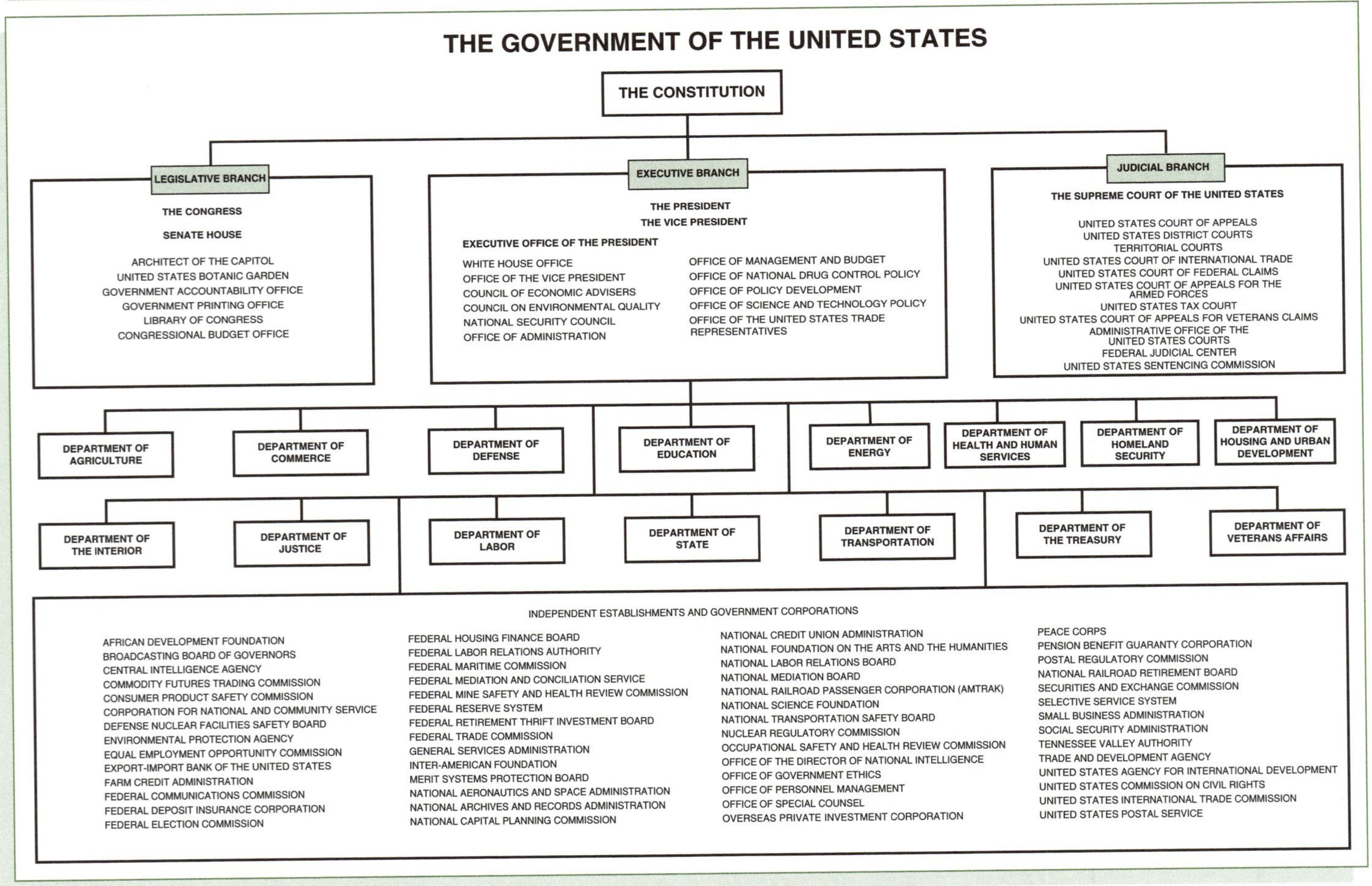

Source: U.S. Government Manual (2007), http://bensguide.gpo.gov/files/gov_chart.pdf.

FIGURE I-3 DHS Organization Chart

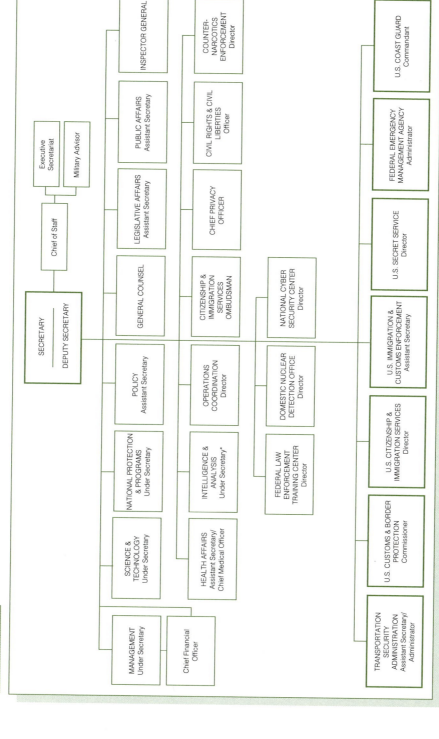

Source: http://www.dhs.gov/interweb/assetlibrary/DHS_OrgChart_2007.pdf.

15

The U.S. Customs Service (Department of the Treasury), Immigration and Naturalization Service (Department of Justice), Federal Emergency Management Agency (General Services Administration), the Transportation Security Administration (Department of Transportation [DOT]), and the U.S. Coast Guard (DOT) were transferred from their former departments (in parentheses) to the reorganized DHS. One of the major functions of the Transportation Security Administration (TSA) is the hiring and training of all of the new federal airport security screeners. In addition, the TSA has many other responsibilities under the Aviation and Transportation Security Act of 2001. Security at U.S. ports as well as safety on other forms of commercial travel is also a responsibility of the TSA. The TSA and DHS Undersecretary for Border and Transportation Security are charged with ensuring the safety of traveling Americans and coordinating efforts with law enforcement so that intelligence gathered concerning possible threats to transportation safety can be shared and appropriate steps taken to ensure security.

Departments are composed of many smaller administrative units with a variety of titles, such as bureau, office, administration, and service. Within DOT, for example, one finds such diverse units as the Urban Mass Transportation Administration (UMTA), the Federal Aviation Administration (FAA), and the National Transportation Safety Board (NTSB). The Bureau of Land Management (BLM) is subsumed within the Interior Department; and the Health Care Financing Administration (HCFA), the Public Health Service (PHS), and (most significant) the Food and Drug Administration (FDA) are all part of the Department of Health and Human Services. The fact that bureaus or offices are located within the same departmental structure does not necessarily mean that they work cooperatively on any one venture; in fact, conflict among agencies within the same department is not uncommon (though efforts such as the creation of a Department of Homeland Security have been made to reduce such conflict). Finally, departments and their subunits generally are responsible for carrying out specific operating programs enacted by Congress; they have, and attempt to maintain, fairly specific program **jurisdiction** and often concrete program objectives. For examples of the various divisions of the DHS, and the approximate percentage of total 2011 budget devoted to each agency or function, see Table 1–1. The U.S. Customs and Border Patrol (CBP), for instance, received the largest share (20 percent) of the total DHS budget; the U.S. Coast Guard (USCG) received 18 percent; TSA was allocated 14 percent; and FEMA 12 percent.

Independent Regulatory Boards and Commissions

Among such organizations are the Federal Trade Commission (FTC), Federal Reserve Board (FRB), National Labor Relations Board (NLRB), Securities and Exchange Commission (SEC), and U.S. International Trade Commission

jurisdiction

in bureaucratic politics, the area of programmatic responsibility assigned to an agency by the legislature or chief executive; also a term used to describe the territory within the boundaries of a government entity such as "a local jurisdiction."

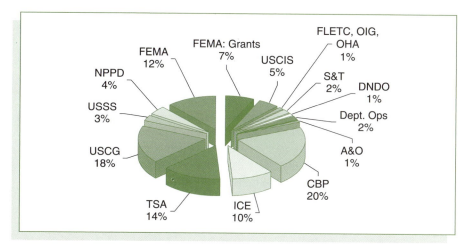

TABLE 1-1

Percent of Total Budget Authority by Organization, U.S. Department of Homeland Security, Fiscal Year 2011.

Note: Departmental Operations is comprised of the Office of the Secretary & Executive Management, the Office of the Undersecretary for Management, the Office of the Chief Financial Officer, the Office of the Chief Information Officer, the National Special Event Security Fund, and the DHS Headquarters Consolidation Project.

Source: U.S. Department of Homeland Security, Budget in Brief, FY 2008, p. 17.

(USITC). These organizations are a second major type of administrative entity and differ from cabinet-level departments in a number of important ways. First, they have a different function—namely, to oversee and regulate activities of various parts of the private economic sector. Second, their leadership is plural rather than singular; that is, they are headed by a board or commission of several individuals (usually five to nine) instead of a secretary. Third, they are designed to be somewhat independent of other institutions and political forces. Members of these entities are appointed by the president with Senate approval (as are senior department officials) but have more legal protection than do Cabinet members against dismissal by the president; in addition, they normally serve a term of office longer than that of the appointing president. In relation to Congress, these entities are supposedly somewhat freer to do their jobs than are departments and their subunits; in practice, this is questionable, but the design does have some impact. Finally, these entities are designed to regulate private-sector enterprises in a detached and objective manner and are expected to prevent abuses, corruption, and the like. Some controversy has existed, however, over just how detached and objective these organizations have been in relation to those they regulate.

Independent regulatory boards and commissions are not, however, the only government entities having regulatory responsibilities. A phenomenon of considerable importance is the growth of government regulation since the 1960s through a wide variety of other administrative instruments. Examples include the FAA, state departments of transportation, the NTSB, and the FDA. These agencies play important roles in their respective policy areas with regard to setting rules and standards for those in the private sector. The increasing incidence of government regulation has spawned rising political discontent over the scope and content of regulatory activity. Former President Clinton and Vice President Gore ordered a cost-benefit analysis (detailed in Chapters 10 and 11) of what were called "important" regulations and recommended the dissolution of those that were deemed "insignificant." They found that it is very difficult in a large bureaucracy to eliminate the bad rules and make the good ones easier to understand. Sorting out the necessary from the unnecessary is a task—involving significant discretionary authority—heavily influenced by private interests, congressional intent, and procedures governing regulatory agencies, boards, and commissions. The Obama administration has attempted to broaden the scope of regulation to include consumer protection, financial institutions, and the provision of affordable health care to millions of Americans. In Chapter 11, we will explore the politics of regulatory reform more fully.

Government Corporations

These are national, state, or local government organizations that are identical to private corporations in most of their structures and operations except one—they are government-owned. Also, while some (such as the National Railroad Passenger Corporation or Amtrak and local public utilities) seek to make a profit, others (such as the Federal Deposit Insurance Corporation [FDIC] and the Lower Colorado River Authority of the state of Texas) do not. These are conceived as corporate entities for a number of reasons. First, their legislative charters allow them somewhat greater latitude in day-to-day operations than other agencies enjoy. Government corporations also have the power to acquire, develop, and dispose of real estate and other kinds of property while acting in their own names (rather than in the name of the parent government). Finally, they can bring suit in a court of law and are legally liable to be sued, also in their own name. Each is headed by a board of directors, much as private corporations are, and is engaged in a wide variety of governmental activities. Three of the newest and largest of such entities are Amtrak, the Corporation for Public Broadcasting, and the U.S. Postal Service (with nearly 550,000 employees, almost one-fourth of all civilian federal workers); two of the oldest, both founded in the 1930s, are the FDIC and the Tennessee Valley Authority (TVA).

Executive Office of the President (EOP)

The EOP is a collection of administrative bodies that are physically and organizationally housed close to the Oval Office and designed to work for the president. Several of these entities are especially prominent and important: (1) The White House Office consists of the president's key staff aides and staff directors. (2) The **Office of Management and Budget (OMB)** assists the president in assembling budget requests for the entire executive branch and forwards them to Capitol Hill as the president's annual budget message, coordinates operating and regulatory programs, develops high-quality executive talent, and improves management processes throughout the executive branch. (3) The Council of Economic Advisers (CEA) is the president's principal research arm for economic policy; it frequently influences the president's economic thinking. (4) Entities such as the National Security Council (NSC), designed originally as forums for generating a broad overview of policy directions, consist of the president, vice president, key cabinet secretaries, and other officials. The formal purpose of these entities is to monitor and assess administration policies. Most of these entities become directly involved in policy making to a greater or lesser degree, according to each president's preferences. As staffs have grown larger, however, actions can be taken without direct presidential supervision, as the Iran–Contra affair during the second Reagan administration (1985–1989) involving the NSC clearly illustrates (for elaboration, see Chapter 6).[11]

Office of Management and Budget (OMB)

an important entity in the Executive Office of the President that assists the president in assembling executive-branch budget requests, coordinating programs, developing executive talent, and supervising program management processes in national government agencies.

Other Independent Executive Agencies

Finally, there are miscellaneous independent agencies that have no bureaucratic departmental "home" but fit no other category we have discussed. Among these are the Office of Personnel Management (OPM) and the Merit Systems Protection Board (MSPB), formerly combined as the U.S. Civil Service Commission, which together oversee the national government's personnel system; the U.S. Mint; the General Services Administration (GSA), the government's office of procurement, property, and supply; the Office of Government Ethics (OGE) discussed in Chapter 5; and the Environmental Protection Agency (EPA).

Foundations of Organization

The foundations of organization, mentioned earlier, are function, geographic area, clientele, and work process. The most common organizational foundation is according to function, indicating that an agency is concerned with a fairly distinct policy area but not limited to a particular geographic area. Organization according to geography indicates that an agency's work is in a specific region; examples include the TVA, the Pacific Command of the Navy, and the Southern Command of the U.S. Army.

Clientele-based agencies are agencies that appear to address problems of a specific segment of the population, such as the (old) Veterans Administration (VA) or the Bureau of Indian Affairs (BIA) and the "new" Social Security

Administration (SSA), which was separated from the Department of Health and Human Services and became an independent agency on March 31, 1995. The label clientele-based agency may be misleading for two reasons. First, every agency has a clientele of some kind—a group or groups in the general population on whose behalf many of the agency's programs are conducted. For example, farmers are clients of the Department of Agriculture, skilled and semiskilled laborers are associated with the Labor Department, and coal interests are linked to the Bureau of Mines. Similarly, the decision to reestablish a separate SSA in 1995 (as an independent agency as it was before merging with the Department of Health, Education and Welfare in 1953) recognized the increasing the political influence of its clientele as well as the importance of domestic spending of about $2.5 trillion for Social Security, Medicare, and Medicaid and other human resources in fiscal year (FY) 2011—over 65 percent of all funds appropriated by the federal government. (According to austere 2011 federal budget estimates, total spending for these three programs and their administrative agencies is estimated to decrease slightly to $2.4 trillion in 2012.)

The label also may be misleading because these clienteles may not always be *satisfied* clienteles. The VA and the BIA are, in fact, excellent illustrations of agencies whose clienteles often have complained about some aspect of agency performance. In 1975, various veterans' groups and individual veterans protested vigorously about the VA's alleged shortcomings in awarding and processing veterans' benefits, to the point that a virtual sit-in took place in the VA director's office. Likewise, the BIA was, for a time, a principal target of the American Indian Movement and others who expressed dissatisfaction with government management of Native American problems on and off the reservation. With both the VA and the BIA, a clientele was the most dissatisfied group—a not uncommon situation in bureaucratic politics. Likewise, the decision to re-create an independent SSA anticipated the intergenerational conflict and continuing controversy over the future of federal Social Security retirement benefits and Medicare, the federally funded health care program for the elderly.[12]

Work process agencies engage predominantly in data gathering and analysis for some higher-ranking official or office and rarely if ever participate formally in policy making. Agencies such as the Economic Research Staff of the Department of Agriculture, the Economic Studies Division of the Federal Energy Regulatory Commission, the U.S. Census Bureau, and the Soils Research Staff of the U.S. Geological Survey fall into this category.

Individual administrators occupying the multitude of positions in the various agencies can be categorized several different ways. For example, most national government administrators are *merit* employees, which means that they are presumably hired, retained, and promoted because they have the skills and training necessary to perform their jobs. Of the approximately 3.2 million full-time civilian employees in the federal government, about 92 percent work under a merit system of some kind. The remaining 8 percent include unionized employees not subject to merit hiring procedures as well as political appointees, some of whom can be removed by the president. In the latter group, numbering some 3,000 individuals, are the highest-ranking officials of the executive branch, including cabinet secretaries and undersecretaries, regulatory commissioners, and EOP personnel (see Chapter 7). Another way of viewing administrative employees is as either specialists or generalists. The term specialist refers to employees at lower and middle levels of the formal hierarchy whose responsibilities center on fairly specific programmatic areas. The term generalist is used to describe those in the higher ranks of an agency whose responsibilities cover a wider cross section of activities within the agency, involving some degree of supervision of various specialists in the ranks below.

The national executive branch, then, is organized primarily into five major types of agencies, with four formal bases of organization (function being the most common) and four broad categories of employees. State and local governments are different, though, and are worth considering briefly for the same reasons that we have examined the national executive branch: the administrative structure has some impact on the way the machinery of government functions and on the content of policies it helps to implement.

State and Local Government Structures

In general, states and larger local governments resemble the national government in composition and organization of their executive-branch agencies. Most states now have numerous cabinet-level departments; states also have a wide variety of regulatory bodies, some government corporations, and miscellaneous agencies. Similarly, most governors have fairly strong executive-office staffs responsive to the governor's leadership (see Chapter 6).

There are more than 88,000 governments within the United States and, except for the federal and state governments, all are local governments such as cities, counties, townships, and school or special districts. Individual state and local agencies are smaller and more numerous than their federal government counterparts. Despite the relatively large number of governments, over 90 percent of all public agencies are comprised of fewer than fifty employees. There are also more elected local officials than state and federal ones: 96 percent of all 513,195 elected officials serve on elected boards or commissions in states or local governments (Table 1–2). These elected governments are small governmental units averaging only about six elected representatives per jurisdiction. States and communities also vary in terms of climate, economies,

TABLE 1-2	Level of Government		Elected Officials		(Percent)
The Number of Governments and Elected Officials in the United States	Federal	1	National	537 ⎫	(3.8)
	State	50	State	18,828 ⎭	
	Local	87,974	Local	493,830	(96.2)
	Special districts	35,356	Special districts	84,089	(17.0)
	Municipalities	19,431	Municipalities	135,531	(27.0)
	Townships	16,629	Townships	126,958	(26.0)
	School districts	13,522	School districts	88,434	(18.0)
	Counties	3,034	Counties	58,818	(12.0)
	TOTAL	88,023		513,195	(100)

Source: U.S. Census Bureau, Governments Division, *Governments Integrated Directory (GID)* (Washington, D.C., 2002); accessed August, 15, 2005 at http://www.census.gov/govs/cog/2002 COGprelim_report.pdf; U.S. Census Bureau, *2002 Census of Elected Officials* (Washington, D.C., 2002) http://www.census.gov/govs/www/gid.html.

geography, population size, topography, type of government, and urbanization, as well as the individual characteristics of residents. For example, the state of Hawaii has only twenty-one governments (and only one municipal or city government) as compared to the state of Illinois with 6,723 governments. Citizens of Hawaii have just 1.7 governments per 10,000 residents, whereas citizens of North Dakota have almost 243 for the same number of residents. These extreme variations among states and local governments reflect a history of independence from the federal government and a tradition of self-governance and local control.

Some state agency structures reflect past or present influences of particular interest groups more than those in Washington do. One example was Pennsylvania's powerful Department of Mines and Mineral Industries, indicative of the role played in that state's economy by coal mine owners over the years. Another is the Illinois Department of Aging, created in response to the emergence of a growing constituency with common problems of senior citizenship. These so-called special interests have "their" agencies in the national government, of course, but a pattern found in many states is the creation of somewhat higher-level agencies in response to constituency pressures. Another distinctive feature of some state executive structures is greater legislative control over some individual agencies' budgets and personnel, in comparison to Congress's hold over national government agencies. This varies, however, from state to state.

Larger cities like New York, Chicago, Houston, Philadelphia, Atlanta, Boston, and Los Angeles have bureaucratic arrangements not unlike those in state and national governments. There is a great deal of administrative specialization, a directly elected chief executive (mayor) with a highly developed executive-office staff, and similar bases of organization.

There are, however, some differences between local governments and state and national governments. Local party politics frequently play a more prominent role in shaping municipal policy making (notably in Chicago, Boston, Philadelphia, and New York), and local public-employee unions have a great deal of influence in many cities. Local government activity is more heavily oriented to providing such essential services as water, sewage disposal and sanitation, and police and fire protection than to broader policy concerns, such as education, health care, welfare reform, and mass-transit development.

In smaller communities, as well as in many counties and townships, bureaucratic structures are not very numerous or sophisticated. This can sometimes mean that professional expertise is not as firmly established in local government as it is in most state governments and the national government. This lack of expertise is often reflected in the limited quantity and quality of programs enacted by many local governments, a pattern particularly visible in some rural county governments, many smaller towns and villages, and most special districts. As noted earlier, many local governments concentrate on providing basic urban services, with less emphasis on the sort of operating programs and regulatory activities that characterize state and national administration. The larger the unit of local government, the more likely its bureaucracy is to resemble state and national administrative agencies.

Politics, Policies, and Organizational Structure

This section reviews several traditional conceptions relating to bureaucratic activity and discusses how our political system has affected American bureaucracies in light of these conceptions. This is an introductory treatment only, for our complex political processes cannot be described adequately in a few words; the same is true of the impacts of political complexity on our public administrative institutions. Even this brief discussion, however, will help to set the stage for a fuller exploration of the political values that underlie our governmental processes, the administrative values that have helped to shape the conduct of public administration, and the many facets of intergovernmental relationships (see Chapter 3).

At first glance, questions of organizational structure may not appear to carry major political overtones. But formal organizational arrangements do not simply appear, and they are anything but neutral in their consequences. The choice of organizational structure may both reflect and promote some interests over others because a particular structure is the product of decisions reached through the political process by a particular majority coalition, whether directly (as through congressional action) or indirectly (as when the president proposes executive reorganization). Those who organize or reorganize an agency in a certain way obviously have reasons for doing so, one of which is usually promotion of their own policy interests. For example, President George H. W. Bush highlighted his concern for our nation's military veterans and expanded the access of veterans' groups to top policy makers in Washington by creating the Department of Veterans Affairs in March 1989. Similarly, the Clinton administration's decision to separate the SSA from the U.S. Department of Health and Human Services highlighted the importance of recognizing the rights of disabled, elderly, and retired persons, and all others who might be eligible for supplemental social-insurance income. In effect, the SSA was protected from future presidents who might seek to change, dismantle, or privatize the agency's basic functions. Despite George W. Bush's concerted lobbying efforts to fulfill his 2004 campaign promise to make fundamental changes in the Social Security system, opposition from bureaucratic interests, among others, contributed to the defeat of several legislative proposals in 2005 to privatize a portion of individual Social Security contributions for younger workers. President Obama has also undertaken major health care reforms that will require significant structural changes.

The Politics of Organizational Structure

Another important dimension of administrative organization is the political setting in which agencies operate; at the same time, structural arrangements can have significant political implications for administrative agencies. Here we will take a closer look at the political importance of structural arrangements, at both the national and local government levels, using as illustrations the establishment of the Department of Veterans Affairs (DVA) by the first Bush administration, the DHS in 2003, and the **Office of the Director of National Intelligence (DNI)** in 2005, both by the second Bush administration. The generalizations cited below apply with equal force to the executive branches of state and local governments.

Organizational form can signify a number of things. First, a particular organizational structure demonstrates commitment to one set of policy objectives instead of another. It can also foreshadow adoption of a distinct policy direction, either in an individual policy area or in broader policy terms. The first President Bush's action to promote the Veterans Administration (VA) to cabinet status as the Department of Veterans Affairs (DVA) was taken in opposition to career administrators and even some influential leaders of the president's own party. It contradicted the general strategy of other Republican policies (such as the New Federalism of the 1980s) that were designed to reduce bureaucracy, save expenses, and weaken federal management of government programs. Despite these concerns and intraparty inconsistencies, however, the DVA was organized, largely in response to pressures from veterans' groups.

Office of the Director of National Intelligence (DNI)

federal office created in 2005 by restructuring fifteen intelligence agencies to coordinate national intelligence-gathering and analysis efforts.

Second, a particular structure helps to order priorities by promoting some programs over others. President George H. W. Bush was a decorated World War II veteran himself, and elevation of existing veterans' services agencies into the cabinet changed both the symbolism and reality of administrative politics. The relatively higher priority of issues affecting veterans was also highlighted by the creation of a cabinet department to deal with them; such status carries with it increased prestige, not to mention visibility, both of which can be very useful to an agency. Furthermore, that sort of commitment from the chief executive, combined with more prominent organizational status, often leads to increased access to committees and influence in the legislature.

Finally, a particular structure may provide greater access to influence for some interests and less for others. Structure and jurisdiction are at least indirectly related and, although changes in jurisdiction may not necessarily be accompanied by a change in structure, any change in structure will inevitably result in some reallocation of program jurisdiction.

Access and jurisdiction are also related. Stakeholders have meaningful access, at best, only to those administrators responsible for the programs with which these groups are concerned. Changes in jurisdiction, however, will often force affected groups to reestablish lines of access. Such changes could cause difficulties for these groups, especially in persuading new working partners to their points of view. Furthermore, stakeholders normally prefer to have all related programs clustered under one administrative umbrella because that allows them to influence the full range of programs. It is also likely that such an arrangement will be managed by administrators sympathetic to programs for which they are responsible. Scattering the same programs among different agencies and administrators may result in more hostile treatment of both programs and interest groups. Executive reorganizations involving the merger of existing agencies and congressional relationships may also create problems for stakeholders.

The politics surrounding structural rearrangements are often highly controversial, as the second Bush administration discovered while implementing its cabinet-level Department of Homeland Security. The tragic events of September 11, 2001 exposed conflicts and lack of coordination and communication among federal, state, and local law enforcement officials, and fragmentation of information-sharing procedures and capabilities. Creation of the Department of Homeland Security, the largest reorganization of the federal government since the Department of Defense was established in the late 1940s, illustrates the dynamics that fostered the very problems the new department is expected to solve (Table 1–1). Combining agencies such as the Federal Emergency Management Agency, the Immigration and Naturalization Service, the U.S. Coast Guard, and the U.S. Customs Services into a single "superagency" did not erase historical lines of communication between constituents, officials, and members of Congress that have existed for decades. Although Congress agreed with the reorganization of homeland security functions, no changes were made in the committee structures responsible for authorization and appropriation of funds for the various components of the new agency.[13]

After several years of congressional debate, extensive public hearings, and the publication of a critical investigating commission report, the Office of the Director of National Intelligence (DNI) was created by Congress in early 2005.[14] Amid similar post-September 11 controversies, the DNI was forged by the merger of fifteen agencies—including various defense intelligence agencies and the Central Intelligence Agency (CIA)—to encourage greater cooperation and coordination among intelligence functions (Figure 1–4). Although the new office now reports directly to the president and controls about 70 percent of the total national nondefense budget for intelligence gathering and analysis, it has yet to define its jurisdictional boundaries. In this case, centralization could negatively impact agency influence and access to congressional authorization and appropriation committees. In addition, some observers note that separating the DNI from the analytical offices of each of the operational agencies may complicate rather than simplify the overall intelligence analysis effort.[15] Despite the additional bureaucracy and centralization of

FIGURE 1-4   Office of the Director of National Intelligence

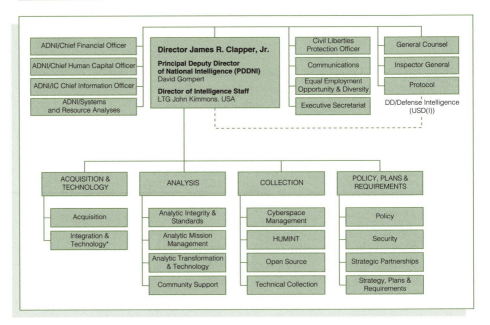

Source: Office of the Director of National Intelligence.

management authority in Washington, the redrawn jurisdictional boundaries are likely to reflect the same conflicts and interests expressed in past arrangements.

When state and local governments reorganize, downsize, or privatize programs and policies, they are also subject to shifting coalitions and political struggles over power and administrative jurisdiction. This is clearly illustrated by the periodic effort in cities and towns across the country to redefine their local government structures. This controversy has its roots in the late nineteenth and early twentieth centuries, when growing concentrations of European immigrants appeared in America's larger cities, as well as some smaller ones. Their arrival was accompanied by more—and more powerful—political party organizations and their "bosses."

Efforts to reform American municipal government, according to the rhetoric of the time, were designed to bring about "economy and efficiency" in government, "to take the politics out of local government," and to promote "good government in the interests of the whole community." Municipal reform, then as now, usually involved one or more of the following structural arrangements: (1) the method of selecting the chief executive, that is, whether to have a popularly elected mayor or a professional city manager chosen by, and responsible to, the city council; (2) the extent of the chief executive's powers—this usually meant whether the office of the mayor was formally strong or weak; (3) whether municipal elections were to have candidates selected by political parties or on a nonpartisan basis; and (4) whether members of the city council were to be elected from specific geographic areas of the city, that is, by districts or wards, or selected at large.

Political rhetoric aside, decisions about these fundamental arrangements carry with them major implications for the distribution of political power. For example, citywide minorities have little chance of winning representation in at-large council elections but a better chance in district or ward elections (provided ward boundaries were drawn up to reflect, rather than fragment, their population concentrations). Similarly, there are numerous instances in which a chief executive elected under the strong-mayor form was almost certain to be more politically sympathetic to ethnic or minority concerns than one chosen under a weak-mayor or city-manager form. It seems clear that group preferences for or against structural reform were not arrived at by chance but arose out of perceived group self-interest. This perception occurs because ethnic voters constitute the political majority in many cities that employ the strong-mayor form. Attempts by mayors in cities or counties without the strong-mayor form of government to reconstitute their governmental systems are likely to be opposed by elected local boards and commissions that have a vested interest in maintaining the status quo.

In sum, there are clear winners and losers in this facet of politics as in all others. Organizational structures, jurisdiction, and access in different settings reflect changing alliances and the relative power of competing political forces, race and ethnic conflicts, and values.

HOW WOULD YOU DECIDE?

The West Wing

The West Wing, an award-winning television series that aired on NBC from 1999 to 2006, took a close look at the organizational structure of American bureaucracy and the politics involved in running the United States of America. The series followed fictional President Bartlet, played by Martin Sheen, and his staff as they negotiated legislative and political issues throughout a presidential administration. Viewers see the Bartlet administration confront domestic terrorism; midterm, primary, and general elections; and legislative battle controversies. As the series progressed, deeper issues were confronted and addressed in connection with events occurring in American life, such as the terrorist attacks on September 11, 2001. Tying the show's topics to current American events demonstrated and conveyed the difficulties that arise in getting administrators and politicians to work together toward a common goal. The show aimed to present viewers with a "real" view of politics and bureaucracy and to create a positive view of public service.

A particular structure helps to order priorities by promoting some programs over others, as shown throughout *The West Wing* and in actual presidential administrations. Shifting coalitions and political struggles over power and administrative jurisdiction lead to major implications for the distribution of political power.

How would you determine the best organizational structures for an administration and thus for a nation?

Source: http://www.nbc.com/The_West_Wing/, accessed April 25, 2011.

---

checks and balances

a governing principle, following from separation of powers, that creates overlapping and interlocking functions among the executive, legislative, and judicial branches of government. These include the president's power to veto an act of Congress (and Congress's power to override a presidential veto by a two-thirds majority), the Senate's power to confirm or reject presidential appointments to executive and judicial positions, and the power of the courts to determine the constitutionality of the actions of other branches.

parliamentary form of government

a form of government practiced in most democratic nations, including France, Germany, the United Kingdom, and Japan, in which the chief executive and top-level ministers are themselves members of the legislature.

The Dynamics of Policy Making in the United States

Governmental power and authority in America are, by design, highly fragmented and scattered, for the Framers of the Constitution feared nothing as much as excessive concentrations of power. Therefore, they did all they could to divide power among the different branches of the national government, and they gave each branch various means of checking the power of the other two. This horizontal division of power is called **checks and balances**. Such a division of power within national, state, and (to a lesser extent) local governments places bureaucracy in the United States in a very different position from the one it occupies in many other countries which have adopted parliamentary systems.

There is little question in **parliamentary forms of government** about how, by whom, and through what channels authority is exercised. In parliamentary governments, the chief executive and top-level ministers are themselves members of the legislature. Parliamentary government is practiced in most democratic nations, and the chief executive (prime minister or premier) is usually the leader of the majority party in the legislature (parliament). In this situation, bureaucratic responsiveness to the chief executive and to the legislature are one and the same thing. In the United States, however, such questions take on added importance because, in our system, there are no similarly convenient answers.

The making of public policy in the United States is characterized by a number of major features. For one thing, the process lacks a centralized mechanism that comprehensively directs traffic. Rather, many centers of power are scattered throughout the executive and legislative branches. This lack of centralization produces a great deal of slack in the decision-making system. That is, in the absence of tight legislative or executive control, there are many opportunities for lower-ranking executives to affect implementation of a law. This phenomenon of administrative discretion is widespread, arising not only from structural separation of powers but also from conflicts that characterize executive-legislative relations and from statutory language that is often broad or even vague.

It follows that there are many **power vacuums** throughout the decision-making process. This is the basis for some, but not all, of the conflict between the president and Congress and between many governors and their legislatures. The existence of a power vacuum also allows those involved in the decision-making process to compete for relatively small amounts of power, thereby increasing their influence a little at a time. Among the most active contenders for these small quantities of power are interest groups and bureaucratic agencies, both of which seek to dominate policy areas of greatest concern to them.

power vacuum

where power to govern is splintered, there will inevitably be attempts by some to exercise that power that is not clearly defined and is, therefore, "up for grabs."

It is not only formal governmental power that is fragmented and scattered in American politics. So, too, is the ability to influence policy making in specific subject areas. The policy-making process is broken into many parts, and responsibility for each component is determined by a combination of factors. In such a setting, it is not uncommon for public administrators to become significant players in the political game, to assume an advocacy stance, and to take initiatives that influence the long-term development of policies, especially in specific programs under their jurisdictions.

Thus, bureaucracy in American government differs from traditional notions of bureaucracy in important ways: it functions in a system in which power is far from centralized; bureaucracy has a great deal of discretionary power in making day-to-day decisions and in dealing with broader policy questions; and accountability is enforced through multiple channels as a result of the fragmentation of higher political authority.

How does all this affect the behavior of public administrators and the growth of bureaucratic institutions? It is impossible to answer that question entirely in a few words, but two general observations suggest the nature of the political environment. Bureaucracies often have independent momentum with which political leaders must contend if they are to influence bureaucratic activity—hardly the conditions suggested by traditional conceptions of bureaucracy. Top executives are not always able to command the civilian bureaucracy to act. Quite the contrary, senior appointed officials are viewed as part-timers, whose influence on the "permanent" bureaucracy is limited. One advantage of this situation, however, is that public bureaucracies can more easily develop continuity in their operations because career employees are directed more by strong "institutional memory" than by the influence of any one appointed senior official (see Chapters 6 and 7). Second, bureaucratic activity focuses predominantly on the respective areas of agency jurisdiction; a bureaucracy will usually contest any significant change in the policy area for which it is responsible. Both of these phenomena indicate the non-neutral stance of American public bureaucracy. This is one of the most important differences between bureaucratic practice and any ideal model of bureaucracy against which its acceptance by the American public might be measured.

Traditional Conceptions of Bureaucracy

Bureaucracy has traditionally been conceived of in terms of implementing directives of other government institutions as a servant of political forces external to it but not as a political force in its own right. This notion of **bureaucratic neutrality** is central to an understanding of the way executive-branch bureaucracies have been designed to function in Western governments for over a century. A number of companion assumptions have also been evident in administrative practice.

Bureaucratic behavior is assumed to follow the intent of the legislature in the form of legislative enactments and guidelines for implementation. With **legislative intent** assumed as a principal guiding force, the bureaucracy's responsibility to the legislature is clearly established: it relies on the legislature for substantive policy direction and for financial and political support. The legislature, in turn, looks to the bureaucracy for faithful and competent administration of the laws.

There is a legitimate function of **legislative oversight**, or supervision, of bureaucratic behavior that logically complements legislative intent. In other words, the legislature is expected to supervise the work of the bureaucracy. Present in both assumptions is the expectation that the bureaucracy is distinctly subordinate to the will and initiative of other parts of the government.

Bureaucratic behavior is assumed to be subject to direction by the chief executive of the government. The apparent contradiction between chief-executive direction and legislative direction of the bureaucracy stems from the fact that these traditional assumptions were derived from parliamentary forms of government, in which the chief executive and top-level ministers are themselves members of the legislature. There is, however, a real contradiction between chief-executive and legislative control of the bureaucracy in a system such as ours. In the United States, the chief executive and top-level executives are independent of the legislature. In fact, they are almost always

bureaucratic neutrality

a central feature of bureaucracy whereby it carries out directives of other institutions of government (such as a chief executive or a legislature) in a politically neutral way, without acting as a political force in its own right; a traditional notion concerning bureaucratic behavior in Western governments; also called *political neutrality*.

legislative intent

the goals, purposes, and objectives of a legislative body, given concrete form in its enactments (though actual intent may change over time); bureaucracies are assumed to follow legislative intent in implementing laws.

legislative oversight

the process by which a legislative body supervises or oversees the work of the bureaucracy in order to ensure its conformity with legislative intent.

prohibited from serving in the legislature at the same time that they hold executive office.

Finally, it was traditionally assumed that the bureaucracy would be a neutral, professional, competent structure staffed by specialists in both general administrative processes and their respective specific policy areas. The notion of a competent bureaucracy responding in a politically neutral manner to the initiatives of executives and legislators external to it seems to conform to the image of administration held by many Americans and has had a powerful influence on administrative design and practice in this country.

Explaining the Growth of Bureaucracy

The reasons for the growth of public administrative functions are not readily apparent. A number of possibilities exist, each of which is worth examining for the influence it has had on the expansion of public administrative agencies.

One explanation commonly cited is that, beginning in the 1800s and continuing today, technological complexity gradually exceeded the capacities of legislative bodies and of political generalists to cope successfully. This view assumes that professional specialization in a host of fields, in effect, invaded the public service just as it assumed far greater importance in society at large. Thus, as both the nation's problems and methods of addressing them became more complex, specialized bureaucracies became more necessary in the process of discharging government's responsibilities. To some extent, technological complexity has had an important effect on bureaucracy, but whether it alone triggered bureaucratic growth is not certain. On the contrary, technological innovations such as the widespread implementation of **electronic government (e-gov)** strategies are designed to increase access to information about government and decrease citizen dependence on bureaucracy. The rapid dissemination of new types of online social networks has provided a framework for the broader application of ICTs in government agencies.

According to a second view, public pressures helped create a diversified and responsive bureaucracy, primarily because economic and social interests (stakeholders) became increasingly diverse throughout our society and government began to recognize those interests. Political scientist James Q. Wilson has referred to the phenomenon of **clientelism**, a term that describes the relationships between individual government agencies and particular economic groupings, a pattern that first appeared at about the time of the American Civil War. Wilson cites another political scientist, Richard L. Schott, who noted that "whereas earlier departments had

electronic government (e-gov)

takes the information technology concept further by integrating disparate information sources into one-stop web "portals" for improving access to information about government; for example, http://www.usa.gov.

clientelism

a phenomenon whereby patterns of regularized relationships develop and are maintained in the political process between individual government agencies and particular economic groupings; for example, departments of agriculture, labor, and commerce, working with farm groups, labor groups, and business organizations, respectively.

been formed around specialized governmental functions (foreign affairs, war, finance, and the like), the new departments of this period—Agriculture, Labor, and Commerce—were devoted to the interests and aspirations of particular economic groups."[16] That trend intensified in the twentieth century to such a degree that it is now entirely appropriate to speak of bureaucratic clienteles or constituencies in the same sense as legislative constituencies. This view, then, suggests that bureaucracies have been created or disestablished in response to popular demand for government action or inaction in specific policy fields.

A third explanation, which has its roots in the disciplines of economics and international relations, maintains that governmental responses to crisis situations, such as economic depressions or military conflicts, cause both revenues and expenditures of government to move sharply upward. More important, after the crisis has passed, the levels do not return to their pre-crisis status, and new ideas of what is acceptable emerge, resulting in new "routine" levels of government activity. As we shall see in Chapter 8 on government budgeting, national government expenditure levels underwent precisely this sort of shift after World War II and also after the September 11, 2001 attacks on the Pentagon and World Trade Center, with political acceptance of the change generally high in both cases. This explanation indirectly emphasizes society's increasing readiness to turn to government for managing responses to major (and, perhaps, not so major) problems. The George W. Bush administration's homeland security and intelligence reorganizations were undertaken to prevent further acts of terrorism and respond to one of the greatest challenges facing public administrators since World War II. The estimated $500 billion to $1 trillion expended on strengthening these functions resulted in the successful operation to capture and kill al-Qaeda leader Osama bin Laden on May 1, 2011. This is a clear example of a response to crisis circumstances prompting bureaucratic and budgetary growth. One final explanation, which also dates back to the late 1800s, overlaps all the previous ones. As the private economy became both more national in scope and more industrial in nature compared to the period before 1850, there developed a need for greater regulation by the national government of private economic activities. Many of those regulative actions spawned new ones that, combined with the other forces at work (particularly crisis-related actions), led to the steady growth of public administrative entities.

All four of these explanations appear to have some merit; together, they paint a clearer picture of how government bureaucracy has reached its present size and scope. Considering "how we got here" may be useful in light of contemporary efforts to deregulate, downsize, privatize, or impose curbs or restraints on administrative agencies. Such explanations may also contribute to our knowledge and appreciation of government agencies and actions at times when civil rights, domestic security, health care coverage, housing values, personal liberties, and retirement savings are threatened.

Social Change and Public Administration

The social setting of public administration, like its structural and organizational arrangements, has both direct and indirect impacts, and changes in that setting, like others, carry with them potentially far-reaching implications. Several **social-demographic changes** during the past sixty years have been of particular importance in shaping contemporary public administration.

The most obvious changes are population growth and shifts in the demographic makeup of the population. We have become a nation of nearly 309 million inhabitants, from less than one-third that many a century ago and just less than half that number (151 million) in 1950.[17] This striking growth in numbers has been paralleled by increases in demands for public services. More often than not, these demands have been directed at administrative personnel, such as police officers, firefighters, teachers and other educators, sanitation workers, and health care workers. Intensifying this increased demand for service is a second development: the continuing concentration of people in urban areas. The greatest population growth occurred in suburban rings around larger cities, mainly in the Southeast, Northwest, and Southwest.

Perhaps more important have been major shifts in both population and economic activity from the Northeast/Midwest (Snow Belt) to the South/West (Sun Belt). During the 1970s, population growth increased faster outside the Snow Belt as states in this region lost nearly 1 million manufacturing jobs. In the 1980s, more than 90 percent of the nation's population growth occurred outside the Snow Belt. Such changes continued during the 1990s and entailed serious social, economic, policy, and administrative implications for regions on both ends of the migration streams. Even within the Sun Belt, growth has been concentrated in particular areas. In Florida, for example, the coastal population doubled between 1964 and 1984. Today, 12 million people live in that state's Atlantic and Gulf Coast counties. Similarly, the population of the seventeen coastal counties of Texas increased by 64 percent in the period 1960–1994 and now numbers 6 million people. Today, a total of nearly 50 million Americans live in counties adjacent to coastal areas. This demographic reality has major implications for large numbers of government programs, including emergency management, flood insurance, beach replenishment, and coastal zoning. Noncoastal states such as Arizona and Nevada have experienced similar increases in

social-demographic changes

shifts in the population and economies of various regions that impact the delivery of public services.

general population. The 2010 census, however, confirmed that the Lost Decade resulted in the slowest population growth and the smallest internal population movement in the United States since the Great Depression in 1940.[18]

Several other important demographic changes also should be mentioned. First, according to the 2010 Census, more than 50 percent of the total population growth in the U.S. in the period 2000–2010 was due to the increase in the Hispanic population. That population group increased by 15.2 million, out of a total increase of 27.3 million. Secondly, about 30 percent of the U.S. population age five or older speaks a foreign language at home, and over 50 percent of those individuals speak Spanish as their first language. Third, the overall minority population grew in every region of the nation, but most significantly in the South and West. In the South, minority populations increased by 34 percent, and in the West, by 29 percent. In the Northeast and Midwest, the corresponding figures were 21 percent and 24 percent, respectively.[19] These changes, and others like them, pose new and complex problems for those who administer government programs in education, economic development, housing, and other social-service areas.

Globalization of the international economy has also permitted mass production and the distribution of durable goods on a larger scale than ever before. Improvements in technology, transportation, and telecommunications now allow literally billions of people to participate in a "networked," that is, less centralized and hierarchical, world economy. Consequently, a number of new concerns have emerged in the field of public management, concerns that have affected managers in both the public and private sectors. For example, it is increasingly apparent that equipment budgets and employee skills within all types of organizations must keep pace with developments in ICTs. All service organizations are coping with **technological change** brought about by the new global economy. Adopting new technologies and adapting to these changes have become increasingly important to public administration. We have experienced a revolution in electronic communications in terms of instantaneously linking widely separated parts of the world via the Internet and satellites. An important outgrowth in this area within the public sector is the emergence of electronic government, to improve access to information and facilitate communication among government agencies and businesses, citizens, and interested consumers. The **knowledge revolution** is another dimension of technological change and is giving rise to both the education industry and the expansion of privately and government-sponsored scientific research. Government regulation of, and participation in, increasingly complex technologies requires more and more sophisticated and specialized bureaucracies. This drastic alteration in technical capacity and responsibilities has had a permanent effect on the nature and course of American politics and public administration.[20]

technological change

rapidly emerging patterns of change (related in part to the **knowledge explosion**) in communication, medical, and transportation technologies, among others, with significant implications both for the societal challenges confronting government and for the means and resources increasingly available to government for conducting public affairs.

knowledge revolution

a global social phenomenon of the past forty years, particularly in Western industrial nations, creating new technologies and vast new areas of research and education; examples include biogenetic engineering, space exploration, mass communications, nuclear technology, mass production, and energy research.

The need for increased specialization is evident throughout much of both public and private administration. Of course, specialization is a core value in traditional conceptions of public bureaucracy; thus, movement toward greater specialization represents the extension of an existing feature rather than an entirely new one. It has been a very important consequence for public administration that specialists both inside and outside of government have been able to be in closer working contact with one another as part of the policy-making process. Technology has allowed for the creation of electronic communication networks such as blogs that make it easier for computer users to communicate with others on the Internet and to exchange data in the **blogosphere**. This reinforces the dual patterns of more informed decision making that results from the use of various knowledge resources that can be brought to bear, and of less centrally directed decision making. Patterns of decentralization have been identified as a significant offshoot of the knowledge explosion that has become so much a part of American life.[21]

The desire for specialization is a major reason for fragmenting and compartmentalizing decision-making responsibility within a bureaucracy. Specialization gives a staff or organization considerable discretionary authority within its jurisdiction. To the extent that personnel systems are based on job-related competence that includes increasingly specialized knowledge, these tendencies toward specialization are likely to be reinforced.

Political decisions to address new problems, or to identify as problems certain conditions already present in society, have almost always enlarged the responsibilities of administrative bodies. This suggests that many of today's challenges, such as climate change, environmental pollution, energy use and conservation, population growth and stability, health care reform, and mass transit, have actually been with us for some time. In all of these cases, changes in societal values preceded identification of the problems. Even though certain situations may not as yet have been widely regarded as areas requiring public action, there is still a need for debate over the scope and nature of particular governmental actions to address them.[22] Administrative entities empowered to deal with these problems are thus drawn into controversies surrounding the nature of the problems themselves as well as the methods used to resolve them.

In sum, the combined effects on bureaucracy of population growth and geographic redistribution, vast changes in our knowledge and technological capabilities, specialization, and the rise of new, complex environmental and social problems have been profound and probably irreversible. Many of these changes are global in nature and impact governance in many different countries (as detailed in Chapter 12). Clearly, change in American society has led to new, unforeseen, and complex pressures on our machinery of government at all levels. Public administration has a history of conflict with its parent discipline (political science), and growing controversy exists over just where public administration belongs intellectually and institutionally. It is within this volatile setting that we take up our study of public administration.

blogosphere

is that portion of the World Wide Web consisting of weblogs or blogs and their interconnections. Community of amateur and professional journalists commenting on a variety of subjects.

Public and Private Administration: Similarities and Differences

Many similarities exist between administrative activities in the public and private sectors. In fact, many elements of public administration have their roots in the private sector. There are those who assume that whatever differences exist are relatively minor and that what works effectively in one setting will also work in the other; thus, for example, the recurring themes that we should make government more businesslike, provide public services equal to the best in business, and bring sound management methods from business into government. But the notion that there are few if any important differences between public and private administration is undergoing intense scrutiny. There is no consensus about the nature of "publicness" in organizations. Scholars are divided over the importance of an organization's public or private status.[23] Along with other factors, this has led to increasing proposals to rely more on nonprofit, faith-based, or "third-sector" organizations to deliver government services. Although some parallels do exist, there are also critical differences among the public, private and non-profit sectors.

First, the similarities. In both settings, managers and those to whom they are accountable have an interest in running programs and other activities that are properly designed, appropriately directed to meeting their intended goals, efficient in expenditure of organizational resources, and effective in their results. Public and private managers are both concerned with meeting their staffing needs, motivating subordinates, obtaining financing, and otherwise conducting their operations so as to promote the survival and maximum impact of their programs. All this involves some "politics," both internal and external to the organization. There are agreements to be reached and maintained, elements of persuasion and coercion to be weighed, and gains and losses to be realized. The president of the Ford Motor Company and the secretary of the Treasury—as well as Ford's chief research engineer and the administrator at the IRS—have to be concerned with many of these same managerial issues, which must be carefully planned for and acted on to promote their organization's interest.

On the other hand, important elements of the managerial environment differ for public, non-profit and private managers.[24] One fundamental difference is that, in the private sector, products or services are furnished to individuals based on their own needs or wants in exchange for a direct (usually monetary) payment—a *quid pro quo* transaction. In the public sector, however, the goal of the manager historically has been to operate programs or provide services on a collective basis (rather than directly to individuals), supported in the great majority of cases by tax revenues, not direct payments (such as user charges or fees) for services rendered. Another key difference is that private organizations define their markets and set their own broad goals, whereas public organizations and managers are obligated to pursue goals set for them by their legislatures. Public managers have relatively little freedom to alter basic organizational goals. Thus, whereas private managers can use an internal measure to evaluate their organization's performance, public managers are subject ultimately to evaluation by outside forces, and it is those outside forces, not open markets, that have the critical last word in judging how well a public organization fulfills its responsibilities. Public managers, moreover, have been evaluated in somewhat nebulous and ill-defined terms. Until recently, for example, many managers have had more incentive to focus on satisfying interested clienteles and on holding and expanding political support than on substantive performance by itself. Meaningful, objective performance measures were largely lacking in the public sector until the mid-1970s, even where managers had sought to use them. New emphases on efficiency, productivity, and accountability for results have produced fresh concern for such measures (see Chapter 10)—another sign of increasing similarity between public and private organizations.

Other differences also exist. For one thing, many public organizations have held a virtual monopoly on providing certain essential public services and, consequently, have been able to survive without necessarily providing the highest-quality performance of their functions. Often, these functions are shared with non-profit agencies such as the Red Cross and United Way. Another difference is that achieving results in the public sector must compete for administrators' attention with political and procedural concerns. Values such as participation and public accountability make it necessary for public managers to divide their attention between the results they seek and how to obtain those results. It is difficult to achieve maximum economy and efficiency while keeping a wary eye on possible political repercussions—and many public managers must do just that.

In contrast to the narrowly focused profit-oriented concern shared by most of private-sector management, there are often conflicting incentives among citizens, elected representatives, and administrative supervisors and leaders. If a consensus is lacking on what is to be done and why (not to mention how, as noted earlier), an organization will not function with the same smoothness it would if incentives were agreed on. Just as economic measures of performance have no counterpart in the public sector, general economic incentives have no parallel either.

Furthermore, most public organizations suffer from diffuse responsibility, often resulting in absence of accountability for decisions made. Separation of powers among branches of government is one factor in this, but fragmented executive-branch authority in most large governments (including those at the local level) is another. In contrast, centralized executive responsibility is a key feature of many profit-oriented organizations. Also, unlike private corporations, public organizations entrust a fair amount of decision-making responsibility to citizen groups, courts, and various types of boards or commissions. Thus, an absolutely clear chain of command may not be possible because of numerous opportunities for outside pressures to influence the power hierarchies.

There are still other important differences. Public-sector managers frequently must operate within structures designed by other groups, work with people whose careers are in many respects outside management's control, and accomplish their goals in less time than is usually allowed to corporate managers. Unlike many private managers, public managers must operate in a gold-fish bowl of publicity in which they are subject to scrutiny and criticism from the press, others outside the agency, and the general public. As for the media spotlight, public managers must cope with critical comments from outside, regardless of how well others understand agency purposes, empathize with operating difficulties, or consider political constraints on the manager. Conversely, the skilled public manager may be able to turn the media, as well as critical stakeholders, to the agency's side, which can make it easier to recruit new staff, acquire more operating funds, or perhaps prevent potential critics from gaining credibility. At times, private-sector managers may have to face the same types of public criticism or have similar opportunities to generate good press. But, for the most part, their activities are significantly less exposed to public view until the final product or service has been delivered and evaluated.

In comparing the changing roles of public, private, and nonprofit sectors, two other dimensions merit consideration. In practice, these sectors are becoming increasingly interdependent: examples of this are the multibillion-dollar government bailout of failed savings and loan institutions in the early 1990s and more recent federal efforts to deal with financial and housing crises triggered by the so-called sub-prime mortgage meltdown since 2007 (see Chapter 9). There is also a growing tendency for governments, especially on the local and federal levels, to enter into contractual arrangements with private firms and non-profit firms for delivery of certain services, such as corrections, homeland security, garbage collection, military security, social services and fire protection. For many, the distinction among the three sectors is becoming less important as functions continue to overlap. There has been a considerable blurring of what many once believed were well-defined boundaries among the three sectors. Nonetheless, a growing body of scholarly opinion holds that public organizations, and the roles of those who occupy key decision-making positions within them, are distinctive in important respects and that we need to develop a broader conceptual understanding of their design, function, and behavior.

Thus, although many administrative activities are common to both public and private sectors, major differences also are evident. As a result, there are obvious limits to how much the public sector can borrow advantageously from the private sector to improve the management of public policies. As we shall see, however, those limits are breaking down as governments everywhere are being asked to do more with less (and, increasingly, to do less with less). At the same time, options are expanding as public administrators are able to choose from a much wider range of strategies to address public problems. This has led to greater interest in, and experimentation with, **privatization**, as well as partnerships and direct delivery of services through faith-based and nonprofit agencies. Even these emerging realities, however, do not change the fact that there are significant differences between public and private management.[25]

Public Administration as a Field of Study

The principal focus of public administration as a field of academic study has changed often since its emergence in the late 1800s. Changing and overlapping conceptions of the subject sometimes reflected and sometimes preceded evolution in administrative practice in the real world of government, and cross-fertilization of ideas between practitioners and academics was prominent throughout the twentieth century. Because so many public administrators were trained in formal academic programs, thus increasing the impact that academic disciplines have had on government administrative practices, it is useful to briefly review major emphases that have characterized and helped shape the academic field.[26]

In its earliest period, from roughly 1887 to 1933, public administration was viewed as distinct and separate from politics, more akin to business and business methods than to anything political. In his classic essay, *The Study of Administration*, Woodrow Wilson wrote that administration "is removed from the hurry and strife of politics. . . . Administrative questions are not political questions. Although politics sets the tasks for administration, it should not be suffered to manipulate its offices."[27] The concept of a **politics–administration dichotomy** was widely accepted during this period, based not only on the writings of Wilson but also on the first textbook in the field, published by Frank Goodnow in 1900 and significantly entitled *Politics and Administration*. Administrative discretion was also an important, though often overlooked, element in the thinking and writing of administrative reformers of a century ago. In his classic essay, Woodrow Wilson argued that administrators should be granted "large powers and unhampered discretion"—both "administrative energy and administrative discretion"[28]—as essential elements of their functioning in accordance with the notion of "political" neutrality. His expectation was that, given the opportunity, administrators would exercise competent professional judgment as they carried out their assigned duties. This would serve the public interest and, in turn, the interests of elected officials of either political party (who could then take the credit for effective governance). In sum, Wilson saw discretion as necessary for administrative *effectiveness* as well as ensuring political neutrality.

The bureaucracy was to administer, in an impartial and nonpolitical fashion, the programs created by the legislative branch, subject only to judicial interpretation. The dichotomy between politics and administration

privatization

a practice in which governments either join with, or yield responsibility outright to, private-sector enterprises to provide services previously managed and financed by public entities; a pattern especially evident in local government service provision, though with growing appeal at other levels of government.

politics–administration dichotomy

originally proposed by Woodrow Wilson in the 1880s, it divides politics and policy making from policy implementation and public administration.

was reiterated in Leonard D. White's *Introduction to the Study of Public Administration*, published in 1926. White summarized the conventional wisdom of administrative theory: politics and administration were separate; management could be studied scientifically to discover the best methods of operation; public administration was capable of becoming a value-free science; and politically neutral administration should be focused exclusively on attainment of economy and efficiency in government.

The next phase in the development of the discipline was the movement toward discovering fundamental "principles" of administration. This offshoot of the scientific approach to administration was based on the belief that there existed certain permanent principles of administration that, if they could only be discovered and applied, could transform the performance of administrative tasks. Publication in 1927 of F. W. Willoughby's *Principles of Public Administration* marked the beginning of a decade in which identifying and correctly applying these principles was the predominant concern of many, both inside and outside of academic circles. Luther Gulick and Lyndall Urwick's *Papers on the Science of Administration*, published in 1937, defined seven principles that have become professional watchwords: planning, organizing, staffing, directing, coordinating, reporting, and budgeting (collectively known by the acronym **POSDCORB**). Gulick and Urwick reemphasized the importance of these administrative principles, declared their applicability to almost any human organization, regardless of what the organization was or why it existed, and stressed the fundamental desirability of efficiency as the underlying goal for administrative "science."[29]

Even as Gulick and Urwick wrote these words, however, the dominant themes of public administration were changing. The willingness of most of those in public administration to "embrace, without basic skepticism, the Wilsonian dichotomy"[30] between politics and administration was no longer as widely shared as it had been. The New Deal of Franklin D. Roosevelt, accompanied by a vastly expanded governmental role and the creation of scores of new administrative agencies in Washington, significantly changed the social and political contexts of public administration and sparked a crisis in the field. There were three major developments in the period 1933–1945: (1) a "drastic expansion in the public conception of the obligations and responsibilities of government in social and economic affairs"; (2) the emergence of an "enduring emphasis upon presidential leadership"; and (3) a change in the nature of the federal system, with a shift to "the national scene [of] the responsibility for most of the important policy decisions" in the economy and society at large.[31] According to political scientist Alan Altshuler, Roosevelt had demonstrated "that patronage might be of great value in aiding a vigorous President to push through programs of social and economic reform."[32] Emphasis on nonpartisan neutrality could have obstructed presidential leadership in achieving social reforms supported by many academics. Blurring the politics-administration dichotomy caused considerable turmoil in the study of public administration as the discipline was

POSDCORB

acronym standing for the professional watchwords of administration: **P**lanning, **O**rganizing, **S**taffing, **D**irecting, **CO**ordinating, **R**eporting, and **B**udgeting.

cast loose from its original intellectual moorings without a clear alternative direction.

In the 1940s, with World War II commanding an even greater commitment in terms of government activity, the turmoil increased. Academics who worked for national government agencies during the war effort took back to their post-war campuses a considerably altered perspective on what was important to teach about administration, especially in relation to the political process and public administration's explicit role in making public policy.[33] During this same period (less than a decade after Gulick and Urwick had published their *Papers*), the principles of administration were coming under increasing fire. Critics claimed that the principles were logically inconsistent and potentially contradictory and that they gave no clues concerning how to choose the one most appropriate for particular situations. For example, one principle held that, for purposes of control, workers should be grouped according to function, work process, clientele, or geography. There was nothing to suggest standards for the use of one instead of another or to suggest whether these were mutually exclusive categories.[34] Critiques of this sort came from many scholars in the field but, in 1946 and 1947, few scholars had greater impact than Herbert Simon. In "The Proverbs of Administration,"[35] Simon likened the principles to contradictory proverbs or paired opposites. For example, Simon pointed out that, whereas "look before you leap" is a useful proverb, so also is "he who hesitates is lost." Both are memorable, often applicable, and mutually exclusive, without any hint of how to choose between them. Simon argued that the principles underlying these proverbs were much the same; that is, they were interesting but of little practical value in defining administrative processes. His book *Administrative Behavior* (1947) developed this line of argument further and contributed significantly to the weakening of the principles approach.

No comparable set of values replaced the POSDCORB principles, but different concerns began to emerge. Through the 1940s and into the 1950s, public administration found its relationship to political science to be one of growing uneasiness. Political science itself was undergoing significant changes in the post–World War II period. Most of these changes were in the direction of developing more sophisticated, empirical (including statistical) methods of researching political phenomena but were always based on the assumption that objectivity in research methodology was of the highest importance.

The problem for public administration in this "behavioral" era was that many functions and processes of administration do not lend themselves to the same sorts of quantitative research as do, for example, legislative voting patterns, election data, and public-opinion surveys. Altshuler points out that administrative decision making is frequently informal and that many decisions are made in partial or total secrecy. He also states that the exact values of administrators and the alternatives they consider are difficult to identify and analyze and that the traditional emphasis on efficiency contrasts sharply with the core concerns of modern political science.[36] Consequently, public administration became, in

Altshuler's words, a "rather peripheral subfield of political science," with many questioning its relevance to the larger discipline. In addition, he questioned whether this direction, as valuable as it was for furthering our understanding of human behavior in an increasingly organized society, resulted in research findings that have political relevance, that is, relevance to the research directions of contemporary political science.[37]

Another related development has been the growth of research into administrative change and organizational behavior—research that seeks to examine all sorts of organizations, not only public entities. This movement began with the assumption that the social psychology of organizations made less important the question of precisely what kind of organization was to be studied and sought to integrate research from not only social psychology but also business administration, information science, sociology, and statistics. This field, currently known as organizational change and development, represents an attempt to synthesize much of what is known about organized group behavior within the boundaries of formal organizations. Organizational change concentrates on the characteristics within a group or team that promote or slow change in response to, or in anticipation of, changes in demands from the external environment, particularly with regard to needs and desires for the services produced by the organization.[38] In contrast, "organizational development" focuses on analysis of organizational problems and formulation of possible solutions.[39] This approach aims at increasing the capacity of an organization to identify, analyze, and solve internal problems as a regular function within its ongoing routines, using social-psychological approaches (see Chapter 4). It conceives of organizations as entities that do not follow a single structure or format from top to bottom, but rather depend on the skill set of particular units within the organization, which are shaped structurally, socially, and technologically in the most appropriate manner. Thus, in large and complex modern organizations, there is likely to be considerable diversity in the arrangements of different units designed to accomplish specific tasks.

Equally important to the context of public administration is social change in, among other things, the makeup of the population, the health of the economy, social relationships, and where people choose to live. Social change is important because emerging social arrangements and patterns of behavior are inevitably accompanied by new problems with which government policy makers must contend. It is also important because, as society changes, so do our values, expectations, and priorities.

Many departments and schools of public administration have attempted to respond to such changes by declaring their intellectual and institutional independence from political science and business administration, moving instead toward the establishment of autonomous departments, programs, or schools. Public administration as an academic field of study, then, is far from a settled discipline.[40] Boundaries between it and other fields such as political science are blurred, and there are many loose ends in terms of what to study and how the study of bureaucracy relates to changes in society.

POINT/COUNTERPOINT

THE ISSUE It is assumed that most of those working in a bureaucracy are professionals in their specialties and that their occupational loyalties rest with their organization rather than with a political party or other external affiliation. Because much of public management in American governments occurs within bureaucratic structures, however, there is a tendency for political perspectives to factor into decisions at times.

Should administrators, who are ideally supposed to remain politically neutral, have political involvement?

Arguments *for* Political Involvement

- Public administers work for, and with, government officials and should thus have some level of political involvement to ensure that the collective bureaucracy is working together as smoothly as possible as opposed to working in opposition to other bureaucracies, to the legislative branch, and to the chief executive.
- Once elected, politicians must inspire and lead government officials to achieve their own policy goals and respond to crises. Getting high-level administrators politically involved will help address policy matters sooner rather than later.

Arguments *against* Political Involvement

- The actions and decisions of public administrators touch the lives of virtually every American and need to remain politically neutral so that the most practical option is chosen, as opposed to following the platform of any particular political party.
- With increasing political uncertainty and strife in the United States over the past few decades, it is important that administrators remain politically neutral and focused solely on the organization of their specialty, doing what they know best.

About This Book

Four essential and recurring themes appear in the pages that follow: (1) increasing the *internal efficiency* and *economy* of using public resources, (2) improving the *performance or results* of public programs—especially through the application of information technology, electronic government, and performance management systems—in the real world of public management, (3) maintaining the *ethics and accountability* of public administrators within the context of the larger political system, and (4) more effectively *anticipating, planning for, and securing the resources necessary* to respond to ever greater complexity in our nation and around the world. An effort is made to treat these issues separately, but it is inevitable that they overlap, both in our treatment of them and in the working environments of public administration.

The discussion of public bureaucracy and management can and does go on at three different (but interrelated) levels of analysis, that is, with a focus on distinct dimensions of the administrative process. One is the role and function of government bureaucracy in society at large—what differences large, complex, and influential agencies make in a nation founded on diffuse notions of popular rule (note the implicit importance of the accountability theme). A second dimension or level of analysis is the management of performance in public organizations, broadly defined as issues and challenges confronting the individual public manager. A third topic is the role of the individual—the contribution, in whatever form, of a person working as a public administrator and the challenges, opportunities, and problems associated with that role. All these are ultimately interrelated, and explaining why that is so is a major purpose of this book.

Summary

Public administration is an influential force in American government and society. Most of us are familiar with bureaucracy, and many of our most pressing current political issues are related to administrative agencies and actions. Public administration is the set of processes, organizations, and individuals associated with implementing laws and other rules enacted by legislatures, executives, and courts. Administrative agencies are involved in the formulation of many of these rules, as well as their application. Public administration is simultaneously an academic field of study and an active field of training. Public administration and its politics involve interactions both internal and external to the formal agency structure. Public administration is also characterized by a distinctly managerial component, focusing on the internal dynamics of public organizations. Public managers must possess certain skills, including an understanding of computers, data analysis, technology, management systems, personnel, and budgeting. A successful public manager must direct both short- and long-term activities and is responsible for defining and bringing about action. Most managers operate within a bureaucratic and political environment that shapes both formal structure and operational policies of their organizations.

Public administration in the national government is characterized by several different types of agencies and ways of categorizing administrative employees; each of these may affect what agencies do and how they do it. The principal agencies are cabinet-level departments, independent regulatory boards and commissions, government corporations, divisions of the Executive Office of the President, and other miscellaneous agencies. These are most commonly organized according to function but can also be organized according to geographic area, clientele served, or work process. Administrative personnel can be classified according to whether they were hired through merit procedures or political appointment and whether they are specialists or generalists.

In larger states and local governments, essentials of organization are the same as those at the national levels. But the influence of local political parties and employee unions and the nature of government activity serve to differentiate local governments from the national government. Smaller local governments usually have less extensive bureaucratic development and less professional expertise than the national government.

Organizational structure is politically significant in a number of respects as it demonstrates commitment, symbolic or substantive, to particular policy objectives; it can signal adoption of specific policy directions; it serves to order political priorities by emphasizing some programs over others; and it provides different degrees of access to decision makers. The politics of organization is also significant in settings other than executive-branch arrangements. Contemporary public administration is shaped by the larger political system of which it is a part, by past and present political and administrative values, and by technology and social change.

The fragmented nature of policy making forces administrators to function in a political environment where there is no central policy coordinator with total control; administrators possess considerable discretion; not all decision-making power or authority is clearly allocated. In such a setting, public administrators are often politically active and take policy initiatives that are not neutral, thus departing from traditional views about bureaucratic roles and functions. Furthermore, bureaucratic activity is organized around jurisdiction over particular policy areas; bureaucracies seek to prevent changes in jurisdiction that might harm their interests or those of their supporters.

Several explanations have been advanced for the rise of government bureaucracy, including technological complexity, public pressures in an increasingly diverse society, and government responses to global, social, and economic crises. In addition to adapting to changing trends in political and economic thought, public administration has also had to adapt to rapid social and technological change. Especially during the beginning of the twenty-first century, public administration must deal with rapid population growth and urbanization, increased specialization, the threat of terrorism, and the possible consequences of complex technological advances. Many similarities, and a number of more significant differences, exist between public and private management. Two of the most important differences are that public managers must pursue broad goals set by others and evaluated by outside forces; neither is true of private managers. In addition, public managers generally cannot design their own organization's structures or control the careers of many subordinates. They generally have far less time than private managers to accomplish their goals and must operate under considerable public scrutiny. Both public and private managers are expected to be similarly competent, effective, and efficient in producing results. There is growing overlap of the two sectors. As an academic field of study, public administration has been shaped by several major and partially overlapping schools of thought.

Discussion Questions

1. How has public support of government bureaucracy changed in recent years? In the past, what has accounted for public support of bureaucracy? What actions can be taken to restore trust and confidence in bureaucracy?

2. How is the American structure of government and public administration different from that of other nations with a parliamentary form of government? Why is it different?

3. How can organizational structure be politically significant? Discuss and cite recent examples. What are public administration's intellectual links to economics? To political science? To sociology? To psychology? To business administration?

4. Discuss the changing roles of public, private, and nonprofit agencies in addressing public problems. What difficulties might a public manager face in trying to implement management techniques borrowed from the private sector?

5. How have technological changes affected government in general and public administration in particular? Discuss the effects of electronic-government (e-gov) on bureaucracies. Be sure to describe changing public expectations as well as the size and structure of bureaucracies in your discussion.

6. What elements of social change have contributed to the expansion of administrative responsibilities in American government? Discuss specific impacts of social change on the scope and activities of administrative agencies.

7. A fundamental assumption of administrative reformers in the late 1800s and early 1900s was that politics could have only adverse effects on administration. How valid is that belief? Why? How, and to what extent, do current administrative structures and practices reflect that assumption?

8. Discuss the contributions to the academic field of public administration made by the following individuals: (a) Woodrow Wilson, (b) Luther Gulick and Lyndall Urwick, (c) Herbert Simon, and (d) Alan Altshuler.

9. During the early 2000s, state and local governments faced severe fiscal constraints. How has this trend affected the field of public administration? If this trend continues, how will it affect the field of public administration? If growth declines, what are the implications for public employment?

10. In recent years, how has the role of the bureaucracy become more apparent in the daily lives of Americans? Is there anything in your own personal or career experience that shows a similar expression of public sentiment? Can you think of areas or agencies in which the public has shown a positive attitude toward government and public administration? Discuss.

Key Terms and Concepts

bureaucracy, *6*

discretionary authority, *7*

entrepreneurial government, *10*

public administration, *11*

stakeholders, *11*

public management, *12*

reverse pyramid, *12*

information communication technology (ICT), *12*

Department of Homeland Security (DHS), *13*

jurisdiction, *16*

Office of Management and Budget (OMB), *19*

Office of the Director of National Intelligence (DNI), *24*

checks and balances, *28*

parliamentary form of government, *28*

power vacuum, *29*

bureaucratic neutrality, *30*

legislative intent, *30*

legislative oversight, *30*

electronic government (e-gov), *31*

clientelism, *31*

social-demographic change, *33*

technological change, *34*

knowledge revolution, *34*

blogosphere, *35*

privatization, *39*

politics–administration dichotomy, *39*

POSDCORB, *40*

Suggested Readings

Goodsell, Charles T. The Case for Bureaucracy: *A Public Administration Polemic*. 4th ed. Washington, D.C.: CQ Press, 2004.

Gore, Albert S. *Earth in the Balance: Ecology and the Human Spirit*. New York: Rodale, 2006.

Greene, Jeffery. *Cities and Privatization: Prospects for the New Century*. Upper Saddle River, N.J.: Prentice-Hall, 2002.

King, Cheryl Simrell, and Camilla Stivers, eds. *Government Is Us: Public Administration in an Anti-Government Era*. Thousand Oaks, Calif.: Sage, 1998.

Mosher, Frederick C., ed. *American Public Administration: Past, Present, Future*. Tuscaloosa, Ala.: University of Alabama Press, 1975.

Nye, Joseph S., Philip D. Zelikow, and David C. King, eds. *Why People Don't Trust Government*. Cambridge, Mass.: Harvard University Press, 1997.

Ostrom, Vincent, and Barbara Allen. *The Intellectual Crisis in American Public Administration*. 3rd ed. Tuscaloosa, Ala.: University of Alabama Press, 2007.

Ott, Steven J. *The Nature of the Nonprofit Sector*. Boulder, Colo.: Westview Press, 2001.

Perry, James L., ed. *Handbook of Public Administration*. Rev. ed. San Francisco: Jossey-Bass, 1996.

Savas, E. S. *Privatization and Public-Private Partnerships*. 2nd ed. Chatham, N.J.: Chatham House, 1999.

Stillman, Richard J., II. *Public Administration: Concepts and Cases*. 9th ed. Belmont, Calif.: Cengage, 2010.

Tolchin, Susan J. *The Angry American: How Voter Rage Is Changing the Nation*. Boulder, Colo.: Westview Press, 1998.

Truman, David B. *The Governmental Process*. 1951. Reprint, New York: Knopf, 1981.

Waldo, Dwight. *The Enterprise of Public Administration*. Novato, Calif.: Chandler & Sharp, 1980.

Wamsley, Gary, et al. *Refounding Democratic Public Administration*. Thousand Oaks, Calif.: Sage, 1996.

White, Jonathan R. *Terrorism and Homeland Security*. 7th ed. Belmont, Calif.: Cengage/Wadsworth, 2009.

White, Leonard D. *Introduction to the Study of Public Administration*. New York: Macmillan, 1926.

Wills, Garry. *A Necessary Evil: A History of American Distrust of Government*. New York: Simon and Schuster, 1999.

Wilson, James Q. *Bureaucracy: What Government Agencies Do and Why They Do It*. New York: Basic Books, 1989.

Public Administration, Democracy, and Bureaucratic Power

The exercise of discretionary power, the making of value choices, is a characteristic and increasing function of administrators and bureaucrats; they are thus importantly engaged in politics.

Wallace S. Sayre,
"Premises of Public Administration:
Past and Emerging," 1958.

The decisions of public administrators do not take place in a vacuum. They are powerfully influenced by broader economic, social, and governmental processes—the constitutional allocations of political power, the exercise of discretionary authority by those inside and outside of government, and the overall roles assigned to elected officials, prosecutors, judges, and appointed administrators in governing the nation. In turn, the *governmental system* (like all other human institutions) is continuously being reshaped by society's values and beliefs (both past and present) about what should be done and how it should be done. These beliefs are defined by the social setting of government, including society's basic values, the extent of popular agreement on them, how directly they relate to the conduct of government, and how government interprets and reflects them. The values of other institutions in society (such as business, courts, military, political parties, schools, religious groups, and the mass media) also shape government and public administration. Conflicting values create demands and expectations that may need to be resolved through government action. For example, the public demands a commitment to fiscal austerity, public safety, national security, and quality education, as well as honest and ethical conduct from elected and nonelected administrators; government is expected to conduct its affairs in a "businesslike" manner, with a high degree of economy, efficiency, and measurable results (see Chapter 10). In addition to the discussion of how the social environment and basic values shape administration, we deal with three principal themes in this chapter. First, we will examine *foundations* of bureaucratic power, especially how expertise in a particular field is used to build, retain, and mobilize support for administrative agencies and programs. Second, we will look at *subsystem politics* and the emergence of *issue networks*, terms that refer to the ways in which bureaucrats enter directly into alliances with others inside and outside of government in pursuit of shared programmatic and political objectives. Lastly, we will consider the challenge of establishing the *accountability* of nonelected government officials (that is, most bureaucrats), identify several limitations on bureaucratic accountability, and suggest how those limitations can be overcome.

Public administration has been sharply affected by changes in values concerning the role of government, in administrative concepts (including renewed concerns about privatization and the use of nongovernmental organizations for government activities) and, in general, social values and public demands. On the one hand, modern bureaucracy is the result of past evolution in theory and practice. Traditionally, institutional change tends to be cumulative: As patterns of behavior come and go, they leave behind carryover effects, which then mingle with, and become indistinguishable from, the patterns that replace them. So it is with contemporary administrative policies and machinery, in which much of what we do today reflects lingering influences of the past. On the other hand, social values and established institutional patterns are undergoing rapid, unpredictable, and turbulent change. Today, many basic values are changing, such as those relating to career choices, marriage and family life, gender roles, freedom of expression, respect for authority, job security, "entitlements," energy consumption, material possessions, the environment, and human rights. For traditional institutions (including bureaucracy) to respond to such social upheaval is a large order, and much recent criticism of bureaucracy focuses on its apparent failure to do so.

Out of all this has come a renewed interest in *democratic values* as they pertain to public trust, responsiveness, and popular control of government institutions. With the expansion of government bureaucracies have come clearer distinctions among *political values*, such as equality, fairness, representation, participation, patriotism, and accountability; *social values*, such as concern for others, civic duty, individual achievement, and morality; and *administrative values*, such as political neutrality, secrecy, economy, efficiency, rationality,

Political Values	Administrative Values	TABLE 2-1
Accountability	Efficiency	Political Versus Administrative Values
Responsiveness	Effectiveness	
Representation	Representativeness	
Participation	Rationality	
Democracy	Professionalism	
Citizenship	Discretion	

Source: © 2013 Cengage Learning.

rule of law, and expertise (Table 2–1). Some of America's traditional values—democracy, equality, freedom of speech and religious expression, and the belief that America has a special moral responsibility to promote these values internationally—have remained constant throughout decades of social change. Other values, such as duty to one's country, social conformity, respectability, accepted norms of sexual morality, and the work ethic, have declined in importance for many people. Values gaining in importance during this same era include respect for diversity, pluralism, greater acceptance of individual differences, wider choices in personal living arrangements, more extended circles of friends, respect for the environment, emphasis on quality of work life, use of social networking, putting family ahead of career and personal ambition, assuming individual responsibility for health care and retirement, and protecting the rights of women and children. As greater numbers of interests espouse different and often conflicting values, it becomes less and less likely that all groups in society as a whole will share a common set of *value preferences*. As always, when different values conflict, it is more difficult to compromise and reach consensus.[1] In the next section, we examine those value conflicts as they pertain to public administration and then deal more extensively with specific problems in this area.

Political and Administrative Values

Our discussion of political and administrative values has three purposes: (1) to understand the fundamental beliefs underlying American government and public bureaucracy, (2) to recognize the impact of values on public administration, and (3) to see the ways in which these values conflict conceptually—and how that conflict affects the conduct of politics and administration.

As used here, the term *political values* refers to basic beliefs and assumptions not only about politics and the political system but also about appropriate government relationships to private activity, especially economic activity. Links to economic activity fall under the heading of political values and are relevant to a discussion of public administration because of increasing governmental responsibility in regulating business and industry.

In general, the United States is regarded politically as a **liberal democracy** and economically as a **capitalist system**.[2] Moreover, the two concepts of **popular sovereignty** and **limited government** are central to the notion of liberal democracy. Popular sovereignty implies some degree of participation in voting and other civic actions. Although this does not necessarily mean mass or universal political involvement, America has, in fact, expanded voting rights over the years. The specific vehicle for popular rule has been representative democratic government. Initially, Americans emphasized legislative

liberal democracy

a fundamental form of political arrangement founded on the concepts of popular sovereignty and limited government.

capitalist system

an economic system in which the means of production are owned by private citizens.

popular sovereignty

government by the ultimate consent of the governed, which implies some degree of popular participation in voting and other political actions, although this does not necessarily mean mass or universal political involvement.

limited government

refers to devices built into the Constitution that effectively limit the power of government over individual citizens.

representation, which is stressed by the Constitution. Concern for political representation and demographic **representativeness** in administrative organizations and processes, which grew throughout the 1960s and 1970s, has diminished in more recent years. These subtle changes in meaning have cumulatively made it more difficult to determine whether democratic or administrative values are being maintained. Conceptual uncertainty about values also makes it more difficult to deal with accusations that we are not living up to our own standards of democratic government. For example, defining representativeness in a particular way might, in effect, include one group while excluding another from decision making, and those excluded might well dispute the existence of representativeness. Public discontent with **affirmative action**, immigration policies, government spending priorities, and preferential hiring has prompted groups in many states to challenge these policies by placing them on the ballot to decide their future through public initiative and referenda. In recent decades, as the public grew dissatisfied with the degree of popular control over bureaucracy, greater representativeness in bureaucracy was seized on as one remedy that had considerable appeal. Political scientist Herbert Kaufman suggested over four decades ago that "the quest for representativeness . . . centers *primarily* on administrative agencies."[3]

The second central concept, *limited government*, reflects the predominant view of those who framed the Constitution that government could pose a basic threat to individual liberties. In their experience with the British government, these men had endured the suppression of their personal liberties, and they wanted to prevent that from happening again. Therefore, they incorporated into the Constitution four devices that effectively limit government: (1) a system of *checks and balances* in which the exercise of even a fundamental power by one branch requires the involvement of a second branch; (2) *separation of powers* among the executive, legislative, and judicial branches of government; (3) *federalism*, a division of powers between government levels in which certain powers are allotted to the national government whereas others are retained by the states (which are to some degree independent of control by the national government); and (4) *judicial review*, the process by which courts can invalidate, on constitutional grounds, the laws and actions of other government entities. In addition to this fragmentation of government powers, the Bill of Rights (the first ten amendments to the Constitution) established broad areas of protection for individual liberties and personal privacy against encroachment by official government actions.

The courts took on a more active role until recent years, under Chief Justice John G. Roberts, Jr.[4] In the words of one observer: "**Judicial review** has passed from matters of procedure to matters of both procedure and substance. . . . Courts have not merely sat in judgment on administrative action but on inaction as well; they have required agencies to do things the agencies themselves had declined to do."[5] Other examples of judicial activism include appointing expert witnesses, dismissing jurors for poor conduct, suggesting areas of inquiry during civil cases, ordering payment of fees for research, and

representation

a principle of legislative selection based on the number of inhabitants or amount of territory in a legislative district; adequate, fair, and equal representation has become a major objective of many who feel they were denied it in the past and now seek greater influence, particularly in administrative decision making.

representativeness

groups that have been relatively powerless should be represented in government positions in proportion to their numbers in the population.

affirmative action

in the context of public personnel administration, a policy or program designed to bring into public service greater numbers of citizens who were largely excluded from public employment in previous years; also, the use of goals and timetables for hiring and promoting women, blacks, and other minorities as part of an equal employment opportunity program.

judicial review

the constitutional power of the courts to review the actions of executive agencies, legislatures, or decisions of lower courts to determine whether judges, legislators, or administrators acted appropriately.

transferring prisoners held in overcrowded city jails to state prisons. Whether such activism on the part of the courts is desirable from all standpoints has been questioned as it runs counter to other political and social values. With the appointment of Supreme Court Chief Justice Roberts in 2005, President George W. Bush fulfilled one of his campaign promises to restore limited government by justices who interpret the Constitution more narrowly and practice judicial restraint, rather that judicial activism.[6]

individualism

a philosophical belief in the worth and dignity of the individual, particularly as part of a political order; holds that government and politics should regard the well-being and aspirations of individuals as more important than those of government.

pluralism

a social and political concept stressing the appropriateness of group organization, and diversity of groups and their activities, as a means of protecting broad group interests in society; assumes that groups are good and that bargaining and competition among them will benefit the public interest.

Two related concepts widely reflected in American society are **individualism** and **pluralism**. Our emphasis on the individual is evident in the complex of protections for civil rights and liberties, but individualism also implies the right to participate meaningfully in the political process. Pluralism stresses group organization as a means of securing protection for broad interests in society. Furthermore, it assumes that groups of citizens have the right to organize to advance their interests, that groups with differing interests will compete and bargain with one another, and that the resulting compromises will benefit the community and the nation as a whole. The rights of all citizens to "organize to advance their interests" links the Bill of Rights, individualism, and pluralism, suggesting that individual freedom includes the unrestricted right to be active in organized interest groups.

Directly related to individualism and pluralism is the capitalist notion of political and economic *competition*, which exists primarily among groups but is also found among individuals. Limited government suggests that economic competition, if regulated at all, will be loosely influenced by government; in theory, market competition itself will establish boundaries of acceptable behavior among the competitors and will allocate the fruits of success. Geared to private profit and general economic growth, these economic doctrines fit very comfortably with capitalist theories. They emphasize maximum freedom for private entrepreneurs (individuals) and minimal government involvement in the decisions and operations of the private economic sector. Two assumptions link capitalism to political values of limited government, individualism, and pluralism: (1) the individual is assumed to be both self-sufficient and capable of being self-governing (thus minimizing the need for government), and (2) the individual is thought to be better off both politically and economically if government intervention is restricted.

During the twentieth century, government's relationship to the economy changed dramatically, and what was once minimal involvement increased. Have limited government and capitalism, then, been lost? Some argue that they have. Others suggest that government programs for economic development, supplemental social insurance and income maintenance, are neither radical nor brand-new ideas, and that governments have a social responsibility within the broader framework of capitalism to ensure economic well-being and social justice, as well as to "provide for the common defense" and to "ensure domestic tranquility."

Our values generally emphasize *how* things are accomplished more than *what* is accomplished, stressing the importance of means, not ends. The end does not justify the means. Rather, procedures are valued for their own sake, and fair procedure lends legitimacy to what is done; hence our commitment to **due process of law**, although there is an inevitable gap in all societies between the ideal and operational reality. Our ideology does not attempt to define specifically what is good or correct public policy. We leave it to the political process to formulate policy while we concentrate on ensuring that the process is characterized by some degree of public access to decision making and decision makers, a certain amount of equity in the distribution of political and economic benefits, and a great deal of market competition among diverse interests. The amount of access, equity, or competition that exists is itself a matter requiring resolution. These values serve as standards against which political reality is measured; only rarely do realities match the rhetoric or thinking. But that does not alter the importance of these political values or their influence on what we may try to accomplish through the implementation of public policy.

due process of law

emphasizes procedural guarantees provided by the judicial system to protect individuals from unfair or unconstitutional actions by private organizations and government agencies.

Representative Democracy

A major political value in America has been **representative democracy**, and increasing emphasis has been placed on democratizing political processes. What that entails has not always been clear, however. Some elements of democracy are universally supported (or nearly so), whereas others are the subject of nearly continuous controversy. Most agree, for example, that *majority rule* and *minority rights* are fundamental. The former enables the political system to make and implement binding decisions through popular control; the latter permits those not in the majority the freedom to voice their political views and otherwise to be politically active. Directly related to these principles are the constitutional guarantees of a "free marketplace of political ideas"—that is, the freedom to speak, write, and publish political concepts and commentaries, including those out of favor with officials and the majority of citizens. (Numerous studies of public opinion suggest, however, that many Americans are inconsistent in their willingness to allow free expression of unpopular ideas.) Most would also agree that democracy requires widespread involvement in the election of public officials by means of voting and active participation in political campaigns.

representative democracy

representatives are nominated and elected from individual districts. They comprise a legislature that makes binding decisions for its society.

One element emphasized in the last half-century as essential to democratic government is *direct participation* in making and administering important decisions by those affected most directly by them.[7] Initially, there was considerable resistance to this idea (both in the abstract and in practice) in light of the extensive reallocation of political resources and power that would be required. Nevertheless, calls for **participatory democracy** in general and participative management in particular have met with increasingly positive responses. Where it has been implemented, direct participation has had the effect of increasing the number of decision makers—such as citizens giving testimony at public hearings,

participatory democracy

a political and philosophical belief in direct involvement by affected citizens in the processes of governmental decision making; believed by some to be essential to the existence of democratic government. Related term: *citizen participation*.

participating in online town meetings, and emerging forms of voluntarism—at the same time that it altered decision-making mechanisms (and very often the content of some decisions). Whether representative democracy requires widespread direct participation is open to debate, but merely raising the question has had an impact on our thinking about democracy and on the ways some government decisions are made.

Another idea about democratic government, closely related to direct participation, was an expanded definition of what constitutes "representativeness" in our major institutions. Numerous groups in the population—women, gays, lesbians, African-Americans, and Latinos in particular—had been regularly excluded from decision making in government, business, industry, the legal system, religious hierarchies, labor organizations, and political parties. It was argued that these institutions had not been sufficiently responsive to the needs, interests, and preferences of such groups. This systematic exclusion from power needed to be corrected, and increased direct representation of these groups in key decision-making positions was advocated as the most appropriate remedy. Not surprisingly, considerable tension has been generated since this policy entered the political arena. Although many governments at all levels have moved steadily to increase representativeness (or diversity) in the workforce, many citizens remain uneasy about full enforcement for a variety of reasons. Compliance was often grudging at best and was accompanied only intermittently by changes in the attitudes and values in question. Furthermore, with the aid of a number of Supreme Court appointments by the Reagan and both Bush administrations (1981–1993; 2001–2009) and several subsequent lower-court decisions, some parts of the policy have been successfully reversed. (The continuing controversy over affirmative action as a public policy is discussed in Chapter 7.)

Furthermore, divisive issues involving economic competition and regulation, compensation, collective bargaining, and popular representativeness have recently tended to center (though not exclusively) on the roles of administrative entities. One crucial debate since President Barack Obama's election has focused on the manner, scope, specificity, and implications of government (mainly administrative) regulation of the economy. There are still other links between representative political values and public administration. One is the diversity of interest groups, which increases the potential for alliances with those in positions of influence in the government. Renewed concern for democratic values and political accountability leads to new questions about administrative discretion, ethics, and effective control of bureaucracies.

Public administration in America has been profoundly affected by the evolution of, and recent upheavals in, political values. It has been shaped in part by actions and concepts that limit government (separation of powers, checks and balances, federalism, and judicial review) while also having an effect on those decisions and devices. In particular, government bureaucracies have both contributed to, and benefited from, what some have called the "tilt" toward the executive branch of government (and away from Congress) during much of the late twentieth and early twenty-first centuries. If public administration had been shaped solely by changing political values and the interplay of political forces, it would have been altered considerably from its earliest forms and practices. Administrative values, however, have also figured prominently in its evolution, and it is on these values that we now focus our discussion.

Administrative Values, Pluralism, and Political Accountability

American public administration is grounded in certain fundamental assumptions that have dominated administrative thinking for more than a century. It has been freely assumed that politics and administration are separate and distinct. Since the reforms of the late nineteenth century, it has been commonly assumed that partisan politics should not intrude on public management processes.[8] Political determinations of broad policy directions and administrative management of public programs were thought of as different processes controlled by different hands. From the founding of the Republic to the early twentieth century, public administrators viewed their role as subordinate and responsive to prevailing majorities in legislatures and to chief executives' proposals and directives. Their duty was not to initiate but to act on the initiatives of others. Administration was to be not only politically neutral but also passive. This conception of bureaucracy is not unlike that of a finely tuned machine that is activated only when someone else pushes the button. These ideas have persisted even though political control of administration was considered entirely appropriate and even consistent with bureaucratic neutrality. It was also assumed, in the early twentieth century, that administrative processes and functions (based on Industrial Age business practices) could be studied scientifically and that such an examination would yield various principles to guide administrative conduct. The purpose of developing a "science of administration" was to increase economy and efficiency in government and to use these principles as measures of administrative performance. Companion values have included an emphasis on merit (instead of political-loyalty tests) as the primary basis for hiring, faith in the work ethic and in statistical evaluations of work performance, and a belief that a basic social consensus (other than the profit motive) underlies public administrative processes.

These values first emerged around 1900, in the era of government reform that followed a period of some seventy-five years in which politics and administration were deeply intertwined. Government administrative jobs had been crudely bartered in exchange for favors and support, and the guiding principle in public personnel administration had been "to the victor belong the spoils of victory." The reform effort was based on the belief that all kinds of politics could have *only* adverse effects on administration and that, therefore, a separation of politics and administration was absolutely necessary.

Heavily politicized administration had indeed been wasteful, corrupt, and inefficient, and there had been undeniably negative effects on the quality and effectiveness of government action. Attempts to separate politics and administration, pursue economy and efficiency, and discover enduring principles of administration were not merely passing fancies. They dominated virtually all the major approaches to administration from the turn of the century until after World War II, and remain present in large segments of the general population even today. Some reformers and others who seek to bring better management practices into government still cling to the doctrines of economy and efficiency almost as a matter of faith.

There are, however, some problems created by administrative values that stress separation of politics and administration while at the same time emphasizing efficiency in government operations. First, these approaches are not all consistent with the political values articulated by the Constitution. Those who drafted that document did *not* seek to establish an extensive bureaucratic structure, nor (as far as we can tell) did they foresee the development of one:

> They placed their faith in periodic elections, legislatures, and an elected chief executive rather than in a bureaucracy, however pure and efficient. There is nothing to suggest that they believed sound administration could compensate for bad political decisions. Redressing grievances and bad political decisions [was] the function of the political process, rather than of administrative machinery.[9]

Thus, the separation between politics and administration probably would have been seen by the Constitution's authors as either undesirable (because government through the political process was central to the constitutional scheme) or impractical. (It is also likely, however, that they would have objected equally to the blatant politicizing of administration that occurred during the mid-1800s.) They would have been suspicious of developments that insulated important decision makers, such as administrators, from effective control by, *and accountability to,* the voters or the voters' elected representatives. Yet the administrative values that we have discussed here seem to create precisely that sort of insulation.

Second, it has become clear, on the basis of a substantial body of research since World War II, that public administration is not merely well-oiled machinery for implementing decisions made by other government institutions. Public agencies and administrators have both the authority and the power to make a host of decisions, both large and small, that have real impacts on public policy. Instituted a century ago in response to unmistakable partisan excesses, protections against undue manipulation have given rise to the possibility of *administrative excesses.* Because control over policy making (in all but the smallest governments) is indirect, it is therefore more difficult for elected leaders and their immediate subordinates to exercise.

Third, there is some tension (if not outright conflict) between the major emphases of the Constitution and those of administrative values. The Framers sought to prevent unchecked exercise of power by any institution of government or by government as a whole and also desired a political system that would freely resort to the political process for making decisions and solving problems and that, when necessary, would be able to act.[10] Changes in particular values have intensified existing pressures on administrative institutions, especially in recent years.

The underlying values of administration, on the other hand, clearly point toward efficiency, not merely as a desirable feature of government operation but as a key standard for evaluating government performance.[11] Reformers who first sought to increase efficiency in government associated most forms of politics with inefficiency (in many instances, rightly so) and consequently were largely "antipolitics." Their values strongly favored political neutrality as a key feature of both the composition and operation of public administrative agencies and, thus, also as a major remedy for inefficiency. (It should be noted, however, that these reform efforts had political effects. In particular, they narrowed channels of access to government employment for those who could not meet criteria of merit, and built public organizations around a predominantly white, middle-class ethic.)

Political scientist Douglas Yates explored more fully the conflicts between these two sets of parallel yet distinctive values. Yates treats them, with somewhat more precision, as normative models of **pluralist democracy** and

pluralist democracy

a normative model of administrative activity characterized by dispersion of power and suspicion of any concentration of power, by exercise of power on the part of politicians, interest groups, and citizens, by political bargaining and accommodation, and by an emphasis on individuals' and political actors' own determination of interest as the basis for policy making; the principal alternative to the **administrative efficiency** model.

POINT/COUNTERPOINT

THE ISSUE Attempts to separate politics and administration dominated all major approaches to public administration until the mid-twentieth century and continue to play an active role in political debates today. The following are some of Douglas Yates's summaries of pluralist democracy and administrative efficiency.[12]

Which model is the most appropriate for managing a modern public agency: pluralist democracy or administrative efficiency?

Arguments *for* Pluralist Democracy

- Power is dispersed and divided; governmental policy making is decentralized.
- There is suspicion of executive power (or any concentration of power).
- Power is given to politicians, interest groups, and citizens.
- Political bargaining and accommodation are considered to be at the heart of the democratic process.
- Emphasis is placed on individuals' and political actors' own determination of interest.

Arguments *for* Administrative Efficiency

- Power is concentrated; governmental policy making is centralized.
- Great emphasis is placed on centralizing power in the hands of the chief executive (for the sake of accountability).
- Power is given to experts and professional bureaucrats.
- There is a strong urge to keep politics out of administration.
- Emphasis is placed on technical or scientific rationality.

administrative efficiency. The "Point/Counterpoint" feature challenges you to take a further look at the merits of the administrative efficiency and pluralist models for managing public agencies.

Both sets of values continue to influence American government and inconsistencies between them have been difficult to reconcile. The result, a structurally fragmented government operating on broadly democratic principles, makes some inefficiency more likely than overall efficiency. On the other hand, efforts to maintain efficiency of operations while holding administrators accountable have met with considerable success. Attempts to reconcile these values merit our continued attention.[13] Conflicts inherent in the application of these explanatory models contribute daily to the operational decisions of public managers (see The Public Manager: An Overview). These models also reveal the complexity of dealing with public issues and reflect citizen expectations (and frustrations) often associated with democratic governance.

THE PUBLIC MANAGER: AN OVERVIEW

Several major points should be made about the public manager's job:

1. The public manager inhabits an intensely political environment. Political processes do not abruptly stop at the door of a bureaucracy; the manager's job and environment are essentially political, requiring a primary emphasis on the task of managing political and administrative conflict.

2. The public manager's job also contains a variety of political dimensions, including building support with the chief executive, dealing with related departments and interest groups, bargaining with the legislature, managing and coordinating a fragmented structure of bureaucratic subunits, and (in the national government) trying to oversee and coordinate policy subsystems extending to the operations of state and city governments.

3. The manager's primary role is to deal with competing organizational pressures and to manage political conflict. In some cases, the manager will employ strategies of conflict resolution. At other times, the task will be to convert the negative, adversary features of conflict into something more positive, namely, cooperation, compromise, and coalition building among both political and administrative actors. (This process of conversion is often what we have in mind when we speak of leadership.)

4. In managing this political conflict, the manager faces many of the same issues that worry an advocate of pluralist democracy and, in a general way, would-be controllers of the bureaucracy. He or she has to worry about the fragmentation of bureaucratic activity, especially where it leads to strongly segmented bureaucratic structures and insulated concentrations of power. No less than the ordinary citizen, the public manager needs to "open up" the bureaucracy in order to achieve any real penetration into its operations. Finally, the public manager, along with the pluralist democrat, must worry about the balance of power among different groups: whether desirable levels of competition and bargaining exist, whether certain interests overwhelm other groups in the policy-making process, whether citizens' complaints and demands are heard and registered. In sum, the public manager, far from being the clerk of a narrow efficiency, faces the problems of both pluralist democracy and administrative efficiency.

Popular control of government has always been a matter of considerable importance in American politics. The Founders emphasized the legislative and, to a lesser extent, executive branches of government—which, in principle, could be held directly accountable to voters through periodic elections. This mechanism did not assume a large bureaucracy or broad-scale participation in anything other than the electoral process. This relatively simple, clear-cut arrangement for **accountability** and popular control has become responsive to other kinds of political pressure. Thus, it is not surprising that there are still concerns about public access to government and influence over what government does, especially in the Internet era where public agencies possess the capacity to collect and restrict access to information as a matter of official secrecy.

accountability

a political principle according to which agencies or organizations, such as those in government, are subject to some form of external control, causing them to give a general account of, and for, their actions; an essential concept in democratic public administration.

Democratic governance requires at least the presence, in a political system, of popular sovereignty, substantial electoral equality among citizens, consultation between government and citizens over proposed major courses of action, and majority rule. Increasingly, *equality of opportunity* is also regarded as a prerequisite for a political system to be truly democratic. In the 1700s, *political participation* referred to voting and holding public office and was limited by such qualifications as property ownership, wealth, education, social status, race, and gender. Beginning in the 1830s, eligibility for participation was broadened, so that today, virtually every citizen eighteen years of age or older can vote and otherwise become involved in politics. Lately, participation has taken on another, more controversial dimension— *mandatory inclusion* of various population groups in governmental decision making.

Debates over the meaning and scope of participation are nothing new and may indeed be inevitable in a democracy. Although participation is a key element of "democratic morality," a number of questions about it still exist.[14] One concerns *who* should participate, with near-universal participation recommended by the true believer in democracy (the pure "democrat"). Another question centers on the *scope* of participation—at what stages of policy making and in what ways participation is to occur. Another dilemma for the aspiring democrat is whether *opportunities to participate* should be afforded equally to those with high stakes in government decisions and those with little interest in specific policies. Such issues complicate the structuring of channels of participation, but a commitment to making participation possible must exist before the issues can be addressed. These questions have taken on increased significance with the widespread use of information communication technologies (ICTs) in political campaigns and administrative processes.

Accountability once meant holding officials generally responsible for their actions through direct elective mechanisms, as in the case of legislators, or through indirect machinery such as independent regulatory boards and commissions in which elected officials held others to account on behalf of the public. Now, however, the meaning and means of accountability are less clear. The issue of *to whom* officials are *actually* accountable is a complex one, making it difficult to determine whether they can, in fact, be made to answer to the general public for what they do, or do not do. Complicating matters still further have been the isolated, but highly publicized, instances of serious abuses of power by major U.S. corporations and federal regulatory agencies. What responsibility, if any, do government mortgage underwriting and regulatory agencies such as Fannie Mae and Freddie Mac, the Pension Benefit Guarantee Corporation (PBGC), or the Securities and Exchange Commission (SEC) have to protect the assets and retirement savings of the employees and shareholders of these publicly operated and regulated corporations? Recent examples of the abuses of power have fueled the debate about public- and private-sector accountability and official misconduct by corporate executives and high-level politicians, as well as by state and local officials.[15]

Disagreement with specific policies notwithstanding, the larger concern is for maintaining democratic norms and practices in a complex governmental system within a diverse and rapidly changing society. Today, many fear that democratic values, however defined, are endangered by government actions that take place *without* popular control and consent. Governmental institutions are clearly under pressure "from the people"— left, right, and center—to stay within the public's political reach. (Witness the intense support for the Pat Buchanan and Ross Perot populist movements during the 1992 and 1996 elections, Ralph Nader's Green Party influence on the 2000 and 2004 presidential elections, and the so-called Tea Party candidates during the 2010 elections.) Difficulties in maintaining democracy, however, are hardly new. Assuming that democracy implies fairly equitable access to decision makers, widespread opportunity to exert influence in the political process, and clear public preferences about public policy, the realities of American democracy have fallen short of this ideal for some time.

If policy mandates are vague, the process of defining the "public interest" is even more so. One can argue (as Ralph Nader did in his failed presidential campaigns during 2000 and 2004) that the public is the ultimate "owner" of governmental institutions and that institutions should serve the owner's interest—the public interest—but defining and gaining agreement on what that is as a practical matter is not easy. In a pluralist democratic society, various contesting forces claim to be acting in and for the public interest, and each may have a legitimate claim to some part of larger societal values. Also, it is not clear whether the public interest is some generalized view of societal good or the sum total of all private interests, which are themselves inconsistent with one another.

Democracy and Public Administration

Democracy requires mechanisms for both participation and accountability, ensured by an independent judiciary, uncensored media, and free elections. Public administration, however, poses troublesome problems for any such system. It does not accord with the notion of elected public officials because most bureaucrats are not elected, and professional values usually emphasized expertise, limited access, knowledge, and secrecy over accountability, participation, transparency, and democratic control. Growing societal complexity and increasing administrative responsibilities require more specialized bureaucratic professionals, as well as new and varied forms of indirect public administrative activity (contracts, grants, e-loans, performance partnerships, tax expenditures, and regulation). At the same time, disadvantaged groups and others have turned to government bureaucracy more frequently for various kinds of aid—ironically, often while voicing grievances *against* many of the same agencies—and to demand a greater role in making policies that affect them. Often, the result has been a collision between the need for professionalism and technical competence, and insistent demands for citizen participation in more aspects of policy making.[16] Bureaucratic accountability in such a system has to be achieved largely, if not entirely, through *indirect* popular influence via the legislature and chief executive. When technical expertise is required, it is very difficult, though not impossible, to reconcile accountability and participation in the policy-making process. It is always difficult to achieve both popular control and administrative discretion at the same time.

The concerns that have come to center on bureaucracy include, besides issues of accountability and participation, the question of representativeness. In addition, the general disposition of bureaucrats and bureaucracies to operate behind a veil of secrecy has triggered efforts to open their activities to public scrutiny. Two such efforts are state and national FOI laws and the so-called sunshine laws requiring that public business be conducted in open forums.

Freedom of Information and Sunshine Laws

Holding government officials accountable for their actions and that of others is crucial to democratic governance, even more so when substantial responsibility is entrusted to nonelected (administrative) personnel. This rationale underlies the need for openness in government operations, public scrutiny, and freedom of information (FOI) and **sunshine laws**, all of which increase the public's ability to inquire successfully into the activities of bureaucracy and other branches of government. The glare of publicity has long been known as one means of enforcing accountability, by making possible a better-informed citizenry that can then act more intelligently and purposefully. **Sunset laws** add another dimension to accountability. By requiring positive legislative action to renew agency mandates, there is a virtual guarantee that some examination of agency

sunshine laws

acts passed by Congress and by some states and localities requiring that various legislative proceedings (especially those of committees and subcommittees) and various administrative proceedings be held in public rather than behind closed doors; one device for increasing openness and accountability.

sunset laws

provisions in laws that government agencies and programs have a specific termination date.

performance will take place. Routine reviews and near-universal renewals of agency authorizations will not serve the purposes of sunset legislation. Only careful, thorough, and demanding examinations will do.

The use of sunset laws, in particular, as an instrument of accountability is part of legislative efforts to hold executives accountable. Once again, the public seems to be looking to its legislative representatives to bring about greater popular control over executive-branch agencies. In both state and national government, increasing numbers of legislators are responding positively to public pressures and, in some cases, to lead public opinion as well as follow it. Further, legislative entities [such as the Congressional Budget Office (CBO) and U.S. Government Accountability Office (U.S. GAO)] that analyze budget requests, conduct general oversight activities, and issue critical reports, have been granted increasing authority to discipline administrative agencies. Agencies such as the Office of Management and Budget (OMB) and state bureaus of the budget ("mini-OMBs") are increasingly active in seeking to hold operating bureaucracies more accountable. These, too, have acquired more authority to carry out that function.

The importance of the relationship between access to information and government accountability was recognized five decades ago. Congress, in the Administrative Procedure Act of 1946, attempted to open up the bureaucracy by encouraging distribution of information to the public on a need-to-know basis. The burden rested with the inquiring citizen to demonstrate that information was needed from the bureaucracy; the presumption was that information could be secured unless a strong case was made to the contrary. As long as popular trust of bureaucracy remained high and no major interests felt harmed or threatened, that arrangement was satisfactory. Bureaucratic secrecy went largely unchallenged and little information filtered out of government when agency personnel decided to restrict it.

By the mid-1960s, the situation had changed. Increasing government activity bred rising citizen concern about administrative decision making, which, in turn, sparked calls for greater access to hard-to-get information. Congress responded, after some delay and without strong presidential leadership, by passing the **Freedom of Information Act (FOIA)** in 1966, based on the principle that the "timely provision of information to the American people, upon their own petition, is a requisite and proper duty of government."[17] The law presumed a right to know, with some limitations on information to be made available (most relating to national security). The effect of this statute was to increase the potential for citizen access to a wide variety of government records and files. This statute is increasingly recognized as a means of exposing mismanagement.[18]

The FOIA records of recent administrations have been somewhat mixed.[19] Proponents of greater access to government information have seen some of these developments as very positive; other developments are viewed less favorably; and there have been frustrating instances of invasion of privacy that are cause for concern. During the 1992 presidential campaign,

Freedom of Information Act (FOIA)

passed by Congress and some state legislatures establishing procedures through which private citizens may gain access to a wide variety of records and files from government agencies; a principal instrument for breaking down bureaucratic secrecy in American public administration.

Bill Clinton was praised for pledging openness in government and, in October 1993, fulfilled that pledge by reversing a twelve-year policy of withholding government information from the press. Attorney General Janet Reno issued new FOIA regulations that, among other things, established a presumption of openness in the executive branch and directed that the Justice Department no longer defend other executive-branch agencies challenged under provisions of the FOIA. The OMB created a new policy under which executive-branch agencies must make government information, in electronic form, accessible to scholars and librarians, among others. And in mid-1993, the U.S. Supreme Court ruled in *U.S. v. Landano* (508 U.S. 165) that FBI records are not automatically confidential, especially if a criminal defendant seeks access to relevant records as part of an effort to establish his or her innocence.

The George W. Bush administration attempted to suspend full implementation of the FOIA in the interests of national security, and limited access to sensitive information about the activities of the armed forces and domestic intelligence agencies in the war on terrorism. Not surprisingly, requests for information dramatically increased, creating a huge backlog of unprocessed FOIA applications. Federal agencies receive over 2 million FOIA requests each year. FOIA allows agencies broad discretion in the release of information. If the agency declares that releasing the data would threaten national security, the information will remain a secret. Documents can be released completely, denied completely, or released partially. Other issues have emerged that further complicate full release of information. First, access to electronic data is thought by most observers, including many members of Congress, to be protected under the FOIA, but many troubling questions remain to be answered (some with privacy implications).[20] Second, there is growing unease that contracting out government services diminishes public access to information about those services, because FOIA provisions do not automatically extend to private-sector entities (see Chapter 10). Nearly forty states have also passed FOIA statutes, with varying degrees of effectiveness. Free and open exchange of information is crucial for both accountability and access. Clearly, freedom of information continues to have substantial importance, in the eyes of both government officials and those who, for myriad reasons, wish to monitor what government does. In addition, unnecessary secrecy inhibits organizational communication and policy implementation. Former Vice President Al Gore argues that withholding such information from the American people may also damage democratic values:

> The historic misjudgments that led to the tragedy of America's invasion of Iraq were all easily avoidable. The [Bush] Administration's arrogant control of information and the massive deception perpetuated on the American people in order to gain approval for a dishonest policy led to the worst strategic mistake in the history of the United States. But the damage they have done to our country is not limited to the misallocation of military and economic and political resources.

Nor is it limited even to the loss of blood and treasure. Whenever a chief executive spends prodigious amounts of energy in an effort to convince the American people of a falsehood, he *damages the fabric of democracy* [emphasis added] and the belief in the fundamental integrity of our self-government.[21]

Sunshine laws, which have been passed at all levels of government and apply mainly to legislative proceedings, have also been enacted for administrative agencies. Regulatory agencies at the national level operate "in the sunshine," although they are required to do so by judicial rather than legislative action. In all fifty states, open-meeting laws are on the books and records of most public hearings applying to state legislative committees, state executive branches and independent agencies, and local governments. The greatest potential beneficiaries are organized groups of citizens who seek to monitor and influence the decisions of administrative agencies. City councils, county commissions, and local school boards have been at the center of controversies over open meetings at least as often as state or national entities. Government behavior can be changed only gradually, if experience with these devices is any guide.

There is also growing concern that government and bureaucracy are not doing enough to protect individual privacy and to ensure that government records concerning affairs of private citizens are fair and accurate. This is a particularly sensitive issue in view of electronic information capabilities. Prior to the widespread availability of ICTs, information might have been available to government, but it was costly and time-consuming to have it on hand or to organize it. Computers, however, make retrieval and cross-referencing of information not only possible but quick and convenient. A principal concern is the extent and diversity of personal information that is now stored on computers of public and private organizations—Social Security data, credit ratings and transactions, driver's license information, medical records, military and State Department communiqués, income figures, and so on. The website **WikiLeaks**, founded in 2006, claims to have access to several million leaked diplomatic and military documents. In July 2010, Wikileaks released a compilation of more than 76,000 documents about the war in Afghanistan not previously available for public review. This set off a firestorm of protests from the Obama administration that such sensitive records may jeopardize the lives of U.S. and coalition soldiers serving in the region.

Both national and state governments have acted to better safeguard an individual's right to privacy and fair treatment. Legislation at the national level includes the Freedom of Information Act, the Fair Credit Reporting Act, the Family Educational Rights and Privacy Act, the Privacy Act of 1974, and the Fair Credit Billing Act. Congress has established the Privacy Protection Study Commission to look into intrusions on individual privacy by agencies outside the national executive branch. The Obama administration created the **Bureau of Consumer Protection (BCP)** to protect buyers from unfair, deceptive

WikiLeaks

website founded in 2006 with access to several million leaked diplomatic and military documents. Wikileaks has released thousands of leaked documents about the war in Afghanistan not previously available for public review. In 2010, this set off a firestorm of protests from the Obama administration that such sensitive records may jeopardize the lives of U.S. and coalition soldiers serving in the region.

Bureau of Consumer Protection (BCP)

federal super-agency created in 2011 to protect consumers and buyers from unfair, deceptive and fraudulent business practices.

The Most Dangerous Man in America: Daniel Ellsberg and the Pentagon Papers

The Most Dangerous Man in America: Daniel Ellsberg and the Pentagon Papers is a documentary film that follows Daniel Ellsberg, a former U.S. military analyst, and explores events leading to the publication of the *Pentagon Papers*, which exposed top-secret military history of U.S. involvement in Vietnam from 1945 to 1967.

The Vietnam Study Task Force was founded in 1967, for the purpose of writing a history of the Vietnam War. Analysts used files from the Office of the Secretary of Defense to create the final product, keeping the study secret from political leaders in Washington. Classified as "Top Secret," the study was never meant to be shared publicly.

Daniel Ellsberg knew the analysts involved in conducting the study and had access to the files. Ellsberg opposed the Vietnam War and attempted to disclose the study's contents to President Nixon's National Security Advisor, Henry Kissinger, among other federal government agents, but was turned away until approaching the *New York Times* in 1971.

The *Pentagon Papers* revealed that the United States had escalated and expanded the Vietnam War by bombing Cambodia and Laos, raiding North Vietnam, conducting Marine Corps attacks—none of which had been reported to the American public. The Papers further revealed that each administration from Truman to Johnson had purposefully neglected to share its full intentions behind actions in Vietnam, compromising the U.S. account of the war, as well as eroding the public support for the Vietnam War.

Ellsberg was eventually charged for his actions as the source of the leak, but all charges were dropped. Ellsberg continued his career as a political analyst.

There is a growing perception that government should do more to protect individual privacy and ensure that individual records and files are fair and accurate. What basic issues are involved in this debate, and how might such privacy guarantees be instituted? Compare the Pentagon Papers with current incidents of the release of classified information such as the WikiLeaks case. How are they similar? Do they differ?

Source: http://www.mostdangerousman.org/ accessed March 13, 2011.

and fraudulent business practices. Over half a dozen states have enacted privacy laws, and an even larger number have adopted their own versions of the Fair Credit Reporting Act. There has been considerable government activity in this area, but concern persists that Big Brother still may have too much access to personal records. Indeed, there are growing fears that "hackers" in *both* the public and private sectors may be capable of invading our privacy and stealing our identities to a far greater extent than ever before. (Note, again, the potential links to freedom of information and national security policy regarding access to electronic data.)[22]

Dimensions of Democratic Administration

The following section examines in greater depth selected areas in public administration that pose particular challenges for the maintenance of democratic norms and practices. We will consider each of the following: (1) citizen participation, (2) bureaucratic representativeness, (3) bureaucratic responsiveness, and (4) administrative effectiveness as a possible threat to personal freedom.

Citizen Participation

The ideology of citizen participation has firm roots among our political values, especially *participatory democracy*. The push for greater citizen participation in government decision making was reborn in the 1960s out of related movements for civil rights and decentralization of urban government structures. It originated in demands by minorities for a larger voice in determining policies and programs directly affecting them. The urban poor, at least during the 1960s, concentrated on organizing themselves and confronting those in power with demands for change. Their participation was formally incorporated in both the planning and implementation of federal Model Cities and community-action programs.

Forms and practices of citizen participation are numerous, ranging from advising agencies to attending hearings to actual decision making. In addition to making statements at meetings held by administrative agencies, individuals may take part in budget and other legislative hearings, and in initiatives and referenda; serve on advisory committees; participate in focus groups and respond to citizen surveys; and, in some cases, sit on governing boards of operating activities funded by government entities. Also, in the delivery of human services, individuals act as *coproducers* of the services by their involvement in program operations (this refers to services such as unemployment compensation, job assistance, garbage collection, and education).[23] The same kind of active role is an essential ingredient in the more contemporary attempts to provide improved customer service and empower local communities to act in their own interests. Viewing citizens as coproducers is a different but highly relevant conception of participation that has expanded with the wider use of electronic communications in government. Strategies for citizen participation are directed generally toward reducing citizen alienation from government. Although some of these purposes may be mutually incompatible, this form of grassroots involvement can also be used to hold public officials accountable.[24]

Ideological differences about the extent of citizen participation and debates over its place in governing are related conceptually to the continuing debate in American politics over centralization and decentralization of administrative authority (see Chapters 3 and 4). Particularly as practiced in the federal system, citizen participation represents an application of the decentralist principle, which assumes value and purpose in delegating decision-making authority to affected persons and groups. Decentralization as a mode of operation clearly permits wider participation; it gives greater assurance that the existing spectrum of opinion will receive a hearing; and it lends more legitimacy to both the process and the outcomes of decision making. Because federalism itself was designed as a bulwark against intrusive centralization, the concept of decentralization obviously has a place in operations under a federal system. Citizen participation, fostered by many national programs, has been a key mechanism used to promote decentralization of operating responsibility.

The concept of participation has been applied in different ways to varying problems. **Community control** focused on neighborhood management of schools and delivery of other essential urban services. Neighborhood and citizen-action organizations sprang up for the purpose of "preserving neighborhood character" and sometimes redevelopment of physical structures in the neighborhood. For example, there have been concerted efforts to prevent construction of interstate highway projects that would cut through, or perhaps level, parts of established urban neighborhoods; cattle ranchers in western states joined forces with Native Americans and antinuclear groups to oppose uranium mining by energy conglomerates; citizen groups protested toxic-waste disposal; and residential associations have tried to attract (or repel) commercial enterprises such as Home Depot and Wal-Mart.[25]

Citizen participation also has been incorporated into formal mechanisms for decision making. At the national level, for example, public participation in regulatory proceedings has been increasing, although with considerable variation in regulators' responses and opportunities provided to citizen groups, such as consumer protection and environmental organizations. Agencies and commissions undoubtedly have legal discretionary authority to decide just how much public participation (if any) to permit and, particularly, whether and how to finance participation by those with limited resources. Nonetheless, there has been considerable frustration on the part of so-called **public interest groups** (**PIGs**), which have been slow to gain access to regulatory proceedings. And, at the local level, participation is now more regularized, especially in building code and zoning enforcement, environmental protection, and planning and design of urban communities.

Some other dimensions of citizen participation are worth noting. First, the matter of who is to participate and to what extent is not only a problem of democratic ideals; it has potentially important implications in a strictly operating sense. In antipoverty programs of the mid- and late 1960s, "maximum feasible participation of the poor" was called for, but there was bitter debate over who constituted "the poor," and how they were to be selected and incorporated into program operations. Furthermore, in almost all studies of citizen participation, it has been found that

> groups of individuals active in such programs (1) represent organized interests likely to have been previously active in agency affairs, (2) include a large component of spokesmen for other government agencies, (3) represent a rather limited range of potential publics affected by programs, and (4) tend toward the well-educated, affluent middle- to upper-class individuals. Viewed in terms of the ideological program goals, programs seldom appear to . . . produce a great socioeconomic diversity among participating interests.[26]

Community control

legal requirements that groups affected by political decisions must be represented on decision-making boards and commissions.

public interest groups (PIGs)

organized lobbying groups that represent primary noneconomic interests in influencing public policy. Examples are Common Cause and Greenpeace.

co-optation

a process in organizational relations whereby one group or organization acquires the ability to influence activities of another, usually for a considerable period of time.

Second, there is a distinct possibility that officially sponsored citizen participation will tend to be **co-optation** and tokenism rather than true representation. On more than one occasion, what began as a good-faith effort to build greater participation into a decision-making process ended up as more show than substance, symbolic politics at its worst, with the newer groups occupying a place of greater visibility but little increased power. In developing relationships between some urban community-action groups and municipal administrations (for example, "city hall"), leaders occasionally have succeeded in co-opting a group's leadership by agreeing to some of their demands and giving them greater political visibility in exchange for moderating other demands. Compromises such as these have occurred in communities like Chicago that have well-entrenched local political organizations, where community-action groups choose to settle for "half a loaf" rather than risk forfeiting all chance to have some impact on the way decisions are made and resources allocated. In addition, co-optation can work both ways, in that a government agency might be co-opted by stronger nongovernmental, private-sector, groups. Either way, co-optation involves surrender by a weaker entity to a stronger one of some power to shape the course of the weaker entity's long-term activities.

Third, decentralizing and localizing control over governmental programs may not guarantee either increased participation at the local level or more democratic operations. Indeed, there is always a chance that local government may be *less* democratic than in a larger and more diverse political system. The dangers of domination by a small minority of elite local citizens are very real, regardless of official mandates or unofficial expectations. It also has been observed that citizen participation can become a "bureaucratic ideology" to be used "against the elected officers of representative government."[27] All such observations clearly imply a hazard inherent in citizen participation: the potential for citizen interests to become primarily self-serving rather than representative of broader interests in the community or society.

A fourth concern is that agency personnel, in their enthusiasm for satisfying immediate citizen-action demands, may initiate responses that prove to be shortsighted when judged by more rigorous criteria over time. Compounding this potential difficulty is a tendency for citizen groups to scorn cost-benefit analysis as an instrument of evaluation of their own proposals. Cost-benefit analysis is not always an appropriate evaluative tool, but it can often strengthen one's case, particularly under conditions of fiscal stress, or at least increase a group's credibility in a political dialogue.

Fifth, if citizen participation is designed to help keep bureaucracy accountable to the general public, it has had a mixed record of success. Citizen groups seem to have the greatest impact when they have the political power to make bureaucrats listen and when group values most nearly match those of the bureaucracy.

Sixth, citizen participation and its impact will be affected by the degree to which contacts with those in government are characterized by confrontation as opposed to negotiation, by a sense of "us against them" as opposed to a perceived community of interests. Tension in a political system is not uncommon, but a democratic system virtually requires that tension not be constant. Barring fundamental shifts in the locus of power in a particular decision-making system, continuous confrontation will soon reach a point of diminishing returns for those seeking access and influence.

Finally, a widely accepted concept affecting participation is citizen *input*, about which a cautionary note is in order. Many of us seem to assume that we should seek "greater input" into the mechanisms of decision making. (The term is borrowed from computer science, where input makes a major difference in results.) However, the concept of input involves an implicit acknowledgment that *somebody else* is running the machine. In other words, those who seek input are admitting to a *subordinate* position in decision making. How to get action with too many voices "in action" is a real dilemma for decision makers. There are other possibilities—coproduction, **empowerment**, partnership, and full control, for example—for which input is an inappropriate concept. To think only in terms of input, in short, serves to limit the variety of ways that participation can occur and to confirm the power of those already holding it.

Citizen participation, in sum, has dramatically modified decision making in a host of policy areas and has taken its place as a major feature of democratic administration. However, nothing is automatic about the manner in which participation and representation are practiced. Although those in positions of power have often yielded only grudgingly to citizen groups, it is unlikely that the gains that have been made will be rolled back.

empowerment

approach to citizen participation or management that stresses extended customer satisfaction, examines relationships among existing management processes, seeks to improve internal agency communications, and responds to valid customer demands; in exchange for the authority to make decisions at the point of customer contact, all "empowered" employees must be thoroughly trained, and the results must be carefully monitored.

Bureaucratic Representativeness

There are, first of all, several approaches to representation.[28] Should constituents' opinions and preferences be conveyed to government officials and reflected faithfully in legislative voting, or should a representative exercise independent judgment and individual conscience in making decisions? The former, which has been labeled the "delegate role," maximizes the public's impact on decision making but does not take advantage of the representative's potentially superior knowledge of details and of subtleties in making choices. The latter, labeled the "trustee role," emphasizes the representative's capabilities and the public's trust that their interests will be faithfully served (thus the label "trustee"). In both instances, we are depending on our representatives to somehow serve the public interest. Unfortunately, it is rarely clear how elected officials make their decisions and to whose voices they listen when they do act as delegates. Thus, in its most basic dimension, there is ambiguity concerning representation.

That ambiguity is complicated considerably when the focus shifts to the administrative context. Because bureaucracies in American politics are acknowledged to have a representative function, it follows that answers to the same sorts of questions must be found. But, historically, bureaucratic agencies have served narrow clienteles with specialized interests (see Chapter 1). An agency's representation of those interests—and its accountability to them—can be quite complete without its serving the larger political system. How, then, can these administrative patterns be reconciled with democratic values that emphasize broad popular representation? Central to the argument is the following proposition: "The attainment of the democratic ideal in the world of administration depends much less on majority votes than on the inclusiveness of the representation of interests in the interaction process among decision makers."[29] The process can be called "democratic" only to the extent that interaction is broadly inclusive at two levels of decision making: first, at the level of political superstructure, where basic decisions on rules for society and roles for actors in the administrative state are made, and second, at the level of program specialization to which much of the decision making of the administrative state has been committed. Interaction should include several types of leaders from diverse segments of the community who, in their participation and the influence of nonleaders upon them, represent the many and varied interests within society.

Thus, the degree to which representation is *inclusive of existing interests in the society* is, in this view, a key test for how democratic administrative processes will be. Underlying this is another concern: the extent of effective access afforded to those not already a part of the interaction process, consistent with the norm of inclusiveness. Both access and regularized interactions are crucial to democratization of administration, especially regarding the opportunity for newer or weaker groups to gain a hearing for their interests and grievances.

Another essential difficulty in representation concerns the delegation of authority. In a fundamental sense, we delegate our authority to Congress and to state and local legislatures to make our laws, knowing as we do that representation of our every view is imperfect. Legislatures, in turn, have delegated vast amounts of authority to bureaucracies (and to chief executives), further removing decision-making power from the source of authority—that is, the people. When authority is delegated, it must be either very precisely defined and limited, which tends to be impractical and defeats the purpose of delegating, or else discretionary, with those who exercise it largely deciding how it should be used.

Once discretionary authority enters the picture, which it clearly does in nearly all forms of administrative decision making, the representational quality of decisions may be diminished. This is especially true where expertise, technical competence, and rationality are highly prized values, as they are in much of our bureaucratic structure. We come back, then, to a dilemma that troubles much of democratic administration: the conflict between professionalism and participation/representation. In recent years, "the people" have grown to resent "somebody else" making a judgment about what is best for them. Most of the time, that "somebody" is a professional operating within a bureaucracy. Thus, discretionary authority exercised by bureaucratic "trustees" increases the chance that the general public's feelings will not be as well represented as they might be under conditions of reduced (professional) discretion.

Another aspect of discretion should be noted. If, as one observer has pointed out, "good administration consists of making [bureaucracy] *predictably and reliably responsive*" to the wishes of the public, then large areas of discretionary authority clearly get in the way of predictability. [30] The only way to make bureaucracy more predictable, given our past history of delegating authority, is to reduce dramatically the discretion technical experts in the bureaucracy are permitted to exercise. This would require a fundamental reassessment of the kind of bureaucracy—and expertise—we want.

Finally, bureaucratic representation is inhibited by longtime practices insulating administrative personnel from direct political pressures. Conceptually, politics and representation of the public's feelings are virtually synonymous, and to hamper political interchange is to place limits on popular representation.[31] Whether the U.S. civil service is, in fact, representative of the population at large is a debatable—and debated—issue.

Several studies suggest that national government civil servants are imperfectly representative of the public at large in demographic (and perhaps political) terms, as senior civil servants certainly are. Yet, given the professional nature of their work, we might expect that to be the case—at least concerning income, education, and certain issue positions. Considering the changes already in motion regarding recruitment, promotion, pay freezes, and the like, it is not surprising that we are seeing less demographic representativeness. Although career civil servants are likely to be affected by the presence of a presidential administration that has "a substantial degree of coherence in its overall program goals and its personnel system, and [that] appears for the moment to have strong political momentum," the views of career employees still do not "exactly mirror those of the presidential administration."[32] Strong partisan ideologies dominated executive–bureaucratic relationships during the second Bush administration (2001–2009).

The issue of representativeness obviously has many sides to it. Women, gays, and ethnic minorities, in particular, have taken the virtually unanimous position that greater representativeness is needed to enhance general understanding within the civil service of problems confronting women, homosexuals, and minority groups. Furthermore, theirs is a call for *advocacy* of their cause as a central activity of female and minority administrators. In general, the effort to increase representativeness based on gender and race is founded on the belief—perhaps quite valid—that government would otherwise ignore their concerns in program design and management. Other groups such

Neo-Conservatives

those who subscribe to the philosophical-ideological basis for the George W. Bush administration's policy decisions favoring preemptive military action, privatization, lower taxes, and cutbacks in domestic social programs.

as evangelical Fundamentalist Christians, **Neo-Conservatives**, and the so-called Tea Party have taken similarly strong stances in favor of including more of their ideology, representatives, and interests in national politics.

Bureaucratic Responsiveness

Responsiveness of public officials to popular sentiments depends on the presence of several factors in the governmental process. It depends fundamentally on the people's assumptions about what *is* and what *should be* in the conduct of government and public-policy making. It is not only a matter of what we establish very loosely as our governmental and societal objectives (and those objectives will conflict), it is also what we take for granted in our expectations about governmental activity.

Second, responsiveness requires meaningful access to the right decision makers and a legitimate opportunity to be heard. Access is a key step in the policy process and, without it, responsiveness cannot be ensured. A key issue regarding access, is—and will continue to be—whether it should be granted or denied by virtue of an individual's (or group's) payment of a "retainer" in the form of a pre-election campaign contribution. Citizen inputs are likely to have a limited effect in attaining bureaucratic responsiveness because of restrictions on citizens' expertise, time, and access to decision makers.

Third, government and its agencies have to be able to respond to potential emergencies, and ongoing policy and program demands, in new ways to meet new threats. Politically, financially, and administratively, agencies must be equipped to deliver services or otherwise satisfy public demands placed on them. These demands have escalated following September 11, 2001, Hurricane Katrina, and the *Deepwater Horizon* British Petroleum (BP) oil spill in the Gulf of Mexico, with the need for comprehensive planning to minimize the impact of natural and man-made disasters and prevent the actions of known domestic and international terrorist groups. In addition, agencies must introduce fundamental changes in the police power of government that may compromise strict interpretation of civil liberties.

There are two major constraints on responsiveness. The first concerns public expectations. Ideally, public expectations should be realistic, reasonable, and manageable. Admittedly, anyone in government can hide behind excuses of unrealistic, unreasonable, or unmanageable public desires to avoid tackling hard problems that may, by objective standards, need attention. But the point here is that there may actually be conditions that, for legitimate reasons, are difficult to deal with—for example, crime, environmental pollution, offshore oil spills, poverty, or nuclear-waste disposal. If people assume that a problem can be solved and it is not solved, the government may be accused (not entirely fairly) of being unresponsive to public wants. Despite our skepticism, inability to act can be an operating reality for a government agency—perhaps as a result of lack of jurisdiction, limited funds, managerial ineffectiveness,

CHAPTER 2 ■ Public Administration, Democracy, and Bureaucratic Power   73

political opposition, or merely difficulties in "making the ordinary happen" (see Chapter 9).

The second constraint on responsiveness is that government agencies cannot—or, at least, do not—respond equally to all societal interests. Inevitably, some groups view government as unresponsive because it does not respond to *them*. And they are often correct in that assessment. The main point, however, is that government is not simply responsive; it is *responsive to* specific sets of interests and preferences that exist in society at large. Especially in the context of limited resources (fiscal and otherwise), government cannot respond to each and every interest or need, and it is rarely able to satisfy fully those interests to which it does respond.

Administrative Effectiveness and Personal Liberty

It is increasingly possible that, as government machinery strengthens, it acquires additional potential for diluting individual liberties. This does not necessarily occur as the by-product of deliberate decision in the highest councils of government. It can result simply from overzealous implementation of perceived mandates by an individual agency or bureaucrat. It is an even greater possibility when strong public sentiment supports an agency such as the Office of the Director of National Intelligence in doing a job that inherently threatens individual liberties. Examples are potential actions by the border patrol, immigration, law enforcement, transportation and national security agencies. In their zeal for securing our borders, preventing further acts of terrorism, and "fighting crime," there is danger that agencies like the FBI, state law enforcement agencies, or local police may infringe on Bill of Rights protections. This is a serious concern of many people, involving such issues as domestic surveillance by U.S. intelligence agencies, search and seizure procedures, wiretapping, profiling ethnic and racial groups, and balancing the priorities of national security versus individual privacy. Civil libertarians are concerned about the **USA PATRIOT Act**, which loosens the procedures and rules of evidence for surveillance, investigation, spying, and jailing of terrorist suspects. President Bush signed the act into law on October 26, 2001, just five weeks after the September 11 attacks on New York and Washington. It is a large, complex, and hastily drafted law that was passed by Congress over the objections of civil liberties groups on both ends of the political spectrum. The act gives the executive branch extensive powers and a wider range of tools to limit freedoms of speech, privacy, and due process. The essential point is that, as the machinery of government grows stronger—whether or not it is supported by popular majorities—the *potential* for infringement of all sorts on individual rights grows apace.[33] This causes operating problems for those in public administration but, because of the basic values at issue, all of society is ultimately involved. Nonetheless, Congress reauthorized the Act in 2011 amid renewed concerns for homeland security.

USA PATRIOT Act

short title of the controversial post-9/11 antiterrorist legislation (P.L. 107-56) "**U**niting and **S**trengthening **A**merica by **P**roviding **A**ppropriate **T**ools **R**equired to **I**ntercept and **O**bstruct **T**errorism" that increased central government powers to investigate, detain, and wiretap persons suspected of engaging in terrorist activity.

The Political Environment of Bureaucratic Power

Like most other government institutions, administrative agencies function within complex and overlapping frameworks of widely scattered legal and political power. Both the formal structure of governmental power and the actual competition for power reflect a *lack of centralization* in the political system. Competition for power includes conflicts among and within the branches of government (especially within Congress), factional conflict within the two major political parties, and continual jockeying for position and influence among interest groups. This dispersal of power is sustained and supported by the noncentralized nature of the American economy and society, with its strong cultural emphases on capitalism, individualism, and pluralism. This prevailing political culture is accompanied by acceptance of individualism and group competition as appropriate mechanisms for achieving success in politics and other pursuits.

Wide dispersal of political power both constrains and creates opportunities for stakeholders—diverse interested individuals, groups, and institutions—to seek and acquire leverage in a policy arena. The major problem facing any group or agency is that competition for influence in a particular subject area is usually fierce because, at the same time, many other groups and agencies are also seeking to have their preferences adopted as public policy.

Take, for example, proposed changes in government health care policy. This area is of considerable interest to stakeholders such as the medical profession, pharmaceuticals manufacturers, hospitals, medical equipment dealers, insurance companies, patients, the uninsured, and consumer groups. Others with a stake in health care policy include labor unions whose members are covered by company-paid health plans, stockholders of drug companies, allied health professionals employed by health care providers, and government agencies—such as the national Department of Health and Human Services (DHHS) and state and national health regulatory commissions—that have responsibilities affecting, and affected by, decisions on health care policy issues. In March 2010, President Obama signed the **Patient Protection and Affordable Care Act of 2010** (**PPACA**) and the **Health Care and Education Reconciliation Act**. These laws are compromised versions of the health care reform agenda of the Democratic Congress and the Obama administration. They include numerous health-related provisions which will take effect over a four-year period: incentives for businesses to provide benefits to employees, expansion of Medicaid eligibility, health insurance exchanges, subsidies for insurance premiums and support for medical research. The statutes also prohibit insurance companies from denying coverage based on pre-existing conditions. The costs of these provisions are offset by a variety of taxes, fees, and cost-saving measures, such as new Medicare taxes for high-income beneficiaries and fees on medical devices and pharmaceutical companies; there is also a controversial tax penalty

Patient Protection and Affordable Care Act of 2010 (PPACA)

health care reform law signed by President Obama on March 23, 2010 along with the **Health Care and Education Reconciliation Act of 2010.**

Health Care and Education Reconciliation Act

compromise legislation signed into law by President Obama on March 23, 2010 with the **Patient Protection and Affordable Care Act of 2010 (PPACA)** addressing comprehensive healthcare and student loan reform.

for citizens who do not obtain health insurance (unless they are exempt due to low income or other reasons). Provisions of the act have been challenged by 20 states in the federal courts as violations of the separation of powers clause. As of this writing, two federal court cases brought by the states have upheld the law and two (Florida and Virginia) have overturned some of its provisions.[34]

The key to understanding why bureaucratic agencies are forced to play political roles is the lack of cohesive political majorities within the two houses of Congress and the resultant "fuzziness" in programmatic mandates often enacted by Congress.[35] Political scientist Norton Long, writing over fifty years ago, observed that "it is a commonplace that the American party system provides neither a mandate for a platform nor a mandate for leadership. . . . The mandate that the parties do not supply must be attained through public relations and the mobilization of group support."[36] Long went on to suggest that the parties fail to provide "either a clear-cut decision as to what [administrative agencies] should do or an adequately mobilized political support for a course of action."[37] He continued:

> The weakness in party structure both permits and makes necessary the present dimensions of the political activities of the administrative branch—permits because it fails to protect administration from pressures and fails to provide adequate direction and support, makes necessary because it fails to develop a consensus on a leadership and a program that makes possible administration on the basis of accepted decisional premises.[38]

Thus Congress, lacking majorities that can speak with clear and consistent voices for sustained periods of time, is characterized instead by shifting political coalitions, the composition of which varies from one issue (and even one vote) to the next.

Another factor contributing to the lack of clarity in legislative mandates to government agencies is the inability of legislatures as institutions—and of individual legislators—to define precisely the exact steps required to put into effect a desired policy or program:

> Legislators, not being technical experts, frequently write laws embodying goals that are exemplary but [that] lack details. Skeletal legislation, as it is frequently called, is phrased in occasionally grand and, therefore, fuzzy terms. The implementing agency is told by the legislature [in national, state, or local government] to provide a *safe* environment for workers, to see that school children are served meals with *adequate* nutritional content . . . to *assist the visually impaired*, to maintain *adequate* income levels, and so on.[39]

Most of the time—but especially when basic statutory language is ambiguous—legislators delegate to administrators the authority necessary to breathe life and specific meaning into such provisions of the law and then to implement them. (Ambiguous language can also be the result of political compromises. For example, it is always easier to agree on support for "affordable health care" than to define exactly what that is.) For whatever reason, then, the usual pattern is legislative enactment of statutes that are phrased in general terms, accompanied by legislative delegation of authority (to define and implement those statutes) to administrative agencies.

Thus, agencies are obliged to make judgments about legislative intent and program management. These decisions carry with them significant political implications. Congress, however, does not simply leave bureaucrats to their own devices. *Legislative oversight* is a legitimate function of Congress, one that can result in fairly strict control by a legislative committee or subcommittee of actions taken by administrators under its jurisdiction. (Other potential controls will be examined in the discussion of bureaucratic accountability later in this chapter.)

Presidents, who might be expected to provide leadership for bureaucracy from a relatively solid base of political support, ordinarily lack the sort of backing that would permit them to take unequivocal policy positions. Presidents have the largest constituencies and therefore must be, if not all things to all groups, at least many things to many of them. Administrative decisions are inevitably impacted by the need to serve so many diverse and varied interests. This can also pose a considerable challenge to administrators seeking to carry out directives from the chief executive as well as the legislature.[40]

Before discussing the principal political resources of administrative agencies, some other generalizations concerning the political environment of bureaucratic power should be noted. First, formal definitions of agency power or responsibility are not likely to reveal the full scope of actual power or influence. Second, although bureaucratic agencies generally occupy a power position somewhere between total independence from the president and Congress and total domination by either or both, the amount of independence they have in any specific situation is also heavily influenced by the power relationships they have with other political actors and institutions. Agencies with relatively low political standing may be dependent on the support of Congress or the president in order to function adequately, thus running the risk of allowing others to dominate their decisions. Those with higher standing or stronger backing from other supporters are better able to stand on their own in relation to Capitol Hill and the White House. These generalizations also hold true in state and local politics.

Third, the acquisition and exercise of bureaucratic power are frequently characterized by conflicts among agencies over program *jurisdiction*, the area of responsibility assigned to an agency by Congress or the president. The study of **bureaucratic imperialism**, that is, the tendency of agencies to expand their program responsibilities, suggests that such expansionism arises because

bureaucratic imperialism

the tendency of agencies to try to expand their program responsibilities.

administrative politicians need to maintain a sufficient power base for their agencies. "*Power is organized around constituency and constituency around jurisdiction.*"[41] In their quest for "sufficient power," bureaucratic agencies seek support from permanent and semi-permanent coalitions of constituency groups—that is, **interest groups**—which in turn are organized to pursue policy objectives of their own. To secure backing from such groups, administrative agencies must manage government programs of interest to these potentially supportive constituencies. Thus, agencies always seek to obtain control over programs that have strong support from influential constituencies. Bureaucratic imperialism, however, is neither universal nor automatic; for example, an agency may deny, in its own interests, that it has legal authority to exercise powers within some specified "unpopular" area of jurisdiction. The point is not that agencies are inherently imperialistic or non-imperialistic but rather that an agency's decisions regarding program jurisdiction usually take into account potential repercussions. Thus, conflicts over agency jurisdiction are serious contests for political power.

> **interest groups**
>
> private organizations representing a portion (usually small) of the general adult population; they exist in order to pursue particular public policy objectives and seek to influence government activity so as to achieve their objectives.

Finally, governmental institutions, including administrative agencies, play at least two roles in the exercise of power and decision-making authority. These roles overlap but are conceptually distinct and can sometimes conflict. On the one hand, institutions may act as *unified entities* seeking to maximize their influence and their share of available political rewards and benefits. On the other hand, government institutions also serve as *arenas of political competition*, within which various forces contend for dominant influence in decision-making processes. This is especially evident in Congress, where rival political coalitions are frequently in noisy dispute over well-publicized issues. Media reports that "Congress voted today to . . ." really mean that a majority coalition was successfully formed on a given vote. Also at issue every time Congress makes a decision is control of the way the question is presented, possible amendments, use of numerous tactics to speed up or delay consideration, and other tactical questions. There is far less visible conflict in the bureaucracy than in Congress, but this pattern of conflict resolution is much the same, complete with conflict over shaping the issue, moving it along or foot-dragging, and so forth. Like Congress, the bureaucracy operates within a complex web of political forces and must respond to the external (and frequently internal) pressures brought to bear on the administration of government programs.

Ordinarily, administrative agencies try to strike a manageable balance between, on the one hand, what they *can* and *want to* do to further their own programmatic interests and, on the other, what they *must* do to ensure their survival and prosperity, however that is defined. Achieving such a balance requires a willingness to compromise, a sure instinct for deciding when to seek a larger or smaller share of the pie, and an ability to read both long- and short-term political forecasts accurately. In addition to those internal skills, however, an agency must first have and maintain the two crucial foundations or sources of bureaucratic power mentioned earlier: expertise in the subject matter of its program responsibilities and political support. Let us consider each of these in turn.

Foundations of Power: Bureaucratic Expertise and Political Support

One of the major foundations of bureaucratic power is the collective expertise an agency can bring to bear on programs for which it is responsible. As various facets of society have become more complex and interdependent and as technological advances have followed one another with astounding speed, the people with know-how—the experts—have acquired increasing influence because of their specialized knowledge. Government is obviously subject to the same forces as the rest of society; this is especially true of particular governmental functions such as intelligence gathering that are uniquely affected by technological change. As a result, government experts now play larger roles in numerous public-policy decisions.

Political scientist Francis Rourke has suggested that the influence of experts rests on five major components: (1) full-time attention by experts to a problem or subject-matter area; (2) specialization in the subject; (3) a monopoly on information in the subject area that, if successfully maintained by only one staff of experts, makes these specialists indispensable in any decision making involving their subject; (4) a pattern of increasing reliance on bureaucratic experts for technical advice; and (5) increasing control by experts of bureaucratic discretion.[42]

The last three of these components deserve discussion. Although a monopoly on information is desirable from a particular agency's point of view, it is rarely achieved in practice. This is partly because no single agency controls all governmental sources of information on any given subject, partly because government does not control all information sources in society, and partly because information—itself a source of power and influence—is the subject of intense interagency competition. Thus, when expert staff members have a monopoly on information relevant to making a given decision, their influence increases. Conversely, influence can be more effectively contested when there is greater diversity of information sources.[43]

Reliance on expert advice, although on the increase, is not without limits; the influence of experts, therefore, is similarly constrained. Not every agency decision revolves around technical criteria or data. Even when an issue does involve technical data, top-level administrators, for political or other reasons, may prefer a decision that is not the best according to technical criteria (see Chapter 5). Thus, in many agencies, expert advisers play a role that, although important and influential, also has its limitations.

Two aspects of the experts' increasing control of bureaucratic discretion are worth noting. First, by exercising discretion, an expert maximizes the ability to decide just how vigorously or casually to implement the public policies over which the agency has jurisdiction. Second, bureaucratic discretion enables agency experts to influence policy decisions by defining the decisional alternatives from which higher-level officials choose the course to be followed. To the extent that responsible policy makers permit bureaucratic experts to define available alternatives, they strengthen the experts' influence through the power to decide what is and is not included among the alternatives presented to those policy makers.

Experts possess another useful resource: their ability to employ the language of their respective trades, speaking in terms and concepts unfamiliar to most of us. This use of **specialized language** (some might call it *jargon*) has become a common phenomenon among experts inside and outside of government, and poses problems for the layman who seeks to understand complex developments and issues. By using jargon, bureaucratic experts make it very difficult for others to challenge them on their own territory, so to speak; if we cannot fathom what they have proposed, how can we argue against it? This resource, moreover, has been greatly enhanced by the fact that, in countless cases, proposals put forward by experts have yielded very positive and beneficial results. This combination of obscurity of means and clarity of results can help to strengthen the position and influence of experts in government agencies.

specialized language

technical vocabulary used by bureaucratic agencies, one effect of which is to restrict access and outside influence.

In recent years, however, the obscurity of means that previously was a source of strength for experts has contributed to growing public disenchantment with big government, bureaucracy, public employee unions and experts in general, especially as salaries and fringe benefits in the private sector have declined. With the increasing desire for broader public involvement in decision making has come a greater unwillingness to take the experts' word and a more insistent demand that experts make clear to the general public exactly what they are doing, proposing, and advocating. In the long run, public reactions and attitudes may have more effect on the influence and power of government experts than any characteristics or actions of the experts themselves.

Political support for an administrative agency has a number of key dimensions. First and foremost, the legislature is a major potential source of support that must be carefully and continuously cultivated. In most instances, an agency derives its principal backing from one subdivision (usually a committee or subcommittee with authority to fund and oversee the agency's operations) rather than from the legislature as a whole. Most agencies are faced with the task of continually generating and maintaining the support of committees, subcommittees, and even individual legislators. They attempt to do this in a number of ways, including (1) responding promptly to requests for information, (2) effectively promoting and managing programs in which legislators are known to have an interest, (3) cooperating administratively with legislators' electoral needs, and (4) anticipating legislative preferences regarding the operations of particular programs.

A second major source of support is the executive branch, which is composed of the president, governor, or mayor and other administrators and agencies formally lodged in the executive hierarchy. Executive influence can be decisive in determining success or failure, and an agency will make every effort to win favor in both the short and long run. An important corollary of presidential or vice presidential backing at the national level is favorable reviews of agency budget requests by the Office of Management and Budget (OMB), which molds the executive-branch budget proposals submitted to Congress each year. Although the OMB does not itself allocate funds to the agencies, its support can enable an agency to concentrate on persuading Congress (which does hold the purse strings) to back its programs financially. The best position for an agency to be in is one in which its programmatic responsibilities have a high priority on presidential policy agendas year in and year out, but few agencies enjoy this kind of support. Far more common is a pattern in which agencies and their programs compete for support and settle for a "win some, lose some" record. Support for an agency can be earned by giving stronger agency support to programs that are consistent with the current administration's policy priorities; by sharing, at least on the surface, chief-executive concerns about how programs are managed; and by avoiding public conflict with the chief executive over policy and program priorities.

A second means of acquiring executive-branch support is by allying with another agency or agencies in quest of common objectives. Such interagency alliances tend to be limited in scope and duration because most agencies are very protective of their program jurisdictions and there is an element of risk that a cooperating agency might also be a potential rival. An example of such a bureaucratic alliance is the periodic coalition formed by the military services in opposition to cuts in defense appropriations, even as each is contending with the others for a greater share of the fiscal pie. But these are occasional alliances brought about by specific and passing needs; they do not usually outweigh more enduring differences among agencies. In sum, although cooperation with other agencies may indeed be a means of acquiring support, it has its limitations. The agencies with which cooperation would be most logical in terms of programmatic interest are the very ones with the greatest potential for conflict over jurisdictional responsibilities.

A third major source of support is constituent or clientele groups that depend on the agency for satisfaction of their policy demands. These interest groups represent an organized expression of political opinion by a portion—usually a small one—of the adult population.[44] They tend to be groups directly affected by the agency's operations, which therefore have a tangible stake in its policy decisions, rule making, or programmatic output. The political relationship that usually develops between an agency and such a group is one of *reciprocity*, in which each has some political commodity from which the other can benefit. The agency's greatest strength is its expertise and the control it exercises over particular government programs that are of interest to the group. In turn, the group has political resources that it makes available to the agency in return for agency attention to its needs and desires. The group may provide linkages to other influential individuals and groups, help the agency sell its program to Congress and the president, or aid the agency in anticipating changes in the political environment that would present problems or provide opportunities.[45]

Administrative agencies often have more than one constituent group, creating both advantages and disadvantages. A principal advantage is that, with multiple sources of support, an agency can operate more effectively in the political process without having to rely too heavily on any one source of assistance. A corresponding disadvantage stems from the fact that various clientele groups often have differing interests, which lead them to demand different things from an agency or to demand the same things but not in the same order of priority. Not infrequently, an agency faces a situation in which satisfying one group's preferences will seriously interfere with its ability to satisfy those of another. An agency must also deal with Congress as a whole or a specific committee as though it were a clientele group with demands and expectations that must be satisfied. An agency is well advised to consider congressional clientele groups as among its most important, especially when it is confronted with conflicting sets of demands. In other words, it is unwise to regularly disregard the demands of Congress, even if this means making other (private) clientele groups unhappy. In state politics, agencies are frequently tied even more closely to private interest groups. When the governor has somewhat limited formal powers or informal influence, or when the state legislature is relatively passive or weak, support from interest groups is often the greatest (and sometimes the only) source of strength for an administrative agency. Even in states with strong governors and legislatures—such as New York, California, Illinois, and Michigan—the support of key interest groups can benefit an agency significantly.[46]

For example, the Illinois Agricultural Association, the state component of the American Farm Bureau Federation, is a vital source of political strength for the state Department of Agriculture; in California, farm organizations help sustain both the Department of Agriculture and the Department of Water Resources. In return, these agencies are expected to advocate and defend the interests of their supporters, such as irrigation for California's farmers. These relationships often become at least semipermanent.

One other aspect of agency–clientele relationships is quite important. Administrative organizations cherish, and thus strive to maintain, their control over particular programs. Sometimes, however, an agency may have to give up some of this control to outside influences, such as legislators or private clientele groups, in return for continuing political support. If this surrender is temporary, an agency loses little and may gain a great deal in the long run. If the agency fails to regain control, however, it is said to have undergone co-optation, whereby a set of outside interests acquires the ability to influence the agency's long-term policies. If this happens, all the agency's substantive policies may be subject to influence, not just those of most direct concern to the outside group or groups.

A fourth source of political support or opposition for an administrative agency is the general public. The potential influence of the unorganized public is great; if mobilized and concentrated on a particular issue, such as public employee salaries and benefits, public opinion can decisively tilt the political balance of power in one direction. The problem for any stakeholder is to mobilize the public successfully, which is no easy task. Ordinarily, most Americans pay scant attention to public issues unless and until the issues affect them personally. The public's attention can be directed to a pending major policy decision, and feelings about it can be aroused. Expression of public opinion can force a decision to be made—for example, withdrawing troops from an unpopular war, combat environmental pollution, and taking steps to reduce government budget deficits. Without broad public demand and backing, these policy directions could not have been proposed or sustained through the political process. In short, public support can be a valuable political asset to strengthen the positions of those in government. Numerous public-opinion studies have suggested that, when the general public has strong feelings on a matter of importance to large numbers of people, the governmental response is usually consistent with those feelings. An agency supported by broad public opinion can, by using public sentiment, generate support for itself and its programs.

In political terms, an agency's overall success can best be achieved by controlling its programmatic responsibilities while simultaneously maintaining adequate support for its operations. This must be accomplished without making any of the agency's clientele groups seriously dissatisfied with the way it is performing its functions. This is far from easy to do, and it is the exception rather than the rule when an agency succeeds on all fronts. More frequent is the pattern of agency adaptation to, and accommodation of, particularly strong interests. Political backing can usually be obtained in sufficient strength to outweigh any losses incurred by diminished program support among weaker clientele groups.

Bureaucrats, Interest Groups, and Politicians: Subsystem Politics in America

There are certain important parallels between the national government bureaucracy and the U.S. Congress. These institutions have three features in common that are important in this context. First, within both, there is a well-established pattern of division of labor; that is, the work to be done is divided among numerous smaller, specialized units. In Congress, these units are the committees and subcommittees of each chamber; in the bureaucracy, they are the multitude of bureaus, staffs, branches, and divisions that make up larger executive agencies. Second, the divisions within both Congress and the bureaucracy are organized primarily according to function and deal with general areas of policy concern, such as education, housing, labor, or defense. Third, the specialized nature of these smaller units is the principal source of their influence in the policy-making process.

It is a pervasive unwritten rule of Washington political life that, all other things being equal, larger institutions defer to the judgments of their more specialized units. This pattern of regularized respect for experts means that, in the great majority of cases, these units tend to be focal points of important decision making. In Congress, although bills passed by the full House and Senate must be identical, committee proposals usually form the core of bills that are eventually passed. Amendment of committee proposals is possible, but the initial form of legislation carries some weight, and key committee and subcommittee members often influence the entire process of deliberation in the full chamber. In the bureaucracy, specialized personnel (the experts described earlier) wield considerable influence in the formulation of proposals that make their way up the formal hierarchical ladder (and to Congress as well) and into the daily processes of program implementation.

In short, it is misleading to assume that influence is concentrated only "at the top" in either Congress or the bureaucracy. The fine details of lawmaking, and of legislative oversight of executive departments, are the responsibility of subject-matter committees and subcommittees of Congress, each assigned jurisdiction over particular administrative agencies and their programs. Only rarely do such matters engage the attention of the full House or Senate. Similarly, the nuts and bolts of administration are normally concentrated in the lower levels of government organizations, not at the top or even very near it. Thus, in the broad picture of policy making in Washington, there is a high degree of fragmentation, with many small centers of influence operating in their respective areas of expertise.

Plainly, bureaucratic expertise is a source of bureaucratic power. Members of Congress also seek to become specialized, for two reasons. First, they are encouraged to do so by constituent interests on the grounds that this is the best route to influence in Congress. Second, they quickly recognize that by becoming influential they can do more for their voters back home. For sound political reasons, most seek to join and eventually lead congressional committees that have jurisdiction over areas of public policy affecting their electoral constituencies. For example, a representative from a constituency with sizable concentrations of low-income and minority groups in a large city would be likely to seek assignment to the Financial Services Committee (especially its subcommittee on Housing and Community Opportunity), or perhaps to the Education and the Workforce Committee; these deal directly with the problems of urban constituents. Likewise, a senator from a state with a major port or a rail transportation center would cherish a seat on the Commerce, Science, and Transportation Committee. And so it goes, all through Congress.

Obviously, members of Congress do not always get their first choices of assignment. But in pursuit of their own electoral fortunes and policy objectives, legislators are attracted to those committees in which they can have the most impact in policy areas that interest them personally and in which they can maximize their influence in support of **constituency** interests that could be decisive in their reelection bids. (Note that this implies selective attention to constituency interests, often focusing on objectives and preferences of influential friends and allies before—or at the expense of—objectives and preferences of others less powerful who live in the same constituency.) This naturally leads to increased contact between legislators and others interested in the same policy areas; administrators in agencies with jurisdiction over relevant programs; interest groups that, even more than legislators or bureaucrats, have specialized interests at the core of their existence and activities; and other members of Congress with one or more similar public-policy interests.

Interest Groups and "Iron Triangles"

This coalition of shared specialized interests produces the potential for pooling political resources by individuals and small groups in different parts of the policy-making arena in order to achieve common purposes. Hundreds of quiet, informal alliances have grown up in this manner, with the term *policy subsystem*—or simply *subsystem*—used to describe them.

What is a **subsystem**? It is defined here as any political alliance uniting some members of an administrative agency, a congressional committee or subcommittee, and an interest group with shared values and preferences in the same substantive area of public-policy making (see Figure 2–1). Subsystems are informal alliances or coalitions that link individuals in different parts of the formal policy structure.[47] Their members usually have some influence in the policy-making process, in part because of their formal or official positions—bureau chief, committee or subcommittee chair, or committee member. The essential strength of a subsystem, however, lies in its ability to combine the benefits of bureaucratic expertise, congressional leverage, and interest group capabilities in organizing and communicating the opinions of those most concerned with a particular public issue. All subsystems have that potential; some, of course, are far more powerful than others.

One example of a very influential subsystem is the medical-industrial complex, composed of doctors, hospitals, insurance companies, pharmaceuticals and medical equipment manufacturers, the U.S. Department of Health and Human Services staff, influential members of House and Senate health and social affairs committees, and each chamber's appropriations subcommittee on Medicare and Social Security expenditures. Parallel executive departments, private insurers, health care professionals, and legislators at the state

constituency

any group or organization interested in the work and actions of a given official, agency, or organization, and a potential source of support for it; also, the interests (and sometimes geographic area) served by an elected or appointed public official.

subsystem

in the context of American politics (especially at the national level), any political alliance uniting some members of an administrative agency, a legislative committee or subcommittee, and an interest group according to shared values and preferences in the same substantive area of policy making; sometimes called an **iron triangle.**

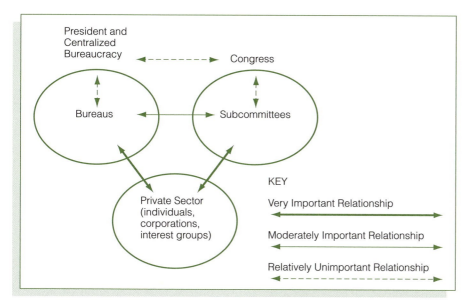

Source: Randall B. Ripley and Grace A. Franklin, *Congress, the Bureaucracy, and Public Policy,* 5th ed. (Pacific Grove, Calif.: Brooks/Cole, 1991), p.102.

and local government level are also active stakeholders in this subsystem. The presence in this subsystem of large industries supplying hospital and medical equipment, prescription drugs, and public health care assistance to the poor (through Medicaid) and the elderly (through Medicare) significantly expands the number of affiliated legislators. Numerous public and private interest groups, such as the American Medical Association (AMA), the AARP (formerly known as the American Association of Retired Persons), and the American Hospital Association (AHA), direct their lobbying efforts toward key members of congressional committees.[48] Members of these committees are not the only legislators who might belong to a subsystem; other legislators may belong to a subsystem in order to advocate the interests of their constituencies.

Another example of a very powerful subsystem is the "highway lobby." Members of the House Public Works and Transportation Committee, officials of the Bureau of Public Roads, and such powerful interest groups as auto manufacturers, auto workers' unions, long-distance truckers, tire companies and their unions, road contractors and their unions, and oil companies and their unions, as well as members of Congress from these groups' states, have a common interest in maintaining and expanding highway usage as well as discouraging mass transit. States represented in this subsystem include (among others) Michigan, Missouri, California, Texas, and Oklahoma, and some key legislators come from those states. It is not surprising, then, that Congress has only reluctantly allocated funds collected from gasoline and road taxes to be used for the expansion of mass-transit systems. This political subsystem ardently opposes gasoline tax increases as a source of federal, state, or local government revenue. Not surprisingly, these same groups opposed a temporary *reduction* in the gasoline tax in order to relieve consumer complaints about the high costs of fuel.

Subsystem activity tends to remain behind the scenes. Policy decisions are reached in a spirit of friendly, quiet cooperation among various interested and influential persons; many of their decisions turn out to be key. Bureaucrats derive considerable benefit from this arrangement because they can usually count on adequate support both from inside government (Congress) and from outside (interest groups). Sometimes referred to as the **iron triangle**, the three-sided relationship (Figure 2–1) allows any one component of the subsystem to activate an effort toward common objectives with the full cooperation of the others. Unless challenged from outside—by other subsystems, the media, or perhaps the president—a subsystem is often able to dominate a policy-making arena.

Admittedly, however, even a strong subsystem cannot ignore the possibility that rivals may emerge. For example, the powerful tobacco lobby has lost considerable influence in the continuing controversies over required health warnings on cigarette packages, payments for the health care of individuals afflicted with smoking-related illnesses, and sales of its products to teenagers; similarly, automobile emission controls, fleet mileage requirements, and air bags were imposed over the objections of auto manufacturers. Under routine circumstances, however, subsystems, including their administrative supporters, exercise decisive influence in the policy-making process.

Several changes in the environment of subsystem politics have become increasingly noticeable, especially in the past dozen years. One is the process by which House and Senate leaders refer a bill to more than one congressional committee; this is known as **multiple referral**.[49] Whereas the Senate requires unanimous consent for such a step (a rare occurrence in that chamber), the practice has become more common in the House. The chamber leadership may refer bills *jointly* (that is, concurrently) to two or more committees; a referral may be *sequential*, going first to one committee, then to another; or a *split* referral may occur, with different parts of the same bill being considered by different committees. One effect of multiple referrals is to strengthen the influence of the chamber's leaders (the Speaker of the House and the Senate majority leader), at the expense of committee—and therefore subsystem—control over the decision-making process regarding a particular bill. Therefore, to the extent that multiple referrals become even more common—which is, of course, uncertain—subsystem influence might be reduced still further.

There are other developments that, like multiple referrals, point to a continued weakening of subsystems as pressures rise for more sharply focused, and therefore more *centrally directed*, congressional responses to a wide variety of policy challenges. One such challenge most evident in debates over

iron triangle

see **subsystem.**

multiple referral

a legislative tactic that has strengthened the power of Congress over policy subsystems.

budgetary issues is the increasing influence of votes in the full chamber rather than in subcommittees and committees. Another challenge, which was especially noticeable in the weeks of **gridlock** between President Clinton and the Republican-controlled Congress in late 1995, resulted in the increased use of what one observer calls special crisis-focused leadership summits. These are also employed at the expense of committee influence in shaping both decision agendas and decisions themselves. Finally, the role of **partisanship** in congressional decision making has become a great deal more prominent in recent years. This indicates that members of Congress may be subject to stronger pressures to respond to *party* rather than to *committee* leaders, thus weakening members' committee and subsystem decision-making roles. This pattern of congressional decision making has been especially apparent since the Republicans regained control of the House of Representatives in 2011.

For several reasons, the influence of similar alliances is often less extensive in state and local policy making, even taking into account the changes in national politics just discussed. First, in many state legislatures, individual committees do not have the same degree of independent standing or jurisdictional control over policy areas that U.S. congressional committees have. Policy making is more centralized in the hands of legislative leaders, making any interest group relationship with an individual committee less productive. Second, in many states and localities, the policy-making process is dominated by less diverse groups than is the case nationally and the process lacks the intense competitiveness for access, influence, and power that characterizes Washington politics. Therefore, the necessity to develop close working relations with an individual committee or agency is not as great. Third, especially in local government, the policy process is not only less visible but much more informal than at the national level. For many established interest groups (particularly the stronger ones), there are fairly regular opportunities for consultation on policy preferences, so that the influence of these groups is often felt throughout local government, not in just one part of it. Thus, though some elements of subsystem politics can be found in state and local governments, the general patterns identifiable in the national policy process do not operate to the same extent on other governmental levels.

"Issue Networks" and Subsystems: Similarities and Differences

Subsystem politics has been the subject of informed discussion since the late 1950s. Several observers have noted still another pattern of interaction developing in the policy process: the phenomenon of so-called **issue networks**, which, like subsystems, involve a variety of political actors attempting jointly to influence the course of public policy. Unlike subsystems, however, issue networks are more open and fluid groupings of individuals both inside and

gridlock

derived from term referring to traffic that is so congested that cars cannot move; government is so divided that no consistent policy direction can be established.

partisanship

political-party pressures on elected members of Congress, state legislature, or local boards and commissions.

issue networks

in the context of American politics (especially at the national level), open and fluid groupings of various political actors (in and out of government) attempting to influence policy; "shared-knowledge" groups having to do with some aspect or problem of public policy; lacking in the degree of permanence, commonality of interests, and internal cohesion characteristic of subsystems.

outside of government. In political scientist Hugh Heclo's words, an issue network is "a *shared-knowledge* group having to do with some aspect [or problem] of public policy"[50]—but without the degree of permanence characteristic of subsystem alliances. Such a "floating" network may exist only when a policy question emerges that activates a wide range of interests; members of the network may not deal with one another regularly outside their network contacts; and, significantly, they may not agree on the nature of the policy problem or on possible solutions to it. In all these respects, issue networks differ from subsystems.

Examples of issue networks include the various groups and public officials involved in specific policies, such as those dealing with AIDS research. These include university medical research departments, state medical associations, hospitals and hospital organizations, U.S. Public Health Service personnel, and nutrition specialists, among others. Also involved are homosexuals in the military, Department of Defense program managers, gay rights groups, and civil rights groups interested in preventing discrimination and ensuring benefits to dependents of military personnel. In these examples, many of the participants could not reach even general agreement on policy directions merely by activating the network. Rather, once a policy question was perceived as affecting a broad range of interests, groups and individuals advocating those interests jumped into the fray over policy development, thus creating the network as a means of addressing the policy issues at hand.[51]

The foundation of shared knowledge that unites network participants often does not lead to the creation of a "shared-action" coalition or a "shared-belief" (conventional interest) group. Like subsystems, such networks function with relative autonomy but, unlike subsystems, they are rarely controlled in a well-organized way, or even with agreement on policy content among the principals involved. Thus, issue networks contribute further and in somewhat new ways to the fragmentation present in national policy making. The expansion of Internet blogs and social networking has led to an increase in the number of issue networks and shared-knowledge groups.

Bureaucratic Power and Political Accountability

To what extent can bureaucracy be held accountable for what it does or fails to do? The political accountability of a bureaucracy is enforced through multiple channels, both legislative and executive. Political interests in the legislature and in the executive branch are frequently at odds with one another, making it, at best, difficult to enforce accountability consistently or effectively. The situation is made more complex by the fact that most bureaucracies operate under joint authority delegated by both the chief executive and the legislative branch and have considerable discretion to make independent choices. The difficulty is further compounded by the hybrid systems of personnel management found in different parts of the executive hierarchy in the national government and in many states and localities. Frequently, top-echelon executives owe their positions to appointment through political channels, but the bulk of their subordinates are hired and usually retained through job-competence-related merit procedures. In state and local government, the mix of political and merit employees in a bureaucracy varies widely, and the presence of public-employee unions and collective bargaining raises other issues of conflicting political and bureaucratic accountability.

Another factor limiting accountability is the inability of top executives to command wholehearted responses from administrative subordinates. A substantial portion of the work of top executives is inspecting, monitoring, and overseeing the activities of their staffs to bring about as much congruence as possible between executive directives and the performance of agencies. In particular, the executive operates under severe handicaps in this effort. Because of time constraints, the necessity of concentrating on a limited number of general policy priorities, and the complexity of administrative operations, a considerable proportion of bureaucratic activity escapes close examination by the state house or the White House. Furthermore, as noted by the late journalist David Broder, subsystems represent "powerful centrifugal forces" in the nation's capital. Broder wrote: "The interest groups that benefit from specific programs, the agency bureaucracies that run those programs, and the congressional subcommittee members and staffs who create, finance, and oversee those programs are *tenaciously resistant to directives from the president.*"[52] Thus, the task of holding bureaucracy accountable for its actions assumes formidable proportions.

Bureaucratic accountability implies several things. First, in a legal and constitutional sense, it implies that a political entity—in this case, the bureaucracy—is not beyond the control of other entities in a checks-and-balances system or, ultimately, beyond reach of the consent of the governed. Also, accountability implies that, to the extent that such an entity exercises delegated authority and discretion in decision making (as bureaucracy certainly does), it also has some responsibility to adhere to the broad will of the governed, however that will has been expressed. This also assumes that the "public will" and the achievement of accountability can be defined.

Although it may be possible in theory to define these concepts and circumstances, in practice it is difficult to do so with certainty or finality. One approach is to interpret election results as reflecting the will of the majority and to define bureaucratic accountability as responsiveness to the chief executive (president, governor, mayor), who is dominant in setting policy directions and standards. Opponents of a given chief executive or of executive power in general would resist such definition, however, looking instead to legislatures and sometimes to the judiciary to lay out broad guidelines for measuring bureaucratic accountability. Political conflict over criteria of accountability ensures less than complete adherence to whatever standards prevail at a particular time.

Bureaucratic accountability

principles of political accountability applied in an effort to control bureaucratic power.

Therefore, it is not simply a matter of bureaucracy being or not being "accountable." Rather, bureaucracy and all other institutions of government can be accountable only to officials or to institutions *outside* themselves. Furthermore, the question, *to whom for what?* must also be answered in meaningful ways for a discussion of program evaluation methods and techniques. Also, the bureaucracy cannot be viewed as a whole; its many subparts have institutional bases, lives, and priorities of their own. All these factors act as constraints on the political accountability of bureaucratic power.

Is it impossible, then, to speak in practical terms of accountability? No, it is not. Allowing for limitations such as those just outlined, it is possible not only to prescribe in theory but to describe in fact some forms and aspects of accountability that characterize political relationships between bureaucracy and other parts of the U.S. polity—although these, too, have their limitations.

First, both the president and Congress have many instruments of control at their disposal. The president's arsenal includes (1) powers of appointment and dismissal, restricted to the very top positions, which give him or her the ability to staff key leadership posts in the executive branch; (2) considerable initiative in lawmaking, which helps shape the legislative environment surrounding bureaucratic implementation of congressional enactments (this includes congressional delegation of authority to the president to formulate rules and regulations under which the bureaucracy functions); (3) by exercising power through the Executive Office of the President (EOP), presidents can make known their preferences and intentions to the bureaucracy, directly and indirectly; (4) specific entities of the EOP, notably the White House Office and the Office of Management and Budget (OMB), which carry the full prestige of the presidency when they interact with the bureaucracy and, in the case of OMB, can exert financial leverage that can be persuasive; (5) access to the mass media, through which presidents can generate favorable or unfavorable publicity; (6) power to initiate bureaucratic restructuring, an unwelcome course of action for most agencies though, in the past, it has been used sparingly (see the comments earlier in this chapter regarding structure, jurisdiction, and clientele politics); and at the state level (7) the **line-item veto**, a favorite way for conservatives to trim budgets. Shrewd presidents have used these instruments to win support for their initiatives, though the process often requires significant expenditure of political capital. In general, governors, local executives, and state and local legislatures have less extensive powers over their bureaucracies.

Congress also has many tools at its disposal with which to conduct legislative oversight of administration.[53] These include (1) appropriations power, the classic power of the purse, and the implied (sometimes real) threat that it can represent to an agency's fiscal well-being; (2) power to conduct legislative postaudits of agency spending and program effectiveness through the Government Accountability Office (GAO), headed by the comptroller-general

---

line-item veto

a constitutional power available to more than forty of America's governors with which they may disapprove a specific expenditure item within an appropriations bill instead of having to accept or reject the entire bill.

and operating under the direction of Congress; (3) hearings before congressional committees in which bureaucrats may have to answer very specifically for their actions (most notably during budget hearings before appropriations committees and subcommittees); and (4) occasional devices such as senatorial confirmation of presidential appointees and special committee investigations. These are not perfect instruments, but they do afford Congress many opportunities to look into details of bureaucratic activities and to maintain a degree of control over the administrative apparatus.

Partly because of bureau–clientele ties, a number of studies have questioned whether legislative oversight—as currently conducted—is even minimally effective as a means of holding bureaucracies accountable to the political system at large. The core concern of those raising this possibility is that changes within Congress itself have produced a markedly reduced capacity for congressional supervision of administrative activities. These changes include an emphasis on wider participation by members of Congress in policy-making processes, a resultant dispersion of power within Congress from its standing committees to much more numerous, and more autonomous, subcommittees, and a tendency to devote more of their time to constituent services or **casework** in pursuit of their own reelection. Casework provides a form of "feedback" between citizen and legislator, and may assist in the early identification of problems with government programs. There has also emerged a generalized pattern of behavior in which legislators regularly call on administrative agencies (and their clientele groups) to facilitate the rendering of services to the public. Administrative agencies benefit during the appropriations process from effectively responding to members' requests for service to their constituents.

casework

refers to services performed by legislators and their staff on behalf of constituents.

Formal responsibility for legislative oversight has also passed from full committees to subcommittees but, although more hearings have been held and more pages filled with testimony, the net effect has been one of less effective oversight. This is attributable to members of Congress simultaneously becoming (1) more dependent on agencies and interest groups as they call on these groups for increased constituent service and (2) less inclined to "challenge the existing relationships between agencies and interest groups" and, thus, "less likely to investigate agencies' implementation of policy unless that implementation flies in the face of these major interest groups."[54]

If congressional supervision of the bureaucracy via subcommittees is indeed less reliable now than in the past, bureaucratic autonomy may be greater than is ideal. We might describe this pattern and others like it as cases in which the *micro-institutions* (committees and subcommittees) within Congress are unable or unwilling to hold agencies accountable for their actions. But it appears that, as a *macro-institution*, Congress is also rather limited in its oversight capabilities. This limitation exists principally because legislators often lack incentive to use available oversight instruments (and frequently have incentive not to use them) and because some instruments of congressional control have proved to be fairly "weak reeds." This is especially true with regard to appropriations: individual members jealously guard their own capacities for largesse but fail to oversee expenditures as a whole.[55] This is perhaps testimony to the strength of our commitment to the concept of checks and balances and to separation of powers, and also to our long-standing belief that Congress is obligated to use a variety of instruments to ensure that laws are faithfully executed by administrative agencies.

In sum, although there may be telling weaknesses in legislative oversight of government bureaucracies, they are not beyond remedy, and there may be alternative means of supervising administrative agencies. This discussion highlights one aspect of the situation that merits explicit emphasis: If we are not content with administrative agencies' behavior, we might do well to pressure Congress to make the desired changes. Indeed, one authoritative observer argues that Congress has already strengthened its own oversight capacity, leading to congressional oversight that is more consistent and effective than many seem to believe.[56] In any event, as political scientist Morris Fiorina notes, "United States congressmen gave us the Washington establishment. Ultimately, only they can take it away."[57]

Some other mechanisms of accountability also exist. Bureaucracies are legally accountable to the courts for their observance of individual rights and liberties, whether in their investigative capacities (especially where regulatory agencies are concerned) or in the course of routine administrative activities. In this respect, they hardly differ from the president and Congress, in that the courts have the ultimate say in defining acceptable legal boundaries of governmental behavior. It is symptomatic of the growth of the bureaucracy and of its impact on our national life that the most rapidly expanding area of court litigation has been in administrative law, in which cases arise out of administrative rules and regulations and their application to individuals, groups, and public and private enterprises (see Chapter 11).

Accountability is hampered by the prevalence of technical subject matter in government decision making. In many respects, this limits the potential for accountability to policy experts capable of understanding an issue and the implications of different proposed solutions. A case in point is energy policy, where one thing that stands out is a need for more and better information for decision maker and citizen alike. Few among us comprehend all the intricacies of supply and demand for electrical power, natural-gas pricing, the politics of oil supply here and abroad, and so on. If we the people cannot monitor corporate or government actions, who can be held accountable for them? There is no easy answer.

Accountability also is made more difficult by the fact that administrators must frequently face situations in which competing criteria for decisions are very much in evidence. For example, it has been noted that, in allocating public housing, there are contradictory goals that create conflicts in the possible approaches to decision making: *equity* (treating like cases alike on the basis of rules) and *responsiveness* (making exceptions for persons whose needs require that rules be stretched). How does one reconcile these desirable but conflicting objectives? By one set standard to which all adhere? By situational ethics? By following dictates based on the kinds of need? Again, there is no single or easy answer. Note, also, that the "equity-responsiveness" tension can be found in numerous other settings as well (for example, personnel management, making grants and loans, and the college or university classroom).

Bureaucratic agencies are also held to account, as part of our constitutional scheme, by the mass media. The news media's interest in bureaucratic activity is founded on a basic premise of free government and on a powerful ethic of American journalism: that a free press, acting in an adversarial relationship to public officials, serves as a watchdog over government actions. In particular, the investigatory potential of the news media makes bureaucracies wary. Part of an agency's strength is good public relations, and adverse publicity resulting from a media investigation—even if unwarranted and even if successfully counteracted—can damage an agency's political standing. Thus, the mere possibility of such an inquiry is enough to prompt most agencies to exercise considerable caution. Increasing numbers of governments, notably state and local institutions, have employed "media consultants" or public relations specialists to handle the volume of such inquiries.

As in the case of bureaucracy–legislature interactions, relationships between administrators and the media are often two-sided. This creates the possibility that the press, far from maintaining a critical and objective perspective, may become involved in continuing relationships, the principal product of which is an ability to publicize agency programs. Under such circumstances, it is still possible for a reporter, editor, or publisher to investigate or critique agency performance. But if an agency official continually provides good copy for a reporter and also provides inside tips or leads on stories that the reporter can take credit for "breaking," it is less likely that an agency will be subjected to the feared spotlight of publicity. This is politics on an intensely interpersonal level, but it can matter a great deal in determining how much and what kind of information will come to public attention about a given agency.[58]

Finally, the advent of the Internet revolution has brought some measure of bureaucratic accountability directly to the public. Although the general populace rarely has direct access to, or control over, a given bureaucratic entity, a widespread public outcry over bureaucrats' actions can have an effect. Ordinarily, this requires public pressure on other divisions of government to get them to restrict the actions of an agency. Such pressure must be sustained over a sufficient period of time and with sufficient intensity to overcome resistance from the agency and its supporters, but it can be done.

Administrative Discretion and Political Accountability: Alternative Perspectives

In discussions of how concerned citizens might hold bureaucrats and their agencies accountable, there is often an implicit assumption that more accountability and control are needed in order to keep these officials in line and that their natural tendency is to go astray unless they are closely watched. There is no question, of course, that, in our system of checks and balances, every government entity (executive, legislative, and judicial) must ultimately be held to account. In recent decades, however, that principle (as applied to administrative agencies) seems to have acquired an additional dimension that is not necessarily accurate. Many people seem to assume—wrongly—that administrative discretion can *only* be abused, at the expense of the public interest, and can serve no useful or constructive purpose. Many also bemoan the fact that neither Congress nor the president is able or willing to control administrative actions fully or effectively. This point of view seems to suggest that elected officials can act only beneficially whereas administrators can be expected to act only in a narrowly focused, inefficient, destructive, and otherwise irresponsible fashion. (Recall Charles Goodsell's remarks about perceived bureaucratic shortcomings compared to the realities, quoted in Chapter 1.) There is, indeed, reason to wonder how much truth there is in this view of discretion.

If exercised positively, administrative discretion has one very positive aspect: program managers are often better able than legislators or judges to make decisions on the basis of the broader public interest—and, according to Wilson's nineteenth-century view, most administrators are capable of doing so most of the time (see Chapter 1). Interference with administrative discretion by congressional restraints and controls actually brings about the kind of narrow responsiveness to private interests that such controls seem designed to prevent. There are two reasons for this. First, interest groups often usurp public power through the manipulation of iron-triangle relationships (see Figure 2–1), exercising considerable influence through both committees and issue networks. Second, as noted previously, legislators are strongly inclined to look after their own policy priorities and constituency interests; in the process, they pressure administrators to conform to their wishes. Thus, it is possible that if oversight of administration is left to legislators acting primarily in their committee roles, the actions taken by administrators may be more narrowly conceived and implemented than would be the case if those same administrators were given more freedom.

This is not, by any means, a call for the complete autonomy of administrators. There is ample reason to be as concerned about "discretionary" abuses of power or fraud or corruption among public administrators as among any other government officials. However, we might do well to place greater implicit faith in administrators than we now do if we want them to be able to act responsibly. Under these circumstances, it would still be possible to hold them ultimately accountable, consistent with our scheme of government and with public expectations for accountability, at least as effectively as we do at the present time.[59]

Summary

Politically, our system of government is a liberal democracy; economically, it is based on free enterprise and capitalism. Throughout our history, key political values have included popular sovereignty, limited government, individualism, and pluralism. We have also emphasized individual liberty and democratic principles such as majority rule, minority rights, and the free exchange of political ideas. Two related concepts—representation and representativeness—have taken on new meanings, leading to definitional uncertainty.

Major objectives of a politically neutral "science of administration" are separation of politics and administration, adherence to scientific management and administrative principles, and, most important, attainment of economy and efficiency in government.

Our political and administrative values, however, are not entirely consistent with each other. One set of values is based on the assumption that individual liberty and the public interest are best served by keeping government restrained—and therefore unable to infringe upon our freedoms. The other set of values, however, is geared toward improving the ability of government agencies to operate efficiently—and also in the public interest. Participation and professionalism often conflict, and it is difficult to incorporate both accountability and access into administrative policy making. Freedom of information and sunshine laws have been enacted to help legislative bodies hold executive-branch agencies accountable. Accountability is made more difficult by the technical subject matter in so much government activity.

Major dimensions of democratic administration include (1) citizen participation, (2) bureaucratic representativeness, (3) responsiveness, and (4) administrative effectiveness as a threat to personal freedoms. Bureaucratic representation is ambiguous, although democratic morality is best served by promoting broadly inclusive representation of interests in interactions among decision makers. Representativeness of women and minorities has increased in the civil service, although with what effects is not entirely clear. Effectiveness of administrative machinery may pose a threat to individual liberties under some circumstances. Concerns about public administration and democratic government include the possible misuse of secrecy, a traditional feature of bureaucracy, to violate the constitutional rights of individual citizens. Recent emphasis has been on the need to protect individual privacy against government invasion and against misuse of personal information. Widening access to the Internet and its capabilities for fraud and identify theft make this an increasingly vital issue for public scrutiny.

Bureaucratic power is exercised in the context of widely dispersed political power. Neither the legislature nor the chief executive has a power base that is consistently strong enough to permit decisive control over the bureaucracy. Administrative agencies build power bases of their own and seek to acquire programs that bring with them constituency support for their activities. Sources of political support include key legislative committees and subcommittees, chief executives and their staffs, other executive agencies (especially those directly under the chief executive), clientele groups that follow agency affairs because of their own interest in the same program areas, the mass media, and the general public, which can occasionally be mobilized on behalf of particular agency objectives.

Subsystem politics in America is built around coalitions that bring together interest group representatives and government officials who share common interests and policy preferences. Because both Congress and the bureaucracy generally divide work among subunits whose expertise they respect, quiet, informal alliances (subsystems) of specialists often dominate their respective policy arenas. Bureaucrats contribute expertise to their subsystems and receive in return an opportunity to share control of a policy area. Promoting accountability of bureaucratic power is not an easy task. Because bureaucracies operate under delegated executive and legislative authority, tight controls from either are difficult to impose, and tight controls from both would be likely to conflict. Accountability suggests that bureaucracy is, or should be, answerable for its actions to other institutions and to the public. This is difficult to put into practice because of the noncentralized nature of both government and bureaucracy. All instruments of accountability have some impact on bureaucratic behavior, but none is perfect. It is also possible that more, not less, administrative discretion would serve the political system well, providing for pursuit of both the broader public interest and administrative accountability.

Discussion Questions

1. What are the basic democratic values that underlie our society? How have they changed in recent years? How have these changes affected public attitudes toward democratic government and public administration?

2. Discuss the political values central to "liberal democracy." In your judgment, which elements stand out as most important? Why? Has the constitutional principle of limited government been lost? Why or why not?

3. Discuss the key problems and issues associated with the value of "representation" in governmental

decision making, including the need for efficient, rational, and neutral policy making by government officials.

4. What is the importance of "citizen participation" as a basic component of democratic administration? Identify and discuss various forms of citizen participation that have been employed over the past three decades to increase access and representation.

5. What steps can be taken to secure and perhaps increase governmental accountability to the people? In your opinion, how effective is each of the devices likely to be? Why?

6. Compare the role played by each of the following in keeping public administration accountable to the public and to elected officials: (a) freedom of information laws, (b) sunshine laws, and (c) sunset laws.

7. In Anytown, U.S.A., a citizens' group is clashing with the city government over the imminent zoning of a large plot of vacant land. (a) Imagine that you are a bureaucrat. At what level of participation would you want the citizens to engage? Why? (b) Imagine that you are an elected official. What level of citizen participation do you favor? Why? (c) Imagine that you are a member of the citizens' group. What level of participation would you want? Why?

8. Discuss how an administrative agency seeking to maximize its political support should manage its clientele group relations. To whom should it look for support? What can it offer to supporters? What should it try to avoid?

9. How do bureaucratic and legislative specializations contribute to the phenomenon of subsystem politics? Explain the power of subsystem politics and how they contribute to the "iron triangle" of mutual responsiveness among administrative agencies, congressional subcommittees, and interest groups.

10. Can bureaucrats and bureaucracies be made accountable? If so, to what extent and to whom? By what means? Why are there no clear-cut answers to these questions? Discuss.

Key Terms and Concepts

liberal democracy, *50*

capitalist system, *50*

popular sovereignty, *50*

limited government, *50*

representation, *51*

representativeness, *51*

affirmative action, *51*

judicial review, *51*

individualism, *52*

pluralism, *52*

due process of law, *53*

representative democracy, *53*

participatory democracy, *53*

pluralist democracy, *57*

administrative efficiency, *58*

accountability, *59*

sunshine laws, *61*

sunset laws, *61*

Freedom of Information Act (1966), *62*

WikiLeaks, *64*

Bureau of Consumer Protection, *64*

community control, *67*

public interest groups (PIGs), *67*

co-optation, *68*

empowerment, *69*

Neo-Conservatives, *72*

USA PATRIOT Act, *73*

Patient Protection and Affordable Care Act of 2010 (PPACA), *74*

Health Care and Education Reconciliation Act (HCERA), *74*

bureaucratic imperialism, *76*

interest groups, *77*

specialized language, *79*

constituency, *84*

subsystem, *84*

iron triangle, *86*

multiple referral, *86*

gridlock, *87*

partisanship, *87*

issue networks, *87*

bureaucratic accountability, *89*

line-item veto, *90*

casework, *91*

Suggested Readings

Behn, Robert. *Rethinking Democratic Accountability*. Washington, D.C.: Brookings Institution Press, 2001.

Berry, Jeffrey M. *The Interest Group Society*. 5th ed. New York: Longman, 2008.

Box, Richard C, ed. *Democracy and Public Administration*. New York: M.E. Sharpe, 2009.

Browne, William P. *Groups, Interests, and U.S. Public Policy*. Washington, D.C.: Georgetown University Press, 1998.

Chandler, Ralph Clark, ed. *A Centennial History of the Administrative State*. New York: Free Press, 1987.

Davidson, Roger H., and Walter J. Oleszek. *Congress and Its Members*. 11th ed Washington, D.C.: CQ Press, 2009.

Fiorina, Morris P. *Congress: Keystone of the Washington Establishment*. 2nd ed. New Haven, Conn.: Yale University Press, 1989.

Garvey, Gerald. *Facing the Bureaucracy: Living and Dying in a Public Agency*. San Francisco: Jossey-Bass, 1993.

Gore, Albert S. *An Assault on Reason*. New York: The Penguin Group, 2007.

Kaufman, Herbert, with the collaboration of Michael Couzens. *Administrative Feedback: Monitoring Subordinates' Behavior*. Washington, D.C.: Brookings Institution, 1973.

Kearns, Kevin P. *Managing for Accountability: Preserving the Public Trust in Public and Non-Profit Organizations*. San Francisco: Jossey-Bass, 1996.

Martin, Roscoe C. *Grass Roots*. Westport, Conn.: Greenwood Publishing Group, 1978.

———, ed. *Public Administration and Democracy*. Syracuse, N.Y.: Syracuse University Press, 1965.

Peters, B. Guy, and J. Pierre, eds. *Handbook of Public Administration*. Thousand Oaks, Calif.: Sage, 2007.

Pfeffer, Jeffrey. *Managing with Power: Politics and Influence in Organizations*. Boston: Harvard Business School Press, 1994.

Riccucci, M. Norma. *Public Administration: Traditions of Inquiry and Philosophies of Knowledge*. Washington, D.C.: Georgetown University Press, 2010.

Redford, Emmette S. *Democracy in the Administrative State*. New York: Oxford University Press, 1969.

Rohr, John A. *To Run a Constitution: The Legitimacy of the Administrative State*. Lawrence, Kans.: University Press of Kansas, 1986.

Rosen, Bernard. *Holding Government Bureaucracies Accountable*. 3rd ed. Westport, Conn.: Greenwood Press, 1998.

Seidman, Harold, and Robert Gilmour. *Politics, Position, and Power: From the Positive to the Regulatory State*. 4th ed. New York: Oxford University Press, 1986.

Sheldon, D. R. *Achieving Accountability in Business and Government*. Westport, Conn.: Quorum Books, 1996.

Smith, Steven S., Jason M. Roberts, and Ryan J. Vander Wielen. *The American Congress*. 5th ed. New York: Cambridge University Press, 2007.

Stillman, Richard J., II, ed. *The American Constitution and the Administrative State: Constitutionalism in the Late 20th Century*. Washington, D.C.: University Press of America, 1989.

Thurber, James A., ed. *Rivals for Power: Presidential-Congressional Relations*. 3rd ed. Lanham, Md.: Rowman & Littlefield, 2005.

Waldo, Dwight. *The Administrative State: A Study of the Political Theory of American Public Administration*. 2nd ed. Piscataway, N.J.: Transaction Publishers, 2006.

Wamsley, Gary L., et al. *Refounding Public Administration*. Thousand Oaks, Calif.: Sage, 1990.

Wood, Dan B., and Richard W. Waterman. *Bureaucratic Dynamics: The Role of Bureaucracy in a Democracy*. Boulder, Colo.: Westview Press, 1994.

Yates, Douglas. *Bureaucratic Democracy: The Search for Democracy and Efficiency in American Government*. Cambridge, Mass.: Harvard University Press, 1982; paperback edition, 1987.

Federalism and Intergovernmental Relations

In the contemporary United States, and contrary to Bill Clinton's 1999 assessment, federalism is most assuredly *not* a "substitute for a sleeping pill." In both the George W. Bush and Barack Obama presidencies, issues concerning the relative authority—and debates about the *proper* authority—of state and national governments have surged to the forefront of our national political dialogue. In early 2009, for example, the Obama administration proposed (and Congress enacted) the **American Recovery and Reinvestment Act** (**ARRA**), which was designed to stimulate new economic activity in the private sector in the midst of a steep recession, and which came with a $787 billion price tag. Many detractors of the president objected, and continue to object, to this assertion of national government authority, which they view as both unprecedented and unjustified. Another instance of debate over national and state authority surfaced in 2010 when Arizona Governor Jan Brewer initiated a restrictive state-level immigration policy, arguing among other things that the national government had not fulfilled its responsibilities to create a nationwide immigration policy. Also in 2010, Texas Governor Rick Perry announced his intention of *not* seeking enactment of state appropriations necessary to implement health care reform in the state. At about the same time, Virginia Attorney General Ken Cuccinelli asserted, as a formal legal doctrine, that the state government can constitutionally prevent the implementation of health care reform legislation within the boundaries of Virginia (a legal doctrine, first articulated in the mid-1800s, known as "nullification," and a key issue leading up to the Civil War of 1861–1865). At a conference of state governors in early 2011, there was considerable debate over the desired amounts of national government aid to state governments, especially within very tight budgets at both levels of government (national and state). Political and policy

> *I think it is quite an interesting thing that we have this impressive array of people to come to a conference on federalism, a topic that probably ten or twenty years ago would have been viewed as a substitute for a sleeping pill.*
>
> Bill Clinton
> Forum of Federation Conference,
> Mont-Tremblant, Canada
> October 8, 1999

American Recovery and Reinvestment Act (ARRA)

an economic stimulus package proposed by President Obama and enacted by the 111th U.S. Congress in February 2009. The stimulus bill was intended to create jobs and promote investment and consumer spending to help recover from recession.

"battle lines" were drawn over such issues, and others like them, suggesting that the nature of U.S. federalism is not merely the subject of abstract or conceptual debate (although it is that, too).

federalism

a constitutional division of governmental power between a central or national government and regional governmental units (such as states), with each having some independent authority over its citizens.

Federalism is a widely recognized feature of American government. The federal system consists of a national government and state governments existing independently of each other in the same territory while commanding the loyalties of the same individuals as citizens of both state and nation. Under the Constitution, the powers of all governments are drawn from the same fundamental source—the sovereign people—and are exercised concurrently. States, in turn, are composed of numerous subjurisdictions, such as cities, counties, municipalities, townships, and special districts, which are dependent entities chartered by the state. The original rationale for establishing a federal system in the United States was to prevent the concentration and misuse of power by a strong national government. The states were viewed as counterweights and protectors of individual liberties against the national government—and many are again coming to view the states in that light.

The nature and operation of federalism have been the subject of much controversy since the founding of the Republic. Referring to our basic governmental structure, former Vice President Al Gore observed that "America was born angry at government. We were so sick of the [distant and insensitive] English crown . . . we quit colonialism before we had something else lined up."[1] Indeed, this nation was later torn by civil war that resulted from conflict over the twin issues of slavery and the extent of the states' authority to oppose the national government. Since the New Deal in the 1930s, and with rising emphasis in the last few years, many Americans (including public officials of both major political parties) have expressed concern about the wide-ranging authority of the national government—perhaps most prominently, in 2009, relating to the economic stimulus package and, in 2010, to financial regulation and health care reform. These concerns focus on, among other things, how the expansion of that authority has affected state and local government powers. In turn, the states' relations with—and influence over—their respective local governments have increased in importance. There have also been growing concerns about citizens' power to retain a significant measure of control over governmental structures at all levels in the federal system.

Public administration is at the heart of many of the questions and controversies that have characterized contemporary federalism. The two have had a reciprocal effect on one another. The administration of national government programs requires recognition of, and accommodation to, the existence, prerogatives, and preferences of states and localities that have their own decision-making apparatus and political majorities. At the same time, the growth of bureaucracy at all levels of government has helped to reshape the federal system.

intergovernmental relations (IGR)

all the activities and interactions occurring between or among governmental units of all types and levels within the U.S. federal system.

In this chapter, our concerns will include (1) the definition of federalism and a brief historical review of its evolution; (2) the rise of **intergovernmental relations (IGR)**, the multitude of formal and informal contacts among governmental entities throughout the federal system, and the ways in which these have modified federalism as a formal concept; (3) the expansion, after 1960, of financial assistance from the national government to states and localities, with accompanying shifts in leverage exerted by the former over the latter, and since 1980, changes in national government aid, together with *reduced* leverage in the hands of national officials for pursuing national goals through state and local action; (4) administrative and political consequences of increased intergovernmental aid, especially administrative complexity and bureaucratic controls accompanying national government grants, and the resulting political conflicts, including a rising public backlash against both government **unfunded mandates** and the professional public administrators responsible for managing intergovernmental programs; (5) growing concern about managing homeland security and antiterrorism initiatives within the existing IGR and grants system; and (6) questions about the future course of IGR, including the impacts of diminished national government fiscal support for many of its own activities as well as those at state and local levels.

unfunded mandates

federal (or state) laws or regulations that impose requirements on other governments, often involving expenditures by affected governments, without providing funds for implementation.

Two comments are in order about key terms in this discussion, namely, *federal* and *federalism*. First, technically, *federal* describes the formal relationships among different levels of government and various qualities or characteristics of those relationships. In a more colloquial sense, however, many people refer to the national government as "the federal government." Such usage, which has roots in debates over ratification of the Constitution in the 1780s, can lead to confused thinking about contemporary federalism and IGR. In this chapter and elsewhere, when reference is made to the *national government*, that is generally the phrase employed; *federal* is used in its more technical sense, for the sake of clarity.

Second, *federalism* has been used to refer to *one variety* of federal practice—namely, with the main emphasis on states and state authority (by implication, at the expense of national government authority). In contrast, when we use the term *federalism* in this chapter and elsewhere, we will be referring to the fundamental distributions of power between national and state governments rather than to any particular version or "brand" of federalism.

The Nature of Federalism: The Formal Setting

The most elementary definition of federalism suggests that it is a *constitutional* division of governmental power between a central or national government and a set of regional units (such as the American states, Canadian provinces, and Swiss cantons); that, under a federal arrangement, both the national and regional governments have some independent as well as some shared powers over their citizens; that neither government owes its legal existence to the other (as local governments in the United States do to the states); and that, as a matter of law, neither may dictate to the other(s) in matters of structural organization, fiscal policies, or definition of essential functions. This definition clearly implies that the regional governments have substantial independence from the national government but that both may exercise powers of government directly over their citizens. It leaves unanswered, however, some pertinent questions about how authority is to be exercised *simultaneously* by different units of government sharing jurisdiction over the same territory and citizenry.

Federalism is also an explicitly *political* arrangement. This relates in important ways to how power in a governmental system is distributed, structured, and exercised. A federal arrangement is designed to restrain and counteract centralized power through multiple centers where decisions are made in widely scattered geographic regions. Such a system, with separate, legitimate, and authoritative government units operating individually within the same overall territory, makes it less likely that a central government could achieve an excessive concentration of power, which might endanger individual freedoms. Finally, federalism has an increasingly important *fiscal/administrative* dimension. This pertains both to the operations of government programs that have impact on at least one other level or unit of government and to the growing complexity and interdependency of programs created, funded, and managed by different governments. Later in this chapter, we will treat the phenomenon of intergovernmental fiscal relations in considerably more detail.

In the early 1800s, the U.S. Supreme Court defined some essential boundaries in national-state relations, with long-term implications. The fundamental issue was the scope of national authority, particularly when it overlapped and conflicted with state powers. Specific questions included whether states could tax national government agencies (they cannot, under *McCulloch v. Maryland*, 4 Wheaton 316 [1819]); whether the national power to regulate interstate commerce superseded state regulatory actions, setting up conflicting rules (it does, with some exceptions); and whether the states could interfere in any way with national enforcement of national laws (they cannot—though in recent years, as we shall see shortly, the Supreme Court has handed down a series of rulings that have changed the rules of the game in this regard). Some other issues were resolved in Congress and by presidential action. The question of slavery, however, proved unsolvable through the political system. This failure, coupled with irreconcilable differences (related to slavery) over national versus state sovereignty, resulted in the secession of the South and the creation of a confederation of eleven states. The Civil War followed, culminating in a Union victory that was both military and political: slavery was ended, the Union was preserved, and a federal—not confederate (state-centered)—system was reaffirmed.

The next half-century was a time of transition in American federalism. Many basic decisions affecting the legal structuring of federalism were resolved and, as government generally became more active in dealing with problems of society, some forms of joint or overlapping governmental activities became more common. A number of new national programs combined participation by (especially) state governments with use of the first cash grants-in-aid from the national government to the states; early examples included agricultural extension programs in 1914, federal aid for state highways in 1916, and the Vocational Education Act of 1917. Fundamental structural-legal questions were receding in importance, but modern IGR was still being defined within the broader federal context.

Intergovernmental Relations: The Action Side of Federalism

Intergovernmental relations is a relatively new term, having come into common usage only in the past sixty years. It designates "an important body of activities or interactions occurring between governmental units of all types and levels within the [U.S.] federal system."[2] In the words of the late political scientist Deil Wright, IGR embraces "all the permutations and combinations of relations among the units of government in our system."[3] These include national-state and interstate relations (the areas traditionally emphasized in the study of federalism), as well as national-local, state-local, interlocal, and national-state-local relations. In addition, other key features of IGR are worth noting.

One is the fact that the consequences of IGR are often unpredictable and decision making is hidden from public view. There is no direct electorate and decisions shift from year to year with no particular direction. There is no policy-making body, no executive, no legislative, and no judiciary to oversee the results of billions of dollars transferred to states and local governments from the federal government. Predictably, this lack of consistency leads to considerable inequities in the distribution of federal money to states and cities.

A second feature of IGR is that, although we speak of IGR in the abstract, the individual actions and attitudes of elected and appointed officials determine what kinds of relations exist between units of government. Understanding IGR has to be formulated largely in the context of human relations and human behavior. Who the officials are, the roles they play in the governmental process, their policy views, and the interests they seek to promote all have a bearing on the conduct of IGR.

Third, IGR does not refer only to occasional interactions, single contacts, or formal agreements. Rather, it is a continuous series of informal contacts and exchanges of information and views among government officials aimed at solving shared multigovernmental problems. Virtually all policy areas have an intergovernmental dimension, and some are almost totally the product of shared policy formulation, implementation, or

No Child Left Behind Act (NCLB)

a controversial statute that reauthorized the Elementary and Secondary Education Act in 2002 and established national assessment standards for annual testing of students and yearly accountability reports on progress toward meeting objectives for individual schools.

financing. Examples of such policy areas include homeland security, air and water pollution control, criminal justice, agriculture, education (a prominent example was the **No Child Left Behind Act [NCLB]**), and transportation. The fact that policies are fashioned through intergovernmental processes, however, does not always mean that government officials agree with one another on all or even most major aspects of a program. IGR can be cooperative, competitive, conflicting, or a combination of all three and still be IGR.

Another key feature of IGR is the involvement of public and private, government and nongovernment, officials at all levels. Clearly involved are chief executives and legislators in Washington, state capitals, county seats, and city halls, because they formally promote and enact the programs that constitute IGR. As appointed administrators at all levels of government have assumed greater responsibility and as IGR has become more pervasive, intergovernmental *administrative* relations have taken on ever greater significance. And, although we speak of inter*governmental* relations, many public purposes are accomplished through nongovernmental institutions and organizations. Thus, IGR, properly understood, also includes the public functions of organizations not formally part of any government, such as voluntary action groups, civic organizations, and the United Way.

Action in the federal system is often taken on selected parts of a general problem rather than on the total problem area; that is, decisions are *fragmented* rather than *comprehensive*. Governments are prone to act in response to relatively specific pressures for narrow objectives and find it difficult and politically "unprofitable" to do otherwise. Thus, although government policies exist in areas such as water quality and air pollution control, no *single* policy governs the nation's approach to environmental quality. Similarly, there are policies concerning urban mass transit and public housing, but there is no *one* overall urban policy. A major reason for this is the ability of literally hundreds of governmental agencies at all levels to act independently of one another. When a policy emerges, it is usually in incomplete form and, in the majority of cases, lacks a centrally coordinated direction.[4] Contributing to this, of course, is the fact (discussed in Chapter 2) that the national government itself is far from a monolithic entity. According to Russell L. Hanson:

> The structure of intergovernmental relations is . . . a federal one in which the powers and responsibilities of government in general are shared among specific governments. However, *the sharing of power and responsibility is not equal, nor is it unalterable.* As a result, the structure of authority [in IGR] tends to be rather loose, and it invites frequent clashes between governments over the right to make certain kinds of decisions. *Conflict often arises in the course of day-to-day interactions between governments* as they seek to define and redefine their relationships with one another in order to satisfy the demands of their respective citizenries.[5]

Because a wide spectrum of political opinions and issue preferences are reflected in the multitude of national government activities, it is inaccurate to speak of what "the national government" desires, intends to do, or is actually doing. The same may be said, though perhaps to a lesser extent, of many state and local governments as well. Thus, when different governments do try to integrate their efforts through cooperative activity, their joint undertakings may well be based on a foundation of programs that are not consistent in intent, design, or execution. IGR is characterized both by this lack of central direction and by some efforts in recent decades to overcome it.

Thus, IGR involves virtually all governments and public officials, it is highly informal and very dependent on human interactions, and it involves the nonprofit and private sectors. A vivid example of IGR at work dates back to the mid-1950s, when President Dwight Eisenhower secured enactment in Congress of legislation creating the Interstate Highway System—a major expansion of the existing system of roads. All "federal" highways, but especially the interstate system, involve national, state, and local road officials (as well as highway contractors and many others) in continuing and frequent contacts—not to mention chief executives and legislators at all levels who are involved in funding and management decisions on a regular basis.

HOW WOULD YOU DECIDE?

The Crumbling of America

The History Channel's 2010 documentary *The Crumbling of America* examines the decaying infrastructure of American roads, bridges, sewer and water systems, and electrical grid. The documentary, released during the same year the *Deepwater Horizon* oil spill in the Gulf of Mexico occurred, is designed to call attention to the weakened and undermaintained necessities of infrastructure across the United States. Expert interviews, on-location filming, maps, and graphs are used throughout the documentary to emphasize the urgent need for federal, state, and local government attention and collaboration.

Intergovernmental relations factors greatly into the decisions made (or not made) concerning things such as rebuilding bridges, repaving streets, cleaning the water supply, and eliminating unnecessary health hazards caused by deteriorating infrastructures. Federal, state, and local governments must work together in order to pass legislation and move forward with rebuilding and restoring America. Legislation concerning maintenance, rehabilitation, and replacement has not been passed in a timely or efficient manner, leading to delayed response—or lack of response completely. Policy makers are hesitant, or unwilling, to address the grave issue often because of cost, both political and financial.

The involvement of public and private, government and nongovernment, officials at all levels is needed to accomplish goals as encompassing as rebuilding a nation's infrastructure. Appointed administrators at all levels of government have assumed greater responsibilities as IGR has taken on even more significance in recent years.

When faced with a nationwide crisis such as a crumbling infrastructure, what issues need to be addressed and resolved within IGR in order to bring about change?

Source: http://shop.history.com/the-crumbling-of-america-dvd/detail.php?p=104694, accessed April 18, 2011.

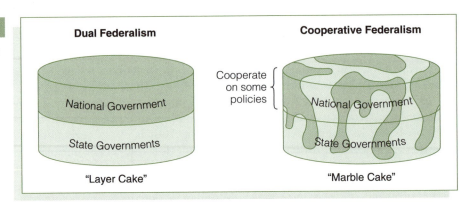

Source: © 2013 Cengage Learning.

Historically, the evolution of federalism and the emergence of IGR have been accompanied by continuing disagreements and tensions over just how national and state governments were to relate to each other. Scholars and others who have studied federalism often have referred to two competing concepts or models, in distinguishing between two broadly different viewpoints. Figure 3–1 illustrates these concepts, known as "dual federalism" and "cooperative federalism." Under the dual federalism approach symbolized by a "layer cake" analogy, the functions of national and state and governments are separate and distinct from each other. On the other hand, under the cooperative federalism approach, symbolized by a "marble cake" analogy, the functions of national and state governments are mingled—some say, deeply intertwined—and exhibit widespread patterns of cooperation and mutual support. Disagreement exists among both scholars and practitioners about the extent to which each of these models has existed, in our history—let alone which one is to be preferred over the other!

The Courts and Intergovernmental Relations

The role of the courts (especially the U.S. Supreme Court) in shaping federalism has been very significant throughout much of our history. But if anything, it has become more prominent in the past sixty years, and especially since 1990. Indeed, both national and state judiciaries have been called on to resolve federalism-related disputes. Especially under the leadership of the late Chief Justice William Rehnquist (1999–2005), the U.S. Supreme Court handed down significant rulings directly affecting the relative authority of state and national governments. Most, though not all, of these rulings favored state authority at the expense of both national authority and citizen rights and remedies. Among other things, the Supreme Court "curbed congressional power under the interstate commerce clause,"[6] and "limited congressional legislative authority to protect minority groups under Section 5 of the

14th Amendment."[7] These decisions dealt with issues as diverse as age and gender discrimination, handgun control, minimum wage, employment conditions, and civil rights. Some have even suggested that the Supreme Court has been engaged in a so-called "federalism revolution," in which a central goal "has been to more firmly fix the boundaries of national versus state authority."[8] As part of that effort, the Court frequently has acted to "restrict statutory claims against state and local governments"—in effect, further strengthening the freedom of state governments to act on their own, without legal challenge.[9]

For example, in 1992, in *New York v. United States* (505 U.S. 144), the Court ruled unconstitutional a 1985 federal statute that in the majority's view exceeded the legal boundaries for national government activity established in the Tenth Amendment to the Constitution. The statute, dealing with low-level radioactive waste, had directed state governments to implement a federal regulatory program. Three years later, in *United States v. Lopez* (514 U.S. 549), the Court took a similar position with regard to the Gun-Free School Zones Act of 1990. Congress had enacted this statute on the basis of its authority to regulate interstate commerce, but the Court ruled that provisions of the statute went beyond the scope of the commerce clause, and were therefore in violation of Congress's powers.

In the case of *Alden v. Maine* (527 U.S. 706 [1999]), the legal question at issue was whether the state of Maine could be sued in its own (state) courts under the federal Fair Labor Standards Act. Again, the majority opinion favored state over national authority by holding that the powers delegated to Congress under Article I of the Constitution do not include the power to subject nonconsenting states to private suits for damages in state courts. This decision was in keeping with a 1984 ruling, when the Court sharply limited the power of lower federal courts to order state officials to obey state laws. That earlier decision had greatly expanded the scope of the Eleventh Amendment, the relatively obscure provision giving state governments immunity from being sued in U.S. courts without the states' consent. The *Alden* ruling reaffirmed the earlier ruling, and strengthened the legal reasoning set forth in that decision.

In *United States v. Morrison* (529 U.S. 598 [2000]), the Court ruled that Congress's right to regulate interstate commerce does not include permitting women to sue their alleged abusers in federal court, when alleged private acts of violence do not cross state lines. The net effect of these and similar Supreme Court rulings (many of them by narrow 5–4 majorities) has been to limit the national government's legal and administrative authority, and to place more discretionary authority in the hands of state (and, by extension, local) officials.

Not all Supreme Court decisions have invalidated or narrowed national government authority. For example, early in 2004 the Supreme Court ruled that the U.S. Environmental Protection Agency (EPA) has authority, under the Clean Air Act of 1970, to "override state officials and order some anti-pollution measures that may be more costly." Although state officials can make some decisions involving facilities within their borders, the EPA retains significant enforcement authority regarding the 1970 statute.[10] In addition, this decision is an example of a growing phenomenon known as **preemptions**—legal actions by federal courts or agencies to preclude enforcement of a state or local law or regulation. These direct assumptions of power have increased significantly during the past three decades, even as prevailing judicial philosophies have pointed in very different directions.[11]

And in mid-2005, in a highly controversial decision, the Court greatly expanded the power of local governments in relation to the property rights of private citizens. In *Kelo v. New London* ([Connecticut] No. 04-108), the Court ruled that local governments may seize people's homes and businesses—even against their will—for private economic development. It was a decision "fraught with huge implications for a country with many areas, particularly the rapidly growing urban and suburban areas, facing countervailing pressures of development and property ownership rights."[12] The New London residents who challenged the loss of their property had contended that while the city government could properly take private property for a "clear public use, such as roads or schools, or to revitalize blighted areas"—under the well-established power of **eminent domain**—it should not be able to take private property "for projects such as shopping malls and hotel complexes, to generate [local] tax revenue."[13] But the Court (again in a 5–4 decision) ruled against the property owners and in favor of this exercise, by the city of New London, of eminent domain power—sparking, among other things, a growing number of *state legislative* efforts around the country to place limits on local authority, in this regard.

Three trends are worth noting with regard to recent Supreme Court federalism-related decisions. First, "the Court did not invalidate any congressional statutes on federalism grounds after 2002."[14] Second, under Chief Justice Roberts the Court has allowed the Rehnquist Court's decisions in this area to stand with virtually no change. And third, while decisions of the Rehnquist Court were often supportive of state government authority, the Court did not overturn a single judicial precedent that supported the basic elements of either the Franklin Roosevelt New Deal of the 1930s and 1940s or Lyndon Johnson's Great Society of 1965–1969.

The courts, then, have been highly influential in shaping the organization and operation of—and within—the federal system. The continuing expansion of IGR has served only to increase the reach of judicial decision making because more governments and their actions are potentially affected by any given ruling. This expansion is testimony to the increased complexity within American federalism, and it is that subject to which we now turn our attention.

---

preemptions

the assumption of state or local program authority by the federal government.

---

eminent domain

power of governments to take private property for a legitimate public purpose without the owner's consent (although governments are required to pay an owner "just compensation" [a fair price]).

Contemporary Intergovernmental Relations: The Rise of Complexity

It was under the presidency of Franklin Roosevelt, a Democrat, that national government activity underwent a quantum leap in terms of scope and diversity, and IGR became more closely interwoven with general (and more centralized) governmental undertakings. With little fanfare, but steadily, intergovernmental aid and joint efforts became more important components of public policy making. Thus, for example, national government grants for rural highway construction and maintenance (begun in 1916) became more numerous; grants for urban renewal became more widespread; and direct aid to urban governments for airport construction and other transportation purposes also appeared on the scene.[15] After the Great Depression, federally funded state and local social welfare, along with farm support and public-assistance bureaucracies, gradually replaced voluntary sources for aiding those in need. In the 1950s, under Republican Dwight Eisenhower, the pace of national government expansion slackened but did not stop completely. Significantly, it was just after Eisenhower took office in 1953 that the Department of Health, Education, and Welfare (HEW) was created, paving the way for later expansion of grants and other provisions relating to social services. Throughout the period 1930–1960, increased national government activity and the rising importance of IGR paralleled one another and often coincided. With the advent of the 1960s, however, IGR experienced its own quantum leap into new forms and new impacts.

In the last five decades, the structure of IGR has been transformed by the rapid proliferation of financial transactions among different levels of government; by the development of new and often permanent linkages among program administrators at all levels; by the establishment of new forms of government at what is called the "substate regional level," such as local-level "special districts" (providing many services, including water, education, and transportation), economic development districts, and health planning agencies; and by the issuance of literally thousands of rules, guidelines, and regulations—collectively known as mandates and often accompanying fiscal aid packages—to hundreds of governmental units (see Chapters 9 and 10). This expansion of national government power has sparked political controversy of various kinds, resulting from the complexity associated with increasing numbers of federal grants and their accompanying regulations. Despite the best efforts of state and local elected officials to keep pace with the rapidly changing rules of the game, there is growing concern that the national government may have acquired excessive influence over state and local decisions. Also, many citizens apparently believe that these same complexities have weakened the people's control over many of the activities and decisions of government that affect their daily lives either directly or indirectly.

It is also true, however, that we rely heavily on state and local governments to implement domestic policies, including those established by the national government. That is one reason that IGR, in general, and especially its fiscal side, is so important to understand. In recent years, IGR has been affected (though more indirectly) by another change: the growing service-delivery roles of nonprofit community organizations and various for-profit organizations in the private sector. Since 2009, the broad policy initiatives of the Obama administration, combined with greater fiscal constraints and pressures at all levels of government, have introduced significant new dimensions to the operations of the U.S. federal system. These developments have posed immense new challenges to those responsible for effectively administering government programs in a constantly changing environment. That these developments have been largely interrelated has made coping with them all the more difficult.

Several principal themes stand out. One is the importance, in this context and in broader terms, of government purposes organized by *function*. Functional alliances have tended to dominate contemporary IGR (much as they have done in "subsystem politics" at the national level) and, as a result, have become centers of ongoing controversy. A second theme, closely linked to the first, is the growing political and managerial struggle between elected public officials and administrative/functional specialists (and their respective political allies) for control of major IGR program directions. A third, broader theme focuses on the tensions between forces promoting greater centralization in the general governmental system and those favoring decentralization (including a lessening of national government regulation of state and local government activity). Nowhere is that issue more crucial than in the federalism/IGR realm, since a prime purpose of federalism is to prevent excessive centralization of governmental authority. Deliberate efforts both to centralize and to decentralize government programs have been numerous. Calls for downsizing, decentralization, and deregulation have been gaining ground in the past thirty years, and reinventing government implicitly (if not explicitly) puts considerable emphasis on decentralizing government functions in order to put them within easier reach of popular control. All these themes have fiscal, administrative, and political dimensions.

Intergovernmental Fiscal Relations

fiscal federalism

the complex of financial transactions, transfers of funds, and accompanying rules and regulations that increasingly characterizes national-state, national-local, and state-local relations.

Intergovernmental fiscal relations, also referred to as **fiscal federalism**, have been central to contemporary IGR for some time. Although there have been some forms of financial aid from one governmental level to another throughout U.S. history, the scope of such transactions has expanded rapidly and dramatically since 1961. This applies to national government aid to states and localities and, to a lesser extent, to state aid to local governments.

Intergovernmental aid has taken on greater importance for a relatively simple reason. Traditionally, many state and local governments have had weaker economic bases and less productive systems of taxation than the national government has. Yet the former provide the great bulk of public services in health, education, welfare, housing, highway construction, law enforcement, police protection, parks and recreation, conservation, and agricultural services. The national government, with far stronger fiscal resources and revenue-generating capacity, *directly* delivers relatively few public services.[16] These include Social Security benefits, postal services, federal law enforcement, veterans' payments, and farm subsidies. In essence, the national government, with the greatest tax resources, delivers the fewest direct services; local governments, with the narrowest and weakest tax bases, are frequently the most heavily laden with costly service obligations such as police, emergency management, fire, streets and roads, sewage and sanitation, water, and utilities; the states fall between them on that spectrum. It should be noted that the national government—through *mandated* grants, contracts, loans, regulations, and the like—now has many avenues of *indirect* service provision.[17]

There are two basic reasons for the revenue-raising disparity among different governmental levels. First, local and state governments have limited geographic areas—often dependent on one or two products or services—from which to extract revenues (for instance, tourism in Florida and coal in West Virginia). A more diversified economy is a more stable and productive source of government income, and only the national government has access to the nation's full range of economic resources.

Second, different types of taxes yield different amounts of revenue from the same income base. The most responsive, or *elastic*, tax (a tax that shows the greatest increase in revenue for a given percentage increase in taxable income) is the graduated income tax (so called because the tax rate rises as income increases). Somewhat less elastic is the sales tax, which levies a flat percentage rate on the price of purchased goods; some sales taxes are general and allow few exemptions, while others are selective and apply only to certain items. Least elastic is the personal property tax, which is levied on real estate and other personal belongings. The national government is the principal user of the graduated income tax. States rely heavily on sales and other excise taxes, though, increasingly, state revenues are also derived from nongraduated or "flat-rate" income taxes. Local governments, including special districts, depend most heavily on personal property taxes, though sales and wage taxes have come into increasing use by many local governments.[18]

Thus, the government with the broadest tax base (the national government) also uses the most efficient generator of revenue, while the governments with the narrowest and least diversified tax base (local governments) employ the least elastic tax, with the states again falling between the two. The result is a **fiscal mismatch** between the service needs and fiscal capacities of different levels of government, and among different governments at the same level in

fiscal mismatch

differences in the capacities of various governments to raise revenues, in relation to those governments' respective abilities to pay for public services that they are responsible for delivering.

terms of their varying abilities to pay for needed public services (for example, wealthy school districts versus less affluent ones). Rising service demands on government at all levels have placed a particular strain on those governments least able to expand their tax revenues rapidly, that is, local units. The consequence of all this has been increasing demand for aid from higher levels of government to help pay for government services.

Grants-in-Aid

The growing needs of state and local government during the first half of the twentieth century coincided with rising congressional and executive-branch interest in expanding and upgrading available public services at all levels of government. By the 1960s, the stage was set for the national government (and some state governments) to utilize financial assistance on a much larger scale than before as a means to expand public services. The principal device adopted to bring all this about was the grant-in-aid, which had been an established mechanism for thirty years and was now to be given a substantially enlarged role.

grants-in-aid

money payments furnished by a higher to a lower level of government to be used for specified purposes and subject to conditions spelled out in law or administrative regulation.

Grants-in-aid are money payments furnished by a higher to a lower level of government to be used for specified purposes and subject to conditions spelled out in law or administrative regulation. Cash transfers are used most widely by the national government, although states also make some use of them. When John F. Kennedy was inaugurated in 1961, only 45 separate grant authorizations existed. Under each authorization, multiple allocations of funds can be made. But in the period 1965–1966, when Lyndon Johnson commanded decisive Democratic majorities in both chambers of Congress, he took advantage of the opportunity to legislate a host of new federally directed grant programs as he pursued his vision of the "Great Society." By the time Richard Nixon entered the White House, only eight years after the start of Kennedy's term, the number of grants had mushroomed to about 400. Using the criterion of separate authorizations, the U.S. Advisory Commission on Intergovernmental Relations (ACIR) estimated that almost 540 grant programs existed in fiscal year (FY) 1981. During the Reagan administration, the number of grants dropped to about 400 by FY 1985, with significant adverse implications for state and local delivery of many public services and for the fiscal well-being of many state and local jurisdictions. The number increased again, however, to 478 grant programs in FY 1989 and to upwards of 600 such programs in FY 2008. Grants have financed state and local programs in virtually every major domestic policy area—urban renewal, highway construction and maintenance, mass transit, education, criminal justice, recreation, public health, and so on.

Equally dramatic is the increase in dollar amounts appropriated under national grant programs. In FY 1960, the figure was about $7 billion; by FY 1970, it had risen to $24 billion; by FY 1981, it was just under $95 billion; by FY 1990, it had reached $135 billion; in FY 2001, it was approximately

$318 billion; and in FY 2008, it had reached approximately $461 billion. In FY 2009–2011, the total amount of grant program aid increased sharply: $538 billion in 2009, $608 billion in 2010, and $625 billion in 2011. After President Reagan's success in slowing the rate of growth in spending for grants, Presidents George H. W. Bush, Bill Clinton, and George W. Bush presided over significant increases in the number of grant programs, along with the funds appropriated for them (see Figure 3–2). Early in 2011, however, the Obama administration proposed a number of dramatic aid reductions for FY 2012 and 2013.

National grants-in-aid were originally enacted to achieve certain broad purposes.[19] These included establishing minimum nationwide standards for programs operating in all parts of the country; equalizing resources among the states by redistributing proportionately more money to poorer states; improving state and local program delivery; concentrating research resources on problems that cross government boundary lines (such as air and water pollution) or that attract interest from numerous governments; and increasing public services without enlarging the scope of the national government or its apparent role in domestic politics. Other purposes have included improving the structure and operation of state and local agencies (such as merit personnel

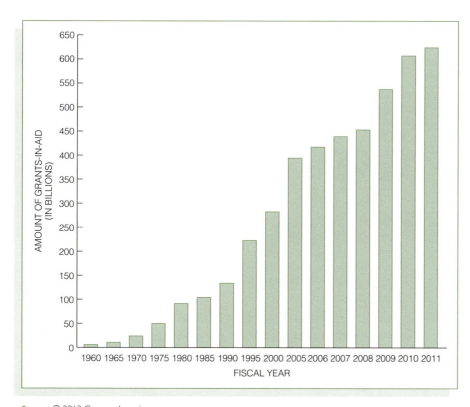

FIGURE 3-2

Historical Trends of Federal Grants-in-Aid, 1960–2011

Source: © 2013 Cengage Learning.

practices or better planning), demonstration and experimentation in national policy, encouragement of general social objectives (such as nondiscrimination in hiring), and provision of services to otherwise underserved portions of the population.

In the 1970s and 1980s, federal grants-in-aid loomed large in the total picture of all government domestic programs (including those at state and local levels). During those two decades, these grants provided about one-fourth of state-local revenues each FY, while at the same time comprising between 12 and 17 percent of all national government outlays. Those proportions began to decline in the early 1980s, following Ronald Reagan's election to the presidency, and continued at a reduced level (especially the proportion of federal outlays) during George H. W. Bush's administration. Between FY 1982 and 1991, the proportion of total federal outlays devoted to grant programs hovered in the range of 11–12 percent before beginning to rise again after the election of Bill Clinton in 1992. The proportion stayed between 14 and 16 percent of outlays for the rest of the decade (even after the Republican takeover of Congress in the 1994 elections), and increased, during the second Bush presidency, to around 17 percent in 2005—1.5 percent higher than the proportion that existed in FY 1980 (see Figure 3–3). At the same time, however, state and local governments became more active in raising their "own-source" revenues (taxes and other

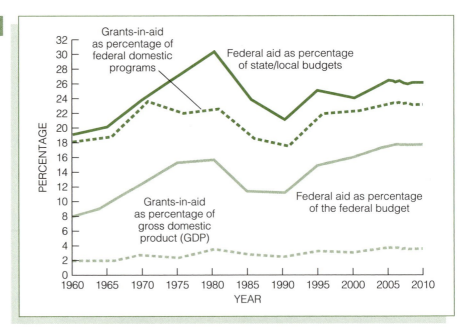

FIGURE 3-3

The Rise and Fall of Federal Assistance, 1960–2010

Source: U.S. Office of Management and Budget, Budget of the United States Government, Fiscal Year 2010, Analytical Perspectives (Washington, D.C. Government Printing Office, 2009). Table 8.3, p. 131; U.S. Bureau of Census, Sastisical Abstract of the United States, 2007 (Washington, D.C., Government Printing Office, 2007), Table 421. Retrieved at: http://whitehouse.gov/sites/default/files/smb/budget/fy2012/assets/hist.pdf.

revenue generators that they establish by law); nonetheless, in 2010, federal grants still provided about one-third of all state-local revenues despite the fact that grants-in-aid as a percentage of federal domestic programs declined.

The advantages attributed to grant-in-aid programs are numerous. First, the national government affords a single focal point for bringing about a greater degree of concerted action on a policy problems. Second, political minorities in states and localities, such as African-Americans and Hispanics, have an opportunity to seek some measure of national support for their policy demands. Third, grants-in-aid are an appropriate way to deal with nationwide problems; many policy questions are interrelated in terms of their impact, such as those linking highways, urban transportation, and air pollution or education, unemployment, poverty, and welfare. Although a fully coordinated attack on such sets of problems has yet to be mounted (and is not likely to be), a greater degree of consistency is possible at the national level than among fifty separate states and 87,000 local governments.

Finally, and perhaps most important, it has been suggested that national funds assist states and localities with programs and projects that benefit citizens outside the borders of the recipient government. These so-called ripple effects—more formally known as **externalities**—justify national monetary support for state or local efforts because of the wider benefits realized from them. Three examples illustrate the point: (1) a state job-training center, whose graduates may find employment in other states; (2) a state park system that attracts tourists and vacationers from a much wider geographic area; and (3) local education systems that, in a mobile society such as ours, are undoubtedly investing in the future productivity and contributions of persons who will reap the benefits of their education elsewhere. Because the nation as a whole gains from such investments of state and local funds, it is agreed that there is good reason to add grant funding from the national treasury.

Grants-in-aid have taken several forms; we "can usefully categorize grant programs along two dimensions"[20]: the degree of discretion national government administrative officials possess in distributing funds and the "degree of restriction imposed on the use of [national government] funds."[21] Administrative discretion in distributing funds is smallest under **formula grants**, which are created by legislation that clearly specifies the criteria for determining eligibility to receive the funds. Depending on the purpose of a grant, these criteria might include population, unemployment rates, or the percentage of the population living in poverty. Administrative discretion is much greater in the case of **project grants**; with these, agency officials have wide latitude in deciding which states or local governments will receive funding and how much each will get. Formula and project grants are subtypes of **categorical grants**, the most commonly used kind of national government assistance programs to state and local governments. Of the approximately 600 categoricals in existence, three-fourths are project grants, available by application; the remaining one-fourth are formula grants, for purposes such as aid to the blind

externalities

the economic consequences or impacts of federal grants-in-aid at the regional and local level.

formula grants

type of national government grant-in-aid available to states and local governments for purposes that are ongoing and common to many government jurisdictions; distributed according to a set formula that treats all applicants uniformly, at least in principle; have the effect of reducing grantors' administrative discretion. Examples are aid to the blind and aid to the elderly.

project grants

form of grant-in-aid available by application to states and localities for an individual project; more numerous than formula grants but with less overall funding by the federal government.

categorical grants

a form of grant-in-aid with purposes narrowly defined by the grantor, leaving the recipient relatively little choice as to how the grant funding is to be used, substantively or procedurally.

and disabled. On the other hand, although individual project grants outnumber formula grants, the dollar amounts available under formula grants exceed those of project grants.

Grants also can be distinguished with regard to how freely recipient governments can use national government funds. Under categorical grants, states and local governments can spend the money only for certain clearly designated "categories" of expenditure, leaving very little room for adjustments on the part of a recipient government. The extreme specificity of categorical grants has been described as "hardening of the categories," which

> created such proliferation of minutely targeted grants that . . . a local government wishing to improve its recreational amenities ha[s] to make separate applications to several different agencies if its total program include[s] buying land for park purposes; building a swimming pool on it; operating an activity center for senior citizens; putting in trees and shrubbery; and purchasing sports equipment. In the area of urban transportation, there are [or have been] separate categorical grant programs covering car pool demonstration projects; urban transportation planning; urban area traffic operations improvement; urban mass transportation basic grants (based on a formula for fund distribution); and mass transit grants (on a project application basis).[22]

Thus, the categorical grant business has become immensely complicated, and is difficult for even experienced professionals to comprehend at times.

With grants-in-aid of all types, the proportion of total expenditures paid by the national government varies considerably. Congress defines some grants as representing important nationwide initiatives and sets the national government share at 100 percent. Other grants require dollar-for-dollar matching funds by the state/local government, which doubles the total amount of money available. Some other grant allocations require recipients to share the burden to some extent but not fifty-fifty (sometimes as little as 1 percent of the total). The national share for all types of grants-in-aid, then, is at least one-half and can cover the total.

One other observation should be made with reference to federal grants and grant-funded state/local programs. Throughout the 1990s and the first decade of the twenty-first century, a mere twenty-one categorical grant programs accounted for 80 percent of total spending for categoricals, and an additional two dozen programs accounted for another 10 percent of spending. These included, among others, the **Medicaid** program (with 55 million poor and disabled recipients), child nutrition grants, wastewater treatment plant construction, Aid to Families with Dependent Children (AFDC), training and employment programs, low-rent public housing, and community development programs. Under the Welfare Reform Act of 1996, the old AFDC programs—now known as Temporary Assistance for Needy Families (TANF)—were to be administered as formula grants by the states, with federal standards. Still, nearly

Medicaid

federal health care program operated by the states to assist the poor.

90 percent of the funds allocated for categoricals were expended by the largest forty-five programs, fewer than 10 percent of the total number of programs.

Expansion of grants-in-aid was accompanied by qualitative and administrative changes: there were increasing numbers of project grants, and an increased variety of matching-grant formulas; Congress broadened the eligibility of grant recipients and increased joint-recipient possibilities; aid was concentrated in large urban areas and directed to the urban poor in numerous new ventures; there was increased national aid not only to governments but also to private institutions, including corporations, universities, and nonprofit organizations; and the national government made funding available specifically to assist state and local jurisdictions in improving both their planning capabilities and their actual planning activities. All these changes grew out of an expanding emphasis on achieving national goals under the direction of the national government.[23]

Prior to the 1960s, aid had been used primarily to supplement the policy actions of states and localities. Under Kennedy and then Johnson, however, presidential and congressional initiatives were couched more in terms of *national* purposes. Given this emphasis, it was deemed entirely appropriate to write into grant legislation substantive and procedural requirements that would promote those purposes.[24] Administration of these programs remained predominantly in the hands of state and local governments, but the national role in defining the uses of grant funds was clearly becoming decisive in determining general policy directions and many specific state and local program activities. In the 1990s, funding for grants-in-aid increased from 11 to 16 percent of total federal spending; grant-in-aid funding constituted just over 17 percent of total outlays in FY 2005, before falling to 16 percent again in FY 2006 and 2007, and to 15.3 percent in FY 2009. The percentage of total outlays jumped sharply in FY 2010, to 17.6 percent, but is projected in FY 2012 federal budget documents to fall back under 16 percent in the next few years.[25]

While major changes were unfolding in national categorical programs, state aid to local governments continued to expand assistance programs as well. Not only were states contributing increasing amounts to local government functions (especially to school districts and to the growing suburbs), but they also were making much of the funding available in the form of revenue sharing, that is, funds drawn from the respective state treasuries and allocated to local governments with few if any "strings" attached. Many states also established the practice (still in use across the country) of returning to each local government a portion of state sales-tax revenues, in proportion to the amount of sales-tax revenue collected within each locality. Thus, from the local perspective, state and national governments, in their differing methods of organizing fiscal assistance to local governments, have moved in somewhat opposite directions during the past forty years. This is not to say, however, that states have given their local governments free rein to allocate funds—far from it. Nevertheless, key features of state aid, especially categorical grants, differ in significant respects from those of national aid.

Categorical Grants and Administrative Complexity

In the preceding discussion of grants-in-aid, we noted a number of administrative dimensions, including the objectives of providing more and better public services, with growing emphasis recently on efficiency and effectiveness—both squarely in our administrative traditions; establishing minimum uniform programmatic standards nationwide; enhancing both the procedure and the substance of state and local programs; and strengthening the planning function. How all of this should be accomplished, however, was and still is a serious question. The use of categorical grants rather than some other instrument of assistance contributed directly to increased interdependence, reliance on political bargaining, and the rise of administrative complexity. This is so because of historical patterns in grants management that are worth reviewing.

Today, states receive more than two-thirds of all formula grants and act as conduits for the majority of project grants to local governments. As Congress deliberated over expansion of successive aid programs, a principal concern was ensuring that the national purposes of programs were not lost by dividing up administrative responsibility among fragmented state agencies. One way to prevent such jurisdictional jostling would have been through the assertion of strong **gubernatorial** prerogatives, whereby the appropriate state agencies were designated to receive given grant funds and to administer program activities under congressional authorization. Most governors, however, were ill equipped to serve that function, especially in the early years of grant activity, when the operations of state executive branches often lacked unified direction and were hampered by partisan politics and administrative chaos.

One response from the national level was the **single state agency requirement**. Only one agency is designated to administer any individual grant and to establish direct relationships with its counterpart in the national government bureaucracy. This provision first appeared in the 1916 Highway Act and was duplicated the following year in the Vocational Education Act. Currently applicable laws either name a specific state agency or call for one to be designated in policy areas such as child welfare, library services, urban planning, water pollution control, civil defense, and law enforcement assistance. Thus, for most of the twentieth century (and continuing into the twenty-first), the administration of grant funds was largely in the hands of professional administrative personnel in individual agencies.

As the grant-in-aid system grew more specialized, national agency personnel came to work even more closely with their state and local counterparts. Partly as a result of national grant policies, the latter were now much more professionalized than they had been in the past, operating under state merit systems that had created a contingent of administrators whose backgrounds, interests, and professional competencies were similar to those of national government administrators. Parallel relationships

gubernatorial

a term that refers to anything concerning the office of a state governor—for example, gubernatorial authority or gubernatorial influence.

single state agency requirement

a requirement contained in federal grants designating only one state agency to administer national grants, and to establish direct relationships with its counterpart in the national government bureaucracy.

were formed between officials of the Bureau of Public Roads and state and local highway department personnel; national educational administrators and their counterparts in state departments of education and officials in local school districts; and Agriculture Department staff with state and, especially, county agricultural officials. This process of strengthening intergovernmental administrative linkages led to a situation largely invisible to the general public but fraught with consequences for the governmental process. Political scientists Harold Seidman and Robert Gilmour, among others, have suggested that what we have in a number of important functional areas are "largely self-governing professional guilds"[26] composed of bureaucrats at all levels with common programmatic concerns. The ACIR, describing the same phenomenon, coined the term **vertical functional autocracies**, the autocracy label signifying not only the agencies' operating autonomy from chief executives and legislators but also the extent of agency control over essential program decisions.[27]

The development of intergovernmental administrative ties gave rise to a new label for the federal system. Previously, dual federalism was likened to a layer cake, with different levels of government clearly distinguished from one another, and growing cooperation was likened to a marble cake, with functions of different levels of government intermingled. The new vertical administrative patterns gave rise to the term **picket-fence federalism**, illustrated in Figure 3–4.

vertical functional autocracies

informal associations of federal, state, and local professional administrators who manage intergovernmental programs; also referred to as **picket-fence federalism**.

picket-fence federalism

a term describing a key dimension of U.S. federalism— intergovernmental administrative relationships among bureaucratic specialists and their clientele groups in the same substantive areas; suggests that allied bureaucrats at different levels of government exercise considerable power over intergovernmental programs. See also **vertical functional autocracies**.

FIGURE 3-4

Picket-Fence* Federalism: A Schematic Representation

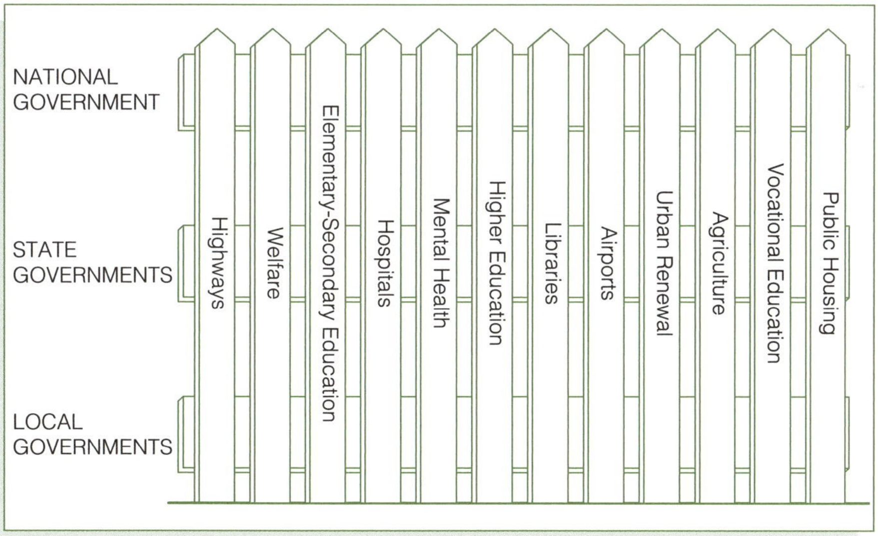

*Each picket represents the political and administrative ties among specialists in each policy area at all three levels of government.

Source: Adapted from *Understanding Intergovernmental Relations*, 3rd ed., by Deil S. Wright. Copyright © 1988, 1982, 1978 by Wadsworth, Inc. Reprinted by permission of Brooks/Cole Publishing Company, Pacific Grove, Calif. 93950.

Former North Carolina Governor (and later U.S. Senator) Terry Sanford provided this definition:

> The lines of authority, the concerns and interests, the flow of money, and the direction of programs run straight down like a number of pickets stuck into the ground. There is, as in a picket fence, a connecting cross slat, but that does little to support anything. In this metaphor it stands for the governments. It holds the pickets in line; it does not bring them together. The picket-like programs are not connected at the bottom.[28]

Bureaucratic officials within each of these pickets, together with their clientele groups at all levels, do not always agree, of course, on the substance and procedures of programs they administer. But the responsibility for formulating many basic policies and for resolving many of the conflicts that arise rests largely—and often exclusively—within the discretion of these functional groupings. How that situation can be reconciled with democratic values of public accountability and control is an important question and one not easily answered. One hopeful sign, however, has been noted: The pickets may have already been somewhat altered. Only ten years after Sanford used the picket-fence label for the first time, David Walker of the now defunct ACIR suggested a variation, namely, *bamboo-fence federalism*. Walker asserted that this new label more accurately "captures the vertical functionalism, continuing professionalism, [and] greater flexibility and realism" of contemporary public administrators, even though most still give primary emphasis to their functional concerns, including the protection of programmatic interests as a high priority.[29]

Categorical Grants: Growing Dissatisfaction

The tremendous proliferation of grants, the rise of vertical functional autocracies, picket- or bamboo-fence federalism, and particularly the duplicative and overlapping nature of so many available grants soon led to a growing chorus of concern about management of grants and about the impacts they were having on recipient governments.

These criticisms suggest several dimensions of the politics of grants.[30] One is provision of essential public services, and equality or inequality among (and sometimes within) jurisdictions in the levels of those services. Another concerns tensions among different levels and units of government over setting program priorities, and program management. A third dimension is the procedural pitfalls that can hamper applicant governments in their efforts to obtain grant assistance. Many state and local officials tell horror stories about rejection of applications on seemingly narrow technical grounds, about having to resubmit applications because a relatively minor section was improperly filled out. Underlying all such concerns, however, is a common theme: considerable conflict between elected state and local officials and the specialists of their own bureaucracies as well as those in the national government's administrative agencies (see Figure 3–4). Much of the criticism came from state and local chief executives and legislators, and was directed explicitly toward the greater control that bureaucrats at all levels were coming to have over government aid programs. As the criticisms grew in intensity and became a partisan issue dividing Democrats and Republicans, the critics increasingly gained the attention of the Congress and, significantly, the president.

Increasing attention was also given to the problem of grant coordination that resulted from the sheer number of grants and the variety of grant sources within the national bureaucracy. The availability of urban transportation grants from different national agencies for similar, often overlapping, purposes made it difficult to select the most appropriate grant program. Also, many general development projects in states and communities had component parts funded independently by separate national agencies. As a result, a grant applicant was faced with applying separately for each part of the overall project, thereby running the risk of applications being approved for some portions of the project but not for others.

Furthermore, most national aid-granting agencies did not have much (if any) knowledge of what other programs were being funded by other agencies; at the other end of the aid pipeline, most recipient governments knew or cared little about what funds other governments were receiving, or even applying for. Grant applications were being reviewed and approved or rejected by national agencies with no means of keeping track of which states and localities were asking for aid, for what purposes it was requested, and how much aid was distributed. Nor were there any provisions for systematically monitoring which agencies were responsible for programs with similar purposes or for determining the actual results, if any, of grant funds. Meanwhile, state and local officials were chafing under what many considered unreasonable guidelines for spending grant money, as well as the problems they encountered in obtaining funding in the first place.

The problems of coordination have been compounded at the recipient end of the aid pipeline by growing intergovernmental administrative linkages in *horizontal* as well as vertical dimensions. Various types of contracting arrangements, consortia, cooperative agreements, regional interagency councils, commissions, multijurisdiction functional agencies, ad hoc planning groups, temporary clearinghouses, and a multitude of other intergovernmental structures have been created to administer federal programs. Interstate compacts, such as the Port Authority of New York and New Jersey, have come into greater prominence; other regional bodies crossing state lines, created by either state or national governments, have also been established.

Likewise, there has been an increase in the phenomenon of substate regionalism.[31] Special districts of all kinds (excepting school districts) have proliferated in recent years—many in response to national government encouragement—for a variety of purposes, such as planning, review of grant applications, economic development, public health, and provision of care for the aging. Here, again, the picket-fence analogy is evident because national, state, and local administrative officials all have active roles in substate regional functions. The formation of these nearly independent federal-local government systems poses considerable administrative difficulties because it frees districts to compete (often successfully) for grant monies available to all other types of local government. Thus, these systems are also woven into the pattern of functionally organized administrative relationships but, at the same time, they are among the most invisible and least accountable of all forms of government.

POINT/COUNTERPOINT

Should the national government truly be the "Senior Partner" in the U.S. "federal partnership"?

THE ISSUE For nearly a century, the national government has distributed increasing amounts of grant funding to state and local governments, for wide-ranging policy and program purposes. In more recent decades, the national government also has increasingly engaged in intergovernmental regulation of states and localities. The national government courts, especially the U.S. Supreme Court, have handed down many rulings that have helped define both requirements and restrictions on state and local action.

Arguments *for* the National Government Being the "Senior Partner"

- Since enactment of the graduated income tax in 1913, the national government has had fiscal resources superior to those of individual states and localities. Its tax base, for obvious reasons, also is superior. It follows logically that when states and localities are in need of assistance, the national government is the "place to turn."

- Nationwide purposes can be pursued, and nationwide needs met, through a single (albeit diverse and cumbersome) government entity. Those purposes and needs must be defined by Congress and the president, but when they are defined, it is easier to track expenditures and programmatic successes and failures than it would be to do such tracking across fifty separate state governments and 87,000 units of local government.

- By using categorical grants, the national government is in a better position to target geographical and programmatic areas across the nation for assistance.

- State and local political interests are well represented in the U.S. Congress, thus providing ample opportunity for state/local policy preferences to be incorporated into national government actions.

Arguments *against* the National Government Being the "Senior Partner"

- Throughout the twentieth century and into the twenty-first, the national government has increasingly tried to utilize grant assistance to influence the course of state and local government activity in policy and program directions that are consistent with the purposes of presidents and congressional leaders. That has tended to weaken the states as "independent actors" in a federal system of shared authority.

- The "national purposes" said to be defined in Washington may or may not be in line with preferences of statewide or local majorities "back home," creating considerable potential for conflict among national, state, and local majorities and their elected leaders.

- What the national government, through Congress and the bureaucracy, chooses to target may be too narrowly targeted to suit many who do not benefit from national government financial assistance.

- The state and local political interests represented in Congress may ignore, or conflict with, other interests that command majority support among state and local voters.

Grant Reform: Multiple Efforts, More Complexity

By the late 1960s, pressures were mounting for changes in the grant-in-aid system, particularly in grants management. Although various concepts and options had been explored from time to time, few actions had been taken. The changes that followed, and that have continued up to the present, have emphasized efforts to reduce the programmatic influence of the national government, through both fiscal and administrative reform. We will consider these, and their major components, in turn.

Fiscal Reform: General Revenue Sharing

During the late 1960s, political reaction mounted to the strings (conditions and specifications) attached to grant-in-aid funding. Increasingly, state and local elected officials sought financial assistance that would permit them greater discretion in spending decisions. The Nixon proposal for general revenue sharing (GRS) appeared to meet such demands. GRS de-emphasized concern for national policies, goals, and standards; defined state and local rather than national majorities as the key decision makers about program spending; and built into the intergovernmental fiscal system greater discretion for state and local elected officials. But, despite attracting quite a following among state and local officials, GRS never lived up to its advance billing.

The principle behind revenue sharing was a simple one: A portion of tax revenues would be returned to states and to general-purpose local governments according to a prescribed formula defined by Congress and automatically followed each year. Revenue-sharing funds would be allocated with no strings attached, and recipient governments could use the money for almost any purpose. There would also be no need for a state or locality to apply for the funds; once the formula was determined, the funds would be available with no uncertainty and no delay. Such an arrangement seemed to respond directly to the sharpest criticisms of the grant-in-aid system. In particular, revenue sharing seemed to represent a way for local political majorities, through their elected officials, to reassert their priorities in local and state spending and not to be bound to grant programs with which they increasingly disagreed on both policy and procedural grounds.

One of the reasons, of course, for its appeal was precisely that GRS would allow officials of recipient governments to exercise wide latitude in deciding how to spend the funds; however, some of those officials proved wiser than others. For example, some communities applied GRS monies to special projects, usually construction projects of limited scope or duration, while others, often out of necessity, incorporated GRS funds into their operating budgets. Those who confined their funding to capital improvement turned out to be better off when the flow of funds stopped in 1986.[32]

Even when GRS was most strongly supported at the White House, it represented only a small proportion of total spending for intergovernmental aid (less than 5 percent). Ronald Reagan, however, opposed extending revenue sharing, and Congress did not renew the program. Reagan's willingness to allow GRS to lapse was apparently due to two policy preferences: (1) an overriding interest in reducing national government spending and growing annual budget deficits and (2) a commitment to another alternative to categoricals, namely, block grants.

Fiscal Reform: Block Grants

If GRS represented a departure from existing categorical aid and its attendant problems, block grants were a more modest attempt (at least initially) to "decategorize" federal grants and "devolve" authority to states and localities.[33] **Block grants**, while also given out for use in a specific policy area (such as community development, public assistance, or health care), leave much more discretion and flexibility in the use of such funds in the hands of recipient governments. They represent a middle way between the alleged restrictiveness of categorical grants and the elimination of all national-level influence and responsibility in intergovernmental aid.

block grants

a form of grant-in-aid in which the purposes to be served by the funding are defined very broadly by the grantor, leaving considerable discretion and flexibility in the hands of the recipient.

In general, block grants have the following features: (1) recipient jurisdictions have fairly wide discretion within the designated program area; (2) administration, reporting, planning, and other program features are designed to minimize grantor supervision and control; (3) most allocation provisions are based on a formula, which is also intended to limit grantor discretion as well as to decrease fiscal uncertainty for the grantees; (4) eligibility provisions are fairly precise, tending to favor general local governments as opposed to special districts, and generalist officials over program specialists; and (5) matching-fund requirements are usually relatively low.[34] The original block grant concept retained the notion that national goals were to be pursued in a program area through expenditure of allocated funds; the ACIR noted that block grants "do not imply a hands-off [national] role, nor one confined to purely procedural matters."[35] These observations were clearly descriptive of the block grants of the 1960s and 1970s.

Under Ronald Reagan, block grants took some sharply different directions: limiting the use of categorical grant programs, shifting away from pursuing national government purposes, spending less for categorical grants, and so on. For example, the number of categorical programs dropped from 534 in FY 1981 to 404 in FY 1984—a decrease of about 24 percent.[36]

Also, there is evidence that the block grant strategy was used implicitly to cut spending and not only to alter the degree of program control exercised by government administrators through categorical grants. None of Reagan's successors, however, adopted that course of action, at least to the same extent. Block grants have been allowed to operate as more of a "freestanding" form of fiscal assistance—although reliance on such grants signals an implicit, if not explicit, federalism-related aid strategy.

Under the administration of President George H. W. Bush, the shifts (both ideological and administrative) toward a stronger state role were reaffirmed and consolidated—although, significantly, not expanded. In FY 1991, for example, Bush proposed increasing block grant funding by the modest sum of $15 million, with the explicit proviso that state governors be given exclusive responsibility for deciding how the funds would be used. This proposal typified the overall approach of the Bush administration toward intergovernmental change: the allocation of generally small amounts of money to these programs in a manner consistent with the philosophical directions defined in the previous administration. The total amounts appropriated for both categoricals and block grants increased somewhat but with more attention to budgetary constraints than to explicitly intergovernmental concerns.

Likewise, President Bill Clinton had to grapple with budgetary concerns and seemingly tried to do so with only minimal attention to IGR. Early in his first term of office, Clinton advocated terminating or consolidating some 150 existing grant programs. In the FY 1995 budget, however, the president proposed a combination of programs in selected programmatic areas that represented some expansion of funding to state and local governments. These included assistance for education, job training, and public works. Interestingly, during President George W. Bush's first term, the administration presided over a fairly significant increase in intergovernmental funding, with FY 2004 budget documents showing continued upward trends in both total dollars allocated and the proportion of total federal outlays going to state and local governments (it should be noted that the majority of the funding was in the form of payments to individuals for Social Security or to institutions, such as hospitals, for medical expenses). That trend was not sustained entirely, however, in budget proposals for FY 2005–2008. While total dollars allocated were projected to increase, intergovernmental aid as a proportion of total federal outlays was projected to level off or to decrease somewhat, as already noted.

Early in 2011, President Barack Obama and his administration proposed significant cuts in national government aid to some of those in need, in larger cities. Fiscal (and political) pressures on Obama will, in all likelihood, cause him to be more reluctant to push for intergovernmental aid than he might otherwise be.

Fiscal Reform: Impacts of Change

Various studies of GRS and block grants have suggested the following patterns of how they were used: (1) more funding was allocated to existing operating programs than to new ones; (2) the largest category of use in smaller communities was capital expenditures—for new municipal buildings, waterworks, even public golf courses; (3) keeping tax rates stable in inflationary times was a major concern of many local decision makers in considering how to use these funds; (4) local political majorities became, if anything, stronger and more entrenched; and (5) alleviating poverty in larger cities, a major aim of many categoricals in the 1960s, was not a primary purpose of either GRS or block grants. A major consequence of the shift to this form of aid was a decline in public-policy concern for needy minorities, many of whose members were concentrated in the poorest central cities. The distinction between local political majorities and minorities as primary beneficiaries of GRS/block grants and categorical grants, respectively, was a significant one; the effects of the grants on each of these recipients form a crucial corollary to debates over types of national government assistance. The politics of fiscal federalism overlaps policy fields such as urban policy and civil rights. To "increase the flexibility of state and local governments" is to de-emphasize the policy concerns (much more prevalent in the 1960s than now) with problems of urban minority groups and, more generally, with problems of poverty.[37]

In addition to these general impacts, neither generation of block grants operated precisely in the manner predicted by their strongest advocates. Soon after being enacted, the early block grants showed signs of what some called "creeping categorization"—a pattern of various abuses discovered in the course of grant implementation, followed by the gradual reassertion of national agency control in order to prevent further abuse.[38]

During the George W. Bush administration in 2005–2009, some patterns of policy and management evident in previous years began to reassert themselves. For example, President Bush (like President Reagan) used spending reductions in intergovernmental programs as part of a larger strategy of budget reductions. However, President Bush differed from President Reagan in at least three respects. First, the president targeted specific intergovernmental programs for reductions, rather than attempting across-the-board cuts (in intergovernmental programs only). Second, particularly with respect to funding for national government antipoverty efforts, the president "pushed for increased funding for religion-based groups while proposing deep cuts for many traditional anti-poverty programs."[39] And finally, the president experienced some significant failures in his efforts; one notable example came in the spring of 2005, when the U.S. Senate voted by 68–31 to restore "funds the White House wanted to eliminate for Community Development Block Grants (CDBG)" (a favorite of local officials ever since their inception in the mid-1970s).[40] Even that vote, however, does not change the fact that "[w]hen adjusted for inflation, spending on CDBG is at its lowest point ever, less than half the fiscal 1978 funding level."[41]

Thus, echoing patterns of the 1980s, it is possible to suggest that some of the current debates over federalism and IGR (at least with respect to intergovernmental aid) are essentially debates about government budgets and spending reductions. It can be said with more certainty that national budget considerations have played a role in shaping the course of funding for states and localities—and to that extent have influenced the relationship of the national government to states and localities.

Both GRS and block grants achieved, at least in part, what their proponents intended for them—to loosen the conditions attached to aid from Washington. Powerful forces, however, will continue to support increases in categorical aid. This fact is reflected in the perpetuation of nearly 600 such programs; together, they still make up about 75 percent of all intergovernmental funding by the national government. This reflects congressional interest in defining and targeting national aid in ways favored by members of Congress, even though their decisions may or may not match the preferences of state and local elected officials, or even those of the public at large. Thus, the debate is likely to continue for some time over the direction of intergovernmental aid.

Administrative Reform: Multiple Initiatives and Shifting Tides

Other efforts to reduce national government influence in IGR have taken numerous—and often contradictory—directions. One early effort was the movement for *citizen participation* in administrative decision making, especially where decisions on expenditures of grant funds were concerned. By incorporating such requirements into a large number of grant authorizations, Congress was responding to substantial pressures from previously underrepresented constituencies, notably poorer urban minority groups (see Chapter 2). The underlying assumption was that government officials had been insensitive to the needs of aid recipients in the past and that, as aid categories multiplied, it would be necessary to expand clientele representation. Thus, in many grants as well as GRS, provision was made for public hearings, and sometimes for more formalized participation, at crucial points in the decision-making process. The promise of citizen participation may well have been greater than the realization of it, not least because some administrators may have succeeded in co-opting potential adversaries from citizen groups.

Another approach to bringing the grants system (and functional specialists) under better control centered on achieving better *coordination* among proliferating aid programs. The earliest efforts focused on coordination among aid applicants and stressed regionwide coordinative mechanisms. A number of efforts were made to promote better communication among aid applicants (especially at the local level). Despite some protests, these efforts were deemed necessary by many in Congress and federal agencies because of widespread local and state unwillingness to consider the effects of their own programs and planning on those of neighboring jurisdictions. Improving coordination through better communication was a consistent theme in the IGR arena.

Emphasis also has been placed on more information and training. Information resources currently available to grant seekers include the "bible" of grantsmanship, the Catalog of Federal Domestic Assistance (CFDA), published by the national government containing descriptions of 1,400 separate assistance programs administered by fifty-seven federal agencies, and available online at *http://www.cfda.gov*; a computerized information system based largely on the CFDA, known as the Federal Awards Assistance Data System (FAADS); and publications of the Grants Management Advisory Service in Washington and the Grantsmanship Center in Los Angeles.

Yet another broad example of multiple initiatives and shifting tides concerns the various approaches of different U.S. presidents in the past thirty years. For example, more than any other president, Ronald Reagan actively sought to change the way national government agencies conducted their intergovernmental activities. By making frequent use of presidential executive orders, he attempted to alter many features of national-state and national-local relations that existed when he first took office. During his second term (1985–1989), President Reagan took more explicit steps to promote his conception of "New Federalism"—a view of the federal system that, if fully adopted, would limit executive agency activities in contemporary IGR and instead return to a position that favored heightened state government activity and influence. National government departments and agencies were told to consider the effects of their regulatory and legislative policies on state and local governments in an effort to improve the management of state-administered federal programs. During the presidency of George H. W. Bush, executive-branch agencies were advised

> to pursue further . . . relief to State and local governments by providing administrative flexibility, promoting efficiency through Governmentwide common rulemaking, cutting . . . red tape, decentralizing the decision-making process, and seeking State and local government views in the development of [national government agency] rules.[42]

In all these formulations, there is the clear assumption that national programs and procedures have had generally adverse effects on state and local governments, and that both states and localities should be in the forefront of planning and managing future intergovernmental programs.[43]

The Clinton administration came to office in 1993 without the same ideological commitment to state and local government predominance that the two previous administrations had, but Clinton (like Reagan, a former governor) was eager to apply to the national government many lessons learned during his experience with state government. In addition, President Clinton (in part from budget/deficit concerns) exhibited some of the same inclinations as Reagan and Bush did toward downsizing, and devolving functions from, the national government. Nevertheless, President Clinton strengthened some national government initiatives for funding intergovernmental activities, especially in policy areas such as education, environmental protection, transportation, and infrastructure improvements. Significantly, however, the Clinton administration spoke consistently of moving decision authority "closer to the people" by allowing state and local governments greater flexibility in managing their programs.

George W. Bush came to the presidency articulating a program designed to lessen the tax burden, reduce national government spending, and promote actions by state and local governments over those of "Washington." By the early years of his second term, however, it was obvious that President Bush's federalism-related record was a mixed one. On the one hand, the president succeeded in reducing national government revenues through lower taxation; he also made considerable headway in redirecting many national government efforts in more philosophically (and programmatically) conservative directions. On the other hand, there was some concern—particularly, and perhaps ironically, among many conservative supporters of the president—that in pursuit of some conservative policy objectives, the president expanded the role of the national government—contrary to long-standing conservative inclinations "to downsize government and devolve power to the states."[44] The concern, on the part of "Republicans inside and outside the White House," was that the president was "fostering what amounts to an era of new federalism in which the national government shapes, not shrinks, programs and institutions to comport with various conservative ideals."[45]

During the Bush administration, the national government moved into more of a predominant position in many aspects of our lives—albeit in a more philosophically (especially socially) conservative direction. One example was the Bush effort to achieve enactment of a constitutional amendment banning gay marriage. Although this effort is supported by many social conservatives, regulations concerning marriage and divorce traditionally are state, not national, government matters. Another example (somewhat more obscure, perhaps) was the proposal—supported by the president and many other Republicans—for the national government to place a cap on punitive damages in medical liability cases. This proposal, if enacted, would have achieved a long-sought policy objective—but in the process, would also usurp some state government powers (for example, significant regulation of both the medical profession and the insurance industry). The problem for the president, and others, is that many proposals would "require conservatives to sacrifice one principle to accomplish another"—never an easy dilemma for any government official, of any persuasion or philosophy, to resolve.[46]

The cuts to the CDBG program, referred to earlier, were yet another example of dilemmas faced by the Bush administration, because of the strong resistance encountered from local elected officials—many of whom were Republicans. And their resistance made it more difficult to accomplish something more fundamental that the president wanted to do.

One other Bush administration initiative should be noted—an initiative with major implications for increased national government spending. In

Medicare Prescription Drug Act

passed by Congress in December 2005 and provides supplemental (Part D) prescription drug coverage for seniors eligible for Medicare.

December 2005, Congress passed by a slim margin the controversial (and costly) **Medicare Prescription Drug Act**. Creation of a prescription drug benefit under the Medicare program was the first new federal "entitlement" program since the 1960s; the drug benefit went into effect in January 2006. An "entitlement" is a government program under which total spending is heavily influenced by the total number of eligible individuals who take advantage of the program, with no fixed ceiling established by law on the overall dollar amounts available to support the program. The federal government, late in 2005, estimated that the total costs of the drug benefit in the first ten years would be $725 billion—a substantial spending commitment, especially for an administration publicly committed to limiting government spending.

Another dimension of federalism under George W. Bush was the emergence of a new activism at the state and local levels—an activism that clearly has continued into the Obama years. Although this is hardly the first time in our history that state and local governments have assumed an activist role, the reasons for that happening in the past twenty years are complex. They included, among other things, national government budget deficits in the mid- and late 1980s (and larger deficits again in recent years), combined with reductions in aid to states and localities—what one observer has labeled "fend-for-yourself federalism."[47] Another reason, in the early twenty-first century, is the greatly increased level of state and local responsibilities in the wake of the September 11, 2001, attacks—especially under tighter budget constraints.

The Obama Administration and Contemporary Federalism

The Obama administration assumed office in January 2009 with what many regarded as a popular mandate for change, a principal theme of the president's election campaign throughout 2008. But even many Obama supporters were not prepared for the scope and intensity of some early, key initiatives that the president undertook—most notably the American Recovery and Reinvestment Act (ARRA), a "stimulus package" with a $787 billion price tag, which was designed to spark renewed economic activity across the board, especially in the private sector. That statute provoked both widespread support and considerable opposition, representing as it did a significant expansion of national government activity and authority.

Under Obama, there have been many developments such as ARRA and health care reform with direct impacts on, and implications for, our federal arrangement of governments. Thomas Gais, director of the Rockefeller Institute of Government, State University of New York at Albany, has identified seven key features of Obama-era federalism[48]:

1. *More money for state and local governments than in any previous national government stimulus effort.* Of the $787 billion appropriated under ARRA, $246 billion went to or through state governments, which was more than twelve times the amount sent to states in the Jobs and Growth Act of 2003 (a more modest stimulus initiative under George W. Bush). Among other purposes, these dollars were directed to Medicaid, the **Race to the Top** education program, infrastructure spending, social and economic "safety net" programs (for example, Food Stamps, Head Start, and unemployment insurance), and energy programs. State governments can expect more national government dollars for higher education expenditures, university research funding, and more grants under NCLB. Also, various health care–related undertakings have received more fiscal support from the Obama administration.

2. *Direct efforts to control state budgets, policies, and administration.* Much of the money "comes with strings attached," continuing a long-term trend under both Republican and Democratic presidents and Congresses. Under ARRA, states had to retain existing Medicaid eligibility rules and current K-12 and higher education spending levels. Under health care reform (provisions of the Patient Protection and Affordable Care Act [PPACA] of 2010), states must maintain current Medicaid/Children's Health Insurance Program (CHIP) eligibility levels for children until 2019. States also must maintain current Medicaid eligibility for adults until health care exchanges are fully operational.

3. *Expanded use of project grants.* The number of such grants is especially noticeable in PPACA/health care reform and the Elementary and Secondary Education Act (ESEA); Race to the Top also included many project grants.

4. *Blurred, entangled, uncertain, and varied division of responsibilities.* In other words, "marble cake" federalism is taken to new heights. This is particularly a result of enactment of PPACA/health care reform. Responsibilities will be interwoven between federal and state governments.

5. *Influence of the president and other national government administrators.* Beginning with the Reagan administration, presidents have used "a growing variety of executive powers to influence the states: from waivers to rulemaking, memoranda, demonstration projects, [and] grant conditions."[49] The use of competitive grants in ARRA and PPACA gives national government administrators considerable influence. Obama's Department of Education insisted that states document education reforms required under ARRA.

6. *Strong interest in reducing disparities across state and local governments in outcomes and resources.* A leading example of this interest is demonstrated in the "Blueprint for Reform," which mandates that high-poverty and low-poverty school districts receive comparable funding. The "Blueprint" would also classify high-poverty schools, districts, and states into "Reward" and "Challenge" categories, based on student performance. Flexibility in operations, policies, and reporting as well as financial rewards would follow. This would have the effect of focusing national government resources on areas of greatest need.[50]

Race to the Top

the Obama administration's $4.35 billion U.S. Department of Education program designed to encourage reforms in state and local district K-12 education. Funded as part of the ARRA of 2009.

7. *Continues stress on accountability based on measured "results" but with emphasis on evidence-based practices and greater concern about data quality and comparability.* Three elements of practice have been altered since 2009. First, Obama's administration has moved away from state-developed tests toward "more comparable interstate measures of graduation rates and readiness for postsecondary programs." Second, there is a "new emphasis on research and diffusion of evidence-based practices—i.e., practices in education and health care that have been evaluated and found to be more effective than others." Finally, a new focus on how goals are to be pursued represents a change from earlier "devolution" practices where the national government was said to be "loose on means, tight on goals." Defining means more specifically is to be done before those means are used at the state and local levels.[51]

In summary, many policy initiatives in the first two years of the Obama administration were characterized by a strong tendency toward "centralization—using [a] combination of controls and selective flexibility to advance [the national] government's views of appropriate policies and budgets."[52] However, this centralization trend differed from those during some previous presidencies, involving "money, targeted assistance, executive control, federal entanglement in state policies and operations, and interest in using states to identify and diffuse 'effective' practices across the entire system."[53]

After Republicans gained majority control of the U.S. House of Representatives and increased their numbers in the U.S. Senate in 2010, President Obama had more difficulty in pursuing the directions taken in 2009–2010. According to Gais, divided government gives states a wider range of opportunities to influence the national government, and makes it harder for Congress and the president to resolve a wide range of issues, and this clearly has been the case since the beginning of 2011.[54] Pressures for *less*, not more, national government activity built during Obama's first two years in office. It is likely that the broad debate concerning national versus state authority, initiative, and control—a debate as old as the Republic—will not only continue but also intensify in the immediate future.

State and Local Activity in Contemporary Federalism

In the past few years, officials at the state and local levels have been unmistakably more active, even assertive, relative to the national government, even as the national government has itself expanded many areas of its own policy activism. Examples include the following:

• In Parkland, Florida, where the motto is "Environmentally Proud," the city began in 2008 to dispense cash rebates to its 25,000 residents for being more environmentally friendly. The city of Baltimore offers at least $2,000 toward closing costs for people who buy new homes close to where they work. Residents of Albuquerque, New Mexico, get fast-track building permits and other perks if they agree to make their homes more energy efficient. And in Arizona, many cities pay residents to replace grass with artificial turf or plants that use less water. Scottsdale, outside Phoenix, will pay homeowners up to $1,500 for such improvements. "We're in the middle of a desert, and water is absolutely the most precious resource we have," said city spokesman Mike Phillips.[55]

- A joint investigation of mortgage-lending companies' foreclosure— involving all fifty states and the District of Columbia—led to greater compliance by those companies with state foreclosure laws. Almost pre- dictably, there has been some variation in the patterns of compliance across the states, but the general trend has been in the direction of greater compliance, and, as a result, more equitable foreclosure processes for millions of homeowners.[56]

- On Election Day 2010, voters in all ten California cities with a referen- dum on the ballot dealing with taxing marijuana sales approved new or higher taxes. This happened on the same day that California voters re- jected Proposition 19 that would have legalized recreational marijuana use statewide.[57]

- In Washington, the notion of using a "cap-and-trade" system to reduce greenhouse gases is a major point of contention between liberals and con- servatives, and between many Democrats and many Republicans. But in 2008, ten northeastern and Middle Atlantic states formed the Regional Greenhouse Gas Initiative (RGGI), which "imposed a cap-and-trade re- gime on large power plants in Delaware, Maryland, New England, New Jersey, and New York." In December 2010, the results to that point were considered to be largely a success.[58]

- According to a 2010 National League of Cities survey, most U.S. cities face worsening economies, and local governments will have to cut person- nel or stop construction over the next few years, even though the national economy was recovering from the deep recession. Three in four city of- ficials reported that overall economic and fiscal conditions worsened in 2009 and 2010, and more than six in ten said poverty intensified. Ninety percent of officials said unemployment was a problem for their commu- nities and that joblessness had mounted. Underlying these problems is the fact that local (and state) economies take more time to recover from a recession than the national economy does, because demands for public assistance rise just as tax revenue falls.

- Some state governments deliberately took action *against specific national government proposals, policies, and/or enactments.* For example, a substantial number of states filed suit in 2010, seeking to overturn PPACA/health care reform. The essence of their argument (both legal and political) is that the national government vastly exceeded its constitutional authority by enacting PPACA. They took issue, especially, with the provision that makes the purchase of health insurance mandatory for individuals. On another front, officials in the state of Texas announced, in late 2010, that they would not comply with greenhouse gas regulations that took effect in early January 2011. One consequence was that EPA took "the unprecedented step of directly issuing air permits to industries in Texas." (In an unrelated, but parallel, action, Texas Governor Rick Perry announced that he would not ask the Texas legislature to appropriate funds to implement state action associated with national health care reform.) Also, Arizona, in 2010, and Utah, in 2011, have adopted statutes that would allow a police crackdown on illegal immigrants. Arizona Governor Jan Brewer justified her state adopting the statute in part on the grounds that in the absence of national government enactment of a new immigration policy, the states have every right to step in. As of early 2011, the Arizona statute was on hold, pending resolution of a lawsuit filed by the U.S. Justice Department in federal court. Finally, many political conservatives, including dozens of state lawmakers, have supported a proposal to amend the U.S. Constitution that would allow states to repeal or void pieces of congressional legislation with which they strongly disagree. Virginia's Attorney General, Ken Cuccinelli, has taken the public stance that as the chief legal officer of his state, he has the constitutional authority to initiate such an action.[59]

- On the other hand, the continuing controversy surrounding health care reform "has largely overshadowed some states' efforts to use the law to help them move as fast as possible to insure more people and increase control over insurance companies."[60] Among others, Minnesota, Connecticut, Maryland, Vermont, and Oregon have moved aggressively on one or more fronts contained in PPACA, in the interests of leveraging more national government dollars for coverage of childless adults (in Minnesota and Connecticut), for providing preventive care (in Oregon), and for constructing an online infrastructure for an insurance marketplace (also in Oregon). Four other states, each of which elected a Republican governor in 2010, also are using grant funds to build the same sort of online infrastructure Oregon is pursuing, putting them in the ironic position of accepting money to implement parts of the law while joining with other states in seeking to overturn PPACA in federal court.[61]

All of this, of course, is in addition to state activism in a variety of other policy areas, in recent years—for example, state attorneys general who pursued, and won, a major settlement from tobacco companies; and a few governors (and some others in state government) who have actively sought to import pharmaceuticals (especially from Canada) in defiance of both

Congress and the Food and Drug Administration (FDA). Small wonder that, over the years, many observers have described the states as "laboratories" of government.[62] And plainly, those "laboratories" have been playing an increasing role in the overall governmental scheme of things.

Prospects and Issues in IGR: A Look Ahead

Any attempt to forecast even the near future in IGR is a highly speculative venture. But there are already certain indications. One issue that has been addressed by both academics and politicians is the extent to which intergovernmental *regulation* has become part of IGR.[63] Intergovernmental regulations, which have become far more numerous since the 1960s, have been enacted as part of national government bureaucracies' efforts to direct implementation of categorical grant assistance programs. In most instances, the regulations are designed to implement other national government legislation aimed at achieving wide-ranging social and economic objectives. Political scientist Donald Kettl explains the rise of **regulatory federalism**:

> The [national] government cannot constitutionally order state and local governments to examine the environmental impact of projects they propose or to keep their financial records in specified ways. The . . . government can, however, set those standards as conditions for [both categorical and block] grants.[64]

regulatory federalism

an approach to intergovernmental relations under which federal agencies use regulations as opposed to grants to influence state and local governments.

Literally hundreds of such regulations now exist. An examination of a small sampling of them may help to convey the scope of this regulation. Under statutory authority from Congress, for example, the EPA may prescribe the treatment local governments must give to their drinking water, as well as the inspections some states must conduct on automobile emission controls. Health care regulations govern the operation of Medicaid programs run by state governments with shared funding by the national government. National mine-safety regulations set standards for the operation of state and local gravel pits. One reason for the creation of new special-purpose local "quasi governments" (such as regional health planning organizations) was a regulatory requirement imposed by agency officials who distrusted—and therefore wanted to bypass—traditional local political institutions. Professor Kettl summarizes the consequences:

> In all of these areas, the [national] government has spun out elaborate requirements about who can make decisions, who must be consulted,

and even how records of performance must be filed. Rules stipulate who must benefit from [nationally] aided programs, and how state and local governments must administer those benefits. These regulations have created a wide channel of [national] influence over the most intimate details of state and local operations. They have also made state and local governments front-line administrators for numerous national programs.[65]

The point has been made, however, that such regulations often have positive substantive aspects as well; the experience of numerous states has suggested how important and useful national government requirements often turn out to be. The central challenge for reforming IGR is to reduce the number of so-called unproductive regulations without abolishing those serving important national (and sometimes *state*) purposes.

Two varieties of regulations have developed. So-called *crosscutting rules* apply across the board to many national aid programs. *Program-based rules* apply to individual programs. Some rules, such as the 1931 Davis–Bacon Act, govern administrative and fiscal policy; other rules, such as those accompanying the 1990 Americans with Disabilities Act, the 1993 Family and Medical Leave Act, and the NCLB of 2002, impact social and economic policy.[66]

Two particular aspects of regulatory federalism deserve mention. One is the concern that many mandated activities are costly—for example, paying prevailing wages (determined by the U.S. Labor Department) on construction projects receiving national government funds, or providing "reasonable accommodation" for access by the physically handicapped—and that governments imposing such mandates have not been supplying necessary funding. This has placed numerous local governments and private organizations in increasingly difficult financial positions because the intergovernmental aid they receive is not sufficient to pay for mandated activities. The federal government has little systematic data concerning the cumulative costs it imposes on state and local governments. Several studies in the past twenty years suggest, however, that an average of 10–15 percent of all municipal budgets is devoted to meeting the financial obligations associated with mandates. These unfunded mandates (legal requirements that states and local governments must undertake a specific activity or provide a service meeting minimum national standards) cover a very wide range of public-policy areas, including community development, environmental pollution, transportation, public health and safety, and public housing. Perhaps predictably, many state and local officials increasingly objected to this practice; one response was enactment of the Unfunded Mandates Reform Act of 1995, which made it more difficult for Congress to impose new laws, rules, or regulations that would add significantly to state or local government costs.

The other aspect of the mandating question, however, is the widely shared impression that national government mandates have been the hardest to bear. Though there is obvious variety among the fifty states, a study commissioned by one state legislature intended to highlight the extent of federal mandates on local governments found instead that four-fifths of the burden (in this case, in the education field) was imposed by state rather than national government law. This does not downgrade the significance of the mandating issue in general; it does, however, suggest that grouping national and state mandates together may foster false impressions about some aspects of the extent of the problem. Since the 1990s, increased attention has been paid to such problems of intergovernmental regulation, and steps have been taken to ease the burden, especially that on local governments. For example, many of the more detailed (and, many say, more burdensome) regulations have been eliminated; also, government regulatory agencies have been directed to cut obsolete regulations and to act like partners with affected businesses, states, and local governments.

Another issue area affecting IGR is the phenomenon known as **devolution**—referring to shifts of governmental authority from the national government to state governments (and possibly from states to localities as well). In the 1980s and especially the 1990s, many advocates joined in promoting devolution, contending that it would "provide more efficient provision and production of public services; better alignment of the costs and benefits of government for a diverse citizenry; better fits between public goods and their spatial characteristics; increased competition, experimentation, and innovation in the public sector; greater responsiveness to citizen preferences; and more transparent accountability in policymaking."[67]

There is evidence, however, that devolution has not "taken hold" as its supporters hoped it would. "Analysts seeking evidence of the impact of devolution have not been able to uncover much."[68] In the late 1990s and the early twenty-first century, new federal mandates were imposed; at least one survey of city officials found strong feelings that very little devolution had taken place; and as noted above, federal intergovernmental aid expenditures rose, rather than fell, for a time—not what one might expect to find in an era of devolution.[69] "The devolution that has occurred has tended to be of an administrative variety (for example, the federal government's granting of a waiver to a state implementing a federal statute); meaningful substantive devolution is notably absent."[70] Regardless of the future of devolution, these and similar issues concerning the nature of federalism will almost certainly continue to be debated. For example, improving the capacity of state and local governments to provide greater homeland security already has prompted significant

devolution

a process of transferring power or functions from a higher to a lower level of government in the U.S. federal system.

changes in IGR. These include, among other things, increased financial, legal, operational, and political resources for national, state, and local agencies, and new methods of interaction involving those agencies, many of which are less familiar with horizontal coordination than with vertical communication.[71]

Intergovernmental Relations and Public Administration

The diffuse nature of federalism (which is perhaps not as diffuse now as it was in the past) has combined with growing intergovernmental ties in all directions to create an unquestionably complex situation. Public administration has been altered, perhaps permanently, by rapid changes in IGR.

For example, it is clear that the patterns of political influence termed *subsystem politics* in the national government (see Chapter 2) have been extended into intergovernmental politics. Despite recent efforts to gain greater control of their bureaucracies, most chief executives have failed to stem the growth of vertical functional bureaucratic linkages—the picket-fence "autocracies" originally referred to by ACIR. One reason for the inability of a president or governor to overcome the institutional strength of multilevel bureaucracies is precisely that the latter can call on political support from at least one other level or unit of government much more easily than a chief executive can. Intergovernmental administrative relations, in other words, have served to strengthen existing bureaucratic autonomy at every level of government. (Whether that general pattern will continue without change— or without external efforts to *impose* change—is an important and intriguing question.)

A second area of serious concern for public administration is fiscal relations, especially the financial difficulties of some American governments. State and local government revenues have been severely affected by the economic downturn of recent years. Even though the private economy has been showing signs of recovery since late 2010, it is very likely that (as in past recessions and recoveries) government revenues will lag well behind private-sector economic activity in returning to fiscal strength and stability. Adding to these difficulties is the fact that about one-third of the states suffer from *structural* budget imbalances resulting from revenue growth that is chronically slower than increases in the costs of services those states must provide. Also, problems like those experienced at various times in New York City, Miami, Detroit, and Cleveland, as well as other major cities and counties (and some smaller ones), may come to hound political leaders, administrators, and citizens in other communities as they struggle to avoid fiscal chaos caused by antitax sentiments among voters, declining property-tax bases, and escalating service costs. Although intergovernmental aid can do much to bail out a city here and a suburb there, a real question exists as to whether costs imposed by inflation, tax limitation movements, and rising service needs can, in fact, be met over the long term by infusions of aid. At the core of the problem is the fact that recipient governments can easily develop a continuing dependency on such aid (whether from national or state sources), which may not always be available. Programs funded in whole or in part through intergovernmental aid face more sharp cuts or even curtailment as funding declines or ceases, and in states facing their own increasing fiscal stress, that possibility is growing stronger. Program cuts, efficiency, priority setting, strategic planning, and "entrepreneurial thinking" are relatively new concerns in public administration—in degree, at least—arising out of the very real fiscal crunch enveloping all levels of government.

A third area of concern is control over grants-in-aid and other funding. A stark reality of IGR is the existence of bureaucratic, and "interbureaucratic," controls on much of the money flowing from one level to another. These controls raise questions about public accountability and about the ability of chief executives to coordinate spending effectively. Public administrators have considerable discretionary authority over public spending; this authority has affected the age-old issue of fiscal responsibility and accountability. A related concern is that, until the last decade, some government institutions (such as state legislatures) have lacked any real access to key decision makers or any impact on decisions regarding intergovernmental funding. For the most part, bureaucrats are in the driver's seat when it comes to categorical grant funding, still by far the largest part of intergovernmental aid. Whether the situation will stay that way is unclear, given new pressures on both intergovernmental aid and the administrators in charge of intergovernmental programs.

Other emerging patterns in contemporary IGR include some decline in the relative prominence of fiscal and grant-related issues and a corresponding rise in the importance of intergovernmental regulatory issues (among others), and the key role of the courts in settling federalism-related questions (such as health care reform and immigration policy, among many others). There is also growing recognition of a disturbing possibility that increased coordination among local governments—a worthwhile objective—may prove to be elusive in the long run. Finally, scholars in the field of federalism will, in all likelihood, continue their efforts to bring some intellectual order out of the seeming chaos that has occurred in IGR just in the last fifty years. For example, there have been spirited debates about the degree of centralization appropriate as a remedy for bureaucratic control of categorical grants; also at issue is the question of just how functional or dysfunctional contemporary IGR has become. It is no exaggeration to suggest that few areas of governance in this country are as complex or as challenging as this one has proved to be.

Summary

Federalism, in its original meaning, defined an arrangement of governments in which a central government and regional units each had some independent standing in the governmental system. Federalism has important constitutional, political, fiscal, and administrative dimensions. Our federal system has evolved through a variety of choices and changes, and today, IGR is predominant on the federal scene.

In the past fifty years, contemporary IGR has become highly complex. Contributing to the complexity are the present grants system, functional alliances among program administrators, and continuing tensions between political executives and functional specialists (and their respective clienteles). Bureaucratic activity at all levels is central to IGR and to fiscal federalism. Categorical grants are the most widely used form of fiscal assistance, though greater political resistance has emerged to "categoricals." Besides being used to achieve a wide range of programmatic purposes, these grants also have served to encourage a number of changes in the behavior of recipient governments. From the early 1960s to the late 1990s, categorical grants of both project and formula types were increasingly used to promote explicitly national purposes.

That led to considerable administrative complexity. Political and administrative choices made early in the history of cash grants set a precedent for single state agency relationships with national agencies in charge of a given grant program. A sequence of events was thus set in motion that led to the creation of self-governing guilds (also called vertical functional autocracies) and picket- or bamboo-fence federalism. These allied interests gradually consolidated control over grant programs, causing a political reaction that sparked a continuing search for ways to control those guilds. Coordination is increasingly difficult to achieve, however, given the proliferation of politically potent government units and of both horizontal and vertical linkages among them.

Grant reform has occurred in several ways. Fiscal reforms included the use of GRS and block grants (though neither has ever approached categorical grants in scope or funding). Since the presidency of Ronald Reagan, block grants have assumed new importance. Administrative reforms have taken the form of either decentralization (in particular, through increased citizen participation) or efforts to improve coordination and management of the grants system. Improved information and communication have also been stressed. In recent years, state authority clearly has grown, due both to many favorable decisions of the U.S. Supreme Court and to an emerging state-level activism that frequently leaves at least some states at odds with the national government in important policy areas.

The Obama administration has both undertaken key initiatives, such as ARRA and health care reform, and introduced new controversies to modern federalism and IGR. Hallmarks of federalism in Obama's first term included more money for state and local governments; direct efforts to control state budgets, policies, and administration; expanded use of project grants; blurred, entangled, uncertain, and varied division of responsibilities between national and state governments; strong interest in reducing disparities across state and local governments in outcomes and resources; and continued emphasis on accountability based on measured "results" but with emphasis on evidence-based practices and greater concern about data quality and comparability.

Issues to be dealt with in the immediate future include the continuing and perplexing problem of unfunded mandates, prospects for further reductions in both national and state aid, and changes in the extent of bureaucratic autonomy at all levels of government. Also important will be questions of continuing fiscal constraints facing government across the board, IGR-related policy directions of the current administration, and the challenge of maintaining governmental accountability in the federal system. Continued complexity in IGR is a certainty.

Discussion Questions

1. In defining the scope of national government authority, especially regarding conflict and overlap with state authority, what issues have had to be resolved—in our early history, in more recent decades, and very possibly in the years ahead?

2. Identify the key features of IGR in contemporary American politics and discuss their significance. What major themes may be said to exist in contemporary IGR?

3. What "fiscal mismatch" exists in modern federalism? Why does it exist? What solution(s) is(are) currently implemented? Does the "mismatch" need to be "solved"? Are there better solutions? If so, suggest what one or more might be.

4. As trust in the national government declines, will trust in local governments increase? Why or why not?

5. What role has the Supreme Court played in defining contemporary IGR?

6. How did the proliferation of categorical grants lead to administrative complexity?

7. What administrative and fiscal problems arise from problems associated with lack of grant coordination? What steps have been taken to prevent such problems from occurring and to deal with them when they do arise?

8. Compare and contrast block grants, categorical grants, project grants, and formula grants. What are they and what are the political consequences of each (referring to questions of political and administrative control, and different patterns of programmatic benefit and lack of benefit for each type of program)?

9. Discuss the use of regulations by administrative agencies as a vehicle for intergovernmental control and how changes in administrative autonomy at all levels of government affect IGR.

10. What political and administrative patterns in federalism/IGR are associated with the presidency of Barack Obama?

Key Terms and Concepts

American Recovery and
    Reinvestment Act (ARRA), *99*

federalism, *100*

intergovernmental relations
    (IGR), *100*

unfunded mandates *101*

No Child Left Behind Act
    (NCLB), *104*

preemptions, *108*

eminent domain, *108*

fiscal federalism, *110*

fiscal mismatch, *111*

grants-in-aid, *112*

externalities, *115*

formula grants, *115*

project grants, *115*

categorical grants, *115*

Medicaid, *116*

gubernatorial, *118*

single state agency
    requirement, *118*

vertical functional
    autocracies, *119*

picket-fence federalism, *119*

block grants, *124*

Medicare Prescription Drug Act,
    130

Race to the Top, *131*

regulatory federalism, *135*

devolution, *137*

Suggested Readings

Anton, Thomas J. *American Federalism and Public Policy: How the System Works*. Philadelphia: Temple University Press, 1989.

Chemerinsky, Erwin. *Enhancing Government: Federalism for the 21st Century*. Stanford, Calif.: Stanford Law/Stanford University Press, 2008.

Conlan, Timothy J. *From New Federalism to Devolution: Twenty-Five Years of Intergovernmental Reform*. Washington, D.C.: Brookings Institution Press, 1998.

Conlan, Timothy J. "American Federalism in the 21st Century," in Chris Bailey, Bruce Cain, Gillian Peele, and Guy Peters, eds., *Developments in American Politics 6*. London: Palgrave Macmillan, 2010.

Elazar, Daniel J. *American Federalism: A View from the States*. 3rd ed. New York: Harper & Row, 1984.

Feeley, Malcolm, and Edward L. Rubin. *Federalism: Political Identity and Tragic Compromise*. Ann Arbor: University of Michigan, 2008.

Gray, Virginia, and Russell L. Hanson, eds. *Politics in the American States: A Comparative Analysis*. 9th ed. Washington, D.C.: CQ Press, 2007.

Hamilton, Michael, ed. *Regulatory Federalism, Natural Resources and Environmental Management*. Washington, D.C.: American Society for Public Administration, 1990.

Kettl, Donald F. *The Regulation of American Federalism* (paperback text edition). Baltimore: Johns Hopkins University Press, 1987.

LaCroix, Alison L. *The Ideological Origins of American Federalism*. Cambridge, Mass.: Harvard University Press, 2010.

Miller, Lisa Lynn. *Perils of Federalism: Race, Poverty, and the Politics of Crime Control*. Oxford: Oxford University Press, 2010.

Nugent, John Douglas. *Safeguarding Federalism: How States Protect Their Interests in National Policymaking*. Norman: University of Oklahoma, 2009.

O'Toole, Laurence J., ed. *American Intergovernmental Relations: Foundations, Perspectives, and Issues*. 4th ed. Washington, D.C.: CQ Press, 2006.

Peterson, Paul E. *The Price of Federalism*. Washington, D.C.: Brookings Institution Press, 1995.

Peterson, Paul E., Barry G. Rabe, and Kenneth K. Wong. *When Federalism Works*. Washington, D.C.: Brookings Institution Press, 1986.

Posner, Paul L. *The Politics of Unfunded Mandates: Whither Federalism?* Washington, D.C.: Georgetown University Press, 1998.

Riker, William H. *The Development of American Federalism*. Boston: Kluwer Academic Publishers, 1987.

Rivlin, Alice. *Reviving the American Dream: The Economy, the States, and the Federal Government.* Washington, D.C.: Brookings Institution Press, 1992.

Schapiro, Robert A. *Polyphonic Federalism: Toward the Protection of Fundamental Rights.* Chicago: University of Chicago, 2009.

Sutton, Robert P. *Federalism.* London: Greenwood Press, 2002.

Stephens, G. Ross, and Nelson Wikstrom. *American Intergovernmental Relations: A Fragmented Federal Polity.* New York: Oxford University Press, 2006.

Walker, David B. *The Rebirth of Federalism: Slouching Toward Washington.* 2nd ed. New York: Chatham House, 2000.

Wright, Deil S. *Understanding Intergovernmental Relations.* 3rd ed. Monterey, Calif.: Brooks/Cole, 1988.

PART II
Managing and Leading Public Organizations

Public organizations are being asked to do more, yet with fewer resources; thus, it is necessary to focus greater attention on internal behavior, dynamics, and leadership within organizations. This section deals with efforts to improve public management, addressing related subjects of organization theory and behavior, decision making, ethics, and administrative leadership.

Chapter 4 reviews the evolution of organization theory, beginning with late-nineteenth-century writings and following developments in theory and practice until the present Internet-driven, decentralized, and networked era. Organization theory has moved from a centralized, formalistic, relatively mechanistic view of organizations to more diverse and comprehensive concepts, reflecting increasingly complex awareness of human behavior and the need for everyone in an organization to learn as they respond to their environments. In addition, important internal dynamics of organizations are discussed, including communication, coordination, centralization and decentralization, line and staff functions, "tall" and "flat" hierarchies, and alternative forms of organization structure.

Chapter 5 examines administrative decision making—the formal and informal considerations that enter into decision processes and how decision makers deal with them. Ethics, the meaning of *rationality*, alternatives to the rational approach, the impact of personal and organizational goals, and other influences in the decisional environment are reviewed.

Chapter 6 focuses on chief executives and their leadership of bureaucracies at national, state, and local levels, and analyzes administrative leadership tasks within organizations. Similarities and differences are given careful attention, particularly with regard to policy development, implementation, changing leadership styles, and coping with declining resources. In addition, we summarize the characteristics and behaviors that facilitate effective leadership in public agencies. How chief executives interact with those in administrative agencies, what defines a good leader, and how their actions affect bureaucratic operations are also discussed.

Organizational Theory

Organization theory deals with the formal structure, internal workings, and external environment of complex human behavior within organizations. As a field spanning several disciplines, it prescribes how work and workers ought to be organized and attempts to explain the actual consequences of organizational behavior (including individual actions) on work being performed and on the organization itself.

The formal study of organizations—which spans the fields of business administration, economics, political science, psychology, statistics, sociology, as well as public administration—has evolved for over a century. Assumptions about work and workers in an organizational setting have changed; numerous (and often contradictory) hypotheses and research findings have emerged about what motivates workers in different work environments and how different incentives affect various tasks, employees, and situations; and a variety of views exists regarding the reciprocal impacts of organizations and the environments in which they operate. Some of the following discussion will be familiar to anyone who has worked in an organization—which, in our society, is most of us.

Categorizing major organization theories is not easy. On one level, they can be distinguished according to whether they concentrate on the needs, objectives, methods, problems, and values of management; on the personal and social needs and values of workers within organizations; or on the attempts by organizations to adapt to their social, political, or economic environments. On another level, it is possible to identify numerous specific theories, each with its own principal assumptions and emphases. Some of these theories overlap to an extent, sharing certain values and viewpoints while differing significantly in other respects. We will examine four major theories of organization: (1) formal theories, (2) the human relations school, (3) organizational humanism, and (4) modern organization theory.

> *As a citizen interested in government and as a former legislator, I had long believed that too many governmental programs are botched because they are started in haste without adequate planning or establishment of goals. Too often they never really attack the targeted problems.*
>
> Jimmy Carter, (then governor of Georgia)
> National Governors Conference,
> June 1974

Formal Theories of Organization

Although formal organization theory, as we understand it, originated in the late nineteenth century, some formative thinking on the subject dates back many centuries. In fact, such concepts of organization were largely derived from the highly structured arrangements of military forces and from rigidly structured ecclesiastical organizations. Most notably, the idea of a **hierarchy**, found in the great majority of contemporary organizations, springs from ancient military and religious roots. Some other features of formal theory (such as the need for control and for defining certain set procedures) also originated in very early organizations. The most prominent model of bureaucracy as an explicit form of social organization, however, was formulated by German sociologist Max Weber (1864–1920) late in the nineteenth century. Although widely known in Europe during the early twentieth century, Weber's work was not translated into English until the 1940s.

hierarchy

a characteristic of formal bureaucratic organizations; a clear vertical chain of command in which each unit is subordinate to the one above it and superior to the one below it; one of the most common features of governmental and other bureaucratic organizations.

Max Weber and the Bureaucratic Model

Weber's model was intended to identify the components of a well-structured government bureaucracy. He prescribed the following five key elements:

1. *Division of labor and functional specialization*—work is divided according to type and purpose, with clear areas of jurisdiction marked out for each working unit and an emphasis on elimination of overlapping and duplication of functions.
2. *Hierarchy*—a clear vertical chain of command in which each unit is subordinate to the one above it and superior to the one below it.
3. *Formal framework of rules and procedures*—designed to ensure stability, predictability, and impersonality in bureaucratic operations (and thus equal treatment for all who deal with the organization), as well as reliability of performance.
4. *Maintenance of files and other records*—to ensure that actions taken are both appropriate to the situation and consistent with past actions in similar circumstances.
5. *Professionalization*—employees are (a) appointed (not elected) on the basis of their qualifications and job-related skills, (b) employed full-time and in a career-oriented civil service, and (c) paid a regular salary and provided with benefits such as health insurance and a retirement pension.[1]

In addition to these explicit components, Weber obviously intended a government bureaucracy of the type just described to be endowed with sufficient *legal* and *political* authority to function adequately. His model of bureaucracy is, in fact, based on both legal and *rational* authority derived from a fixed central point in the political process and is assumed to function under that authority.[2] It is important to understand that Weber's formulation should be viewed in the context of the late nineteenth century and the rampant **patronage** systems that existed at the time. His model proposed a solution to the existing situation and a blueprint for professional and efficiently managed merit-based organizations (see Chapter 7).

This model of bureaucracy represented an effort by Weber to both describe and prescribe what he saw as the ideal form of organization then emerging in early-twentieth-century Europe. It is clearly a formalistic model and lacks dimensions later recognized as important, such as informal lines of authority, internal communication, customer feedback, concern for individual workers, equitable distribution of resources, and motivation in the bureaucracy. Also, Weber himself indicated that the model was not meant to apply to all conceivable organizational situations. It represented only a broad framework rather than an all-encompassing model, complete in every detail. Despite these limitations, however, the Weberian model was the first effort to define systematically this new form of social organization and to prescribe or explain its operations in abstract and theoretical terms.

One of the central goals of Weber's model was to make possible an optimum degree of *control* in an organization. The quest for control lay at the heart of virtually every element of the model. In particular, the *formalism* suggested by rules, procedures, and files, along with the exercise of authority through a hierarchy, point to Weber's overriding concern for organizations that would be both smoothly functioning and effectively managed. In this **formal theory of organization** and in others proposed at the time, to the extent that management concerns are emphasized, the ultimate goal is control from the top down over all organizational activities and needs. Consequently, in order to facilitate control, there is a preoccupation with encouraging *uniformity* rather than permitting diversity—in values as well as behavior—within the organization. In today's complex, diverse, network-based, and regulated society, this generalization has important political, as well as managerial, applications and implications, especially for well-educated "knowledge workers" in large service-oriented bureaucracies.

Nonetheless, a comparison of the Weberian model to contemporary American public administration illustrates the model's attractiveness as a yardstick against which to measure actual administrative practices, and the limitations on its applicability to very different times and circumstances. American public bureaucracies have operated within a formal framework of vertical hierarchy; extensive division of labor and specialization; specific rules, procedures, and routines; and a high degree of professionalization, complete with extensive merit systems, career emphases, and salary and fringe benefits. Yet, in spite of these similarities, there are equally prominent differences.

First, although the formal bureaucratic structure is hierarchical, those within that hierarchy respond to commands, incentives, and political decisions that arise from outside it. Thus, the hierarchy is often only one of the chains of command active in the bureaucracy (a reflection of our political diversity).

patronage

selection of public officials on the basis of political loyalty rather than merit, objective examination, or professional competence.

formal theory of organization

stresses formal, structural arrangements within organizations, and "correct" or "scientific" methods to be followed in order to achieve the highest degree of organizational efficiency; examples include Weber's theory of bureaucracy and Taylor's scientific management approach.

functional overlap

a phenomenon of contemporary American bureaucracy whereby functions performed by one bureaucratic entity may also be performed by another; conflicts with Weber's notions of division of labor and specialization.

merit system

a system of selection (and, ideally, evaluation) of administrative officials on the basis of job-related competence, as measured by examinations and professional qualifications.

Second, Weber's division of labor and specialization were designed to reduce **functional overlap** among bureaucratic units, so that any functions performed by a given entity were the responsibility of only that entity; in Weber's view, this was in the best interests of efficient operation. In contrast, American bureaucracy is shot through with functional overlap in spite of its specialization. This reflects (among other things) overlapping political jurisdictions and societal interests. For example, an occupational retraining program could logically be placed under the authority of either the Department of Labor (because the program is vocationally focused) or the Department of Education (because it emphasizes training, a DOE responsibility in programs not related to labor). Furthermore, functional overlap is practically guaranteed in a federal system in which separate governments organize their bureaucracies independently. (As described in Chapter 3, managing intergovernmental programs is especially challenging for many public administrators.) Yet, modern bureaucracies are increasingly required to act cooperatively and cross-functionally to resolve multidimensional problems.

Third, the kind of professionalization foreseen by Weber has been only partially achieved in American bureaucracy; this has been due in part to matters of definition. Weber's European "professionals" were so defined because they were making the bureaucracy their lifelong careers, were competent to perform the tasks for which they were hired, and were paid in the manner in which other professionals were paid. American bureaucracy differs from this European ideal in at least one key respect. There is a wide variety of personnel systems, ranging from the fully developed **merit system**, in which job-related competence is the most important qualification for employment, to the most open, deliberate patronage system in which political loyalty and connections are the major criteria in personnel decisions. The U.S. Civil Service, several states (such as Minnesota, California, and Wisconsin), and many cities headed by professional city managers make personnel decisions largely on a merit basis. Patronage is found in many other states, as well as in numerous urban and rural governments throughout the country—sometimes even when a merit system appears to be in operation.

The fourth departure from the Weberian ideal of professionalism is that more and more specialized professions in the private sector—law, information technology, medicine, engineering, social and physical sciences, and business management—are represented among government employees. Whereas Weber seemed to envision a *professional bureaucrat*, the American experience has produced *bureaucratic professionals*—specialists trained in various private-sector professions who find careers in the public service. Weber's conception appears to be narrower than the American reality with regard to the scope and diversity of skills of bureaucrats, as well as the variety of their professional loyalties. A further implication of professionalization is that employees of a Weberian bureaucracy would be judged by their *continuing competence* in their jobs. In this regard, American merit systems also diverge from Weber's model.

In the majority of cases, those who secure a merit position need only to serve a probationary period (usually six to eighteen months) before earning job security. How rapidly one rises through the ranks or how easily one can transfer to a new position may well be affected by periodic evaluations of competence, but it is still the exception rather than the rule to find a public employee dismissed solely for incompetence on the job.

Finally, Weber placed considerable emphasis on career employment. It is only since 1955, however, that the national government and some states and localities have attempted to structure their personnel systems so as to foster a career emphasis as an integral part of public-sector employment (see Chapter 7).

In summary, even though American public administration has emulated many elements of Weber's model, the applicability of that model in the United States is limited in important respects. In contrast to Weber's ideal model, the U.S. bureaucracy was not designed principally for efficiency, but for accountability and equity, with divided lines of authority and considerable discretionary power. Such deliberate inefficiency was largely dictated by the U.S. Constitution and the existing decentralized political culture (described in Chapter 2). The fundamental strength of Weber's model is that it defined and described bureaucracy as a structure of social organization and as a means of promoting hierarchical control, and that it paved the way for further theory, explanation, and prescription regarding large and complex organizations.

Frederick Winslow Taylor and "Scientific Management"

The development of Frederick W. Taylor's (1856–1915) theory of **scientific management** marked the beginning of the managerial tradition in organization theory.[3] Taylor's theory was designed to assist private-sector managers in adapting production practices to the needs of an emerging industrial economy in the late 1800s and early 1900s. Prior to Taylor's research, there was little systematic organization of work in private industry; his writings became the principal source of ideas on the subject. Unlike Weber, Taylor focused on private industry and prescribed a "science" of management that incorporated specific steps and procedures for implementation. (Weber's more abstract model of bureaucracy did not specify actual guidelines for operations.) Both men, however, emphasized formal structure and rules, dealt hardly at all with customers or with work environments, and directly or indirectly reinforced the command-and-control hierarchy by equating the values of those at the top with the needs of the organization as a whole.

The theory of scientific management rested on four underlying values. The first was *efficiency* in production, which involved obtaining the maximum benefit or gain possible from a given investment of resources. The second was *rationality* in work procedures, which addressed the arrangement of work in the most direct relationship to objectives. The third was *productivity*, which meant maintaining

scientific management

formal theory of organization developed by Frederick Winslow Taylor in the early 1900s; concerned with achieving efficiency in production, rational work procedures, maximum productivity, and profit; focused on management's responsibilities and on "scientifically" developed work procedures, based on time-and-motion studies.

the highest production levels possible. The fourth was *profit*, which Taylor conceived of as the ultimate objective of everyone within the organization. These values formed the framework within which the remainder of his theory was applied.

Taylor made several other critical assumptions. He viewed organizational authority as highly centralized at top management levels and separate from those at the bottom of the hierarchy. He assumed a hierarchy of midlevel managers and supervisors through which top management conveyed orders to those below. And he thought that, at each level of the organization, responsibility and authority were fixed at a central point. Taylor also believed that there was only "one best way" to perform a particular task, and that, through scientific research, that method could be discovered and applied. Taylor maintained that the ideal method for performing a certain task could be taught to workers responsible for that task and that selection of workers for their capabilities would be the most rational way to achieve the organization's overall objectives.

According to Taylor, management needed to do three things to increase productivity (and thus profits). First, the most efficient tools and procedures had to be developed and applied. Here, Taylor relied on so-called *time-and-motion studies*, which concentrated on identifying the most economical set of physical movements associated with each step of a work process. Taylor was a pioneer in such studies, although he was only one of a number of researchers in this area.[4] Second, in teaching the new techniques to workers, emphasis was to be placed on *standardizing procedures* in order to enable workers to discharge their responsibilities routinely yet efficiently. Third, criteria that emphasized *task-related capabilities* needed to be developed for, and applied to, the worker selection process. Note, again, that top management was to be entirely responsible for implementing this "science" of administration.

As with any model or theory, there were shortcomings in the application of scientific management to industry and, later, to government. A theoretical shortcoming that received considerable attention from later scholars was that, under scientific management, workers were seen as mere cogs in the industrial machine, with motives and incentives that were purely financial and with no other needs on or off the job that were worthy of incorporation into the theory. This narrowly focused theory failed to account for productivity losses resulting from workers who are experiencing health and family problems. An important alternative perspective on Taylor and his work argues that Taylorism's obsession with efficiency failed to include important elements that would later emerge and significantly impact both human relations and organizational humanism.[5] (Although Taylor also viewed management in rather one-dimensional terms, critiques of his theory—and of Weber's—have concentrated on the consequences of viewing workers too narrowly.)

Taylor's theory encountered significant difficulties when American industry tried to implement it. Taylor had assumed that management and labor would share the same objectives and that there would be no conflict or disagreement over organizing to achieve them. He believed that management would naturally seek efficiency, rationality, and productivity in order to maximize profits. Taylor thought that labor would support those same goals because, at the time, laborers were paid by the piece (that is, they received a certain sum for each item produced) and would therefore earn more money as production increased. Thus, Taylor projected a united labor–management interest in his science of management. The problem was that this unity of interest was assumed without accounting for how it might be affected by the law of supply and demand. Taylor projected that demand for a product would always keep pace with supply and, thus, that maximum productivity would always be a goal of both management and workers. In practice, however, production levels sometimes exceeded market demand for a product. When this occurred, management laid off some workers, retaining only the number needed on the job for each to maintain maximum productivity without causing total output to exceed demand. This touched off vigorous opposition by workers who were "downsized" and by their labor unions (then in their infancy). Most industrial managers had enough power to withstand labor's reaction, but Taylor's theory came under increasing criticism.

Nevertheless, Taylor and his many disciples had inaugurated a new direction in organization theory and management practice. Scientific management took hold not only in the private sector but also in public administration. For a time, the values of efficiency, rationality, and productivity were virtually official doctrine in the national bureaucracy; eventually, an important body of theory in public administration evolved largely from Taylor's work. Scientific management has had a lasting influence on organization theory. It has directly shaped the values and structures in numerous private and public enterprises, and has indirectly influenced organization theory as other theories either followed from it or developed in reaction to it. In particular, scientific management is generally regarded as having had tangible and lasting impact on the principles approach to public administration.[6]

The "Principles" and Other Early Writings

Leonard D. White, in his *Introduction to the Study of Public Administration* (1926), was clearly influenced by Taylor in asserting that management procedures could be studied scientifically to discover the best method of operation. This was not only White's view—it was commonly held by most scholars of public administration of that period. Together with the politics–administration dichotomy, the quest for economy and efficiency, and the notion of public administration as a value-free science, the scientific study of management practices was at the core of public administration theory.

Other elements of Taylorism appeared in the *principles of administration approach*, which became prominent in the 1930s. The very effort to discover principles was itself derived from the scientific approach to management, and individual principles reflected Taylor's continuing influence on the study of organizations, both public and private. The writings of

Henri Fayol, F. W. Willoughby, and the team of Luther Gulick and Lyndall Urwick set forth the essential themes of the principles approach.[7] The major themes were as follows:

1. *Unity of command*—direction by a single individual at each level of an organization and at the top of the structure.
2. *Hierarchy*—the vertical ordering of superior–subordinate relations in an organization, with a clearly defined chain of command.
3. *Functional specialization*—division of labor and subject-matter specialization as a main contributor to work efficiency.
4. *Narrow span of control*—each supervisor having responsibility for the activities of a limited number of subordinates.
5. *Authority parallel with responsibility*—each responsible official endowed with the authority necessary to direct operations in the particular organizational unit.
6. *Rational organizational arrangement*—planning the organization according to function or purpose, geographic area, process performed, or people served (clientele).[8]

As they were applied to more organizations, the principles were increasingly criticized as being inconsistent and inapplicable and eventually became outdated by developments in both theory and practice. These developments were not limited to public administration. In particular, new approaches in psychology and sociology focused attention on those who made up the workforce of an organization. The **human relations** approach constituted the next major phase in the evolution of organization theory and signaled the advent of the informal tradition. Those who embraced this approach did so because they were increasingly dissatisfied with one or more dimensions of scientific management. This triggered an intense controversy over the nature of organizations and over what aspects of organization were most appropriate as building blocks for successful management. In a sense, that controversy, begun in the late 1920s and early 1930s, continues to the present day.

human relations

theories of organization that stress workers' noneconomic needs and motivations on the job, seeking to identify these needs and how to satisfy them, and focusing on working conditions and social interactions among workers.

The Human Relations School

The informal and formal traditions differ from each other in both major assumptions and principal research directions. Whereas formal theories assumed that workers were rational in their actions and motivations and sought to maximize their economic gains, informal theories looked beyond economic motivations and viewed workers as having noneconomic needs on the job and as being motivated (at least potentially) through satisfaction of those needs. Thus, researchers in the informal school sought to determine which noneconomic factors in the work situation, broadly defined, might have an impact—and what kinds of impact—on workers and their performance.

The Hawthorne Studies

The first major studies of the human relations approach were conducted at the Western Electric Hawthorne plant in Cicero, Illinois, between 1927 and 1932.[9] Elton Mayo and his associates at the Harvard Business School began the study to measure the effects of worker fatigue on production. But their research was expanded over a period of five years and resulted in a set of findings about motivation, productivity, and other job-related factors not based solely on economic reward. Specifically, the Hawthorne studies centered on how workers reacted to actions of management, how variations in physical working conditions affected output, and how social interactions among workers affected job performance. It is significant that, initially, Mayo did not intend to examine all these relationships; an investigation of them became necessary after early results of the study did not turn out as expected.

In one experiment, male workers making parts of telephone switches were paid by the piece and, hence, according to Taylor's theory, were expected to try to maximize their production output. To the surprise of both Mayo and the management of Western Electric, production stabilized well below the expected level, primarily because of the workers' reluctance to increase it beyond a certain point. This appeared to be a result of their fear of layoffs, and nothing management did or said could change their attitude—or their level of productivity. This turn of events was totally unexpected and was not explained by anything in the theory of scientific management.

Another experiment involved varying the physical surroundings of a group of female telephone-relay assemblers and observing changes in output. It was predicted that improvements in working conditions would lead to greater output and that changes for the worse would cause a drop in productivity. This same experiment was also conducted with the men making switches. The results, however, did not conform to expectations on two counts. First, the women's production levels rose after each change in working conditions, regardless of whether conditions had been improved (better lighting, bigger working area, more frequent rest breaks) or worsened. Apparently, the women were responding to the attention they received as the subjects of an experiment. Such a reaction has become known as the **Hawthorne** or **"halo" effect**. More to the point, as long as management consistently paid attention to the women and their work, they seemed ready to produce at steadily higher levels. The second unexpected result was that the members of the male work group reacted entirely differently from the way that the women did. No matter what changes were made in working conditions, the men seemed to lag behind their previous level of productivity. These findings, which ran counter to the concepts of scientific management, suggested that a new explanatory theory was needed.

Mayo and his associates concluded that, within the formal organizational framework, there was an *informal* social substructure of groups and teams that tangibly influenced the behavior and motivations of the workers. There was also, quite clearly, peer pressure to conform to the group's production target

Hawthorne or "halo" effect

tendency of those being observed to change their behavior to meet the expectations of researchers; named after a factory in Cicero, Illinois, where studies took place in the late 1920s and early 1930s.

level in preference to any levels set by management. Among both men and women, there was pressure to regard oneself as a team member and to react to management in those terms rather than strictly as an individual. This was very important in light of contrary assumptions made about workers by Taylor and other formal theorists. The work of the Mayo researchers also revealed the importance of noneconomic incentives and motivations on the job, in contrast to the "rational economic" assumptions of formal theorists.[10]

In sum, the Hawthorne studies opened the way to investigate factors other than formal organizational structure and operations, and established the importance of social structure and worker interaction. These studies became the basis for the human relations school of organization theory, which stressed the social and psychological dimensions of organizations, particularly the satisfactions workers derived from the work situation and effective motivating forces on the job.

Leadership in Organizations

A major emphasis in the human relations school during the 1930s was the study of organizational leadership, and how—if at all—leadership affected workers' behavior and the organization's general performance. Two of the most influential scholars in the field were Chester Barnard and Kurt Lewin. Barnard examined the nature of authority within organizations, concentrating on leader–follower interaction; Lewin studied different leadership styles and their effects on subordinates.

Chester Barnard spent his professional life in executive positions in the private sector (for example, as president of the New Jersey Bell Telephone Company). Writing on the basis of that experience, he theorized that leadership could not be exercised by those at the top of a hierarchy solely at their discretion. Rather, leadership's effectiveness depended largely on the willingness of others (that is, followers) to accept and respond to it. Barnard maintained that workers had a social-psychological **zone of acceptance** (or "zone of indifference").[11] His main point was that followers can greatly influence the nature and effectiveness of leadership over them. (This perspective is linked to the rise of teams, quality circles, group rewards, and other types of empowered work groups, treated later in this chapter.) Whatever the amount of legal, political, or organizational authority leaders possess, their *operating* authority is granted, in effect, by followers.

Barnard's view of leadership also included the idea that leaders and followers each had something sought by the other and could, in effect, bargain to their mutual advantage. Organization leaders could offer appropriate incentives to workers, and workers could contribute to the welfare of the organization through improved job performance. This early version of what has come to be known as exchange theory reflected Barnard's opinion that coercive leadership relying on negative incentives, such as punishments or wage

zone of acceptance

the extent to which a follower is willing to be led and to obey the leader's commands or directives; concept originally proposed by Chester Barnard, who wrote about leadership in the 1930s.

reductions, was less effective than supportive leadership offering positive inducements.[12] In other words, Barnard thought that, as a motivator, the carrot was more effective than the stick.

Kurt Lewin, founder of the Group Dynamics School at the University of Iowa in the 1930s, conducted a series of experiments designed to test the effects of different types of leaders on the work output and group atmosphere of ten-year-old boys.[13] Lewin and his associates trained adult leaders in three leadership styles and then rotated the different leaders among groups of boys who were making masks. The leadership styles were (1) *authoritarian*—a threatening, intimidating, coercive leader who permitted no nonsense in the work group (thus suppressing the natural high-spiritedness of young boys), who specialized in finding fault with individual workers, and who resorted to scapegoating when things went wrong; (2) *laissez-faire* (hands-off)—a distant, nonthreatening leader who gave no direction, said nothing concerning cooperation among the workers or the need to keep on working, and gave no encouragement to the boys; and (3) *democratic*—a leader who stressed the job "we" had to do, maintained a relaxed and informal atmosphere, was very positive and supportive, encouraged the boys to do their best, lavished praise for work well done, and encouraged those who were more proficient at mask making to assist those who were still having some difficulty.

To the extent that it is possible to draw firm conclusions from a study in which ten-year-old boys were the subjects, the principal findings in the Iowa experiments were revealing. First, productivity was greatest under the authoritarian leader, with the democratic leader second, and the laissez-faire leader third. The only exception to this pattern was during "leader-out" periods, during which the leader left the group on its own. In those periods, groups under democratic leadership maintained the highest levels of production, and the production of authoritarian-led groups fell off sharply (as expected) without the coercive motivation of the authoritarian leader. Second, interaction among group members and levels of group satisfaction with the work experience varied dramatically according to the style of leadership. Democratic leadership was clearly the most conducive to interpersonal cooperation, group integration, and worker satisfaction. Authoritarian leadership led to considerable hostility among some group members, apathy on the part of others, and very high tensions. Laissez-faire leadership had the smallest impact on worker behavior and attitudes.

As in all such research, there are limitations on the findings of these experiments, chief among them the extent to which the findings can be applied to other, more complex situations. Many tasks in business, industry, and government are more complicated than making masks, and the personal and psychological needs of adults differ from those of ten-year-old boys. Hierarchical organizations with multiple layers of leaders and followers present different problems of group motivation, and a workforce of adults that is socially, economically, ethnically, and professionally diverse is far more difficult to deal with than a homogeneous group of boys.

Yet the findings of this experiment and the conceptions suggested by Barnard both pointed to the possible importance of leadership as another variable in getting the most and the best out of workers. Like the concern for working conditions and social interaction, this represented a fertile new field of inquiry, with some reason to think that "better leadership" might well help to make a better organization (see Chapter 6). That the Iowa results may not be universally applicable does not, by any means, reduce their significance in the study of organizations.

Critiques of the Human Relations School

More recent scholars have devoted some attention to shortcomings in the human relations school of organization theory. The principal criticisms have revolved around three points. The first and most commonly noted charge is that this theory fails to take into account the potential for conflict between workers and managers.[14] Critics have pointed out that, although "good human relations" are advanced as the remedy for just about any difficulty between employers and employees, it is not enough simply to make the worker feel important in situations that involve basic conflicts about conditions of employment, such as the extent of control, long-range goals, promotions, work methods, and specific task assignments. In this respect, human relations proponents and formal theorists were guilty of the same oversight—that is, neither approach seemed to acknowledge that work-related conflict was a real possibility that had to be dealt with.

Second, the human relations school seemed to discount almost entirely the effects of formal structure on the members of the organization. Also, the rational-economic incentives so much in favor with formal theorists were given little if any emphasis in these later formulations. This is not surprising because it was formal theory with which the human relations school was in sharpest conceptual disagreement. The human relations approach, after all, produced the first body of theory to take issue with the Weber–Taylor–Fayol–Gulick approach. Even so, there is some accuracy in such criticisms. Other studies confirmed that organizational structures, monetary incentives, and wage or salary differentials affected the amount of conflict and tension between labor and management.

Third, the kind and complexity of technologies employed in an organization may be considerably more important in shaping informal social structure and human interaction than the factors that Mayo, Lewin, and others regarded as pivotal. Robert Blauner, in particular, made this point persuasively, stressing impersonal factors (that is, technology) as crucial.[15] It is possible, however, that this does not really contradict the findings of human relations studies. Blauner was observing an organizational environment in the 1960s in which technology played a much bigger part than it had during the 1930s, when emphasis on human relations first emerged. Still, this view does suggest that, as factors in the work situation change, theories that previously were useful for analyzing organizations may have decreased applicability. New technologies in particular—such as database management, advanced fiber optics, videoconferencing, and data compression—are having an even greater impact in the workplace and are affecting on-the-job individual and group relationships.

These are not, however, the first critiques of the human relations approach. Another body of research, begun in the 1940s and 1950s, contributed a different perspective on the worker's place in the organization and on what satisfactions and motivations existed in the work situation. Known as organizational, or industrial, humanism, this approach was concerned with the organizational factors that contributed to the psychological and psychosocial health of the worker. In particular, it defined the worker's relationship to the work itself as an important variable in maintaining motivation and job satisfaction; this approach differed significantly from those that had emphasized worker–supervisor or worker–worker interactions. **Organizational humanism** marked a turning point, serving as something of a bridge between the human relations approach and what we refer to as modern organization theory.

Organizational Humanism

Organizational humanism was based on several assumptions that differed from those of both formal organization theory and the human relations school. The first was that work held some *intrinsic* interest that would itself serve to motivate the worker to perform it well. According to the second, individuals worked to satisfy both off-the-job and on-the-job needs and desires. This suggested that workers sought satisfactions in their work, and that achieving those satisfactions was a separate and distinct objective related to the most fundamental reasons for working. The third assumption was that work was a central life interest to the worker, not merely something to be tolerated or endured for *extrinsic* rewards. A fourth assumption, following directly from the notion of the centrality of work and of on-the-job satisfactions, proved to be a harbinger of things to come in contemporary organization theory.

It was assumed that this theory of management was better able to promote positive motivation (through delegating responsibility, permitting discretion and creativity on the job, and involving the worker in important policy decisions affecting the work environment) than to conclude that workers were inherently uninterested in their work and would avoid doing it if possible. The latter pessimistic view of workers was an implicit part of formal theories of organization, and even human relations scholars seemed to share it to some extent. Organizational humanists, however, assumed the opposite. They did so in light of their research findings, which showed that authoritarian management practices designed to control lazy, irresponsible, and undisciplined employees resulted in unhappy and frustrated workers, and poor work performance for all employees.

organizational humanism

a set of organization theories stressing that work holds intrinsic interest for the worker, that workers seek satisfaction in their work, that they want to work rather than avoid it, and that they can be motivated through systems of positive incentives, such as participation in decision making and public recognition for work well done.

Theory Y

model of organizational behavior that stresses self-motivation, participation, and intrinsic (internal) job rewards.

Theory X

model of behavior within organizations that assumes that workers need to be motivated by extrinsic (external) rewards or sanctions (punishments).

Douglas McGregor, who was among the pioneers of organizational humanism, argued that workers could be self-motivating from their own interest in the work and their own inclination to perform it.[16] McGregor's **Theory Y** was in sharp contrast to what he called **Theory X**, which maintained that workers were lazy, wanted to avoid work, and needed to be forced to do it; see Table 4–1 for summaries of Theories X and Y. Another major figure among organizational humanists was social psychologist Chris Argyris, whose view of work as a central life interest was fundamental to this approach.[17] Argyris also pointed out that the need of workers to identify with their work is another source of motivation to perform it well.

The writings of Rensis Likert emphasized employee participation in as many phases of management as possible, directed by a leader or leaders in the democratic mold (which was consistent with the findings of earlier human relations scholars). And Frederick Herzberg, in a study of over 200 accountants and engineers and some nonprofessional employees in a Pittsburgh firm, found that motivators such as salary, fringe benefits, good lighting, and adequate facilities served only to meet workers' minimum expectations, without producing real satisfaction on the job. What did yield personal satisfaction were things such as recognition for good job performance, opportunity to take initiative and exhibit creativity, and responsibility entrusted to individual workers and groups of workers. Because they were the most satisfying aspects of the jobs, these intangibles (according to Herzberg's study) proved to be far better motivators than tangible features such as salary or fringe benefits.[18]

TABLE 4-1	Theory X and Theory Y: A Summary

Underlying Belief System: Theory X
1. Most work is distasteful for most people.
2. Most people prefer close and continuous direction.
3. Most people can exercise little or no creativity in solving organizational problems.
4. Motivation occurs mostly or only as a response to bread-and-butter issues—threat of punishment—and is strictly an individual matter.
Underlying Belief System: Theory Y
5. Most people can find work as natural as play, if conditions permit.
6. Most people prefer and can provide self-control in achieving organizational objectives.
7. Most people can exercise significant creativity in solving organizational problems.
8. Motivation often occurs in response to ego and social rewards, particularly under conditions of full employment, and motivation is often dependent upon groups.

Source: Reproduced by permission of the publisher, F. E. Peacock Publishers, Inc., Itasca, Illinois. From Robert T. Golembiewski and Michael Cohen, eds., *People in Public Service: A Reader in Public Personnel Administration*, 1970 copyright, p. 380.

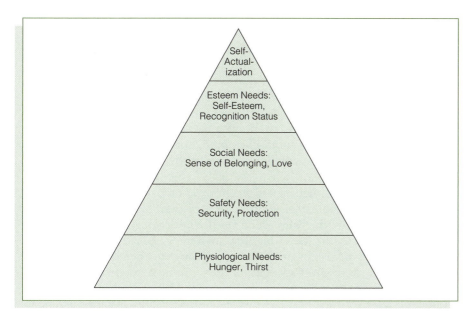

Source: © 2013 Cengage Learning.

FIGURE 4-1

Maslow's Hierarchy of Needs

Some of the most important research in organizational humanism was done by Abraham Maslow. He wrote of "self-actualizing" workers who achieved the highest degree of self-fulfillment on the job through maximum use of their creative capacities and individual independence.[19] According to Maslow, the worker had a **hierarchy of needs**, in which each level had to be satisfied before the individual could go on to the next one (see Figure 4–1). The first level of the hierarchy included *physiological needs* such as food, shelter, and the basic means of survival. Next was minimum *job security*, in the form of a reasonable assurance (but not necessarily a guarantee) of continued employment. After these essentials came *social needs*, which included group acceptance both on and off the job, as well as positive and supportive interpersonal relationships. *Ego satisfaction* and *independence needs* represented the fourth level of Maslow's hierarchy; these were derived from accomplishments in one's work and public recognition of them. (A management practice of some importance in this regard is "public praise, private criticism" for an employee.) Finally, Maslow's highest level was *self-actualization*—feelings of personal fulfillment that resulted from independent, creative, and responsible job performance.

As the worker satisfied the needs of one level, he or she was seen as being further motivated to work toward satisfying the needs of the next higher level. Thus, Maslow placed his emphasis on interactions among the essential needs of the employee on and off the job, the work being done,

hierarchy of needs

psychological concept formulated by Abraham Maslow holding that workers have different kinds of needs that must be satisfied in sequence—basic survival needs, job security, social needs, ego needs, and personal fulfillment in the job.

the attitude of both management and employee toward work performance, and the relationships among employees in the work situation. In a sense, Maslow incorporated into a larger and more complex scheme those aspects of the human relations approach that centered on interpersonal interactions among workers. Like other formulations in organizational humanism, the hierarchy of needs assumed that worker satisfaction could be affected by many factors in the organization, both close to the work situation itself and more distant from it. It should be noted, however, that Maslow did not assume that all employees would be motivated by the same essential needs and interactions.

Organizational humanism did not escape criticism, however. Robert Dubin found, for example, that fewer than 10 percent of the workers he studied in an industrial work group preferred the informality, job-centeredness, and independence on the job so highly valued in organizational humanism.[20] He suggested that different workers have widely varying needs and that no one approach could successfully meet all of them. Some workers needed strong direction from a leader, not independence; lack of direction caused them to be anxious and frustrated in their work. Some really did work for the money. Others simply did not get along with their coworkers; in these situations, an emphasis on group interaction tended to cause additional problems instead of solving existing ones. Still others did not especially want to participate in organizational decision making. Finally, there were those who sought to achieve certain needs without continuing to strive for higher-level satisfactions, thus posing motivation problems for managers relying on Maslow's formulations. (Maslow had acknowledged the possibility that such a situation could arise.) In sum, Dubin suggested that placing too much faith in "one-size-fits-all" organizational humanism should be avoided. The varied needs of employees had to be taken into account.

Another critique of organizational humanism came from two sociologists who questioned some assumptions about the need for workers to "self-actualize" in their jobs and to participate in organizational decision making. H. Roy Kaplan and Curt Tausky maintained that some of the assumptions of organizational humanism seem to have been grounded more in ideological beliefs than in empirical data and that, according to mounting evidence, they did not stand up to empirical research and testing.[21] According to Kaplan and Tausky, many organizational humanists mistakenly viewed employee motivations and satisfaction one-dimensionally and failed to recognize that, for some, work was not intrinsically interesting and fulfilling, creativity and independence were not valued, and monetary and other tangible benefits were of the first order of importance. Kaplan and Tausky's is a wide-ranging challenge that echoes, to some degree, Dubin's earlier critique.

A third, related criticism of organizational humanism was that the *kind* of work being done—routine or nonroutine, individualized or small-group or assembly-line—greatly affects the possibilities for motivating and satis-fying workers. It often appears that the more routine the task, the greater the possibility for worker dissatisfaction (or, at least, for frustration and boredom). That phenomenon alone limits the applicability of organiza-tional humanism.

On the other hand, there may be ways to combat this problem. One approach is to make more systematic the recognition for employees do-ing routinized tasks; recognition such as the Employee of the Month award, complete with a prime parking space or the individual's photograph hung in the front office, is a familiar example of this. Another device is to alter the routine work situation, such as on an auto assembly line, and give workers the opportunity to form their own work groups, which then pro-ceed to assemble a single automobile (or other product) from the ground up. This may reduce on-the-job boredom and frustration while increasing the sense of participation in, and identification with, the service provided or the product being turned out—in the best tradition of organizational humanism. Such programs in auto factories are in wider use in parts of Western Europe than in the United States; whether they could successfully be put into practice on this side of the Atlantic is not clear. Nevertheless, when examined separately from the kind of supervision or the backgrounds of the workers, the nature of particular tasks appears to be relevant in explaining the success or failure of organizational humanism in different work situations.

HOW WOULD YOU DECIDE?

Wal-Mart: The High Cost of Low Price

Wal-Mart: The High Cost of Low Price, a documentary made by Robert Greenwald, takes a close look at the negative economic impact that the installation of Wal-Mart stores can have on local communities. The film opens with Lee Scott, the president and CEO of Wal-Mart Stores, Inc., presenting record sales and earnings information, promis-ing that Wal-Mart will only continue to grow in size and revenue.

The film then presents the personal stories of indi-viduals directly impacted by the business practices of Wal-Mart. Despite annual $400 billion-dollar corporate revenues, Wal-Mart pays its employees little, leaving them to struggle to pay for health insurance, as it is too expensive for most to afford. Women and racial minorities seldom rise to management positions. Local communities struggle with the consequences of the corporation com-ing to town, as it puts smaller, family-owned companies and stores out of business.

Greenwald's aim of the film is to bring awareness to the economic policies and social attitudes of the U.S. gov-ernment and big corporations such as Wal-Mart, focusing on how they affect the daily lives of individual employees.

Given the condition of the economy and complexity of today's work environment, is it possible or realistic to "humanize" an organization to achieve higher levels of personal satisfaction on the job? Discuss the condi-tions under which application of organizational human-ism may be limited.

Source: http://www.walmartmovie.com/about.php, accessed April 1, 2011.

Modern Organization Theory

modern organization theory

body of theory emphasizing empirical examination of organizational behavior, interdisciplinary research employing varied approaches, and attempts to arrive at generalizations applicable to many different kinds of organizations.

Modern organization theory differs from all previous approaches in four key respects. First, rather than assuming that management systems are apolitical, there is a deliberate effort to separate facts from values (assuming that is possible) and to study organizational behavior empirically. Proponents of earlier approaches made quite a few assumptions that were grounded in the predominant economic or social values of the time, the perceived needs of management or labor, anecdotal evidence, or simple common sense. In contrast, modern organization theorists make every effort to minimize the impact of their own values on the phenomena under study. Second, modern organization theorists make extensive use of previously unavailable empirical research methods. These include the use of statistics, information retrieval systems, computer simulations, customer surveys, and quantitative techniques. Such methods permit more sophisticated insights into the operation of organizations and the needs of all customers, not just those occupying official positions within administrative agencies. Third, modern organization theory is constructed on an interdisciplinary basis, broadening the perspectives that can be developed concerning organizational behavior and the management of large, complex enterprises. Fourth, modern organization theory attempts to generalize about organizations in terms sufficiently broad to encompass many different kinds of enterprises, including businesses, hospitals, government agencies, universities, interest groups of all kinds, labor unions, voluntary agencies, and community-based organizations. In order to make such generalizations, it is necessary to use abstract formulations that can account for characteristics common to dissimilar organizations. Thus, features such as information generation and transmission, informal group processes, power relationships, environmental stability or turbulence, and decision making become the currency, so to speak, of generalized organization theory. We will examine briefly some of the major approaches that have been developed.

The modern period of organizational theory was ushered in by a pioneering study conducted by John Pfiffner and Frank Sherwood that described organizations as being characterized by a series of interrelated networks superimposed on a formal structure.[22] They also discussed, among other features, formal and informal communications systems, group dynamics, relative power of different parts of the organization, and decision processes. Theirs was the first comprehensive effort to integrate a variety of approaches, and it set the stage for a tremendous expansion in information about organizations and in specific approaches to studying them.

All modern organizational theories share a general descriptive approach known as **systems theory**. In the context of modern social science, a *system* refers to "any organized collection of parts united by prescribed interactions and designed [at least ideally] for the accomplishment of a specific goal or general purpose."[23] This definition is equally applicable to an

systems theory

a theory of social organizations, holding that organizations—like biological organisms—may behave according to inputs from their environment, outputs resulting from organizational activity, and feedback leading to further inputs; also, that change in any one part of a group or organizational system affects all other parts.

automobile engine, a hospital, the Department of the Interior, or a major industrial firm. (The last three, of course, are *social* systems that are subject to sociological, political, and psychological analyses of their functions and effectiveness.) For any biological, mechanical, or social entity, the systems approach generally assumes the existence of *inputs*, *some means of responding* to those inputs, *outputs*, *feedback* from the environment in response to system outputs, and *further inputs* into the system stemming from feedback; see Figure 4–2 for an application of this approach to politics. For an organization, inputs might consist of demands for some action, resources to pursue organizational objectives, underlying values of those outside the organization (and within it), and support for, or at least passive acceptance of, the organization's essential structure and goals. The means of responding to inputs would include all formal and informal decision mechanisms, judgments about how—or even whether—to respond to particular inputs, the history of the organization in similar circumstances, the organization's inclination (or lack of it) to follow precedent, and the availability of necessary resources. Outputs could refer to the rendering of services by the organization, symbolic steps taken to maintain favorable images of the organization, rules and regulations for which it has proper authority, and adjustments to demands for change or to reallocations of resources (by a legislature, for example).[24] Under this formulation, it is critical to establish and maintain reliable and valid measures of results.

A crucial distinction that has been drawn regarding the application of systems theory to complex organizations is between closed and open systems.[25] **Closed systems** are essentially simple systems that have very

closed systems

organizations that, in systems theory, have very few internal variables and relationships among those variables, and little or no vulnerability to forces in the external environment.

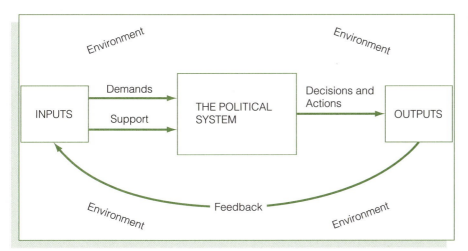

FIGURE 4-2

A Simplified Model of a Political System

Source: David Easton, *A Framework for Political Analysis.* Copyright © 1965, 1979 David Easton, reprinted with permission of the University of Chicago Press.

few internal variables and relationships among them and little or no vulnerability to forces in the external environment. The primary objectives of those managing closed systems are the elimination of uncertainty, optimum use of resources that contribute to the overall result, and maximum predictability of outcomes. Many formal (closed-system) theories focused on the concepts of *planning* or *controlling* behavior within organizations. Control, stability, and predictability were the cornerstones of these theories of organization, which may once have worked effectively in a relatively simple and predictable world, with few external factors impacting internal processes.

open-systems theory

a theory that views organizations not as simple, "closed" bureaucratic structures separate from their surroundings, but as highly complex entities, facing considerable uncertainty in their operations, and constantly interacting with their environment; assumes that organizational components will seek an equilibrium among the forces pressing on them and their own responses to those forces.

Open-systems theory proceeds from very different logical premises, which many scholars argue are more appropriate to the study of contemporary organizations (including public administrative agencies) than the premises that underlie closed-systems theory. Open systems are seen as highly complex, interdependent, with overlapping boundaries, and characterized by an *expectation of change* and *uncertainty*, internally and externally. This view is based on the fact that, in organizational theorist James Thompson's words, "a system contains more variables than we can comprehend at one time, [and] some of the variables are subject to influences we cannot control or predict."[26] As a result, the elimination of all types of uncertainty is not considered a viable organizational objective, and the very nature of an organization is vastly different. Again, quoting Thompson:

> Approached as a natural [open] system, the complex organization is a set of interdependent parts which together make up a whole because each contributes something and receives something from the whole, which in turn is interdependent with some larger environment. Central to the natural-system approach is the concept of *homeostasis*, or self-stabilization, which spontaneously, or naturally, governs the necessary relationships among parts and activities and thereby keeps the system viable in the face of disturbances stemming from the environment.[27]

An obvious difference between closed and open systems is the way each allows external environments to impact the organization. Open-systems theory, like some other modern theories, assumes considerable interdependence between organizations and their environments, with changes in the latter triggering adaptive responses within the organizations. Thus, a private firm will alter its marketing priorities in response to changing consumer preferences; a government agency can turn public criticism in its favor by providing more points of access for citizen or employee participation in decision making. In such instances, the formal "boundaries" of the organization do not exclude others who are not formally members of it; in fact, those inside the organization are willing to change their activities to meet externally imposed needs or wants. Also, because open systems continuously interact with their environments, there is a constant need to seek **homeostasis**, or equilibrium, by balancing pressures and responses, demands and resources, and worker incentives and contributions (to use Barnard's formulation). All this is in the long-term interest of organizational stability, which permits continued functioning in the manner expected by leaders, workers, customers, and other external clienteles. In sum, open-systems theory—in sharp contrast to Weber's self-contained, closed bureaucracy—defines organizations as a great deal more than just independent formal structures, interpersonal relations, or worker involvement in the job. It treats organizations as whole beings, complex in their makeup and constant in their interactions with the surrounding environment.[28] Working collaboratively and effectively within the flexible boundaries of open systems requires new skills for public managers and new performance management strategies.[29]

Other approaches that are based on the systems framework deal with organizations in a similarly broad-gauged fashion. For example, **information theory** is based on the view that organizations require information to prevent them from evolving to a state of chaos or randomness in their operations. **Game theory** addresses itself to competition among members of an organization for gains and losses, in terms of resources and access to resources; game theory is distinctly mathematical in orientation and methods. The concept of the self-regulating organization is advanced in **cybernetics** (see Table 4–2).[30]

More recently, three other emphases have emerged in modern organization theory. One bears the label **Theory Z** and refers to patterns of organization and operation characteristic of many contemporary Japanese corporations (and some Japanese municipal governments).[31] Proponents of Theory Z assume that productivity is a problem of social or managerial organization; rather than by technological change, productivity can be improved by greater communication, feedback, and involvement of workers. Once the organization is committed to real involvement of employees in self-managed work teams, the key ingredients become trust, subtlety, and mutual support. The key values and characteristics of Theory Z are summarized in Table 4–3.

Theory Z is suggestive of some beliefs present in our earlier thinking and is decidedly different from others. For example, the involvement of workers is reminiscent of organizational humanism, and the positive consequences of workers having confidence and trust in their managers echo the human relations approach. On the other hand, American theories put little or no emphasis on managers knowing the private lives of employees (the so-called holistic or all-encompassing approach), generalist career paths, or collective accountability. Nevertheless, the perceived successes of Japanese manufacturing firms have drawn international attention to extended and

homeostasis

describes organizations in a state of equilibrium, by balancing pressures and responses, demands and resources, and worker incentives and contributions with external environmental factors.

information theory

modern theory of organization that views organizations as requiring constant input of information in order to continue functioning systematically and productively; assumes that a lack of information will lead to chaos or randomness in organizational operations.

game theory

a modern theory viewing organizational behavior in terms of competition among members for resources; based on distinctly mathematical assumptions and employing statistical data collection methods.

cybernetics

emphasizes organizational feedback that triggers appropriate adaptive responses throughout an organization; a thermostat operates on the same principle.

Theory Z

Japanese management system that stresses deliberative, "bottom-up" collective accountability and decision making, long-term planning, and closer relationships among managers and workers.

| TABLE 4-2 | Common Characteristics of Open Systems |

Characteristic	Examples
1. Open systems import some form of energy from the external environment.	1. Cells receive oxygen from the bloodstream; the body takes in oxygen from the external world; organizations must draw renewed supplies of energy from other institutions or people or the material environment.
2. Open systems transform the energy available to them.	2. The body converts starch and sugar into heat and action; organizations create a new product or process materials or train people or provide a service.
3. Open systems "export" some product into the environment.	3. Biological organisms export carbon monoxide; the engineering firm constructs a bridge.
4. The pattern of activities of the energy exchange has a cyclical character: the product export furnishes the source of energy for the repetition of the cycle of activities.	4. Industry utilizes raw materials and human labor to turn out a product that is marketed, and the profit is used to obtain more raw materials and labor to perpetuate the cycle of activities; the voluntary organization provides satisfactions to its members, who are further motivated to continue their activities.
5. To survive, open systems must arrest the process of inevitable degeneration (entropy) by acquiring more energy from the external environment than they expend.	5. Prisoners on a starvation diet husband their energy to stretch their limited intake of food; organizations attempt to acquire a comfortable margin, or reserve, in their needed resources.
6. Open systems receive information and negative feedback from their environments and must simplify all such data by coding it into a limited number of recognizable categories.	6. Individuals receive instructions, warning signals, pleasurable feelings, and the like; a thermostat regulates room temperature by a feedback mechanism; an automated power plant supplies and distributes electricity also through feedback.
7. Open systems maintain some constancy in energy exchange, and in relations among their respective parts, so that the essential character of the system is preserved (even if it expands).	7. Body temperature remains the same, despite varying external conditions; human physiological functions are maintained evenly by endocrine glands.
8. Open systems tend toward differentiation and elaboration.	8. The human body evolves from very simple cells; organizations move toward greater specialization of functions (e.g., medicine).
9. As differentiation proceeds, it is offset by two processes that bring the system together for unified functioning: integration and coordination.	9. In small groups, integration is achieved through shared norms and values; in large organizations, coordination occurs through fixed controls, such as setting priorities, establishing routines, and scheduling activities.
10. Open systems can reach a final state from differing initial conditions and by a variety of paths.	10. Some biological organisms can develop from a variety of initial forms.

TABLE 4-3	Values and Characteristics of Theory Z

Values	**Characteristics**
1. Emphasis on trust, subtlety, and intimacy	1. Permanent rather than short-term employment
2. Increased involvement of workers leads to increased productivity	2. Slow rather than rapid promotions
3. If workers have confidence in their managers and believe their organizations are just and equitable, they will function well in uncertain environments, take risks for their organizations, and make personal sacrifices	3. General rather than specialized career paths
	4. Collective decision making
	5. Collective accountability
4. Good managers know the private lives of their employees	6. Decision making is "bottom up"
	7. Decisions are made slowly at each level, but final plans are rapidly implemented

Source: Adapted from Clyde McKee, "An Analysis of 'Theory Z': How It Is Used in Japan's Public Sector," delivered at the 1983 annual meeting of the American Political Science Association, Chicago, September 1983. Reprinted by permission of Clyde McKee, Trinity College, Hartford, Conn.

modified versions of Theory Z and to its extension, **total quality management (TQM)**. The concepts supporting TQM have been applied in a number of different settings, including many in the United States.

Reflecting a long-term trend toward participatory (Theory Z) management in American society, TQM is based on the idea that the greater the involvement that individual employees (or teams of "empowered" employees) have in determining and implementing organizational goals, the more committed they will be to achieving those goals. By providing incentives to increase the success of the whole enterprise, TQM encourages organization-wide commitment, empowerment, teamwork, and better quality results. A management system developed in private industry and based on **statistical process control (SPC)** techniques, TQM is aimed at satisfying customer expectations by continuously working across an organization to improve internal and external processes. Theory Z and TQM echo elements of earlier American organization theories (such as improving relationships between supervisors and workers). This is not surprising because the underlying principles of **systems analysis** and SPC were taught by Americans recruited to assist the Japanese in rebuilding their war-torn economy following World War II. Key elements of a typical TQM system include the following:

- Top-level support and commitment
- Focus on customer satisfaction
- Written productivity and quality goals and an annual improvement plan

total quality management (TQM)

management approach that encourages organization-wide commitment, teamwork, and better quality of results by providing incentives to increase the success of the whole enterprise. Elements of TQM include commitment to meeting customer-driven quality standards; employee participation or empowerment to make decisions at the point closest to the customer; actions based on data, facts, outcome measures, results, and statistical analysis; commitment to process and continuous quality improvements; and organizational changes and teamwork to encourage implementation of the above elements.

statistical process control (SPC)

the use of statistics to control critical processes within organizations; frequently used with **TQM** and **Theory Z** Japanese management techniques.

systems analysis

analytical technique designed to permit comprehensive investigation of the impacts within a given system of changing one or more elements of that system; in the context of analyzing policies, emphasizes overall objectives, surrounding environments, available resources, and system components.

- Productivity and quality measures and standards that are consistent with agency goals
- Use of the improvement plan and measurement system to hold managers and employees accountable
- Employee involvement in productivity and quality improvement efforts
- Rewards for quality and productivity achievement
- Training in methods for improving productivity and quality
- Retraining and outplacement for employees who might be negatively affected by improvement efforts
- Reducing barriers to productivity and quality improvement

Public managers realize that performance measurement alone does not necessarily lead to quality improvement. Likewise, merely training employees in the use of quality techniques and tools, without guidance on how to apply them to their specific environments, does not guarantee improved quality service or better results. All the elements described above are necessary but are insufficient by themselves to continuously manage performance systems and improve customer service. Structural as well as attitudinal barriers must be overcome to sustain any total quality improvement effort.

Total quality management is based on internal regulation and worker self-management commonly known as *empowerment* (see Chapter 2); its strategies are designed to reduce internal competition, foster teamwork, improve decision-making processes, and reduce costs. In the competitive manufacturing sector, these techniques have produced remarkable gains in quality, productivity, and competitive position. In public administration, quality management was communicated as an attitude that stresses customer satisfaction, encourages employees to examine relationships among existing management processes, improves internal communications, and responds to valid customer demands. In exchange for the authority to make decisions at the point of customer contact, all empowered employees must be thoroughly trained, and results (at least until new systems are in place) must be carefully monitored. Governments at all levels are finding it increasingly necessary to provide training for service quality improvement, especially for citizen-contact employees who have the most direct relationship with citizens/customers/taxpayers.

Despite resistance, quality management theories were applied to improve a wide range of federal executive agencies, educational institutions, hospitals, public utilities, and state and local governments.[32] One observer has argued, however, that "pure" quality initiatives are ill suited to public-sector organizations, citing four key limitations: (1) defining the customers of government is ambiguous; (2) public administrators are service rather than product oriented; (3) public agencies are input rather than output oriented; and (4) politics works against long-term leadership and constancy of mission.[33] In addition, political leadership is necessary to achieve any change and governments are organizations that must respond to customers who typically do not pay directly for services received. Nonetheless, during the 1990s, the Office of Management and Budget (OMB) provided leadership for a joint public- and private-sector quality improvement effort, designating TQM as the official management improvement system for all federal executive agencies. (Although TQM is no longer the "official" management system for federal agencies, many continue to apply its principles to implement results-driven government.)

Together with TQM and process re-engineering, "organizational learning" and "continuous learning theory" reflect significant change in the evolving discipline of organizational behavior. These theories suggest that all organizations, like individuals, have the capacity to learn and grow from interactions with their environments. Those committed to fostering continuous learning can create opportunities, policies, and resources to support individual growth and development. Organizational behavior can be transformed in the same way in which individuals learn from contacts with systems, processes, expanded training, and educational opportunities. **Learning organizations** are built on many of the same assumptions as those of earlier theories, including shared vision, consistent values, dedication to organizational mission, and competence. Vital elements that must be taught include systems thinking, personal mastery, shared visioning, team-based learning, and problem solving. When combined with delivery systems such as electronic government, information technologies, and the Internet, learning theories can provide a platform for enhancing a wide range of public services.[34] Creating a *continuous learning environment* is becoming important as more service organizations, including governments, evolve into networked, nonbureaucratic, boundaryless, and decentralized organizations in the twenty-first century.[35]

As useful as organizational theories are in explaining many aspects of human behavior within organizations, they cannot possibly encompass all the dynamics of actual operations within large and complex enterprises. They do, however, suggest a theoretical framework for understanding a wide range of internal variables related to organization design, communication, coordination, and effective leadership styles.

learning organizations

concept of organizations that emphasizes the importance of encouraging new patterns of thinking and interaction within organizations to foster continuous learning and personal development; see *http://www.brint.com*, a commercial business technology and knowledge management site for information about knowledge management and learning organizations, and *http://www.learningorg.com* to find out more about learning organizations.

Organizational Dynamics and Behavior

In the course of daily activities, many possibilities exist for assigning work, deciding how managerial objectives are transmitted to others, delegating responsibility, and making many similar choices. Moreover, the way subordinates are regarded by managers affects the modes and styles of communication that are used to convey directives (that is, whether managers issue "marching orders" or set out program objectives with flexibility in how best to achieve goals). The application of Theory X, Y, or Z would dictate the operating responsibility that management chooses to delegate to others. In most public organizations, proponents of these theories interact simultaneously and often conflict, reflecting individual managerial experience and styles.

communication

vital formal and informal processes of interacting among and between individuals and units within an organization, and between organizations.

coordination

the process of bringing together divided labor; efforts to achieve coordination often involve emphasis on common or compatible objectives, harmonious working relationships, and the like; linked to issues involving communication, centralization/decentralization, federalism, and leadership.

formal communication

official written documentation within an organization, including electronic mail, memorandums, minutes of meetings, and records; forms the framework for organizational intent and activity.

informal communication

all forms of communication, other than official written documentation, among members of an organization; supplements official communications within an organization.

These concerns are part of the dynamics of organization and affect both individual and group behavior. Two topics can be classified as *process issues:* (1) **communication**, a vital function in organizational life; and (2) **coordination** of activities internally or across organizational boundaries. Both are central not only to traditional thinking and effective operations in practice but also to processes of change within organizations. Four other topics to be discussed are appropriately labeled *design issues* because they are relevant to the formal structuring of organizations. They are (1) line (substantive or policy-focused) and staff (support or advisory) activities, and how they are related—and differentiated—in practical terms; (2) centralization versus decentralization in assigning responsibility and in overseeing operations; (3) the implications of tall versus flat hierarchies for managing a workforce (that is, the practical differences between organizations having few structural layers and those having many); and (4) the possibilities of alternative forms of organization.

Communication: Formal and Informal

Few topics have received more attention in both academic and practitioner literature than communication. (In this discussion, "communication" refers to the *field* and *process* of communication, whereas the plural, "communications," refers to individual *messages* sent or received.) In the contexts of large and small groups, interpersonal relations, communication theory, the general political realm, and even relations between nations, communication has been the focus of intensive research as well as practical application.[36] This attention is not unprecedented, however, particularly in the context of public organizations. Every major theory of organization has included (explicitly or implicitly) assumptions about the nature, roles, and processes of communication in various organizational settings. Observers of organizations traditionally approached the subject by attempting to define the types and flows of communication. More recently, as the Internet has altered the scope and substance of the field, more attention has been given to social and psychological dimensions aiding or retarding effective communication.

There are many types of organizational communications. One of the most important distinctions is between formal and informal. **Formal communications** (1) originate in the authority of an organization official who attempts to influence some element of collective activity, (2) are directed to a particular audience within the organization, (3) follow proper organizational channels to the audience, and (4) constitute a building block in the continuing effort to officially state organizational policies, purposes, missions, strategies, and tactics. Formal communications are usually written, so that they become part of a permanent record of activity. They range from broad policy statements to specific operating memorandums.

Informal communications, on the other hand, take varied forms: (1) They may come from many sources (not necessarily individuals acting in an official capacity); (2) although they are directed toward a selected audience, others may also become aware of the message; (3) they may follow official channels of communication, but often those who send them deliberately avoid those channels; and (4) they are concerned with organizational life and activity (like formal communications), but reflect a wider range of thinking and actions on the part of members of the organization. Informal communications supplement official messages and can even become a more reliable guide to what organizations actually do. Formal memorandums are the skeletal framework of organizational intent and activity. Less-structured contacts, such as those among friends and coworkers or through friends discussing agency projects or the last staff meeting over lunch, facilitate the multitude of actual operations built around the policy directions set in formal communications.

In a bureaucracy with a vertical chain of command, established communication routes traditionally follow hierarchical lines of authority. That is, formal communications are more closely associated with the arrangements and structures on the organization chart than informal communications are. However, it should be noted that formal communications are not confined to vertical organizational channels. A common and increasing phenomenon is **lateral or cross-functional communication**, which cuts across the vertical hierarchy yet is still conducted relatively formally. Thus, even as the chiefs of different (and potentially competing) divisions within an agency pursue their respective programmatic objectives, discovering that they have a common objective can prompt them to stay in touch, both formally and informally, in an effort to promote their mutual interests.

Messages do not merely travel top to bottom in an organization, given the presence of both formal and informal lateral communication possibilities. Still more important, however, is *upward* communication, which goes against the traditional direction of formal channels but is becoming ever more crucial to the effective functioning of organizations large and small. This has a number of important dimensions.

First, every organization has *feedback* mechanisms—some means of transmitting information from those who received messages to those who sent them. Virtually every communication system provides for feedback, at least in theory; these feedback mechanisms can be highly formalized and sophisticated or they can be informal. The problem for the top-level manager and others is to ensure that they will be able to learn via feedback what effects their own communications have had. Feedback mechanisms can range from suggestion boxes, individual conversations, or an open-door policy by supervisors to regularized consultations between management and subordinates, surveys of employee opinion, or surveys of citizens about the quality of the services provided by a public organization. These "voice of the customer" surveys are becoming increasingly useful to senior managers as feedback mechanisms from internal employees who provide services, as well as from external recipients of services.

lateral or cross-functional communication

patterns of oral and written communication within organizational networks that are interdisciplinary and typically cut across vertical layers of hierarchy. See also, interoperability.

A second factor, complicating the feedback process, is the strong tendency for good news to travel freely up the line but for bad news to be suppressed, rerouted, or rewritten. The desire of lower-level units and personnel to present a favorable image to those higher up accounts for this phenomenon. But, in the interest of their own effectiveness, higher-level managers ordinarily need to know both good and bad news. Managers must have a clear understanding of all that is going on in their organization in order to be able to correct existing problems, anticipate future difficulties, and iron out internal conflicts that may hamper organizational activity. Too often, those who have knowledge that might be deemed negative do not report it to their supervisors for fear of the consequences.

To overcome the natural reluctance to report bad news to superiors, managers can initiate something akin to a "no-fault" or forgiving information policy (within limits). Such a policy encourages employees to bring problems that are unmanageable at lower levels to the attention of higher management but without fear of retribution or faultfinding as a penalty. To be successful, such feedback would have to develop in the context of positive, supportive, trust-based interactions between superiors and subordinates; the open democratic leadership style is more conducive to this sort of communication than other styles. Negative feedback is often lacking precisely because the types of general organizational relationships that would facilitate it have not been developed and maintained. Top management must take deliberate steps to make such feedback possible, regardless of the possible consequences. (In this regard, see discussion of "whistle-blowers" in Chapter 5.)

In this era of more democratic and participatory management in both the public and private sectors, all employees are being asked to address a wider range of organizational problems. Whether formal or informal, upward flows of communication have increased in importance and can contribute measurably to the effective functioning of an organization. Without accurate feedback from employees, the probability increases that management decisions will be based on false, incomplete, or misleading information.

Dimensions of Communication

Although achieving better communication is a goal to which many subscribe almost on faith, it may be useful to consider various aspects of the process; such an examination may yield a fuller understanding of the potential and the pitfalls. We will briefly examine (in order) the prerequisites, purposes, obstacles (and their remedies), and consequences associated with better communication.

There are, first of all, several kinds of *prerequisites*, including the transmitter of a message, the message itself, the medium through which it is sent, and a receiver mechanism of some sort. Considerable research has been done on how the medium and especially the receiver influence the understanding of messages sent; the late Marshall McLuhan's work is a leading example of this kind of research on mechanistic communication models.[37] Other kinds of prerequisites, however, are equally important, including the individual desire to communicate clearly, a shared interest in achieving common understanding among those communicating with one another, and organizational arrangements that facilitate message transmittal. In short, simply wanting to improve communication is not enough. This is especially true in a diverse work environment where those involved may lack common definitions of the terms employed or shared understanding of the concepts and assumptions underlying the information transmitted. (That problem significantly affects all types of organizations having difficulty communicating with those receiving services. In the college classroom, for example, professors and students sometimes have communication problems.)

The *purposes* of communication may seem obvious, yet they can be as varied as the people communicating. Many of us may use communications for purposes less constructive than achieving human understanding and organizational effectiveness or promoting the public interest. Sometimes communications may be carefully calculated by those employing them; the more they confuse potential opposition, the more they may be able to *de*fuse it. Furthermore, the intentional use of disinformation is a tactic to gain and maintain power. The same may be said of the use of professional jargon, or what has been labeled "bureaucratese." Jargon may be one way to fend off criticism; if listeners cannot understand what is said, they cannot take issue with it.

On the other hand, the crisp memo is a weapon of considerable potency in bureaucratic politics. It is widely acknowledged in all large organizations that one can be influential through carefully conceived, well-written, and brief memorandums to key decision makers. In many respects, the potential benefits of memo writing represent everything **gobbledygook** does not: clarity of expression, sharpening understanding of available options, and the deliberate shaping of opinions. How clear the meanings of communications are, then, depends heavily on how clear senders intended them to be—and why!

Obstacles to effective communication can be found among both senders and receivers of messages. One obstacle, already noted, is lack of clarity on the part of the sender as a result of poor word choices, failure to explain the purposes of the communication, inadequate explanation of actions to be taken, and the like. Another problem is lack of accurate or complete relay of a message (as in the games "telephone" and "rumor clinic"); the more layers there are in the structure of an organization, the more likely it is that messages will be distorted (and the more difficult it will be to determine the impacts of the messages sent). A third obstacle is failure of the receiver to listen or to read, a human failing related to our tendency to screen out negative or unwanted information; related to this is reluctance to accept the contents of the message if it goes against the receiver's opinions on the subject of the message. Still another problem is failure of the receiver to act appropriately on the

gobbledygook

misleading jargon or meaningless technical terms often used purposely to obscure the meaning of communications within organizations.

message if he or she fails to comprehend its importance fully. Numerous *remedies* are available to the communication-conscious manager, but they must be chosen carefully; none can be counted on to completely overcome all obstacles to communication. One remedy is formal training in communication skills for all employees. Another is more specifically targeted training for higher-level managers, designed to make them sensitive to the need for continual monitoring of messages passing through their divisions; this might be coupled with a program of incentives for improving communication flows. A third device, which can be used by top management personnel, is spot-checking activities at lower levels of the organization to be sure that directives have been received and are being acted on. (All electronic or e-mail systems now allow the sender to check the exact time a message was received.) If such monitoring from the top occurs through normal channels, it may suffer from the same problem posed for regular communications, namely, imperfect relaying. Modern information technologies aid in shortening the distances among decentralized, often isolated agencies and public-service functions, allowing managers to go outside the usual channels in following up on their directives. But perhaps the most important factor in improving communication is a clear perception on the part of employees that top management is committed to maintaining effective flows of communication and that the process is explicitly valued for the contributions everyone can make to organizational operations.

The *consequences* of communication, like its purposes, cannot simply be assumed. Although many people think that better communication will solve problems and conflicts, that is not necessarily true. At the root of most communication problems are perception and credibility issues. Certain attitudes and behaviors are essential to break down mistrust and establish clear lines of communication. It is possible, of course, that improving communication will produce beneficial results in an organization, in the ways that have already been discussed. On the other hand, communicating more clearly can complicate matters as well. The circumstances of communication strongly influence which kinds of results actually occur.

Of most relevance to the public administrator, the communication processes in public bureaucracies generally occur within the context of what some have labeled the **bargaining or conflict model** of communication. To the extent that public administration is viewed as a distinctively political process, this model of communication seems to apply. Administrators do seek monopolies on key information; they do conduct their communication activities with an eye toward maximum political gain; and so on. According to this conception, the communication process becomes another weapon in the administrator's political arsenal; clear communication of ideas, actions, or intentions could easily conflict with attaining political objectives.

On the other hand, an alternative model of communication that is equally relevant to public administration merits attention. Although the conflict

bargaining or conflict model

communication model that assumes the presence in an organization of considerable sustained conflict, strong tendencies toward secrecy, and motives of expediency on the part of most individuals.

model is widely applicable, a **consensual or consensus-building model** may be useful at some points in the administrative process. Under such circumstances, it is useful to communicate openly about both differences and areas of agreement. In this setting, communication should be open and clearly inclined toward sharing rather than guarding information, even if doing so leads to recognition of disagreement. The key to successful use of this model is the common will to understand and overcome differences. There may be political risks in employing this approach, but a judgment must be made about whether those risks are worth taking.

A manager choosing between these communication models must take several things into consideration. Among them are the relative probabilities of achieving organization goals with one or the other approach, the chances of reaching consensus with another agency (or agencies), and the sensitivity of information that would be shared if the consensus-building model is used. Other concerns could include the longer-range needs of the organization for political support from others, the agency's credibility in the administrative-political process, and the reliability of potential allies as working partners.

What, then, is the importance of communication? Clearly, the basic processes serve to facilitate management of large enterprises in a number of ways. These include the following:

1. Defining and fulfilling objectives
2. Determining the division and assignment of responsibilities across the full range of functions in the organization
3. Identifying problems and opportunities in ongoing programs
4. Anticipating long-term and short-term options
5. Motivating employees and pinpointing morale problems
6. Soliciting ideas from individuals throughout the organization
7. Resolving conflicts as (or before) they occur

As with many other human activities, the particular styles and mechanisms of communication may influence the content and purpose of the message, the degree of effectiveness, and the consequences for the organization as a whole.[38]

consensual or consensus-building model

communication model which assumes that by cooperation instead of power struggles and political trade-offs, administrators may seek to reach agreement with potential adversaries as a means of furthering mutual aims.

Coordination

Like communication, the concept of coordination has almost universal appeal in the abstract. Obviously, a large and complex organization must achieve a minimally adequate degree of coordination in its multiple activities if there is to be any chance of consistency in the impacts of those activities. Put another way: If the right hand is ever to know what the left hand is doing, activities need to be coordinated at various points in the process. The need for coordination varies according to the type of service provided and the geographic location of the public agency. Coordination problems become more serious as organizations undergo growth, increase in complexity, cope with external threats, and experience internal differentiation of functions. Organizational communication can be important here, it should be noted. And coordination can occur in different ways.

What exactly is *coordination*? Various definitions have been advanced, most of them emphasizing notions such as common goals and interests, compatible objectives, and harmonious collaboration among different groups or organizations.[39] Essentially, coordination is the process of bringing together divided labor. It is the opposite of division of labor and the organizational cure for it where it is necessary to integrate the activities of different entities—whether separate agencies of the same government, agencies of different governments (or governments themselves), or elements of the public and private sectors. Having compatible objectives or working jointly may help to facilitate the co-ordinative process, but the basic task can still be carried out even under less than favorable conditions (such as conflict, hostility, and apathy).

If we consider coordination in light of prerequisites, purposes, obstacles, remedies, and consequences, as we did with communication, some similarities—but also some differences—are evident between the two phenomena. At the risk of oversimplification, it may be said that the prerequisites are virtually the same—channels and mechanisms for coordination must be purposefully established and carefully maintained, just as for communication. The difficulty of accomplishing this varies with the degree of organizational autonomy possessed by the entities being coordinated. As far as purposes are concerned, there is probably less variety in the objectives of those who desire coordination than in the objectives of those who seek to improve communication. Whereas communication can serve to mislead or confuse as well as to clarify, coordination is almost always designed to clear away difficulties in organizational activity.

It should be noted, however, that many individuals and groups may resist would-be coordinators' efforts to clear away perceived difficulties. For their own reasons and priorities, some people both inside and outside of organizations may prefer to engage in their assigned activities without bending their purposes to some larger, better-coordinated undertaking. Such behaviors demonstrate the validity of the observation that "coordination is rarely neutral. To the extent that it results in mutual agreement or a decision on some policy, course of action, or inaction, inevitably it advances some interests at the expense of others or more than others."[40] Thus, those who seek better coordination must deal with those who would plant obstacles in their path. Those obstacles to coordination merit our attention, as do their remedies.

One obstacle is differing perceptions of program goals. This, in turn, leads to varied degrees of commitment to a coordination process that assumes substantial goal consensus among major participants. Other obstacles are divergent preferences on major or minor aspects of implementation;

conflicting priorities, even when substantive agreement on the total program exists; unequal fiscal capabilities; conflicting political pressures on program agencies; poor organization; breakdowns in communication; and inept leadership.[41] In addition, *legal autonomy* can lead to a situation in which some or all of the obstacles mentioned may be present but little can be done to cause the relevant officials to coordinate their efforts; this is especially evident when many separate local government jurisdictions exist in a single metropolitan area. In other words, coordinating across organizational (including governmental) boundaries is more difficult than intraorganizational coordination. Prior to the reorganizations that created the Department of Homeland Security and the Director of National Intelligence, federal agencies such as the FBI and the CIA had few incentives to cooperate and share information regarding terrorist activities and other threats to domestic security. One of the consequences of this lack of cooperation was that both agencies failed to act on evidence of al Qaeda's preparations for the September 11, 2001 hijackings.[42]

Overcoming these obstacles is not easy, but a number of remedies do exist. One is improved communication; that can be an implicit reason for focusing on communication problems. In the abstract, there is every reason to hope that better communication—on objectives, tactics, perceived problems, or opportunities—can indeed lead to a better "meshing of the gears" among agencies and their activities. But whether better communication actually facilitates coordination depends to a large extent on the amount of conflict (both real and potential) present in the entities' relationships. Limited areas of conflict would permit the use of the consensus-building model of communication, which would tend to improve coordination. Significant conflict, however, would probably lead to use of the bargaining model of communication and, in that event, the impulse to hoard information would work against the effort to coordinate more fully. Even in the absence of conflict, however, the will to improve coordination must be present among key personnel in the affected organizations or units.

Another remedy for coordination problems is the exercise of leadership in at least two important ways. First, responsible managers can devote leadership resources and exert their influence in support of coordination, clearly demonstrating their concern for improving it. Relevant managerial functions include goal setting and building consensus supportive of common goals; conflict management aimed at containing and resolving internal disputes before they reach a level of intensity harmful to organizational effectiveness; and information management. Second, on an interpersonal level, managers of different organizations or agencies can initiate efforts to coordinate activities of their respective entities, thus establishing the context for a more formalized coordinative process. Their success ultimately depends on their personal commitment and their ability to go back to their organizations and build support there for coordination in the manner described above.

Organizational arrangements for strengthening coordination fall into two principal categories. One is *central coordination*, in which decisions are rendered by a coordinative entity or individual. The other is *mutual adjustment* (sometimes termed *lateral coordination*), in which there exist "consultation, sharing of information, and negotiation among equals."[43] (Note the presumption of the consensus-building model of communication.) A third possibility also exists, "a combination of these—a process in which lateral coordination is expedited, facilitated, and even coerced by leadership and pressure from an independent or higher-level coordinator."[44]

Overall, then, coordination, like communication, is often highly prized but just as often is achieved only with conceptual and operational difficulties. The more complex the organization, the greater the challenge to those who would achieve coordination of activity among its various parts.[45]

Line and Staff Functions

line functions

substantive activities of an organization, related to programs or polici es for which the organization is formally responsible, and usually having direct impact on outside clienteles; the work of an organization directed toward fulfilling its formal mission(s).

staff functions

originally defined to include all of an organization's support and advisory activities that facilitated the carrying out of "line" responsibilities and functions; more recently, redefined by some to focus on planning, research, and advisory activities, thus excluding budgeting, personnel, purchasing, and other functions once grouped under the "staff" heading.

The notions of **line functions** and staff functions in an organization can be traced back to very traditional treatments of formal organization. They deal with programs or policies having *direct impact* on outside clienteles and are ultimately accountable to a superior in the performance of substantive responsibilities. This definition has been widely accepted in public administration ever since the principles approach emerged during the 1930s. In the same period, **staff functions** were originally defined as consisting of support and advisory activities undergirding the ability of line personnel to carry out their duties. These could be, for example, financial and budgetary, personnel administration, planning, purchasing, and legal counsel. More recently, however, the notion of staff activities has undergone some revision (it should be noted, however, that these revisions have not been accepted by all experts in the field and outside observers). With the work of Leonard D. White, the term *staff* came to mean the planning, research, and advisory activities essential to the long-term well-being of an organization.[46] A new term— *auxiliary*—was coined to describe the remaining activities that would need to be performed in all units (such as budgeting, personnel, and purchasing). The interrelationships among line, staff, and auxiliary activities (especially between the first two) have continued to be an important concern in public administration.

Several areas of interaction among functions are important in public administration organizations. First, the activities of such diverse units in any organization require some degree of coordination. The likelihood of conflict is greatest between line and staff personnel; the most obvious point of potential clash is in their very different time perspectives and their order of priorities. Line personnel are usually concerned with the immediate, the concrete, the here and now, and the substantive aspects of activity, whereas those engaged in longer-range planning typically concern themselves with where the agency may be going five or ten years hence. Thus, top management must at least integrate their activities, if not directly attempt to link them operationally.

Second, some kinds of conflicts between the different types of personnel are virtually unavoidable. For example, an agency budget officer, who is responsible for reducing costs and keeping budget requests in line with projected estimates, may have to cut funds, which may result in a variety of complaints. The bureau chief may believe that top management is not sufficiently aware of, or sensitive to, the importance of the bureau's work. At the same time, the budget officer may come to regard the bureau as a reckless spender of scarce departmental dollars. In another example, a reform-minded city manager's attempts to centralize the purchasing function may infuriate department directors who have their own arrangements with suppliers and resent giving up their authority and discretion.

Finally, these traditional distinctions are increasingly seen as less important in an era of rapid change inside and outside of organizations. In particular, as long-term strategic planning has taken on greater legitimacy—and has become a more significant part of the thinking of top-level line managers—the planning function has become more closely integrated with daily operations. Reciprocal understanding is growing, blurring old distinctions between line and staff. In their demands for more and better program analysis before policy commitments are made, many political leaders have further enhanced the position of staff personnel vis-à-vis their line counterparts. Thus, as societal demands and management techniques have changed, the distinctions between line and staff functions have become increasingly less significant.

Centralization and Decentralization

The degree of **centralization** in an organization affects all other aspects of organizational life. Traditional management approaches have stressed how top managers exercise their powers in the interest of economy, efficiency, or effectiveness. The easy assumption of this thinking has been that it is entirely appropriate to centralize authority in an organization. Especially in recent years, however, much has been said, written, and accomplished in support of the value of **decentralization** in administration. It is useful to understand what each concept means before going on to discuss why decentralization has become so much more acceptable.

In its extreme form, centralized management means that all essential decision making and implementation are the concentrated responsibility of those at the top of the organizational hierarchy. Communication and coordination become one-way streets, from the top down (except for structured feedback). Nothing of any consequence goes on that is not under the direct control of

centralization

an organizational pattern focused on concentrating power at the top of an organization.

decentralization

an organizational pattern focused on distributing power broadly within an organization.

top management. Some entities still function in this way, but many others at all levels of government and in the private sector do not. As the scope and complexity of many organizations have increased, it has become necessary to delegate considerable amounts of operating authority to line managers (and occasionally to others), whose position in the organization is some distance from top management.

In general, most employees seek a larger voice in organizational affairs. The decentralization of decision-making authority effectively responds to this desire without forcing top management to relinquish command authority or oversight capacity. Even if employees of a public agency have not pressed for internal decentralization, the national government has encouraged it by responding to the demands of external clienteles, especially in cases involving the poor, and by increasing citizen participation in decision making. Concepts of citizen participation, neighborhood empowerment, and community activism trace their origins in part to congressional decisions intended to broaden opportunities for citizens to become more self-sufficient and less dependent on government. Thus, decentralization strategies often result in increased internal complexity.

Although ultimate policy and administrative responsibility remain with top managers, many day-to-day operating decisions are delegated to others at lower ranks within the organization. Depending on the degree of decentralization, some or all of the programmatic activities are supervised by middle-level managers operating under discretionary authority from senior management. Communication becomes a multichannel affair, with all manner of messages, directives, and informal contacts. Although still partly a central responsibility, coordination is also more likely to involve lateral (or cross-functional) coordination to a significant degree. It is also probable that top management will show greater willingness to include a wider range of employees in mapping out long-term strategies.

If centralization is analogous to *centripetal* force—that is, gravitational force that pulls all objects to the center—decentralization has as its analogue the *centrifugal* aspects of physics, in which the major thrust of the system is away from the center. In practice, a decentralized system of organization is one with *both* centripetal and centrifugal forces at work. It might be noted that these issues were—and still are—central to the continuing debate over American federalism, as well as to specific forms of administrative organization. Initiatives aimed at reinventing government stressed employee empowerment, devolution, and decentralization, together with teamwork, participatory management, labor-management cooperation, customer service, and employee enrichment programs. Much of what is said in the following section about the significance of centralization and decentralization also applies to the foundation and operation of the federal system.

Significance of Centralization and Decentralization

There can be little doubt that the degree of centralization in an organization (or, for that matter, a political system) can make a difference in how things are done. But what is that difference? What purposes and values are served by greater or lesser centralization?

Clearly, effective control and internal program consistency are enhanced by centralization; so, too, is accountability for actions of individuals within organizations. If authority is highly centralized, there can be little question as to whose values and assumptions shape organizational goals. Centralization also decreases the likelihood that management prerogatives will be challenged directly from below. Orderly operations within an organization are similarly facilitated whenever management responsibility is centralized.

On the other hand, centralization—even as it may facilitate control—often carries with it a certain lack of flexibility and adaptability, especially in large enterprises. According to many observers, one of the advantages of decentralization is that it enables middle-level managers in the field to act as organizational *sensors*—able to detect new problems or opportunities, in a position to respond on the spot to particular policy needs, and so on. Especially in an age of diversity and change, organizational adaptiveness may depend in large measure on the speed with which changes in the environment are detected and brought to the attention of top management, and subsequent adjustments provided for. In many settings—large government bureaucracies, private corporations dependent on changing markets, local government service-delivery mechanisms faced with changing citizen demands—the need for this sort of adaptive capability is so great that it demands some sacrifice of central control. In short, the most important need is an organization's ability to adapt itself for survival amid uncertainty and change.

Another function served by decentralization pertains to a political-philosophical question: To what degree are the members of an organization or other system meaningful participants in affairs of governance? Political systems, both ancient and modern, have confronted this question and have responded in many different ways. In democratic systems, suspicion of centralist control runs very deep, prompting many to equate decentralization in government with popular rule in one form or another. In our society, that doctrine has recently been joined to theories about organizational life; the result has been considerable emphasis on greater participation (through decentralization) by many who were previously excluded from organizational decision making. In general, it is thought that democratic participation enhances the quality of decisions reached and increases the probability that affected clienteles or "customers" will accept those decisions. Whether those expectations are realistic or well founded is another question.

Here again, however, there is another side to the coin. For just as top management might have to choose between control and flexibility, those who preach the virtues of decentralization must be alert to the possibility that, in a decentralized organization, it will be more difficult to hold accountable those who actually make decisions. The astute leader may find it possible to put through desired policy while avoiding accountability by pointing to the decentralized nature of the decision-making process in which many others also took part. There is the further prospect that co-optation will occur, thus reducing criticism or opposition by giving critics or opponents a stake in the decision process. Their co-optation would have important political consequences for the maintenance of meaningful opposition and the existence of informed, critical debate over proposed policy directions.

Thus, decentralization is far from an unmixed blessing and should not be viewed as a panacea that will solve all of an organization's ills. Note, in this connection, the conceptual links between our discussion of centralization and decentralization and our treatment in Chapter 2 of citizen participation, and of the administrative efficiency and pluralist democracy models. Advocates of centralization seek to apply the administrative efficiency model, whether consciously or not; arguments in favor of one are virtually identical to arguments in favor of the other. Similarly, those committed to decentralization implicitly favor the democracy model and its underlying assumptions and rationales.[47] Equally important is the fact that the centralization–decentralization debate cuts across a wide spectrum. It is as appropriate to questions of large-scale political arrangements (such as democratic governance or federal systems) as it is to smaller-scale organizational concerns, including the extent to which practices like democratic or participative management are encouraged within an organization.

In any discussion of decentralization, the caveat of the late Paul Appleby (former assistant to the Secretary of Agriculture and a leading scholar in public administration) is well worth noting. He wrote that nothing can be decentralized until it has first been centralized.[48] This suggests—or should suggest—that a central authority capable of *decentralizing* is also theoretically capable of *recentralizing*! Thus, decentralization can occur only in the context of previous centralization—not the most comforting thought for those who place their faith in decentralization as the appropriate remedy for abuse of centralized power. In many instances, the "center" can assume responsibilities that had been delegated elsewhere if decentralized operations are interfering with other values or objectives that are deemed important by those at the center. It is one of the pitfalls affecting the whole concept of decentralization in organizations.

The feeling is still widespread, however, that decentralization has sufficient advantages to warrant taking the attendant risks. It is significant that many top-level managers share that opinion.

Flattening Organizational Hierarchies

Most people associate bureaucracy with a distinct vertical chain of command through which a number of essential tasks can be effectively coordinated. These include exerting managerial control, providing for division of labor, and sending and receiving communications. Much of the literature on the subject assumes that a bureaucratic structure implicitly embraces many layers of organization in a "tall" hierarchy. Only in more recent decades has much attention been given to "flat," or "delayered," hierarchical arrangements, and to some of the differences between flat and tall organizations.[49]

Tall hierarchies evolved out of a combination of circumstances and organizational factors present in many early bureaucracies. Among the most important was, first, the diversity of tasks being performed within the same organization, therefore requiring significant horizontal and vertical differentiation of each division or unit from all others. Second, the principle known as narrow **span of control** combined with task diversity and interdependence of activities to encourage the growth of tall hierarchies. Third, that higher-level employees in many early organizations were regarded as more professional than those at lower echelons gave impetus to the tendency to differentiate clearly between top and bottom in the organization structure. Finally, the growing complexity of internal tasks and the expanded capacities of Internet Communication and Information Technologies (ICTs) to connect with external environments have spurred more modern organizations to exhibit intensified patterns of decentralized hierarchy.

Flat hierarchies were not unknown even in the early 1900s, however, and recently have become more common. A flat hierarchy is one in which either top management is conducted in a collegial, board of directors fashion, or all subordinate units below the highest level of the organization are regarded as hierarchical equals, or both. An early example of a flat hierarchy was the commission system in some local governments, in which each commissioner was the organizational equal of all the others and responsibility for municipal leadership and management was shared coequally. A more contemporary organizational example is that of the scientific research team; although there is probably a division of labor among team members and a coordinator of team efforts, no one leader is officially designated or informally acknowledged as such by team members. Also, decision making is a function shared on the basis of mutual respect for each other's expertise (to some extent, this is similar to organizational humanism and quality circles). Another example is the small professional staff in a nonprofit social-service agency (such as a local Girl Scout office), which depends on the active participation of dedicated volunteers in the community. Other examples are found in state and national advisory commissions, research organizations, and blue-ribbon citizens' panels (see Figure 4–3).

span of control

the number of people an individual supervises within a subunit of the organization. Each supervisor should have only a limited number of subordinates to oversee; this expands the chain of command to produce the needed ratio of supervisors to subordinates at each level, in the interest of overall coordination.

FIGURE 4-3

Tall and Flat Hierarchies

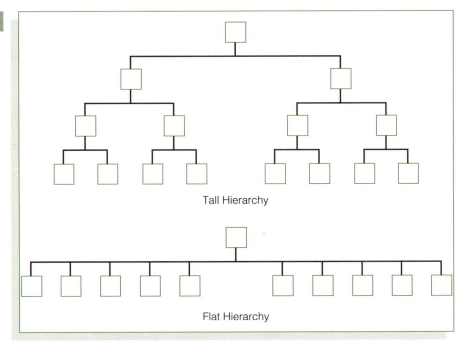

Tall Hierarchy

Flat Hierarchy

Significance of Tall and Flat Hierarchies

Among the most important differences between these two types of structures, communication problems in a tall hierarchy stand out. In general, the more layers an organization has, the less likely it is for messages to reach all levels undistorted. For lower-level employees and customers, the problem of access to those at higher ranks is closely related to this difficulty in communication. Obviously, these problems are greater in taller hierarchies and create the very real possibility that many employees will be alienated from organization leadership. Furthermore, as already suggested, problems of coordination are usually greater in the presence of organizational complexity; a tall hierarchy can contribute to the development of both those situations. Finally, issues of centralization and decentralization are more pressing in tall than in flat hierarchies.

Flat hierarchies are not, however, without their drawbacks. If organizational tasks become more diverse, there may not be enough flexibility in the structure to permit the reflection of that diversity, resulting in operating problems among individuals and staffs that are too closely crowded together. A second possible disadvantage lies in the existence of interpersonal hostilities on the same operating level of a flat hierarchy; again, there may not be

POINT/COUNTERPOINT

THE ISSUE Tall hierarchies evolved out of a combination of circumstances and organizational factors present in many early bureaucracies. These hierarchies provide a distinct vertical chain of command through which essential tasks and projects can be effectively coordinated. Given the complexity of modern organizations, is it inevitable that this is the best approach?

Are "tall" hierarchies inevitable in complex organizations?

Arguments *for* Tall Hierarchies within Organizations

- The diversity of tasks being performed within modern organizations makes it necessary to have a distinct chain of command and division of labor.
- The distinct chain of command provides a more efficient organization, with employees knowing their respective places and performing their specific tasks, without getting lost in the intricacies of different positions.
- The growing complexity of internal tasks and external responsibilities has forced organizations to exhibit centralized management systems, concentrating power with employees at the higher levels of the organization.

Arguments *against* Tall Hierarchies within Organizations

- The more layers an organization has, and the more complex the chain of command, the greater the potential for messages to arrive distorted.
- Tall hierarchies create the possibility that employees will be alienated from organization leadership, as lower-level employees are further removed from decisions made by higher-level management.
- A distinct chain of command has the potential to leave many employees dissatisfied with their own positions within the organization, as distance from the higher-level management creates a sense of "disconnect" and lack of appreciation for daily tasks performed and responsibilities fulfilled.

enough distance to shield an organization effectively against the adverse consequences of such feelings, thus allowing the functioning of the organization as a whole to be disrupted. Finally, flat hierarchies, particularly in smaller organizational settings that have some sort of chain of command, could produce too many leaders and not enough followers. It is not unknown for individuals operating on roughly equal footing to attempt to take charge of a portion of the agency's overall tasks; in the process, they demonstrate that no other individual possesses either the formal or the personal authority to counteract the attempt effectively. On the other hand, such a development can be dealt with in a tall hierarchy—and with potentially greater impact—partly because there are channels designed to handle such situations. Thus, we find that neither choice of structure is without its problems and that the choices that are made can predictably affect the life of the organization.

Alternative Forms of Organization

Traditional formulations about bureaucratic organization assumed (among other things) a division of labor, specialization, and an absence of functional overlap among the various units within an organization. Apart from the question of whether these conditions are always present, another set of issues has emerged to challenge the most basic assumptions about the appropriateness of bureaucracy as an organizing principle. Specifically, three developments have taken place that have encouraged informed thinking about various alternatives to bureaucracy as a form of organization.

First, the rise of new technologies such as smart phones and broadband and wireless access to the Internet has significantly altered and expanded the capability to perform substantive tasks in both public and private organizations. Scientific and other professional research and expertise, in a host of fields, have affected so much of public-policy making that it is difficult to imagine climate change, emergency management, transportation, conservation, agriculture, urban planning, housing, or national defense without them. The technologies involved in operating an organization such as wireless communications, psychological profiles and testing, computer applications, and other quantitative aids have themselves spawned a number of new specialties in the field of management alone. The result has been a proliferation of new and different collaborative and cross-functional organizational units devoted to functions that were unknown in most organizations just a few years ago. It has also spawned the development of software to address these problems. Examples of how technological change has affected organizations include the following: An insurance company contains a medical rehabilitation unit that concentrates on support services for vocationally disabled individuals insured by the company; almost any large state government department has within it an Office of Planning and Analysis whose job it is to look past immediate challenges and anticipate the future; and a corporate legal office includes a paralegal unit that assists in research and administrative services essential to providing high-quality legal work. Much of this technology allows public administrators to "work smarter, not harder" while concentrating their efforts in other areas of importance.

Second, the growth of complex knowledge has been characterized by increasing interdependence of fields of knowledge; the same is true of the staffs of specialists in those various fields. Thus, in the university setting, interdisciplinary plans of study and research are increasingly common. So also are interdependent teams of experts acting as consultants to industry or government organizations. Under such circumstances, hierarchical channels of authority would be highly dysfunctional and would tend to interfere with the accomplishment of stated objectives. Other organizational forms have had to be developed.

Third, the rise of professionalism in many occupations has triggered an emphasis on professionalism itself in public organizational activities. Consequently, this has strengthened organizational tendencies toward diversity and created the need for different styles of management among diverse professionals. By itself, professionalism might have made bureaucratic hierarchy somewhat inappropriate as a principle of organization but, in combination with the factors mentioned above, many claim that such a hierarchy has been made all the more unworkable.

What, then, are some of the alternative forms of organization? Several directions have been suggested. One is the call for "an end to hierarchy and competition,"[50] a clarion call for sweeping change in the ways we approach both structure and incentive systems within modern organizations. A second approach has been suggested by public administration scholar Warren Bennis, who has argued that a Weberian-style bureaucratic structure may have been entirely adequate and appropriate for dealing with routine and predictable tasks in a stable environment (such as the early 1900s) but that, given the unpredictable nature of contemporary organizational life, coupled with a far more turbulent social environment, organizations need new forms of management and leadership.[51] Bennis sees an end to hierarchical leadership because no one leader is capable of mastering the complex and diverse technologies present in so many organizations. And, because of technological needs, managers will increasingly become coordinators or facilitators among teams of experts operating within a decentralized and horizontal chain of command. According to Bennis, this clearly suggests a participative style of management; if the chain of command runs horizontally, it virtually requires a view of organization members as equals, not as superiors and subordinates.[52] The concept of a "series of interconnected and networked teams" already operates in many computer software companies, aerospace industries, blue-ribbon commissions, and numerous professional consulting firms that have considerable influence on the policy-making process.

One other possibility, referred to in Chapter 1, is that public organizations might come to reflect the reverse pyramid associated with knowledge workers (those whose work centers around communication and information technology) in service-providing organizations, including intelligence gathering and law enforcement.[53] Rather than a top-down vertical hierarchy characteristic of traditional bureaucracies, this reverse structure defines managers as sources of support, principally for their frontline employees who deal directly with those receiving services provided by the organization. Such a structure assumes a greater degree of accountability, decentralization, independence, and participatory management than is found in most traditional hierarchies; it also implicitly assumes an open rather than a closed system, one that is in nearly constant interaction with its surrounding social environment. Because of the changing nature of organizations and the growing service demands on many government organizations, the reverse pyramid may indeed be found in increasing numbers of government structures.

Organization Theory and Behavior in Perspective

The theories and realities of organization are all in a state of continuous change. In this chapter, we have seen many proposals for organizational arrangements; none of them, however, solves all the problems that existed before or is free of its own shortcomings. Yet we seem never to cease trying to devise the communication channel that is one step better, to bring about coordination of programs and projects that will be truly effective, and to establish a nonhierarchical structure that will not suffer from lack of formal direction and leadership. In the midst of such variety and richness in the possibilities available, it may be that our single biggest problem is learning how to select the proper devices, forms, and tools to fit particular organizational and functional needs. That would require broadening management skills and training in directions that are not now clearly perceived; it also has implications for our choices on larger questions of power, authority, and self-governance. Increasingly, choices made that pertain directly to administration will be made in the larger "force field" of values that surrounds all our institutions. It is evident that both general and specific values are in an evolutionary process.

In spite of its intellectual diversity, the subject of organizational theory has been characterized by a unifying theme: the attempt to identify the elements in an organization's existence that are most important to the successful attainment of its goals. What those elements are, what the goals are, and even what constitutes the organization itself have not been agreed on. The overlapping series of schools or approaches has given us a wide range of ideas from which to choose. Furthermore, the evolution of organizational theory has reflected changing emphases in a host of academic disciplines, in business and industry, and in society at large concerning what is important and how to go about achieving it.

Several general comments are in order. First, the various approaches to organization theory have clearly overlapped chronologically and, more to the point, intellectually. The human relations school, though departing significantly from Weber and Taylor, assumed the existence of the same formal, hierarchical structure. Organizational humanism borrowed from the human relations approach. TQM, Theory Z, and learning organizations have incorporated some elements of organizational humanism. Learning theory encompasses aspects of systems thinking and TQM. Thus, various strands of theoretical development have often been woven together as parts of different fabrics, so to speak. Each theory is neither self-contained nor totally self-explanatory.

Second, although various approaches may fall out of favor among organization theorists of a particular period, those approaches do not necessarily cease to have any influence. On the contrary, the influence of organization theories is generally cumulative; at any given time, one may find in existing organizations some offshoots of earlier belief and practice. For example, although Weber's and Taylor's ideas of formal theory no longer predominate among contemporary scholars, they have had a powerful influence in shaping many public and private institutions and, significantly, are still influential (however indirectly) in the thinking of many people. The same is true of the principles of administration and the human relations approach, both of which still carry some weight in theory and practice.

Furthermore, the modern tradition avoids the closed- versus open-system dilemma and views the organization, in James Thompson's words, as a "problem-facing and problem-solving phenomenon . . . focusing on organizational processes related to choice of courses of action in an environment which does not fully disclose the alternatives available or the consequences of those alternatives."[54] Thus, most organizations are neither fully closed nor fully open systems. In an increasingly interdependent world, the former is impractical, if not impossible; the latter, although still possible, would produce a situation in which any organization would be overwhelmed by the inflows of energy and information, rendering it ineffectual at best. In this mixed view of organizations, then, external environments are regarded as very important; at the same time, organizations are seen as attempting to cope internally with enormous uncertainty as they try to learn from the environment and successfully cope with change.

Finally, the evolution of organization theory has included a marked shift in assumptions about organizational leaders and followers—from a formal hierarchical relationship in which orders were transmitted and obeyed without question to much more diverse and diffuse network arrangements in which more participation and team direction are accepted as a matter of course. The command-and-control emphasis has had to yield to other values, further complicating our understanding of how organizations can be effectively operated and posing new challenges for managers themselves.[55]

Organization theory and practice have grown more complex over the years as they paralleled actual developments in organizations throughout modern society. As more knowledge has been brought to bear, it is not surprising that today we are confronted by both greater diversity of approaches and less certainty about the nature of large-scale organizations and the behavior of people within them. That trend is likely to continue.

Summary

Organization theory focuses on formal and informal structures, internal dynamics, and surrounding social environments of complex human organizations. Spanning several academic disciplines, it has emphasized, at different times, the needs of management, the needs and motivations of workers, and the relationships between organizations and their environments. Four major areas of organization theory are (1) formal theories, (2) the human relations school, (3) organizational humanism, and (4) modern organization theory.

Weber's formal model of bureaucracy incorporated the concepts of hierarchy, division of labor and functional specialization, detailed rules and procedures, maintenance of files, professionalization, and adequate legal and political authority. Control was a central purpose of this model. American public administration differs from the formal model as a result of commands from outside the formal hierarchy, the extent of functional overlap among agencies, less than complete operation of merit personnel systems, diversity of substantive professional expertise, loose requirements for continuing competence, and late development of a career emphasis. Early in this century, scientific management theories were proposed to meet the growing needs of private industry. Authority was concentrated in management's hands, and there was "one best way" to perform each task; efficiency, rationality, productivity, and profit were highly prized. The human relations school, the first of the "informal" theories, was launched with the Hawthorne studies in the late 1920s and early 1930s. A major emphasis of the human relations school was the effect of leadership on worker performance and social interaction. The leadership function was viewed as offering positive incentives to workers in exchange for their contributions to the organization and its work.

Organizational humanism was founded on four central assumptions: (1) work was (or could be made) intrinsically interesting to the worker; (2) workers sought satisfactions in their jobs; (3) work was a central life interest to the worker and not merely a means to financial gain; and (4) greater worker involvement in management could serve as positive motivation to improve worker performance and satisfaction.

Modern organization theory is characterized by an effort to separate facts from values, apply empirical research methods (including the use of statistical data and computers), incorporate information from diverse sources, and respond to complexity in the formulation and application of theory. Contributions to modern theory have come from concepts such as open-systems theory, information theory, cybernetics, organization development, Theory Z, TQM, and learning theories. All are systemwide theories and strategies used by thousands of governments for improving processes and achieving agency goals.

The dynamics of organization help shape how daily activities are carried on within organizations and include (1) communication, (2) coordination, (3) line and staff functions, (4) centralization and decentralization, (5) tall and flat hierarchies, and (6) alternative forms of organization.

In recent years, alternatives to the bureaucratic form of organization have been suggested more frequently on the grounds that formal bureaucracy is no longer an appropriate way to structure organizations. Organization theory seeks to identify the elements crucial to organizational success. There has been both chronological and intellectual overlap from one body of theory to the next, and most theories have left their imprint on society even after passing from prominence among theorists. The complexity of modern organization theory parallels the complexity of real-world organizations in an era of accelerating change.

Discussion Questions

1. Discuss the similarities among the Weberian bureaucratic model, scientific management, and the "principles" approach to studying public organizations. Describe the basis of each theory and its impact on the development of American public administration.

2. What were the principal findings of the "Hawthorne" experiments (in the late 1920s and early 1930s) and how did they subsequently influence organization theory and application in American public administration? What did these findings suggest about practices of leadership, motivation, and supervision of employees that were current at the time?

3. The human relations school challenged the formal approach in a number of ways, including its enhanced concern with an informal social structure within organizations. What are the criticisms of this school and how have they influenced its acceptance and application in public agencies?

4. Discuss the values underlying modern organization theory. What are the major elements and implications of a "systems" approach to overcoming complexity, uncertainty, and isolation from the surrounding environment?

5. What are the common characteristics of "open" and "closed" systems of organization? How do open systems facilitate organizational development and change?

6. What is the central theme or purpose of organization theory? How can the various theories of organization be applied within the context of public administration to better achieve the goals of public agencies?

7. Discuss how senior public managers can encourage "feedback" within their organizations. What problems or difficulties might such managers encounter, and how might they deal with them?

8. Why would some individuals in organizations resist efforts to "improve coordination" among various units and activities? How might those intent on improving coordination overcome such resistance? Discuss.

9. What are the respective advantages and disadvantages of centralization and decentralization in an organization (or laterally across organizational lines)? How might a manager decide how to strike a balance among the various benefits and drawbacks? Discuss.

10. Why have organizational decentralization and greater employee participation become more widespread? What are the positive and negative consequences of this twenty-first century Internet-driven megatrend?

Key Terms and Concepts

hierarchy, *146*

patronage, *147*

formal theory of organization, *147*

functional overlap, *148*

merit system, *148*

scientific management, *149*

human relations, *152*

Hawthorne or "halo" effect, *153*

zone of acceptance, *154*

organizational humanism, *157*

Theory Y, *158*

Theory X, *158*

hierarchy of needs, *159*

modern organization theory, *162*

systems theory, *162*

closed systems, *163*

open-systems theory, *164*

homeostasis, *165*

information theory, *165*

game theory, *165*

cybernetics, *165*

Theory Z, *165*

total quality management (TQM), *167*

statistical process control (SPC), *167*

systems analysis, *167*

learning organizations, *169*

communication, *170*

coordination, *170*

formal communication, *170*

informal communication, *170*

lateral or cross-functional communication, *171*

gobbledygook, *173*

bargaining or conflict model, *174*

consensual or consensus-building model, *175*

line functions, *178*

staff functions, *178*

centralization, *179*

decentralization, *179*

span of control, *183*

Suggested Readings

Argyris, Chris. *Integrating the Individual and the Organization*. Piscataway, N.J.: Transaction, 1990.

———. *Knowledge for Action: A Guide to Overcoming Barriers to Organizational Change*. San Francisco: Jossey-Bass, 1993.

Ban, Carolyn. *How Do Public Managers Manage?* San Francisco: Jossey-Bass, 1995.

Barnard, Chester. *The Functions of the Executive*. Cambridge, Mass.: Harvard University Press, 2007.

Beam, George. *Quality Public Management: What It Is and How It Can Be Improved and Advanced*. Chicago: Rowman & Littlefield, 2001.

Bozeman, Barry. *All Organizations Are Public: Bridging Public and Private Organizational Theories*. San Francisco: Jossey-Bass, 1987.

Brudney, Jeffrey L., Laurence J. O'Toole, and Hal G. Rainey, eds. *Advancing Public Management: New Developments in Theory, Methods, and Practice*. Washington, D.C.: Georgetown University Press, 2001.

Davis, Charles R. *Organization Theories and Public Administration*. Westport, Conn.: Praeger, 1996.

Downs, Anthony. *Inside Bureaucracy*. Boston: Little, Brown, 1967; reprint edition published by Waveland Press, Prospect Heights, Ill., 1993.

Fry, Brian R., and Jos C. N. Raadschelders. *Mastering Public Administration: From Max Weber to Dwight Waldo*. 2nd ed. Washington, D.C.: CQ Press, 2008.

Garnett, James L. *Communicating for Results in Government: A Strategic Approach for Public Managers*. San Francisco: Jossey-Bass, 1994.

Goldhaber, Gerald M. *Organizational Communication*. 6th ed. Madison, Wis.: Brown & Benchmark, 1993.

Graham, Cole Blease, Jr., and Steven W. Hayes. *Managing the Public Organization*. 2nd ed. Washington, D.C.: CQ Press, 1992.

Hummel, Ralph. *The Bureaucratic Experience: A Critique of Life in the Modern Organization*. 5th ed. New York: M.E. Sharpe, 2007.

Likert, Rensis. *New Patterns of Management*. New York: McGraw-Hill, 1961.

March, James G., Herbert A. Simon, and Harold S. Guetzkow. *Organizations*. 2nd ed. Cambridge, Mass.: Blackwell, 1993.

Maslow, Abraham H. *Motivation and Personality*. 3rd ed. New York: HarperCollins 1987.

Meyer, C. Kenneth, and Charles H. Brown. *Practicing Public Management: A Casebook*. 2nd ed. New York: St. Martin's Press, 1989.

Ott, Steven J., Sandra J. Parkes, and Richard B. Simpson. *Classic Readings in Organizational Behavior*. 4th ed. Belmont, Calif.: Wadsworth, 2008.

Rainey, Hal G. *Understanding and Managing Public Organizations*. 4th ed. San Francisco: Jossey-Bass, 2009.

Senge, Peter M. *The Fifth Discipline: The Art and Practice of the Learning Organization*. New York: Currency, 2006.

Senge, Peter M., Charlotte Roberts, Richard Ross, Bryan Smith, and Art Kleiner. *The Fifth Discipline Fieldbook*. New York: Currency Doubleday, 1994.

Simon, Herbert A. *Administrative Behavior: A Study of Decision-Making Processes in Administrative Organizations*. 4th ed. New York: Free Press, 1997.

Stivers, Camilla. *Gender Images in Public Administration: Legitimacy and the Administrative State*. 2nd ed. London: Sage, 2002.

Stupak, Ronald J., and Peter Leitner. *Handbook of Public Quality Management*. Boca Raton, Fla.: CRC Press, 2001.

Thompson, James D. *Organizations in Action: Social Science Bases of Administrative Theory*. Piscataway, N.J.: Transaction, 2003.

Vecchio, Robert P. *Organizational Behavior: Core Concepts*. 6th ed. Mason, Ohio: South-Western, 2005.

Decision Making in Administration

The making of decisions is at the heart of public administration. How decisions are made, by whom, by what standards, at what cost, and for whose benefit are questions of continuing interest as well as occasional controversy. The scramble for influence over decisions, the accessibility of decision makers, the actions of those making and affected by government decisions, the ethical standards maintained and the values applied by public administrators, as well as the accountability of decision makers, all attest to the importance attached to the decision-making process.

The substance of decisions, as well as the procedures by which they are made and applied, leave a lasting imprint on administrative politics. In this chapter, we will discuss the general nature of bureaucratic decisions, principal approaches to decision making, the impacts of different kinds of goals, ethical considerations of decision making, major features of the surrounding environment that ordinarily enter into the process, and how different sorts of political pressures affect the way many administrative decisions are made.

decision making

a process in which choices are made to change (or leave unchanged) an existing condition and to select a course of action most appropriate to achieving a desired objective (however formalized or informal the objective may be), while minimizing risk and uncertainty to the extent deemed possible; the process may be characterized by widely varying degrees of self-conscious "rationality," or by willingness of the decision maker to decide incrementally, without insisting on assessment of all possible alternatives, or by some combinations of approaches.

The Nature of Decisions

Organizational **decision making** involves making a choice to alter some existing condition, choosing one course of action in preference to others, expending some amount of organizational assets or individual resources to implement the decision, and acting with the expectation of gaining something desirable. Some decisions are made to maintain the *status quo*, but theoretically the mere fact that a decision was called for *not* to change something alters the overall situation. The definition of decision making suggests that a decision is not a single, self-contained event; rather, it is

> the product of a complex social process generally extending over a considerable period of time. . . . Decision making includes attention-directing or intelligence processes that determine the occasions of decision, processes for discovering and designing possible courses of action and processes for evaluating alternatives and choosing them.[1]

Thus, a decision entails a series of other choices that may rightly be regarded as part of it.

It is assumed that a decision maker selects the course of action most appropriate to achieving a desired result or objective; deciding what is most appropriate, however, is often difficult. There is always some uncertainty as to the eventual outcome of a decision; as a result, a degree of risk (however small) is involved in implementing that decision. Concerns that are central to the decision-making process, therefore, include (1) increasing potential gains, (2) monitoring the ongoing decisional process, and (3) reducing the resource expenditure, uncertainty, and risk involved in achieving whatever gains are made.[2]

In this chapter, we will discuss decisions about relatively important, even fundamental, matters in organizational life. But it should be noted that the great majority of all decisions are more or less routine and based on previously adopted policy. Routine decisions have the advantage of requiring little time or mental energy to make; they can be made according to regular schedules (Should we hire our usual extra summer help?) or where clear need exists (Should we send out the snowplows?), without having to start from scratch each time. The central risk involved in routine decision making is that decision makers may fail to perceive a need to reconsider existing policy or program assumptions on which routine decisions are based.

For example, in an agency dependent on extra personnel to meet seasonal demand (such as the U.S. National Park Service), the number of extra people needed should not *automatically* be based on prior experience. If, say, the price of park admission rises $15 per person, the Park Service personnel director may reasonably assume that fewer staff aides will have to be hired because the flow of visitors is very likely to diminish. Similarly, sending out the snowplows as a routine response to a midwestern snowstorm might have to be re-examined if a city is confronted with a fiscal crunch (as many now are). Work crew layoffs, reduced gasoline allocations, fewer streets plowed, fewer plows in operation—under nonroutine circumstances, all these options might have to be explored. Thus, maintaining routines that are inappropriate to changing conditions may only complicate the problems to which they were first addressed and may lead to new problems.

Approaches to Decision Making: Concepts and Controversies

Few issues have occupied such a central place in the literature of public administration or have generated so much debate as the question of *how* to make decisions. Arguments have raged over issues such as the importance and relevance of goal setting, the capacities of decision makers to absorb information and use it objectively, the scope and types of data that decision makers ought to use in order to make good decisions, and the consequences of employing different approaches to decision making. Models that are applicable to administrative organizations have been derived from a variety of disciplines, notably economics, philosophy, and political science. Some have stressed statistical techniques, utilizing quantitative data and (allegedly) value-free criteria for decision alternatives. Others, said by their advocates to be both more realistic and more effective, suggest that decisions can and should be made without first having to define every purpose that might be served by a given action; these models also recommend the use of more informal measures of decision choices. Still other models have been advanced to integrate the strong points of existing models into new perspectives on, and approaches to, decision making.

The debate surrounding how decisions should be made is marked by intense disagreement. Issues of decision making are far from settled, and new contributions to the literature continue to appear. New controversies and directions have recently emerged, especially in government, that are reshaping many long-standing assumptions about how decisions should (and can) be made. These include efforts supporting empowerment of citizens, better service to government's customers, and devolving decision-making power to nongovernmental entities. Other issues (such as the cumulative impacts of past decisions on a current choice) also affect decision making and further complicate matters. The complexity and importance of the subject make it imperative that students of public administration understand the nature of the controversies surrounding decision making, as well as key aspects of the process itself. The following section explores the principal approaches to decision making and criticisms of each, considers other dimensions of the process, and concludes by examining a consciously political approach to decision making.

Rationality in Decision Making: The Classical/Economic Model

The **rational approach** is drawn from economic models of decision making. According to this classical outlook, decision makers are consciously rational; that is, they order their behavior so that it is "reasonably directed toward the achievement of conscious goals."[3] Another crucial dimension of economic

rational approach

an approach to decision making that is derived from economic theories of how to make the "best" decisions; involves efforts to move toward consciously held goals in a way that requires the smallest input of scarce resources; assumes the ability to separate ends from means, rank all alternatives, gather all possible data, and objectively weigh alternatives; stresses rationality in the process of reaching decisions.

rationality is the concept of *efficiency*, or in political economist Anthony Downs's words, "maximizing output for a given input [of scarce resources], or minimizing input for a given output." Downs defines the rational decision maker as "a [person] who moves toward his [or her] goals in a way which, to the best of his [or her] knowledge, uses the lease possible input of scarce resources per unit of valued output."[4]

In terms of actual behavior, a rational person (1) can always make a decision when presented with a range of alternatives; (2) knows the probable consequences of choosing each alternative; (3) ranks all alternatives in an order of preference, so that each is preferred, equal, or inferior to other options included in the ranking; (4) always chooses the highest-ranked alternative; and (5) always makes the same decision each time the same alternatives are available. Such an individual would normally try to separate ends (goals) clearly from means (methods) while concentrating on one or a few primary goals; pursuing too many goals simultaneously would frustrate efforts to attain them and to measure the efficiency and rationality of the process. Also, the rational decision maker would seek to gather all possible data pertaining to the range of alternatives and objectively weigh alternative solutions before selecting the best possible one (maximizing). The analysis and methodology must be comprehensive, with precise evaluation procedures, quantification of measures and relative values, and appropriate use of statistics.

Important also are the relationships that are assumed to exist between means and ends (and that enable the decision maker to choose the most rational means for achieving the specified end), and the relationships between costs and benefits involved, in the interest of efficiency. **Cost–benefit analysis** and specification of **cost–benefit ratios** for each alternative presume the ability to assign a quantitative value to each alternative in a ranking and to distinguish clearly among the values assigned. In theory, this makes it possible to determine the optimum ratio of benefits to costs, thus enabling the decision maker to make the final best choice.

This model essentially stresses the rationality of the decision-making process as *value-neutral* without reference to whether goals are also rational. The test of a good decision is that "it can be shown to be the most appropriate means to [achieving] desired ends,"[5] judging in long-term perspectives. It is *procedural* criteria that must be satisfied in order to assess decision making as being rational; the decision outcome is distinctly secondary. (The analytical steps in the method are similar to the seven-step policy analysis approach outlined on page 393.) For several decades, the rational model has had a powerful influence on decision theory and on the art and craft of practical decision making. It was not until the late 1950s that questions and criticisms began to be raised about the model and alternative approaches to decision making were suggested. Two principal themes were sounded: (1) that the rational model lacks practical applicability outside the realm of economic theory, and (2) that it is less desirable

cost–benefit analysis

technique designed to measure relative gains and losses resulting from alternative policy or program options; emphasizes identification of the most desirable cost–benefit ratio, in quantitative or other terms.

cost–benefit ratios

the proportional relationship between expenditure of a given quantity of resources and the benefits derived therefrom; a guideline for choosing among alternatives, of greatest relevance to the rational model of decision making.

than other possible models as a mode of operation, especially in public administrative organizations.

Critiques of the Rational Model

The practicality of the rational model has been questioned on numerous grounds.[6] Most critiques are based on the proposition that it is not possible—and never has been—to construct a purely rational, value-neutral, decision-making process for any but the simplest, lowest-level decisions. Among the impediments to rationality suggested by the model's critics are the (1) impossibility of distinguishing facts from values and of analytically separating ends from means, (2) improbability of obtaining agreement among decision makers on predetermined goals, (3) changing and ambiguous nature of many political and administrative goals, (4) pressures of time to make a decision when it is needed, and (5) ability of decision makers to handle only a limited amount of information at any one time. Other problems associated with the rational approach include the difficulty of giving one's undivided attention to a single problem or decision; the costs of information acquisition; failure to secure all possible data because of time constraints, excessive cost, or oversight; defects in communication processes; and the inability to predict all the consequences of a given choice, which contributes to inevitable uncertainties during and after the decision process. Competition for resources among analysts and decision makers and their organizations prevents any single entity from achieving maximum utility. Moreover, the need to deal with different aspects of the same problem—for example, the funding and location of new public sports arena or capital and operating budgets for mass-transit systems—presents uncertainties in sociopolitical environments that affect substantive problems and the availability of both alternatives and resources.

The other major criticism of the rational model is that it requires activities and calculations that are not possible in governmental decision-making processes. The first and principal spokesman for this view was political scientist Charles Lindblom, who first articulated his position in 1959.[7] Lindblom argued that decision makers do not have to seek prior goal consensus in order to make sound decisions for the short run; furthermore, because goals can rarely be agreed on in advance, even trying to achieve consensus makes the pursuit of reasonable decisions just that much more difficult. Lindblom referred to this facetiously as the science of "muddling through" a decision, also noting that the means–ends analysis called for in the rational model is impossible if means and ends are confused (as, he suggested, they inevitably are). Also, public administrators cannot look to the general public to set and articulate meaningful policy goals (see Chapter 9) because public opinion is highly ambiguous, inconsistent, and diverse; even if identifiable goals do exist, they do not serve as clear guides to administrative decision making. Finally, many broad public goals may conflict with one another.

Incrementalism and Mixed Scanning: Response and Counterresponse

As we have seen, major criticisms of the rational model center on several of its basic assumptions. A number of scholars have expanded on these criticisms and have argued that individual decisions, and change in general, are produced by an "incremental" process. **Incrementalism**, in contrast to rationality, emphasizes decision making through a series of limited, successive comparisons within a relatively narrow range of alternatives rather than a comprehensive range; it uses the status quo, not abstract goals, as the key point of reference for decisions. Incrementalism focuses primarily on short-term rather than long-term effects, on the most crucial consequences of an action rather than on all conceivable results, and on less formalized methods of measuring costs and benefits.

Differences between rationalists and incrementalists are very sharp. First, the rationalist attempts to maximize benefits in all phases of decision making, whereas the incrementalist tries to *satisfice* (to use economist Herbert Simon's term). To satisfice is to reach a decision that is satisfactory, yielding benefits that suffice to meet the situational needs of the decision maker. In other words, a decision maker who satisfices is one who is willing to "settle for good-enough answers in despair at finding best answers."[8] The incremental decision maker accepts that it may not be possible to get everything out of a given decision and that settling for "half a loaf" is not unreasonable. Furthermore, the incrementalist maintains that it is *irrational* to expect success every time a decision is made, because doing so increases the risks—and consequences—of failure and expends resources too rapidly, and because rationality itself would not be cost-effective (assuming, again, that rationality is possible).

Second, although incrementalism does not dismiss the importance of long-term consequences, it emphasizes short-term needs and problems. Incrementalists are comfortable filling the role of troubleshooters, responding to immediate pressures and seeking to alleviate the worst of them. Charles Lindblom, perhaps the leading spokesman for this school of thought, speaks of serial analyses—that is, repeated and ongoing analyses—rather than one comprehensive analysis as called for in the rationalist view. He maintains that making *continual incremental adjustments* in both the definition of a problem and the formulation of solutions is a reasonable and effective method of solving problems and making decisions.

Third, Lindblom and others suggest that the emphasis in the rational model on comprehensive evaluation of how a given decision would affect all other decisions is unrealistic. They contend that it is impossible to account in advance for all the ways in which a particular course of action will affect other decision-making processes and their outcomes.

Incrementalism may also have a practical advantage for public administrators as they try to deal with executive orders or legislative requirements,

incrementalism

a model of decision making that stresses making decisions through limited, successive comparisons, in contrast to the rational model; also focuses on simplifying choices rather than aspiring to complete problem analyses, on the status quo rather than abstract goals as a key point of reference, on "satisficing" rather than "maximizing," and on remedying ills rather than seeking positive goals.

which often are ambiguous. Making decisions incrementally may enable administrators to satisfy minimal expectations while gaining time to determine more specifically what effects the directives will have in practice. Under time pressures and conditions of uncertainty of all kinds, it is difficult at best to pursue a classical/economic rational course.

Most important, those who advocate the incremental approach reject the notion that only "efficiency" models of decision making are legitimate. They argue that noneconomic models and modes of decision making have intrinsic value and that, in some circumstances, using economic models might well be inappropriate. Furthermore, they claim that the incremental model allows for measures of costs, benefits, and side effects of decisions that are not economic or even necessarily quantitative. Incrementalists acknowledge that this approach permits *subjective values* to influence decisions, but they justify that on the grounds that subjectivity can never be eliminated entirely. They maintain that it is better to openly incorporate sound subjective judgment than to attempt self-consciously to exclude all traces of subjectivity. At the same time, incrementalists strongly endorse the need for adequate and good-quality data, for choosing sound courses of action, and so on. The difference is that they are prepared to make decisions even when the ideal conditions called for by the rationalists do not exist, which, they maintain, happens in an overwhelming majority of decision-making situations.

The incremental approach itself has come under fire. Two critics, in particular, stand out—one for identifying a serious shortcoming, the other for elaborating on the criticism of the first and outlining a third approach to decision making. Yehezkel Dror, in a pointed response to Lindblom, emphasized that marginal changes acceptable to incrementalists may *not* suffice to meet real and growing policy demands and that, as policy needs change, decision makers may have to develop innovations bolder than those apparently contemplated by supporters of the incremental approach.[9] Dror's message is that if incrementalists focus solely or even primarily on small-scale changes designed to meet disjointed and short-run needs, they are likely to overlook larger needs and demands, with subsequent decisions even more likely to "miss the mark" in one or more policy/problem areas.

Dror also criticized incrementalism for making more acceptable the forces in human organizations that tend toward inertia and maintenance of the status quo. His comments suggest that, in incrementalism, one can find justification for the behavior of Anthony Downs's "conserver"—the bureaucrat who is chiefly interested in maintaining power, prestige, and income and who takes a cautious, low-risk approach to decision making. Dror clearly leaned toward a view of bureaucratic behavior that encourages both responsiveness to larger-scale needs and innovativeness in seeking solutions; he found incrementalism wanting in both respects.

Amitai Etzioni expanded on Dror's criticisms of the incremental model and offered an alternative approach, which he labeled **mixed scanning**.[10]

mixed scanning

a model of decision making that combines the rational-comprehensive model's emphasis on fundamental choices and long-term consequences with the incrementalists' emphasis on changing only what needs to be changed in the immediate situation.

Etzioni's chief criticism of the incremental approach was its apparent failure to distinguish between fundamental and non-fundamental decisions. He suggested that, for non-fundamental decision making, the incremental approach was entirely valid and appropriate but that, in making fundamental decisions, a wider perceptual horizon was needed. More important, he believed that incrementalists tended to decide only non-fundamental matters—stemming from their emphasis on the troubleshooter approach to solving problems—and, as a result, promoted a general aimlessness in overall policy. Etzioni suggested a twofold or mixed approach to decision making that incorporates some elements of both the rational-comprehensive and incremental approaches.

Etzioni's mixed-scanning model can best be understood through his analogy involving a high-altitude weather satellite in orbit around the earth. Onboard the satellite are two cameras—one equipped with a wide-angle lens that can scan a large area and record major weather patterns and the other equipped with a narrow-angle lens capable of zeroing in on turbulence and examining it in much finer detail. Examination by the narrow-lens camera is contingent on the wide-lens camera having first discovered large systems of turbulent weather. Conversely, the wide-lens camera is incapable of detailed analysis of storm centers and other phenomena. In sum, either camera without the other would supply some useful information, but much more can be obtained when they are used in combination. Further, the analysis provided by the narrow-lens camera is more intelligible when meteorologists have some idea of the total weather system's size, location, and boundaries—that is, when they have a meaningful context for the detailed data. So it is with decision making:

> Fundamental decisions are made by exploring the main alternatives the actor sees in view of his conception of his goals, but—unlike what rationalism would indicate—details and specifications are omitted so that an overview is feasible. *Incremental decisions are made but within the context set by fundamental decisions (and fundamental reviews).* Thus, each of the two elements in mixed-scanning helps to reduce the effects of the particular shortcomings of the other; incrementalism reduces the unrealistic aspects of rationalism by limiting the details required in fundamental decisions, and . . . rationalism helps to overcome the conservative slant of incrementalism by exploring longer-run alternatives.[11]

This prescription for decision making has, in turn, been criticized in several ways. First, it is difficult to identify "a big or little decision" because the consequences often are unknown or unpredictable at the time a decision is being made. From that, one might infer that, although fundamental decisions may be relatively easy to recognize, problems can develop when a seemingly minor choice turns out to have led to unexpectedly significant outcomes. In this context, perhaps too much emphasis has been placed on differences between fundamental and incremental decisions, implicitly undercutting the mixed-scanning model.

Contrary to the interpretation given it by many observers, incrementalism is not, by definition, concerned with change only in small steps, nor is it biased against large-scale alterations in the status quo. Change by increments, according to this view, is a matter of degree as well as substance. Lindblom acknowledged criticisms that "doing better usually means turning away from incrementalism" by arguing that incrementalists "believe that for complex problem solving, it usually means *practicing incrementalism more skillfully* and turning away from it only rarely."[12] Contrary to the assumptions underlying the rational model, no one can hope to analyze a complex problem completely, and calculated analytic strategies designed to simplify complex problems hold more promise of success than do attempts at comprehensive "scientific" analysis. Incremental analysis can and should focus on immediate problem solving rather than long-term goals. It is that line of reasoning that challenges the mixed-scanning model. Incrementalists believe that relying on rationality produces worse analysis and decisions than does strategic analysis. In sum, Lindblom would fault mixed scanning for its failure to reject the rational model completely, while defending incrementalism as a viable approach to decisions of either large or small consequence.[13]

We will return to these models later in this chapter. Now we turn to other dimensions that also merit discussion.

Decisions in the Balance: The Environment of Choice

In addition to questions concerning assumptions and models, a number of other considerations are involved in reaching decisions. First is the matter of the resources necessary to implement a decision. The decision maker must consider both what kinds and what quantity of resources will be expended in pursuing a particular course of action. A decision to take some organizational action may require expenditures of time, personnel, money, and what scholar Robert Putnam referred to as *political capital* (budget, influence, prestige, and so on). The responsible official must have a reasonably clear idea of just how much it will cost in terms of all these resources.

Decision makers also must establish whether potential benefits are worth probable costs. This requires answering some difficult questions: Do we have sufficient time to devote to this policy, such as continuing the war in Afghanistan, given our other domestic and international priorities and responsibilities? Will our allies and political supporters go along with us despite the costs, or will we encounter pressure to do it differently or perhaps not at all? Are we sufficiently certain about the probable benefits we can expect from maintaining the current course? At times, decision makers may have to choose between two mutually exclusive benefits (either this gain or that one, but not both), to decide whether to seek something now or later (entailing the risk that it might be difficult now, but impossible later), and (especially in government) to weigh the impact of values such as promoting democracy in the Middle East that are not central to the specific decisional equation (setting a bad political precedent, losing faith and trust in elected officials, damaging democratic traditions in other countries, and so on). The Obama administration has confronted the same set of issues in its response to upheavals in Bahrain, Egypt, Libya, Syria, Tunisia, and Yemen. A corollary concern is how to measure both costs and benefits or to ascertain whether meaningful measures are even available. One of the most tangible measures is in dollar terms, particularly regarding costs. Were the benefits received from the $950 billion, nearly 5,000 American lives, and thousands of Iraqi lives expended to topple the Saddam regime and occupy Iraq worth the costs in American resources and lives? They may have been, or they may *not* have been, but *how do we measure that?* There has always been considerable debate, both in the academic community and in government, over different ways to measure costs and benefits, separately and in relation to each other, and over the political implications of using different sets of measures.

Finally, decision makers may base their decisions on different grounds, singly or in combination. Three such grounds are most prominent. One is *substantive* grounds, with decisions made on the merits of the question. For example, a decision concerning the design of a highway linking two major cities, using efficiency criteria, would focus on the "shortest distance between two points" in terms of mileage, travel time, and construction costs and time. A second basis is *political* grounds—that is, net gain or loss measured by changes in political support or resources. In the example of the highway, the decision as to a specific route might be affected by the discovery that following a straight line between the cities would take it across some valuable farmland owned by an influential politician or a contributor to the election campaigns of incumbent officeholders. In this case, the "shortest distance" might well include a generous curve around the perimeter of the farm property, even if this meant that total dollar costs, mileage, and construction time would increase. Also relevant to political grounds for decision making are values such as popular representation and accountability. A third basis for decision is *organizational.* For example, if the government's highway engineers felt strongly that a detour around the farm property would detract from economy, efficiency, sensible roadway design, and scenic value, the responsible decision maker would have to weigh the possible effect on the engineers' morale of deciding to build the curve anyway.

Note that different considerations produce the need for a prior decision—namely, which factor(s) should be given predominant weight in the final decision. The question in the highway example is: can the organization better afford to have on its hands an angry politician, demoralized professional employees, or displeased consumers (users of the highway)? There is no easy or automatic solution to such a dilemma. Other factors would have to be taken into account, such as who else would be pleased or displeased with a particular decision. In hundreds of administrative decisions—some routine, some not—the same sorts of considerations apply. The less routine a decision is, the more carefully such questions must be weighed.

Various types of decision makers are likely to be concerned with the different grounds for decisions. Normally, organizational experts (such as highway engineers) have as their highest priority the substance of a decision or issue rather than concerns of politics or of the organization as a whole. This is in keeping with the main task of substantive specialists—to concentrate on the subject matter of their area of expertise. Those more highly placed in an organization, however, whether higher-ranking specialists or so-called political generalists, ordinarily have a different order of priorities, giving greater weight to political and organizational aspects of decision making. This is not to say that top-level officials are ignorant of, or oblivious to, the merits of a question, or that specialists care little for politics. It is to say, however, that generalists are often inclined toward more of a balancing process, weighing and choosing from among a greater number of decisional criteria.

Many generalists are appointed directly through political channels or are otherwise politically connected to a greater extent than most experts are; consequently, they are under more constraint to act with sensitivity toward their political mentors and allies (and adversaries). At the same time, their concern for the organization as a whole prompts them to be watchful of the morale of specialists who are likely to be dissatisfied with political decision making (and sometimes interference) that runs counter to their expert opinion and preference. Some tensions within a bureaucracy are due to these variations in approaches to decision making in different parts of the organization.

In addition to the considerations already discussed, there is normally a time factor in decision making. Time is a key resource in both making and implementing a decision; it is therefore necessary to allow for sufficient time at every stage of deliberation and action. There are two significant time considerations. First, the amount of time in which to reach a decision is not unlimited. Time constraints—especially during an emergency or crisis—can profoundly affect the ability of decision makers to gather and analyze information and to project and compare consequences of different alternatives, ultimately affecting the course of action selected. Second, the outcomes of decisions can be more or less predictable with long-term and short-term consequences that may have to be dealt with. For instance, anticipated benefits frequently are long-term, whereas costs are short-term; thus, in the immediate future, the latter will probably outweigh the former. A case in point is job training for the unemployed; it takes time for them, as with any new worker, to become fully productive employees, and per capita costs of training can run very high. How quickly and with how much certainty benefits will be derived would have to be considered. Politically, a decision that yields some gain right away and carries with it the promise of better things to come is the most defensible. The essential point is that time is a relevant consideration in assessing the costs and benefits of a given course of action.

Information Quality and Decision Analysis

Central to all these decision-making elements is the quantity and quality of information available. All decision makers need enough information to serve as a basis for making reasoned choices, and most try to gather as much information as possible before making a final decision. The ideal situation (the rational-model setting) would be one in which an official had total access to, and could verify the accuracy of, all data directly related to the decisional alternatives under consideration, including comprehensive projections of all possible consequences resulting from each proposed course of action. In practice, decision makers must "muddle through," consciously settling for less than complete information, usually because a decision is needed promptly. If decision makers postpone a decision, pending the acquisition of more information, that may reduce the risk of making mistakes. Even officials or agencies enjoying strong political support seek to accumulate hard data to back their decisions; a recurring pattern of faulty or inadequate data could endanger that support. Accurate information, in sum, is needed to make decisions that are supportable both objectively and politically.

The uses to which information is put are also important. The role of **decision analysis** has assumed great prominence in the last forty years, relying on a wide variety of new techniques. Herbert Simon noted advances through which "many classes of administrative decisions have been formalized, mathematics has been applied to determine the characteristics of the 'best' or 'good' decisions, and myriad arithmetic calculations are carried out routinely to reach the actual decisions from day to day."[14] Simon and others have noted two significant developments that have facilitated use of such techniques: the improvement and wider use of survey sampling techniques (to gather empirically defensible information on the public-policy issues and problems) and the rapid increase in the information processing and technical capacity of computers and software (which seem to go through new "generations" every two or three years).[15]

In addition, much greater use has been made of the experimental method in investigations of decision making and multi-linked information and communication systems. In short, the need for information, though growing rapidly, has been joined to burgeoning technologies, such as personal computers, broadband communications networks, smart phones, satellites, and social networking. All this has resulted in vastly expanded information gathering, data analysis, and decision-making capabilities.

Technology may also have created an illusion of greater capabilities than we actually have. For example, malfunctions in both humans and computers can, and do, occur in the myriad technological systems that underpin decision making. When these malfunctions happen, data necessary for an informed decision can be inaccurate, with the predictable consequence that, at a minimum, the decision reached will be inappropriate to the problem because the problem will

decision analysis

the use of formal mathematical and statistical tools and techniques, especially computers and sophisticated computer models and simulations, to improve decision making.

have been incorrectly defined and presented. Such a malfunction could have grave consequences, as in the case of the Bush administration's assertion that Iraq under Saddam Hussein had attempted to purchase nuclear materials from an African country. This "fact" was used to justify the invasion, but later turned out to be based on either faulty or deliberately misinterpreted intelligence.[16]

Limitations on human and computer capabilities may also blind us to the simple reality that human judgment is still valuable in making decisions and that computers are no substitute for it. Although very useful, computers should not be relied on totally as a basis for decisions.[17] It is also important to remember that computers are no better than the people who manufacture them, program them, or input and interpret the data. Experience can contribute to one's judgmental capacity; so, too, can breadth of training, perceptiveness, sensitivity, and capacity for continued learning. It is the integration of individual competencies and computer technology that leads to the most effective decisions.

There are several other significant limitations on the acquisition and use of information. Two troubling examples in the Information Age are computer hacking and viruses that could infect all the data contained in personal computer files. Perhaps most important is the fact that we live in a world of imperfect information. It is futile to mount a search for literally *all* the information that might be obtained on a subject, and most decision makers have somewhat more modest ambitions. Compounding the problem, communication of information is often less than clear and is subject to human error at the point of origin and at the receiving end, even when both parties desire full mutual understanding (see Chapter 4).[18]

Another crucial limitation on information resources has been the cost of obtaining information. Information costs include the personnel and time that must be devoted to its acquisition, organization, and presentation. Acquisition costs, in particular, can become prohibitive. The greatest value of the computer as an information storage and retrieval system—and of online data services—is the enormous saving in time and money they make possible in obtaining a quantity of data compared to the investment necessary to gather the same amount of data by older methods. (This, incidentally, is a clear example of long-term benefit making worthwhile a high short-term cost—in this case, the cost of installing computerized information systems and training competent analysts to operate them.)

The last major limitation stems from the conscious and (especially) unconscious biases of those who send, relay, and receive information. We tend to attach high importance to objective information, yet there is great difficulty in interpreting information with complete objectivity. Even the most fair-minded individuals have subjective values that color their perceptions of data, images, or phenomena. Existing preferences can shape responses, or even receptiveness, to particular information. Thus, pure objectivity in data interpretation is an impossibility and, as a result, absolutely objective information is beyond our grasp.

Finally, there is the problem of deliberate distortion of information. Information is a source of power, and it is often in the best interests of an agency or official to provide only information that will have a positive political effect. We may debate the utility and wisdom of political interference with objectivity in information, but it is undeniably a significant constraint. With enough effort, deliberate distortions can be discovered and corrected, but that effort can require large investments of resources and, consequently, is made only irregularly. In sum, motives of self-interest can seriously impair objective use of data.

Decision makers also face other kinds of problems. For one thing, decision making is strongly influenced by previous decisions and by policies already in effect. In other words, some alternatives are not available because of past decision making. Instead of starting with a clean slate, decision makers must work within the confines allowed by past choices. An example would be a decision to implement an affirmative action plan in local government hiring, which might effectively foreclose any contrary options five or ten years later. The same would be true of a local decision to sell bonds for a capital construction project, or for the army to change its basic emphasis on the weaponry it needs for ground warfare.

Another problem is unanticipated consequences in spite of efforts to foresee all the outcomes of each decision. Sometimes the projected outcome does not occur; sometimes there are unintended side effects that develop along with the projected outcome; sometimes only the side effects occur. If these unanticipated results turn out to be serious, they can cause intense problems and political repercussions. This happened in California during the early 1990s as a result of speculative investments in high-risk bonds used to finance capital improvements in 180 local governments. The resultant $2 billion loss in Orange County, California lowered bond ratings, hampered growth, and affected millions of taxpayers. Predictions for similar adverse developments have been made recently and refer to the fragile conditions of the federal budget, as well as many state and local budgets (see Chapter 8).

Yet another potential pitfall in decision-making processes is the phenomenon of **groupthink**, defined by social psychologist Irving Janis as "a mode of thinking that people engage in when they are deeply involved in a cohesive in-group, when members' strivings for unanimity override their motivation to realistically appraise alternative courses of action."[19] This phenomenon is most likely to be evident in small groups of decision makers. The two basic elements in most potential groupthink situations are group cohesiveness and a tendency toward unanimity, or at least toward making any dissident member feel conspicuous and uncomfortable. Two other factors are the degree to which a cohesive group of decision makers becomes insulated from other influences in the decision-making process and the extent to which a cohesive group's leader promotes one preferred solution (even when that leader genuinely does not want group members to be "yes-men" and the members try to resist unanimity). In essence, any cohesive "in-group" of individuals

groupthink

a mode of thinking that people engage in when they are deeply involved in a cohesive in-group, when members striving for unanimity override their motivation to realistically appraise alternative courses of action; facilitated by insulation of the decision group from others in the organization, and by the group's leader promoting one preferred solution or course of action.

ONE WAY TO COMBAT "GROUPTHINK": LESSONS FROM THE STATE DEPARTMENT

An institutionalized practice for the encouragement and preservation of dissent has been in effect since 1972 at the State Department. Known as the "Dissent Channel," it provides that employees here or abroad who dissent from policy recommendations of their superiors can invoke a special channel for memoranda or messages. This channel ensures (1) that top-level officers in the secretary's office will know about the dissent; (2) that the dissenter gets an acknowledgment within a week; and (3) that the dissenter gets a substantive response after senior decision makers (often including the secretary, who gets a copy of each message) have reviewed the dissenter's views and reasons. The strongest admonitions are made to departmental superiors never to penalize dissenters for taking advantage of this channel. Ten to fourteen messages per year are sent through this channel, and it clearly has enriched the State Department's policy process.

Source: Adapted from testimony of Charles Bingham, member, Special Panel on the Senior Executive Service, American Society for Public Administration, February 28, 1984; *The Senior Executive Service*, Hearings before the Subcommittee on Civil Service, Committee on Post Office and Civil Service, U.S. House of Representatives, 98th Cong., 2nd sess. (Washington, D.C.: U.S. Government Printing Office, 1984), pp. 284–85.

who generally think along similar lines can be a breeding ground for group-think; some politicians seem to surround themselves with advisers fitting this description. Familiarity with the "agendas" of one's high-level advisers can facilitate the advisory process but can also repress critical analysis—the thoughtful dissenting voice that can cause those in the majority to re-examine their assumptions and commitments—with consequent errors in decisional outcomes.

Finally, decision making involves **sunk costs**—certain irrecoverable costs resulting from commitment of past resources. The realities of sunk costs raise the stakes in decision making. The term has two meanings. First, a given resource or commodity, once spent, cannot be used again. For example, a piece of land committed to use as an approach ramp to a superhighway obviously cannot also be used as an elementary school site. Second, sunk costs suggest that once a decision has been made to proceed in a particular policy direction, certain costs would be incurred if that direction were to be reversed later. An analogy would be an administrator investing in an office computer network with a company that is known for poor installation and inadequate maintenance. If the administrator makes the wrong choice (as seems likely in this case), it will take extra time, money, and lost productivity before another provider can be found, this time with a stellar reputation and a quality product. Investment of extra resources and some political risk are required to reverse a policy direction. It is often easier to maintain a given policy course than to change it; to a degree, this explains why administrative agencies resist having to modify what they are doing.[20] If, however, the costs of *not* changing direction approach or exceed

sunk costs

in the context of organizational resources committed to a given decision, any cost involved in the decision that is irrecoverable; resources of the organization are lessened by that amount if it later reverses its decision.

the costs of changing, an agency would be far more likely to adapt its policy. In any event, sunk costs represent an additional factor to be taken into account in the course of making and implementing decisions.

Implications of the Decision Environment

Given the variable nature of goals—and of elements in the decision environment such as resource availability, competing grounds for decision, information constraints, and sunk costs—it would appear that the requisite conditions for the rational decision model are found rarely, if at all. However, though rationality as process is unlikely to be found in administrative decision making, reasonable, sensible, and productive decisions are not only possible, they occur frequently. Decision makers face difficult problems, particularly in a social and political environment filled with uncertainty and change. They can and must try to reduce the effects of that uncertainty so that decisions are useful and appropriate in solving the problems at hand and in anticipating longer-term needs. Multiple methodologies might help them in their efforts. But the rational model, as a whole process, is likely to be applicable only in very limited instances.

Decision Making: Links to Organization Theory

As all organizations try to cope with the uncertainty thrust on them by the external environment, they must develop processes for searching and learning, as well as for deciding. They must try to set limits on how the external environment defines situations—and make decisions within the framework of **bounded rationality**. This notion of bounded (limited) rationality, so crucial to the recent reshaping of organization theory, overlaps the incrementalist and mixed-scanning approaches to decision making, with acceptance of satisficing rather than maximizing very much at the heart of it.[21] Thus, developments in the art of making decisions have been paralleled—indeed, caused in part—by evolving conceptions of complex organizations.

With the rise of so many new pressures on government decision making—and especially for enhanced accountability of public administrators—it seems clear that the continuous-learning model may be applicable to a greater extent than ever before (see Chapter 4): continuously reinventing government calls for potentially major changes in the decision routines of literally thousands of government entities at all levels. Empowerment of administrators and citizens (whether or not directly a part of agency clienteles) means that policy and program preferences of many individuals and groups outside public agencies will become intermingled with those of agency personnel. And any efforts to streamline or scale back government activity (meaning government organizations and the personnel employed there) have a disruptive effect—for better or worse—on the manner in which decisions are considered and made. To the extent that

bounded rationality

the notion that there are prescribed boundaries, controls, or upper and lower limits on the decision-making abilities of individuals within organizations.

these various pressures impact administrative decision making, it is less likely that anything close to goal consensus can be achieved, either internally or externally. Without goal consensus, of course, pure-form decisional rationality is impossible—according to the criteria used by the rationalists themselves.

The Problem of Goals

One does not have to subscribe to the rational model of decision making to acknowledge that, in one form or another, all programs are managed, agencies receive and spend public funds, individuals engage in myriad activities, and administrative routines are carried on in order to fulfill some kind of purpose or purposes. In this sense, the goals of various organizations range from the most concrete to the most ambiguous formulations; they may be substantive or symbolic, individual or organizational or suborganizational, and they may be held by those inside the organization or imposed from outside. Agency personnel may consciously select particular objectives, or others outside the agency may come to regard it as pursuing certain goals because of its programmatic choices (incrementalists argue that the latter occurs quite frequently). Formally, of course, the goals pursued by a public agency are defined in the first instance by legislatures (as noted previously). Similarly, measures of success or failure in achieving formal agency goals are devised and applied by at least some outsiders.

The types of goals that can be pursued by agency personnel acting collectively or by individuals seeking their own ends through administrative action (or inaction) vary greatly. We will seek to give some order to this subject by examining organizational goals, broadly defined, and then considering impacts of personal goals of employees in public agencies.

Organizational Goals

Many casual observers of government organizations seem to believe that they exist to achieve only certain kinds of goals, such as substantive programmatic objectives (for example, adequate health care or safe, reasonably priced air travel), and that they act out of a desire to satisfy a broad public interest. Other observers assume, in contrast, that government bureaucracies act as interest groups, are concerned only with their own survival, and take a limited view of the public interest. Neither view is totally wrong, but both fail to account for the complexity of goals and how they are attained within government agencies.

Survival and maintenance are indeed principal goals of virtually all organizations, governmental or otherwise. (To draw an analogy to human behavior, survival is a fundamental instinct but not the sole purpose of our existence.) Administrative agencies, like other organizations, have as one of their goals maintenance of their own position. Such inward-oriented goals, which have been termed "reflexive," are supported by those aspects of an organization's behavior and programs that have primary impact internally rather than externally. Agencies pursue such goals by trying to persuade a significant constituency that their functions and purposes are essential either to society at large or to an important segment of society.

Administrative agencies are, of course, concerned with **substantive goals**. All government organizations seek to achieve program objectives, whether popular or unpopular, visible or obscure, major or minor. Program objectives appear to be the *raison d'etre* (the reason for existence) of administrative agencies and, in many cases, they constitute a powerful argument for an agency's existence. Goals can also lend **legitimacy** to organization activities both within and outside the formal organizational structure. Thus, goals become the rationale for legitimizing those serving the organization and for those seeking to understand the courses of action that the organization follows. This type of goal has been labeled "transitive" in that there is an intended programmatic impact on the environment beyond the organization itself. In advancing its cause through the political process, an agency will emphasize substantive goals—their importance to particular clienteles and to the whole society—and the agency's performance in pursuit of them.

Political scientist Lawrence Mohr has suggested an alternative conception of organizational goals that narrows and sharpens what is meant by the terms. In Mohr's view, we may accurately label as "organizational goals" only those on which there is widespread consensus of intent (agreement as to purpose) among a large majority of organization members, and that relate to "mainstreams" of organizational behavior.[22] Mohr maintains that these goals must be identified on the basis of empirical investigation rather than superficial reading of official pronouncements, informal discussion with leaders or members, or intuitive judgments. He raises the possibility of being able to identify such organizational goals empirically and precisely, and he stresses the necessity of doing so. Without identifying goals in this manner, Mohr says, the result of any inquiry into the goals of an organization are likely to be misleading, or at best incomplete. The implication of this conception of goals is this: If organizational goals are formulated by achieving a consensus of intent, then by definition there is substantial overlap between personal and organizational goals. Were this the commonly accepted and applied definition of organizational goals, the leader's task in this regard would be virtually nonexistent.

Research in the human relations school of organization theory, as well as later studies, suggest that where there are differences between an organization's official and actual goals, it is group norms among members that account for those differences and designate *actual* goals. Where leaders rely heavily on member preferences as part of goal definition, chances are greater that personal and organizational goals can be reconciled at least to some degree. This is because the followership can be expected to respond favorably to a leadership willing to "include them in" on so basic a question as the goals of *their*

substantive goals

an organizational goal focusing on the accomplishment of tangible programmatic objectives.

legitimacy

the acceptance of an institution or individual such as a government, family member, or state governor as having the legal and publicly recognized right to make and enforce binding decisions.

organization. Leaders are therefore well advised to focus on the task of goal definition. If the results here are positive, other leadership tasks will be more readily accomplished.

Pursuit of program goals is not without its subtleties, however. In practice, an agency may emphasize substantive goals and others that are largely "symbolic." **Symbolic goals** (and some substantive goals) are valuable because of the political support they can attract; in effect, the agency adopts the goals of persons outside it (see Chapter 10). Frequently, an agency goal can be both substantive and symbolic, with merit in objective terms as well as beneficial political consequences. Finally, it is common to find agencies saying that they are trying to accomplish a worthy but unreachable goal—for example, total eradication of illiteracy in the United States—yet continued pursuit of that objective yields benefits to both the agency and society. Many citizens and public officials support efforts to wipe out illiteracy and are willing to appropriate public funds to agencies with jurisdiction to carry on the struggle, which benefits at least some of those who cannot read or write.

Another dimension of substantive goals is the tricky question of goal attainment. How do we know when a goal has been met, and what happens to the agency in charge of a program when its goal has been reached? Achievement of organizational goals can be detrimental to an agency's continued operation. If an agency accomplishes its purposes, some might question the further need for it. On the other hand, if, in order to avoid that embarrassing dilemma, an agency does not act vigorously to solve the problem, it risks the wrath of supporters in the legislative and executive branches, as well as clientele groups. Fortunately for most agencies, the dilemma is not unsolvable because of the breadth of many goals and the different dimensions of goal attainment situations.

For many public agencies, it is highly probable that goals are not objectively attainable. It is possible to view organizational goals conceptually as *aims*, or sets of values to be pursued, rather than as tangible objectives to be achieved. In this sense, goals are sets of broad policy directions in which organization members seek to move without necessarily expecting to accomplish them, whereas objectives are more limited, achievable purposes that are related to the larger goals. Affordable and universal health care, for example, are abstract goals; concrete objectives that move the organization (or community or state or nation) closer to such goals include control over health insurance companies and doctors' fees, and increased competition among health care providers. Using this example, is it possible to reach the goal of affordable health care so that efforts to achieve it may cease? Not really, for two reasons. One is that definitions of "affordability" have to be agreed upon through the political process. There will be continuing disagreement about the government's role in controlling costs and, consequently, about whether the goal is in fact achievable in a free market economy. The other reason is that, even if it can be agreed that universal coverage and cost control are worthy social goals, ongoing programs will be required to keep it that way. (Note that

---

symbolic goals

organizational objectives reflecting broad, popular political purposes; frequently unattainable.

the latter observation implicitly undercuts the rational model, because many public policy goals are never really "achieved," once and for all.)

There may be political advantage in deliberately stating agency goals in general terms. The goal of "improving the quality of our schools" is far less likely to cause problems for an education department than is a goal of ensuring that high school graduates are equipped with specific reading and writing skills and are qualified for entry-level jobs or eligible for colleges and universities according to a prescribed entrance test score. Also, the more generalized a goal statement, the more widely supported it is likely to be, with less chance of concerted political opposition.

Legislative language establishing agency goals can be imprecise as a result of uncertainty about specific meanings and the frequent need for compromise. For example, a health program in the U.S. Department of Health and Human Services could have minimizing heart disease and related ailments among adult Americans as its overall goal. This is a laudable goal; no one would quarrel with it. But who is to say that the minimum has been reached and by what measures? Such language is quite common in legislation and administrative regulations. Under these circumstances, all an agency with such responsibilities needs to show is that it has had some success in putting across its message (get more exercise, stop smoking, have regular checkups, and so on), with some resultant reduction in heart disease and related ailments, and it is likely to be able to sustain itself and its programs. Most agencies start with a combination of goals, and many branch out into new but related areas. Thus, agency goals may undergo substantial and permanent modification at the instigation of decision makers outside the agency.

One other major point should be made about organizational goals. When public bureaucracies are repeatedly criticized for failure to reach their goals, they may develop a tendency to articulate publicly goals that they know they can reach. This strategy is often referred to pejoratively as "lowering the bar" and is guided as much by political as it is by administrative considerations.

Bureaucracies also know that they may suffer politically from excessive attachment to goals that turn out to be unpopular. In short, politics may influence the choice of official or unofficial organizational goals. An agency may adopt as official goals only objectives that, in the judgment of its leaders, will produce the requisite political support for its operations. This does not happen universally, but the fact that it *can* happen should serve as a warning not to view goals as abstract, permanent, or sacred statements that are above politics or somehow separate from the interests of the agencies.

Integrating Personal Goals with Organizational Mission

In addition to organizational goals, the personal motivations of employees must be considered. Most individuals have personal goals. Besides the basic drives for earning a decent living and job security, individual motivation may relate to opportunities for professional advancement or personal self-improvement. Or, as Anthony Downs and Arnold Meltsner each noted, job performance can be related to an overzealous attachment to a particular policy direction.[23] In other words, personal goals can affect an organization's goals in two ways: (1) individuals might devote more time and energy to pursuing their own goals than those of the organization and (2) they might come into conflict with others in the organization over matters such as advancement through the ranks or policy-related organization activities.

Downs has suggested five types of bureaucratic mind-sets, each characterized by a particular combination of goals.[24] Two types, *climbers* and *conservers*, act purely out of self-interest. Climbers are interested in increasing their power, income, and prestige; conservers seek to maximize their job security and maintain the power, income, and prestige that they already have. The three other types are, in Downs's words, "mixed-motive officials, [who] combine self-interest and altruistic loyalty to larger values. The main difference among the three types of mixed-motive officials is the breadth of the larger values to which they are loyal."[25] Downs calls them *zealots*, *advocates*, and *statesmen*, who focus, respectively, on relatively narrow policies or concepts, on a set of wider functions or on a wider organization, and on the general welfare or public interest, broadly defined.

Although Downs's formulation is admittedly hypothetical and idealized, Meltsner's analysis of federal bureaucrats found noticeable similarities to Downs's typology.[26] The essential point here is that the greater the variety of bureaucratic types and motives, the more difficult it is to attain official organizational objectives because so many other unofficial objectives are present. Also, potential for internal conflict and weak leadership is increased with the variety of bureaucratic types, and a higher level of conflict will inhibit attainment of both official and unofficial goals.

Goal articulation is a critical function of organizational management and leadership. How goals are defined and communicated may trigger strong reactions from individual members. If reactions are negative—because of conflicting personals goals, substantive disagreement, lack of consideration for members' views, or inadequate preparation—gaining members' support will be that much more difficult. Leaders often have to devote a significant amount of time, energy, and resources to winning member support for group goals, and they do not always succeed. Realistically, not all members are capable of personal commitment to the goals of the organization; some members of any group may have different goals and priorities. Very often leaders must settle for grudging or reluctant cooperation, which is a far cry from genuine support.

Enlightened leadership requires a clear vision of, and dedication to, organizational goals that outweigh any personal objectives—and this selfless commitment must be perceived as such by followers. Leaders should not underestimate the difficulty of convincing others that their direction is the proper one. Successful leadership requires sound theory, consistency, hard work, and discipline, and it may entail confronting some unpleasant realities

goal articulation

process of defining and clearly expressing goals generally held by those in an organization or group; usually regarded as a function of organization or group leaders; a key step in developing support for official goals.

about the basic structure of the organization. Above all, a personal commitment to achieving the mission of the organization is required.

The types of bureaucrats Anthony Downs labeled climbers and conservers—those interested in, respectively, achieving and preserving power, prestige, and income—attest to the possibility that highly personalized goals may predominate among some organization members. The larger the proportion of total membership that falls into these molds, the more difficult the task of directing the organization's activities toward larger goals. A related problem is determining the true state of affairs in this regard, that is, knowing what members' goals really are. Organizational goals can be separate from personal goals and from the feelings, values, and preferences of an organization's members. From this perspective, goals seem to exist independently of organization members—as something determined by persons outside the organization, as self-defining in the course of organization activities, or as the product of articulation by the leadership.

From the standpoint of an organization's ability to fulfill its official objectives and manage its programs effectively, the ideal situation is one in which there is a high degree of **goal congruence** among all organization members. If leaders are agreed on objectives and priorities and can count on unified support from employees in attaining shared objectives, an organization's chances of success are obviously enhanced. Such congruence, however, is the exception rather than the rule, even within the leadership. Also, within the framework of an organization at large, there are likely to be numerous small groups, each with its own particularistic goals, which may be given greater weight than those of the wider organization. The importance of small-group goals has been emphasized in the findings of Elton Mayo and his associates in the Hawthorne experiments and by John Pfiffner and Frank Sherwood in their studies a quarter of a century later (see Chapter 4).[27] All this makes it even less likely that substantial goal congruence will exist. Moreover, goal congruence can become too much of a good thing by discouraging fresh thinking about organization directions and actions and stifling the sort of open dialogue that often gives rise to creative and useful new ideas.[28] (See the discussion of groupthink earlier in this chapter.)

goal congruence

agreement on fundamental goals; refers to the extent of agreement among leaders and followers in an organization on central objectives; in practice, its absence in many instances creates internal tensions and difficulties in goal definition.

Ethical Dimensions of Decision Making

In pursuit of personal (and even organizational) goals, it is not uncommon to find examples of administrative behavior that raise serious questions about the ethical propriety of tactics used or courses of action followed. Such instances, fortunately, do not make up the bulk of administrative decision making, but they occur frequently enough to warrant discussion here. Evaluating decisions according to standards of ethical behavior has a long history in American government. In recent decades, it has become a matter of greater urgency and concern for many, in and out of government—especially as we have become aware of numerous examples of behavior widely characterized as unethical.

But just what is ethical behavior? Unfortunately, as noted in Chapter 2, there is no single answer to that question. Yet several efforts have been made to define, in sufficiently broad terms, the ethical behavior that a majority of Americans would perceive as acceptable in the public service. Another effort was made in the mid-1980s by the **American Society for Public Administration (ASPA)**, which formally adopted a **Code of Ethics** applicable to official conduct in virtually any administrative agency or setting (Accessible at: *http://www.aspanet.org/scriptcontent/index_codeofethics.cfm*). Foremost among the provisions of the ASPA Code of Ethics are imperatives for public administrators to "serve the public, beyond serving oneself"; to conduct themselves in a manner that inspires "public confidence and trust"; to strengthen organizational "capabilities to apply ethics, efficiency and effectiveness" in serving the public; and to exercise discretionary authority "to promote the public interest." Such provisions clearly emphasize the *public* and *ethical* obligations of government administrators—a theme that is the underlying foundation for this, and perhaps any, workable code of ethics.

Some years ago, political scientist Stephen K. Bailey suggested that people need certain attitudes and moral qualities in order to behave ethically in the public service. The first attitude is an awareness of moral ambiguity in decision making. The second attitude is appreciation of the contextual forces at play in decision situations. The third attitude is a conception of the "paradox of procedures," that is, an understanding of the need for orderly and rational procedures balanced against an understanding that procedures (red tape) can sometimes be an impediment to responsiveness and public accountability. The moral qualities are (1) *optimism*, including a willingness to take risks; (2) *courage*, including the courage to avoid special favors, the courage to make decisions that are unpopular, and the ability to decide under pressure; and (3) *charity*, that is, being fair and placing principle above personal needs for recognition, status, and power.[29]

Obviously, such considerations are ignored when public officials (at any level) engage in various forms of questionable behavior. There are countless examples of unethical behavior involving public officials, dating back decades (and even centuries). A relatively recent example of unethical behavior involved Bernard "Bernie" Kerik, who served as police commissioner of New York City from 2000 to 2001 under former Mayor Rudy Giuliani. In December 2004, President Bush nominated Kerik as U.S. Secretary of Homeland Security. A week later, Kerik withdrew his nomination, explaining that he had employed an illegal immigrant as a nanny; subsequently, numerous other more serious allegations surfaced which would likely have led to a confirmation battle. In 2006, Kerik pleaded guilty to two unrelated ethics violations after an investigation by the Bronx District Attorney's Office. In early November 2007, a federal grand jury issued a 16-count indictment alleging

American Society for Public Administration (ASPA) Code of Ethics

effort by the nation's leading professional association of public administrators to draw up and enforce a set of standards for official conduct.

conspiracy, mail fraud, wire fraud, and lying to the Internal Revenue Service (IRS). Kerik initially pleaded not guilty to all charges, but after his bail was revoked, he agreed to a plea bargain with prosecutors, admitting guilt to 8 of the charges. On February 18, 2010, Kerik was sentenced to four years in federal prison; a year later, he lost an appeal to reduce his sentence because of alleged bias by the sentencing judge.

Then there was the case of I. Lewis "Scooter" Libby, a former assistant to President Bush, Chief of Staff to Vice President Cheney, and Assistant to the Vice President for National Security Affairs during President Bush's first term. Libby was indicted, tried, and convicted on four counts of obstruction of justice and perjury in connection with the CIA identity leak known as the Plame Affair. Although President Bush commuted Libby's 30-month prison sentence, his conviction stood and he was required to pay a $250,000 fine and perform 400 hours of community service.

Yet another example concerns the actions of some staff members at the Federal Emergency Management Agency (FEMA), who in late October 2007 staged what appeared to be a press conference at which Deputy Director Harvey Johnson was asked about agency assistance to the victims of Southern California wildfires, earlier in the month. It turned out that the so-called press conference was a phony, with the "reporters" actually being FEMA employees themselves. They had been coached to ask gentle and unchallenging questions leading to answers that put the agency in a very favorable light. Homeland Security Secretary Michael Chertoff labeled this venture "one of the dumbest and most inappropriate things" he had seen in his long and distinguished government career, and as one result a top FEMA employee apparently lost his chance to become public information officer with the National Director of Intelligence.

All such behaviors are unethical for several reasons. They involve violating basic values, such as telling the truth and making decisions based on the objective merits of a case. They clearly suggest a callous disregard for the concept of the public interest, which public servants are obligated to promote and pursue. Finally, they harm essential public-service concepts such as operating within the laws of the land and remaining accountable to higher levels of authority (and to the legislature) for one's official actions. (We should keep in mind, however, that, as serious as these cases were, the great majority of decisions made by public officials—at all levels—do *not* involve breaching the public trust.)

Another aspect of ethics is the question of **internal (personal) checks** versus **external (legal-institutional) checks** on the behavior of individual administrators. Over the years, a debate has gone on about whether one or the other type of control is more effective for ensuring ethical behavior, accountability, and responsibility. The classic exchange on this subject took place more than seventy years ago between political scientists Carl Friedrich and Herman Finer.[30] Friedrich essentially argued that administrators are responsible if they are

internal (personal) checks

personal values of, and actions taken by, individuals who are concerned with behaving in an ethical and moral manner.

external (legal-institutional) checks

codes of conduct, laws, rules, and statutes that serve as safeguards to ensure that individual actions are ethical.

responsive to two dominant factors: technical knowledge and popular (majority) sentiment. He urged reliance on these criteria for assessing responsibility, laying little if any stress on mechanisms for ensuring adherence to those standards. Finer, writing a year later, criticized the absence in Friedrich's formulations of any institutional safeguards for administrative responsibility. Whereas Friedrich defined responsibility as a "sense of responsibility, largely unsanctioned, except by deference or loyalty to professional standards," Finer regarded it as "an arrangement of correction and punishment even up to dismissal both of politicians and officials."[31] Finer went on to warn that "sooner or later there is an abuse of power when external punitive controls are lacking."[32]

Thus, the central question, as framed in this exchange, is whether responsibility can be achieved by reliance on internal checks primarily or whether it requires political checks and sanctions in addition to the individual administrator's own ethical sense. Recent commentaries take the position that both types are needed. One central point made by a number of observers has been summed up as follows: "The public has to be able to rely on the self-discipline of the great majority of public servants. Otherwise *the official restraints and sanctions must be so numerous and so cumbersome* that effective public administration is impaired greatly."[33] The essential point is that, although there may be some things we can—and perhaps must—do to try to ensure ethical actions in the public service, the ultimate safeguard is in the character and inclinations of bureaucrats themselves.

A crucial distinction in this regard is between private and public morality. John Courtney Murray, the great American Jesuit philosopher, wrote that "one of the most dangerous misconceptions of the modern world is the idea that the same standards that govern individual morality should also govern national morality."[34] Behavior offensive to private morality, for example, could conceivably be moral according to standards of public morality. But what is "public morality"? For an answer, we must look to a basic distinction between those clothed with the authority of official position and all others; a crucial difference is that government has a monopoly on the legitimate use of force. This means that government may use force when necessary to apprehend suspected criminals, that it may utilize the death penalty as long as it is constitutional to do so, and that it may order its soldiers to kill those of another country in wartime. We judge these acts by standards very different from those applied to private citizens because the contexts of governmental versus individual actions are different. With power, of course, should go responsibility—some sense that there are different sorts of limits on behavior because of one's *public* obligations.

Joseph Califano, a former White House counselor and secretary of Health and Human Services, provides a Watergate-related example:

> Patrick Gray can equivocate in statements to the press, campaign while Acting FBI Director for the Republican Presidential candidate, and destroy "politically dynamite" documents, but his Catholic upbringing and schooling did not permit him to lie under oath because that

involves personal morality and perhaps serious sin. The Haldeman and Ehrlichman letters of resignation pay lip service to public morality, but protest their private morality as though *that were the ultimate standard by which their exercise of the public trust* should be judged.[35]

And that is the point: The public trust and its exercise add an entirely different dimension to what individuals do in official capacities or in matters related to government decisions. The public trust imposes obligations on public officials over and above those arising from private moral codes. This may explain why President Clinton, despite the eventual admission that he lied about the Lewinsky affair, never suffered a major loss of public trust in opinion polls measuring his job performance as president. In this case, what was deemed public, and what was considered private, were different. On the other hand, President Bush led an exemplary private life after becoming president, yet suffered more negative public opinion of his job performance than any other recent president since Richard M. Nixon.

One other example further illustrates confusion of public and private morality. The case involved the late Mayor Richard J. Daley of Chicago and two of his sons, who were employed by an insurance firm in suburban Evanston. It came to light that the firm had been awarded millions of dollars' worth of Chicago city government insurance contracts without competitive bidding. When questioned by reporters about this, Daley explained that any father would do what he could to help his sons. True enough and, by Daley's strict personal moral code, entirely appropriate. But because of his public position and power, there were at least some who regarded this as a breach of public trust because other insurance firms were also (corporate) citizens of Chicago and public morality requires a government to deal equitably with all its citizens. And that, Daley clearly had not done.

What, then, can we say of **political corruption**? Corruption is offensive to many traditions of private morality, yet rooting it out is very difficult. There is one overriding truth about corruption: According to the standards many of us apply, corruption is universal in the sense that virtually every political system has had its share of political favoritism, private arrangements between public figures, and out-and-out thievery and bribery. We find this offensive—it runs counter to our Western standards; but without trying to justify it, we should note that not everyone reacts the way we do. In many parts of the world, what we call corruption is part of the routine of entrepreneurial politics—and business and other enterprises, for that matter. Yet it is appropriate to combat it if, in fact, corruption violates our expectations of what our officials should and should not do.

Corruption is commonplace in government, and many states and localities are impacted. Deals are made quietly, contracts awarded, jobs created, votes bartered for (and occasionally stolen), offices bandied about, power exerted, contributors rewarded, and so on, all on the basis of various forms of favoritism. The battle over municipal reform (Chapter 1) has centered

political corruption

all forms of bribery, favoritism, kickbacks, and legal as well as illegal rewards; commonly associated with reward systems in which partisan patronage is in use; more generally, patterns of behavior in government associated with providing access, tangible benefits, and so on, to some more than others, on an "insider" basis.

on making it possible to stamp out corruption in government. Our image of corruption seems to emphasize big-city politics, but the fact is that, in rural America, there is the same kind of favoritism toward friends and rewards for political loyalty as in the city. Patronage is rampant in some states, barely visible in others. The remarkable thing is that so much has been done to make the conduct of government more honest and transparent.[36]

One other observation is in order. Corruption, as a practical matter, is a *form of privilege* indulged in by those in positions of power, wealth, and influence for mutual gain. As such, it is inherently antidemocratic and unethical because it concentrates power and its benefits in relatively few hands. If democracy is founded in large part on a premise of political equality, corruption is offensive to that value as well as to ethical values. Ultimately, this is another good reason for being concerned with corruption in a democratic government, one at least as relevant as ethical considerations.

The Ethical Setting: New Emphasis on an Old Challenge

One of the most pressing problems confronting public managers in the early twenty-first century is the challenge of defining, establishing, and maintaining a high level of ethical behavior among government employees. This is an especially sensitive problem for government, perhaps even more than for business or other private-sector institutions. Almost by definition, government is designed—and widely expected—to serve the needs and interests of the full range of society, not just those who may seek a particular product or service as they might from the private sector. Ethical behavior on the part of public servants can enhance workforce effectiveness, improve employee morale, and promote better public relations. It may also serve to set a standard for the behavior of others outside government (though that might not be viewed as a major purpose). Indeed, in recent decades, ethical behavior has taken on new importance, in part because of the widespread public cynicism about government, a pervasive distrust that almost invites government employees to be anything but ethical in their daily activities and operations.[37]

There have been impressive efforts on the part of government employees and (significantly) many employee associations to raise the ethical standards of conduct in the public workplace. In addition to the ASPA Code of Ethics, the International City/County Management Association (ICMA) has established and widely circulated an organizational code of ethics.[38]

Administrators have made, and continue to make, systematic efforts to familiarize public employees with these codes, to train employees in what is expected of the ethical public servant, and to monitor employees' behavior for compliance. First and foremost, of course, it has been necessary to identify what is meant by "behavioral ethics" or "ethical standards." Although there is room for debate, substantial consensus currently exists on some essentials. Furthermore, there appears to be considerable agreement about how to make codes of ethics operational in the workplace. We will address each of these efforts in turn.[39]

Many observers of administrative ethics suggest that professional conduct, personal honesty, and concern for serving the public and respecting both the law and democratic principles are at the center of those beliefs. Among other things, ethical conduct describes an employee's actions regarding professional excellence, merit-based employment decisions, commitment to government service, professional development, conforming to professional codes (such as the legal or medical profession's canons of ethics), and interpersonal skills. Other professional duties might also be cited, such as protecting the health, safety, and welfare of the public; promoting safety in the workplace; and acting with empathy and understanding toward others (both coworkers and those who seek to use the services offered by a particular agency). Other responsibilities might include ensuring employee privacy, applying fairness in making job assignments, monitoring and preventing sexual harassment, maintaining honesty and accuracy in financial reporting, protecting so-called **whistle-blowers** (those who publicly report cases of fraud, abuse, or mismanagement in their organizations), and providing employees with leaves of absence for education or child care.

Ethical behavior emphasizing personal honesty and integrity calls for avoiding any personal gain that results from the fulfillment of one's duties (these conflicts of interest, though, can sometimes be difficult to define and monitor), dedicating oneself to honesty and integrity, maintaining open and truthful relationships, and respecting the confidentiality of information. (Note that it is possible, as in the case of confidentiality, for some ethical standards and behaviors to be regarded as both professional and personal.) In general, it can be said that standards of personal honesty in the government workplace involve many of the same elements as they do in private life. Public standards, however, are usually of greater importance than private standards because of the nature of government work, which takes place in an open setting, where personal dishonesty may have impacts far beyond one individual's behavior or punishment.

Finally, respect for the law and democratic principles (what has been termed the "political" aspect of ethics) may be said to underlie both professional and personal dimensions. This refers to what might generally be expected of public employees in their official capacities as public servants—by their superiors, their subordinates, and the people they serve. These aspects involve a commitment to maintaining open (and usually participatory) modes of decision making, conducting official business in a consensus-building fashion whenever possible, complying with all relevant laws and regulations (and encouraging others to do likewise), and impartially distributing the benefits and burdens associated with the agency's services. That this list of ethical considerations is long indicates the scope of concern presently found in the public service, as well as the difficulty confronting an individual administrator in living up to all these ethical standards.

whistle-blowers

those who make any disclosure of legal violations, mismanagement, gross waste of funds, abuse of authority, or dangers to public health or safety, whether the disclosure is made within or outside the formal chain of command.

Implementing Standards of Ethics

How, then, do public managers concerned with ethics go about promoting appropriate attitudes and behaviors within their workforce? Not surprisingly, there is no single, easy answer; a number of approaches have been employed. One is formal adoption of a code of ethics or policy statement in order at least to signal an organization's seriousness of intent regarding the promotion of ethical conduct. A related phenomenon is development of codes of ethics by professional associations (as noted earlier); these codes can affect the actions of association members (such as attorneys) who are employed in the public sector. Another approach that has come into greater use is the requirement of financial disclosure in order to minimize the possibility of monetary conflicts of interest. A fourth approach prohibits employees from accepting outside honoraria (payments for individual services, such as giving lectures); a fifth approach requires administrative approval of professional activities outside of the organization; and a sixth approach establishes in-house ethics training for all employees (on a mandatory or voluntary basis). Perhaps the most important element in strengthening ethical conduct in government agencies, however, is what some have called the "moral leadership" of both top-ranking organization leaders and those in middle management. In other words, leading by example appears to hold the greatest potential for leaders to influence public administrators in the desired ethical directions. These ethical considerations may be said to constitute the ethical environment of public administrators' everyday activities.[40]

HOW WOULD YOU DECIDE?

Casino Jack and the United States of Money

This documentary traces the career of Washington, D.C., lobbyist Jack Abramoff, who was involved in a corruption scandal that eventually led to his own conviction, as well as the conviction of two White House officials, former House Majority Leader Tom DeLay (R-Texas), Representative Bob Ney (R-Ohio), and nine other lobbyists and congressional staffers.

Nicknamed "Casino Jack" for the multimillion-dollar dealings with Indian casinos that led to his downfall, Abramoff was investigated by the Senate Indian Affairs Committee, chaired by Senator John McCain (R-Arizona), in late 2004. Abramoff and partner Michael Scanlon sought to con Indian casino gambling interests out of an estimated $85 million in fees. In 2006, Abramoff pleaded guilty to three felony accounts: conspiracy, fraud, and tax evasion. Abramoff was convicted and received a six-year sentence, of which he served three and a half years before being released in December 2010.

The documentary uses actual footage of events and centers on the world of Washington lobbyists, who influence every major decision made in the Capitol. In such a high-stakes environment, ethics come into play daily.

What factors account for the increased concern with ethics and ethical behavior of public officials?

Source: http://casinojack-movie.com/accessed March 8, 2011.

Political Rationality: A Contradiction in Terms?

We have been speaking for the most part of decision makers in the abstract and of models of decision making applied to theoretical situations. We now take up a question relevant to our overall concern in this book: whether it is possible to achieve any sort or degree of rationality in a public administrative system permeated by political influences and pressures. Can administrators who act at least partially in response to political stimuli be said to be acting rationally, in any sense, when they make decisions? Can politics and rational decision making be made to coexist or, at least, not totally contradict each other?

Much of the literature on rational decision making in economics and political science suggests that the answer to such questions is no. Politics is frequently represented as *interfering* with rational processes, outweighing more objective considerations, and overriding "neutral" or "nonpolitical" measurements, requirements, and data. When political considerations predominate in decision making, as they frequently do, the stigma of irrationality is attached to the process and the outcomes. To dispute this characterization of *politicized* decision making requires a significant modification of the meaning of rationality. In particular, what must be changed is the "currency" of rationality, the criteria by which rationality is defined and measured.

Plainly stated, rationality has traditionally been an economic measure, and the currency has been implicitly or explicitly quantitative. For many years, most economists—and many others—have assumed that economic-quantitative rationality is sufficient as an overall definition of the concept. Recently, however, the possibility has been raised that there may be other, equally valid, forms of rationality, specifically **political rationality**.[41] This is to say that political and economic choices are often conceived of in different terms and directed toward fulfilling different kinds of objectives, and should therefore be evaluated according to different criteria. More to the point, it is not rational—by any standard—to pursue the politically impossible.

In a political setting, a decision maker's need for support assumes central importance, and the political costs and benefits of decisions are crucial. Political benefits that might accrue to a decision maker are self-evident: obtaining short-term policy rewards; enhanced power over future decisions; added access to, and earlier inclusion in, the decision-making process (given that both access and involvement are meaningful); and so on. Political costs, however, are less obvious and need explicit categorization, which political scientist Aaron Wildavsky provided:

> *Exchange costs* are incurred by a political leader when he [or she] needs the support of other people to get a policy adopted. He has to pay for this assistance by using up resources in the form of favors

political rationality

a concept advanced by Aaron Wildavsky suggesting that behavior of decision makers may be entirely rational when judged by criteria of political costs, benefits, and consequences, even if irrational according to economic criteria; emphasizes that political criteria for "rationality" have validity.

(patronage, logrolling) or coercive moves (threats or acts to veto or remove from office). By supporting a policy and influencing others to do the same, a politician antagonizes some people and may suffer their retaliation. If these *hostility costs* mount they may turn into reelection costs—actions that decrease his chances (or those of his friends) of being elected or reelected to office. *Election costs*, in turn, may become *policy costs* through inability to command the necessary formal powers to accomplish the desired policy objectives. [We] may also talk about *reputation costs*, i.e., not only loss of popularity with segments of the electorate but also loss of esteem and effectiveness with other participants in the political system and loss of ability to secure policies other than the one immediately under consideration.[42]

It is apparent that, as stated here, political benefits are rarely measurable in quantifiable terms. The one set of political costs that might be measurable numerically is re-election costs, but it is difficult to determine from voting data how particular actions by politicians affect the ballot choices of thousands of voters. This lack of easy measurability, however, does not diminish the impact political costs have on the behavior of governmental decision makers, including those in bureaucracy.

There is a widespread tendency, even among some political scientists, to scornfully dismiss or downgrade as "irrational" any behavior or decision not clearly directed toward achieving the "best" results. But if criteria of political rationality were to be used—that is, establishing cost–benefit ratios in political terms—such behavior and decisional outcomes might be perfectly "rational." Perhaps most important, decisions made and measured by even the most objective economic-quantitative criteria have political implications; for example, an economically rational tax reform law will benefit some more than others. The mistake all too frequently made in and out of government is ignoring or denigrating those implications because they somehow "pollute" the "truly objective" decisions based on only the most "neutral" of considerations.[43] In every instance, *the choice of criteria* by which to measure decisional outcomes has political significance because of the ever-present possibility that adherence to a particular set of criteria (including quantitative data) will ultimately favor the interests of one group over those of other groups.

Another observer who has made a similar point from a different perspective is Martin Landau.[44] He questions the traditional inclination to minimize organizational duplication and overlap in the name of efficiency, and he points out that such practices, rather than being rational, may prove to be quite irrational. He suggests, first, that duplication of organizational features may make overall performance more reliable in the event that any one part breaks down. As an example, he cites an automobile with dual braking systems; the secondary system may seem to be just so much extra baggage, so uneconomical, so wasteful—until the primary braking system fails![45] Within human organizations, training more than one individual or staff member in essentially the same tasks fits the same description of "rational duplication"; the alternative is increased risk of organizational breakdown, should any one part fail. Second, Landau asserts that overlapping parts may improve performance by allowing for greater adaptability within the organization as a whole. His examples of rational overlapping include biological organisms that can adapt and survive in the face of a failing part and, significantly, the U.S. Constitution.

Why the Constitution as an example of rational overlap? Because our framework of government was calculated from the outset to be overlapping (and, for that matter, duplicative) in the interest of preventing political tyranny, that most efficient of governmental methods. Separation of powers and checks and balances were both designed to prevent any one branch of government from becoming predominant. And what are checks and balances except *deliberately designed overlap* in the execution of essential government functions? Similarly, our structure of federalism is clearly duplicative, yet the purpose is the same: to prevent undue concentration of power. From Landau we can infer that in working toward the accomplishment of clearly delineated political goals (in this example, preventing concentration of power), some structural and behavioral arrangements may be politically rational and defensible even though they might appear quite irrational in economic or other "value-neutral" terms. Above all, both Landau and Wildavsky challenge the application of economic criteria to the measurement of political phenomena,

POINT/COUNTERPOINT

THE ISSUE Administrators act at least partially in response to political stimuli on a daily basis. In a political setting, a decision maker's need for support assumes central importance, and the political costs and benefits of decisions are crucial. Is it possible to achieve any sort of rationality in a public administrative system permeated by political influences and pressures?

Can politics and rational decision making be made to coexist?

Arguments *for* Politics and Rational Decision Making Coexisting

- The U.S. Constitution was calculated from the beginning to be overlapping in the interest of preventing political tyranny.

- Loyalty to elected political officials expedites policy implementation.

- Elected officials are accountable to voters for policy failures.

Arguments *against* Politics and Rational Decision Making Coexisting

- Politics is frequently represented as interfering with rational processes, outweighing more objective considerations.

- Professional, trained administrators are better able to implement policies.

- Political influences are inherently corrupting.

as well as the assumption that economic rationality is, by definition, superior to political rationality.

In sum, then, *political rationality* is not at all a contradiction in terms. We can accept the propositions that politics is legitimately concerned with enabling the decision processes of government to function adequately, that basing decisions on political grounds is as valid as basing them on other grounds, and that rationality according to the currency of politics is as defensible as rationality in economic terms. Political rationality, when appropriately conceived and applied, can be a useful tool for evaluating both the processes and the outcomes of organizational decision making.

Organized Anarchies and Uncertainty

One other perspective on decision making explains many of the gaps left by the preceding perspectives. Michael Cohen, James March, and Johan Olsen studied decision processes of organizations confronted with ambiguity in the organizational setting—that is, in circumstances in which organizations have "goals that are unclear, technologies that are imperfectly understood, histories that are difficult to interpret, and participants who wander in and out."[46] Terming such entities **organized anarchies**, Cohen, March, and Olsen developed the *garbage can theory* of organizational choice (their term): such "organized anarchies" operate under conditions of pervasive ambiguity.

The garbage can theory appears to have two principal emphases. First, under conditions of **pervasive ambiguity**, organizations behave in ways that contradict conventional assumptions about organizational choice. Second, so many organizations now operate under conditions of ambiguity and behave so unpredictably (in light of traditional theories) that the garbage can explanation might account for collective behaviors that deviate from expected patterns. The garbage can model, in short, assumes that pervasive ambiguity introduces so much uncertainty into decision processes that the assumptions of traditional theories about coping with uncertainty do not apply. As a result, decisions made in the "garbage can" must be more flexibly implemented than decisions made under conditions of greater certainty, for there will be more uncertainty in the implementation as well.

In short, the organized anarchy/garbage can model refers to almost random streams of "people, problems, and solutions." Because these three streams are treated in the model as independent of each other, the choice of an appropriate solution to any given problem, or an appropriate decision maker to resolve the problem, is as much a product of chance as it is of rationality in some settings—and perhaps more so. In light of recent events in and surrounding many public organizations, this model may be the most appropriate perspective (even more than "bounded rationality") from which to understand the complexity of government decision making in the twenty-first century.

organized anarchies

organizations in which goals are unclear, technologies are imperfectly understood, histories are difficult to interpret, and participants wander in and out; decision making in such organizations is characterized by pervasive ambiguity, with so much uncertainty in the decision-making process that traditional theories about coping with uncertainty do not apply.

pervasive ambiguity

a situation of long-term uncertainty that pervades the decision-making environment of an organization.

Summary

Decision making involves attempts to bring about a change to achieve some gain by means of a particular course of action requiring expenditure of a certain amount of resources. There is some unavoidable uncertainty and, therefore, some risk involved, and most decision makers seek to minimize both. Most decisions are of a relatively routine nature, though care should be taken not to allow routines to dominate. A significant debate, still ongoing, surrounds how actually to make decisions. The rational model assumes that decision makers pursue known goals and seek to achieve them in the most efficient manner possible. There are criticisms of the model, however, centering on its lack of practical applicability as a method of administrative decision making. Two major alternatives to the rational model have been suggested: incrementalism and mixed scanning.

There are major considerations in the decision analysis process, and, on balance, these considerations seem to point toward a decision process in which the rational model cannot prevail. The debate over appropriate models of decision making is part of the larger evolution of contemporary organization theory—as well as an indicator of the many changes currently taking place inside and outside of most government organizations.

Organizational goals, though often ambiguous, can influence administrative behavior and can, in turn, be affected by political considerations. Key goals may include agency survival and maintenance (reflexive goals), accomplishment of substantive program objectives that influence the external environment (transitive goals), and symbolic goals. Agencies seek to articulate their goals in relatively general fashion and may be deliberately unclear about some of them to preserve political support. Efforts to achieve certain kinds of goals may have to be ongoing because of the nature of the problem. Also, some goals may be determined by the extent political support can be generated for them. The personal goals of agency employees usually vary considerably, thus making goal congruence between individuals and organizations difficult to achieve.

Ethical considerations in decision making have assumed greater importance in recent decades despite some uncertainty in defining what constitutes ethical behavior. Efforts by professional associations to define codes of ethics for administrators emphasize the public obligations of public administrators. The personal character of bureaucrats is a crucial factor, but legal-institutional checks are also needed to promote morality and responsibility in the public service. In addition, there are differences between private and public morality. The latter is based on the idea that special responsibilities accompany exercise of the public trust and legitimate use of force. Among government employees, ethical behavior has come to be regarded as an increasingly important aspect of administrative activity. Professional conduct, personal honesty, and respecting the law and democratic principles are at the heart of concerns about ethical behavior. Another critique of rationality is founded on the premise that economic-quantitative measures may not always be appropriate in determining what is rational. By using a set of explicitly political measures, political rationality is possible. What is politically rational may not be economically rational, and vice versa, and applying economic concepts of rationality to political phenomena may be misleading. The garbage can theory of organizational choice suggests an alternative perspective on the effects of decisional ambiguity on an organization's activities—ambiguity that, if anything, is on the increase.

Discussion Questions

1. Discuss the problems and ambiguities involved in "achieving the goals of the organization." How important are different kinds of goals in actually determining organizational success or failure?

2. Compare and contrast the different kinds of goals that can exist within an organization. How is each type likely to affect organizational behavior?

3. What are the major considerations involved in decision making? How are they interrelated?

4. How should a decision maker choose the appropriate basis for decision making (substantive, political, or organizational)? Can any general guidelines be suggested? What factors enter into this kind of decision? Discuss.

5. Under what kinds of pressures are decision makers forced to operate? What, if anything, can be done to cope with these pressures? Discuss.

6. Compare and contrast the rational decision-making approach and incrementalism, stressing the advantages and disadvantages of each (in theory and in practice).

7. Explain what is meant by "mixed scanning" and indicate how it acts to reduce the alleged weaknesses in both rational and incremental decision making.

8. Discuss the phenomenon of "groupthink," explaining the factors in the group situation that appear to be associated with it, how it might affect the making of decisions, and what (if anything) might be done to combat it.

9. What is "political rationality"? How does it compare to traditional economic rationality? Give examples of situations in which a decision might be rational by one set of criteria but not by the other, and in which a decision might be considered rational in both senses.

10. How have recent presidential decisions responded to public concerns about creating jobs, domestic security, economic growth, and the war on terrorism?

Key Terms and Concepts

decision making, *194*

rational approach, *196*

cost–benefit analysis, *197*

cost–benefit ratios, *197*

incrementalism, *199*

mixed scanning, *200*

decision analysis, *205*

groupthink, *207*

sunk costs, *208*

bounded rationality, *209*

substantive goals, *211*

legitimacy, *211*

symbolic goals, *212*

goal articulation, *214*

goal congruence, *215*

American Society for Public Administration (ASPA) Code of Ethics, *216*

internal (personal) checks, *217*

external (legal-institutional) checks, *217*

political corruption, *219*

whistle-blowers, *221*

political rationality, *223*

organized anarchies, *226*

pervasive ambiguity, *226*

Suggested Readings

Adams, Guy B., and Danny Balfour. *Unmasking Administrative Evil.* Rev. ed. Armonk, N.Y.: M.E. Sharpe, 2004.

Allison, Graham, and Phillip Zelikow. *Essence of Decision: Explaining the Cuban Missile Crisis.* 2nd ed. New York: Longman, 1999.

Bowman, James S. *Ethical Frontiers in Public Management: Seeking New Strategies for Resolving Ethical Dilemmas.* San Francisco: Jossey-Bass, 1994.

Cohen, Michael D., James G. March, and Johan P. Olsen. "People, Problems, Solutions, and the Ambiguity of Relevance." In James G. March and Johan P. Olsen, eds., *Ambiguity and Choice in Organizations.* Bergen, Norway: Universitetsforlaget, 1976, pp. 24–37.

Downs, Anthony. *Inside Bureaucracy.* Boston: Little, Brown, 1967; reprint edition published by Waveland Press, Prospect Heights, Ill., 1994.

Frederickson, H. George, and Richard K. Ghere, eds. *Ethics in Public Management.* Armonk, N.Y.: M.E. Sharpe, 2005.

Garofalo, Charles, and Dean Geuras. *Ethics in the Public Service: The Moral Mind at Work.* Washington, D.C.: Georgetown University Press, 1999.

Heineman, Robert A., William T. Bluhm, Steven A. Peterson, and Edward N. Kearny. *The World of the Policy Analyst: Rationality, Values, and Politics.* 3rd ed. Chatham, N.J.: Chatham House, 2002.

Huberts, Leo W. J. C., Jeroen Maesschalck, and Carole L. Jurkiewicz. *Ethics and Integrity of Governance: Perspectives across Frontiers.* London: Edward Elgar Publishing, 2008.

Janis, Irving L. *Groupthink.* 2nd ed. Boston: Houghton Mifflin, 1982.

Koteen, Jack. *Strategic Management in Public and Nonprofit Organizations: Managing Public Concerns in an Era of Limits.* 2nd ed. Westport, Conn.: Praeger, 1997.

Menzel, Donald C. *Ethics Management for Public Administrators: Building Organizations of Integrity.* Armonk, N. Y.: M.E. Sharpe, 2007.

———. *Ethics Moments in Government: Cases and Controversies.* Boca Raton, Fla.: CRC Press, 2009.

Moore, Mark. *Creating Public Value: Strategic Management in Government.* Cambridge, Mass.: Harvard University Press, 1997.

Moore, Mark, and Malcolm Sparrow. *Ethics in Government: The Moral Challenge of Public Leadership.* Englewood Cliffs, N.J.: Prentice Hall, 1990.

Rohr, John A. *Ethics for Bureaucrats: An Essay on Law and Values.* 2nd ed., revised and expanded. London: Routledge, 1989.

———. *Public Service, Ethics, and Constitutional Practice.* Lawrence: University Press of Kansas, 1999.

Simon, Herbert A. *Administrative Behavior: A Study of Decision Making Processes in Administrative Organizations.* 4th ed. New York: Free Press, 1997.

Simon, Herbert A., Riccardo Viale, Robin L. Marris, and Massimo Egidi. *Economics, Bounded Rationality, and the Cognitive Revolution.* Softcover ed. Northampton, Mass.: Edward Elgar, 2008.

Svara, James H. *The Ethics Primer for Public Administrators in Government and Non-Profit Organizations.* Boston: Jones and Bartlett, 2006.

Swan, Wallace. "Decision Making." In Thomas D. Lynch, ed., *Organization Theory and Management.* New York: Marcel Dekker, 1983, pp. 47–79.

Van Wart, Montgomery. *Changing Public Sector Values.* New York: Routledge, 1998.

Chief Executives and the Challenges of Administrative Leadership

The quality and style of leadership practiced by elected officials and appointed public administrators are key factors in how public agencies perform their duties and achieve their goals. Some aspects have already been examined including the importance of decision making, management and leadership, various styles or theories of motivation, and the effects that leaders have on the work of their subordinates in a variety of organizational settings. These examples focus on leadership in formal settings, in which those in charge of a work group or unit had close contact with those they supervised. Another dimension of leadership with important consequences for public administrative activity is how elected or appointed chief executives (and their immediate subordinates) influence administrative behavior from a more distant position (in organizational terms) and how those executives interact with the bureaucracies they attempt to lead.

The roles played by chief executives (presidents, governors, mayors, city managers, and county executives) as leaders of their governments' bureaucracies have not been studied as fully as some of their other functions. Yet, as the presence of public bureaucracies and their effects throughout society have grown, accountability, character, efficiency, and results have become salient concerns.[1] More to the point, chief executives (together with judges and legislators) have increasingly been regarded as logical choices for the task of maintaining some measure of operational control and accountability within their administrative establishments. To a great extent, electoral outcomes—that is, whether elected executives remain in office—are determined by public perceptions of these leadership criteria.

We will consider various challenges of leadership as they affect what elected officials and public administrators do. Keep in mind that, in bureaucracies where the "value-neutral professional model" predominates, various leadership dimensions are distinctly different in how these agencies operate and in how public administrators respond to both appointed and elected officials' efforts to lead them. In addition, we address ways in which chief executives seek to lead their respective bureaucracies and how definitions of roles of leaders in the ranks of administrators are changing.

The Context of Administrative Leadership

American chief executives stand apart from the executive-branch agencies they are expected to lead. Unlike most modern bureaucrats, these leaders and their immediate subordinates obtain their positions through elections (either partisan or nonpartisan) or are answerable directly to elected officials (cabinet secretaries and undersecretaries, other high-level political appointees, county administrators, and city managers). These officials are responsible, in the eyes of most of the public, for the operations of the bureaucracies that make up their respective executive branches. Historically, they have also taken much of the "heat" for programmatic failure. At the same time, however, they are not really a permanent part of their bureaucratic structures, which are highly fragmented by function, operate autonomously within our diverse system of federalism (see Chapter 3), and depend on chief executives for only some of their political support.

Chief executives are clearly expected to set general policy directions and to provide the leadership necessary to manage government agencies and programs. If they are to fulfill those expectations, they need some measure of effective influence, if not control, over bureaucratic agencies that may not be primarily interested in the executive's political success or failure. Chief executives require deliberate strategies and various forms of leverage in dealing with administrative agencies, if they are to succeed in directing administrative behavior toward fulfillment of their policy objectives.

Certainly, in the formulation of broad policy directions, executive leadership has been evident, especially in the past five decades; presidential, gubernatorial, and local executive initiatives have been commonplace and have come to be regarded as marking the opening round of policy deliberations on many issues. The ability of individual chief executives to influence their bureaucracies significantly cannot, however, be taken for granted. Where the chief executive controls most of the key mechanisms of governmental and political-party power—such as party nominations for office, patronage in government hiring, and awarding of government contracts—we can expect to find relatively responsive bureaucracies. Examples of such chief executives are Governor Huey Long of Louisiana during the 1930s and the late Mayor

Richard J. Daley of Chicago.[2] The degree of chief-executive control over the bureaucracy may vary with the extent of such powers—comparisons among state governors are revealing in this respect—but there are other factors involved as well.[3]

Chief executives' control over the bureaucracy is frequently challenged by the legislative branch, the judiciary, the mass media, and others such as opposition-party spokespersons who also seek a voice in agency decisions. More important, in many instances, their authority to lead is challenged from within, by members of their own political party, members of the courts, legislature, interest groups, or bureaucrats themselves. Presidents (and most governors and many mayors) have diverse and frequently disunited coalitions of political support that do not enable them to operate with a free hand or to speak with a consistent voice on all issues. Bureaucracies, on the other hand, have a limited range of policy interests because they are more specialized with narrower bases of support. By concentrating its efforts in one policy area, an agency can develop clientele support and expertise and can convert these diverse interests into political resources. These resources, in turn, gain the support of those in the legislature and the public who seek favorable agency treatment of their interests. Thus, agency responses to executive directives are usually calculated in terms of their effect on agency interests rather than on the interests of the chief executive. (Note that the "iron triangle" depicted in Chapter 2 does *not* include the chief executive as a major player.) Because, in most cases, an agency is not beholden to the chief executive for its political survival and because the chief executive is unlikely to risk either political resources or political defeat every time an agency fails to follow orders from above, executive leadership is much more the product of **political persuasion or "jawboning"** than of any clearly defined command authority.[4]

political persuasion or "jawboning"

power of chief executives to convince legislators, administrators, and the general public that their policies should be adopted; jawboning is quite literally the primary tactic, that is, talking, used by presidents, governors, or mayors to achieve this goal.

To persuade public bureaucracies to follow their lead, chief executives must convince agency personnel that there will be reciprocal political and fiscal support for their specialized program interests as long as those programs are integrated acceptably within the executives' broad policy directions. A variation of the same approach involves the chief executive singling out one favored program within an agency for support, keeping alive agency hopes that other programs will be similarly favored by the executive later. In other cases, when agency programs clearly occupy a low priority on a chief executive's policy agenda, the agency may adapt *procedurally* to the executive's priorities—such as trying to economize under an executive (at any level) who is emphasizing spending reductions. Even if policy differences continue to exist, both agencies and chief executives advance their interests by such a tactic; this is indicative of the agency's fear of retribution from an unfriendly or hostile chief executive. Direct conflict, of course, is another possibility, although usually a last resort for both sides.

Two elements of chief executive–bureaucracy relationships shape how the former operates to influence the latter's activities. One is the general nature of linkages between the two; the other is the specific instruments a chief executive can employ in the quest for control over bureaucratic behavior. Control from one or the other side is rarely complete, but the conflict over control and power is ongoing.

Chief Executive–Bureaucratic Linkages

Interactions between chief executives and their administrative bureaucracies take various forms but all have some impact, both on the executive's political and policy decisions and on bureaucratic behavior. It is possible to speak of policy development and policy implementation as distinct phases of chief executive involvement with their bureaucracies (see also Chapter 9). We shall use that approach in discussing these linkages.

Policy development in broad outline is what chief executives intend to do in their capacity as leaders of bureaucracy. Yet even executives with extensive formal and political power, such as second-term presidents and some popular governors, must still depend on professionals in the bureaucracy for program advice, for evaluation, and for proposing program reductions. The chief executive's dependence on experts varies among different policy areas, such that "the more technically complex the work of a bureau and the more structurally autonomous it is, the less impact [the chief executive] has on its policy development."[5] Policy areas such as energy conservation, environmental protection, national defense, nuclear power, public health, or transportation require more specialized technical expertise than most chief executives possess. Another factor affecting executive dependence on bureaucracy for policy development is the diversity of information sources within the chief executives' staffs, and among those that can be called on outside government as well (for example, from issue networks). Political considerations can often reduce dependence on experts; for example, physicians' recommendations on health care policy may be offset by motives of self-interest. There may also be some choice as to which bureaucracy a chief executive relies on. But, in virtually every case, some bureau or agency helps direct policy at both the formulation and implementation stages.

Policy implementation makes chief executives even more dependent on bureaucracies. Influence over implementation is generally limited to fairly broad-gauged actions (such as budget cuts, proposed reorganizations, and personnel measures) and is related to existing institutional resources. At the national level, for example, the U.S. Office of Management and Budget (OMB) has placed greater emphasis on management improvement, including introducing specific results-driven productivity-enhancement techniques. This creates at least the potential for more effective control over program implementation by elected chief executives. Similar developments have taken place at the state level, with the creation of departments of administration,

policy development

general political and governmental process of formulating relatively concrete goals and directions for government activity and proposing an overall framework of programs related to them; usually but not always regarded as a chief executive's task.

policy implementation

general political and governmental process of carrying out programs to fulfill specified policy objectives; a responsibility chiefly of administrative agencies, under chief executive and/or legislative guidance; also, the activities directed toward putting a policy into effect.

new budget systems, and centralized planning increasingly available to governors as management tools. In recent years, large local governments (both municipal and county) have moved in this same direction.[6]

Thus, most chief executives, including presidents, governors, and mayors, must contend with a dual difficulty. They must rely on bureaucratic expertise for much of the content of policy and, at the same time, they must seek agency compliance in implementing and evaluating policy as they desire (see Chapters 9 and 10). Strengthening the tools available to chief executives for program management, coordination, and policy evaluation has brought about some change, but most chief executives, as outsiders, still must induce cooperation from bureaucracy rather than being able to count on it as a matter of course.

Making the overall task of bureaucratic leadership more complex—but also possibly strengthening the chief executive as bureaucratic leader—is the fact that chief executives generally exercise leadership in three distinguishable but overlapping arenas: (1) the *public* arena, in which the chief executive commonly seeks to "set the agenda" for public discussion of policy issues and concerns; (2) the *legislative* arena, in which a chief executive plays a major role in proposing specific legislation and influencing the course of legislative deliberations; and (3) the *administrative* or bureaucratic arena, in which chief executives must attempt to move administrators to effectively manage programs and policies as the chief executive wants them implemented. When leaving office, elected executives have often expressed frustration with their inability to assert their leadership over administrative agencies. Upon leaving office in 1961, Republican president Dwight David Eisenhower poignantly warned against the then emerging power of the "military–industrial complex" to impact foreign policy, legislation, and program management.

Because of the political dynamics linking these three arenas, the actions of executives in one arena may have impact in at least one other. For example, a series of major legislative successes may create a political "halo," whereby chief executives encounter somewhat less bureaucratic resistance to their initiatives. Though our focus is on bureaucratic leadership, we also will take note of significant features of each of the other two arenas as we proceed.[7]

Chief Executives and Bureaucracies: The Instruments of Leadership

instruments, or tools, of leadership

various mechanisms such as legislative support, policy initiatives, and emergency decision-making powers available to chief executives to help direct bureaucratic behavior.

The ability of chief executives to lead their bureaucracies effectively depends on a number of **instruments, or tools, of leadership**, but there is considerable variation in the ability of any one leader to wield these instruments, singly or in combination. Governors and mayors especially have widely varying degrees of legal powers available to them (the legal authority of mayors often varies even within the same state). Also, not all chief executives (including presidents) are inclined to use the leadership tools available to them in the same way or to the same degree.[8] Nevertheless, particular leadership instruments can prove useful to a chief executive intent on steering agency behavior in particular policy directions.

Three factors (apart from specific instruments or tools) can help to shape the leadership environment. First is the chief executive's support in the legislature, such as Congress, state legislature, city council, or county commission. *Legislative support* or *opposition* can affect leadership over a bureaucracy because administrators are more inclined to follow the executive's lead if they know that members of the legislature also support that lead; the legislature, after all, is a key source of political and fiscal support for bureaucratic agencies.

Second is the degree of (or the potential for) *policy and program initiative* exercised by the executive leader. During the twentieth century, this became a much more visible part of the chief executive's function than in the past, in part because the public at large has clearly come to expect it of elected executive leaders. This power to initiate provides an important advantage because the way in which a question or proposal is first put forward can significantly affect the outcome of the decision process.

Another source of strength is the capability of chief executives to *respond to crisis situations*. That capacity is reinforced by public expectations that a chief executive will effectively coordinate and direct governmental actions in the wake of ongoing threats to national security and other crises requiring governmental responses, including hurricanes, floods, and serious outbreaks of violence. Perhaps one of the best examples of effective leadership response came in the aftermath of September 11, 2001, when former New York City Mayor Rudy Giuliani—with strong support from then New York Governor George Pataki and the Bush administration—attempted to lead a coordinated intergovernmental response to the horrors of those terrorist attacks. Giuliani's efforts in this regard were heavily criticized by firefighters and others searching for bodies of victims in the rubble of the twin towers.[9] However, the Bush administration's inept efforts to assist Hurricane Katrina victims in 2005, following the wind damage and flooding on the Gulf Coast and in New Orleans, forced resignations and led to a major reorganization of the Federal Emergency Management Agency (FEMA).[10] The Obama administration was faced with a similar ecological disaster when the *Deepwater Horizon* oil rig exploded and despoiled the Gulf of Mexico for three months in 2010. The reorganized FEMA, together with thousands of federal, state, and local officials as well as volunteers, directed cleanup efforts while ensuring that food, shelter, and moral support were made available as necessary to affected residents.[11] The Obama administration demanded that BP pay for the cleanup; BP is overseeing management of the cleanup in the Gulf by hiring thousands of formerly unemployed (due to the spill) workers in Louisiana and Mississippi.

Presidential power has been called on regularly in times of disaster, economic, and military crises—for example, Franklin Roosevelt's economic leadership during the Great Depression of the 1930s, Richard Nixon's supervision of wage and price controls in an effort to control inflation in 1970, George H. W. Bush's Operation Desert Storm campaign against Iraq during the 1990–1991 Persian Gulf war, and Barack Obama's decision to use military force to assist Libyan rebels in March 2011. As a rule, powers created or invoked to meet specific crises do not disappear entirely after the crisis has passed. Hence, each time the president is called on to deal with a crisis, presidential powers are further enhanced. A vivid demonstration of that phenomenon came in 1978, when a law took effect (passed in 1976 at Gerald Ford's initiative) that ended a continuous state of national emergency dating from 1933. Presidential powers during that time had included power to seize property, to organize and control the means of production, to declare martial law, and to restrict travel. It is significant that such emergency powers can last so long after a crisis has ended. For example, during Operation Desert Storm in 1990, emergency war powers were restored and numerous civilian airline crews and aircraft were drafted into service temporarily to transport supplies and personnel to Kuwait and Saudi Arabia.

None of these sources of strength is an unmixed blessing, however. The degree of legislative support for chief executives may vary during their term; policy initiatives may be greeted with resistance by the public and the legislature, or a crisis may not be handled well, thus damaging a chief executive's image and prestige. President George W. Bush's administration was criticized for engaging the military in an indefinite struggle in Iraq without proper planning for postwar occupation. Apart from the ebb and flow of political influence in the public and legislative arenas, a chief executive's influence over administrative agencies is likely to depend more directly on other factors—factors that have much more influence in the everyday operations of agencies.

The Budgetary Role

Of greater significance to virtually any chief executive is a central role in formulation of the executive budget—the proposals submitted by the president to Congress, and by most governors to their respective legislatures, for dollar amounts to be allocated to executive-branch agencies. Local chief executives often, but not always, play a similar role; we will focus on the president's budgetary role for purposes of illustration. The president's programmatic and budgetary priorities form the guidelines by which the OMB—working directly with and for the president—evaluates each agency's request for funds, so that it is possible for the president to influence substantially how much money is included or cut in budget recommendations to Congress for every agency in the executive branch. Congress, of course, is not bound by presidential recommendations for agency budgetary allocations, but it ordinarily appropriates an amount not appreciably different from, although usually lower than, that requested by the president and the OMB.[12] Exceptions to this general rule have occurred in recent years as agencies favored by the administration and

Congress must cope with unusual expenditures. The Department of Veterans Affairs, for example, has experienced cost overruns because of the larger than expected number of Afghanistan and Iraq war veterans seeking additional medical help.

When Congress is controlled by the Republicans, it frequently clashes with Democratic presidents over spending priorities and amounts, with the Senate often voting larger sums for domestic programs than the president had asked for. Under Richard Nixon (1969–1974), this precipitated bitter conflicts over presidential vetoes and over Nixon's impounding (withholding authority to spend) funds appropriated by Congress (see Chapter 8). President Jimmy Carter (1977–1981), a Democrat with a Democratic Congress, faced less friction on budget matters than Nixon had, although some of his proposals were treated unfavorably. Ronald Reagan, a Republican with a Republican Senate and apparent public backing (especially during his first term, 1981–1985), nevertheless encountered congressional resistance to his spending control initiatives. President George H. W. Bush took on a more conciliatory role as efforts to reduce annual budget deficits intensified in the early 1990s. The elder Bush got into trouble with members of his own party when he violated a "no new taxes" campaign pledge by compromising with congressional Democrats on budget priorities. Despite relatively high job approval ratings and success as commander-in-chief during the Gulf War, the elder Bush was defeated in 1992 by a then unknown former congressman and Arkansas governor, Bill Clinton.

President Clinton worked with Democratic congressional leaders, and often with reluctant Republican members, before Congress accepted his budget proposals by the slimmest of margins. This legislation included a budget deficit reduction agreement that was intended to reduce national government annual deficits by nearly $500 billion by 1996. The budget conflicts between President Clinton and Congress were so intense and the divisions so deep that the proposal barely passed the House of Representatives (218–216) and Vice President Al Gore had to cast the deciding vote in the Senate to break a 50–50 tie. In 1995, the federal government was twice shut down because the Democratic president and Republican-controlled Congress failed to agree on budget priorities. The deep involvement of the president testified to the role any president can assume in the budgetary process—and to the sharing of responsibility that characterizes that process. President Obama modified his 2011 budget priorities and legislative agenda after Republicans won a majority of U.S. House seats in the 2010 midterm elections. In sum, the president has considerable influence over the amounts of money received by executive agencies, but his or her influence—and even legal authority—cannot be said to be absolute. There is continual competition for control of agency funding, with the president occupying a major leadership role.

A second function related to budgetary coordination emerged for the OMB in the 1970s, chiefly at the instigation of President Nixon. When the old Bureau of the Budget (BOB), which had existed in the Executive Office of the President (EOP) since 1939, was transformed into the OMB in 1970, the change in title was not merely cosmetic. It signaled Nixon's intent to gain greater mastery over the operations and management practices of the sprawling federal bureaucracy. Even though Nixon's effort suffered from lack of an explicit strategy, he did succeed to some degree in modifying management practices and establishing presidential authority to monitor them. This set a precedent for later efforts by Reagan, Bush, and Clinton to deregulate agency authority, reduce budget deficits, and consolidate grant programs.

When administrators propose legislation for consideration by Congress, **central clearance** with the OMB is a required formality. This gives the president an opportunity to review proposals for their consistency with his legislative program. Agencies and their administrators may deal informally with Congress but, as a matter of routine, most agencies seek clearance and do not openly defy the president and OMB if clearance is denied. Toward the end of the Carter administration in the late 1970s, the OMB began to involve itself in numerous efforts to manage agency activities more fully. One device was limiting the paperwork requirements agencies impose on other governments and the private sector.

With passage of the Paperwork Reduction Act in late 1980, a new Office of Information and Regulatory Affairs within the OMB was established, charged with reviewing all requests for information from the public made by government agencies.[13] Other steps primarily affected regulatory agencies—a focus of central concern during the Reagan administration. Early in his term of office, Reagan put heavy emphasis on central clearance of proposed regulations and issued several directives that enhanced the position of presidential leadership (and control) in this regard. Other proposals, some of which were adopted in whole or in part, included requiring cost–benefit analysis of proposed regulations as well as so-called inflation impact statements. The role of the OMB as presidential staff coordinator of regulatory clearance became more clearly defined as Reagan, the elder Bush, and President George W. Bush pursued policies of scaling down the national government's role in economic and social regulation (see Chapter 11).

During the first months of his administration, Ronald Reagan demonstrated just how great an impact a president can have on bureaucratic agencies through his successful efforts, supported by a conservative Congress, to make deep cuts in the national government's domestic spending. The president's fierce determination to significantly alter the nature and scope of national government activity was reflected in tax reductions and the billions of dollars cut from executive budget submissions and projections. The impacts of these cuts, combined with fundamental changes in philosophy and program emphasis issuing from the White House, put the entire bureaucracy on notice that it could no longer expect to conduct business as usual. Clearly, influence over the budget gave this president tremendous leverage over the fortunes of individual agencies. Indeed, the uses

central clearance

key role played by the Office of Management and Budget (OMB) regarding review of agency proposals for legislation to be submitted to Congress, with OMB approval required for the proposals to move forward. A similar role or pattern exists in many state governments and some local governments, in the relationships among chief executives, administrative agencies, and legislatures. Central clearance also is practiced with regard to submission of budget proposals from executive-branch agencies to legislatures, during the budget-making process.

of presidential authority in this regard exceeded what many observers had thought was possible, even if only as a short-term strategy for a new president intent on achieving significant change in the manner in which the nation was to be governed. On the contrary, but consistent with expanded executive authority, President Obama has actively pursued the use of regulatory policies to implement his administration's policies.

The budgetary influence of governors and local chief executives is predictably varied but, in general, few state or local executives can match the president's sustained impact on budget-making processes. This is true at the state level even though **executive budgets** exist—with direct involvement of the governor—in forty-four of fifty states.[14] In addition, most governors have acquired significant new budgetary powers under recent revisions in state constitutions. Although their powers have increased, most governors are still not nearly as strong in budget making at the state level as the president is at the national level.[15]

executive budgets

budgets prepared by chief executives and their central budget offices for submission to the legislature for analysis, consideration, review, change, and enactment.

Many governors find their positions defined—and often restricted—by formal legal and political factors. The most important of these is of state constitutional origin, reflecting the earlier age in which many constitutions were drafted and in which powerful political and social forces favored sharp restrictions on gubernatorial powers. Among the restrictions still facing most governors are term limitations, lack of appointment power (as many cabinet officials are elected separately), and limited budgetary control over legislatures. The late Terry Sanford, former governor and U.S. senator from North Carolina, commented that "the American governorship was conceived in mistrust and born in a strait jacket."[16] In many instances, state government power was tightly constrained across the board, with all branches and entities given only authority that could be rigidly defined.

In recent decades, there has been considerable change in state constitutions, most of it favorable to the exercise of stronger gubernatorial leadership—including leadership of state bureaucracies. More than half of the states have comprehensively revised their constitutions or have streamlined their amendment processes, making it easier to adjust the constitutional framework as the needs of state government required. As amending the constitution was made easier, efforts increased to update provisions bearing on the exercise of governors' powers, including some that are budget related. Though many constitutional constraints still curb the power of governors and other officials, the executive branches of most states are in a much stronger position today than they were twenty years ago.

Another constitutional feature that is still in force in many states is the specific mandating of programs or allocation of funds (or both)—requirements that reduce the ability of the governor (and everyone else) to make policy choices based on the best estimates of current societal and programmatic needs. Specified in the constitutions of some states, for example, are very detailed budgetary allocations that can be changed only by a constitutional amendment. Although constitutional provisions elsewhere may not be as restrictive, they nevertheless limit gubernatorial freedom of action beyond the usual constitutional and political checks and balances.

One leadership instrument available to the president and to governors as a source of budgetary influence is the **veto power**. The president may veto any legislation after Congress has passed it, but presidential veto power is limited by the requirement that the president must approve or disapprove an entire bill. That is, even if most of a bill was acceptable to the president, with only one or a few unacceptable provisions, the president still had to sign or veto the whole bill. For this reason among others, presidents vetoed relatively infrequently, making the veto power less significant than it might have been. That is one of the reasons why recent candidates as well as presidents and the Republicans' short-lived "Contract with America" called for the presidential **item veto (or line-item veto)**. The Contract was part of the 1994 Republican takeover of Congress that included policy proposals designed to redefine the relationship between the government and the people. Congress passed, and President Clinton signed, legislation authorizing a restricted version of the presidential line-item power, limited solely to discretionary spending measures, at the time representing about one-third of the total federal budget. However, in 1998, the Supreme Court declared unconstitutional the presidential line-item veto power. President George W. Bush enjoyed so much congressional support that it was almost seven years before Congress succeeded in overriding one of his vetoes for the first time in November 2007. During his first two years in office, Barack Obama enjoyed considerable success in persuading Congress to accept his domestic policy agenda. He has been less successful, however, with economic policy and job creation.

All but one of the governors have a similar veto power. More importantly, however, forty-three governors also have an unrestricted line-item veto, enabling them to disapprove specific provisions of a bill while signing the rest of it into law. Illinois, in addition, provides for an amendatory veto, permitting the governor not only to disapprove a provision but also to propose alternative language to the legislature; this could mean rewriting the content and even the intent of legislation if the legislature goes along with it. Two other states permit their governors to use this power for what are labeled *technical corrections*, without always distinguishing between content-related and technical changes.

Item-veto power enables most governors to exert control with something resembling surgical precision. It permits intervention in budgetary and other matters of interest to functional specialists in a particular program area without forcing the disapproval of entire spending provisions, program authorizations, or other interests. Essentially, it allows a chief executive greater control over spending decisions in individual program areas.[17] That is why it has more potential as a leadership tool that truly matters to program administrators in the bureaucracy and to their allies in the legislature and among interest groups.

veto power

constitutional power of an elected chief executive to overrule an appropriation, bill, or decision by the legislature. At the national government level, requires a two-thirds majority of both houses of Congress to override.

item veto (or line-item veto)

constitutional power available to more than forty of America's governors, under which they may disapprove some provisions of a bill while approving the others.

In sum, the budgetary role of many governors resembles, in important respects, that of the president—but with some important differences as well. Most but not all of the differences favor presidential influence compared with that of most governors, but governors have emerged in recent decades as far more important budgetary actors in their respective states, and they are virtually certain to continue in that role.

At the local level, few mayors enjoy such influence in budget making; in many American cities and towns, the office of mayor is more a ceremonial one than that of a working chief administrator. City and county managers, on the other hand, play key roles in formulating budget proposals and often succeed in winning council approval for these proposals.[18] One contributing factor is the manager's expertise and the legitimacy this provides; another is the fact that managers are full-time professionals and, in many instances, mayors and city council members are part-timers. The growing professionalization of county government has led, in many cases, to similar patterns of expertise—and budgetary influence—among county administrators and county managers. Still, the budget role of local executives is somewhat more modest, relative to their respective bureaucracies, than that of either governors or presidents.

Personnel Controls and Chief-Executive Leadership

A second important set of tools that chief executives may use to influence their respective bureaucracies is personnel management—overseeing the rules, organizations, and activities involved in filling administrative positions throughout the executive branch and in managing the people hired for those positions and the many tasks they perform. As in the case of budgetary practices, there is considerable variety in types of personnel systems (see Chapter 7), for example, patronage and merit systems. Patronage emphasizes political party or policy loyalty as a basis for making personnel decisions—hiring, on-the-job evaluation, promotions, transfers, and so on. The concept of merit, on the other hand, is the basis for a system under which the employee—as a career civil servant—is hired and later evaluated (and promoted, and so on) on the basis of career-focused job-related competence. The merit employee is thus presumed to place much more emphasis on career development and much less emphasis on loyalty to an individual leader. Patronage makes it easier for chief executives to exert their will over larger segments of a bureaucracy because, in a patronage system, loyalty and responsiveness to the policy preferences and directions of a chief executive are more routinely expected of employees by top leaders and by employees themselves. Many states prohibit by statute any elected official from ordering an appointed career civil servant to perform certain specific acts. For example, the mayor is not allowed to contact police officers directly for services other than those authorized by city ordinances or by the police chief.

Until 1883, presidents enjoyed extensive discretionary powers over appointment and dismissal of administrative employees, a power that has been largely unavailable to presidents since that time because of merit reform. The president has the power to appoint some 3,000 executive-branch employees out of a total of some 3 million civilian employees. (Establishment of the Senior Executive Service, under the Civil Service Reform Act of 1978, increased both presidential appointment authority and the potential for presidential influence over high-ranking career bureaucrats; see Chapter 7.) Still, the president's power to appoint is more significant in the long-range execution of public policy than is his power to dismiss, because not all appointees are removable and those who are seldom find themselves actually fired. Often, but not always, the president has been able to guide the activities of these appointees, but his ability to control their respective bureaucracies through them has usually been more limited.

Limitations on presidential influence over political appointees, and on the influence of presidents and appointees alike over the bureaucracy, are complex and deserve examination. An essential element, already implied, of presidential–bureaucratic interactions is that they are not direct: There are layers of both political and career personnel between the White House, statehouses, city halls, and their respective bureaucracies. Another important factor is that cabinet officers are not merely "extensions of the presidency [with] no competing loyalties."[19] The president cannot automatically assume perfect obedience (or anywhere near that) even from a high-ranking political appointee who also has to work with the bureaucracy in order to be reasonably effective in departmental leadership. Cabinet secretaries are often pulled in opposite directions by competing political forces—the president and their own departments—because of the more focused policy interests of the latter. Secretaries of cabinet-level departments cannot be expected to act strictly as "the president's men (or women)"; as a result, a unified cabinet is unlikely. But, at the same time, a president "should [safeguard] the powers and prestige of his department heads as . . . those of his own office." To the extent that the status and authority of any department head are downgraded, he or she "is *less able* to resist the pressures brought upon him [or her] by constituencies, congressional committees, and the bureaucracy."[20]

Political appointees, in turn, have had their own difficulties in directing the activities of their respective bureaucracies. One explanation for this is that these appointees make up a "government of strangers"—certainly to their departments, often to each other and to White House staff members, and sometimes even to the president who appointed them.[21] It is more than simply a case of bureaucrats being in government longer than most political appointees, though that is part of it. Rather, newly appointed executives have to spend part of their limited time in office—two years or less for many secretaries, undersecretaries, and assistant secretaries—learning both the formal and informal rules of the game in their departments.[22] Thus, implementation of presidential policy initiatives is delayed for significant periods of time within cabinet departments—and, in politics, delay can signify ultimate defeat for a presidential appointment, policy, or program.

Once having become acclimated to Washington politics, political appointees (and new presidents) are often rudely confronted with other operating realities of bureaucratic politics. One major reality is that there are important differences between modes of operation of political leaders and career officials. The former seek to accomplish many things in a short time, with what they hope is overt political appeal; they are thus interested in quick, dramatic actions and results, especially on first taking office. Career bureaucrats, on the other hand, are predisposed toward behaviors that have been described as gradualism, indirection, and political caution, and a concern for maintaining relationships. *Gradualism*—moving slowly—has the advantage of decreasing the possible fear associated with change. *Indirection*, or avoiding direct confrontations, is aimed at minimizing the potential number of sources of opposition to a program, personnel action, or implementation strategy. *Political caution* is designed to prevent unintentional or unwarranted identification of a career official with particular political appointees; this could easily compromise an official's career status and reputation. Finally, *maintaining relationships* is especially crucial for career employees, whose professional existence and effectiveness depend centrally on developing cross-agency networks.

Inevitable tensions are generated as a result of interactions among officials with these divergent approaches to discharging their public responsibilities. In particular, criticisms of the bureaucracy or of bureaucrats—across the board—are voiced by political leaders anxious to see movement in key policy areas and frustrated by a bureaucratic environment many do not understand. Among the kinder terms used to describe bureaucrats and their agencies are *slow-moving*, *unresponsive*, and *disloyal* (to the chief executive). But there is a lesson here—namely, that what are regarded as inherent deficiencies of bureaucracy "are often its strengths. Effective functioning [of government] requires a high degree of stability, uniformity, and awareness of the impact of new policies, regulations, and procedures on the affected public."[23] Bureaucrats are usually in a better position to assess such impacts than are Washington's executive "strangers." Moreover, civil servants can perform a valuable public service by resisting the demands of their political bosses. **Bureaucratic resistance** based on expertise, knowledge, and concern for program effectiveness—as opposed to simple obstructionism—may be the only viable alternative to letting things go wrong, and then being responsible later for correcting the problem. Hugh Heclo, a longtime observer of administrative politics, sums up these tendencies this way:

> It is not simply a question of civil servants resisting any confrontations or change but of preferences for fights that do not lead to too much unnecessary antagonism and uproar—changes that do not extend uncertainty in too many directions at once. [These sorts of behavior] go beyond conventional images of bureaucratic inertia. Such tendencies

bureaucratic resistance

feature of administrative agencies that emphasizes gradualism and political caution when dealing with newly selected political leadership in the executive branch.

can find a *good deal of justification* in an environment of complex and uncertain political leadership on the one hand and long agency tenures and individualistic job protections on the other.[24]

Some recent presidents have been surprised by the inability of their highest-level departmental political appointees to overcome these patterns of bureaucratic behavior. Because departmental appointees work more closely than presidents or White House staff with their bureaucracies, they have a tendency to take on the perspectives of their departments, often at the expense of what might be called "presidentialist perspectives."[25] This can lead to a very frustrating situation for presidents, who may have expected the sort of control over appointees that others have and who find instead that cabinet members serve more as "ambassadors" *from* the departments than emissaries *to* them. One consequence can be conflict among not only departments but also the secretaries themselves over program jurisdiction. Another more serious result is a drain on presidents' time and resources if they choose to mediate a succession of internal conflicts. More than likely, they will delegate responsibility for mediation to the vice president or to others on the White House staff, or they will resign themselves to having to work around such conflicts. None of these choices is especially attractive.

Under the Reagan administration, there were developments in Washington executive politics that may have represented the start of a long-term shift in some of the patterns just discussed.[26] Ronald Reagan, more than any other modern president, came to Washington with an explicit management strategy and firm determination to change the operations of the national government bureaucracy. Political scientist Richard Nathan, writing in 1983, described the principal elements of this strategy:

> The key ingredient has been the appointment of loyal and committed policy officials. But this is only one dimension. The internal organization and operation of the White House staff is another. Loyal "Reaganites" have been placed in key White House policy-making positions, with experienced Washington hands assigned to parallel posts to promote the administration's policies in the legislative process and in the media. *Appointed policy officials in agency posts have penetrated administrative operations by grabbing hold of spending, regulatory, and personnel decisions.* From the beginning, these and other administrative tactics have been used aggressively by the Reagan administration.[27]

There are several important points to be made here. First, actions taken by Reagan staff regarding career personnel demonstrated that chief executives need not rely on the ultimate instrument of dismissal to make significant changes in the behavior of career officials. Many positions were eliminated and those filling them reassigned (though there were some layoffs). These

reductions-in-force (RIFs) sent a signal throughout the bureaucracy that, unlike some presidents, Reagan was absolutely serious about making cuts in the scope and size of government. It also indicated that the relative security of the career civil service could and would be breached if such breaches contributed to advancing the policy goals—especially in domestic policy—of the Reagan administration. Second, a number of Reagan's subcabinet officials remained in their positions for well over two years, reducing the impact of their being "strangers" in the executive branch. Third, the combination of budgetary and performance management strategies (see Chapters 8 and 10) had the effect of disrupting some of the behavior patterns associated with senior careerists. It is much more difficult to practice gradualism or indirection, for example, when executive-branch political leadership is clearly intent on *accelerating* change and *creating* confrontation in administrative operations.

These Reagan strategies, taken together, raised an issue of significant importance—namely, whether these steps constituted excessive (and long-term) politicizing of the bureaucracy. Some critics charged that the president, in the interests of his own policy agenda, wanted presidential control to reach down to levels of the bureaucracy that previously had been largely the domain of career civil servants, thus compromising the value-neutral position of the civil service. There is a major difference between a president trying to influence the bureaucracy through personnel appointments, on the one hand, and seeking to cement into the ranks of the bureaucracy supporters committed to one and only one policy agenda, on the other. Whether President Reagan deliberately intended to achieve the latter is not clear, but the pattern of his personnel appointments was disturbing to many observers, some of whom strongly supported the Reagan domestic policy agenda.

One other negative aspect of this management strategy has been noted by critics of the Reagan presidency: the possibility that it may have contributed to the Iran–Contra affair.[28] This episode, which involved the sale of weapons to Iran through third-party intermediaries and the subsequent diversion of some of the proceeds to the U.S.-backed Contra rebels in Nicaragua, involved four unpleasant possibilities. The first was that federal laws had been broken—laws banning further aid to the Contras. The second was that National Security Council officials had lied to congressional committees investigating these transactions. The third was that these officials had acted in every respect with the confidence that their president would have approved of what they were doing even if they had not been ordered to take these actions and had not even informed the president of their activities. The fourth possibility, of course, is that Ronald Reagan—as well as then vice president and successor George H. W. Bush—did, in fact, know of these activities but denied (then and later) that a link of any kind existed between the sale of arms to Iran and aid to the Contras.

As president, George H. W. Bush was less aggressive than Ronald Reagan in attempting to direct administrative activities partly because he perceived

reductions-in-force (RIFs)

systematic reductions or downsizing in the number of personnel positions allocated to a government agency or agencies; usually the result of higher-level personnel management policy decisions related to other policy objectives, including budget cuts and executive reorganizations.

less need to move as decisively as President Reagan had moved. Another possibility is that Bush chose to take a less threatening path in dealing with the career civil service because he had previously held a variety of top positions in the bureaucracy, including ambassador to China and director of the Central Intelligence Agency (CIA). As an insider, he had considerable personal experience working with career administrators—and perhaps a better understanding of their modes of operation. For whatever reason, his authority vis-à-vis the Washington establishment was weakened.

As a Washington outsider, President George W. Bush experienced similar problems with some of his cabinet officials, particularly former Secretaries of State and Treasury, Colin Powell and Paul H. O'Neill. Secretary O'Neill had served with distinction in the private sector and had held other high-level bureaucratic posts, including deputy director of OMB and systems analyst with the Department of Veterans Affairs. Nonetheless, he was asked to resign in December 2002, following public criticism and statements contrary to Bush administration policy. Although the White House cited his failure to implement Bush economic policy as the reason for his departure, O'Neill (as well as other former administration staff) later alleged that decision making for the Iraq invasion began just weeks after Bush's inauguration, months before the September 11, 2001 terrorist attacks. Bush's victory over John Kerry in the 2004 election provided a convenient and politically favorable occasion to replace nearly his entire cabinet, with the exception of former Secretary of Defense Donald Rumsfeld (who resigned about a year later), in a symbolic show of executive leadership and reinforcement of presidential loyalty.

Upon election in 2008, President Obama sought to surround himself with like-minded cabinet members who would help push through his policy agenda. Various cabinet members have stepped down during his first years in office, including White House chief of staff, Rahm Emanuel, who was elected mayor of Chicago in 2010. (This role transition was seen by many as one of the first strategic steps in Obama's 2012 presidential campaign.) Obama has been criticized for being aloof and detached from policy makers, even many within his own administration, leading to reports of strained relationships in need of repair and policies in need of attention. He was criticized in March 2011 for taking his family on a South and Central American diplomatic junket while at the same time launching massive air attacks to assist Libyan rebels. His Secretary of Defense, Robert Gates, a holdover from the Republican Bush administration, announced his retirement and departed Washington in the summer of 2011. Former President Bill Clinton even chided Obama to become more actively involved in motivating his appointees to achieve policy goals.

At the state and local levels, there are, once again, some concerns similar to those at the national level—and some substantial differences. For many governors, there are limitations on powers of appointment and dismissal for subordinate executive-branch positions; not even the president has unlimited authority in this respect, but the authority of individual state governors seems considerably less extensive by comparison. In many states, there are boards and commissions created by the legislature to which the governor cannot name members. In other instances, appointees cannot be removed by the governor except under the most extraordinary circumstances. And most governors face the political necessity of at least tolerating appointees sponsored by political-party or interest group supporters. In fact, in some predominantly rural states, a bureau or department head may be selected by a committee made up entirely or in part of people the agency serves. Governors' control over executive-branch personnel is reduced still further by the simple fact that many states elect at least one other top-level executive official (state attorney general, treasurer, secretary of state, comptroller, or even—in a few cases— lieutenant governor) separately from the governor. The net effect is to reduce the leverage that a governor has over subordinates, thus frustrating efforts to develop and implement consistent policies.

The local level presents a mixed picture, especially as local governments have become increasingly professionalized. The stereotypical image of a local boss controlling all personnel matters is now the rare exception; more common is the local government in which a merit system represents the formal mechanism for personnel management. Yet political party influences are often still felt in the local personnel process, especially in large cities. To the extent that vestiges of patronage persist, local executives may still be able to name some administrative personnel. On the whole, however, local chief executives are less influential in this respect today than in the past.

Executive-Branch Reorganization

A third instrument of chief executive control is periodic **reorganization** of administrative agencies. Like budgetary coordination, reorganization authority is a legacy of the reform movements of the early 1900s. Traditionally, reorganization was aimed at increasing economy and efficiency, clarifying chains of command, and the like. And, with few exceptions, presidents (and governors) who possess generous reorganization authority have approached their efforts with those objectives in mind.

Proponents of reorganization often seem to regard it as a cure-all for correcting bureaucratic ills. Reorganizations have, at various times, been touted as a means of eliminating waste and saving billions of dollars, restoring to economic health a chronically ailing maritime industry, reducing airport noise, and controlling crime.[29] Yet there is reason to suggest that such rationales may have been "oversold"—that reorganizations, although useful, have higher political costs and fewer benefits for a chief executive than many imagine.

One important reason for the failure of reorganizations to deliver on their promises is that the "standard reorganization strategies for rationalizing and simplifying the executive branch often clash with one another."[30] Political

reorganization

authority delegated by the legislature to the chief executive to add or subtract staff positions, or to restructure organizational arrangements, to achieve policy goals as well as increased economy, efficiency, and effectiveness of bureaucratic agencies.

scientist Herbert Kaufman lists seven basic prescriptions for reorganization: (1) limiting the number of program subordinates under a given executive, (2) grouping related functions under a common command (as happened in the creation of both the Defense Department and the Department of Education), (3) increasing the number of executive staff positions, (4) granting extensive reorganization powers to elected or appointed executives, (5) insulating career public servants against political pressures, (6) decentralizing administration, and (7) expanding opportunities for public participation in the administrative process.[31] In the name of economy, efficiency, and responsiveness, these have been tried repeatedly in one form or another.

One must be selective as to which prescription to use, depending on circumstances and on the objectives. The first four prescriptions tend toward centralization of authority; the last three tend to promote dispersal of authority. More importantly, these prescriptions in combination involve trade-offs of advantages and disadvantages. It is impossible to reap only benefits from reorganizing without also having to cope with attendant disadvantages, and hard choices must be made about which disadvantages will be accepted in order to gain other benefits. For example, grouping related functions under a common command is at odds with protecting an agency from political pressures; similarly, increasing decentralization and public participation clashes with limiting the number of subordinates effectively involved in program administration. Adding staff positions goes against decentralization; insulating administrators against political pressures interferes with executive reorganization authority; decentralization, coupled with protection from political pressures, can severely reduce the command authority of the chief executive. Reorganizations matter most in terms of the distribution of influence, the flows of communication, and the course of policy—not in terms of economy and efficiency. Therein lies the appeal of this device for the sophisticated executive, and "the genius of the reorganizer is to know which trade-off to make at a given time."[32] As President George W. Bush and his advisers learned, their proposals to combine all or part of twenty-two existing federal agencies into a new Department of Homeland Security (DHS) was no easy job. Despite the reorganization of homeland security and intelligence agencies, all jurisdictional issues among the DHS, Director of National Intelligence (DNI), and the Defense Department have not been resolved. There are still questions about which agency is in charge if the United States is again hit by a terrorist attack. Under the **Posse Comitatus Act of 1878**, U.S. military forces are forbidden from taking part in domestic law enforcement. Despite the creation of additional homeland security and intelligence bureaucracies, the final authority to respond to a national emergency is still unresolved.

Most recently, President Obama has initiated plans to eliminate and reduce the overlap that has developed within the federal government, by focusing on reorganization. In his January 2011 State of the Union address, Obama stated that "In the coming months, my administration will develop a proposal to merge, consolidate, and reorganize the federal government in a way that best serves the goal of a more competitive America."[33] Similar to prior presidential attempts at reorganization, Obama's plan continues to prove challenging. There is a significant difference between being able to propose a package plan, subject only to legislative veto by one or both houses, and having to submit reorganization plans as part of the usual legislative process. Allowing a legislature to amend, revise, and otherwise tinker with the proposals, even to the point of completely rewriting them, is a form—and a sign—of chief-executive weakness compared to the package approach. The president and many governors now have the option of proposing reorganization packages.

Information Resources

Control over information represents a fourth broad approach to maintaining chief-executive influence over bureaucratic agencies, as well as in the policy-making process. It is said that knowledge, or now *information*, is power and, in an era of intensive specialization and greater access to information, that holds true as never before. The more complex the bureaucratic structure of any given executive branch, the greater the challenge to the chief executive in terms of information gathering and use. For purposes of this discussion, we will focus on the presidency, but it should be noted that state and local chief executives interacting with relatively complex bureaucracies will find their situations not unlike the one that confronts the president.

The president, of course, must deal increasingly with a highly specialized and expert bureaucracy (inside as well as outside the presidential establishment).[34] How then are presidents to gather the facts and figures necessary for informed decision making without being dominated by, or becoming excessively dependent on, their sources of information?

To a large extent, the president is dependent on specialized bureaucratic agencies and also on information supplied by the network of presidential advisers, both those within the EOP and those having independent status. The president's ability to keep this network functioning adequately while avoiding dependence on any one source of information is crucial to retention of political leadership and policy initiative. Franklin Roosevelt was perhaps the master of this art. He ensured a constant stream of facts, ideas, suggestions, and countersuggestions by (1) centralizing decision-making responsibility in the Oval Office, (2) delegating responsibility for proposing policy alternatives rather widely so as to involve large numbers of administrators in the process of brainstorming for ideas, (3) actively encouraging open debate and discussion among members of his administration, and (4) leaving just about everyone somewhat uncertain as to whose ideas might be acted on in any given situation. He also took care to follow suggestions from a variety of sources, thus demonstrating his intention to take useful ideas and follow them up irrespective of the source.[35]

Roosevelt's technique had the effect of generating more ideas than he could use, but it was to his advantage as a political leader to have that volume of information, combined with a carefully cultivated ability to make the final choices himself. Presidents since Roosevelt have had a far more difficult task in this regard, as a result of the growth of virtually every major institution in the executive branch and the increasing power of special-interest "lobbies." There is more information than any one person can absorb and utilize; there are more competitors, both institutional and personal, for access to, and control of, information; and the greatly increased quantities of information generated by others for their own use and political advantage pose an obstacle to presidential policy direction that is difficult to surmount. For example, as lead advocates and spokespersons for health care reform in the mid-1990s, former President Bill Clinton and U.S. Secretary of State (at time of publication) Hillary Rodham Clinton were defeated by a highly successful media campaign mounted by large insurance companies opposed to their proposals. President Barack Obama succeeded in passing health care reform legislation, but had to compromise with Republicans on key provisions to the final bills.[36]

Recent presidents have tried to deal with their growing information needs by (1) increasing the information capabilities of the EOP; (2) creating specialized staffs, or **task forces**, with corresponding increases in the political and programmatic responsibilities entrusted to them; and (3) delegating greater operating authority to EOP personnel. These changes have improved the president's information base for assessing alternatives and making choices, thereby creating something of a counterforce to the information generated in other parts of the bureaucracy and elsewhere. Furthermore, the proliferation of presidential staffs has permitted more specialization within the EOP, thus strengthening the president's policy-making effectiveness vis-à-vis the expertise of the bureaucracy. Finally, by broadening the authority of assistants, the first lady, the vice president, and staffs to speak and act on behalf of the president, George W. Bush enhanced his ability to transmit and acquire information through his immediate subordinates, especially Vice President Dick Cheney. This is important because presidents and other chief executives frequently encounter difficulty in transmitting and receiving accurate information through the bureaucratic hierarchy.

The strength of a governor's staff and executive-office resources, including information capabilities, must also be assessed. In recent decades, many states have made considerable progress in these areas, with a consequent increase in gubernatorial effectiveness. Most states have a department of administration to assist the governor in directing the bureaucracy's operations, and in a number of other states, the governor's personal staff has been expanded to include qualified subject-matter specialists, who strengthen the reservoir of expertise available in the executive office itself.

Transmitting information from one level in a hierarchy to the next can present major obstacles because of the tendency for a portion of the

task forces

temporary cross-functional teams responsible for achieving a particular goal, often drawn from several departments within a larger agency; typically disbanded after the goal is accomplished.

information to be screened out by those who receive it and, in turn, send it on. This may be done in a deliberate attempt to frustrate the will of the official sending the information, or it may be done unintentionally without any particular motive—perhaps even unconsciously. Depending on how many levels there are in an organizational structure, a great deal of information can be distorted and even lost in this manner.[37] A chief executive, or any other top-level official, cannot casually assume that his or her communications—including instructions, statements of policy, or major program directives—travel down the hierarchy simply on the strength of their having been issued. There must be follow-up to ensure that communications have been received and accurately understood by those for whom they were intended (see Chapter 4).

Obtaining reliable information that gives a clear, complete picture of what is going on in the bureaucracy is the other side of the coin. Unless there is some disruption in the normal routine of administration, the chief executive does not have to be informed about the details of administrative activities. Such an assumption is justified on the grounds that the chief executive's responsibilities are broader than the activities of a single bureaucratic agency and that his or her attention should be directed to individual entities only if there is some special reason for doing so. In traditional administrative thinking, this assumption is called the **exception principle**, suggesting that only exceptions to routine operations merit involvement of the chief executive. But the exception principle does not always work well in practice. For one thing, there is a strong, if natural, reluctance to communicate bad news through the hierarchy and, least of all, from an immediate subordinate to a superior official of that agency. Also, for its own reasons, an agency may prefer not to call attention to activities that are likely to be unpopular with its nominal superior. Therefore, for the president or other chief executive to have accurate, comprehensive information requires a successful effort to overcome built-in fear and resistance to a free upward flow of communication.

Among the ways of coping with problems in acquiring information are (1) making use of external sources of information (newspapers and other media, interest groups, and so on); (2) creating overlapping substantive areas of responsibility within or among bureaus, resulting in multiple channels of information sources and presumably more reliable information; (3) using informal channels to supplement formal ones; and (4) deliberately bypassing formal structures and intermediate layers of bureaucracy to contact directly the person or people who have the information being sought.[38] Franklin Roosevelt and John F. Kennedy frequently telephoned lower-echelon bureaucrats to get information that was moving too slowly, or not at all, through formal hierarchical channels. Such an informal practice has two effects, both desirable from the president's point of view: it gets the particular information into his or her hands more quickly and it signals the rest of the bureaucracy that he or she is prepared to bypass the usual channels when the president deems it necessary. The latter is likely to reduce the time required to transmit communications

exception principle

assumption in traditional administrative thinking that chief executives do not have to be involved in administrative activities unless some problem or disruption of routine activity occurs—that is, where there is an exception to routine operations.

through channels; the threat of being bypassed can motivate those responsible for forwarding information to the president to do so with a minimum of delay, outweighing any contrary motivations to obstruct or distort.

By simply withholding all or some information, a president can decisively influence the shape of internal deliberations, media reports, public debate, and even global confrontations. This device, however, has its limits, and failure to control information can also have major policy implications. A classic illustration involved President Kennedy's explanations of just what was promised to anti-Castro Cubans who wanted to invade Cuba at the Bay of Pigs in 1961. The invasion became a fiasco for the United States because, first, air cover promised for the landing on the beaches never materialized and, second, Kennedy's spokesmen—particularly a Pentagon press officer with years of experience on the job—initially denied any American involvement in either the planning or the execution of the abortive invasion. These spokesmen followed up their denials, once they were known to be false, with claims that the national interest had both *required* and *justified* their giving out false information.

A president, on the other hand, can find himself or herself forced to react to a situation in which he or she lacks information vital to an impending decision. One such case was the Cuban missile crisis in 1962. President Kennedy needed to establish beyond doubt that Soviet missiles had been installed in Cuba before deciding what actions to take—actions that might have led to global nuclear war. But, despite the terrible urgency, he had difficulty obtaining the necessary photographic evidence because of the time consumed by bureaucratic processing of the information and at least one interagency squabble—over whose pilots (Air Force or CIA) would fly whose planes over the western end of Cuba, where the missiles were ultimately spotted.[39] If presidents are unable to acquire information readily in the most extraordinary circumstances, even in a potential nuclear crisis, they clearly cannot depend on routine flows of information.

Another example was the attempted break-in at the Democratic election headquarters in the Watergate apartments in Washington, D.C., during the presidential election campaign in 1972. The documented falsehoods of the Nixon White House in regard to the "Watergate affair" also demonstrated the power of the president to influence the course of public discussion, as well as the dramatic consequences of not maintaining complete information control. Like some previous presidents, Nixon invoked the doctrine of **executive privilege** to justify withholding confidential communications between himself and senior advisers. Although subsequent presidents including George W. Bush have also claimed the need for confidential information to remain so, Nixon's refusal to release tape recordings of private White House meetings was ruled unconstitutional in *United States v. Nixon* (418 U.S. 683, 1974).

President Bush's case for war with Iraq was based on two major intelligence failures: the first was the finding that Iraqi leader Saddam Hussein

executive privilege

the claim, largely unsupported by the federal courts, made by presidents that confidential information exchanged between themselves and their advisers cannot be released without the president's approval.

had connections to al-Qaeda, which was never verified; the second had less to do with a vision for a "democratic Iraq" and more to do with the fact that the United States had lost a potentially powerful ally in the war on terror—Saddam Hussein himself. He was a man whose ideas were very much Western in their roots. He believed in secularism rather than theocracies or religious fundamentalism and was not a religious extremist, but rather a military dictator, not unlike others in the region. It is important to consider these facts to realize just how extreme the American *casus belli* (justification for acts of war) was at the time. The Iraqi government under Saddam even tried back-channel communications with the U.S. government prior to the invasion in an effort to convince Washington that Iraq had no weapons of mass destruction (WMDs). Irrespective of these facts, the Bush administration had already decided to go to war with Iraq, WMDs or not. The lack of conclusive evidence of Iraqi ties with al-Qaeda terrorists did not dissuade Bush from "finishing the job" that his father had started during the 1991 Gulf War.[40] During the 1980s, prior to his invasion of Kuwait, Saddam had a mutually advantageous relationship with the United States—one of four powerful allies in the region, even receiving funds from the CIA. After going to war with Saddam and vilifying him in the media, the United States would have looked ridiculous had we continued using him as a weapon against terrorism.

Contrary to the intelligence findings of numerous career intelligence officers, the Bush administration failed to heed the facts presented to it. The CIA officers who actually presented accurate and factual intelligence on the question of WMDs in Iraq silently and subsequently resigned under pressure from the White House. During this time, the administration's attention was selective—and favorable—to intelligence that supported its plan to invade Iraq. It ignored evidence that Saddam actually did have a WMD research facility that was being modeled after the Manhattan project, although it had been shut down for about ten years. The only reason the CIA was aware of this was that they sent Iraqis living in the United States to Iraq prior to the war to talk to family members who were working for, or supposedly research scientists employed by, Saddam's regime. The scientists advised their family members and tried to get the message across to the United States that there were no WMDs, at least not anymore. (At one point, they did say that there was an ongoing research project but that facilities had been destroyed during a Desert Storm bombing raid in 1991.) This information apparently was either ignored or never reached the White House.

Finally, the ultimate goal for invading Iraq may have been a smokescreen for the U.S. media and citizenry to change focus from al-Qaeda to Hussein. Unfortunately, most of Bush's extreme right-wing supporters went along with the notion that there must be some linkage between al-Qaeda and the Hussein regime, providing the administration all the support it needed to go into Iraq. This was consistent with the Bush administration's decision-making model of always basing its decisions on backing from its strongest supporters. The

POINT/COUNTERPOINT

THE ISSUE Control over information is an approach to maintaining chief-executive influence over bureaucratic agencies and the policy-making process. With the rise of modern technology, which provides individuals with instantaneous information, how are presidents to gather facts and figures necessary for informed decision making without being dominated by their sources of information?

Under what circumstances should presidents, or other chief executives, overrule the advice and intelligence received from bureaucrats?

Arguments *for* Executive Overrule

- Greatly increased quantities of information generated by others for their own use and political advantage pose an obstacle to presidential policy direction.

- The ever-increasing number of assistants, confidantes, and bureaucrats associated with a chief executive leads to an overwhelming number of opinions without a unanimous agreement being reached.

- The difficulty in transmitting and receiving accurate and timely information through the bureaucratic hierarchy makes it hard to determine what data or which fact is absolute truth and which position should be taken.

Arguments *against* Executive Overrule

- In an era of intensive specialization, bureaucrats are the most informed individuals working for the chief executive and thus have a much better, deeper understanding of a given situation.

- There is more information available to individuals now than any one person can absorb and utilize; thus the chief executive must depend on knowledgeable bureaucrats.

- The creation of task forces or specialized staffs ensures that chief executives have trusted individuals working for and with them, so that time is not wasted.

objective of the administration was to build support for the next presidential campaign and win re-election in 2004. Why else would they go into Iraq telling the world that there were WMDs only to eventually admit that they were wrong, and, in the process, lose a great deal of worldwide credibility and political capital? The aims of the administration surely must have been domestic in nature; the means of accomplishing the domestic political agenda entailed demonizing Hussein and invading Iraq.

Just how effective, then, are budgetary, personnel, reorganization authority, and information control in the total picture of presidential leadership? The answer is mixed. In terms of public and congressional leadership by the president, control of information can be a crucial instrument. But with respect to the bureaucracy, presidential leadership is subject to greater constraints, if for no other reason than that the president's control of information is less secure. Individual administrators in key positions within bureaucracies could have more to do with shaping the available alternatives for presidential decisions through provision of information on program failures and successes than any other institution or person.

Commonalities and Differences in Leadership Resources

The institutional, legal, and personal factors that facilitate strong executive leadership seem to operate at all levels of government, though somewhat less clearly and predictably for local executives. Strong chief executives draw much of their strength from the following general features.

A chief executive's political strength in the legislature, and as leader of a political party or faction, adds substantially to leadership capability in office. Research in congressional voting behavior, and to a lesser extent in state legislatures, suggests that many legislators are responsive to the initiative of the chief executive, particularly when party loyalty is invoked. Other considerations (such as policy preferences, constituency interests, and individual conscience) also play an important part in legislative decision making, but many votes are cast strictly along party lines. If a governor is strongly supported by legislators of the same party, it adds measurably to gubernatorial effectiveness. If, on the other hand, a governor must constantly struggle to gain the support of his or her own partisans in the legislature, leadership capability is a good deal more constrained. The same principle holds true with equal import for local executives and presidents. It is important to note that strength in the legislature is usually tied to the amount of popular support for the chief executive.

The power to initiate policy proposals and see that they are carried out politically is a key element of executive leadership. Legislatures at all levels ordinarily lack central policy formulation capabilities so that a chief executive who wishes to see his or her "public agenda" passed into law can do so in most cases. This assumes, of course, an executive leader who seeks to lead actively—an assumption that is usually, but not always, valid.

The capacity to respond to crisis situations (which, by their nature, require immediate, coordinated direction) has strengthened chief executives' positions. For one thing, the public has come to expect chief executives to exercise this prerogative. Also, especially in the case of the presidency, some residual emergency powers have remained in force after particular crises have passed.

More important are specific leadership tools. A central role in executive budget making strengthens the overall influence of the chief executive. If budgetary "central clearance" exists, executive agencies must pay heed to the preferences of the elected executive, at least during key stages of the budget cycle.

A crucial resource is control over executive-branch personnel decisions. The more extensive the authority to decide appointments and dismissals, the greater the political hold over actions of those whose tenure in office depends on pleasing their "patron" (hence the term *patronage*). Few chief executives, at any level, currently enjoy that kind of personnel domination.

The ability to propose agency reorganizations enhances the chief executive's power, particularly if the legislature must accept or reject the proposals as a package. This power, however, is effective more as an implied or occasional threat because reorganization is a major step. A chief executive who attempted more than one reorganization within a short time span would encounter either the likely defeat of the proposals or reduced credibility with the legislature (or both). Reorganization authority is thus a political leadership resource of rather limited potential. Still, it is better to have it in reserve than to lack it entirely or to have to subject any reorganization proposal to the normal legislative mill.

Chief-executive information resources constitute a source of potential strength. This depends on institutional arrangements in which provision is made for adequate staff; on the skills of individuals who make up the staff; and on considerations of information availability, transmission, and control. Chief executives are generally more dependent on, rather than independent of, information sources in the bureaucracy—and, increasingly, within their own executive establishments as well. Even so, information can be a key source of executive influence. Several specialized institutes provide information and research on how executives can better manage and lead their respective organizations.[41] Some chief executives have particular advantages and disadvantages that should be noted. Presidents, for all their difficulties with semiautonomous bureaucracies, are better off than many governors and mayors in that fewer constitutional restrictions are placed on presidential leadership. Many governors have a more flexible veto power than the president, whereas many mayors lack veto power altogether. Presidents appoint their cabinet; governors often must work with high-level elected officials from the opposition party. Both presidents and the majority of governors are their party's acknowledged leaders, a situation many mayors may envy. Most governors and local executives are limited, in a broad sense, by the fact that their governments' fiscal and administrative capabilities generally lag behind those of the national government. Moreover, many of them depend to some extent on national government assistance for a portion (sometimes a substantial portion) of their revenues. Although fiscal dependence is an indirect impediment to the autonomy of executive leaders, it can, in some ways, have even more adverse long-term effects on state or local policy initiatives.

The Organizational Setting of Leadership

Leadership has attracted great interest in both ancient and modern times from scholars, generals, politicians, and more casual observers. Virtually every culture, from the most primitive to the most complex, has operated within some sort of framework in which leadership functions are differentiated, identified, and exercised by some and not others. Styles of leadership have been studied and restudied; prescriptions for leadership have been written and revised; exercise of leadership has been carefully analyzed and often sharply criticized. Despite all this attention, the question of what it takes to be an effective leader is still far from settled. More research has been done in this century, paralleling the expansion of knowledge in related fields such as social psychology, sociology, organization theory, and political science. The subject has taken on particular urgency in the past two decades, however, as popular discontent has grown regarding the failure of leadership in existing political and social institutions.

Administrative leadership is exercised within specific organizational settings as well as in the context of the larger environment; both can significantly influence the behavior of leaders. We will first consider the impact of organizational settings, move next to traditional approaches to the study of leadership and some of the findings, and finally examine a number of roles and challenges that are, or can be, a part of the leadership function.

To focus our consideration on the exercise of leadership, we make several assumptions. First, the leader attains his or her position through legitimate means and remains the leader through the acquiescence of the "followership." In most cultures, groups tend to accept more readily leaders whose characteristics and abilities facilitate accomplishment of the specific tasks—for example, the quarterback on a football team is likely to be both a good player and a good motivator. It is also assumed, however, that the leader's legitimacy is not automatically continued and that the leader's actions contribute to, or detract from, the legitimacy the group accords him or her.

Second, the principal interest here is in leaders within administrative hierarchies, where advancement through the ranks or appointments from outside the organization by top-level, often elected, superiors constitutes the main method of filling leadership slots.

Third, it is assumed that organization members have at least a minimal interest in carrying out both the organization's overall responsibilities and their own particular responsibilities. Furthermore, we assume that the members' job performance can be affected by the ways in which top leaders and immediate supervisors conduct themselves in the course of discharging their responsibilities. There is ample evidence supporting the view that the relationship between leaders and followers, as well as followers' personal feelings about leaders and the way they lead, can have major consequences for work performance and the general work atmosphere (Chapter 4).[42]

Finally, the leadership roles and challenges discussed center on leaders who are in a position to influence significantly what happens in an organization. This is mentioned explicitly because it is frequently *not* the case; that is, some leaders are in a relatively weak position as a result of group structure and the nature of the work to be done.[43] One example of this would be a research team of equally competent and well-known scientists in which one member informally assumes overall direction of team tasks. As "first among equals," this leader would have to guide others through persuasion and participative decision making. Our concern, however, is with leaders who are significantly involved with the totality of a group's or organization's existence, activities, and sense of identity, and whose leadership is accepted and acknowledged by group members.

In administrative hierarchies, leadership is a multidimensional function because of multiple levels of organization, wide variation in specific tasks and general functions, and numerous situations requiring leadership of some kind. The job of a leader within the administrative framework, therefore, is not constant. The particular combinations of needs within groups being led are rarely the same from one set of circumstances to the next.

A useful conceptual approach to the organizational setting is sociologist Talcott Parsons's suggestion that "organizations exhibit three distinct levels of responsibility and control—technical, managerial, and institutional."[44] These are analogous to the distinctions drawn previously among types of decisions made by different kinds of bureaucrats and among the varying grounds for reaching decisions (Chapter 5). Leadership in complex organizations is greatly affected by the variations in responsibility and control identified by Parsons; to understand why that is, we will elaborate on what each level signifies.

The technical level, or suborganization, deals with problems "focused around effective performance of the technical function"—for example, teachers conducting their classes, a transit authority employee operating a bus on the prescribed route and running on time, or a government tax office processing income tax returns. Major concerns at this level are the nature of the technical task and "the kinds of cooperation of different people required to get the job done effectively."[45] The second, or managerial, level performs two functions for the technical suborganization: (1) mediating between the lower level and those who use its services and (2) acquiring the resources necessary for carrying out technical functions, such as purchasing, hiring, and general operations. In these senses, the managers control, or administer, the technical suborganization—although such control is not strictly a one-way street. Line workers are increasingly encouraged and expected to participate. The institutional level of the organization develops long-term policy and provides top-level support to achieve group goals. The relationship between this level and the others bears on our earlier discussion of the relationships between chief executives and bureaucracies: In terms of "formal" controls, an organization may be relatively independent, but in terms of the meaning of the functions performed by the organization and hence of its "rights" to command resources and to subject its customers to discipline, it is never completely "independent."

The significance of this observation is that, in operating terms, suborganizations at the technical and managerial levels may possess considerable autonomy and responsibility, but with ultimate responsibility and accountability vested at higher levels. (Note the further parallel between this observation and those made about the existence of considerable discretion in the making of public policy in our governmental system.)

How is administrative leadership affected by all this? One part of the answer is that, at each of the points dividing the levels of organization (institutional from managerial and managerial from technical), "there is a qualitative break in the simple continuity of 'line' authority *because the functions at each level are qualitatively different. Those . . . at the second level are not simply lower-order spellings-out of the top-level functions.*"[46] In other words, one of the principal challenges of leadership is overseeing processes of defining, organizing, supporting, and monitoring multiple functions at multiple levels of organization, which by their nature tend to defy uniform methods of supervision. Responsibilities at each level must be clear enough to ensure that basic functions appropriate to that level or unit are, in fact, carried out. Particularly for elected or appointed chief executives, but for virtually any top official, these challenges must be of paramount concern.

These conceptions of organization help clarify another problem relevant to leadership, one discussed by Mary Parker Follett (1868–1933), an early student of leadership, almost eighty years ago.[47] The problem is one of *distance* within organizations, of difficulties encountered when directives must traverse a *tall* hierarchy (see Chapter 4).

According to Follett, "One might say that the strength of favorable response to [an] order is in inverse ratio to the distance the order travels."[48] Follett was speaking not only of physical or geographical distance but also of the need for collaborative effort, or teamwork, between superiors and subordinates. She maintained that this could best be accomplished through face-to-face interaction, lessening both the physical distance and the tensions involved in giving orders. Such an observation, made during the 1920s (the heyday of scientific management), takes on greater significance in light of the more varied organizational functions that now exist and of Parsons's analysis of organization levels. Today, it is equally desirable, if not more so, to bridge the distances within complex organizations by using enhanced information technologies such as the Internet.

Thus, if leadership is to be effective, a deliberate effort must be made to overcome inevitable barriers inside organizations. Bear in mind, also, that the individual who may be a follower relative to higher-level officials may be a leader to others occupying subordinate positions. Multiple sets of leaders and followers operating at different levels in complex organizations complicate the tasks that each set and each leader must carry out. Thus, leadership development is equally important for followers who may "share" or coproduce some good or service within an organization.

Traditional Approaches to the Study of Leadership

The earliest efforts to analyze leadership employed two principal approaches, centering on the individual leader and on the leadership situation. The **traits approach** sought to explain leadership in terms of personality characteristics, such as intelligence, ambition, ego drives, and interpersonal skills. Considerable emphasis was placed on leadership traits during the early years of the twentieth century but, in numerous studies since then, the traits approach has been found to explain little. Furthermore, contrary to the most basic assumption of this approach, leaders were not found to possess common characteristics. The traits

traits approach

traditional method (now used less widely by scholars) of analyzing leadership in a group or organization; assumes that certain personality characteristics such as intelligence, ambition, tact, and diplomacy distinguish leaders from others in the group.

approach was discarded by most scholarly observers by the 1950s. Attention shifted to a seemingly more promising avenue of exploration, namely, analysis of leadership situations and how situational factors were related to what was required in a leader in a particular set of circumstances. (Interestingly, Follett had stressed the importance of situational factors in the 1920s.)

situational approach

method of analyzing leadership in a group or organization that emphasizes factors in the particular leadership situation, such as leader–follower interactions, group values, and the work being done.

The **situational approach** has become the general framework of analysis in most subsequent leadership studies. This approach does not try to explain leadership success or failure, particular styles of leadership, or why one person becomes a leader whereas another does not in terms of variations in personal skills and character. Rather, the situational approach emphasizes leader–follower interactions, the needs of the group or organization in the time period under study, the kind of work being done, general group values and ethics, and the like. From this, it follows that leaders in one situation may not be cut out to be leaders in other situations. Some years ago, a successful businessman who headed the European division of a large multinational corporation was asked to serve as dean of a business school at a large private research university on the basis of his experience. The university struggled for some years to find an acceptable candidate before he took the position. But, shortly thereafter, the faculty rebelled and the university governing board realized it had made a mistake—the successful businessman was an abject failure as a dean. Not only were the specific duties different but so, too, were the types of people involved and their values and expectations, as were the dean's interactions with university personnel as opposed to company employees. The point is that variations in the times, in circumstances, and in group characteristics help determine the most appropriate kinds of leadership and, to an important degree, who will lead. Personality, skills, ambition, and the rest make some difference but only in the context of the social environment, the leadership setting, and demands arising from the group.

Another general dimension of leadership is how specific styles of management affect the distribution of power, influence, and freedom of action of leaders and followers in an organization. Figure 6–1 illustrates a continuum of leadership behavior, suggesting the range of possibilities open to leaders in choosing management techniques. (Recall the discussions of Theories X, Y, and Z in Chapter 4, especially Tables 4–1 and 4–3.) Such choices, like leadership effectiveness, are conditioned to a considerable extent by the nature of the organization, the tasks to be completed, and nature of the group relationships between leaders and followers.

Group situations vary according to (1) *position power* of the leader, defined as the authority vested in the leader's official position; (2) *task structure* of the group, the degree to which assignments can be programmed and specified in a step-by-step fashion; and (3) leader–member *personal relationships*, based on affection, admiration, and trust of group members for the leader. Leaders who are liked and respected by a group and have a clear-cut task and high position power are in a more favorable position than leaders who have poor relationships with group members, an unstructured task, and weak position power.[49]

| FIGURE 6-1 | The Continuum of Management Behavior: Relations between Managers and Leaders |

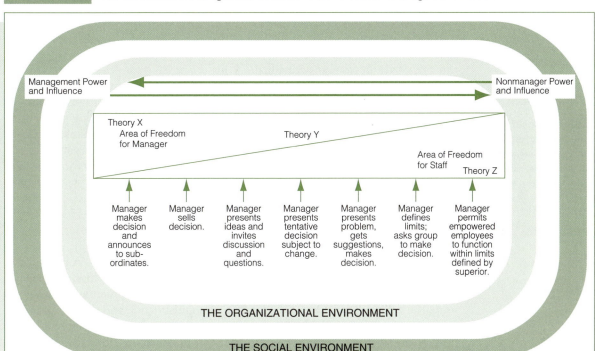

But how to choose the particular leadership style most appropriate to a given situation? Recent research suggests that leadership comes from the interaction among people in a work situation and requires a combination of interpersonal and group-situational skills. For example, if tasks are clear-cut, if relations between leader and members are positive, and if official position power is considerable, a leader is best advised to be strongly directive rather than democratic and nondirective. An All-American quarterback does not call the plays by taking votes in the huddle. By the same token, the chairperson of a voluntary community-service committee cannot order group members to vote in a certain way or to act according to his or her directions. This theory of leadership is important for what it suggests about what *can* be changed to improve leadership effectiveness (rank, task structure, concern for followers) and what *cannot* be changed (leader personality, work situation, organizational characteristics). Leader traits (within limits), situational dynamics, and relationships dictate the most effective leadership style. The relationship among personal traits, personality, and the situation describes the most common approach to studying leadership. The most successful style must be determined almost on a case-by-case basis; it is anything but preordained.

Leadership in a nonhierarchical organization is defined as a property of the social system in which individuals, groups, leaders, and followers interact. Leadership is "an outcome of *collective* meaning-making, not the result of influence of vision from an individual . . . [it] is created by people making sense and meaning of their work together, and this process, in turn, can bring leaders into being."[50] This model of **relational leadership** encourages responsiveness to customers, grants increased nonroutine decision-making power to people with direct customer contact, and makes everyone accountable for the outcome of their work as well as for fulfilling the mission of the organization. These ideas more closely fit the model of learning organizations introduced in Chapter 4, requiring a flexible concept of leadership in an open system that emphasizes continuous developmental and adaptive change. These concepts also reflect the notion of the reverse pyramid (discussed in Chapters 1 and 4), and are reminiscent of the thinking of Chester Barnard (Chapter 4).

In the early 1980s, research findings appeared that, ironically, gave renewed emphasis to the importance of personality characteristics in potential and actual leaders. This is suggestive of the traits approach, which has been out of favor among most students of leadership for some time, but there are important differences. One is the far greater sophistication and understanding we now possess of individual and group psychology. Another is the explicit link assumed in the recent research between personality and leader behavior, making assessment of personalities more meaningful. And there has been a systematic effort to identify different dimensions of leader personality in much greater detail.[51]

> **relational leadership**
>
> leaders must not only be competent at traditional skills such as goal setting, conflict management, and motivation, but also be able to acquire information from group members and adapt their leadership styles to fit the needs of followers.

Challenges of Administrative Leadership

As anyone with managerial responsibilities already knows, attempts to change or direct group behavior can be frustrating. It is difficult enough to change individual behavior; it can be extremely difficult to change the behavior of an organizational subgroup made up of diverse individuals. For a leader to overcome member resistance requires the ability to convey a sense of the larger issues, mission, and needs that justify the existence of the organization. In essence, this means (1) broadening the horizons of members to include a fuller picture of the organization and reconciling personal and organizational goals; (2) persuading others to do what is in the best interest of the organization for their own reasons; (3) coordinating and integrating specialized staff functions; (4) stimulating group action toward common goals; (5) serving as model of organizational behavior; and (6) defending the organization and, if necessary, managing crises that threaten group cohesion (see Table 6–1). The result, ideally, would be that, when actions are proposed that affect specific work units,

TABLE 6-1   Roles of Administrative Leadership

1. DIRECTING AND RECONCILING PERSONAL AND ORGANIZATIONAL GOALS
- Bringing coherence to the multitude of diverse activities within an organization
- Defining the nature of problems to be addressed
- Reconciling personal and organizational goals
- Persuading those responsible to direct their work toward common organizational objectives

2. MOTIVATING OTHERS TO DO WHAT IS BEST FOR THE ORGANIZATION
- Inspiring followers in the most positive fashion
- Using a combination of incentives appropriate to the interests of those doing the work
- Building cohesiveness in the organization through member satisfaction
- Raising customer service quality standards
- Persuading others to think less in traditional bureaucratic terms than as coaches, teachers, or facilitators of change

3. COORDINATING AND INTEGRATING ACTIVITIES
- Coordinating and integrating the varied functions and tasks of increasingly specialized staff members
- Delegating and relying on the competence of subordinates as they attempt to organize efforts of staff members into a coherent whole
- If the tasks of directing and motivating members have been carried out effectively, coordinating and integrating their efforts should follow naturally
- Conceptually, there are a number of factors to be considered

4. INNOVATING AND POINTING THE WAY
- Serving as a "spark plug" or the "one who makes it happen"
- Stimulating group action without coercion
- Knowing when the group is ready to be directed, and when members expect to be told what to do
- In these circumstances, the tasks to be performed may be short-term and clearly defined; those responsible will succeed or fail within a limited time period

5. SERVING AS EXTERNAL SPOKESPERSON—AND "GLADIATOR"
- Representing the organization's views and interests in the external environment
- Articulating formal organizational positions to those outside
- Serving in an advocacy role when the organization seeks to secure additional resources or to maintain the resources it has (a task that has become more important as budgets have become more constrained)
- All leaders must periodically defend their organizations

6. MANAGING CRISES
- Responding to crises of various kinds—military, economic, or natural disasters
- Dealing with the occasional serious problem or difficulty that arises in their units or that affects one of their clienteles
- Defending the organization against external attempts to downsize or eliminate
- Crises, even major ones, are generally limited to particular suborganizations or governments and, at least, have a definable end point

members of those units—by understanding larger organizational purposes—would be more inclined to accept, and even to take an active part in, what their leadership is trying to do. Willingness to actively participate in work re-design requires a high level of trust between members and supervisors, often lacking in many organizations.

leader as director

refers to the challenge of bringing some unity of purpose to an organization's members.

The key to a leader's efforts as **director** is to reconcile personal and organizational goals and to create as much psychological overlap as possible between the two. If a leader can induce individual members to internalize general objectives of the organization, most of this task will have been accomplished. This might be done by direct and indirect persuasion, by example, or by developing members' understanding of rationales for pursuing particular objectives or adopting specific tactics. To the extent that there is conflict over goals, of course, this challenge will remain an ongoing one, with considerable potential for difficulty. The optimum situation is one in which members see pursuit of organizational goals as consistent with, and supportive of, achievement of their personal goals. There is a substantial body of research suggesting that coercive measures aimed at motivating employees by fear of punishment may have short-term impacts, but are not effective in the long run.[52]

leader as motivator

key task centering on devices such as tangible benefits, positive social interaction, work interest, encouragement by job supervisors, and leadership that is self-confident, persuasive, fair, and supportive.

Motivation continues to be a complex task of leadership. People respond to leadership that is clearly defined and, at the same time, persuasive, fair, and supportive. But no rule is universally applicable; exceptions are frequent, and leaders have to remain alert if they expect to cope with the full range of motivational problems that could arise in their organizations. Using the analogy of the carrot and the stick, the stick is definitely our second choice, especially in organizations that encourage participation. On the basis of research conducted over several decades, there is reason to believe that emphasis should be given to incentives such as offering attractive salaries, fringe benefits, and working conditions; creating positive social interaction among groups of workers; and making the work as interesting and challenging as possible. The problem is that different incentives work for different people, and leaders face the continuing challenge of tailoring these motivators to the needs, preferences, and attitudes of organization members or member groups.[53] More and more organizations are also realizing the importance of selecting and evaluating supervisors. Thus, leaders should be concerned about the quality of face-to-face supervision, as well as tangible benefits and incentives and the intrinsic interest the work offers.

leader as coordinator

(and integrator) involves bringing some order to the multitude of functions within a complex organization.

Another dimension of leadership is **coordination** and integration of organizational activities in order to mesh the leader's own tasks with those of the remainder of the organization. The need here is to avoid working at cross-purposes, making certain that leaders and followers generally share the same vision, or understanding, of the organization's mission and its intended goals. This directly relates to the leader-as-director challenge in the effort to create constancy of purpose and psychological overlap among several different sets of goals. It is also linked to the role of leader as motivator in the creation of inducements designed to move members in particular directions.

Most important is to recognize the tendency for individuals concentrating on their own particular work environment to develop **tunnel vision**, through which they see the worth of their own tasks but fail to appreciate the importance of other aspects of the organization's activity. For example, a leader attempting to change the operations of a division, staff, or branch, for the purpose of strengthening the organization's overall capacities or performance, may encounter resistance from members in that subsection who believe that their procedures and output are adequate for their purposes. Their frame of reference is *their* work, defined as the work of the subsection, whereas the leadership's responsibilities encompass the work of the entire organization.

Mechanisms for generating ideas for work redesign include focus groups, surveys, newsletters, suggestion boxes, question-and-answer sessions, and advance communication of proposed actions to members. This amounts to regularized **brainstorming** for ideas, a process that, by involving members, is likely to make final decisions more palatable to more people in the organization. Circulating information about actions already taken can also be beneficial. Not circulating information widely can result in built-up resentments, which can linger and affect subsequent organizational activities.

Even in the best of circumstances, leaders will have to manage diverse operations on a smoothly coordinated time schedule. Personnel, materials, financial resources, services to consumers of the organization's output (however defined), and so on, all have to be integrated into the organization's ongoing activities. In this respect, advance planning is a key leadership function to ensure that the necessary components are on hand as needed. Every organization in existence faces that common need, and every leader is expected to meet it.

In addition, leaders are required to serve as a "spark plug" or the "one who makes it happen"—an idea that is widespread in the conventional wisdom about groups and organizations, and it appears to have some validity. But the particular conditions prevailing in the group situation may strongly affect a leader's opportunities to stimulate group action. An example is the situation of the captain of an aircraft in its final approach before landing, when leadership decisions, instructions, and actions are crucial and no one would realistically want him or her to discuss or evaluate proposed options with the flight crew. Other examples of well-structured tasks for which a leader is the catalyst for group action include rescue operations after a disaster, infantry combat, and a football team's last-minute drive for the winning touchdown.

Many tasks, however, are less structured, more routine, and more time-consuming. Here, too, a leader may be a successful **catalyst**, provided that members understand and support organizational objectives and that the leader has made clear how individual activities help promote those objectives. For example, an academic department chair concerned about financial support for the department from the university administration may encourage faculty members to pursue research interests as well as excellence in teaching. Published articles, books, and research papers enhance a department's prestige

tunnel vision

results from a fear of mistakes, missed deadlines, and focus on a narrow work environment, which limits the ability to see an organization's activities as a whole.

brainstorming

free-form and creative technique for collecting and discussing ideas from all participants without criticism or judgment.

leader as catalyst (and innovator)

formalized conception of the "spark plug" role in a group setting. As part of the catalyst role, a leader is also expected to introduce innovations into an organization.

outside the university, providing a strong argument for continued internal support. Even though such activities are conducted largely on an individual basis, a chair can relate them to departmental well-being and thus attempt to motivate faculty members in those terms.

innovation

the introduction of something new into an organization.

The process of **innovation** is tied to the role of a leader as catalyst because, in many instances, an organization's routine operations do not require very substantial direct participation. Indeed, delegation of authority is a critical leadership function. When normal procedures are all that is required, the leader is ordinarily in the background—and is best advised to remain there so as to permit members to function with some measure of independence. However, changes in existing routines must usually be initiated outside the group or subgroup because the routines may serve a stabilizing function inside the group and have the support of its members. Furthermore, routines frequently evolve in a way that reflects values and preferences of the group regarding not only the mechanics but also the very purposes of group activities. Thus, group members may interpret a proposed change in routine as a comment on their purposes as well as their procedures (which may be true). The challenge to the leader, then, is to justify adequately to group members any proposed change he or she deems necessary in the context of the larger organization.[54] Clearly, the catalyst role is important if innovation is to be brought about.

One of the most challenging roles for leaders is serving as spokespersons regarding budgetary (and other policy-related) decision making, in which favorable portrayal of the organization can be decisive in influencing those who make decisions for the next fiscal year that can have real impact on the agency. This, however, is only the most visible kind of leadership opportunity. In fact, the task for the **leader as gladiator** is ongoing—standing up for the organization and its members when there is a complaint about its operation, anticipating and preparing for changes in the external environment that might adversely affect the organization, or simply keeping abreast of developments in the larger organization as they relate to the values, work, and well-being of the unit.

leader as gladiator

leadership role in which the leader seeks to promote the work of an organization, often in an effort to secure additional resources, as well as defending the organization in the external environment.

Few things are better for group morale than a leader who willingly and effectively defends the group's collective and individual welfare. Aside from the practical benefits such advocacy can produce, a leader's active support and defense of the organization represents, in concrete form, faith in staff members and their work. The leader, in acting as gladiator, is demonstrating that he or she is a part of the organization rather than aloof from it. In addition, the leader as gladiator is, in effect, carrying out one of the cardinal principles of good management: Bestow praise publicly! Defense or advocacy on behalf of the organization constitutes collective rather than individual praise, but it indicates positive feedback in a strategically important form, and that is usually not lost on members of an organization.

A recently emergent dimension of leadership, however, goes beyond this sort of problem. It has to do with growing fiscal pressures on many public entities, particularly in state and local governments. Linked to all the other five roles, the **leader as crisis manager** must cope with an unpleasant new reality—that economic and other resources are not without limits. Such problems, although not minor, are generally limited to particular suborganizations or governments and, at least, have a definable end point. However, some elements of crisis management reflect deeper and more enduring fiscal problems. And because it is clear that many citizens are unwilling to pay higher taxes in order to meet rising costs of government and that resource scarcity will be with us for some time, these leadership challenges *lack* the kind of end point characteristic of more immediate difficulties. In recent years, various responses to scarcity have been developed for administrative leaders to implement.

One is the growing practice of **downsizing**, which poses special difficulties for the leader responsible for carrying it out. With slower growth in the economy, and perhaps with significant contractions in the public sector, leaders must deal with unfamiliar situations that require new strategies and methods for rendering them acceptable to organization subordinates. Various tactics exist for downsizing, addressed to the political and economic/technical needs of the organization, both internally and externally. Tactics designed to resist organizational decline include mobilizing dependent clienteles, diversifying programs, targeting high-visibility programs for elimination (to make it politically costly for those making the decision), adopting user charges and other means of direct funding for services when possible, retaining internal *esprit de corps* and morale by developing a siege mentality, and improving productivity. Tactics designed to make downsizing smoother include cutting programs having low prestige or those providing services to politically weak clienteles or those run by weak subunits. It is also possible to vary leadership styles at each stage in the downsizing process, to ask employees to sacrifice by deferring raises or by taking early retirement, and to shift programs to other agencies, thus reducing overall expenditures. How effective any or all of these are, of course, is another question.

The other leader roles are profoundly affected by changes brought about by decline and the need for downsizing. For one thing, members of any organization may experience a shift in personal goals, tending toward the conserver mentality that is bent on "holding on if we can." The branch chief within a government bureaucracy, the manager of a plant within a large manufacturing conglomerate, and the academic department chair within a college structure headed by a dean share a periodic need to go to bat for their organizations under such circumstances. To some extent, that can be useful, but a leader must try to channel that motivation into useful and productive directions. The motivator role is obviously affected, for, in the face of deteriorating employee morale, the leader must be able to "rally the troops" in order to continue essential activities at an acceptable level of performance. The coordinator role must be fulfilled even more effectively—with the resource base of the organization shrinking, ever more careful coordination of human and material resources is necessary. The role of catalyst/innovator likewise is more sensitive than ever because it falls to the leader to stimulate and direct the changes that must be made. Ideally, this

leader as crisis manager

involves coping with both immediate and long-term difficulties, more serious than routine managerial challenges.

downsizing

current fiscal pressures on public organizations have spawned the need for downsizing in many places, forcing leaders to use a variety of new tactics. At the same time, they must strive to maintain organization morale and performance levels, while holding to a minimum the negative effects of organizational decline. See also **reductions-in-force (RIFs)**.

should include the leader having previously anticipated problems of decline, so that resource reserves have been acquired as "organizational insurance." In this respect, foresight and keen judgment are valuable leadership assets. Concern for innovation must also be manifested in another way. Because of the possible tendency toward conserver behavior referred to earlier, organization leaders must resist pressures to conduct only "business as usual" at the very time when complex and interdependent problems in the organization's environment cry out for innovative efforts at solving them. Leaders and their organizations are truly on the horns of a dilemma in this regard: declining resources evoke pressures for retrenchment and holding ground, but social and economic complexities underlying resource decline demand vigorous and innovative responses. No easy solutions exist to this basic dilemma, but efforts to develop answers are essential in the immediate future. Finally, and perhaps most important, the crisis manager role calls for a leader's best efforts in order to reduce as much as possible adverse consequences of organizational decline for the administrative unit.

shared vision

foundation of core values within which leaders, managers, and employees interact and on which everything else in the organization is based.

In sum, organizations comprising diverse specialties and functions require efforts at the top, as well as throughout the ranks, to bring about satisfactory coordination and integration of goals. Organization members need some sense that their different functions somehow fit into a larger **shared vision** of the mission of the organization. And leaders must take responsibility for instilling that view.

What Makes an Effective Leader?

We come back, then, to the persistent question that is at the core of most inquiries into the subject of leadership. Without claiming to have found the answers, let us suggest a number of general considerations relevant to achieving effective leadership (see Figure 6–2).

First, it appears that a leader is wise to convey to members that they are regarded as valuable to the organization and competent in their work. Many are, of course, quite competent, but the point here is that competent workers will appreciate that management has taken note of their worth, and less competent workers may work harder to live up to the leadership's expectations. The expectation of competence may, in fact, be a key factor in developing motivation to be competent.

Second, there is strong evidence that, if staff members of an organization perceive the leadership as being receptive to ideas, feedback, comments, and even complaints from below, they will be far more willing to respond to leaders' directives.[55] For one thing, communication from members gives leaders the clearest picture of what is important to employees and of their general attitudes and aspirations. This cannot help but make it easier for the leaders to communicate meaningfully. More important, the leaders' willingness to listen to, and act on, useful ideas from the ranks builds a sense of cohesiveness among the members that is likely to increase each member's commitment to the organization's well-being. Without such feedback, it is virtually impossible for leaders to make the changes necessary to improve work performance.

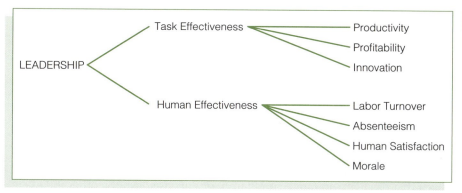

FIGURE 6-2

Effective Leadership

Source: © 2013 Cengage Learning.

Third, several studies suggest that the democratic leader is more effective in the broad view than any other type, with member satisfaction clearly higher in democratically led groups, and interaction among group members distinctly more relaxed and mutually supportive.[56] At the same time, the democratic leaders in these studies did not abdicate leadership functions but managed them in an open, participative, and supportive way. There is some reason to believe that such a style may work more effectively with some types of followers than with others (for example, professionals and some staff members in flat hierarchies with less formal structures) and perhaps with some types of personalities than with others. The general pattern seems to be one of fairly successful leadership direction under democratic conditions.

Fourth, a study of a work group in private industry suggests indirectly some of the leadership features to which employees may respond favorably. The study indicated that the more highly employees rated supervisors on a number of key attributes, the less employees expressed a desire for unionization. The attributes mentioned were fairness, use of authority, the ability to handle people, giving credit, readiness to discuss problems, and keeping employees informed. This combination suggests the scope of abilities demanded in many leadership situations.

At the risk of oversimplification, it is worth pointing out several other important qualities of leadership:

1. Ideally, a leader should be clear, reasonable, and consistent concerning expectations of, and standards of judgment for, member performance.
2. A leader is advised to deal openly, fairly, and equitably with all members, making distinctions among members only on work-related, not personal or lifestyle, criteria.
3. A leader should maintain a fairly firm hold on the reins of leadership, at the same time fostering a genuinely constructive two-way flow of communication by explaining rationales for proposed courses of action and by acting on worthwhile suggestions from members.
4. A leader should move carefully and democratically to secure consensus—more than merely a majority vote—on significant actions. One tactic is to strive for consensus by means of an extensive consultative process, which requires formal votes only when absolutely necessary.

5. A wise leader will try to prevent "empire building" and other divisive tendencies within the ranks. The goal is to prevent disunity as one step toward building cohesion within the group.
6. A leader should absolutely avoid cronyism (partiality to friends and associates) and favoritism.
7. Perhaps hardest of all, a leader can greatly influence the whole course of events in the organization by setting the tone of interactions with the members. He or she must behave in a manner consistent with the goals set for the entire organization or work group.

Although *tone* is admittedly a vague term, the leader sets some behavioral standards that often are imitated, consciously or unconsciously, by other members of the group. Clearly, this will not happen in all instances. However, where a leader has, in general, acted constructively, the chances are greatly improved that members will respond in kind, both in their attitudes and behaviors toward the leader and in their general demeanor toward one another. These generalizations have their exceptions but, as standards for positive and enlightened leadership, they appear to have much to recommend them.[57]

Of course, there are some obstacles to effective leadership. The situational potential for leadership may vary according to the organizational level and experience of a particular group leader. It may also vary according to the flexibility that higher-level leaders permit within the rest of the organization. The tighter the rein held on subordinates by superiors, the less chance subordinates will have to exercise leadership within their own organizational subunits. In addition, if an organization is highly structured—some would say bureaucratized—the possibilities of leadership in the manner we have described are more limited. This is so because more of the decisions concerning management of organizational affairs are already settled questions and thus are not ordinarily subject to being reopened. In this sense, bureaucracy is not conducive to leadership.

Individual goals may simply remain beyond the reach of the leaders' influence, though cooperation could more easily be induced from less secure members than from those with seniority, tenure, and the like. The leadership will probably have to accept some disparities between what it seeks and what individual members are willing to contribute.

Fighting tunnel vision and articulating a shared vision (among both members and leaders) may turn out to be a frustrating job. In organizations undergoing staff reductions, it is especially difficult to focus attention on anything other than job security. It is also difficult to innovate in highly structured organizations, and a body of professional opinion holds that traditional management values—of the scientific-management school and its conceptual descendants—hamper development of conditions conducive to innovation.[58] Additionally, values and preferences of organization members may prove to be so entrenched that leaders may have to coerce staff members to use new procedures and may fail entirely to instill new attitudes. In the face of stiff resistance, a leader must weigh the costs of coercion against the projected benefits of innovation.

Green Zone

Green Zone, a 2010 film starring Matt Damon, centers on the task of American soldiers to find weapons of mass destruction (WMDs) in Iraq. The existence of WMDs justified American involvement in Iraq, according to American political leaders at the time the movie takes place (2003). Damon plays U.S. Army Chief Warrant Officer Roy Miller, who leads his squad of soldiers on the dangerous investigation of local buildings and sites, said to possibly store such weapons. They are continually confronted with empty warehouses and abandoned sites—and no WMDs.

Information leads Miller to the Green Zone, also known as the International Zone of Baghdad. There, he seeks the truth regarding the existence of WMDs and discovers that there had been no program since the Persian Gulf War and that the suggestion that such weapons existed was simply used as an excuse to invade Iraq. Miller shares this revelation with American media sources as the movie closes.

Green Zone has been charged with being anti-American, as it addresses the controversial subject of United States involvement in Iraq. Many see it as a topic in need of further discussion, however, as President George W. Bush, and his administration, made the executive decision to send troops to war and to spend billions of dollars on divisive war. Equally difficult are decisions to withdraw troops after they have been deployed to a combat zone.

Keeping the qualities of leadership in mind, how does a chief executive make a decision such as going to war? What is the role of a chief executive in developing and implementing a policy? Refer to news media coverage of President Obama's decisions to launch air strikes against the regime of Libya's Col. Muammar el-Qaddafi in March 2011 and to raid Osama bin Laden's compound in pakistan.

Source: http://www.greenzonemovie.com/, accessed March 21, 2011.

A gladiator will not always succeed in protecting his or her organization from the external environment; depending on the mix of failure and success, this could work to the leader's disadvantage both inside and outside the organization. Part of a leader's skill should lie in knowing when to fight and when not to.

Finally, effective leadership is conditioned by the particular combination of people, tasks, and organizational dynamics present in each situation. Virtually all of these leadership tasks face obstacles to their being fully achieved—in the organization's dynamics, the mix of members, and the nature of the external environment. Despite what we know about leadership, it is still not possible to construct an all-inclusive set of leadership guidelines that will cover every leadership situation. Although leadership operates within many contemporary constraints, it still occupies a place of considerable importance in organizations.

Leadership in contemporary organizations clearly operates under greater restraints from several standpoints—diminished legitimacy, declining resources, pressures for greater diversity in the workplace, public distrust, and rising turbulence internally and externally, to name only a few. Yet many still aspire to positions of leadership, and there is no question that effective leadership is essential in our attempts to cope with rapid change. Despite many things that are very different from the past, there is continuing and justifiable interest in leadership roles.

Summary

Leadership of bureaucracies makes a vital contribution to the success or failure of administrative organizations, especially from the standpoint of promoting accountability, ethics, efficiency, and results. Executive leadership differs from leadership within the ranks of administrators themselves in several different ways. American chief executives are highly visible to the public and are perceived as being able to provide both political leadership and policy initiative; they are also usually considered responsible for the operations of executive-branch bureaucracies. Most chief executives lack specialized knowledge and must rely on persuasion rather than on command authority.

Linkages between chief executives and bureaucracies come into play in policy development and policy implementation. In policy development, chief executives depend on the expertise of professionals in the bureaucracy for both general program advice and specific proposals. Executive dependency increases with program complexity and bureaucratic autonomy. Bureaucracies play an even greater role in policy implementation. General factors that can contribute to chief executives' influence over bureaucracy include support in their legislatures, the degree of policy and program initiative that chief executives exercise, and their capacity to direct governmental responses to crisis situations.

Other, more tangible factors that affect daily administrative operations are crucial to executive leadership. A chief executive is strengthened by having a central role in formulating the executive budget; related functions include forging a stronger role for the budget office in management coordination, requiring central clearance for legislative proposals, and exerting greater control over the regulatory process. The president's influence is greater at the federal level than that exercised by most governors, although many governors have had their budgetary powers strengthened in recent decades. Many local executives do not have comparable influence in local government budget making; city managers stand out among those who do play key budgetary roles.

Personnel controls represent a second major instrument of chief-executive leadership. Executives usually have greater impact working under a patronage system than when merit systems are in effect. Interactions among presidents, their top-level political appointees, and senior career officials are complex, involving different sets of assumptions and modes of operation on the part of each. Governors often have less control over budget and personnel than does a president, due to greater limitations on appointments and dismissals, and the fact that many states elect at least some other executive-branch officials separately from the chief executive. Reorganization of administrative agencies may have higher costs and fewer benefits for a chief executive than is generally thought. Reorganization strategies may clash, requiring care and sophistication in their use.

A major factor in chief-executive influence is control over, and the uses of, information. The president and other chief executives may be dependent on bureaucratic sources of information but there are ways of overcoming this dependency. Governors are in a stronger position now than in the past with regard to their information capabilities. Chief executives must closely monitor information transmittal and must also make deliberate efforts to promote feedback from those in the administrative hierarchy.

In complex organizations, administrative leadership is multidimensional; it is sensitive to the changing nature of the work environment, and recognizes distinctions at the technical, managerial, and institutional levels. Leaders in such settings must direct multiple functions at each level. They must also make an effort to overcome various kinds of distance within the organization.

Traditionally, leadership has been studied through two approaches. The traits approach emphasized the personality and aptitudes of individuals who were leaders, in an effort to isolate leader characteristics. This conception was followed by the situational approach, which views all organizational circumstances—structural, interpersonal, task-related, and value-based—as crucial to the kind of leadership that comes to exist. Currently, a combination of the two approaches, with emphasis on the relationships between leaders and followers, is most common in studies of leadership.

Variations in group situations may significantly affect leader effectiveness. Factors in the group situation important in this regard are position power of the leader, task structure of the group, and leader–member personal relationships. To be effective, leadership must vary with circumstances in the group and the work situation.

Discussion Questions

1. If chief executives are expected by the public to direct government bureaucracies effectively, yet are unable to assert the kind of leadership expected, what are the implications for public trust in executive leadership?

2. Discuss how and why executive power seems to increase after every emergency or crisis situation. Why doesn't executive authority simply revert to what it was before the crisis occurred?

3. What expectations, interests, and behavior patterns might be said to characterize newly installed political appointees in formal positions of leadership in executive agencies? How do many, if not most, appointees interact with the senior career

officials in their respective agencies? With the chief executive who appointed them? Discuss.

4. According to Hugh Heclo, what informal behavior patterns seem to be followed by many bureaucrats? What justifications or rationales might be advanced in support of those behaviors? In your judgment, are these adequate, defensible rationales? Why or why not?

5. It is said that in politics, knowledge—and therefore information—is power. Discuss how chief executives can assure themselves of an adequate flow of accurate information.

6. What are the principal instruments that can be used to make a chief executive "strong"? Even if

all are available to an individual chief executive, are there any constraints on executive leadership? If so, what are they?

7. Discuss the commonalities and differences in leadership resources among chief executives at the federal, state, and local levels.

8. If "leaders are made, not born," what "makes" them leaders? How much difference does individual personality make? What about circumstances in the individual leadership situation? What factors seem to you to be most important? Why? Discuss.

9. Discuss how position power, task structure of the group, and leader–member personal relationships interact to influence the choice of leadership style. Can generalizations be drawn confidently in this regard? Discuss.

10. How are leadership style, group morale, and overall group performance interrelated? Identify the leadership factors most important to group morale, and discuss the links between morale and performance.

Key Terms and Concepts

political persuasion or "jawboning", 232

policy development, 233

policy implementation, 233

instruments, or tools, of leadership, 234

central clearance, 238

executive budgets, 239

veto power, 240

item veto (or line-item veto), 240

bureaucratic resistance, 243

reductions-in-force (RIFs), 245

reorganization, 247

Posse Comitatus Act of 1878, 248

task forces, 250

exception principle, 251

executive privilege, 252

traits approach, 259

situational approach, 260

relational leadership, 262

leader as director, 264

leader as motivator, 264

leader as coordinator, 264

tunnel vision, 265

brainstorming, 265

leader as catalyst (and innovator), 265

innovation, 266

leader as gladiator, 266

leader as crisis manager, 267

downsizing, 267

shared vision, 268

Suggested Readings

Abramson, Mark A., and Paul R. Lawrence, eds. *Learning the Ropes: Insights for Political Appointees.* Lanham, Md.: Rowman & Littlefield, 2005.

Allison, Graham, and Phillip Zelikow. *Essence of Decision: Explaining the Cuban Missile Crisis.* 2nd ed. New York: Longman, 1999.

Antonakis, John, Anna T. Cianciolo, and Robert J. Sternberg, eds. *The Nature of Leadership.* Thousand Oaks, Calif.: Sage, 2011.

Barge, J. Kevin. *Leadership: Communication Skills for Organizations and Groups.* New York: St. Martin's Press, 1994.

Bennis, Warren, and Bert Nanus. *Leaders.* 2nd ed. New York: Harper Business, 1997.

Berman, Larry, ed. *Looking Back on the Reagan Presidency.* Baltimore: Johns Hopkins University Press, 1990.

Beyle, Thad L. *Governors and Hard Times.* Washington, D.C.: CQ Press, 1992.

Bryson, John M., and Barbara C. Crosby. *Leadership for the Common Good: Tackling Public Problems in a Shared-Power World.* 2nd ed. San Francisco: Jossey-Bass, 2005.

Campbell, Colin, and Bert A. Rockman, eds. *The Clinton Legacy.* New York: Seven Bridges Press, 2000.

Cronin, Thomas E. *The State of the Presidency.* 3rd ed. Boston: Little, Brown, 1990.

Edwards, George C., III, and Stephen J. Wayne. *Presidential Leadership: Politics and Policy Making.* 8th ed. Belmont, Calif.: Wadsworth/Thomson Learning, 2009.

Ellis, Richard, and Aaron Wildavsky. *Dilemmas of Presidential Leadership: From Washington through Lincoln.* Piscataway, N.J.: Transaction, 1989.

Fisher, Louis. *The Politics of Shared Power: Congress and the Executive.* 4th ed. College Station: Texas A&M University Press, 1998.

Gardiner, John W. *On Leadership.* New York: Free Press, 1993.

Graham, Bob, with Jeff Nussbaum. *Intelligence Matters: The CIA, the FBI, Saudi Arabia, and the Failure of America's War on Terror.* New York: Random House, 2008.

Guest, Robert H., Paul Hersey, and Kenneth H. Blanchard. *Organizational Change through Effective Leadership.* 2nd ed. Upper Saddle River, N.J.: FT Press, 1986.

Hunt, James G. *Leadership: A New Synthesis.* Newbury Park, Calif.: Sage, 1991.

Johnson, Craig E. *Meeting the Ethical Challenges of Leadership: Casting Light or Shadow.* Thousand Oaks, Calif.: Sage, 2008.

Jones, Charles O. *The Presidency in a Separated System.* 2nd ed. Washington, D.C.: Brookings Institution Press, 2005.

———. *The Trusteeship Presidency: Jimmy Carter and the United States Congress.* Baton Rouge: Louisiana State University Press, 1988.

Kernell, Samuel. *Going Public: New Strategies of Presidential Leadership.* 3rd ed. Washington, D.C.: CQ Press, 2006.

Kouzes, James M., Barry Z. Posner, and Tom Peters. *The Leadership Challenge: How to Get Extraordinary Things Done in Organizations.* 3rd ed. San Francisco: Jossey-Bass, 2002.

Lynch, Richard. *Lead! How Public and Nonprofit Managers Can Bring Out the Best in Themselves and Their Organizations.* San Francisco: Jossey-Bass, 1993.

Maranto, Robert. *Beyond a Government of Strangers: How Career Executives and Political Appointees Can Turn Conflict to Cooperation.* Lanham, Md.: Lexington Books, 2005.

Martin, David L. *Running City Hall: Municipal Administration in America.* 2nd ed. Tuscaloosa: University of Alabama Press, 1990.

McClellan, Scott. *What Happened: Inside the Bush White House and the Culture of Deception.* New York: Public Affairs Books, 2008.

Nathan, Richard P. *The Administrative Presidency.* New York: Prentice Hall, 1983.

Neustadt, Richard. *Presidential Power and the Modern Presidents.* New York: Free Press, 1991.

Pfiffner, James P., ed. *The Managerial Presidency.* 2nd ed. College Station: Texas A&M University Press, 1999.

Risen, James. *State of War: The Secret History of the CIA and the Bush Administration.* New York: Free Press, 2007.

Rockman, Bert A. *The Leadership Question: The Presidency and the American System.* New York: Praeger, 1984.

Rockman, Bert A., and Richard W. Waterman. *Presidential Leadership: The Vortex of Power.* New York: Oxford University Press, 2008.

Rosenthal, Alan. *Governors and Legislatures: Contending Powers.* Washington, D.C.: CQ Press, 1990.

Sabato, Larry. *Goodbye to Good-Time Charlie: The American Governorship Transformed.* 2nd ed. Washington, D.C.: CQ Press, 1988.

———. *The Sixth Year Itch: The Rise and Fall of George W. Bush's Presidency.* New York: Longman, 2007.

Seidman, Harold, and Robert Gilmour. *Politics, Position, and Power: From the Positive to the Regulatory State.* 4th ed. New York: Oxford University Press, 1986.

Selznick, Philip. *Leadership in Administration: A Sociological Interpretation.* Berkeley: University of California Press, 1984.

Smith, Peter B., and Mark F. Peterson. *Leadership, Organizations, and Culture.* Newbury Park, Calif.: Sage, 1988.

Suskind, Ron. *The Price of Loyalty: George W. Bush, the White House, and the Education of Paul H. O'Neill.* New York: Simon & Schuster, 2004.

Van Wart, Montgomery. *Dynamics of Leadership in Public Service.* 2nd ed. Armonk, N.Y.: M. E. Sharpe, 2011.

Van Wart, Montgomery, with Paul Suino. *Leadership in Public Organizations: An Introduction.* New York: M.E. Sharpe, 2007.

Waterman, Richard W. *Presidential Influence and the Administrative State.* Knoxville: University of Tennessee Press, 1989.

Wildavsky, Aaron. *The Beleaguered Presidency.* New Brunswick, N.J.: Transaction, 1991.

PART III

The Core Functions of Public Management

THIS SECTION covers three functions central to the conduct of public administration: (1) public personnel administration and human resources development (including public-sector collective bargaining); (2) the budgetary process; and (3) public-policy and program implementation. Each of these represents a fundamentally important set of activities in administrative practice. Together, they form the core processes of public-sector operations.

The personnel and human resource development function, treated in Chapter 7, concerns, among other things, criteria and methods for hiring individuals into the public service in national, state, and local government; for training and skill development; for promoting and transferring them within the workforce ranks; for strengthening labor–management relations; for contracting out and privatizing certain positions; and, on occasion, for dismissing unqualified individuals from their jobs. Politically charged issues such as collective bargaining, pay and benefits, outsourcing, patronage, privatization, and affirmative action pose difficult questions that must be answered within the domain of public personnel administration. There also have been significant changes in the national government's basic approaches to personnel administration, stemming from attempts to create new federal departments initially without union representation; privatize portions of the federal workforce; "pay gaps" resulting from differences in public and private salaries; and the opening of more federal grants and contracts to nongovernmental, private, nonprofit, and faith-based organizations. In response to severe budgetary and fiscal constraints, President Obama froze federal civilian employees' salaries for 2011–2012. Furthermore, collective bargaining and union membership have become highly contentious subjects in public-sector labor–management relations at all levels of government, but especially in state and local governments, where public-employee unionization and bargaining are divisive issues.

The budgetary process, discussed in Chapter 8, is obviously important because of rising deficits and debt, and because of increased costs of providing government services and political conflicts over allocation of limited public funds. It is important also because control over major aspects of budgeting processes represents crucial political power. In the past half-century, the political stakes in the budgetary game have risen steadily. In recent years, government officials at all levels have paid considerable attention to assessing the results of expenditures, reducing budget deficits, and gaining greater control over public spending. Recent proposals call for major reforms in entitlement spending, Social Security benefits, and taxation.

Chapter 9 explores the vital subject of administering public policies and programs. This includes planning activities, program analysis, legislation, implementation, and program evaluation, in an era of downsizing political mistrust and chronic fiscal stress. At the same time, we have seen the emergence of concerns and innovations—among them, a renewed commitment to training and customer service, greater use of technology by public employees, managing for results, and increasing concern for institutional security—that reflect both increased complexities and new challenges for government at all levels. Policy problems have become far more complex, and this entire area reflects the need for more sophisticated recruiting, training, and systematic approaches to job enrichment and performance management.

Public Personnel Administration and Human Resources Development

I don't think it does anybody any good when public employees are denigrated or vilified or their rights are infringed upon. We need to attract the best and the brightest to public service. These times demand it. We're not going to attract the best teachers for our kids, for example, if they only make a fraction of what other professionals make. We're not going to convince the bravest Americans to put their lives on the line as police officers or firefighters if we don't properly reward that bravery.

Barack Obama
Washington, D.C.
February 28, 2011

diversity

reflects the goal of many affirmative action programs to diversify the workforce to reflect the population demographics (makeup) in the affected jurisdiction.

From the time the first executive-branch agency opened its doors, even before ratification of the U.S. Constitution, the personnel recruitment, selection, training, and promotion functions were vital parts of American public administration. They have evolved from relatively obscure, often routine, functions of government to a prominent, frequently controversial area of administrative practice. Since the early 1800s, there has been considerable variation in rules and regulations governing personnel policies and practices to respond to the changing values, expectations, and assumptions of society pertaining to proper methods of filling government positions.

Three values predominant in our approach to government have had strong, but shifting, impact on personnel practices: (1) the quest for strong *executive leadership*, (2) the desire for a *politically neutral*, competent public service, and (3) the belief that the composition of the public service should generally mirror the *demographic composition* of American society.[1] Strong executive leadership and greater representativeness often have occurred together (see Chapters 2 and 6). For example, when a strong mayor practices patronage in hiring, drawing political supporters into local bureaucracies from an ethnically diverse majority coalition, it has the effect of increasing political loyalty to the mayor in the ranks while enhancing representativeness. In such a case, both *representativeness* of social groupings and *representation* of the political majority are served through administrative appointments. Greater **diversity** in the workforce—which is representativeness in another form—has been a value of increasing importance in the public service. We will discuss aspects of diversity later in this chapter.

On the other hand, the quest for **politically neutral competence**—involving formal disregard of race, gender, ideology, or political-party ties in filling administrative posts—has usually been carried on in opposition to advocates of strong leadership and representativeness. For example, supporters of civil service (merit) reform in the late 1800s and early 1900s harshly attacked both political "bosses" and the patronage systems that enabled them to dominate many states and cities. Significantly, most merit reformers also feared the potential influence of ethnic immigrants in many boss-run cities; part of their fervor was based on a strong desire to exclude recent immigrants from a share of political power. In short, the reformers opposed representativeness for emerging potential rivals on the economic, political, and social horizon. At the present time, those opposed to affirmative action, diversity, immigration reform, and quotas to achieve racial balance argue that race, ethnicity, and gender are similar to political criteria, and should not be used as factors for hiring and promotion.

> **politically neutral competence**
>
> idea that appointments to civil service positions should be made on the basis of demonstrated job competence, and not based on age, ethnicity, gender, politics, or race.

The case for politically neutral competence rests on the assumption that public managers should be hired and promoted solely on the basis of job-related skills, professionalism, and knowledge. Advocates of this approach contend that public programs are better administered, elected executives better served, and public funds better spent if those in charge possess demonstrated competence in the particular program area, along with management expertise and *institutional memory*—that is, the ability to apply the lessons of past experience profitably to current tasks. Those holding this view believe that considerations such as political-party loyalty, especially in hiring decisions, interfere with the quest for true managerial competence.

In response, patronage advocates stress the importance of a chief executive's ability to rely on the absolute loyalty of his or her subordinates throughout the executive branch in order to ensure efficient and effective program implementation. Without dismissing the importance of competence or professionalism, those favoring political loyalty as a key factor in making personnel decisions argue that reliance on neutral competence creates public bureaucracies less subject to control by elected political leaders. The accountability demanded by an increasingly frustrated public suffers, under this scenario. This issue has been a part of public administration virtually since its founding, though it has been debated more intensely at some times than at others. With recent Republican victories in Congress and in a number of state governors' races, the debate has intensified once again.

> **public personnel administration (PPA)**
>
> policies, processes, and procedures designed to recruit, train, and promote people who manage government agencies.

The terms **public personnel administration (PPA)** and **human resources development (HRD)** are used to describe various personnel functions, such as training, staff development, and virtual learning (e-learning) that are increasingly necessary to improve service quality and productivity in complex public organizations (see Chapter 10). In the public sector, these functions differ from

> **human resources development (HRD)**
>
> training and staff development of public employees designed to improve job performance.

those in business and industry in important respects, most prominently in the need to conduct the functions of personnel administration within constraints set by other formal political institutions, by agency clienteles, by professional associations of employees and other interest groups, and by political parties and the mass media.[2] Today, PPA and HRD are no longer regarded, as they once were, as separate from the general processes of public-policy making and performance management; there are two reasons for this. First, decisions made in the personnel area have a direct bearing on who makes and implements government policies. Second, such decisions have themselves become policy matters, reflecting demands for effective program administration, improved productivity, employee rights, collective bargaining agreements, and traditional merit reforms. To a great extent, personnel policies and training practices have become an extension of partisan political value conflicts, and the political dimension of PPA and HRD has taken on increasing importance in recent years.

Another widely recognized problem is that rules and regulations sufficient to cover government employees in the past are no longer flexible enough to accommodate newer, more customized service-delivery models. For example, separate salary schedules have been established in selected personnel grades for professionals in engineering and architecture, medicine and nursing, metallurgy, and veterinary medicine, among others. Another issue concerns the fact that the total size of the bureaucracy has stabilized in recent years, but the cost (mainly in salaries and benefits) has risen dramatically, which is attributable both to inflation and to a larger proportion of higher-level administrators (with higher salaries) in the civil service. Past attempts to reform the rules and regulations covering various personnel systems have met with some successes.[3] Nonetheless, the numbers and diversity of skills and training among government employees make it difficult to implement reforms in personnel procedures, such as simplification of job classification, pay for performance, and performance evaluation.

The sheer diversity, size, and scope of contemporary government make human resources and personnel concerns more important than ever before. Although the issue of "big government" is not directly tied to personnel policies, political pressures for reducing or controlling bureaucratic size affect personnel administrators and many of their decisions. This is especially important because Americans seem to mistrust large institutions (such as business, labor, and government), in part, simply because they are big. Furthermore, "whenever surveys [measuring citizen confidence in institutions] have dealt with different size levels of the same institution, they have found greater hostility to the 'big' or 'large' versions than to smaller ones."[4] This may explain the consistently higher approval ratings given by citizens to local governments over both states and the federal government.

The image of a "bloated" national bureaucracy, however, may not be completely accurate. First, since 1951, civilian employment in the national government has remained relatively stable, whereas state and local government employment increased dramatically (see Figure 7–1). Total state and local employment quadrupled, increasing from fewer than 4 million in 1951 to almost 17 million in

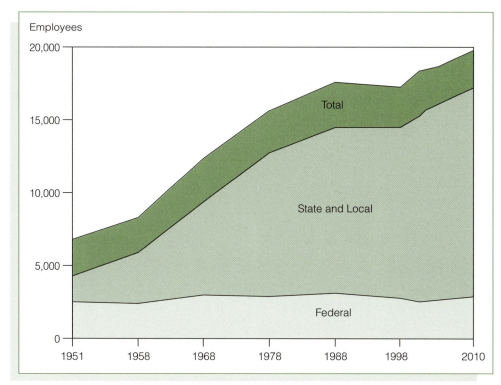

FIGURE 7-1

Government Civilian Employment, 1951–2010 (in thousands)

Source: http://www.census.gov/govs/www/apes.

2010, both full-time and part-time. The figure for **full-time equivalent (FTE) employees** was 16.8 million in January 2010 (see Table 7–1). Nearly 80 percent of all state and local employees work as teachers, nurses, police officers, and firefighters or other criminal justice or correctional officers. Over 9 million work in elementary, secondary, and higher education. Consequently, as compared to the federal government, a much higher proportion of state and local budgets are expended on salaries and benefits. During the same period, the number of national government civilian employees fluctuated, ranging from a low of 2.37 million in 1954 to just over 3.1 million in the early 1990s; in 2010, FTE civilian employees numbered nearly 2.9 million. In addition, there were 2.6 million military personnel: 1.4 on active duty and another 1.2 million in the reserves.

Second, the number of national civilian employees as a percentage of the total workforce has also fluctuated considerably in that same period. From a high of 10 percent following the World War II buildup, it dipped in the mid-1950s, then rose sharply again until the 1960s before beginning another decline that brought the ratio down to its lowest levels in the late 1990s, before rising again in the 2000s (Figure 7–2). Federal civilian employment in 2010 was still less than 2 percent of the total domestic workforce, whereas combined civilian and military represented 2.84 percent of total employment.

full-time equivalent (FTE) employees

actual number of full-time government personnel plus the number of full-time people who would have been needed to work the hours put in by part-time employees.

TABLE 7-1	State and Local Government Employment, by Function, January, 2011	

Function	Total	Percentage*
Total	16,807,109	100%
Education	9,045,057	54%
a. Elem & Sec	6,937,017	41%
b. Higher Educ	2,020,795	12%
c. Other Education	224,467	1.3%
Police	954,068	5.6%
Hospitals	1,002,546	6.0%
Transportation		
a. Air Transportation	48,289	0.2%
b. Highways	542,015	3.2%
c. Water and Terminals	13,208	0.1%
d. Transit	241,176	1.4%
Corrections	751,531	4.5%
Public Welfare	526,188	3.0%
Health	439,227	2.6%
Judicial and Legal	431,385	2.5%
Financial Administration	401,065	2.0%
Other Government Administration	287,920	1.0%
Natural Resources and Water	360,890	2.1%
Firefighters	348,610	2.0%
Parks and Recreation	276,072	1.6%
Sewerage and waste management	243,068	1.4%
Housing and Community Development	114,282	0.6%
Electric and gas	92,612	0.5%
Social Insurance Administration	81,207	0.4%
State Liquor Stores	8,177	0.05%
Libraries	136,902	0.8%
All Other and Unallocated	461,622	2.8%

*May not equal 100% because of rounding.

Source: U.S. Bureau of the Census, "State and Local Government Employment and Payroll Data," January, 2011.

The Clinton administration (1993–2001) reduced civilian federal government employment by eliminating several layers of supervisory positions in nearly all federal executive departments. Under President George W. Bush, *total* federal employment increased by 7.4 percent between 2002 and 2009, but most of that was limited to homeland security, national defense,

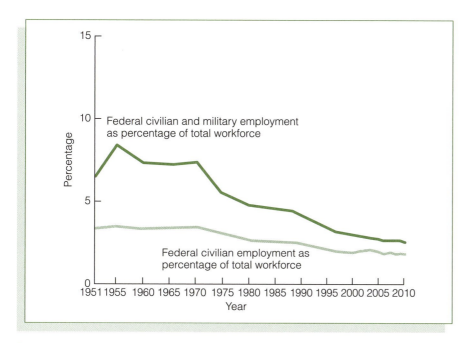

FIGURE 7-2

Employees in Federal Civilian Service and in the National Workforce, 1946–2010

Source: Employment Projections Program, U.S. Department of Labor, U.S. Bureau of Labor Statistics. http://www.bls.gov/emp/ep_table_101.pdf.

and federal criminal justice, with other functional areas absorbing deep cuts (see Table 7–2). The Department of Homeland Security (DHS) grew by 17 percent from its inception in 2002 with 158,000 to a projected 185,000 employees in fiscal year 2010; the Justice Department increased by 16 percent over 1992. For specialized mission-critical agencies, increases have been even more dramatic: since 2001, the personnel for border security (the U.S. Customs and Border Protection division under DHS) doubled from 9,000 agents to 18,000. During the same period, other executive agencies experienced critical shortages of key personnel, resulting in major policy failures and significantly contributing to waste, fraud, and abuse.[5] Yet, even with expanded hiring for such critical purposes, increases in national government civilian employment have not kept pace with population growth (see Figure 7–2).

Another development in the area of PPA has been increased turnover rates among those remaining in the civil service. As uncertainties abound, individuals often try to anticipate changes in their agencies by voluntarily seeking other posts. Like most other areas of government activity, the civil service felt keenly the effects of initiatives to reduce government spending. Limited entry into the career civil service thus has been the rule since the

TABLE 7-2 National Government Civilian Employment by Function: 1992 and 2009

	1992	2009	Percentage Change
Total-all functions	3,046,873	2,823,777	−7.32%
Financial administration	137,744	124,059	−9.93%
Other government administration	28,966	24,611	−15.03%
Judicial and legal	50,768	62,097	22.31%
Police	87,616	178,537	103.77%
Corrections	23,818	36,802	54.51%
Highways	4,110	2,832	−31.09%
Air transportation	53,937	47,070	−12.73%
Water transport and terminals	14,725	4,628	−68.57%
Public welfare	10,385	8,127	−21.74%
Health	144,339	152,013	5.32%
Homeland Security*	157,862	182,001	15.29%
Hospitals	73,860	192,876	161.14%
Social insurance administration	68,787	64,954	−5.57%
Parks and recreation	27,156	25,464	−6.23%
Housing and community development	28,006	15,156	−45.89%
Natural resources	232,124	180,800	−22.11%
National defense and international relations	984,226	729,222	− 25.91%
Postal service	774,028	703,861	−9.06%
Space research and technology	25,339	18,354	−27.57%
Other education**	13,790	9,992	−27.54%
Libraries	4,945	3,871	−27.72%
Other and unallocable	58,200	238,451	309.71%

* The Department of Homeland Security was formed in 2003, drawing its 157,862 employees from the U.S. Coast Guard, U.S. Secret Service, Bureau of Customs and Border Protection, Federal Emergency Management Agency, Transportation Security Administration, and other agencies.
** Includes Department of Education and the National Science Foundation, plus parts of the Bureau of Indian Affairs.

Source: U.S. Bureau of the Census. "Federal Government Civilian Employment by Function: March 2009." http://www2.census.gov/govs/apes/09fedfun.pdf (accessed April 13, 2011). U.S. Census Bureau, Federal Government Civilian Employment by Function: March 2009.

early 1980s. Closely related is the imposition of reductions-in-force (RIFs) on most domestic agencies. The number of positions allocated to many agencies was reduced, resulting in a net decline in total national government civilian employment of just over 7 percent since the early 1990s (see Table 7–2). As part of efforts both to reduce costs and to strengthen agency command structures, "downsized" higher-seniority civil service employees can "bump" employees at lower ranks in different agencies. Spending reductions, personnel cuts, and pay freezes for many agencies and civil servants contributed to each of the phenomena just mentioned, as well as to significantly undercutting employee morale.

Many former members of the armed forces have bumped lower-seniority civilian employees; some transferred to other agencies, but many civil service workers were permanently "downsized" (that is, terminated). Moreover, the potential long-range impacts on civil service are significant if the net effect is to lessen the attractiveness of government employment, damage the management capacities of executive agencies, and reduce the effectiveness and productivity of government programs. For example, could agency understaffing—at all levels of government—be a contributing factor to increased incidents of airline passenger complaints, child abuse, fraud and waste, environmental pollution, juvenile crime, or tax evasion?

The rates of change in these respects have increased somewhat, and the immediate effects on government personnel are obvious. For some functions within various agencies, the changes have been significant, from *decreases* in water transport and terminal workers, to *increases* in federal police forces, secret service personnel, and so on. Other entities with noticeable personnel increases included federal agencies responsible for maintaining homeland security and national defense (Justice, Defense, and Homeland Security) and conducting international affairs (State Department, Agency for International Development, and the new Bureau of Citizenship and Immigration Services [formerly the Immigration and Naturalization Service] within DHS).

These figures, however, do not truly reflect all that has happened in the past half-century, either in terms of the numbers of public employees working under direct funding or contracts with the national government, or in terms of the scope of their activity. More than thirty years ago, Joseph Califano, then Secretary of Health, Education, and Welfare (now Health and Human Services), observed that his department employed some 144,000 people, but *indirectly* paid the salaries of nearly *1 million* more in state and local governments, through myriad grant-in-aid programs. It was estimated at the time that if all personnel dependent on national government funds—state and local personnel, private contractors paid indirectly, consultants, and the like—the total payroll would include about *8 million people* (and the number of federal "dependents" has certainly increased since then).[6] If we consider the scope and impact of national government actions in this light, combined with unfunded mandates, grant-in-aid requirements, military deployments, and expanded state and national regulatory responsibilities, we see that public concern about the size of government bureaucracy is not entirely groundless. It may be somewhat misplaced, however, in that government roles have changed substantially in the past decade. Nonetheless, concerns about budgets, salaries, and size persist and that clearly affects personnel management.

At the state and local government levels, the personnel picture has worsened because of budget cuts. Over half of all state and local government FTE employees work in primary, secondary, or higher education, an area hard-hit by budget cuts resulting from the prolonged economic recession and the mortgage meltdown.[7] State employees not in education accounted for about 20 percent, and the remainder were noneducation employees in city, county, and other local governments. Expansion of public employment at the state–local level was due in large part to a sharp rise in educational employment during the 1960s, but other state–local functional areas, such as health and hospitals, police, corrections, and fire protection, also benefitted at that time. Many states mandated costly expansions in various public programs, creating the need for more police, correctional officers, teachers, transit workers, and homeland security employees.

Another feature of PPA that is not reflected in head counts of government employees is the changing nature of the workforce. Especially in the national government, increasing numbers of bureaucrats have become older, more specialized, better educated, and more highly paid than many of their predecessors. Governments are now managed by better-credentialed, more competent professionals and technocrats.

The national government's role—and its relationship to states, localities, nonprofit organizations, and private consultants and contractors—has been affected as well. It has been suggested that it is increasingly state and local governments, along with private contractors, that actually translate national government directives into public realities (recall a similar implication in Chapters 1 and 3 regarding devolution, privatization, and decentralization in intergovernmental relations). Expertise is not confined exclusively to the national government but, wherever it is found, its significance has become unmistakable—and is related much more closely to the expanding role of government than simply to numbers of people directly or indirectly supported by a government payroll. Indeed, the public and private sectors are increasingly dependent upon one another for **interoperability** of information and communication technologies, joint missions, mutual responsibilities, and financial support. We will deal further with the rise of public-service partnerships, professionalism, and specialization later in this chapter.

interoperability

the capacity of governmental organizations to share and integrate information using common standards to use the full power of existing technologies to achieve higher levels of two-way interactions with businesses, citizens, or other governments.

Evolution of Public Personnel Administration

The evolution of PPA from 1789 to the present did not occur in a social or political vacuum. Rather, development of the personnel function and of specific practices was related to other changes in public administration and society. The following seven major phases in the evolution of federal personnel administration have been identified, with the most recent phases highlighted in Table 7–3:

1. Government by "gentlemen" reflected the powerful influence of the American quasi-aristocracy on all of politics and the use of **nepotism** within political participation.
2. Government by the "common person" resulted from a movement toward a more **egalitarian** political system. The **Civil Service (Pendleton) Act** of 1883 created a bipartisan commission responsible for organizing open competitive examinations for civil service positions.
3. Government by the "good" focused on elimination of corruption in hiring practices and equality of access to competitive entrance examinations.
4. Government by the "efficient" was characterized by maintenance of the merit system and of political neutrality and by the pursuit of management efficiency.
5. Government by "administrators" saw the development of an activist political role for public administrators. The **Brownlow Report** in 1937 called on the president to assume greater responsibility and authority within the executive branch, and the **Second Hoover Commission** in 1955 helped set the stage for the eventual establishment of the **Senior Executive Service (SES)** of upper-level career executives serving administrative positions.
6. Government by "professionals" was a period of greater concern for recruiting, testing generalized skills of job applicants, and meeting the challenges of, as well as the opportunities for, increased professionalism in the public service.
7. Government by "citizens, experts, and results" is driven by changes in technology, such as e-government facilitated by the Internet, and calls for increased accountability, improved performance, and expanded minority participation. The advent of networked technologies and e-government has brought about nearly "real-time responses," and access to information on the Internet has brought about a more informed and participatory citizenry.[8]

The growth of professionalism and specialization in the public service contributed not only to higher government salaries but also to overly narrow job classifications. In some cases, this has resulted in professionals having a direct voice in public-policy making, with adverse consequences for popular control and accountability. One classic study identified five major avenues to political power: (1) election or appointment to high office, which is generally dominated by lawyers; (2) effective control (if not a near monopoly) by an individual profession of important managerial functions in an agency—for example, educators in the Office of Education, engineers in public works agencies, or foreign-service officers in the State Department; (3) a professional

nepotism

form of favoritism based on hiring family members or relatives.

egalitarianism

philosophical concept stressing individual equality in political, social, economic, and other relations; in the context of public personnel administration, the conceptual basis for "government by the common person."

Civil Service (Pendleton) Act

a law formally known as the Civil Service Act of 1883 (sponsored by Ohio Senator George Pendleton), establishing job-related competence as the primary basis for filling national government jobs; created the U.S. Civil Service Commission to oversee the new "merit" system.

Brownlow Report

recommendations for reform of the federal bureaucracy from a 1937 committee, appointed by President Franklin Roosevelt and chaired by Louis Brownlow, that included respected scholars and practitioners in the emerging discipline of public administration.

Second Hoover Commission

1955 blue-ribbon commission appointed by President Eisenhower and chaired by former president Hoover to study higher-level positions in the civil service.

TABLE 7-3	Changes in Public Bureaucracy since 1955

Government by Professionals (1955–1995)

- The Federal Service Entrance Examination (FSEE) was established in 1955; it was designed to provide a single point of entry into the U.S. civil service, make it possible for public servants to transfer more easily from one agency to another, and allow the Civil Service Commission to engage in more systematic recruiting, especially on college and university campuses.
- Professionalism has become widespread in the public service, so that the career needs of individuals within their professions conflict, to some extent, with the traditional emphasis on the administrative job itself.
- Contemporary personnel administration must take account of the needs of both public agencies and their professional employees.
- The increasing power of various professions became a force to be reckoned with in the administrative process.

Government by Citizens, Experts, and Results (1995 to present)

- Federal Blue Ribbon Commissions set goals for results-driven government and "wired" access to public services.
- Adoption by government of information technology with the Electronic Government Act of 2002 allowing greater numbers of citizens direct access via World Wide Web portals; one-stop customer-centered "shopping" for public services.
- Increased demand for information-technology specialists in government.
- State-sponsored websites and adoption of e-government allow citizen access to wider range of information.
- Government agencies become more market-driven and results-oriented; citizen relationship management recognized as legitimate function of government.
- Increased concerns about privacy and protection of individual records.

Source: © 2013 Cengage Learning.

Senior Executive Service (SES)

established in the national Civil Service Reform Act of 1978; designed to foster professional growth, mobility, and versatility among senior career officials (and some "political" appointees); incorporated into national government personnel management broad emphasis on performance appraisal and merit pay concepts as part of both the SES and the broader merit system reform; see **Civil Service Reform Act of 1978.**

presence in an agency but without professional domination (all agencies have legal counsel, budget officials, information technology specialists, planners, and personnel specialists); (4) an ability to generate pressure on decision makers from fellow or allied professionals outside the governmental structure; and (5) an ability to operate through the system of intergovernmental relations by collaborating with fellow professionals in other units of government (through the "guilds," picket fences, or vertical functional autocracies described in Chapter 3).[9] Licensing of professions at the state level (such as physicians, lawyers, insurance agents, mortgage brokers, and realtors) and regulatory processes at the national level are two areas in which professional influence is strong—too strong, according to some.

Professions such as banking, law, medicine, and civil engineering have been described by different observers as enjoying excessive influence in formulating and implementing public policy. The lack of public accountability of such professional associations is central to criticisms of their role. There is also the possibility that loyalty to professional associations (such as the American

Medical Association for medicine or the American Bar Association for law) may supersede loyalty to an agency as the standard by which professional employees judge their own work.[10] Individual loyalties to widely varying professional standards can create tensions within an agency that are very difficult to resolve from a broader public-policy perspective.

Merit and Patronage in Perspective

Politics has always played a role in personnel administration. Andrew Jackson is remembered as the father of the patronage system, though Thomas Jefferson was the first president to view partisan loyalty as an important criterion in the selection of public servants. Moreover, Jackson insisted on some competence in government employees and was not nearly as abusive in his patronage tactics as some later presidents were (notably James Buchanan and Abraham Lincoln). Franklin Roosevelt established the tradition of a strong executive who emphasized political loyalty as well as professional competence. His use of a "brain trust" of politically loyal policy advisers enhanced the respect for policy analysis and policy analysts in government.

The merit versus patronage debate arouses deep passions in many of us. The devotion of so many people to what they see as interconnected values of integrity, efficiency, economy, political neutrality, and ethical standards fosters a strong preference for merit system practices, often accompanied by contempt for patronage. Both have a rich history in American PPA and, until the recent recession, merit has clearly held favor among middle- and upper-class citizens, who are the chief beneficiaries of such a system.

The distinctions between merit and patronage systems become clearer in defining job qualifications. Those who favor merit are fond of saying that you do not have to be qualified to get a patronage job, but that is not always true—the qualifications are usually partisan-based rather than job-related, but they are job requirements just the same. Put simply, merit judges *what* you know, whereas patronage is more interested in *whom* you know (or who knows you) and how you can help politically. Each system has some clear advantages. The most obvious advantage of a merit system is its ability to bring into the public service individuals who are considered competent (by management's standards) to perform the tasks required in a given position. Doing one's job well is valued in any organization, and it is the root of the merit system. There is also some value in having continuity and stability in the public service (that is, institutional memory) instead of the dramatic, and sometimes traumatic, turnovers in personnel experienced at the beginning of virtually every new presidential administration between 1829 and 1881. On the other hand, a patronage system also affords some advantages. The most important one is that the chief executive can command the loyalties of bureaucratic subordinates much more effectively. Every local, state, and national "boss" has had that ability, and the effect in each case has been to buttress chief-executive leadership (see Chapter 6). This approach yields a vastly different kind of bureaucracy and often a different set of social, economic, and political priorities in public policies. But to the extent that we value strong leadership, we may favor patronage.

The tensions between merit and patronage are rooted in a deeper philosophical and political conflict affecting how jobs are filled and how the work of any government entity is organized. The merit concept is built around the use of **achievement-oriented criteria**—that is, making personnel judgments based on the applicant's demonstrated, job-related competence. By contrast, in patronage systems (and in some other approaches to personnel decision making), judgments are based on **ascriptive criteria**—that is, attributes or characteristics of the individual other than his or her skills and knowledge. Ascriptive criteria include patronage (in which personnel decisions are based at least in part on the applicant's political party or other organizational loyalties), affirmative action (in which one's race or gender is given strong consideration), veterans' preference (based on military service), and nepotism (choice influenced by kinship). Though all such approaches seem to conflict with merit principles, each is said to have certain advantages—not only for the individuals affected but also for the personnel selection system and perhaps society at large. For example, military service to one's country is generally accepted as a commitment to public service, so it is not unreasonable to consider such service in evaluating a candidate's qualifications for a civilian government position. Eventually, all managers must find ways to deal with pressures generated by such conflicting values.[11] Are merit and patronage, then, permanent and inevitable opposites? Surprisingly perhaps, the answer is no. In practice, neither merit selection nor patronage exists in a pure form. Partisan influence is not entirely unknown in merit systems although it is usually subtle. In some states and cities, the appearance of a merit system may mask an effectively functioning patronage arrangement. Knowing someone is still useful to the candidate for a merit position. By the same token, traditional patronage practices have been severely constrained by governments' need to hire individuals with specific high-level technical skills, by reduced reliance on campaign workers in an era of media campaigns, by decreased availability of government jobs, and by a number of Supreme Court decisions limiting patronage hiring.[12] The era of the "party hack," if not gone forever, has been significantly transformed by the changing needs and restrictions of a complex technological society.

achievement-oriented criteria

standards for making personnel judgments based on an individual's demonstrated, job-related competence.

ascriptive criteria

standards for making personnel judgments that are based on attributes or characteristics other than skills or knowledge.

Formal Arrangements and Tasks of Personnel Administration

All civil service systems are not created equal, but the national government arrangements will serve as an illustrative model for discussion of the structure of most merit personnel systems. Many state arrangements, among the nearly forty states that have merit systems, closely resemble the national government format, with some variations.

About 90 percent of all national executive-branch employees are currently covered by some merit system, most under the system administered by the **Office of Personnel Management (OPM)**, which replaced the Civil Service Commission in 1979. The proportion of national executive employees working within competitive merit systems has risen steadily, if gradually, from about 10 percent in 1884 (one year after passage of the Pendleton Act) to over 90 percent for the first time during the 1970s. Partly in response to prodding from the national government, state governments have gradually extended—or established—merit systems in their executive branches. For example, Congress requires states to organize **merit pay** systems in single state agencies designated as grant-in-aid recipients; the tremendous proliferation of grants has thus had the spin-off effect of strengthening merit principles in state government. The Intergovernmental Personnel Act (IPA) of 1970 greatly reinforced that requirement; most states now have many merit features built into their personnel arrangements. Local governments have been similarly affected but to a lesser extent.

The system of classifying positions is central to any personnel structuring. In the national government, jobs are classified according to ten grades, or levels, that make up the **General Schedule (GS)**. Established in 1949, the GS is based on the idea that employees should be rewarded for longevity (length of service) and commitment to the public service through pay raises and promotions rather than rigid performance standards, as is typically the case in the private sector. Under the GS pay system, federal employees receive annual pay increases for satisfactory performance within a given period of time. Within each grade (GS-1 to GS-15) there are ten "steps," which are based on years of service. (For a current list of salaries for each GS grade, see http://www.opm.gov/oca/11tables/html/gs.asp.)

At the top of the personnel structure is the **Executive Schedule**, occupied by the highest-ranking career officials, those who interact on a regular basis with politically appointed administrators (see Chapter 6). Approximately 6,700 SES executives are eligible for performance bonuses within their pay grades and, in 2010, top pay was limited by Congress to $179,700. The federal government spent about $180 billion, less than 5 percent of its total budget, for salaries and benefits for all federal workers. The average wages and benefits for all federal civilian workers in 2010 was estimated to be about $120,000. Promotion from one grade to the next is not automatic and, at the outset of one's career, retention in the service itself is not guaranteed. A probation period of six to eighteen months must be served before full merit protection is attained, and not all employees are put under merit. Failure to achieve promotion in that time is a virtual invitation to leave the civil service.

Consistent with emphasis on general preparation and technical skills, it is not difficult for an employee in the public service to transfer from one agency to another—or even from one merit system to another. Employees with greater seniority have "bumping rights" over others with less service, as noted

Office of Personnel Management (OPM)

key administrative unit in the national government operating under presidential direction; responsible for managing the national government personnel system, consistent with presidential personnel policy.

merit pay

approach to compensation in personnel management founded on the concept of equal pay for equal contribution; related to, and dependent on, properly designed and implemented performance appraisal systems; applied to managers and supervisors in grades GS-13 through GS-15 in the national executive branch, under provisions of the Civil Service Reform Act of 1978.

General Schedule (GS)

pay scale for federal employees, based on grades and steps.

Executive Schedule

compensation schedule for the federal Senior Executive Service.

earlier. OPM has had reciprocal agreements with the Tennessee Valley Authority and Panama Canal Zone, for example, that permit employees to transfer to the other systems, and vice versa, with no loss of pension benefits or grade level. This interagency mobility has advantages not only for employees but also for agencies looking for varied combinations of skill and experience.

In some state merit systems, it has been possible to move up the ladder very rapidly. In Illinois, for example, competitive examinations for higher-level jobs—open only to those already holding state positions—were given with some frequency. A capable individual who landed a first job could take the examinations every time they were administered and, if successful, could achieve significant career advancement in a relatively short time. Pay freezes and budget cuts, however, have slowed the pace of upward mobility for most public employees, at all levels of government.

The formal tasks of personnel administration have traditionally included position classification, recruitment, examination, selection, and compensation. More recently, as management of complex organizations has become more challenging, administrators (including personnel administrators) have had to become better grounded in human resources planning, employee training, counseling, motivating employees, labor relations, interpersonal skills, social and behavioral psychology, disciplining employees, and dealing with legal constraints.

Position Classification

position classification

formal task of American public personnel administration, intended to classify jobs in different agencies that have essentially the same types of functions and responsibilities, based on written descriptions of duties and responsibilities.

The major purpose of **position classification** is to facilitate performance of other personnel functions across a wide range of agencies within the same general personnel system. Many positions in different agencies have similar duties, so that it makes sense to group into one classification jobs with essentially the same responsibilities. Otherwise, recruitment and examination would be far more complex. Both these tasks have greater flexibility and value if potential employees can be evaluated in terms of their suitability for the general duties and responsibilities. Pay scales also can be set only if positions are grouped so that it is possible to award equal pay for equal work, which has been an underlying, if not completely implemented, rationale of position classification since passage of the Pendleton Act in 1883.

A written description of the responsibilities involved in a position is the basis for its classification and distinction from other jobs. But there are many obstacles to effective classification. Description of duties is relatively easy, but the exact responsibilities of a position (supervisory tasks, evaluating the work of subordinates, and expectations for initiative, innovation, or suggestions) can be elusive. How challenging the duties and responsibilities are is another ambiguous aspect of position descriptions. In an effort to counteract these problems, some weighting of the various job features—frequency of supervision, difficulty and complexity of each task, and so on—has been tried, so that classifications reflect as accurately as possible the true nature of each position. Such obstacles are not easily overcome, and many classification systems consequently (perhaps inevitably) contain some "soft spots" that require continuing attention.

There are a number of problems with position classification, even under the newer, smaller, and more responsive government structures of the 2000s. Although an agency is responsible for classifying, according to existing schedules, the positions in that agency, there is a legitimate interest in maintaining some consistency from one agency to the next. Consequently, most states and localities, as well as the national government, provide for *reviews* and *audits* by a central personnel office with authority to change, if necessary, agency classifications that are out of line. There is also concern that *narrow specialization* in many job descriptions has hampered efforts to attract into the public service qualified individuals who lack *exactly* the right combination of skills for a given position. In this respect, position classification may be said to interfere with the merit principle itself, in that job-related competence is defined too narrowly. There is always the possibility that, without adequate monitoring, an existing classification system will become outdated as a result of rapidly changing job requirements. It has been argued that, as task-oriented groups (for example, quality-improvement teams) become more common, position classification geared to hierarchical organization will itself become obsolete. These are problems that bear watching but, because most government organizations are still arranged hierarchically, position classification is likely to remain both appropriate and useful—although with some changes almost certainly in store.

An important development was the set of recommendations regarding position classification emerging from a number of different sources, which examined (separately) personnel management at national and state-local levels. A common theme present in the work of both the National Performance Review (NPR) and the National Commission on the State and Local Public Service (the Winter Commission) was the need to reduce the existing complexity in classification, especially the sheer number of separate classifications (the Winter Commission noted that the problem was particularly acute in state governments).[13] Both commission reports emphasized **broadbanding** job classification; that is, the recommendations urged personnel managers to consolidate existing classifications into a far smaller number, thus reducing complexity and also increasing flexibility and mobility for employees. The George W. Bush administration proposed significant changes in federal position classification, including elimination of the GS system and greater use of pay bands. The Department of Homeland Security, for one, struggled with attempts to modify the traditional GS pay system with broader pay bands, replacing annual longevity pay adjustments with a pay-for-performance system based on an assessment of the local labor market and geographic location.[14]

broadbanding

the consolidation of existing job classifications into fewer and broader categories, reducing complexity and specialization in job classifications.

Recruitment, Examination, and Selection

Attracting, testing, and choosing those who join the public service have been systematic activities of government personnel administration for a relatively limited period of time. Concerns and issues involved in these areas overlap one another to some extent but deserve separate discussion.

Recruitment has been something of a problem for far longer than it was recognized as such. During the early decades of the last century, a combination of low pay and low prestige—not unrelated—made working for the government distinctly unattractive. The prestige problem was a matter of public values and attitudes toward government generally; even among those who favored strong administrative capabilities, "politics" was seen as unsavory, to be tolerated rather than actively joined. Generally, the prestige of government service has decreased significantly over the past few decades. Compensation differentials between the public and private sectors have contributed to that change in prestige. It has thus become more difficult to arouse the interest of skilled and competent individuals in government service, and a considerable effort has had to be made to attract younger workers who possess critical skills. In 2007, the federal government estimated that nearly 200,000 "mission critical" jobs were needed to fill existing vacancies.[15]

The most important developments were the establishment of systematic ties to recruiting services on college campuses, in search of the professionally trained student as well as the liberal arts graduate, and to professional associations. At the same time, a host of requirements (filing fees, residency, and the like) that had acted to constrict access to the public service were dropped, and open competitive examinations were adopted. In a word, the recruitment process was democratized.

In recent years, the recruitment picture has changed dramatically in a number of respects. In general, it is necessary for most federal agencies to go out and "beat the bushes" for prospective employees. The number of civilian jobs in the national government often outnumbers the pool of available applicants, and competition from private employers offering higher salaries makes it even more difficult to recruit qualified applicants. Merely because the government job market, like that of the private sector, has tightened does not mean that there is no need to recruit for specific positions. The demand for qualified employees still exceeds supply in selected occupational areas (engineers, scientists, and, occasionally, secretaries and clerks) and in different parts of the country. This has encouraged some government agencies to offer incentives such as housing assistance and signing bonuses to prospective recruits. As more private-sector jobs are "outsourced" and the civilian job market tightens, it is expected that greater numbers of students will consider public employment opportunities.

The examination process is a complex and decentralized one. An examination must be broad enough to test adequately for skills that may be used in widely varying agencies yet still precise enough to be meaningful in testing specific skills and competencies. Many national agencies, as noted earlier, supplement general examinations with more specialized tests, interviews, written work submitted by the applicant, and so on. In state and local government, similar examinations are often used, with many of the same problems as well as advantages.

Most government entrance examinations are written, although it is becoming more common to incorporate both written and oral portions. Also, not unlike standardized college and graduate school entrance exams, most tests attempt to measure both aptitude and achievement. As alternative methods of measuring competence, it is common practice to give weight to education and experience, and, in some instances, enough of one or both can substitute for taking the initial examination. Graduates with the Master in Public Administration (MPA) degree, for example, typically receive "fast-track" appointments because of their recognized achievements. In the great majority of cases, a combination of written and oral examinations, personal interviews, education, experience, and written statements is used as the basis for evaluating prospective employees.

A central concern is the validity of examinations, that is, how well they actually test what they are designed to test. Another consideration is whether tests should measure specific work skills or factors such as imagination, creativity, managerial talent, and the capacity to learn and grow on the job. Clearly, for some positions, work skills deserve major emphasis, whereas, for others, the second set of abilities should also be considered (see the set of sample questions for New York City police examinations on page 296).

Of growing concern in the past four decades has been the matter of bias in testing—specifically, whether examinations have exhibited an unintentional cultural bias that has unfairly discriminated against members of minority groups. Past federal civil service examinations became the focus of lawsuits brought by African-Americans and Hispanics who alleged that they were culturally biased and tested for general knowledge not required for the 118 job categories for which they were used. Carter administration officials negotiated with the plaintiffs over plans to phase out the exam, and to replace it with up to 118 separate tests designed to measure specific skills for each position. Shortly before President Carter left office, the Justice Department filed its plan in U.S. District Court in Washington as a consent decree to settle the suit, and the Reagan administration abolished the tests in August 1982.

Subsequently, OPM established a new system (known as Schedule B hiring authority) pending development of alternative competitive examining procedures. However, that interim lasted well into Ronald Reagan's second term. Some viewed this (noncompetitive) hiring method as a threat to the competitive merit system. Others argued that agency use of Schedule B meant that there was no central point in the national government to which individuals could apply for jobs. Gradually, however, the picture changed; OPM developed job-related alternative examinations (in compliance with the consent decree), which accounted for just over one-half of the positions formerly filled

SAMPLE TEST QUESTIONS DEALING WITH ADMINISTRATION FROM NEW YORK CITY POLICE EXAMINATIONS*

1. "Records of attendance, case load, and individual performance are ordinarily compiled for a police department by a records unit." A plan is suggested whereby all patrol sergeants would regularly review summaries of these detailed records, insofar as they concern the men under them. The adoption of such a plan would be

   (A) inadvisable; the attention of the patrol sergeant would be unduly diverted away from the important function of patrol supervision.

   (B) advisable; the information provided by summaries of detailed records would conclusively indicate to the patrol sergeant the subordinates who should be given specific patrol assignments.

   (C) inadvisable; the original records should be reviewed in detail by the patrol sergeant if he is to derive any value from a record review procedure.

   (D) advisable; the patrol sergeant would then have information that would supplement his personal knowledge of his subordinates.

2. In planning the distribution of the patrol force of a police department, one of the following factors that should be considered first is the

   (A) availability of supervisory personnel for each of the predetermined tours of police duty.

   (B) hourly need for police services throughout the 24 hours of the day.

   (C) determination of the types of patrol to be utilized for the most effective police effort.

   (D) division of the total area into posts determined by their relative need for police service.

3. There are some who maintain that the efficiency of a police department is determined solely by its numerical strength. This viewpoint oversimplifies a highly complex problem mainly because

   (A) enlargement of the patrol force involves a disproportionate increase in specialized units and increased need for supervision.

   (B) supervisory standards tend to decline in an enlarged department.

   (C) the selection and training of the force, and the quality of supervision, must also be considered.

   (D) the efficiency of the department is not related to its numerical strength.

*Correct answers: 1-D, 2-B, 3-C.

Source: Modern Promotion Courses publications, New York City.

under the old system.[16] And, under George H. W. Bush, OPM established (in May 1990) a new examination, Administrative Careers with America (ACWA), which expanded still further the coverage of positions filled through this new, centrally administered exam. Although ACWA represented a step forward, those who were critical of Schedule B still considered the situation less desirable than it was during the time when competitive examinations were in place.[17]

Selection processes vary widely from one level of government to another, and here, as elsewhere, the national government was the first to develop systematic procedures. There clearly is no overall pattern; merit systems are not identical, and patronage still operates in many state and local governments. But national government practice suggests what is possible—and also gives some idea of the limitations.

After qualifying through examination, education, or experience, an applicant received a merit rating (GS-7 or GS-9, for example). Applicants' names were placed on a register, meaning that they were officially under consideration for appropriate positions as these became available throughout the bureaucracy. At that point, it was up to each agency to notify OPM as positions opened up. OPM then forwarded to the agency the names of those it found qualified for the particular position, and the agency took it from there.

In this procedure, two guidelines helped to shape the final decision. The first was called the "rule of three," referring to OPM's practice of sending three names at a time to agencies with one position to fill; those individuals were, literally, finalists in the competition. The other guideline, **veterans' preference**, helped determine whose names were included in that vital set of three because it affected total points assigned to each applicant. In many states and localities, both the rule of three and veterans' preference are still required by law. All honorably discharged veterans with the minimum passing score of 70 on the 100-point test got a 5-point bonus (with the exception, after 1979, of nondisabled military retirees at or above the rank of major or lieutenant commander); all disabled veterans received a 10-point bonus, as did Vietnam veterans; and those disabled in Vietnam received a 15-point bonus. In some cases, survivors of veterans killed in action received these bonuses as well. In many states and localities, disabled veterans still receive an absolute preference. Veterans' preference reflects the political strength of veterans' groups, as well as the generally high regard in which America's veterans have been held, although Vietnam veterans did not enjoy the same respect as did those of earlier conflicts or those of Operation Desert Storm (the Persian Gulf War in early 1991), or the more recent Afghanistan and Iraq wars.

It should be noted that veterans' preference—variously considered as both an achievement-oriented and an ascriptive personnel criterion—has had a significant impact on the composition of the national government's workforce: 30 percent of federal employees are retired military personnel or veterans. Defenders of the merit system are hard-pressed to support this kind of noncompetitive generosity, even toward veterans. Many states, and hundreds of local governments as well, employ veterans' preference as a criterion for promotion as well as entry, and a substantial proportion of those in senior grades of the national bureaucracy are veterans. The late Alan K. Campbell, OPM director under President Carter and a key architect of civil service reform, argued that veterans' preference "has damaged the quality of the senior civil service, to say nothing of discriminating against women in the [national] government."[18] There is considerable irony here in that two different ascriptive criteria—veterans' preference and affirmative action—clash with each other as well as with the concept of merit.

veterans' preference

law passed in 1944 that required the federal government to favor those veterans who had served on active duty or were returning from war when hiring new employees in an attempt to recognize their service, sacrifice, and skills; does not apply to positions in the Senior Executive Service or to internal agency actions such as reassignment or promotion.

Compensation and Locality Pay

Deciding how much to pay employees is one of the more difficult and occasionally controversial tasks confronting any government personnel system. In one sense, the task is made easier by the fact that legislatures almost always must provide pay scales and other rules of compensation, but hard decisions about what to propose remain a central responsibility of personnel administration.

There are several key considerations in determining a reasonable level of compensation. One is the necessity of paying employees enough to fulfill their minimum economic needs. Closely related is the question of compensation in proportion to the work done in terms of its importance, quality, and quantity. These can be highly subjective measures, permitting considerable disagreement about what is appropriate. A third consideration is comparability of pay scales. This has two dimensions: (1) ensuring that wages and salaries for a given classification bear a reasonable relationship to others in the same civil service system with comparable complexity, responsibility, and skill and (2) attempting to maintain rates of compensation for government employees that are not dramatically different from wages and salaries paid for similar kinds of work in the private sector.

Another dimension of pay comparability concerns variations in the cost of living throughout the nation, and even within many states, in wage and salary levels paid in business and industry, which makes it difficult to align government salaries with them on a truly comparable basis. There has been a concerted effort—sometimes formalized, sometimes not—to tie government wage and salary levels to changes in the cost of living. As a practical matter, that avoids some tough questions, but the harm it does to the expectation that more skilled individuals will be better paid is obvious. Since the beginning of the recession in late 2007, national government salaries and wages have not changed significantly, but are more stable relative to compensation paid for comparable positions in the private sector. The apparent disparity has resulted from the elimination of private-sector jobs and reductions in wages and fringe benefits for those still employed.

pay gap

the difference between public and private salaries for comparable positions.

The **pay gap** for national government civil servants also has narrowed and ranges from 20 percent to nearly 50 percent, depending on grade and geographic location. The U.S. Bureau of Labor Statistics found an average pay gap of 22 percent; by 2007, the pay gap had increased slightly as federal employees made an average of 23 percent less than their private-sector counterparts.[19] This is not a new problem. In a 1989 survey, the National Commission on the Public Service found that "the gap between what government and the private sector pay has grown far beyond the point where government can hope to recruit and retain qualified staff, even as the federal benefits package has [also] become less attractive."[20] President George H. W. Bush and Congress tried to improve the situation somewhat in 1989. Legislation passed by Congress, together with an executive order issued by the president, provided for salary boosts for top executive-branch officials ranging from about 8 percent to as much as 35 percent (most civil service raises, which took full effect in 1991, averaged just over 4 percent).[21] In certain mission-critical specialties, the pay gap now exceeds 50 percent for comparable private-sector positions, forcing the federal government as well as many states and local governments to offer signing bonuses and other pay incentives to attract qualified workers.

In 1993, the Clinton administration asked OPM to make recommendations regarding **locality pay**. OPM sent its report to the president in November 1993, and a new overall pay system went into effect in January 1994. Under the new arrangement, a total of twenty-eight area pay scales now exist in the federal civil service, for designated high-cost metropolitan (and other) areas. As the new system took effect, about 60 percent of federal employees were covered by one or another of these area scales; the remaining 40 percent are paid according to the "rest of the country" scale.[22]

Of greater concern is the possibility of a "pension bubble" that would negatively impact already stressed public budgets. During the mortgage boom in the early 2000s, many public-pension fund managers switched from more conservative funds to riskier ones that would pay higher returns. Funds that were expected to return 7–8 percent are now barely paying 1–2 percent, creating the potential for major crises in public financial markets. Current retirement investments may not allow public-employee retirement systems to fulfill the promises that have been made, and taxpayers are obligated to make up the difference. As a consequence, public employees are being asked to contribute more for both health care and retirement plans.[23]

Generally, national government employees are substantially better paid and receive more generous benefits than their state and local counterparts. Within that overall comparison, there are other variations. One is the high proportion of state and local government employees working in education, transportation, and health care services (see Table 7–1); another is the greater impact of public-employee unions and collective bargaining on wages and salaries. In making interstate or interlocal comparisons, other factors that help explain variations in level of compensation include the degree of urbanization and industrialization in the government jurisdiction and the extent to which a bureaucracy has become professionalized. It should be noted, however, that in some cases, state and local pay exceeds pay at the national level for similar duties.

In recent years, state and local employees have fallen behind in compensation, compared with their private-sector counterparts and federal workers. From 2000 to 2008, state/local employees received an 18 percent increase in pay and benefits, after inflation adjustments, compared to 31 percent raises for private workers and 58 percent for federal employees during that same period. Starting in 2009, however, according to the U.S. Department of Labor Bureau of Labor Statistics, state and local public employees received an average of nearly $40 per hour, compared to $26 per hour for workers in comparable positions in the private sector. Private-sector workers have been losing pay and benefits because companies are reducing pension benefits and requiring employees to pay a greater share of their health care costs. This discrepancy has become a national issue, triggered in part by politically motivated actions to eliminate collective bargaining rights by Republican governors and legislatures in Wisconsin, Ohio, and Indiana, as well as several other states during the first months of 2011.

locality pay

adjustments to federal pay scales that make allowances for higher- or lower-cost areas where employees live.

Collective Bargaining and Personnel Reform in the Public Sector

collective bargaining

formalized process of negotiation between management and labor; involves specified steps, in a specified sequence, aimed at reaching an agreement (usually stipulated in contractual form) on terms and conditions of employment, covering an agreed-on period of time; a cycle that is repeated upon expiration of each labor–management contract or other agreement.

Since the late 1950s, **collective bargaining** procedures, modeled largely after those then prevailing in the private sector, have replaced traditional management-oriented, and management-controlled, personnel practices in many jurisdictions and at all levels of government. As a result, there have been frequent and significant shifts in effective decision-making authority on personnel matters, changes in the distribution of political and policy influence, and, on occasion, very visible implications for the delivery of the most essential public services. In this section, we will examine (1) the general nature and dynamics of public-sector collective bargaining; (2) reform efforts to strengthen labor–management collective bargaining processes; (3) the sequence of steps involved in the actual process of collective bargaining between employers and employees; (4) the impacts of collective bargaining in the public sector; and (5) current controversies surrounding attempts of several state governors to eliminate the practice.

Government Labor–Management Relations: An Overview

labor–management relations

formal setting in which negotiations over pay, working conditions, and benefits take place.

The term **labor–management relations**, the framework for collective bargaining, suggests something quite specific about the kinds of interactions that take place between managers and their employees. At the very least, it implies that employees have consciously chosen to organize themselves for the purpose of dealing with their superiors concerning terms and conditions of employment. Beyond that, in both public and private sectors, what is suggested is greater sharing of control over what once were strictly management's prerogatives in managing the workplace—that is, a basic reordering of the power to determine distribution of responsibility on the job, levels of compensation for work performed, procedures for airing and resolving grievances, conditions in the workplace, and the like. Viewed another way, labor–management relations represent a form of organizational participation permitting individuals and groups other than formal leaders to have a voice in directing the organization. Many government employees (for example, public safety personnel) have had influence in dealing with their employers in the past. But this newer form of participation is governed rather strictly by contractual provisions arrived at through a joint process and ratified by both management and labor. Thus, an essential element of labor–management relations is the phenomenon of structured relationships between formally organized participants in a shared management process.

This description could apply equally to industrial and governmental labor–management relations. It would be a mistake, however, to overlook significant differences that exist between the two settings.[24] For example, top public managers are chosen through elections and political appointments, both of which are influenced by labor groups and the general public; such is not the case in private management. Another difference is the near impossibility of separating public-sector bargaining from the political process. Thus, the term **multilateral** (many-sided) **bargaining** is increasingly used in the public sector, rather than **bilateral** (two-sided) **bargaining**, reflecting the involvement of many others besides management and labor bargaining teams. A third difference is the obvious contrast in types of services provided by public and private sectors; there are different markets for each, their purposes differ, and (most important to some observers) most public organizations have had a virtual monopoly on the rendering of certain essential public services, such as police, fire, and sanitation, making the nonmonetary costs to public health and safety very high in the event of a strike or work slowdown.

There are important distinctions among some of the catchwords commonly used in dealing with this subject. First, not all employee organizations are formally labor unions. Other historically prominent types of organizations include various employee and professional associations (for example, of nurses and social workers). Early objectives of labor groups included workplace safety, improving the status of members and the well-being of respective professions. Labor organizations have been increasingly drawn into the arena of collective bargaining as a result of pressures from rivals often formed explicitly for the purpose of bargaining. For example, the National Education Association (NEA), representing about 2 million teachers, became significantly more militant in response to the growing success of the American Federation of Teachers (AFT), a self-conscious labor union committed to collective bargaining.[25]

Collective bargaining, as a process, is fairly recent as a significant element in public employer–employee relations. In fact, only since the 1960s has collective bargaining played an important role in PPA. Although strikes are by far the most widely reported, visible, and controversial of all the varied aspects of public-sector labor–management relations, that should not be permitted to obscure the fact that most labor–management interactions, including most collective bargaining processes and outcomes, rarely result in strikes by public employees. The strike issue is one component of the total topic; although feelings often run high on that issue, one should take care to consider other aspects of labor relations as they deserve to be considered.

Neither management nor labor is all-powerful in decision making about management of the public workplace. Especially in recent years, the interest of ordinary citizens has grown considerably in the content and procedures of labor–management relations (see Figure 7–3).

The taxpayer still has to foot the bill (however indirectly) for costs incurred in reaching agreements. Consequently, formal bargaining and other

multilateral bargaining

public-sector collective bargaining negotiations that include the broadest number of affected public-employee and other groups.

bilateral bargaining

collective bargaining negotiations in which only management and labor are represented.

FIGURE 7-3

Dimensions of Bargaining

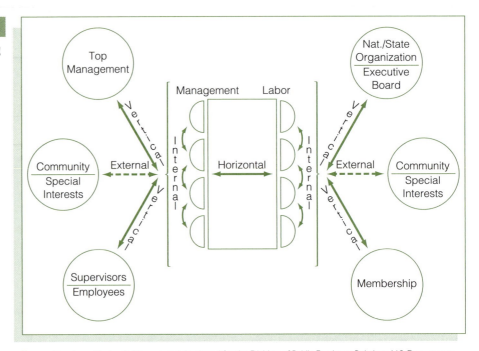

Source: Courtesy of Irving O. Dawson, and developed for the Division of Public Employee Relations, U.S. Department of Labor.

forms of decision making in this area cannot take place without some accounting being made to the ultimate board of directors, that is, the people. This is a central dimension of multilateralism in public-sector bargaining, and it has taken many forms. Two examples from the education arena are instructive. In California, the state sunshine bargaining law requires that proposals be publicly disclosed before school boards begin negotiations with teachers. And Rochester, New York, adopted a "parent involvement policy," which, among other things, invites parent participation in collective bargaining by (1) having parents work with the school board as it prepares its bargaining position before the opening of negotiations and (2) appointing one carefully selected parent to serve on the board's bargaining team. Thus, the larger reality of accountability to the general public is inescapable. And, in ways decidedly different from those of private-sector bargaining, both parties to labor–management agreements must be mindful of the impacts on the citizenry and of possible public backlash against particular provisions or the whole system of bargaining. In this era of shifting public confidence and of tighter government budgets, such concerns merit a great deal of attention from both union officials and public managers—and they are increasingly receiving that attention.

Historical Development of Public-Employee Organizations

Public-employee labor organizations were present in the national government as early as the 1830s, but nothing like modern *union* activity existed before the early 1900s. Although the **National Labor Relations Board (NLRB)** was established in 1935, unionized public-employee organizations were discouraged until the 1960s. A turning point for public-sector labor unions—one that signaled the rapid rise of collective bargaining on a large scale—came in 1962, when President John F. Kennedy issued **Executive Order (EO) 10988**. It extended to national government employees the right to organize and to engage in collective bargaining; among other things it provided for withholding union dues and for advisory arbitration of employee grievances, and prohibited union shops (in which all employees are compelled to be union members). Although this order legally altered only national government policy on bargaining with its own employees, states and local governments were also challenged to re-examine and possibly change labor–management negotiation policies. Thus, although the national government was not the first to establish comprehensive new labor relations policies, Kennedy's action (which redeemed a 1960 presidential campaign pledge) served as a catalyst for change, with nationwide repercussions at all government levels.

Following Kennedy's executive order, there began a period of intensive growth in membership in most unions, spurred by deliberate efforts on the part of various union organizers to increase membership. There was a steady increase in numbers and percentages of national government employees who belonged to labor organizations representing exclusive bargaining units (those represented in negotiations by only one labor group, chosen by majority vote) or who were covered by formal labor–management agreements.[26] By 2009, 1.1 million federal civilian employees (or 33 percent) were represented by over 100 labor unions. The number of union members is not the same as the number of employees having union representation. The latter is almost always considerably higher than the former because those who do not pay union dues can also be represented in collective bargaining and are governed by any contractual agreements reached.

Growth in union membership and representation has not been the only important development in the national government.[27] Three new regulatory entities were created by executive order to centralize decision making that had previously been in the hands of individual executive-branch agencies. These were the Federal Labor Relations Council, the Federal Service Impasses Panel (to aid in resolving negotiating impasses), and a new Assistant Secretary of Labor for labor–management relations, who exercised responsibility for making decisions concerning, among other things, bargaining units, representation, and unfair labor practices. The **Federal Mediation and Conciliation Service** (**FMCS**, already in existence) was given an expanded role in

National Labor Relations Board (NLRB)

independent federal agency created in 1935 to enforce the National Labor Relations Act; conducts secret-ballot elections to determine whether employees want union representation, and investigates and remedies unfair labor practices by employers and unions.

Executive Order (EO) 10988

issued by President Kennedy in 1962, this order extended the right to organize and bargain collectively to all national government employees.

Federal Mediation and Conciliation Service (FMCS)

created by Congress in 1947 as an independent agency to promote sound and stable labor–management relations (http://www.fmcs.gov).

mediating negotiation disputes.[28] Also, a requirement for reporting and disclosure procedures similar to those demanded of unions in private employment was imposed for the first time.

A further significant step was taken with the passage of President Jimmy Carter's **Civil Service Reform Act of 1978**, which reinforced merit system principles, prohibited employment discrimination, and protected federal employees from arbitrary action, favoritism, or political coercion. One of the most important consequences of the act was to place in statutory form (Title VII) many terms of the various executive orders, so that "presidents no longer have the authority to regulate the process on their own."[29] Some specifics pertaining to collective bargaining included creating an independent **Federal Labor Relations Authority (FLRA)**, with powers greater than those of the old Federal Labor Relations Council (including a general counsel authorized to bring unfair labor charges); bringing negotiated grievance procedures into the scope of bargaining; extending labor unions' free automatic dues checkoff if authorized by the employee; requiring any agencies that issue government-wide regulations to consult with unions before taking any action that would make a substantial change in employment conditions; and permitting judicial review of some FLRA final orders.[30] FMCS was created by Congress in 1947 as an independent agency to promote sound and stable labor–management relations. And the **National Labor Management Association (NLMA)** is a national membership organization devoted to helping management and labor work together for constructive change. The net effect of these changes has been to put in place a complex and varied set of regulations governing a wide range of labor–management relations in the national government service. The days of unilateral personnel management, without participation of—and accommodation to—government employees represented by their unions, are long gone.[31]

The Civil Service Reform Act (CSRA) of 1978

In the course of civil service administration throughout this past century, both the advantages and disadvantages of reform became clear. Numerous choices were made that affected personnel management and collective bargaining practices. Each time presidential and other commissions examined the national bureaucracy, personnel problems were on their agendas, but prior to 1978, little in the way of comprehensive change had been brought about. When Jimmy Carter became president, a new effort was begun to alter merit system practices.[32] The principal targets were numerous; each problem had evolved over long periods of time, and solving them posed political as well as managerial challenges. Certainly, one of the most important was the evolution of the merit system from a protection against blatant partisan manipulation to a system that provided what many called excessive job security for employees (competent or not), that made possible virtually automatic salary increases

Civil Service Reform Act of 1978

law designed to reinforce merit principles, protect whistle-blowers, delegate personnel authority to agencies, reward employees for measurable performance, and make it easier to discharge incompetent workers; created the Federal Labor Relations Authority (FLRA), Office of Personnel Management (OPM), Senior Executive Service (SES), and Merit Systems Protection Board (MSPB).

Federal Labor Relations Authority (FLRA)

replaced the Federal Labor Relations Council and increased the strength of the bipartisan, three-member panel to supervise the creation of bargaining units and union elections, and to deal with labor–management relations in federal agencies.

National Labor Management Association (NLMA)

national membership organization devoted to helping management and labor work together for constructive change.

(deserved or not), and that made it difficult for responsible managers to dismiss unproductive employees. This "protected employment system," as it was described by former OPM Director Campbell, was clearly the focus of the Carter reform efforts. More to the point for a management-conscious president, existing arrangements made it difficult at best for public managers to direct the operations of their agencies effectively. (There is always interest within new presidential administrations in increasing the political responsiveness of top career officials.)

Other concerns addressed by the reform legislation included (1) the fact that no statute or executive order had ever spelled out the merit principles that were the foundation of the merit system; (2) what, if any, personnel practices were prohibited (for example, management retaliation against whistle-blowers—those disclosing waste, fraud, abuses, or other mismanagement); (3) the status of veterans' preference; (4) the informal—and often haphazard—manner in which employee performance was evaluated; and (5) the lack of a statutory basis for the conduct of labor relations (specifically, collective bargaining) with national government employees.

Unlike the 1883 Pendleton Act, which was devoted almost solely to eliminating patronage practices, the CSRA incorporated a wide variety of complex and interrelated objectives. For example, the design of the SES included the following: (1) SES members, drawn primarily from the supergrades (GS-16 through GS-18), would be able to work more closely and harmoniously with political appointees at the point of contact between the political head of the agency and the careerists (see Chapter 6); (2) the responsiveness of these senior career officials to presidential policy leadership would thus be enhanced; (3) incentives could be developed for greater productivity on the part of senior executives (especially considering that they would sacrifice substantial job security on joining the SES); (4) financial bonuses—and greater acknowledgment of careerists' policy advisory roles[33]—would serve as those incentives; (5) job performance of senior civil servants could be appraised more systematically; and (6) based on those appraisals, decisions about awarding bonuses could be made fairly and objectively.

Similarly, for the merit pay system for upper management grades GS-13 through GS-15, agencies were required to develop **performance appraisal** systems that included performance standards, and to tie merit pay to performance on the basis of the appraisal process. Underlying both the SES and merit pay were several assumptions: "protected employment" would be diluted, performance of middle- and top-level managers would be better evaluated, and **pay for performance** would serve as a positive incentive to those affected. It was hoped that, as a result of these reforms, the overall productivity and effectiveness of national government programs would be enhanced. Stronger protections for whistle-blowers were designed to achieve the same end.[34]

The early promise of the CSRA gave way instead to considerable frustration. One overriding difficulty was the dramatic change in the political and

performance appraisal

formal process used to document and evaluate an employee's job performance; typically used to reinforce management's assessment of the quality of an individual's work, punish workers who are "below standard," and reward others with bonuses, higher salaries, and promotions.

pay for performance

pay system proposed to replace the existing General Schedule, giving managers more power to award merit pay and weakening the power of unions.

governmental environment that accompanied the transition from the Carter to the Reagan administrations (1980–1981), specifically the Professional Air Traffic Controllers Organization (PATCO) strike, and radical changes at OPM. Civil Service Reform Act implementation went forward, however, in spite of these and other constraints. Some serious difficulties arose from ongoing conflicts between OPM and the agencies and between Congress and the executive branch; still others resulted from the way that many federal executives believed CSRA would affect their careers.

Specific problems included the following. First, performance appraisal suffered from uncertainties about how appraisals would be conducted, how their results would be used, whether OPM would properly monitor and evaluate the new appraisal procedures once they were in operation, and whether factors other than objective performance were the basis for some of the pay adjustments that were to be linked to these appraisals. Second, problems included a salary cap on what SES members could earn, controversy over the size of SES salary bonuses and merit pay increases, and disputes over the degree of fairness in awarding SES bonuses. Lastly, the design of the SES as a meeting ground for political and career executives came into question. Many careerists objected to what they saw as politically motivated decisions that, in their view, adversely affected them and the programs they managed. Furthermore, "relations between career and political people . . . deteriorated" within an atmosphere of frustration and dissatisfaction.[35] Another irony regarding the CSRA is that the act may have served as an example for personnel systems in other governments, with greater impacts than those felt in Washington. Civil service reform was implemented in the governments of twenty-four American states and fourteen other countries at least as fully as it has been in the national government's civil service.[36] Those impacts should be borne in mind, when evaluating the overall effects of civil service reform at all levels of government over the past thirty-five years.

Recent State and Local Government Experience

At state and local levels, the labor relations picture is different in several key respects from that in the national government and the private sector. For one thing, the total number of public employees belonging to labor unions or covered by bargaining agreements exceeds the number at the national level; in percentage terms, state-local unionization covers about 36 percent of all full-time employees. From 1962 to 1987, state and local union membership grew from 1.6 million to 4.9 million. Of that total, some 1.2 million were state employees and the remaining 3.7 million worked for local governments. By 2000, that number had fallen slightly to 42 percent of the local government workforce. The unionization rate for public employees has remained fairly constant since 1987, while membership rates have declined sharply for all major private-sector industries.[37] Unionization rates in the private sector have dropped from 20 percent in 1983 to 6.5 percent in 2009 (see Figure 7–4).

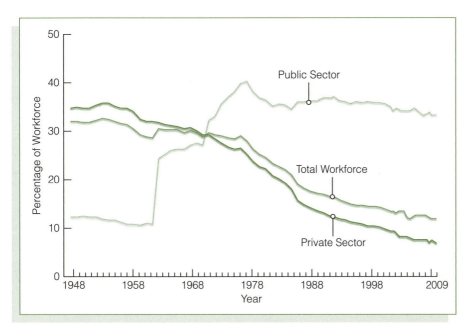

Source: Bureau of Labor Statistics, 2010.

FIGURE 7-4

Changes in Union Membership: 1948–2009

Among occupations, public-sector union rates are highest among police officers, firefighters, and teachers. A higher proportion of black males are members of unions (14 percent) than whites (12 percent), Asians (11 percent), or Hispanics (9.8 percent). On average, unionized worker salaries ($863 per week) were about one-third higher than nonunion employees ($663 weekly) in 2007. School districts alone account for 49 percent of all organized—that is, unionized—local government employees and 37 percent of all organized employees in state and local governments combined. Also, school districts and municipalities together account for over three-fourths of organized local employees, and almost 60 percent of those organized in both state and local governments. The number of public- and private-sector workers belonging to unions rose by 311,000 to 15.7 million in 2007, according to the U.S. Department of Labor's Bureau of Labor Statistics.[38]

The most heavily unionized functions in state government are highways, public welfare, hospitals, and public safety, each with about one-half of all employees organized. The largest state-local employee organization (with about 2 million members) is the NEA; it is perhaps significant that the NEA is traditionally the least militant of the teachers' organizations.[39] A second important difference between the state-local and national settings is the far greater complexity of state and local laws and regulations governing collective bargaining. As political scientist N. Joseph Cayer has noted, "[t]here is no common legal framework under which state and local government labor relations are governed. Labor relations take place under policies made through common law doctrines, judicial decisions, executive orders, and statutes and ordinances."[40] Political scientist Richard Kearney has described the overall situation this way:

> These policies exhibit considerable divergence. State legislation, for instance, ranges from a single comprehensive statute providing coverage for all public employees in Iowa, to coverage of only firefighters in Wyoming, to the total prohibition of collective bargaining in North Carolina. In other states, public employees bargain under the authority of an attorney general's opinion (North Dakota), or civil service regulations (Michigan state employees).[41]

According to the American Federation of Labor and Congress of Industrial Organizations (AFL-CIO), twenty-three states and the District of Columbia extend full collective bargaining rights to all public employees; thirteen states protect bargaining rights for some public employees; and fourteen states do not provide for collective bargaining for any state or local government employees.[42] In sum, "the labor relations situation for public employees is different in every city, county, and state, and *the general status of public sector labor relations is still undefined.*"[43]

Thus, labor–management relations loom larger in state-local personnel management than in the national government in quantitative terms, in complexity, and with regard to use of the strike. States and localities have increasingly looked to full-time labor relations specialists for guidance and expertise. In some government jurisdictions, such specialists are given major responsibility for conducting collective bargaining with employee representatives. With or without the assistance of these experts, however, public managers have had to become more sensitive to, and skillful in dealing with, the needs and preferences—and formal demands—of their respective labor forces. In particular, they have had to learn the art of collective bargaining as a central element of personnel management.

The Collective Bargaining Process

The process of collective bargaining comprises a number of distinct steps and decision points, which are usually specified in some detail in government jurisdictions operating under comprehensive bargaining legislation. In such jurisdictions, the law specifies relevant organizational and administrative arrangements for implementing and enforcing the collective bargaining statute. In cases in which there is no comprehensive statutory authority, many of the same procedural steps are also found, but they lack both the detail and the implementation mechanisms characteristic of more far-reaching legislation.[44]

Whatever the steps in the actual bargaining process, it is standard for bargaining to be supervised by an agency, such as FLRA, with specific oversight responsibility. Here, too, there is considerable variety in the specific form such supervision takes. In state and local governments, a number of different arrangements are possible for supervising the bargaining process. In some states (such as Maine, New York, and Hawaii), an agency is created for the sole purpose of supervising collective bargaining as well as all other aspects of public employee labor relations; in some other states, responsibility is assigned to personnel departments, departments of labor, or personnel boards (as in Alaska, Massachusetts, Montana, and Wisconsin). Another variation involves supervision of the overall process by a state board, but with delegation to individual departments of specific responsibility for bargaining in their respective areas; examples might include a state department of education or a local board of education.

The usual bargaining sequence consists of the following:

1. Labor organizing efforts, followed by the union seeking recognition as the bargaining agent
2. Selection of the bargaining team by both employees and management
3. Defining the scope of bargaining, that is, just what issues will be subject to negotiation and what will not be, within the limits set by statute or executive order
4. Putting forward proposals and counterproposals
5. Reaching agreement at the negotiating table (this assumes that agreement can be reached)
6. Submitting any agreement reached to a ratification vote by both employees and management
7. In the event agreement cannot be reached, attempting to resolve impasses through **impasse procedures** (mediation, fact finding, arbitration, or referendum)
8. Dealing with the possibility—or reality—of a strike
9. Once a contract is signed, collaborating in the implementation of its provisions (contract administration)

This is, in reality, a *cycle* rather than a *sequence*. Except for the very first contractual arrangement between management and labor, these steps are repeated periodically, with considerable incentive for both sides to prepare carefully—during the last step of the cycle, namely, contract implementation—for the next round of bargaining by keeping a complete record of "all problems, disputes, grievances, and interpretations" encountered in administering the previous agreement.[45] After the process has become well established, the first two steps are normally omitted unless there arises strong sentiment among employees for a change in the organization representing them or unless it is deemed desirable by one or both sides to change the composition of their respective bargaining teams.

An important aspect of the collective bargaining environment is the existence in most jurisdictions of a code of unfair labor practices. Although not a formal part of actual bargaining, or even of the scope of negotiations, such codes do play a part by restricting certain kinds of behavior by both sides

impasse procedures

in the context of labor–management relations and collective bargaining, procedures that can be called into play when collective negotiations do not lead to agreement at the bargaining table; these include mediation, fact finding, arbitration, and referendum (in some combination, or following one another should one procedure fail to resolve the impasse).

that would have the effect of poisoning the atmosphere of negotiations if they did occur. Included among prohibited behaviors are (among other things) dismissing employees for union organizing, physical intimidation or attempted bribery to influence the outcome of union representation elections, discriminating arbitrarily against employees for nonmembership in a union, and, of course, refusing to enter into collective bargaining where it is provided for. Under terms of most labor–management agreements, any activity that may violate codes of unfair practices can become grounds for initiating grievance proceedings.

productivity bargaining

labor–management negotiations that link productivity improvements to employee wage increases as an alternative to reductions-in-force.

Another dimension of bargaining that has emerged only in recent years is so-called **productivity bargaining**. Following the example of the private sector, public managers have attempted, with some success, to negotiate contract provisions, whereby employee wage increases are linked to various cost-cutting efforts—including increasing productivity on the job—as an alternative to layoffs. In large cities, such as New York and Washington, D.C., contracts with very specific clauses were signed under which labor unions agreed to help cut labor costs and increase output; in the case of the former, this was part of the mid-1970s fiscal crisis and efforts by all levels of government to prevent New York City from going into bankruptcy. In a period of growing fiscal stress for many American states and municipalities, productivity bargaining is a device that is likely to see increasing future use.

Public-Employee Strikes

The phenomenon of the strike is most evident in state and local government; in fact, only postal workers and PATCO members have actively defied the prohibition on strikes by employees of the national government. Strike activity increased dramatically during the 1960s, but in more recent decades, there have been fewer strikes, relative to the number of employees covered by bargaining agreements and in relationship to the number of agreements that are regularly negotiated at the state and local levels. How the affected public reacts often predicts the success or failure of this union strategy. Sometimes it may even be difficult to say whether a strike has actually occurred. Because strikes are prohibited almost everywhere, a **job action** of some kind—of which strikes are only one variety—may take another form. One hears of the "blue flu" afflicting substantial numbers of police officers or the "red rash" affecting firefighters—all on the same day, with some attendant publicity beforehand—or of teachers' "sick-ins" or sanitation workers' slowdowns. What constitutes an actual strike against government employers, in short, may not be as easy to determine as one might think. Thus, a count of the number of strikes—as distinct from other kinds of job actions—must be received a bit skeptically. The count would be far higher if all types of job actions were surveyed, though that too would pose some difficulties.

job action

any action taken by employees (usually unionized) as a protest against an aspect of their work or working conditions; includes, but is not limited to, strikes or work slowdowns.

The Uncertain Future of Public-Sector Collective Bargaining

It is clear from this discussion that the past fifty years have seen unparalleled— and undoubtedly permanent—changes in many aspects of personnel management. Equally obvious are what N. Joseph Cayer describes as the "clear implications for financial management, budgeting, personnel, and planning, and for the roles of employees and managers in the system."[46] There are also other concerns in the early twenty-first century related to the emphases on performance management and the quest for improved customer service quality.

First, with regard to fiscal implications, two elements stand out: (1) higher personnel costs are associated with collective bargaining and (2) agreements negotiated between labor and management reduce the flexibility of those responsible for drawing up and approving government budgets by creating wage/salary and fringe benefit figures that can be changed only with great difficulty after a contract is ratified by the negotiating parties. Another, broader dimension of the fiscal issue is the fact that labor organizations in comparable jurisdictions (for example, suburban communities within the same metropolitan area) often seek comparability in pay, thus adding pressure to the budgetary process in any one jurisdiction. One response to this problem is the growing phenomenon of multiemployer bargaining. And, to the extent that planning and budgeting are to be coordinated functions, they are under greater constraint because of the need to permit negotiators to decide issues that may have long-term consequences.

Second, the scope of the personnel function is likely to become a subject of future collective bargaining. Because the scope of bargaining can change in successive negotiation cycles, aspects of personnel management that have not been negotiable (for example, merit system principles, job classifications, appeals procedures, and work rules and regulations) could well become so. Thus, depending on how much effort labor organizations make to bargain on such issues, and on management's ability to counter such attempts effectively, the personnel function could well undergo further—and even more fundamental— change. Part of this evolution lies in what many see as the basic philosophical conflict between collective bargaining and merit principles, which, however, is not a universally held position.[47] This translates into an issue of managerial command and control, especially with regard to cash-strapped state and local governments.

For public-sector managers, collective bargaining offers both disadvantages and advantages—the former more readily noted by some observers than the latter. Assuming that management's prerogative to run the operation on its own is entirely legitimate, having to share the power to do so is a disadvantage. An accompanying problem is the difficulty management is likely to encounter in developing a consistent personnel policy among diverse groups of union and management employees in the same agency.

On the other hand, a number of distinct advantages have also been suggested. One is that bargaining requires all those interested in effective public management to deal with the management function in all its dimensions, not just whether enough money is available or whether enough authority has been delegated or whether city council will support top-level managers in this or that conflict. A second advantage lies in having to be prepared for bargaining, which forces managers and their superiors to carefully identify managerial weaknesses, in general, and negotiate on training needs, in particular, and to remedy them; otherwise, the unions might well hold the upper hand in the bargaining process. This is complicated in cases in which supervisory and managerial unions exist—a phenomenon unique to the public sector. Where management has previously labored under the burden of its own structural or procedural shortcomings, it can be said that collective bargaining has served the interests of governmental effectiveness by forcing attention to those shortcomings.

The future of public-sector unions and collective bargaining is likely to be a confrontational one. Past conflict between Republican presidents and federal unions diverted resources and distracted some public employees from ever more important international and domestic security responsibilities. The George W. Bush administration sought to abolish the GS pay system as well as collective bargaining and require that at least part of every pay raise for 1.8 million federal civilian workers would be decided on the basis of annual performance evaluation. The administration was less forthright about how performance would be evaluated, and about who would interpret the results. Many careerists were alienated by proposals to eliminate the GS and replace it with a pay-for-performance scheme that would radically alter career paths and labor–management relations. The new system was to initially apply to about 700,000 Department of Defense (DoD) employees, who would work under broader pay bands (see above) and new rules for promotions within each pay band. That proposal, however, was scaled back to include 11,000 DoD civil service employees who shifted to a new National Security Personnel System (NSPS) in April 2006; another 66,000 DoD employees converted between October 2006 and January 2007. Similar changes were slated to take effect in DHS in October 2005, but were delayed by a lawsuit filed by the National Treasury Employees Union and four other federal unions, which represent 150,000 federal employees in thirty government agencies. Unions representing the affected workers are adamantly opposed to new regulations that would eliminate the decades-old GS system and replace it with a results-based system that would better reward the department's best workers. Several members of Congress agreed with this assessment and viewed the new system as "union busting."

The proposed new system would have extensively revised appeals procedures for employee disciplinary actions and limited the power of unions to bargain collectively over workplace rules. Under the system, a portion of the salary increase pool (about one-half) would be set aside and left to the discretion of the Secretary of Defense to award larger raises to the department's best workers. The objections of congressional representatives and federal employee unions to the NSPS and pay-for-performance systems reflect concerns about the wisdom of such radical changes at a time when the United States is heavily involved with military and homeland security operations. President Barack Obama signed legislation repealing the NSPS in October 2009. Employees under NSPS had until January 1, 2012 to convert back to the previous pay systems without losing pay or seniority as a result of the conversion. In February 2011, the U.S. Senate passed legislation allowing federal DHS officers to unionize, potentially adding 50,000 Transportation Security Administration (TSA) members to federal unions.

POINT/COUNTERPOINT

THE ISSUE The labor relations picture is different at the state and local levels from that existing at the national level and in the private sector. In state and local governments, there are many more public employees belonging to labor unions and covered by bargaining agreements. With many states facing budgetary constraints and deficits, the role of unions has to be discussed more frequently.

Are public-employee unions to blame for budget deficits in several states?

Arguments *for* Public-Employee Unions Causing Budget Deficits

- There is no common legal framework or pattern for state and local government labor relations, causing communities within the same metropolitan area to seek comparable pay, and thus putting pressure on the budgetary process.

- Lack of cohesion in labor relations laws has led states and cities to take on full-time labor relations specialists for guidance and expertise, taking time and money away from other important matters and decisions.

- The ability to strike (or any other form of job action) and collectively demand higher wages challenges the order of states and cities, thus challenging both the authority and the stability of state and local government entities.

Arguments *against* Public-Employee Unions Causing Budget Deficits

- Productivity bargaining has become more prevalent in recent years, in order to negotiate contract provisions that link employee wage increases to various cost-cutting efforts, thereby preventing states and localities from going into bankruptcy.

- Strikes are prohibited almost everywhere, and have continually gone down in number over the years, due to greater coverage of employees by bargaining agreements within a state.

- Bargaining requires all those interested in effective public management to deal with the management function in its totality, not just within budgetary matters.

Developments in Personnel Administration

There has clearly been a great deal of ferment and change in the processes of fulfilling government's need for qualified employees. PPA has become even more susceptible to both internal and external pressures for change and for adaptation to changing values and conditions. Furthermore, the 2000s have seen a variety of significant changes with major impacts on public personnel. Three developments illustrate the scope and potential consequences of recent change in personnel management: (1) the erosion of affirmative action and comparable-worth efforts in hiring, promoting, and equalizing pay for women and members of minority groups; (2) changing guidelines governing patronage and other partisan activity; and (3) new directions in personnel management resulting from massive reorganizations of federal executive agencies.

Affirmative Action and Comparable Worth

In the public service, as elsewhere, there has been emphasis in recent years on hiring and advancement of minorities and women. The rationale behind the affirmative action movement is that some individuals and groups have been unfairly—in many cases, arbitrarily—discriminated against in the past and that seeking to bring them into government service is one effective way to redress old grievances (see Chapter 2). The national government has gone a long way, under executive orders such as **Executive Order (EO) 10925** (1961) and provisions of legislation such as the **1964 Civil Rights Act** and the **1972 Equal Employment Opportunity Act**, to ensure that women and minorities are given at least strong consideration, if not outright preferential treatment, in decisions to hire government employees. The U.S. **Equal Employment Opportunity Commission (EEOC)** was established in 1964 to investigate charges of racial and other arbitrary discrimination by employers and unions, in all aspects of employment, and to enforce equal employment laws with legal action.[48]

The principle of equal pay for equal work was firmly established by the national **Equity Pay Act of 1963**, requiring an end to any gender-based (or other) discrimination in compensation for individuals engaged in similar work. The issue of **comparable worth**, however, goes beyond that principle. It addresses the difficult question of how to set pay levels for individuals doing work that is different, but comparable in value to the employing organization, government, or society at large. Apart from the intrinsic issues, there is a key relationship here to affirmative action because most secretaries, librarians, and nurses are female and lower-paid; most managers, engineers, and truck drivers are male and higher-paid. Some try to justify lower pay for "women's work" on the grounds that, historically, women were not the principal breadwinners; that many younger women were in the workforce only until they married and started a family; or that the forces of labor supply and demand (not gender discrimination) worked to depress compensation levels for nurses, secretaries, telephone operators, teachers, and the like. Others argue that these and similar assumptions represent

---

Executive Order (EO) 10925

issued by President Kennedy in 1961, this EO required for the first time that "affirmative action" guidelines be used to prohibit discrimination in employment by federal agencies and contractors.

1964 Civil Rights Act

landmark legislation prohibiting discrimination by the private sector in both employment and housing.

1972 Equal Employment Opportunity Act

amended Title VII, the Civil Rights Act of 1964; designed to strengthen the authority of the Equal Employment Opportunity Commission (EEOC) to enforce antidiscrimination laws in state and local governments as well as in private organizations with fifteen or more employees.

Equal Employment Opportunity Commission (EEOC)

investigates and rules on charges of racial and other arbitrary discrimination by employers and unions, in all aspects of employment (http://www.eeoc.gov).

Equity Pay Act of 1963

prohibited gender-based (or other) discrimination in pay for those engaged in the same type of work.

comparable worth

extended the "equal pay for equal work" principle to develop criteria for compensation based on the intellectual and physical demands of the job, not market determination of its worth.

social stereotypes of women as inherently less valuable workers. Yet another dispute revolves around the methodology that would be used to determine comparability among diverse occupations. And there are vastly differing perceptions of how practical, or useful, the task of comparing is.[49]

The issues raised by affirmative action and comparable-worth programs are weighty ones. First, if a merit system is viewed as one that goes strictly by the applicant's job-related competence, then affirmative action conflicts with that objective. This has been the basis of many criticisms of such programs. Those who support affirmative action point out, however, that it is entirely appropriate as a remedial effort in light of historic lack of access to jobs suffered by minorities. They also point to features such as veterans' preference, along with failure to enforce standards of competence as vigorously after appointment as before, as evidence of imperfection in existing merit practices. The essence of their contention is that denial of access through omission or systematic exclusion of certain groups is best remedied by practicing systematic inclusion through affirmative action. They also claim that this makes the public service more representative of different groups in the population and, thus, more responsive to their concerns.

Affirmative action is also said to be needed because of past biases in intelligence, employment, and promotion testing. That is, it has been alleged that competitive examinations have often been discriminatory above and beyond the "necessary" discrimination among the various competencies and skills of those seeking employment or advancement. Advocates of this view argue that testing is based on the experience and training of a white, middle-class population (usually in key management and recruiting positions) and inevitably discriminates unfairly against those whose cultural background, experience, and training are dissimilar.

The debate over affirmative action, comparable worth, and quotas—indeed the whole area of what many think of as **reverse discrimination**—is likely to continue, guided by decisions made in legislatures or courts in the immediate future. One indication of the position of the U.S. Supreme Court on this matter was its decision in June 2009 to reverse the actions of the mayor of New Haven, Connecticut, who six years earlier had promoted African-American firefighters over their Caucasian counterparts even though their scores on promotion examinations were lower.[50] The Supreme Court overturned the lower court ruling that had upheld the promotions after finding that there had been no racial bias in the examination process, as alleged.

But what difference has this furor made? There has been a significant increase in the proportion of minorities and women present in the workforces of national, state, and local governments; to that extent, affirmative action employment programs have succeeded. It also is clear that, of the minorities and women in both public and private sector employment, a substantial majority still tend to occupy the less responsible lower-level positions relative to white males, and many are found at entry-grade levels of the civil service hierarchy, with correspondingly lower salary or wage levels. This is a reflection, in part, of the dominance of a generation of military veterans who benefited from preferences on federal service exams for upper-level posts. Interestingly, over one-half

reverse discrimination

unfavorable actions against white males to achieve affirmative action goals to hire and promote more women and minorities.

of all federal workers (including 30 percent of all FBI agents) were eligible for retirement in 2010. As a result, opportunities for greater upward mobility for minorities (and for others) are likely to increase, especially considering the Obama administration's recognition of the importance of federal unions, and the role played by those unions in promoting upward mobility.

Predictably, the picture varies at different levels of government. National government data indicated, for example, that in 2010 women made up more than 44 percent of the total federal civilian workforce, African-Americans held 17.3 percent of federal civilian jobs, and Hispanics represented 7.6 percent of the federal workforce.[51] But despite increases in numbers of women and minorities in the federal civil service, women are still concentrated in lower-echelon jobs. According to one study, women held only 15 percent of the positions in grades GS-13 through GS-15 (though this had increased from only 10 percent a decade earlier).[52] And the Merit Systems Protection Board reported during the 1990s that women and minorities accounted for only 12 and 9 percent, respectively, of the members of the SES, suggesting that a "glass ceiling" still bars women and minorities from rising to the highest levels of the national civil service, as was still the case regarding comparable positions in the private sector.[53]

States and localities present a much more varied picture. There is evidence that white women, as well as minorities of both genders, have made marked gains in government employment generally, but at a slower pace in state and local governments (especially for minorities) than at the national level. Also, as in the case of the national government, white males still predominate in the higher personnel grades and pay levels. Not surprisingly, there is great variation among the states and among the thousands of local governments, as well as among different functional areas.[54]

Clearly, affirmative action has not done all that its proponents hoped it would; it is questionable that it could have tilted the balance as far as some wanted it to. Furthermore, the outlook for the immediate future is mixed; some developments augur well for affirmative action, and others, such as the passage of Proposition 209 in California, decidedly do not.[55] That vote was widely interpreted as a backlash against affirmative action aimed at blacks, immigrants, women, and other ethnic minorities. The California decision was upheld by the federal appeals court and the controversy spread to other states. In 1998, voters in the state of Washington passed a similar ballot measure repealing affirmative action programs. And in February 2000, amid considerable controversy, Florida abolished preferential treatment for minorities in contracting, hiring, and admissions to state universities as part of Governor Jeb Bush's "One Florida" initiative.

Prior to the appointment of conservative Justices to the U.S. Supreme Court in 2005, proponents of affirmative action pointed hopefully to federal court decisions that sustained various practices, or required government actions, that are consistent with the principle of affirmative action. On the other hand, public administration scholar David Rosenbloom correctly predicted some years ago that affirmative action, at least in the national government, would become a relatively less prominent concern. He noted, among other things, the absence of a strong national consensus supporting affirmative action, along with the rise of new personnel concerns (for example, retrenchment and productivity)[56]; other new priorities such as sexual harassment, employee empowerment, and improving service to "customers" also point to diminished attention to affirmative action. Under the George W. Bush administration, the budget and staff of EEOC were cut, resulting in huge backlogs of case investigations.[57] Lacking executive and judicial support, and without additional budget and staff, it is highly unlikely that the EEOC or any other regulatory agency will be able to fully enforce allegations of racial or gender discrimination. Funding and staff reductions occurred in the same time period in which President Bush and Congress shifted more money to national defense and homeland security.

The ultimate success of state efforts to encourage their own affirmative action policies or limit federal ones is likely to be decided not by voters but by the federal courts. Although enforcement of civil rights protections has decreased, it is doubtful that affirmative action will be thrust aside entirely, especially given its statutory foundations and the growing emphasis on encouraging diversity in college admissions and in the workforce. In a 2003 precedent-setting case, the Supreme Court delivered a split decision, upholding the University of Michigan's use of affirmative action factors for law school admissions, but striking down procedures and weighting formulas used to process larger numbers of undergraduate applications.[58]

HOW WOULD YOU DECIDE?

North Country

Academy Award winner Charlize Theron plays single mother Josey Aimes in *North Country*, a film about the need for change and justice in the workplace. In the film, based on a true story from 1984, Josey leaves an abusive husband, taking her two children with her to her hometown in northern Minnesota. In order to support her family, she begins work in the local iron ore mines, a traditionally male-dominated job that pays more than any other job in the area. The mining industry is one in which little has changed regarding gender acceptance and inequality. Josey is prepared for the physically demanding, as well as dangerous, work, but not the extent of harassment and abuse that she and the few other female miners encounter. She is verbally and physically abused, as well as sexually harassed, without any action being taken by her boss, who tells the women that it comes with the territory in a male-dominated career.

Josey eventually speaks out against the treatment that she and the other female miners have endured, but her complaints go unanswered and unaddressed. The belief is that there are separate jobs for men and for women, and that Josey should find another career if she is unhappy with the way she is treated. Josey refuses to stop and files the nation's first class-action sexual harassment lawsuit, which she wins.

Steps within the national government have been taken over the past few decades to address the question of equal pay and equal employment opportunities for individuals, regardless of age, race, or gender. Cases like Josey Aimes's, however, are still prevalent throughout the country, despite recent legislative strides and judicial decisions resulting from various lawsuits.

What role should the three major levels of government play in creating and enforcing legislation that combats age, race, and gender discrimination in the workplace?

Source: http://northcountrymovie.warnerbros.com/, accessed April 1, 2011.

Personnel Policy and Politics

The desirability of linking government personnel practices to partisan politics has been a matter of controversy in this nation for nearly the whole of our political history. It is no different now, and two aspects of this issue have loomed large in recent developments in personnel administration.

One revolves around judicial determinations concerning patronage and, in particular, a number of decisions in which various courts have ruled that dismissal of, or other adverse actions against, non-merit-protected employees solely on partisan grounds could be construed as a violation of constitutional rights protected by the First and Fourteenth Amendments to the U.S. Constitution. In *O'Hare Truck Service, Inc. v. City of Northlake*, 518 U.S. 712(1996), the Supreme Court dealt a further blow to political patronage, making it clear that individuals and companies do not give up their rights to free speech and political association merely because they perform services for the government. These rulings do not apply to confidential policy-making jobs, but the courts have not yet determined where to draw the line between these and other posts. And, even though the courts have spoken regarding patronage, such practices are thought to be too entrenched to disappear overnight. It is clear that patronage—though often in modified form—is still very much with us.

The other dimension of personnel and partisanship is the issue of whether civil servants should be required to maintain partisan neutrality by virtue of their being public employees. This required neutrality, which was a primary objective of merit reformers in the nineteenth century, was embodied in the Political Activities Act of 1939 (the Hatch Act). This legislation, as amended in 1940 and 1966, prohibited any active participation in political campaigns by national government employees, state and local employees working in any nationally funded program, and employees of private organizations working with community-action programs. But as rights of government employees became a more prominent concern in the 1960s and early 1970s, efforts were made to limit or overturn the Hatch Act. The reasoning behind these efforts was that provisions barring political involvement were said to infringe on rights that could be exercised by others, thus rendering government personnel second-class citizens. The right to vote was not enough, it was argued; government employees should have the right to participate in all aspects of politics.

In a series of court cases, several state and local versions of the Hatch Act were challenged, some successfully. The U.S. District Court for the District of Columbia declared the Hatch Act itself unconstitutional on grounds of vagueness and of First Amendment violations in *National Association of Letter Carriers, AFL-CIO v. United States Civil Service Commission*, 346 F. Supp. 578 (1972). But, in 1973, the Supreme Court reversed that lower court ruling on a 6–3 vote, upholding the act and its constitutionality. After that, efforts centered on persuading Congress to loosen restrictions on government employees' political activities. In the early summer of 1990, Congress enacted a revision of the Hatch Act that would have relaxed many of the restrictions on "political" (meaning, mainly, partisan) activities by national government employees, but President Bush vetoed the bill. In 1993, however, Congress again passed repeal of the Hatch Act, and this time President Clinton signed the bill into law. The effect of this change was to permit national government employees to participate in most aspects of electoral politics in the same manner as any other citizens. The only major restrictions are that federal employees may not run for partisan elective office or solicit campaign contributions from the general public.

Two other political aspects of government personnel management are concerns that current efforts to bring about greater responsiveness to political leadership among higher-level civil servants may have gone too far, and that the amount and intensity of partisan criticism aimed at public administrators has reached a level not seen in quite some time.[59] To paraphrase a number of commentaries about the changes, achieving greater responsiveness is one thing; downgrading and gutting the competitive service is quite another.[60] The various steps taken during the George W. Bush years were cause for concern for many who have defended the merit system over the years. Fewer reservations have been expressed about the Obama administration's personnel initiatives. It has been suggested, however, that too much presidential control—even in the name of empowering civil servants—carries with it potentially damaging effects on the civil service as a whole.

The other political dimension has a larger context and perhaps wider-ranging consequences. It has been said, with some justification, that those who find intense criticism of public officials disturbing freely acknowledge that those officials must be held accountable—that we have a legitimate interest in official actions being linked appropriately to established public purposes and policies. On the other hand, the pervasive public habit of blaming government bureaucracy for private market economic failures (among many other things) has become part of our national folklore. It does nothing to promote accountability, and may do a great deal to undermine the morale and self-confidence of conscientious public servants. This denigration (downgrading or deriding) of civil servants has often surfaced in the public utterances of candidates for elective office—including candidates Carter, Reagan, and George W. Bush the first time each ran for the presidency, and candidate Clinton (though somewhat less pointedly) at various times during his presidency. As a result, it is argued, many talented and experienced officials, with a wealth of experience and understanding of public programs, have left government service. Those who replaced them are inevitably less experienced, less informed by past failures and successes, and less familiar with their programmatic and political "territory." The net result may well be a government service less prepared to manage programs involving hundreds of billions of dollars, or to plan responsibly for policy and program needs ten and twenty years hence. Despite negative campaigning aimed at the character of candidates, misuse of taxes, misplaced budget priorities, and wasteful public projects, one positive aspect of the 2008 presidential election was the distinct lack of invective directed at civil servants as a group.

Unfortunately, the tradition was revived in 2010 as major policy differences resurfaced between Democrats and Republicans (who re-established control of the House of Representatives for the first time in four years).

Reforming Personnel Management

The National Performance Review (1993–2001) proposed a series of progressive changes that had far-reaching implications for how the national government managed its personnel systems.[61] Specific proposals were adopted to (1) deregulate personnel policy by phasing out the 10,000-page *Federal Personnel Manual*, together with all agency implementing directives; (2) simplify existing position classification systems by giving more agencies more flexibility in how they classify and pay their employees; (3) permit agencies to design their own performance management and reward systems; and (4) streamline systems for dealing with poor performance, including reducing by one-half the time required to dismiss managers and employees "for cause," that is, for failure to perform their duties in a competent and productive manner. The Clinton administration intended to both *deregulate* and *decentralize* many key aspects of personnel management. What makes such efforts all the more significant is the fact that each one, by itself, points the way to new approaches to managing national government employees.

Several initiatives undertaken by the Bush administration brought about even more fundamental changes in managing executive-branch personnel. Early in his first term, Bush proposed five government-wide strategies, including **competitive sourcing**, which permitted private companies to compete with federal agencies for nearly half a million jobs, including almost 850,000 jobs of federal employees that were already available to private contractors. Federal agencies were ordered to make 15 percent of their jobs open for outside competition. President Bush and many of his appointees believed that most citizens did not care who provided the service and the private sector (they argued) operates for less, creating competition and allegedly leading to savings of 20–50 percent. Paul Light saw the competitive sourcing initiative as part of a "long-standing effort to keep the total headcount of government as low as possible."[62] Bush administration officials acknowledged the potential negative effects on morale of public employees, but were quick to point out that this is not outsourcing of jobs, but "introducing competition" to the federal workforce.

It is still unclear how the former president's vision of competitive sourcing related to government performance and more efficient delivery of public services. With the exception of increasing expenditures for national defense, most federal assistance programs consist mainly of mandatory entitlement transfers for social-insurance payments to individuals, for medical services, or research grants to institutions; relatively few federal agencies perform direct domestic customer-service responsibilities. There have been few large-scale

competitive sourcing

one of the Bush administration's five performance management improvements designed to outsource more federal jobs to private contractors.

public–private competitions among service providers in the federal government. Claims of large savings were based on a limited number of trials, and proved to be exaggerated. Public employees countered that after working in the government for several years, they have proven their efficiency and should not be distracted by unnecessary competition, to determine whether private contractors would do a better job. Consequently, managers are placed in a very difficult position, because they have to accommodate policies of the administration while supporting their subordinates.

How these issues are resolved has obvious financial implications for public budgeting, but also directly affects personnel management, collective bargaining, labor relations, and the push for greater employee productivity. Despite the expanded use of competition, privatization, and a results orientation in the national government, it is still too early to determine the *level* of commitment or the long-term impact of alternative personnel systems (APS) on employee morale or productivity. APS is a commonly accepted term for the host of personnel systems outside of the competitive civil service system that are designed to address long-standing issues in federal agencies, such as performance appraisal and compensation. They may be established under narrowly focused legislation for an agency or a related set of agencies, under the demonstration project provisions of Chapter 47 of Title 5 of the U.S. Code or under new provisions of Title 5, which now allow both DHS and DoD to set up contemporary human resource management systems. There are few reliable studies of the impact of competitive sourcing on citizen "customers," employees, or disabled persons.[63] Consistent with President Obama's budgetary priorities and challenges to public employees, there is a need for more empirical research to determine whether or not reforms lead to fundamental shifts in the administrative values of public officials—and if so, with what consequences.

Perspectives and Implications

The U.S. civil service has existed for more than a century on a foundation of belief and practice clear in intent and quite consistent in manner of operation. Recently, however, all of the assumptions underlying past practice are being seriously questioned. The merit system has been modified to accommodate veterans' preference and, more recently, demographic representativeness. At the same time, efforts are under way to breathe new life into the meaning of *merit* by linking performance to compensation and other incentives such as promotion. The Carter administration sought to achieve a significant degree of change in the merit system in this respect. The Reagan administration undertook other initiatives, designed for the most part to enhance presidential influence over the activities of career civil servants. In terms of the assumptions underlying personnel management, this meant favoring political responsiveness over politically neutral competence, at least to some extent. The resultant uncertainties compounded those associated with civil service reform in the late 1970s. The first Bush administration took some steps to ease the "pay crunch" and to reestablish a systemwide point of entry into the national government civil service (with the ACWA examination). The Clinton administration initiated major efforts to reform the personnel system, pointing in directions that were largely new to the national government. Other dimensions of potential change include the impact of future court decisions on patronage practices, public backlash against hiring quotas and affirmative action, and more contracting out or privatization of public operations to outside consultants and contractors. State and local government personnel practices are also undergoing change, partly in direct response to initiatives from Washington (including the courts) and partly because of forces at work within their respective jurisdictions. In the fall of 2010, under pressure from Congress, the Obama administration proposed freezing of federal salaries for two years, while at the same time supporting collective bargaining at all levels of government.

Recommendations of the National Commission on the Public Service (the Volcker Commission) significantly influenced personnel administration as well. The commission recommended, in general, that steps be taken to address the negative perceptions of public service said to exist among many of our citizens, to deal with managerial issues (such as recruitment and retention of public servants), to strengthen education and training for serving in public-sector positions, and to increase pay and benefits for government employees. More specific recommendations were aimed at improving the work environment, reducing hiring of political appointees, increasing access to job openings, and rewarding executive excellence. Some, but by no means all, of these suggestions have been implemented in the federal civil service; whether more of these will be adopted (or even advocated) remains to be seen.[64]

The second Bush administration attempted to initiate major reorganizations challenging long-established civil service principles. Supporters of these changes considered them necessary to introduce more merit into a pay and cultural system that has not been receptive to these concepts in the past. They argued that pay for performance would increase productivity and job performance, recognize employees for their contribution to the organization, and accelerate salary progression for top performers. On the other hand, critics argued that the new pay system would give rise to managers rewarding favored employees at the expense of others who are doing a good job. It also is seen by many as a thinly veiled "scam to reduce overall employee pay" and benefits.[65] Many of the Bush administration's initiatives regarding pay classification, pay for performance, evaluation, and adverse action appeals reflected an anti–civil service, pro-business approach to personnel selection and performance, with only token participation by all stakeholders, including unions, interest groups, and employees.

President Obama's administration has taken strides toward improving the public's opinion of government employment and civil service. Obama has invited the Director of OPM, John Berry, to regularly attend Cabinet meetings.

Operations that were once outsourced in previous administrations have been brought back into the government, and effort has been made to hire and promote educated, bright individuals. Teams within the administration have been launched to grapple with questions about government merit pay programs, and Obama has requested regular meetings between Berry and other top officials to address personnel issues head-on. Such programs, however, often struggle, and it remains to be seen how the Obama administration will tackle the implementation of such sensitive efforts.[66]

This kind of turmoil in a central area of public administration has affected the quality of job performance and the condition of the public service.[67] The more essential point to consider is the vast uncertainty surrounding public personnel functions, triggered by political pressures from both Republican and Democratic presidents for different sorts of change. As basic concepts and their meanings continue to undergo a long-term process of redefinition and as new concerns command our attention, how PPA will continue to unfold and develop is far from certain.

Summary

Public personnel administration has evolved from a fairly routine function of government to a very controversial one. Personnel practices have varied, reflecting at different times the values of strong executive leadership and political representativeness on the one hand and politically neutral competence on the other.

The public aspect reflects the impacts of other political institutions, including legislative bodies, interest groups, and political parties. The size of government bureaucracies is a matter of concern to both citizens and personnel administrators, as is the competence and diversity of employee skills. National government budget cuts have been felt in the personnel area in the form of limited entry, reductions-in-force, "bumping" of employees to lower ranks, increased turnover, and pay freezes.

Public personnel administration has evolved, at the national level, through a series of stages—from total exclusion of all but the most elite to the broad inclusion of all seeking admittance. In many local governments, the organizational arrangements for personnel management are small, informal, or both. Greater attention to HRD and professionalism is a relatively recent feature of bureaucracy that has implications for the general conduct of public administration. Similar developments have taken place, varying in extent, in state and local governments that have strong merit systems.

Merit systems emphasize competence related to the job and offer some stability; patronage systems favor political connections and loyalties, and permit a chief executive to select loyal subordinates.

Position classification is essential in order to conduct recruitment, administer broad-gauged entrance examinations, and award equal pay for equal work. Recruitment has become both more systematic and less restricted. Examination processes are more complex at all levels of government. Achievement-oriented factors, such as education and experience, and ascriptive criteria have played a role in both examination and selection.

Salary and wage levels in the national government have increased dramatically but have lagged significantly behind those in the private sector for comparable positions, with adverse consequences for the public service. State and local government compensation tends to be lower than that in the national government, though there are exceptions. Efforts to achieve pay comparability with private-sector jobs face formidable obstacles.

Public-sector collective bargaining has emerged as a major force in PPA at all levels of government. Within a framework of labor–management relations, what has evolved is a pattern of unified employee organizations created to share control with management over terms and conditions of employment. Although similar to—and patterned after—collective bargaining in the private sector, bargaining in governmental arenas differs in a number of important respects. Various types of employee organizations—most prominently, public-employee unions—have become involved in collective bargaining.

State and local experience, though much more varied, has included major union gains in membership, extension of collective bargaining rights in both state and local governments, and greater frequency of public-employee strikes and other job actions. Collective bargaining in the public sector has diverse impacts on wages and salaries, service delivery, and employee productivity.

Developments in PPA include civil service reform, the consequences of budget cuts, affirmative action, attempts to determine comparable worth, as well as proposed changes in civil service rules. The Civil Service Reform Act was an attempt to reform the national government merit system by introducing performance appraisal systems and financial incentives for higher-quality performance and greater productivity.

Affirmative action programs have continued to produce gradual increases in the proportions of minorities and women holding responsible government positions. Partisanship, an old issue in personnel administration, has seen some changes recently. Patronage has been challenged successfully in a number of court cases.

For several decades, PPA and HRD have been a dynamic, fluid, even turbulent area of public administration. The outlook is for more of the same. The role of professionals and the future of bureaucracy remain in flux.

Discussion Questions

1. What are the elements of PPA and how do they differ from their private-sector counterparts?
2. Which mode of public personnel administration is preferable: government by "gentlemen," government by the "common person," government by the "good," government by the "efficient," government by "administrators," government by "professionals," or government by "citizens, experts, and results"? Explain.
3. What are the key impacts and future directions of public-sector collective bargaining? What areas of the subject merit further study? Defend either position: that public-sector employees should be allowed to strike or that they should be prohibited from striking, using (but not necessarily limited to) the arguments presented in this book. Consider blogs, newspaper articles, and other sources describing the showdowns between labor groups and elected officials in states such as Wisconsin, Ohio, and Indiana.
4. What differences exist among the three major levels of government (national, state, local) in terms of types of employees that have organized, fractions of employees that have organized, the provisions and atmospheres for conducting collective bargaining, and the percentage of employees covered by collective bargaining agreements?
5. Trace the development of public-employee organizations. What were their functions? What roles did they play in "labor–management" relations? Why was collective bargaining not commonplace in PPA until the 1960s?
6. Should public-sector employment reflect political demographics (that is, workforce 47 percent Democrats if community 47 percent Democrats), ethnic demographics, partisan patronage, political responsiveness, or politically neutral competence? Defend your answer.
7. What were the major recommendations for change in personnel management proposed by the Obama administration?
8. During the early 2000s, the number of federal government employees has grown more rapidly than was the case in many state and local governments. If this trend continues, how will it affect the field of public administration? If growth declines, what are the implications for public employment?
9. Assess proposals to institute pay for performance in federal agencies. What are the consequences of adopting new labor–management procedures at a time when the United States is deeply involved with homeland security and other national security concerns?
10. Discuss APS and their potential impact on traditional civil service systems.

Key Terms and Concepts

diversity, *278*

politically neutral competence, *279*

public personnel administration (PPA), *279*

human resources development (HRD), *279*

full-time equivalent (FTE) employees, *281*

interoperability, *286*

nepotism, *287*

egalitarianism, *287*

Civil Service (Pendleton) Act, *287*

Brownlow Report, *287*

Second Hoover Commission, *287*

Senior Executive Service (SES), *288*

achievement-oriented criteria, *290*

ascriptive criteria, *290*

Office of Personnel Management (OPM), *291*

merit pay, *291*

General Schedule (GS), *291*

Executive Schedule, *291*

position classification, *292*

broadbanding, *293*

veterans' preference, *297*

pay gap, *298*

locality pay, *299*

collective bargaining, *300*

labor–management relations, *300*

multilateral bargaining, *301*

bilateral bargaining, *301*

National Labor Relations Board (NLRB), *303*

Executive Order (EO) 10988, *303*

Federal Mediation and Conciliation Service (FMCS), *303*

Civil Service Reform Act of 1978, *304*

Federal Labor Relations Authority (FLRA), *304*

National Labor Management Association (NLMA), *304*

performance appraisal, *305*

pay for performance, *305*

impasse procedures, *309*

productivity bargaining, *310*

job action, *310*

Executive Order (EO) 10925, *314*

1964 Civil Rights Act, *314*

1972 Equal Employment Opportunity Act, *314*

Equal Employment Opportunity Commission (EEOC), *314*

Equity Pay Act of 1963, *314*

comparable worth, *314*

reverse discrimination, *315*

competitive sourcing, *320*

Suggested Readings

Berman, Evan M., James S. Bowman, Jonathan P. West, and Montgomery Van Wart. *Human Resource Management in Public Service: Paradoxes, Processes, and Problems.* 3rd ed. Thousand Oaks, Calif.: Sage Publications, 2009.

Cayer, N. Joseph. *Public Personnel Administration in the United States.* 4th ed. Belmont, Calif.: Thomson/Wadsworth, 2003.

Dresang, Dennis L. *Public Personnel Management and Public Policy.* 4th ed. New York: Longman, 2001.

Hays, Steven W., Richard Kearney, and Jerrell D. Coggburn, eds. *Human Resource Management: Problems and Prospects.* 5th ed. Upper Saddle River, N.J.: Prentice Hall, 2008.

Huddleston, Mark, and William Boyer. *The Higher Civil Service in the United States.* Pittsburgh: University of Pittsburgh Press, 1996.

Kearney, Richard C. *Labor Relations in the Public Sector.* 3rd ed. Boca Raton, Fla.: CRC Press, 2001.

Klingner, Donald, and John Nalbandian. *Public Personnel Management.* 6th ed. Upper Saddle River, N.J.: Prentice Hall, 2009.

Mosher, Frederick C. *Democracy and the Public Service.* 2nd ed. New York: Oxford University Press, 1982.

Rabin, Jack, Thomas Vocino, W. Bartley Hildreth, and Gerald J. Miller, eds. *Handbook of Public Sector Labor Relations.* New York: Marcel Dekker, 1994.

Riccucci, Norma M. *Public Personnel Management: Current Concerns, Future Challenges.* 4th ed. New York: Longman, 2005.

———, ed. *Public Personnel Administration and Labor Relations.* Armonk, N.Y.: M.E. Sharpe, 2007.

Riccucci, Norma M., Katherine C. Naff, Jay M. Shafritz, and David H. Rosenbloom. *Personnel Management in Government: Politics and Process.* 6th ed. Boca Raton, Fla.: CRC Press, 2007.

Rice, Mitchell F. *Diversity and Public Administration: Theory, Issues, and Perspectives.* 2nd ed. Armonk, N.Y.: M.E. Sharpe, 2010.

Riley, Dennis D. *Public Personnel Administration.* 2nd ed. New York: Longman, 2001.

Risher, Howard, et al. *New Strategies for Public Pay.* San Francisco: Jossey-Bass, 1997.

Rosenbloom, David H., ed. *Centenary Issues of the Pendleton Act of 1883: The Problematic Legacy of Civil Service Reform.* New York: Marcel Dekker, 1982.

Selden, Sally C. *The Promise of Representative Bureaucracy.* Armonk, N.Y.: M.E. Sharpe, 1998.

Sylvia, Ronald. *Public Personnel Administration.* 2nd ed. Fort Worth, Tex.: Harcourt College, 2002.

Thompson, Frank J., ed. *Classics of Public Personnel Policy.* 3rd ed. Oak Park, Ill.: Wadsworth, 2002.

Government Budgeting

The mayor of a financially beleaguered city orders layoffs of many white-collar workers, police and fire personnel, and sanitation workers in a last-ditch effort to balance the budget and avoid tax increases. The governor receives a report from the state comptroller that the state's cash accounts are getting dangerously low because of declining tax revenues and rising unemployment compensation and Medicaid costs. The sheriff in a rural county tells citizens to purchase guns to protect themselves after patrols are cut back due to the high cost of gasoline. The mayor of a large urban county is recalled from office by voters for increasing property taxes and failure to curb spending. The president of the United States asks for, and receives, supplemental funding for a war that an overwhelming majority of Americans believe is misguided. Department heads and bureau chiefs at all levels of government feverishly search for ways to meet projected spending levels—a step made necessary by a general fiscal crunch and political demands for more efficient program management. Legislators seek to satisfy their clientele groups by approving program spending, but they cast a wary eye on a public growing restless with what are perceived to be generous "entitlements" and seemingly out-of-control spending. Everyone agrees that there are serious budget problems, but there is little agreement on how to solve them.

In all of these examples, government budget processes are at the core of both political and managerial controversies, especially in the current era of divided government. Budgeting in the public sector is a process central to politics, particularly to administrative politics and the operation of government agencies and programs. It is the major formal mechanism through which necessary resources are obtained, distributed, spent, and monitored. Competition for a greater share of an ever-shrinking fiscal "pie" has always been keen, but never more so than in recent years. The size and shape of individual agency budgets, and the processes involved in proposing and approving them, are all changing rapidly, with unpredictable consequences for a variety of political interests and government programs.

> *A billion here, a billion there, and pretty soon you're talking about real money!*
>
> Statement attributed to the late U.S. Senator Everett McKinley Dirksen, Republican of Illinois

Foundations of Modern Government Budgeting

Before the U.S. Civil War, budgeting was rather informal and routine at all levels of government. The national budget and number of federal employees were fairly small, amounting to less than $1 billion until 1865, at the height of the Civil War; there were 50,000 federal civilian employees in 1871.[1] The budgetary process was fragmented, with little systematic direction. Beginning with the presidency of Thomas Jefferson (1801–1809), agencies seeking funds had dealt mainly on their own with congressional committees having jurisdiction over their respective operations. The president had no authority to amend agency requests and no institutional means of influencing their formulation. Congress made its appropriations very detailed, both to control executive discretion to transfer funds from one appropriation account to another and to keep spending within the appropriations' limits.[2]

Starting with the Civil War, some important long-term changes began to affect numerous government practices, and the framework of a truly national economy slowly took shape. The war itself was a watershed in national-state relations, as well as in development of the presidency as a predominant force in national politics. During the 1870s and later, several general patterns of government behavior became more prominent, with implications for the rise of the modern budgetary process.

The first of these was growth in the national government's authority to regulate the expanding industrial economy and to exercise the war power and related prerogatives in foreign affairs, in which the president's role especially was enhanced. At the same time, the power to tax was used to a greater degree than ever before. The regulatory power represented government response to the Industrial Revolution and to the emergence of powerful private economic interests. The war power was exercised most visibly in the U.S. Civil War and in the Spanish-American War (1898–1901), and U.S. diplomatic involvement was on the rise as well. The tax power was expanded by ratification of the Sixteenth Amendment in 1913, permitting a federal graduated income tax.

The second pattern—government involvement in the private economy—meant more than simply regulating the flow of commerce. Starting in 1864, when the National Banking Act created a single, unified banking system as another step toward a national economy, the government's role in financial affairs became more regularized. Equally important, the way was paved for expanded government activity. In the twentieth century, this included not only increasing regulation of private economic enterprise, but also greater participation in planning and managing various public enterprises. Since 1933 and the New Deal era of Franklin Roosevelt, fiscal and regulatory policies have been the predominant instruments of the national government in influencing the economy, one that presidents of both parties have not hesitated to use when it has suited their economic and political purposes. Because the consequences of these actions reach far beyond the government itself, it is not difficult to see how budgetary processes have grown in importance.

The third pattern was growth in presidential strength and influence, beginning in the last half of the nineteenth century and continuing to the present. The first enthusiastically activist president was Theodore Roosevelt (1901–1909). Others after him, notably his cousin Franklin Roosevelt (1933–1945), made even more dramatic and significant changes in the presidential role. Presidents Truman (1945–1953), Kennedy (1961–1963), Johnson (1963–1969), and Nixon (1969–1974) all actively supported expansion of presidential prerogatives, albeit for widely varying purposes. Dwight Eisenhower (1953–1961), although not associated with an activist view of the office, presided over a fairly rapid expansion of the role of the executive branch generally, and he did little to roll back changes made before he took office. Action by Congress delegating discretionary authority to the president was a recurring feature of the twentieth century. Gerald Ford (1974–1977) and Jimmy Carter (1977–1981) exercised presidential prerogatives a bit more cautiously, in view of the public's negative reaction to the Watergate scandals, but the office itself remained very strong. Ronald Reagan (1981–1989), intent on reversing expansion of government's overall role, capitalized on the powers of the presidency in his quest to reduce that role—a major change for a "strong" president. George H. W. Bush (1989–1993) was not as strong a president as Ronald Reagan, nor did he pursue as distinct or broad-ranging a policy agenda. The elder Bush was less decisive in his vision of spending priorities than either Presidents Reagan or Clinton. The Clinton administration (1993–2001) took specific actions to measure and manage expenditures, emphasizing performance improvement standards and better reporting systems. The budgetary and economic policies of George W. Bush (2001–2009) were largely driven by additional discretionary spending required to support U.S. armed forces in Afghanistan and Iraq. As already noted in previous chapters, President Obama entered the White House in 2009 with an ambitious domestic policy agenda that included health care reform, tighter regulation of the financial industry, and greater use of information communication technologies (ICTs) to link citizens with government service providers.

Before President Obama was elected, however, the economy had fallen into recession. Officially, the "Great Recession" began in December 2007 and was said to have ended in June 2009. Many Americans, however, have not felt the effects of economic recovery because of lagging job growth. In addition, several years of escalating real estate prices, poor mortgage lending and underwriting practices, and other risky financial market ventures led to a market crash in September 2008, which significantly deepened the ongoing recession. Lower tax revenue (due to slower economic activity) and recession-induced spending for unemployment assistance combined with a large stimulus package and increased defense spending to produce substantially higher federal budget deficits in 2008 and 2009. The national government used a portion of the increased debt to acquire troubled financial assets from the private sector as a way of ameliorating the financial market crisis and assisting the economy. As a result, there were corresponding increases in debt held by the public in 2010 and 2011.

Taken together, these long-term patterns had several important consequences in the development of modern budgetary practice. They raised the stakes of budgetary decision making by increasing the scope and economic impact of such decisions and their effect on political interests as well. They created both the possibility and the necessity of effectively coordinating scattered spending activities of the national government—possibility because of the growing capabilities of the presidential office and necessity because expenditures were rising and some centralization of control seemed appropriate. They prompted the first stirrings of budgetary reform in the early 1900s and focused greater attention on the president as chief economic strategist. Primary among these was the concept of the **executive budget**, with the chief executive placed in charge of developing and coordinating budget proposals for the entire executive branch prior to their presentation to the legislature (at the state level as well as in Washington, D.C.).

executive budget

budgets prepared by the chief executives and their central budget offices for submission to the legislature for analysis, consideration, review, change, and enactment.

Purposes of Budgeting

At its simplest, a budget can be a device for counting and recording income and expenditures; many fiscal and other public-policy functions also can be served through budgeting, some or all of them simultaneously. It may not even be appropriate to label such a document a budget; perhaps *ledger* is more precise. Budgets, however, do include that information. Another function of budgeting is to generate a statement of financial intent constructed on the basis of anticipated income and expenditures.

A closely related function is to indicate *programmatic* intent, showing both preferences and, more important, priorities in deciding what to do with available funds. Budgets should also reflect the mission, or purpose, for a bureaucratic agency's existence. This suggests still another function of budgets, intentional or not: They reflect the political priorities of those who formulate them. In recent decades, the role of the budget in the national government's efforts to manage the economy has increased substantially; that is, many budget decisions are made and evaluated in terms of how they affect general economic growth, as well as specific economic and political interests and concerns.

One other purpose deserves mention: controlling the bureaucracy and shaping agency programs. Legislators who cherish control of the government's purse strings often use that control to influence agency behavior. Ronald Reagan, from the very start of his presidency, used a comprehensive assault on the national government budget as the key to his attempt to reshape the national bureaucracy. Reagan demonstrated convincingly that the most direct way (if not always the easiest politically) to control an agency is to cut—or increase—its budget (George W. Bush learned that lesson well, also). Thus, chief executives who seek to direct bureaucratic operations have a strong and continuing interest in budgets and budget making.

The budget of any organization may be read as something of an index to relative distribution of power in the economic and political systems in which the budget was enacted. This is true whether we are speaking of university decisions to allocate a certain amount for academic scholarships or more faculty, or of state government appropriations for education, health care, transportation, or other priorities. Budgets represent authoritative decisions to spend or reduce money in certain ways in preference to others, and such decisions do not just happen. They are made through a political process in which power and persuasion are crucial to success.

Because the outcomes of budgetary decision making are so important to all participants and beneficiaries, the formal nature of the decision process has long been central to budgetary politics. Throughout much of our history, decisions about public spending could best be characterized as incremental, following the model described in Chapter 5. Changes in annual spending from one year (or biennium—a two-year period) to the next, and in the policies such spending supported, tended to be gradual. Much of the status quo was simply assumed to be beyond questioning; how much more should be allocated was a common theme and a key focus of budget processes. Under the Constitution, all money bills must originate in the House of Representatives, and congressional committee chairs, among other things, jealously guard their prerogatives in the areas of revenue collection and spending.

In recent decades, however, the incremental decision-making model has had decreasing applicability in explaining how budgets are proposed and enacted. Efforts were mounted to make budgeting more "rational," through reducing the influence of politics as usual and strengthening the role of policy evaluation in long-range planning, in hopes of increasing program effectiveness. Another change has been the emergence of legislative formulas as the basis for allocating larger amounts of funds in greater numbers of programs. Partisan conflict over budget priorities, especially in the context of divided government, has dominated budgetary decision making, and has contributed to increased spending for the past thirty years (see Figure 8–1).

The major reason for this is that federal programs for Social Security, Medicare, Medicaid, and veterans' benefits are distributed on a formula basis and, as the number of those eligible for particular government benefits rise, expenditures automatically increase. Such programs are known as **entitlements**, that is, "legal obligations created through legislation that require the payment of benefits to any person or unit of government that meets

entitlements

government programs (mainly for individuals) created under legislation that defines eligibility standards, but places no limit on total budget authority; the level of outlays is determined solely by the number of eligible persons who apply for authorized benefits, under existing law.

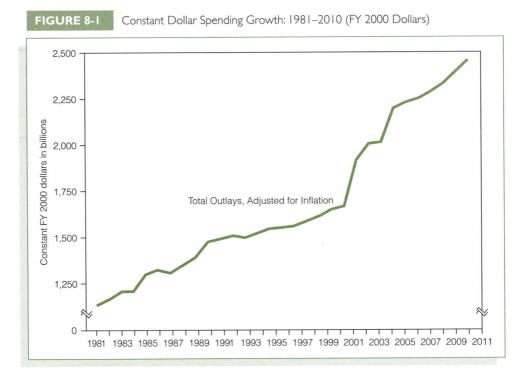

FIGURE 8-1   Constant Dollar Spending Growth: 1981–2010 (FY 2000 Dollars)

Source: http://www.whitehouse.gov/omb/budget/fy2006/sheets/hist0123.xls.

---

mandatory or direct spending

category of outlays from budget authority provided in laws other than appropriations acts for entitlements and budget authority for food stamps.

discretionary spending

category of budget authority that comprises budgetary resources (except those provided to fund direct-spending programs) in appropriations acts.

the eligibility requirements established by law."[3] Over two-thirds of the federal budget (70 percent) is now devoted to entitlements, interest on the federal debt, and defense spending. This **mandatory or direct spending** has reduced Congress's ability to influence the overall budget without changing the law that originally authorized the spending. The range of budgetary choices available after all mandatory allocations have been made is termed **discretionary spending**; this now constitutes a smaller proportion of the total budget than it used to—less than one-third (see Table 8–1), and it is rapidly declining. The net effect of these changes, as well as new requirements for weapons systems, intelligence gathering, homeland security, and additional expenditures arising from the war on terrorism, have combined to dramatically drive up overall government spending and potentially eliminate discretionary spending altogether. It should be noted also that the growth of entitlement programs, accompanied by deficit spending, was largely attributable to the creativity of congressional authorizing committees in circumventing existing controls that had been imposed by appropriations and budget committees.

The rise of new congressional budget processes was designed to enhance Congress's ability to monitor expenditures under the direction of its new budget committees (one in each chamber). The new process was also designed to

| TABLE 8-1 | Projected Spending and Receipts Summary 2011–2015 (in billions of dollars) |

| | **Estimates** | | | | |
	2011	**2012**	**2013**	**2014**	**2015**
Outlays:					
Discretionary:					
DoD-military	733	695	645	662	674
Non-military	547	547	542	546	551
Total, discretionary	1,280	1,242	1,188	1,208	1,225
Mandatory:					
Social Security	748	767	807	842	900
Medicare	494	492	534	564	589
Health	388	373	385	478	541
Income Security	622	554	536	525	519
Other	285	300	320	360	416
Total, mandatory:	2,537	2,486	2,582	2,769	2,965
Net Interest	209	242	320	417	494
Total, outlays	3,817	3,728	3,770	3,977	4,190
Receipts	2,174	2,638	3,009	3,322	3,583
Deficit	−1,643	−1,090	−761	−665	−607

Source: U.S. Office of Management and Budget, Budget for Fiscal Year 2012, Historical Tables.
Table 3.1: Outlays by Superfunction and Function, 1940–2016.
Table 5.6: Budget Authority for Discretionary Programs, 1940–2016.

enable Congress to generate independent information concerning revenues, expenditures, and projected surpluses or deficits through the **Congressional Budget Office (CBO)** rather than relying on information furnished by the president's Office of Management and Budget (OMB). This new process also increased conflict between the president and Congress over budgetary matters. Concern also has risen on the part of legislators and the public over the continuing annual **deficit** in the national government budget. Both political parties often claim credit for efforts to reduce budget deficits, but neither wants to antagonize support groups impacted by budget cuts. Incrementalism has not entirely disappeared, but budgetary decision making is far more complex and unpredictable than it was in the past.

Budgetary decisions and decision processes, and the changes in both, are heavily influenced by their political environments.[4] In recent years, government budget makers have been confronted by growing pressures

Congressional Budget Office (CBO)

created in 1974; the budget and financial planning division of the U.S. Congress; see also the **Congressional Budget and Impoundment Control Act of 1974**.

deficit

amount by which governmental outlays exceed governmental receipts in a fiscal year.

on revenue sources; calls for additional spending to fund wars in Iraq and Afghanistan, and military action in Libya and to prevent terrorist acts; demands for entitlement reform and less deficit spending; and citizen resistance to increased taxes, especially at state and local government levels. These have combined to create pressures on all public budgets, making difficult budgetary choices more necessary than ever. Today, government budgeting has become the object of a battle among choices that delineate the very role of government in our lives. In past years, an underlying public consensus was said to exist about many governmental activities, but that consensus has clearly eroded. It has been replaced by a *dis*sensus (or disagreement) reflecting sharp differences and intense conflicts over debt, deficits, Medicare, taxation, Social Security, and military spending. As the late Aaron Wildavsky put it, "[P]olitics is about grand questions: How much, what for, who pays; in sum, what side are you on?"[5] That dissensus was clearly evident during the spring and summer of 2011, following Republican victories in the 2010 congressional elections, when considerable time, effort, and energy was spent in negotiations with the president over how much to cut spending and reduce the nation's annual budget deficits. Equally serious and parallel negotiations centered on whether to raise the federal government's **debt ceiling**, and how to achieve agreement on that critically important question. In the late summer of 2011, the agreement between Congress and the White House to raise the debt ceiling—but the failure at the same time to take meaningful steps toward reducing federal deficits and the national debt—led to a downgrade of the U.S. government's credit rating and triggered one of the largest stock market declines in recent history.

debt ceiling

the statutory limit on the federal debt; periodically raised by Congress.

Government Budgets and Fiscal Policy

Government budgets are increasingly viewed as instruments for managing national economies. Their impact depends on the relative significance of the public sector in the total economic picture and on the willingness of citizens to accept the authority of governments over the private sector as legitimate. Budgets can be regarded as instruments of **fiscal policy** aimed at "consciously influencing the economic life of a nation."[6] Different governments regard this potential budgetary role quite differently. Similarly, the extent to which national budgets in other countries are treated as tools of fiscal policy varies widely. In many European countries, for instance, the relative share of public resources (as a percentage of total goods and services produced) collected and spent by government is much higher than in the United States (see Figure 8–2).

Fiscal policy, as we use the term here, refers to government actions designed to develop and stabilize the private economy; they include (1) taxation and tax policy, (2) direct budget expenditures, (3) management of the national debt, and (4) indirect tax expenditures. Related to fiscal policy—and, ideally,

fiscal policy

refers to government actions aimed at development and stabilization of the private economy, including taxation and tax policy, expenditures, and management of the national debt; monetary and credit controls are also related to fiscal policy.

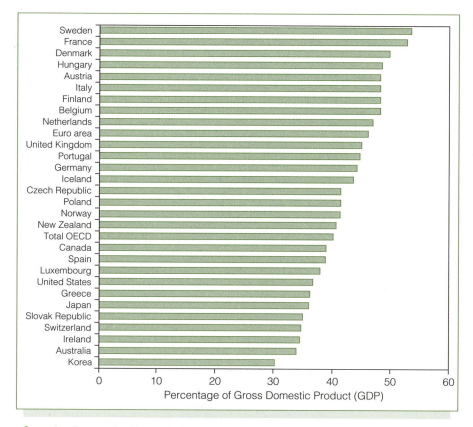

FIGURE 8-2

Government Outlays
as Percentage of GDP

Source: http://www.oecd.org/datavecd/5/51/2483816.xls.

fully coordinated with it—are monetary and credit controls. We will examine these tools and relate them to the budget process. ("The Budget: Mastering the Language" on page 336 provides concise definitions of the basic vocabulary of budgeting at the national level.)

Fiscal Policy Tools

The primary tool of fiscal policy is **taxation**, which has traditionally been viewed simply as a means of raising government revenue. For the past fifty years, however, taxation and tax policy have also been used to influence the volume of spending by private citizens and organizations. Raising taxes has at times been a weapon against inflationary spending because it reduces the amount of disposable personal income; conversely, reducing taxes has been viewed as one means of boosting consumer spending. Such policy was relatively clear-cut until the recent recession. Reducing taxes, for example, to

taxation

primary means by which governments raise revenues for public services; taxes can be collected from individuals and corporations on income (earned and unearned), profits, property value, sales, and services.

THE BUDGET: MASTERING THE LANGUAGE

The budget is the president's financial plan for the national government. It accounts for how government funds have been raised and spent, and it proposes financial policies for the coming *fiscal year* and beyond.

The budget discusses *receipts* (amounts the government expects to raise in taxes and other fees); *budget authority* (amounts that agencies are allowed to obligate or lend); and *outlays* (amounts actually paid out by the government in cash or checks during the year). Examples of outlays are funds spent to buy equipment or property, to meet the government's liability under a contract, or to pay employees' salaries.

The budget earmarks funds to cover two general kinds of spending. *Mandatory* spending covers *entitlement* programs (such as food stamps, Social Security, and agricultural subsidies) that may be used by anyone who meets eligibility criteria. Mandatory spending may not be limited in the appropriations process. *Discretionary* spending is set annually in the appropriations process.

The budget has a twofold purpose: to establish governmental priorities among programs and to chart U.S. fiscal policy, which is the coordinated use of taxes and expenditures to affect the economy.

Congress adopts its version of the budget in the form of a *budget resolution*. This resolution, which is supposed to be adopted by April 15 of each year, sets Congress's overall goals for taxes and spending, broken down among major budget categories, or *functions* (the president's budget is similarly divided by function). An important step in congressional budgeting is the *reconciliation* procedure, when Congress enacts spending reductions and revenue increases (or both) in order to bring existing law into line with spending targets adopted in its budget resolution. Subsequently, if Congress is unable to pass a budget, or to approve major appropriations bills for executive-branch agencies, it may adopt *continuing resolutions*, which authorize expenditures at the same levels as in the previous fiscal year, until formal action is completed on the budget or appropriations.

An *authorization* is an act of Congress that establishes government programs, defines their scope, and sets a ceiling for how much can be spent on them. Authorizations do not actually spend the money. In the case of authority to enter contractual obligations, however, Congress authorizes the administration to make firm commitments for which funds later must be provided. Congress also occasionally includes mandatory spending requirements in an authorization, in order to ensure program spending at a certain level.

An *appropriation* provides money for programs within the limits established in authorizations. An appropriation may be for a single year, a specified period of years, or an indefinite time, according to the restrictions Congress wishes to place on spending for particular purposes.

Appropriations generally take the form of *budget authority*, which can differ from actual outlays. That is because, in practice, funds actually spent or obligated during a fiscal year may be drawn partly from budget authority conferred in that year, and partly from budget authority conferred in previous years.

Source: Adapted with permission from *Congressional Quarterly Weekly Report*, 43 (February 9, 1985). Copyright © 1985 by Congressional Quarterly Inc. Reproduced with permission of Congressional Quarterly Inc. in the format textbook via Copyright Clearance Center. For an interactive version of definitions relating to these and other terms, see http://www.washingtonpost.com/wp-srv/politics/interactives/budget1011.

increase consumption and "spend our way out of a recession," works very nicely, assuming that such spending doesn't trigger increased higher interest rates and inflation. But if any significant increase in spending is inflationary, the old rules don't work anymore. The uncertain condition of the national and the global economies raises new questions about how to use tax policy as an instrument of economic management. These uncertainties did not prevent President Bush from proposing and Congress from approving, early in 2008, a $170 billion economic stimulus package featuring tax rebates for individuals and new depreciation rules for businesses, precisely to try to head off a recession. However, these policies failed to reduce either government spending or the national debt.

As with tax policy, there have been fundamental changes in attitudes toward government expenditures. The traditional view has been that, as governments spent money, the sums expended replaced private-sector spending, representing a last resort when the private sector could not carry on whatever activities the money paid for. Now, however, the government's spending practices are seen as an essential part of total spending for goods and services and as having major "pump-priming" effect on private-sector expenditures. That is not surprising, considering, for example, that the national government budget reached over $3.8 trillion in expenditures for fiscal year (FY) 2011. Although this amounts to 25.3 percent of total **gross domestic product (GDP)**, a much smaller percentage amount than in almost any other advanced industrial democracy, programs funded by these taxes, and those raised separately by states and local governments, can have a major influence on individuals, institutions, and local communities. Nonetheless, the total amount of all government spending is still less, about 33 percent of the GDP, leaving 67 percent to the private sector (see Figure 8–3).

Millions of businesses, individuals, and state and local government institutions depend on federal revenue for basic services and support. For example, governmental decisions to close or not to close several large military installations carry with them crucial economic implications for regional economies. These installations pump millions of new dollars into the local (and state) economies. In many instances, a multiplier, or *ripple effect*, prevails—sales and rentals of housing are brisk; retail and wholesale businesses benefit; there is a sharp rise in demand for goods and services of all kinds. This has the effect of increasing tax revenues in all taxing jurisdictions (both state and local) and, in general, strengthening the localities' financial bases because of new jobs created and increased population.

gross domestic product (GDP)

sum of goods and services produced by the economy, including personal consumption, private investments, and government spending.

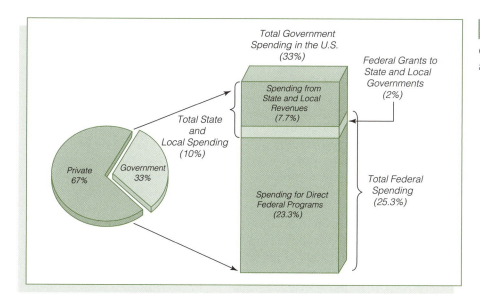

FIGURE 8-3

Government Spending as a Share of GDP, 2011

Source: © 2013 Cengage Learning.

national debt

the cumulative sum of borrowing necessary over time to pay the difference between the amount raised and spent in the annual federal budget. For current estimate, see the National Debt Clock at: http://www.brillig.com/debt_clock.

A third fiscal-policy tool is management of the **national debt**. The national debt is the accumulation over time of the difference between the amounts the federal government spends and collects in taxes. Sale of government bonds and other obligations took on fiscal-policy overtones for the first time during World War II, when the sale of war bonds was touted as another means of holding down consumer spending for scarce goods and services. In selling bonds, "a government changes the composition of privately held assets—converts private assets from money to bonds."[7] The limit on this debt is set by Congress and has an indirect but potentially major impact on the amount and composition of private holdings and on interest rates, income, and spending rates.

In recent years, government borrowing and the national debt have become major political issues. When President Reagan took office in 1981, the national debt was just under $1 trillion ($1,000 billion); when George W. Bush assumed office in 2001, the debt stood at $5.7 trillion; by 2009, when Bush finished his second term, it had ballooned to nearly $10 trillion. Under President Obama, the debt continued to rise, to some $14 trillion—an imposing figure, though some say it should be of less concern because many of the government's creditors are U.S. citizens, banks, and businesses.[8] As important as the size of the long-term debt itself (at least in the short run) is the annual cost of interest that must be paid on the debt. This amount is included as "Net Interest" in the annual federal budget together with appropriations for other federal expenditures (see Table 8–1). Whereas the national debt represents *cumulative* "red ink," the **budget deficit** is the difference between how much the federal government collects and spends in *any one year*. Political leaders continue to argue for reductions in government spending (usually in someone else's district) in the struggle to balance the national government budget. Both the Congress and President Clinton claimed credit during the 1996 presidential and 1998 congressional campaigns for fulfilling a 1992 promise to reduce the budget deficit by 40 percent to under $150 billion by FY 1997. Progress made during the 1990s toward a balanced budget was completely erased by the Bush administration's need for higher national security spending, tax cuts, and the weakened economy. During his first two years in office, President Obama was accused by political opponents of not acting decisively enough to forestall deficit increases resulting from lower tax revenues and increased spending on domestic programs.

budget deficit

the difference between the amount of revenue raised by taxes and the amount of federal government spending in a fiscal year.

In state and local government, debt management is similarly complex if only because many state constitutions require both state and local governments to operate with balanced budgets. Nevertheless, most states and localities have extensive **bonded indebtedness**, meaning that they issue interest-bearing bonds, generally free from federal taxation, to raise funds for specific stated purposes. They must manage the debts they owe to holders of those bonds over the lifetime of the bonds—paying interest on schedule and at stipulated rates and redeeming the bonds at agreed-on times. Several larger, older cities (such as New York and Cleveland in the 1970s, Detroit in the early 1980s,

bonded indebtedness

revenue-raising tool for governments to issue notes or promises to pay a certain amount (principal) at a certain time (maturity date) at a particular rate of interest.

and Miami in the 1990s), as well as newer, more affluent jurisdictions such as Orange County, California, have at times experienced difficulties in meeting their financial obligations. Problems of debt management have become more severe for all governments, as many states, as well as local jurisdictions, have lost property tax revenues due to steep declines in real estate values. There is concern that a "bond bubble" may burst and negatively impact the capacity of states to raise necessary revenue.[9]

Another less visible fiscal-policy tool of increasing importance for all governments is **tax expenditure financing**, the practice of giving favorable tax breaks or creating "loopholes" for certain kinds of spending by individuals, nonprofit institutions, religious organizations, professional sports franchises, and corporate enterprises. For example, the national government permits income tax deductions for interest expenditures on home mortgages, employer health care expenditures, and subsidies for Southern cotton farmers, to mention a few of the most common. Businesses may receive substantial tax credits if they invest in purchases of new equipment or hire new workers from designated "empowerment zones"; the oil industry, in particular, one of the most profitable businesses in the world, benefits from exemptions related to drilling for new sources of oil and natural gas. Local governments do not collect property taxes on land and buildings owned by certain colleges, universities, churches, or synagogues. Bill Clinton proposed, and Congress passed, tax credits of up to $1,500 for students attending community colleges and up to $10,000 for college and university expenses. Both of these deductions are limited to families making below a certain maximum income. In maintaining such tax incentives for special interests, the government must balance revenues lost against broader social purposes or probable gains in private-sector expenditures, along with the tax benefits realized by all levels of government as a result of increased private-sector activity. The 2010 bipartisan **National Commission on Fiscal Responsibility and Reform** (also known as the Fiscal Responsibility Commission or the Simpson–Bowles Commission after the names of its cochairs) proposed the elimination of many of these "loopholes." Regardless of the outcomes of 2011 Congressional budget deliberations, special interests will lobby hard to save these legal deductions, now estimated at $1.1 *trillion* in potentially taxable revenue lost to the federal treasury (in addition to many hundreds of millions of dollars not available to state and local governments).[10]

Monetary and Credit Controls

Monetary controls are ordinarily exercised in two principal forms by national and state governments. First, the Board of Governors of the **Federal Reserve System** regulates the supply of money released into circulation. Restricting the **money supply** has been used to restrain inflation; increasing the supply has been used to lower interest rates and to stimulate economic activity. This function of "the Fed" is carried on outside the direct control of the president; he or she appoints its members but does not have command authority over their decisions.[11]

tax expenditure financing

revenue losses from provisions in the federal, state, or local tax codes that allow a special exclusion, exemption, or deduction from gross income or that provide a special tax credit, a preferential rate of tax, or a deferral of tax liability.

National Commission on Fiscal Responsibility and Reform

established in 2010 by President Obama to identify areas within which to improve fiscal policies and achieve long-term sustainability.

Federal Reserve System

independent board that serves as the central bank of the United States. "The Fed" administers banking, credit, and monetary policies and controls the supply of money available to member banks.

money supply

amount of money available to individuals and institutions in society.

Interest rates charged by lending institutions are subject to regulation by the states, and, as we have seen in recent times, the prime lending rates that banks make available to their borrowers influence business investment, new-home construction, and financing of home mortgages. In somewhat different ways, government loan programs (technically different from the controls just described) make a crucial difference in a wide range of activities, such as FEMA disaster loans for hurricane and flood victims as well as VA or FHA loans for buying or building a house. Poor management of loans and mortgage insurance programs contributed to the financial collapse of 2008–2010 and forced many homeowners into bankruptcy. Loans are controlled in part by the budgetary process in the form of initial appropriations and yearly expenses to continue operation of loan programs. Even small changes in the cost of borrowing money can have major impacts on business, families, and individuals seeking to provide or upgrade housing, create or expand business, or sell property or assets. Furthermore, loan guarantees have become increasingly important for a broader segment of societal interests.

Economic Coordination

Underlying all government activity to influence the private economy is the public acceptance or *legitimacy*, in principle, of that activity. The national government's role in this respect gained wide—although far from universal—acceptance during the Great Depression years and afterward, in a period marked by passage of the Employment Act of 1946 to combat the postwar recession. This act made promoting maximum employment, production, and purchasing power an ongoing governmental commitment. In addition, the act established the president's **Council of Economic Advisers (CEA)**, discussed in Chapter 1. These steps were important both in themselves and as indicators of likely governmental responses to subsequent economic crises.

Council of Economic Advisers (CEA)

U.S. president's chief advisory and research source for economic advice. Consists of three economists (one appointed as chair) and assists the White House in preparing various economic reports.

Central economic coordination has come to mean a dominant role for the president both in determining the existence of crisis conditions and in directing governmental responses.[12] Although the president's authority lapsed later in the 1970s, a precedent was set for future chief executives to exert their power in budgetary matters. Even with all these powers at the president's disposal, however, there is still some question as to whether presidential coordination can be truly effective. Although we expect the president to influence the economy in a positive manner, he or she lacks the tools to manage its performance in all but the most indirect ways. Still, public expectations as well as the president's role in this area have expanded greatly during the last fifty years.

The Reagan, George H. W. Bush, and Clinton presidencies gave rise to several important issues concerning the relationship between government activity and the national economy. One is the role of government spending as an economic stimulus. Since the 1930s, prevailing economic doctrines assumed that government played an important role in periods of economic downturn because of its ability to spark demand for goods and services produced in the private economy. Moreover, since the late 1960s, stimulating private-sector activity has been a consistent and deliberate budgetary objective, regardless of economic cycles, and has become a generally accepted part of the national government's overall economic role. President Reagan's determination to limit government spending (without regard, some maintain, to the adverse economic consequences) clearly led to a reassessment of this aspect of government budgeting. President Obama proposed, and Congress passed, a massive stimulus package in 2009 to correct the negative impacts of recession (see Chapter 3).

The economic impact of continuing budget deficits raises the very real fear that deficits, if left unchecked, will hamper economic recovery and trigger new cycles of inflation and recession. Closely related is the concern that the government's need to borrow money from private lenders will crowd others seeking credit out of the market. Recent history offers some instructive guidelines for policy makers. Among President Clinton's major legislative achievements were the budget deficit agreements of 1995 and 1997, which pledged the executive branch and Congress to make the cuts necessary to reach a balanced budget by the year 2002. These targets were actually reached four years earlier, in 1998, and the federal budget showed a surplus in fiscal years 1998–2002. **Budget surpluses**, however, were wholly eliminated by 2003 through tax cuts, lost revenues due to a weak economy, creation of the Department of Homeland Security, and additional defense spending as a proportion of the **gross national product (GNP)** for the wars in Afghanistan and Iraq. Under the George W. Bush administration, the Department of Defense budget nearly doubled in size from 2001 to 2009.

The economy's performance impacts government budgets and electoral politics. As unemployment increases, government spending on countercyclical measures will also rise (for unemployment compensation, job training, and other assistance programs) at the same time that revenues from sales and income tax receipts usually decrease. Those patterns have always existed. Now, however, instead of the 4–5 percent unemployment that existed thirty years ago (constituting what most economists regarded as full employment), contemporary unemployment levels have held fairly steady at 9–10 percent. Furthermore, there is reason to believe that these levels are the new norm—because more people (such as working women) are entering the workforce and because of basic changes in the kinds of jobs available (more lower-paid service positions and fewer industrial jobs). Higher levels of "structural" unemployment resulting from permanent loss of jobs or **outsourcing** in certain sectors of the global economy (such as automobile manufacturing, customer services, and consumer electronics) are more difficult to deal with. In turn, as a result of larger government payments for unemployment compensation and decreased tax revenue, reducing budget deficits is more difficult. Regardless of how this problem is addressed, the rules of the game in coping with budget deficits have changed within the context of overall economic and fiscal policy.

budget surpluses

occur when government brings in more revenue than it spends.

gross national product (GNP)

the sum of goods and services produced by *all Americans*, wherever they may be located around the world, during a given period of time, typically one year.

outsourcing

reallocation of jobs to more favorable economic environments (that is, lower wages, less taxes, less regulation, and so on), typically seen as movement of jobs from developed countries to less developed ones. See also **contracting out.**

The consistent economic policies of the Clinton administration, relatively low inflation rates, and a growing economy helped create over 20 million new jobs from 1992 to 2000. Since 2007, however, over 9 million jobs have been lost in the United States due to outsourcing, corporate downsizing, a weak global economy, collapse of housing values, and higher fuel prices. Although they lack direct controls to influence the future direction of the economy, incumbent presidents are nonetheless held accountable for its success or failure.

In sum, we now have not only a "mixed" public and private economy in which both sectors overlap considerably, but also the availability of a broad set of economic controls to the national government, with vast potential for decisively influencing virtually every kind of economic activity. At the same time, the kinds of problems confronting government have changed, making economic coordination and stimulation more difficult.

Links to Government Budgeting

Budgetary decisions are connected to all government attempts to influence the national and regional economies. At the same time, debt management and monetary and credit controls have only incidental relationship to the budgetary process—debt management in that debates over budget allocations may hinge in part on whether adequate revenues are available to finance proposed programs without increasing the debt, and monetary and credit controls in that appropriations are needed to pay expenses of ongoing loan programs. Of much more direct consequence to budgeting are tax policy, expenditures, the power of interest groups to create and maintain tax loopholes, and economic coordination.

Tax policy obviously influences how much revenue is available for government programs. Tax decisions, however, are normally made outside the direct focus of budget making and involve a different set of participants, both on Capitol Hill—the **House Ways and Means Committee** and the **Senate Finance Committee**, primarily—and in the executive branch. Tax policy, although significant, lacked any direct relation to the national government's budget until the mid-1970s.

Expenditure policy *is* budget making when all is said and done. The effects of spending decisions on national, state, and local economies can be dramatic—as in the case of closing government installations—or hardly visible. Entire communities that depend on the money generated by military expenditures, for example, become vulnerable when budgets are cut. But large or small individually, their cumulative consequences act to shape or reshape economic activity in significant ways. National government spending is as important for its effects on the nation's economy as for its impact on the operations of government agencies funded through direct budgetary allocations.

The Clinton "investment" strategy was reflected to some extent in budget proposals put forward by the president. The Clinton administration's budgets included more money for education, environmental protection, job training, technology, and public works. At the same time, only marginal cuts were made

House Ways and Means Committee

primary committee in Congress concerned with taxation and fiscal policy.

Senate Finance Committee

principal Senate committee concerned with revenue generation, taxation, and the operations of the Internal Revenue Service (IRS).

in entitlement programs. All these expenditure categories clearly involve some potential impact on the private economy. How much impact and on whose interests, however, is another question, one that has always aroused considerable debate whenever any president has presented an annual budget to the Congress.

Finally, economic coordination in the broadest sense is tied closely to budget making because the budget is a major instrument of the government's—especially presidential—economic policies. The executive budget is also related to economic development not only because it reflects chosen courses of action in existing fiscal policy but also because it can be a major battleground in determining the shape of that policy and, consequently, economic activity in both the public and private sectors. This is why the budgetary process is subject to so much political conflict—control over the content of budgets means the ability to allocate resources to some and not others. Presidents have other means at their disposal to encourage economic growth, but the budget remains an instrument of the highest importance. Even though the federal budget constitutes less than one-quarter of the total value of goods and services produced in the United States, it is a tangible representation of our fears, hopes, and values. Where the money comes from and how it is spent concerns nearly all of us—for different reasons. Over 90 percent of revenues (receipts) are generated from individual, payroll, and corporate taxes. How that money is used becomes a statement of relative priorities for millions of Americans who depend on government for income security, educational advancement, medical care, housing, homeland security, and national defense (see Figure 8–4).

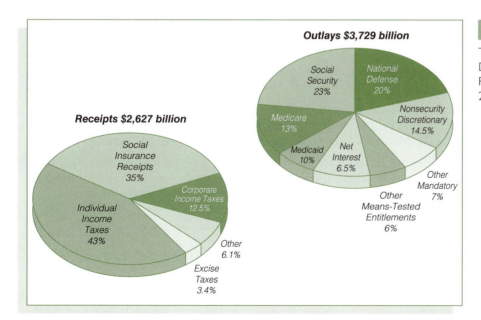

FIGURE 8-4

The Federal Government Dollar—Where It Comes From and How It Is Used, 2012 (estimated)

Source: © 2013 Cengage Learning.

POINT/COUNTERPOINT

THE ISSUE With the national government's debt and deficits so high, state and local governments, as well as individuals and private companies, are struggling to survive the effects of the most recent economic crisis. Entire communities become vulnerable when budgets are cut and economic activity shifts. Control over the content of budgets means the ability to allocate resources and potentially boost the economy. In times such as these, should the federal government step in to help?

Should the federal government use government spending to assist individuals and companies in time of economic distress?

Arguments *for* Federal Government Spending

- Government spending is an essential part of total spending for goods and services and has major pump-priming effects on private-sector expenditures. The federal government is the *single largest purchaser of goods and services* from the private sector in the United States.

- Companies will pay back government loans once they become profitable again.

- At times, profits can be made through government spending, further helping the economy—by 2011, most of the Troubled Asset Relief Program (TARP) loans had been paid back, with interest, and it was a profit for federal lending agencies.

Arguments *against* Federal Government Spending

- Government spending represents a last resort when the private sector cannot carry on, by itself, whatever activities it is trying to maintain; thus companies and individuals risk becoming completely dependent upon the government.

- As the government spends money, the sums expended replace private-sector spending and continue to contribute to the federal deficit.

- Federal assistance can provide only so much support—once the assistance runs out, companies risk returning to where they started, with high debt and the inability to support themselves or employees, making the situation worse than before.

The Process of Budget Making

The role of the executive branch, including OMB and the multitude of operating agencies, is far from the whole story of budget making. In American governments, the essential power of the purse is universally vested in the legislative branch; this extends to the authority to levy taxes, determine spending levels, actually appropriate funds, monitor and audit expenditure activities of executive agencies, and establish a wide variety of formulas by which automatic spending decisions are mandated year after year. The rise of the executive budget has sparked frequent, often intense conflict between the two branches of government over definitions of spending purposes and control of expenditures. As the budget has grown in importance as a tool of policy formulation, legislative–executive conflict has widened to include that dimension as well. Consequently, the role of legislatures has changed in recent years, serving only to complicate further the intricate interactions that take place in budgetary negotiations and decision making.

We will examine the essentials of budget making, focusing primary attention on the national government without overlooking state and local variations. One problem here is that less is known from systematic study about state and local budgeting, although research into that area has increased.[13] Of particular importance are reform of the congressional budget process, begun in 1974, and the emergence of deficit reduction as a top priority, with the Gramm–Rudman–Hollings (GRH) Act of 1985, the Omnibus Budget Reconciliation Act (OBRA) of 1990, and the **Budget Enforcement Acts of 1990, 1997, and 2002** at the center of those efforts. We will discuss essential features of budget making and then review more recent—and crucial—developments.

Essentials of the Process

Nowhere does the fragmented nature of American political decision making have a greater impact on the complexity of the process than in budget making.[14] In addition to institutional conflict between the president and Congress, the House and Senate often treat legislation, including money bills, differently. Committees within the two chambers guard their respective jurisdictions and are sensitive to any perceived "invasion of their turf." In addition, revenue and spending bills are handled by different committees on both sides of Capitol Hill. Tax bills are handled by the House Ways and Means Committee (where all tax bills must originate) and the Senate Finance Committee; appropriations bills are dealt with by the respective appropriations committees. Only since Congress created independent (and potentially powerful) budget committees in each chamber have institutional mechanisms of any sort existed on Capitol Hill for monitoring the relationship over time between revenues and expenditures. Thus, budget making in the national government (as in many states and localities) is characterized by both institutional and political fragmentation, opening the way for influence to be exerted at multiple points during the process—a system that virtually requires compromise as the ultimate basis for most budgetary decisions.

Most governments budget on an annual (twelve-month) or biennial (two-year) basis, though not all funds approved in a given year for expenditure are actually spent in that year. The budget covers a *fiscal year* rather than the calendar year, which runs from January 1 to December 31; currently, the national government fiscal year runs from October 1 to September 30. (In state and local governments, the fiscal year begins most commonly on July 1.) Each stage of budget making is predominantly under the auspices of either the executive or the legislative branch, though few functions in budgeting are exclusively the responsibility of either one.

Time frames of government budgets involve several elements. One is that, even though a government as a whole may budget on an annual basis,

Budget Enforcement Acts of 1990, 1997, and 2002

informal title of the Omnibus Budget Reconciliation Act, signed into law on November 5, 1990, and August 1997; an extension of the Gramm–Rudman–Hollings Act requiring that all new spending be offset by either new taxes or reductions in expenditures; provided for a special five-year process for deficit reduction, made permanent changes in the congressional budget process, changed the treatment of Social Security revenues in the U.S. federal budget, and established limits on federal discretionary spending.

budget obligations

orders placed, contracts awarded, services rendered, or other commitments made by government agencies during a given fiscal period that require expenditure of public funds during the same or some future period.

budget outlays

agency expenditures during a given fiscal period, fulfilling budget obligations incurred during the same or a previous period.

individual agencies within that government may be permitted an alternative arrangement, such as a three-year budget. Another element is the distinction between **budget obligations** (also referred to as *budget authority*) and actual outlays of funds. Obligations against the budget include orders placed, contracts awarded, services rendered, or other commitments made by government agencies during a given period, all of which will require expenditure of funds (**budget outlays**) during the same or some future period. The outlays themselves are expenditures within a given fiscal year, regardless of when the funds were obligated.[15] The significance of this distinction is that it implies *two separate budgets*, each with its own political and fiscal life. As much as one-third (sometimes more) of annual budget expenditures may support obligations from previous fiscal years. Budget planning and revenue requirements, among other things, are affected by this.

Government budgets progress in their annual or biennial cycle through five broad stages. In sequence, they are (1) *preparation*, which is almost wholly internal to the executive branch; (2) *authorization*, principally a function of the legislature; (3) *appropriations*, a legislative function; (4) *execution* (implementation), mainly—but by no means entirely—an executive function; and (5) *audit*, carried out by both legislative and executive entities but ordinarily independently of one another. We will examine each stage in some detail, considering not only the essential procedures of each but also the important budgetary concepts employed at different times. We will focus on the national government for illustrative purposes, although some similarities in processes can be found in many state and local governments.

Office of Management and Budget and Budget Preparation

Preparation of the budget begins at the federal level when OMB, having made some preliminary economic studies and fiscal projections, sends out a *call for estimates* to all executive agencies. This occurs some fifteen to nineteen months before the fiscal year in question begins—in late spring of the previous calendar year. The call for estimates is a request for agencies to assemble and forward to OMB their funding projections for ongoing and new programs in that fiscal year. This requires heads of agencies and of their subordinate units to develop program and fiscal data that make it possible to formulate an estimate of overall agency needs. This information is sent on to OMB, together with supporting memorandums and analytic studies, especially those relating to proposals for new or expanded programs.

Next, OMB calls on the *budget examiners*; each of the 300 examiners is assigned on a continuing basis to an agency or agencies for the purpose of becoming thoroughly acquainted with agency activities and expenditure needs. These examiners, who are, in effect, OMB's field workers, hold hearings with agency representatives on programmatic, management, and budget questions. OMB then issues "circulars" or directives to guide federal agencies in budgetary and management activities. OMB Circular A-11 integrates performance management with budgeting by directing agencies on how to prepare their budgets in accordance with the Government Performance and Results Act (GPRA). (For details, see Chapter 10.) Circular A-76 outlines procedures that federal agencies must follow when contracting out commercial (nongovernmental) activities. The agency's representatives normally include unit heads and agency budget officers, although others also may be included. Whereas budget examiners work *with* agencies, they work *for* OMB; their job is to probe and question every major expenditure proposal that agency leaders regard as important enough to include in a budget estimate. Agencies are required to plan strategically and Circular A-11 provides guidelines for the information that plans must contain. Expenditures requests are reviewed for consistency with the goals and objectives specified in the GPRA plans.

When this process is completed, the examiners make their recommendations to OMB. The director of OMB and the president draft general budget policy, major program directions and emphases, spending ceilings, and other fiscal projections, ultimately developing ceilings for each agency. The examiners' recommendations are incorporated into reviews of each agency's estimates and are often the basis for revision ordered by OMB. After a process that usually takes four to six months, original estimates are generally trimmed, and all agency requests are assembled into a single budget document running to several hundred pages. This becomes the draft of the president's budget message, which is submitted to Capitol Hill shortly after the first of the (calendar) year.

Part of the politics of budget making centers on interactions between each agency and the central budget office (OMB, a state bureau of the budget, or a city finance office). Because the central budget entity speaks and acts for the chief executive, whereas operating agencies usually have markedly different priorities, tensions between their budget priorities are inevitable. Considerable evidence suggests that deliberate strategies must be followed by agencies seeking to increase their allocations and that the preparation stage is an important opportunity for each to press its case.

Authorizations and Appropriations

The *authorization* stage has historically involved determination of maximum spending levels, or caps, for each program approved by the legislative branch. This can occur during or apart from the formal budget process, and it is the responsibility of standing committees in each chamber, such as the Senate Committee on Banking, Housing, and Urban Affairs, and the House Committee on Foreign Affairs. These permanent subject-matter committees make recommendations to the full chambers for the agencies under their respective jurisdictions. After chamber approval, a bill is normally considered by a conference committee, which irons out differences in the amounts authorized by each chamber. Assuming that agreement is reached (which is almost always the case perhaps with the exception of pre-election years), the authorization bills are forwarded to the chief executive for approval.

Authorizations may be enacted for expenditures in the same or subsequent years, making this step highly significant in terms of specific authorization provisions. Furthermore, depending on legislative or presidential politics, individual programs or agencies may be granted standing authorizations for funding—that is, open-ended authority for fiscal support subject only to yearly appropriations and without the need for reauthorization prior to appropriations action. That status signifies considerable influence in the legislature on the part of the agency or program so favored; it also weakens to some degree the control a chief executive can exercise over such an agency's fiscal and political fortunes.

The majority of state governments, and almost all local governments, draw up their budgets without incorporating an authorization stage into their procedures. Thus, as a formal step in determining expenditures, authorization has its greatest role and influence in Congress. This reflects the less formalized budget procedures that exist in many states and localities, as well as the more extensive division of power (between standing committees and appropriations committees) in Congress. The National Association of State Budget Officers (NASBO) is the leading professional membership organization for those concerned with state budgets, and a principal instrument through which states undertake collaborative efforts to advance the quality of their budget practices.[16]

The *appropriations* stage is one of the most crucial to budget making. Appropriations, as distinct from authorizations, grant the money to spend or the power to incur financial obligations, and the appropriations committees in the two houses (of Congress and most state legislatures) play the major role in this phase of the budgetary process.[17] According to existing rules of procedure, no appropriation may be voted on until after an authorization has been approved for a particular program. But it has been known to happen otherwise. On one occasion, the House appropriated funds for development of the controversial neutron bomb—a weapon said to kill by radiation without destroying neighboring populations or property—before any formal authorization had been made. It was a bomb, some said, that nobody knew we had, and the appropriation had been buried in a $10.4 billion water, power, and energy research appropriation bill. This can work the other way as well. Legislation authorizing a certain level of spending for an agency can include language mandating (ordering) that the agency spend this or that amount of money for specified purposes. As an example, a military authorization bill for weapons systems development may contain a provision directing the Pentagon to spend $125 million on research for medium-range missiles. When that happens, it virtually forces the House and Senate appropriations committees to approve that funding because the agency would be violating the law if it did not spend the money as directed. Not surprisingly, this practice, known as **backdoor financing**, is a source of considerable irritation to appropriations committee members (and many others). More important, backdoor financing eliminates discretionary decision-making control from the appropriations stage and forces anyone wishing to challenge such expenditures to seek to amend the authorization. That is often difficult to do politically; as a result, backdoor financing has had the effect of reducing control over the general level of expenditures. The George W. Bush administration effectively used special appropriations to circumvent full congressional budget review processes.

backdoor financing

practice of eliminating discretionary decision-making control from the appropriations stage of the budgetary process.

One other feature of recent congressional behavior that has major implications for authorization and appropriation processes is the dramatic growth of entitlement programs. Entitlement legislation places no limit on the total amount of budget authority for a program; eligibility standards are defined by law, and the level of outlays is determined solely by the number of eligible persons who apply for authorized benefits. (Thus, for example, Medicare, Social Security, and many veterans' benefits programs come under the heading of entitlements.) Furthermore, many entitlements are indexed to the rate of inflation, with benefits rising as the cost of living goes up. The net effect of entitlements, and of indexing, has been to further reduce the year-to-year control Congress might exercise over the rate of growth—and the substantive purposes—of national government spending. While serving as a U.S. Senator from Arizona, 2008 Republican presidential candidate John McCain often voted against further entitlement spending, referring to Medicare and Medicaid expenditures as "unsustainable."

Backdoor financing and annual "off-budget" accounting procedures tend to mask trends in revenue and expenditure projections.[18] Dire forecasts have been largely ignored by the media, leaders of both political parties, Congress, and the president. Following the 1996 election, President Clinton proposed the creation of yet another commission to study the issues surrounding the drain on federal resources expected from baby boomers retiring in the early twenty-first century. Despite the pessimistic forecasts, President Bush spent considerable political capital during 2005 to mobilize public opinion in support of his campaign promise to open Social Security to allow individuals to manage private retirement accounts. That proposal failed because it received little support from either congressional Democrats or Republicans.

President versus Congress: Conflict over Authorizations, Appropriations, and Fiscal Control

As a consequence of the fragmentation of authority in national budget making, the ability of any one institutional actor in the process to effectively restrain the expansion of national government spending has grown progressively more limited. The political impacts of backdoor spending, special orders, and mandatory entitlement programs include obstacles that must be cleared in order to address the fundamental issue of whether such programs should be continued. These questions obviously engage powerful and well-organized political interests at a very sensitive level. Unless a coalition of forces is willing even to raise the issue, thus confronting the collective wrath of those benefiting from the particular expenditure, it is difficult to alter priorities or stem the rise in expenditure levels. The Simpson–Bowles Fiscal Responsibility Commission learned this hard political truth after the lukewarm reception to fiscal austerity recommendations from some of its members and from the president.[19]

Nowhere was the battle between president and Congress joined more vigorously or more significantly than in the fight (during the Nixon Administration, 1969–1972) over efforts to reduce spending by impounding (withholding) funds after they had been authorized and appropriated by Congress. **Impoundment**, unlike the formal veto power (see Chapter 6), is something of a "super item veto" and is not subject to a congressional override. The practice of establishing reserves or of administratively withholding spending authority from some programs dates back at least a century. Under President Nixon, impoundment was a partisan process aimed at funds for programs that had grown out of the Great Society of the Johnson years (1963–1969). Members of Congress, among others, condemned this practice in speeches and press releases. Some were moved to file suit against the president, claiming that impoundment was not authorized by the Constitution and that, although precedents existed, these were not constitutionally sanctioned. But Congress, growing increasingly impatient with lengthy court proceedings, acted early in 1974 to halt impoundment through legislation.

The **Congressional Budget and Impoundment Control Act of 1974** abolished an earlier limited authorization for a president to withhold funds. It also sharply curtailed permissible grounds for deferring spending of appropriated funds, required positive action by both House and Senate to sustain an impoundment beyond a period of forty-five days, demanded monthly reports from either the president or the comptroller general (head of the Government Accountability Office [GAO]) on any deferred spending, and enabled the comptroller general to go to court for an order to spend impounded funds if a president failed to comply with any of the preceding regulations. These provisions seemingly restored a considerable measure of congressional control over appropriations and expenditures. With other developments in Congress's budgetary role, impoundment moved off center stage as a key question in legislative–executive relations.

Congress's Budgetary Role

In the confrontation between President Nixon and Congress over impoundment, another crucial issue was dealt with: whether Congress had the institutional capacity to monitor its own actions in approving expenditures and to put a brake on rising spending totals. Some observers believe that the 1974

---

impoundment

in the context of the budgetary process, the practice by a chief executive of withholding final spending approval of funds appropriated by the legislature, in a bill already signed into law; may take the form of deferrals or rescissions; presidential authority to impound limited by Congress since 1974.

Congressional Budget and Impoundment Control Act of 1974

changed the congressional budget process and revised timetables for consideration of spending bills; created the **Congressional Budget Office**.

law was at least as important for the new congressional budgetary procedures it instituted as for the restrictions it established on presidential authority to impound funds.

The procedures described earlier had left Congress open to various kinds of criticism, including fragmented consideration of the budget, disjointed action on the budget, and failure to take into account financial implications of future expenditure obligations. In addition, two other factors have contributed to growing difficulties in maintaining control over, and accountability for, expenditures.

First, very often a subsystem alliance, or iron triangle—consisting of program managers, interested subcommittee chairs, and outside interest groups—united "to thwart the will of the President and of the Congress as a whole"[20] by effectively controlling the financing and administration of particular programs (see Chapter 2). Second, whereas in the past Congress had routinely cut requests the president made on behalf of the agencies, it gradually came to cut less, and less regularly, than it once had. Appropriations subcommittees were becoming more likely to hold the line at the level requested by the president than to assume that cuts would or should be made. Also, many members of Congress displayed less willingness to defer to the judgments of specialized subcommittees and committees, whose spending recommendations were overturned with increasing frequency on the floor of the House and Senate—usually in favor of higher, not lower, amounts.

The combined effect of these changes was considerably higher appropriations levels in legislation passed by Congress. More important, there was a growing realization by observers in and out of Congress that little meaningful legislative control existed over the totality of the budget, with few legislators having any idea what "whole" was the end product of the "parts." The 1974 budget act represented a comprehensive attempt to deal with these problems. The new procedures mandated by the act can be analyzed in five segments.[21]

First, each chamber established a budget committee that would consider annual budgets in their entirety. Committee membership, particularly in the House, overlapped with membership on the Appropriations and Ways and Means committees (five from each of those committees serve on the House Budget Committee), thus ensuring some integration of effort among those three key entities. Second, the act established the CBO, with a professional staff and a director appointed jointly to a four-year term by the Speaker of the House and the president pro tem of the Senate. The CBO was to assist the budget committees and Congress as a whole in analyzing and projecting from budgetary proposals. It was to serve both as a provider of economic and fiscal data, as the House wanted, and as something of a think tank with a more philosophical approach to spending and an interest in examining national priorities, thus satisfying the Senate. Third, the act established a procedure whereby Congress would enact at least two concurrent *budget resolutions* each year, one in the spring and the other in the fall, for purposes of setting maximum spending levels during the appropriations process. The spring resolution was to set targets for spending, revenue, public debt, and the annual surplus or deficit, and the fall resolution was to set the final figures for each. Fourth, a *new timetable* was put into effect, with the fiscal year beginning on October 1 instead of July 1. Fifth, the act *banned most new backdoor spending* programs, thus extending congressional control over the budget even further. However, because many such programs existed before 1974, backdoor spending has not been eliminated; on the contrary, program costs have increased.

A major factor in the early success of the new procedures was development by the CBO of cost analysis data, relating to proposed legislation, that were seen as objective, straightforward, and timely. These data helped to minimize the "budget-numbers games" that had characterized so much legislative bargaining among the administration, agencies, lobbyists, and Capitol Hill staff. There was some disagreement about CBO's data, but this new situation certainly was an improvement over the previously fluid one, in which whom to believe in forecasting or analysis was itself a major concern.

Another important factor was effective monitoring by both budget committees and the CBO of Congress's revenue and spending actions. Also, the budget committees—through their initial responsibility for projecting total revenues, the annual deficit, and the level of the national debt—could monitor broad-gauge effects of individual committee and floor actions and inform the members. Other factors included the severe recession of 1974–1975, which coincided with the backlash (in Congress and in the country) against presidential excesses and provided an opportunity for Congress to assert itself; general public concern over growth of government spending; partisan jockeying during an election year; provisions of the budget act that provided for adequate staff assistance, enforcement mechanisms for various deadlines in the new budget cycle, and structural coordination among key committees; the determined leadership of the House and Senate budget committee chairs; and a great deal of plain hard work by budget committee members in both chambers.

After a few good years under the new budget process, the usual patterns of diffused influence in Congress gradually reasserted themselves; members paid less attention to the need for restraint and more to their geographic and interest-group constituencies. Because the process challenged established practices in one of Congress's most essential functions—allocation of resources—it should come as no surprise that those practices were resistant to change. Heightened tensions in Congress were a reflection of changes in the budgetary process. Also, political conditions prevailing in both House and Senate became increasingly unstable. President Reagan's vigorous pursuit of deep cuts in domestic spending amplified partisan liberal–conservative splits and intensified pressures on most members of Congress for attentiveness to special interests. Other emerging difficulties in the congressional budget process included an increasing tendency for Congress to ignore—or simply not be able to carry out—a number of the most important functions in the process. One was meeting the deadlines for enacting budget resolutions; Congress missed its own deadlines as often as not.

There were several reasons for this. For one, members of Congress needed to make judgments about the condition of the economy as part of their budget deliberations, and they sought as much information as possible before doing so. Another reason was that many legislators often tried to postpone the tough political choices involved in budgetary decision making until the last possible moment—an often criticized but entirely understandable tendency (at least from their standpoint). A second recurring problem was inaccurate projections of spending and revenue targets for a given fiscal year (an indication of the difficulty in making such projections eighteen months in advance). A third phenomenon, reflecting both mechanical and inherently political problems, was that several fiscal years began without a budget being enacted into law or, at least, without passage of major appropriations bills. When that happened, Congress simply authorized agency expenditures at the same levels as in the previous fiscal year until action was completed on the budget or on relevant appropriations legislation (this has been called, none too kindly, "government by **continuing resolution**").[22] This pattern continued as Congress and the Obama presidency battled to a standstill during 2011.

continuing resolution

a type of appropriation used by Congress to fund agencies when a formal appropriations bill has not been passed.

The Balanced Budget and Emergency Deficit Control Act of 1985 (Gramm–Rudman–Hollings Act)

Even with a new budget process credited by many observers with improving budget making in Washington, the national government's annual deficits grew larger. Pressures on Congress to take some action mounted accordingly. In December 1985, Congress passed the Balanced Budget and Emergency Deficit Control Act of 1985, also known as **GRH Act** after the names of its Senate sponsors Phil Gramm (R-TX), Warren Rudman (R-NH), and Ernest Hollings (D-SC). This act mandated steady reductions in annual budget deficits, mandated a balanced budget by FY 1991, and became the focus of Congress's budget deliberations. A continuing issue from the mid-1980s to the early 1990s was the question of which political interests are best served by a given budgetary approach or emphasis. To get to a zero deficit in FY 1991, the new act specified reductions of $36 billion a year in the deficit beginning with FY 1986. If the appropriations bills failed to achieve the deficit target in any one year, across-the-board spending cuts would be made to eliminate the excess deficit.[23]

GRH Act

informal title of the Balanced Budget and Emergency Deficit Control Act of 1985, which mandated steadily decreasing national government annual budget deficits through fiscal year 1991.

Gramm–Rudman–Hollings also provided that these cuts would fall equally on defense and nondefense programs and that the president had authority to suspend the cuts in a recession or during wartime. However, the legislation also provided that Congress could exempt some programs and expenditures from sequestration and, not surprisingly, *quite* a number of politically sensitive programs were exempted, including Social Security, veterans' compensation and pensions, the Medicaid program, interest on the national debt, the Supplemental Security Income (SSI) program, food stamps, and child nutrition programs. The net effect of these exemptions was to remove nearly 75 percent of national government spending from the threat of seques-trations under GRH, leaving "program areas such as education, student loans, energy assistance, and defense to bear the brunt of the burden, in the absence of increased revenues."[24] This naturally raised questions about Congress's in-tentions, not to mention the statute's likely effectiveness.

Gramm–Rudman–Hollings designated the directors of OMB and CBO as key decision makers to determine the deficit outlook each fiscal year and to recommend whether spending cuts would be needed. These cuts, as noted, would be made only if Congress failed to meet the specified deficit target be-fore each fiscal year began on October 1. Under such circumstances, however, the president was to have the authority to sequester (impose spending cuts), in keeping with the report of the comptroller general.

In 1986, however, in the case of *Bowsher v. Synar* (106 S. Ct. 3181, 92 L.Ed.2d 583), the U.S. Supreme Court ruled that the role of the comptroller general in the **sequestration** process violated separation of powers—that an official re-sponsible to Congress could not set the guidelines for the president to follow in sequestering funds. Congress remedied that problem in its 1987 amend-ments to the original bill, authorizing the director of OMB (with advisory recommendations from CBO) to determine whether sequestration would be necessary.

Gramm–Rudman–Hollings made a number of significant changes in the 1974 Congressional Budget Act by

1. requiring Congress to approve the size of the deficit in each year's concurrent resolution;
2. eliminating the second concurrent resolution entirely;
3. advancing the deadline for congressional action on the concurrent resolution from May 15 to April 15;
4. changing the deadline for completion of the **reconciliation process** from September 25 to June 15;
5. placing "off-budget" government corporations "on budget" (thus including the operating surpluses or deficits of such corporations in deficit-reduction calculations);
6. placing two Social Security trust funds off budget for the first time; and
7. incorporating loans and loan guarantees into the concurrent resolution, thus giving official standing to a credit budget (also for the first time).[25]

Reconciliation involves making adjustments in existing law to achieve con-formity with the annual spending targets adopted in the concurrent resolution. Those adjustments can be spending cuts, revenue boosts, or a combination of the two. The key step, following committee recommendations, is House and Senate action on an omnibus, or all-encompassing, reconciliation bill.

Unfortunately, this effort was no more successful than the 1974 act. Legislative–executive gridlock on budget issues intensified as timetables were ignored, and deficit-reduction targets were moved back. Congress resisted

sequestration

withholding of budgetary resources provided by discretionary or direct spending legislation, following various procedures under the Gramm–Rudman–Hollings Act of 1985 and the Budget Enforcement Acts of 1990 and 1997; the withholding of budget authority, according to an established formula, up to the dollar amount that must be cut in order to meet the deficit-reduction target.

reconciliation process

important step in congressional budgeting, when Congress makes adjustments in existing laws to achieve conformity with annual spending targets adopted in each year's concurrent resolution; these adjustments can take the form of spending reductions, revenue increases, or both.

across-the-board cuts and failed to relinquish control over distribution processes. In 1987, GRH was amended to revise deficit targets downward while postponing the deadline for achieving a balanced budget from FY 1991 to FY 1993. Some saw those decisions as realistic; others wondered if it was going to be truly possible to come to grips with the problem of continuing budget deficits. (It is discouraging to note that—in light of worsening deficits, deep political divisions over what to do about them, and little optimism that workable solutions were at hand—the 1985 deficit-reduction bill was described as "a bad idea whose time has come" by former New Hampshire Republican Senator Warren Rudman—one of the bill's cosponsors![26])

The Budget Enforcement Acts and the OBRA of 1993

The Budget Enforcement Act of 1990 made several changes in the federal budget process by amending both the Congressional Budget Act of 1974 and the GRH Act. It amended the GRH Act to work from "baseline" budgets rather than outlays and gave the president much more authority to enforce deficit-reduction targets. The act further revised the GRH Act's deficit-reduction estimates and extended the sequestration process through FY 1995. Further, it set limits on discretionary spending for three categories—defense, international, and domestic expenditures—and created a **pay-as-you-go (PAYGO)** procedure requiring that increases in direct spending (the so-called *uncontrollable* appropriations) be offset by decreases in annual appropriations so that there is no increase in the deficit.[27] This principle formed the basis for congressional–executive-branch budget "summits" in the mid-1990s to compromise on conflicting priorities.

The **OBRA of 1993** extended the Budget Enforcement Act through FY 1998, established tighter spending limits, limited discretionary budget authority to FY 1993 levels, and extended PAYGO procedures to a broader range of entitlements. President Clinton signed two budget reconciliation acts into law in August 1997 as part of a plan to balance the federal budget by FY 2002. The Budget Enforcement Act of 1997 made technical corrections in the law and extended provisions of the 1990 act through FY 2002. Under pressure from the White House in the months following September 11, 2001, Congress failed to reauthorize PAYGO. Lapsing of the PAYGO provision of the Budget Enforcement Act was viewed by many as the beginning of the current era of conflict between the executive and legislative branches, resulting in opposing priorities, gridlock, massive budget deficits, and uncontrollable spending.

Subsequent events may have served only to force a short-term compromise on deficit-reduction targets, without agreement on priorities for the long-term role of government in fiscal-policy making. At this point, however, we turn to the budget functions of execution and audit to complete the overall discussion of the budget cycle.

pay-as-you-go (PAYGO)

procedure requiring that spending increases be offset by other decreases in annual appropriations so as not to increase the deficit. Congress failed to reauthorize in 2002.

OBRA of 1993

extended the provisions of earlier legislation through 1998 and established stricter limits on discretionary spending.

Execution and Auditing of the Budget

Budget execution is the process of spending money appropriated by Congress and approved by the president. Money is apportioned from the Treasury, covering three-month periods beginning October 1, January 1, April 1, and July 1. Spending of funds is monitored by an agency's leadership, OMB, standing committees of Congress with jurisdiction over the agencies, and, periodically, GAO, the auditing and investigative arm of Congress.

Administrative discretion in spending funds is considerable. Agency personnel, in the course of program operations, may transfer funds from one account to another, reprogram funds for use in different though related ways under established budget authority, and defer spending from one fiscal quarter to the next in order to build up some cash reserves. Administrative conduct is influenced in these respects and others by legislative committees with jurisdiction over the given agency; committee review and clearance are frequently obtained prior to many such spending decisions. Similarly, the president may seek to defer spending of funds as a means of influencing agency or program directions. Congress or the president may also seek to rescind budget authority for funds previously approved for a given fiscal year. Since 1974, any deferral of spending must be reported to Congress by the president in a special message; proposed rescissions (cancellations) must also be transmitted by the president in the same manner. A deferral takes effect unless Congress passes a law overturning it, which the president must sign; for a rescission to take effect, however, both chambers of Congress must approve it within forty-five days of the president's special message.[28]

One other procedural element should be noted, a consequence of the quarterly apportionment arrangement mentioned earlier. Most agencies will try not to spend all their quarterly allotment in that quarter in order to maintain something in reserve—for emergencies, for unforeseen expenses, or simply because costs are higher during some parts of the year than others. For example, the National Park Service's expenses in the spring and summer are far greater than during the winter. In the last quarter of the fiscal year, however, this reserve buildup can lead to a strange but widespread practice. Agencies do not want to return money to the Treasury at the end of the year; thus, in the last few weeks, they will attempt to spend all but a small portion of their quarterly allotment plus any reserve accumulated through the first three quarters. The reason for reluctance to return money to the Treasury is that agencies fear being told, when next appearing before an appropriations subcommittee, "You didn't need all we gave you last year, so we'll just reduce your appropriation accordingly this year." Whether that would actually happen in every instance is not clear, but the fear is strong enough to produce behavior that is a bit surprising; one might think that agencies would be proud of having demonstrated concern for the taxpayer's dollar. But most of the time, this is not how it works out.[29]

The audit stage involves several functions divided among different auditors and carried out during different time periods. Informal audits are ongoing within agencies—they have to be in order to generate fiscal data necessary to demonstrate proper spending of funds and programmatic efficiency. Formal audits are under the direction, at various times, of agency auditors (or of private auditing firms with which agencies contract), of OMB, and of GAO. In some states, an auditor general or auditor of accounts is responsible, full-time, for maintaining a check on agency expenditures. Also, legislative oversight amounts to an ongoing informal legislative audit, though for somewhat different purposes—for programmatic concerns as well as those of expenditure control.

In recent decades, the focus and purpose of audits have shifted—in some cases, dramatically. The original purpose of auditing was to ensure financial accuracy and propriety; changes came about as budgeting, and management, generally, became more systematic. A managerial focus developed hand in hand with emphasis on program efficiency. And, in the past three decades, performance audits have become more common, stressing (as with planning–programming–budgeting [PPB] in the 1960s) program effectiveness and overall agency performance. Unlike PPB, performance auditing has taken firm root in many agencies and is increasingly used by central budget offices in the executive branch to enhance budgetary control by the chief executive.

In summarizing the five stages, we should note that, at any given time, an agency head or budget officer can be giving attention to as many as four fiscal years. By way of illustration, in the late spring of 2011 (the third quarter of FY 2011 for the national government), audits of FY 2010 were nearing conclusion, expenditures in FY 2011 were well under way, budget submissions for FY 2012 had already occurred, and preliminary preparation of estimates for FY 2013 had already begun. And, to illustrate the political turmoil that can interfere as it frequently does with the formal budget process, in FY 2011 Congress failed to approve spending authority for President Obama, so the national government operated on a series of short (two- to three-week), continuing resolutions. This kind of interference with the budget process is not uncommon prior to a presidential election year.

Budget Approaches in the Executive Branch

The growing importance of the executive budget has been a hallmark of American national politics in this century. As the national government budget became an instrument of economic policy, it became steadily more important to have a central budget clearance mechanism that could respond to changing economic conditions and needs. Budget reform has been a recurrent theme, stressing, at first, control of budget expenditures, then performance measures aimed at rational procedures to improve management, followed by deficit reduction to achieve a balanced federal budget, and, more recently, output-oriented budgeting for results.

Line-Item Budgeting

The first actions for budget reform were taken at the local level as part of a larger movement for general reform of local government, including the drive to establish the city-manager form of government.[30] By the mid-1920s, most major American cities had adopted some form of budgeting system, in most cases, strengthening the chief executive's budgetary role. At the state level, a strong movement for reform was under way between 1910 and 1920, centering on making "the [chief] executive accountable by first giving them authority over the executive branch."[31] By 1920, budget reform had occurred to some extent in forty-four of the then forty-eight states and, by 1929, all the states had central budget offices.

Throughout this same period, action was also being taken at the national level, triggered by President William Howard Taft (1909–1913), whose **Commission on Economy and Efficiency** was established in 1909 and made its final report to the president three years later. That report recommended that a budgetary process be instituted under the direction of the president, a proposal greeted with considerable skepticism by those who feared any such grant of authority to the chief executive. Among these was Woodrow Wilson (1913–1921), who, as president, vetoed legislation in 1920 that would have set up a Bureau of the Budget (BOB) in the executive branch and a General Accounting Office as an arm of Congress. One year later, President Warren Harding (1921–1923) signed virtually identical legislation into law, and a formalized federal executive-budget system was instituted. The 1921 act vested in the president exclusive authority to consolidate agency budget requests and to present an overall recommendation to Congress.

The central purpose in all these developments was control of expenditures, with emphasis on accounting for all money spent in public programs. **Line-item budgeting** was the first modern budget concept to gain acceptance, and it remained the predominant approach to budgeting through the 1930s. In this period, budgets were constructed on a line-item, or *object-of-expenditure*, basis, indicating very specifically items or services purchased and their costs. The emphasis was on control—that is, detailed itemization of expenses, central supervision of purchasing and hiring practices, and close monitoring of agency spending. The focus was on how much each agency acquired and spent, with an eye to completeness and honesty in fiscal accounting.

Performance Budgeting

The next broad phase of reform involved a conceptual change and further structural adjustment. Beginning with the New Deal, when management of national programs became centrally important, the line-item budget was partially replaced by performance budgeting. **Performance budgeting** differed from the previous control orientation in several ways. First, it was directed toward promoting effective management. Second, it dealt not only with the quantity of resources each agency acquired but also with what was done with

---

Commission on Economy and Efficiency

established in 1909 by President William Howard Taft (1909–1913); recommended that a national budgetary process be instituted under direction of the president.

line-item budgeting

earliest approach to modern executive-budget making, emphasizing control of expenditures through careful accounting for all money spent in public programs; facilitated central control of purchasing and hiring, along with completeness and honesty in fiscal accounting.

performance budgeting

approach to modern executive-budget making that gained currency in the 1930s and then again in the 1950s, emphasizing not only resources acquired by an agency but also what it did with them; geared to promoting effective management of government programs in a time of growing programmatic complexity.

those resources. Third, it called for redesigning expenditure accounts, developing work and cost measures, and making adjustments in the roles of central budgeters and in their relationships with the agencies.

Performance budgeting demanded a greater degree of centralized coordination and control. In that connection, BOB was transferred from the Treasury Department, where it had been lodged by the Budgeting and Accounting Act of 1921, to the newly established Executive Office of the President (EOP) in 1939. (The EOP was itself a product of the movement for consolidation of executive control over administrative activities.) Ironically, under performance-budgeting procedures, control and planning functions were dispersed to agency heads rather than being retained in BOB. Alleged agency failures to maintain control and to plan adequately for future activities later led to proposals for centralization of these functions within BOB.

During the performance-budgeting era, which spanned approximately twenty years (1939–1960), a number of noteworthy developments contributed to more systematic executive-budget making. During World War II, both presidential powers and the scope of the national budget expanded markedly—roughly eleven times between 1940 and 1946. As in the period after the Civil War, the budget total dropped sharply from its wartime peak but remained substantially higher than prewar levels. Enactment of the Employment Act of 1946 signaled government intent to utilize fiscal policy and economic planning to an unprecedented degree. The report of the **First Hoover Commission** to President Truman in 1949 on improving government management practices made clear that performance budgeting was preferable to line-item budgeting because it indicated more clearly what agencies were actually doing. The report also recommended expansion of BOB's role in budget and management coordination, again emphasizing growing presidential influence in both aspects of administrative operations.

In 1950, Congress passed the Budget and Accounting Procedures Act, which mandated performance budgeting for the entire national government. Aimed at developing workload and unit-cost measures of activities, it appeared to do little more than simply control and record aggregate expenditures. Although performance budgeting was very good at measuring efficiency of government programs, it did little or nothing to measure effectiveness. The difference is between assessing the efficiency of programs in terms of their internal operations and assessing their effectiveness in terms of impacts of program activities, end products, and results. For example, a school board or a group of citizens might wish to evaluate the local high school for *efficiency* by calculating the number of dollars spent per student or dollars per after-school activity, and so forth. But measures of a high school education's *effectiveness* would need to go beyond the question of dollars spent or square feet of space used or hours of time spent in study hall. Such measures would have to address what students actually learned and perhaps evaluate what was learned in light of larger objectives: Was the student college-bound or on some other track?

First Hoover Commission

(1947–1949) chaired by former President Herbert Hoover, this group tried to reduce the number of federal agencies created during World War II; recommended an expansion of executive budgetary powers.

Was the subject matter relevant to the future needs of society? Although there was little evidence that it was used as a basis for budgetary decisions, performance budgeting "did introduce on a wide scale the use of program information in budget documents as well as the used of performance information for various purposes."[32] Thus, measures of efficiency and effectiveness—indeed, the rationales for measuring them at all—are very different and involve significant concerns for the public manager (for contemporary examples, see Chapter 10).

Planning–Programming–Budgeting: The Rise and Fall of "Rationality"

Planning–programming–budgeting was an instrument of executive budgeting designed to alter processes, outcomes, and impacts of government budgeting in significant ways. As the label implies, it was aimed at improving the planning process in advance of program development and before budgetary allocations were made. It was designed to allow budget decisions to be made on the basis of previously formulated plans and was intended to make programs, not agencies, the central focus of budget making. It would, proponents promised, make it possible to relate budget decisions to broad national, state, or local goals. In the words of one observer, "the determination of public objectives and programs became the key budget function."[33] Put another way, PPB represented an effort to incorporate rationality in budgetary decision making in place of well-entrenched incrementalism. It facilitated assessments not only of agency resources and activities (as under line-item and performance budgeting) but also of the actual external effects of those activities. To accomplish that, it was necessary to create new information systems and, more important, to obtain new and objective information that would demonstrate on a firm factual basis which programs were most likely to achieve their objectives. This required greater attention to policy analysis and evaluation (see Chapter 9). The emphasis of PPB was distinctly economic. Implementation depended on the presence in the bureaucracy and in BOB (later OMB) of individuals skilled in economic analysis—specifically, cost–benefit analysis of programs. Furthermore, in assessing consequences of budget decisions, advocates of PPB called for examination of their economic impacts on society.

Although there is informed opinion to the contrary, it seems apparent that to make PPB work for the entire executive branch would require centralized control over composition of executive-budget proposals, as well as over planning, determination, and evaluation of goals. This, in fact, was one of the arguments made in support of PPB—that it would bring some coherence, consistency, and rationality into a budget process said to be notably lacking in those characteristics. But depending on one's point of view, increased centralization could also be an argument against PPB.

Expectations ran high for PPB in its early stages, during the early and mid-1960s. Some thought it would reform budgeting in the national government so as to bring about greater rationality, less "politics," better and more informed decisions, and so on. But for a variety of reasons, PPB failed to gain a permanent place in national budget making—perhaps because expectations were inflated or because PPB was flawed or because some of those who were to implement it actively resisted it and others were not sufficiently knowledgeable or experienced in planning and analysis, or motivated to make it work. Most likely, all these explanations have some validity.

Congress was one major sources of resistance to PPB for much of this period, especially the appropriations committees. Members of Congress, some of whom had spent years building up their contacts and their understanding and knowledge of agency budgets, were not favorably disposed toward a new budgeting system that, in their view, threatened to disrupt their channels of both information and influence. Even at its peak, budgets were not sent to Congress solely in the PPB format. More important, Congress did not change its appropriations practices to accommodate PPB. Also, Congress objected to the implication that it was up to the executive branch, by whatever method, to determine what the nation's programmatic goals were and what programs were needed to achieve those goals. Finally, a Congress in which political rationality and political consequences of spending were at least as important as economic, cost-effectiveness criteria, where simplifying complex budget choices was a way of life, and where consensus and compromise were preferred to direct conflict over choices was not a Congress likely to be very receptive to a budget system stressing economic "rationality."

By the mid-1970s, most budget watchers had concluded that PPB had not worked. Most agreed that PPB had had some impact on national budgeting but had not achieved its primary goal—"to recast [national] budgeting from a repetitive process for financing permanent bureaucracies into an instrument for deciding the purposes and programs of government."[34] Much of the PPB package may have been dismantled, but some components live on: (1) a basic focus on information, (2) concern with the impact of programs, (3) emphasis on goal definition, and (4) a planning perspective. Implementation of PPB went forward in several states and a number of local governments, many of which tried it in the wake of the national government experience. The actual impacts of PPB were a great deal more modest than some early claims for it. In the 1970s, other concerns began to emerge that drew attention away from PPB and toward different issues in the budgetary process.

Zero-Base Budgeting

Government activities came under increasing pressure in the 1970s for a combination of reasons. One reason was growing public restlessness about particular policy directions, such as the war in Vietnam, civil rights enforcement, and some regulatory activities of the national government. A second reason was the fiscal crunch in which many governments—especially local governments—found themselves, necessitating a more careful choice among competing interests of what would be funded and what would not be. Third, there developed some feeling, reflected in opinion polls, that the public was not getting its money's worth from costly government programs and that a hard look was needed to judge what was working and what wasn't.

Problems of financing activities and evaluating their effectiveness are not confined to government; business and industry have also had to confront these issues. It is no accident that zero-base budgeting (ZBB) developed in industry during the same period, when some in government—notably state government—were installing elements of it there.[35] ZBB involved three basic procedural elements within each administrative entity. The first was identification of decision units, the lowest-level entities in a bureaucracy for which budgets are prepared—staffs, branches, programs, functions, even individual appropriations items. Second was analysis of these decision units and formulation of decision packages by an identifiable manager with authority to establish priorities and prepare budgets for all activities within the administrative entity. The analysis began with administrators providing estimates of agency output at various funding levels (for example, 80, 90, 100, and 110 percent of current amounts), and assessing the cost-effectiveness and efficiency of the unit; it then proceeded to formulation of decision packages by each administrator. The third procedural element was ranking of decision packages from highest to lowest priority. Higher-level agency officials next established priorities among all packages from all units, with the probable available funding in mind. The high-priority packages that could be funded within the probable total dollar allocation were then included in the agency budget request, and the others were dropped.

An important aspect of the process was that each manager prepared several different decision packages pertaining to the same set of activities to allow those conducting higher-level reviews to select from alternative sets of proposals for the same program or function. Packages received higher priority as their cost declined, assuming the same set of activities. In practice, ZBB did not project budgetary allocations at "zero" before analysis of activities was begun or reallocate funds on a large scale from some policy areas to others. In theory, it called for re-examining every item in the budget periodically—every one, two, or five years—but realistically such a schedule would not be workable because budget makers did not have the authority or the tools to conduct these examinations on a regular basis. Although regarded by some as a rational-comprehensive budgetary tool, the evidence suggests that ZBB was essentially a form of incremental (or *decremental*) budgeting.

Recent Presidents and Government Budgets

The Reagan administration attempted to change what it saw as a pattern of "constituency-based" budget decisions, in the interest of creating (and sustaining) a "fiscal revolution" in the national government. Viewing previous budgets as no more than an accumulation of claims on the national treasury made by allegedly greedy special interests, the administration proposed reductions in some strongly supported domestic programs. Also important were the administration's commitments to tax reduction and to balance the budget. These were viewed (according to "supply-side" economic theory) as essential to sparking new, noninflationary expansion of private economic activity, which, it was thought, would result in sustained economic growth and continued reductions in budget deficits. The president persuaded Congress to enact an across-the-board, three-year tax cut with considerable benefit to more affluent taxpayers—which was a continuing source of controversy—on the theory that this would create jobs. Central to "Reaganomics," as this policy was called, was a determination to reduce government spending, especially domestic spending.

The "mix," or composition, of the annual budget was altered considerably during the early years of the Reagan presidency. There were major policy and budgetary successes (in that first year, for example, Congress voted to cut spending by $130 billion). Defense spending was increased substantially; however, in virtually all other functional areas of discretionary domestic spending, budget reductions were vigorously pursued (and achieved). Among the more controversial patterns of budget cutting were efforts to limit health care payments, reduce social-services program funding, freeze pay, reduce pensions for government civilian employees, and cut back levels of national government aid to state and local governments.[36] Adding to the controversy were claims that these expenditure areas were being made to bear a disproportionate share of budget reductions, on the grounds that total nondefense discretionary spending (as opposed to mandatory spending) constitutes as little as 18 percent of the national government's annual budget.[37]

The first Bush administration undertook efforts that pointed in somewhat different directions from those of its predecessor. One was fulfilling a campaign pledge of deficit reduction; another was imposition of modest cuts in military spending; a third was a willingness to increase the number of domestic grant programs to states and localities (but not the constant-dollar amounts supporting those grants). Of course, the first Bush administration was confronted with the entirely nonroutine expenditures associated with the Persian Gulf war and the savings and loan industry bailout, which cost more than $300 billion in so-called off-budget expenses.

The Clinton administration sought to emphasize budget priorities in education, job training, technology, and public works. But the president also was concerned with crime, deficit reduction, drug treatment, the environment, training and better pay for military personnel, and canceling or postponing dozens of military weapons systems. The president was forced to deal with much tighter fiscal constraints than his predecessors, so that proposed dollar reductions for Medicare, weapons systems, and public housing (among many others) became more acceptable to budget makers. The president also proposed eliminating or consolidating several hundred grant programs, and reducing spending for both foreign affairs and agriculture.[38]

More than any other recent president, George W. Bush increased *discretionary spending* to fully support the U.S. military engagements in the Middle East. Whether the threat of Iraqi weapons of mass destruction (WMDs) justified the commitment of dollars and military personnel to this mission became an increasingly controversial political issue, especially during the 2008 presidential campaign.[39] Bush increased spending as a percentage of GDP from 18.4 percent to 22.8 percent, more than under any president since Franklin Roosevelt. Early in his administration, President Bush proposed five government-wide initiatives designed to integrate performance measures with budgeting, focus on results and extensively privatize the federal workforce. These recommendations included few specifics and focused on the following areas: (1) strategic management of human capital, (2) competitive sourcing, (3) financial performance, (4) electronic government, and (5) budget and performance integration.

President Obama's Fiscal Responsibility Commission issued its final report in December 2010 with an ambitious six-part plan to promote economic growth, reduce deficits, and reform entitlements such as Medicare and Social Security. If enacted by Congress, the plan would

- achieve nearly $4 trillion in deficit reduction through 2020;
- reduce the deficit to 2.3 percent of GDP by 2015 (2.4 percent excluding Social Security reform);
- sharply reduce tax rates, abolish the Alternative Minimum Tax (AMT), and cut backdoor spending in the tax code;
- cap revenue at 21 percent of GDP and get spending below 22 percent and eventually to 21 percent;
- ensure lasting Social Security solvency, prevent the projected 22 percent cuts to come in 2037, reduce elderly poverty, and distribute the burden fairly; and
- stabilize debt by 2014 and reduce debt to 60 percent of GDP by 2023 and 40 percent by 2035.[40]

It is significant that—judging by the most frequent reactions to the findings of past presidential commissions—the broader the scope of recommendations, the lesser the chances for full implementation. It is almost certain, however, that the search will go on for other ways to enhance executive-budget control. With the expansion of the number of actors in the budget process, its complexity has greatly increased. But another factor is also having a major impact: the growing need to budget in an era of resource scarcity.

Budgeting and Resource Scarcity

Resources have always been relatively scarce in the sense that there is rarely, if ever, enough to go around to satisfy all the pressures on the public treasury. What is new is the advent of *absolute* scarcity; declining rates of growth, absolute shrinkage of tax bases (not only in larger, older central cities, where that problem has been evident for years, but also in the suburbs as foreclosures increase housing values decline), and rising inflation, coupled with recession, have put governments in a new fiscal squeeze. Getting the most out of existing resources has become a recurring theme, with renewed emphasis on both economy and efficiency, as public agencies adjust to new, harsher realities.[41]

The level of political tension has risen as various interests in the governmental process see all too clearly the possibility of having to defend repeatedly their claims for government support. As long as the total fiscal "pie" was expanding, which was the case for many years, competition for a share of it could be brisk without getting to be cutthroat. Now, however, as the total pie becomes stable or actually decreases in size and costs rise rapidly, the competition greatly intensifies.[42] How much it intensifies depends on the extent of government commitment to costly existing programs, increases in costs, employee demands for wage increases, the condition of the existing fiscal base, political pressures from taxpayers for easing the tax burden, and the like. Thus, hard-pressed cities such as New York, St. Louis, and Cleveland face a much heavier crunch than the expanding states and cities of the West and Southwest, or even the national government. But the differences may be more in degree than in substance; government jurisdictions currently in a more favorable position are well advised to prepare for the fiscal pendulum to swing the other way in their cases as well.

Under these circumstances, controllability of spending becomes a matter of premier importance and political debate. The controllability issue raises questions about government's ability—and the people's resolve—to truly control the purse strings. States, unlike the national government, often have constitutionally mandated expenditures, with specific **earmarking** of revenues for designated purposes (such as elementary, secondary, and higher education; road construction and maintenance; or operating game preserves), leaving the legislature without discretion to change them. And, ironically, as fiscal constraints on government were growing significantly, there was a major rise in the proportion of the national budget accounted for by expenditures that are uncontrollable under existing law. Allen Schick has even suggested that, in practice, some 95 percent of the budget is in fact *uncontrollable*.[43] These outlays are uncontrollable in two senses: (1) expenditures are legally mandated unless Congress changes the law and (2) the level of expenditures is determined by economic and demographic conditions largely outside the immediate control of the president and Congress.[44] The welter of entitlements, formula grants, and the like makes efforts to control spending solely through budget devices seem futile. Controllability of the budget must come through nonbudgetary mechanisms (strictly speaking) and the will to use them. One such approach is improving the efficiency, productivity, and quality of existing programs, which is discussed in detail in Chapter 10.

earmarking

revenues are "earmarked" for designated purposes (such as elementary, secondary, and higher education; road construction and maintenance; or operating game preserves), leaving the bureaucracy without discretion to change them.

Budgeting and the Future: More Questions Than Answers

Considering the magnitude of contemporary financial problems in both the public and private sectors, complex issues in the budgeting arena, and the attention paid to them, one might legitimately wonder why more has not been done to alleviate the worst of the difficulties. It is therefore useful to examine briefly some large-scale dimensions, and questions, concerning budgeting and government spending.

One question worth asking is: Just how high is national government spending? In terms of simple numbers, it would appear to be very high; almost $4 trillion in FY 2011 is not small change. That figure, however, does not take inflation into account—that is, it does not reflect the purchasing power of those dollars, as an inflation-adjusted figure (*constant dollars*) would. From FY 1980 to FY 2009, annual outlays (not adjusted for inflation) increased from $591 billion to $2.9 trillion—more than a fivefold increase. Measured in constant (2000) dollars, however, the increase in outlays during the same period "only" doubled (from $1.2 billion to $2.45 trillion).

Growth in spending, relative to both our nation's population increase and the private economy's growth (measured in terms of the GDP), has been significant but not necessarily excessive. In FY 1970, national government outlays represented just under 20 percent of GDP; these rose to nearly 25 percent in FY 1983, then dropped to just under 17 percent in FY 2003, and rose again to 25.3 percent in FY 2011. Also, it should be kept in mind that between 1950 and 2010, the population of the United States more than doubled—from 151 million to just less than 309 million people. Even if national government expenditures (in constant dollars) had increased only in exact proportion to the population growth during that same period, the net increase would be substantial—and, indeed, it has been just that. Governments in other advanced industrialized countries collect and spend far more as a percentage of their GDPs (see Figure 8–2). What has changed since the year 2000 has been the proportion of spending as a ratio of the amount borrowed to cover the difference between revenues and expenditures (Table 8-1).

Out of these figures comes an important reality—the performance of the private economy is critical to the condition of the national budget. This is, of course, true on the revenue side, because a robust economy generates more tax dollars at the same tax rates than a sluggish economy does. It is also true on the expenditure side, however, because, during periods of slow economic growth, tax collections decline, and payments to individuals increase, thus putting more pressure on a government treasury already suffering from decreased revenues. The recession made it more difficult to move toward a balanced budget; slow growth in the GDP since 2007 has worsened the overall budget picture.

There also have been sizable reductions in income taxes in 1981 and again in 2001 and 2002, under Presidents Ronald Reagan and George W. Bush. It has been estimated that, in the first three years (combined) after the 1981 tax cut,

$135 billion that might have helped reduce budget deficits were not collected—good news for the individual and corporate taxpayer, but bad news for deficit reduction. Congress, in fact, took some potentially unpopular steps to curb the deficit, raising selected taxes (despite resistance by the Reagan administration) in 1982, 1983, and 1984. It has been suggested that increased revenues from these taxes have had the effect of lowering annual deficits from what they would have been otherwise by about $75 billion per year, from FY 1986 onward.[45]

"No new taxes," in turn, became a slogan of the George H. W. Bush campaign for the presidency in 1988. That pledge took on a somewhat hollow ring for many supporters when, in June 1990, he indicated publicly that as part of high-level negotiations between Democrats and Republicans, tax increases were one of many possibilities up for discussion in the negotiations. Some of the president's detractors were quick to point out that they had described the original pledge of no new taxes as ill-advised when it was made. The larger point is that, in the absence of stronger economic performance in the private sector, increased taxes combined with spending restraint may be one of the best options available to combat chronic budget deficits. One difficulty, of course, is that, although we as a nation have long resisted "taxation without representation," lately many of us seem to be almost equally unhappy about the prospect of taxation *with* representation. Another difficulty is that cutting spending continues to have broad popular appeal—even if, under present law, most of the national government's annual expenditures are beyond reach unless entitlements are cut. However, it is increasingly apparent that, if the president and a majority of Congress agree to change present law, no entitlement is guaranteed, and no expenditure is actually uncontrollable.

HOW WOULD YOU DECIDE?

Inside Job

The film *Inside Job* won the Academy Award for Best Documentary Feature in 2011, and it addresses the global financial crisis of 2008. The film offers a comprehensive analysis of the crisis that cost the nation over $20 trillion, caused millions of people to lose their jobs and homes, and contributed to the worst recession in the United States since the Great Depression.

The film centers on the changing financial industry leading up to the economic crisis and the political movement toward deregulation, which allowed for large increases in circumventing traditional regulations intended to control risk. The director, Charles Ferguson, examines the economic crisis as it began, paying close attention to the prevalence of conflict of interest within the financial

sector that affected credit rating agencies and other individuals who received funding from consultants.

At the close of the film, the question is whether the financial system has truly changed as a result of the economic crisis and deep recession. Conservative presidents have attempted to use tax reductions to stimulate the economy. Liberal presidents have applied tax stimulus in attempts to achieve the same economic goals.

Given the fragmented nature of the U.S. economy and the freedom given to private interests, which sector can be trusted more fully to advance policies that are most likely to create economic growth?

Source: http://www.sonyclassics.com/insidejob/, accessed April 13, 2011.

Problems and Prospects

The budget process continues to be a center of attention in the nation's capital, and in many states and localities as well. Still, deficit-reduction efforts have foundered as legislatures fail to place stronger curbs on the growth of public expenditures, budgetary pressures on Congress and the executive branch are increasing, and there is a great deal more uncertainty in agency and congressional operations when the budget process calls for virtually continuous deliberations.

Under the budget-reduction statutes of 1985, 1990, 1993, 1997, and 2002, sequestration was mandated if Congress fails to achieve the deficit target for a given year. That seems straightforward enough, but it has turned out not to be. In 1987, efforts were made to meet the deficit target by backdating expenditures from one year to the previous one, selling major national government assets, and delaying some individual purchases from September 30 to October 1 (so that associated costs would be reflected on the next fiscal year's ledger). Another issue has surfaced concerning calculation of the deficit itself, with accusations being heard that some are engaging in budget gimmickry to arrive at the designated deficit targets, that others are using "blue smoke and mirrors," and so on. Such accusations hurled back and forth between the White House and the Capitol, between Democrats and Republicans, have had the effect of increasing mistrust among large numbers of key participants in the budget process.

A related issue that surfaced in 1989 and 1990 was the elder Bush administration's deficit projections incorporating, on the "plus" side, the substantial and growing surpluses in the main trust fund of the Social Security system. Those surpluses are the result of boosts in Social Security taxes; they are deliberate, and designed to create—over a period of many years—a reserve in the system sufficient to meet the system's payout obligations when especially large numbers of American workers begin retiring (about the year 2012). The administration was roundly criticized for including such trust fund surpluses in its calculations; indeed, the whole issue of calculating surpluses and deficits in subparts of the overall budget was raised by this practice. The major contention was that incorporating trust fund surpluses into calculations about the budget deficit gave a misleading, if not false, impression concerning existing realities. George H. W. Bush came under increasing pressure regarding such calculations, which perhaps contributed to increased willingness to negotiate about future efforts to develop individual retirement accounts.

The possibility of strengthening the chief executive's authority to restrain expenditures selectively has been a favorite issue of fiscal conservatives. Republican Presidents Ronald Reagan and George H. W. Bush, and even Democrat Bill Clinton, advanced proposals dealing with the nation's continuing inability to control government spending. Presidents Reagan and Bush actively supported a constitutional amendment that would require the national government to maintain a balanced budget. They also advocated a constitutional amendment or legislation that would enable the president to exercise a line-item veto over appropriations (see Chapter 6). It remains to be seen whether this power, if judged by the future Supreme Courts not to violate the Constitution, will be used by chief executives to eliminate wasteful and unnecessary spending or simply to promote the interests of their political party.

Congressional involvement in annual budget deliberations as well as in virtually continuous revision in dollar amounts available to the national government's executive-branch agencies has limited the potential for reform.[46] Budget making will command more and more of the attention of government decision makers, possibly crowding off the public agenda other issues and concerns that merit attention as well. Some say that this is exactly what has been happening in Washington as concern about budgets and deficits becomes ever greater. The National Performance Review (NPR) recommended a biennial (two-year) budget, eliminating the need for congressional and White House staff to review budget proposals annually. Congress did not act on this recommendation, nor is it likely to when faced with increasing debt and deficits.

Finally, we come to the phenomenon sometimes labeled **summitry** in national government budget making: the practice of initiating negotiations among leaders of Congress and the White House involving top Democrats meeting with top Republicans (usually away from public view), in efforts to confront more effectively the seemingly intractable budget (and budget deficit) challenges. Summitry did not happen overnight; it represents the culmination of a series of events, dating back more than thirty years. First (it is said), the president's budget message ceased to serve as Congress's starting point in budget deliberations. Then, Congress's own procedures mandated under the 1974 legislation failed to halt the growth of national government expenditures, producing additional frustration at both ends of Pennsylvania Avenue (the Capitol and the White House). A summit held in 1989 succeeded only in producing an agreement no one seemed to like and sowed seeds of further partisan mistrust; neither Republicans nor Democrats wanted to take the blame for failing to deal with the deficit. And in the post-9/11 era, neither side has been willing to engage in domestic diplomacy necessary to compromise on deficits and budget priorities. The fundamental difference between the 2011 White House and Republican budget proposals reflected how each party envisioned the influence of government in the economy, as measured by spending and revenues as a percentage of GDP. Emerging from a deep recession, the Obama administration has portrayed itself as seeking to rebuild the economy with the proposed 2012 budget. But deep differences exist between Republican and Democratic visions of the future, even though both proposed budgets seek to bring the national deficit under control through spending cuts and tax increases.[47]

The significant point is that the United States seems to have reached a condition of near chaos in budgetary decision making, with so many pressures applied on behalf of so many interests from so many different directions that it appears as if summitry may be the only way to deal with the root causes of our difficulties. (At one point in the early summer of 2011, "summitry" took the

summitry

in national government budget making, the practice of initiating negotiations among leaders of Congress and the White House, involving top Democrats meeting with top Republicans (usually away from public view), in efforts to confront more effectively the seemingly intractable budget (and budget deficit) challenges.

form of a golf game in which President Obama and Republican House Speaker John Boehner took part—just the two of them!) In terms of some of the perspectives discussed in Chapters 3 and 4, it might be said that the budgetary process has been burdened with the consequences of a great deal of long-term decentralized participation within our federal system. It can be argued that we have now reached the point at which the need for central direction, to restore a degree of order essential to decision making, has become so great that only at the highest levels of government can individuals holding sufficient influence in the process come together with any hope of resolving what needs to be resolved for the system to function.

Clearly, the nature of budgeting has changed in the past fifty years; it is equally clear that change has not occurred in a social or political vacuum. As Allen Schick has observed, "[t]he budget cannot make order out of chaos, it cannot bring concord where there is unlimited strife. Where there is [political] instability . . . [budget] issues become symbols of larger, unresolvable political conflicts."[48] That view is consistent with the position taken at the outset of this chapter—namely, that government budgets reflect the political preferences and priorities of those who make them—and, by implication, of the citizenry at large. Where those preferences and priorities are very much in turmoil, as they have been in recent years, it is not surprising that the politics of government budgeting is similarly turbulent. It appears certain that we face continuing political and fiscal conflict as we grope for a new national consensus on the proper role of public spending.

Summary

The budgetary process is central to resource allocation in the political system. The nature of decision making has long been an issue of considerable importance, with political influence, policy control, and rationality as key variables. The scope of government spending and its impacts on society have dramatically expanded in recent decades, with new practices and new concerns emerging since the 1970s.

Budgets are tools used by governments to influence the course of private-sector economic activity. The chief instruments related to budgeting include taxing and spending patterns; management of debt: monetary, and credit controls; and economic coordination. Such uses of the budget are of relatively recent vintage, having developed fully only in the last fifty years. Accompanying these changes has been a marked increase in both the role of the national government and the influence of the president in budget and policy formulation. The executive budget has been central to all this, whereas Congress maintains basic control over public purse strings.

Budget formulation in the executive branch has been characterized at different times by various orientations and emphases. The process of budget making is highly fragmented in many American governments and includes choices as to annual or multiyear budgeting, as well as current and future obligations. Budget preparation focuses on the roles of agencies and a central budget office in assembling executive-budget proposals for the legislature. Authorizations are legislative determinations, first, of programs themselves, and second, of maximum spending levels. Appropriations allocate actual funding or obligations, and normally must follow—and be governed by—authorizations. However, a recent tendency has emerged toward backdoor spending authority and entitlement programs that remain in force unless deliberate action is taken to change their provisions. This has simultaneously weakened controls over spending and contributed to rapidly rising expenditures, at least in the national government budget.

Budgeting in an era of resource scarcity is a harsh new reality. Rising costs and limits on taxes have combined with stabilizing or even shrinking resource bases to create a serious fiscal squeeze for many governments. Among the consequences are the increasing importance of budgetary decisions, increasing demands for controllability of expenditures, and emerging practices such as PAYGO, sequestration, and summitry. Important issues, including deficits and chief-executive powers, continue to be associated with budgets and budget making. A consensus on the appropriate government role in fiscal decision making has yet to be achieved.

Discussion Questions

1. Explain how taxation, government expenditures, management of the national debt, and tax expenditures (tax breaks) can be used by national, state, and local governments as tools of fiscal policy.

2. Describe the current budget process at the national level, as amended by GRH and the Budget Enforcement Acts, at each of the five steps of the budgetary cycle. Assess the process's apparent weaknesses and shortcomings, and the prospects for eventually achieving a balanced budget.

3. What factors (general and specific, short- and long-term) explain the rise and fall in expenditures in the national government budget over the past thirty years?

4. The cumulative debt for the U.S. government in 2009 was about three times its annual revenue. Even if budgets are balanced after FY 2012, that debt (and its interest) will still have to be paid. Is the amount of U.S. government spending a problem, and if so, how can it be dealt with?

5. Define—then compare and contrast—incremental budget making, line-item budgeting, performance budgeting, PPB, and ZBB. What are the features, advantages, and disadvantages of each? Which do you think should be used today? Defend your answer.

6. Discuss the relationship between the national economy and national government fiscal activity. Include in your discussion the government's role as a distributor of scarce public resources.

7. Discuss the roles of the president and Congress in budget determination. When did the president get a role, and why was the president given executive budget authority?

8. Why is incremental budget making not used as often as it once was?

9. Explain the relationship among monetary and credit controls, budgeting, and "power politics."

10. What are the possible consequences for the national economy of increased annual deficits, cumulative debt, and threats to not raise the debt ceiling?

Key Terms and Concepts

Suggested Readings

Forsythe, Dall W. *Memos to the Governor: An Introduction to State Budgeting.* 2nd ed., updated. Washington, D.C.: Georgetown University Press, 2004.

Frank, Howard A., ed. *Public Financial Management.* Boca Raton, Fla.: CRC Press, 2006.

Franklin, Daniel P. *The Age of Deficits: Presidents and Unbalanced Budgets from Jimmy Carter to George W. Bush.* Washington, D.C.: Congressional Quarterly Press, 2009.

Hyde, Albert C., and Jay M. Shafritz. *Government Budgeting: Theory, Process, Politics.* 3rd ed. Belmont, Calif.: Wadsworth, 2002.

Jones, Vernon D. *Downsizing the Federal Government.* Armonk, N.Y.: M.E. Sharpe, 1998.

Kettl, Donald F. *Deficit Politics: Public Budgeting in Institutional and Historical Context.* Upper Saddle River, N.J.: Prentice Hall, 1992.

Kettl, Donald F., and John DiIulio Jr. *Cutting Government.* Washington, D.C.: Brookings Institution Press, 1995.

Lee, Robert D., Jr., Ronald W. Johnson, and Philip G. Joyce. *Public Budgeting Systems.* 8th ed. Boston, Mass.: Jones and Bartlett, 2008.

LeLoup, Lance T. *Parties, Rules, and the Evolution of Congressional Budgeting.* Columbus: Ohio State University Press, 2005.

Light, Paul. *Thickening Government.* Washington, D.C.: Brookings Institution Press, 1995.

McCaffery, Jerry, ed. *Public Budgeting and Financial Management in the Federal Government.* Greenwich, Conn.: Information Age, 2002.

Mikesell, John L. *Fiscal Administration: Analysis and Applications for the Public Sector.* 8th ed. Belmont, Calif.: Wadsworth, 2008.

Oleszek, Walter J. *Congressional Procedures and the Policy Process*. 8th ed. Washington, D.C.: CQ Press, 2010.

Panetta, Leon. "Politics of the Federal Budget Process." In James A. Thurber, ed., *Rivals for Power: Presidential-Congressional Relations*. 3rd ed. Lanham, Md.: Rowman & Littlefield, 2005.

Rabin, Jack, ed. *Handbook of Public Budgeting*. New York: Marcel Dekker, 1992.

Reischauer, Robert D., and Henry J. Aaron. *Setting National Priorities*. Washington, D.C.: Brookings Institution Press, 1999.

Rubin, Irene S. *The Politics of Public Budgeting: Getting and Spending, Borrowing and Balancing*. 6th ed. Washington, D.C.: CQ Press, 2010.

_____. *Public Budgeting: Policy, Process, and Politics*. New York: M.E. Sharpe, 2008.

Schick, Allen. *The Federal Budget: Politics, Policy, Process*. 3rd ed. Washington, D.C.: Brookings Institution Press, 2007.

Steuerle, Eugene C., and Melissa Favreault. *Contemporary U.S. Tax Policy*. 2nd ed. Washington, D.C.: Urban Institute Press, 2008.

Thurber, James A. *Rivals for Power: Presidential-Congressional Relations*. 4th ed. Lanham, Md.: Rowman & Littlefield, 2009.

Wang, Xiao Hu. *Financial Management in the Public Sector: Tools, Applications, and Cases*. Boca Raton, Fla.: CRC Press, 2010.

Wildavsky, Aaron, and Naomi Caiden. *The New Politics of the Budgetary Process*. 5th ed. New York: Longman, 2004.

Public Policy and Program Implementation

Our goal is to make the entire federal government both less expensive and more efficient, and to change the culture of our national bureaucracy away from complacency and entitlement toward initiative and empowerment. We intend to redesign, to reinvent, to reinvigorate the entire national government.

President Bill Clinton
March 1993

Discussions of government policy in areas such as agriculture, education, homeland security, emergency management, criminal justice, environmental quality, foreign affairs, health care, transportation, or land-use planning attempt to convey an impression of well-defined purposes—carefully mapped out, sufficient resources marshaled and at the ready, with consistent support through the political process. However, the realities of governing in the United States differ dramatically from this conception.

In our complex and fragmented governmental system, there is often no single dominant political majority capable of determining policy in every instance. Congressional voting coalitions are usually temporary, changing from one issue to the next; presidential election majorities are often fashioned out of very diverse groups in the population, each with policy interests that conflict with others; court rulings may or may not coincide with public sentiment; administrative agencies are not permanently tied to any one political coalition. The combined impacts of these shifting attitudes, institutions, and a very diverse population on the definition, formulation, implementation, and evaluation of public policy often blur rather than clarify policy objectives and content. Instead of being clear and unmistakable government commitments, many policies are "mixed bags" of programs reflecting a variety of past actions and declarations, *ad hoc* responses to contemporary situations, and considerable uncertainty about future policy directions. Cynicism abounds as greater numbers of citizens express reservations about the capacity of executives, legislators, and public administrators to address fundamental and fiscal issues.

Yet there are strong expectations that public problems will be tackled and that the resulting programs will be well managed—that they represent the culmination of deliberate efforts to analyze, plan, design, fund, and operate sets of activities appropriately directed toward accomplishing agreed-upon objectives. There is the further expectation that managers and others will be capable of evaluating the actual achievements of government programs. Although it is difficult to identify or rationalize all aspects of a given policy, managers must focus on discrete tasks involved in organizing and operating programs. This is necessary despite the ever-present swirl of political controversy, media scrutiny, opposing approaches offered by various interests, and bitter partisanship that frequently surrounds much of what governments try to accomplish.

In these endeavors, a particular agency or bureau in the administrative process and the individuals within that organization (as well as other "stakeholders" such as recipients of public services, elected officials, and government contractors) must collaborate in a common effort to achieve policy goals. Managing public programs, individually and as they affect the course of public policies, involves major concerns discussed in previous chapters: expertise, ethics, effective management, executive and managerial leadership, organizational structure, motivation, decision making, personnel selection, and budgeting. All of these impact the roles of bureaucracy and the ultimate success or failure of government problem solving. And with growing sophistication in our capacity to analyze public programs has come a greater awareness of the need and potential for more intelligent, more "rational" conduct of public management processes. At the same time, increasing numbers of narrow-focused special-interest groups, commonly referred to as **single-issue groups**, mount well-funded campaigns on both sides of numerous issues. Therefore, policies are applied through a complicated and fragmented political process that is anything but rational, in classical/economic terms.

In this chapter, we examine the nature of public policies; describe various policy-making processes, particularly as they involve individual administrators and private contractors; program management, planning, and analysis; implementation, including how some policy directions are altered in the course of managing individual programs; how programs are (or could be) evaluated; and the challenges of improving policy by applying analytical processes. The ultimate purpose is to understand how public policies evolve as they do, the role of administrative politics in this process, and the operational realities—including problems—of managing public programs to achieve policy goals.

> **single-issue groups**
>
> ideologically oriented groups that focus on a single issue, such as a woman's right to terminate a pregnancy or abortion rights, to the exclusion of all others. Elected officials who do not support groups on the issue are targeted for defeat.

The Changing Nature of Public Policies

What precisely is **public policy**? Many people regard public policies as deliberate responses or purposive actions to alleviate problems and needs systematically identified by some legitimate means. It is commonly assumed that government policies are intended to solve—or at least cope with—major

> **public policy**
>
> (1) organizing framework of purposes and rationales for government programs that deal with specified societal problems; (2) complex of programs enacted and implemented by government.

social and economic problems. There is typically some disparity, however, between the perception of the average citizen about policy processes and the outcomes and realities of policy making.

Let us consider some of the most common popular assumptions about government policy. First, some people believe that governments have clearly defined policies, well-thought-out in advance, on all or most major issues and problems. Second, many believe these policies are established through some kind of rational choice of better (as opposed to worse) alternatives made by political leaders. Third, some think everything that is done to address a problem or issue follows those policies. Fourth, it is often assumed that the policies of government are clearly perceived and understood by citizens. And fifth, many believe that government policies are widely agreed on and supported—otherwise, how could they remain in force? As appealing or logical as these ideas might be, not one of them is true.

Public policies are generally not clearly defined in the sense that all major problems are anticipated and the machinery of government geared up to meet them before they become unmanageable. That would require the kind of centralized leadership inconsistent with the Constitution and resisted by many of us. Some processes designed to foresee future developments and prepare for them have not accomplished all that they were intended to, and "circumstances beyond our control" often prevail. With the exception of threats to national security and major natural disasters, it is unusual to have a consistent policy for dealing with a specific problem. As a practical matter, governments could not possibly have predetermined policies on all issues, especially accidents, natural disasters such as earthquakes, wild fires, tornadoes, floods, and hurricanes, as well as deliberate acts of terror. Thus, policies are more often the product of responses to particular circumstances or problems rather than the result of deliberate actions. They frequently result from *ad hoc* decisions made at many levels, at different times, by officials and others who see only some parts of the overall problem. Rational policy choice implies a decision-making capacity largely lacking in most of our noncentralized government institutions. The diffuse intergovernmental array of some 87,000 state and local governments, combined with differences of opinion among over 500,000 elected nationwide policy makers, further weakens the capacity for centrally coordinated actions.

Because of this size and diversity, many government activities do not follow official policy directions or support publicly stated goals. Political party platforms, pronouncements by top executives, state and local initiatives and referenda, even Congressional resolutions are often a better reflection of intent than of reality in policy making. What actually takes place often differs from official proclamations of what was supposed to occur. Also, we tend to pay more attention to government activity that is likely to have a tangible impact on our lives, but otherwise it is unusual for large numbers of people to comprehend the intricacies of public policy. A good example is foreign policy. Different ethnic and nationality groups are sensitive to even small changes in what this nation does or contemplates doing regarding their mother countries or other entities with which those groups identify, but most citizens have only a generalized awareness of our overall foreign policy. Another issue that defies easy comprehension is climate change. Although we are generally aware of the ostensible (apparent) effects of climate change on the environment, we tend to view government policy options and actions through the "lenses" of our own experiences. Unless we are personally and immediately affected by climate change (or by any other broad policy concern), we are most likely to accept the status quo, and to question policy proposals that may require us to make significant changes in the ways we live our lives. The visibility of any particular problem or set of issues affects our awareness of proposed public policy. Many domestic policies are also understood only in broad outline. In short, it is not accurate to assume that most Americans are knowledgeable in detail about individual policies.

Finally, it is rarely true that there is widespread, active support for existing public policies, although most have at least passive backing. Policy directions that offend basic values of large numbers of people are not likely to be sustained for very long without at least being challenged. Examples of sharp public reaction to disputed policies include resistance to the Supreme Court ban on prayers in the public schools, opposition to judicial rulings on abortion, challenges to hiring preferences and "quotas" for affirmative action, disagreement over the display of religious symbols such as the Ten Commandments in state facilities, opposition to and support for the use of vouchers for public school students to attend private schools, and expressions of public distaste for some forms of public health and safety regulation. In one sense, policies that exist without widespread challenge may be taken as a barometer of public feeling about what is acceptable, generally speaking. Few policies survive that offend either powerful political interests or large numbers of ordinary citizens, or both. In sum, although support for what government does is not necessarily enthusiastic, policies must have a certain amount of acceptability. However, the most acceptable policies may not be the most effective, and the most effective policies may not be acceptable to a majority or a vocal minority. Some compromise is often necessary to implement most public policies.

It makes a difference *which* situations are defined as problems, *who* defines them, and *why* they deserve attention in the policy arena. Unequal access to affordable health care, for example, was part of the American scene for decades before President Barack Obama defined it as a high-priority problem in 2008. Although the problem was analyzed and various options were formulated by experts using a rational policy approach (see Chapter 5), opponents were successful in labeling the changes as "socialized medicine," assuring its defeat in Congress prior to 2010. Nuclear reactor safety, climate change, crime control, job training, "welfare-to-workfare" reform, sex discrimination, and the AIDS epidemic are examples of issue areas that were defined as policy problems long before any action was taken. Also, policy initiatives can come from many parts of the body politic—the president, Congress, interest groups, the mass media, state or local governments, and so on. Perhaps the only policy maker prohibited in theory from initiating policy changes on its own is the judiciary. Chief executives are usually in the best position to take the initiative, but they have no monopoly on attempting to raise awareness of issues for public and governmental attention. Furthermore, most policy changes come about slowly; it is far easier to *resist* change than to bring it about. American government tends to move in evolutionary fashion; *incrementalism* has generally been the order of the day. Finally, many policy actions are more symbolic than real. *Symbolism* is not without value in politics, but it should be understood for what it is and not be confused with substantive change.[1] State laws punishing desecration of the American flag, legalizing moments of silence to counter federal court decisions banning school prayer, permitting the display of state flags bearing Confederate symbols, and calls for a balanced federal budget amendment to the U.S. Constitution are largely symbolic, but no less important to constituent groups.

symbolic actions

proposals for policy changes that serve some limited political purpose, but do not threaten the current situation.

Because most citizens are unfamiliar with the details of policy, **symbolic actions** are often sufficient to satisfy calls for change without threatening the status quo. The passing of public attention from an issue often signals a slowdown in dealing with it, even if many in government would prefer to move more rapidly. Organized group support and opposition make a major difference in how substantive—or simply cosmetic—policy changes are.

Public policies, then, tend to be haphazard, not widely understood or actively supported, and often inconsistently applied. Not all situations in society that might be classified as problem areas are, in fact, defined as such. At other times, problems that affect only a small, but politically powerful, minority are defined as public issues deserving of broader attention. This happened in 2008, when the Bush administration tried to ease stock market jitters with an ambitious plan to assist banks, corporations, Wall Street firms, and other financial institutions with significant investments of federal loans and loan guarantees to rescue financially troubled companies. And sometimes an unspoken policy exists to take no action on a problem; the decision *not* to act can be just as significant as a stated government policy to those interests that benefit from the status quo. When changes in policy do occur, they tend to be rather slow and unfocused. That any coherent policies exist is often a surprise.

Types of Policies

There is great variety in the kinds of policies pursued by government entities. These can be distinguished on the basis of their essential rationales, their impacts on society, and the respective roles played by administrative agencies in each. Major policy types include distributive, redistributive, regulatory, self-regulatory, and its logical corollary, privatization.[2]

Distributive policies deliver large-scale services or benefits to certain individuals or groups in the population. Examples are loans and loan guarantees provided by the national government to cover private-sector losses, such as those suffered by the commercial airlines following September 11, 2001, and the banking, financial services, and financial services industries in 2007–2008; agricultural price supports, especially those benefitting wealthy farmers; tax deductions for interest paid on home mortgages; loans for college students; subsidies to energy and oil companies (sometimes labeled "corporate welfare"); and government contracts to politically active private firms. These involve policy subsystems or iron triangles (described in Chapter 2) on almost an *ad hoc* basis, with direct beneficiaries who do not pay direct costs. Bureaucracies are often, but not always, involved in both the enactment of such policies and their implementation. President George W. Bush's Secretary of the Treasury, Henry Paulson, was heavily criticized for engineering the "bailout" of politically influential corporations in 2007–2008. The Troubled Asset Relief Program (TARP) bailout was originally estimated to cost taxpayers $300 billion, but current Secretary of the Treasury Timothy Geithner estimated that all but $25 billion of the loans would be paid back by the summer of 2011.

Redistributive policies "involve deliberate efforts by the government to shift the allocation of wealth, income, property, or rights among broad classes or groups" within the population.[3] These efforts are often the source of intense controversy in the political arena, controversy that could significantly impact the execution of a policy as well as its initial adoption. Thus, redistributive policies such as affirmative action, the graduated (or "progressive") income tax, Medicaid for the poor and (to a lesser extent) Medicare for the elderly, and Temporary Assistance for Needy Families (TANF) were all subject to intense debate and conflict during legislative deliberations. This type of policy is most sensitive politically and thus most susceptible to political pressures. It is also very difficult to implement policies that are redistributive across economic classes in society. Many policies that began with this goal have lost much of their redistributive character as a result of changes (for example tax exemptions, lower tax rates, income shelters, and similar loopholes) made in the basic law—some of which were proposed by the agency responsible for its administration! Because of the controversy they generate, redistributive policies almost inevitably draw bureaucracies directly into the policy process, even though many would prefer to remain on the sidelines. In other instances, agencies with jurisdiction over redistributive policies have taken the lead in maintaining their essential character.

Regulatory policies promote restrictions on the freedom to act of those subject to the regulations. The most prominent of such policies pertain to business activities—for example, advertising practices, toy safety, pollution control, natural-gas pricing practices, and product liability. Other regulatory policies are also in effect in areas such as civil rights, job safety, nuclear power

distributive policies

policy actions such as subsidies or tax deductions that deliver widespread benefits to individuals or groups who often do not bear the costs directly.

redistributive policies

deliberate efforts by governments to shift the allocation of valued goods in society from one group to another; highly controversial and often accompanied by bitter political conflicts.

regulatory policies

establish restrictions on the behavior of those subject to the regulations, aim to protect certain groups, range broadly in scope, and are often enforced against businesses.

plants, and local government building and zoning ordinances. These are usually the product of conflict between competing forces—such as producer and consumer—each of which seeks to control the behavior of the other to some degree. Thus, regulatory policies involve greater tension among relevant actors and usually incorporate a larger and more direct role for bureaucracies. The regulative actions of government, especially in the areas of immigration control, homeland security, transportation safety, and antiterrorism, have increased substantially in recent years (see Chapter 11).

self-regulatory policies

protective regulations that either advantage certain professions or classes, or remove from the government the power to regulate.

Self-regulatory policies, or constituent policies, represent a variation on regulation in that policy changes are often sought by those being regulated as a means of protecting or promoting their own economic interests. The leading example is licensing of professions and occupations, such as banking, law, medicine, real estate, cosmetology, and taxi driving. Normally (especially in the case of professions), a legislative body enacts a licensing law, providing for enforcement by a board dominated by members selected from the licensed group. Other bureaucracies, and most other interests, typically take little interest in this kind of policy.

Bureaucratic agencies play somewhat different roles in each type of policy. As already implied, their roles may also vary within a given policy category, as is the case in redistributive policy. Subsystems exert considerable influence in the formation and implementation of distributive policies, although in a highly individualized manner. Depending on the kind of policy at issue, bureaus and their allies may be more or less involved; the degree of involvement hinges primarily on the extent to which formal responsibilities are assigned to a given agency. Self-regulation only sporadically engages the attention of agencies outside a specific profession or occupation (although some subsystem politics is involved).

Public Policy, Politics, and/or Private Management

Governments may try to create new policy-making environments for a variety of purposes, not exclusively to increase administrative efficiency or affect policy outcomes. Some reasons are *ideological* and intended to shift government programs in the direction of rewarding loyal interest groups; examples include the Republican *Contract with America* in 1994 and 2010, school vouchers, privatization, the market-based concept of "public choice," and other theories (some of which are supported by *both* political parties). Others are *pragmatic*, such as the "reinventing government" initiative, customer-service standards, and the National Performance Review (NPR). Still others reflect a *devolutionary* approach, shifting policy-making authority from one level of government to another or to facilitate new **partnerships** with private and nonprofit entities; examples of this sort of initiative include Richard Nixon's general revenue

partnerships

government-funded programs involving a wider range of participants, including private and nonprofit organizations, faith-based groups, and corporations.

sharing, Ronald Reagan's *New Federalism*, and George W. Bush's faith-based initiatives. Those who advocate less government, more privatization, and outsourcing or **contracting out** typically presume that business-oriented, market-driven alternatives are best because they are less costly, more efficient, and result in better service delivery and results. Often, this assertion is a self-serving statement of ideological faith rather than empirical fact. Supporters of privatization tend to view government as an inherent part of a larger problem, rather than as a co-partner for improving public administration. Thus, prescriptions for change often mirror ideological preferences, rather than reflecting fact-based judgments about ways to reach the most satisfactory policy outcomes.

Conflicting opinions about the content of policy and the role of the private sector in public policy making also reflect differing definitions of policy, administration, and management. As noted in Chapter 1, "public management" is a practical rather than theoretical discipline, emphasizing accountability, political control of public agencies, and managerial concerns related to operations, planning, organizational maintenance, information and communications systems, budgeting, personnel management, performance evaluation, and productivity improvement. In fact, public policies result from a complex network of fragmented, intertwined public, private, and nonprofit interests designed to address special interests as well as specified larger-scale societal problems. "Public administration" is a broader concept and variously defined by leading scholars as

> the use of managerial, political, and legal theories to fulfill legislative, executive, and judicial mandates for provision of regulatory and service functions . . . the organization of government policies and programs . . . the reconciliation of various forces in government's efforts to manage public policies and programs . . . all processes, organizations and individuals associated with carrying out laws and rules adopted by legislatures, executives, and courts . . . or simply the "accomplishing" side of government.[4]

During its 120-year history, the discipline of public administration (and more recently, public-policy making) has reflected conflicting normative views about the interactions of politics and administration within formal government arrangements. Its most influential thinkers view the relationship, referred to as the politics-administration dichotomy, as a conflict between *political values*, such as accountability, control, and responsiveness, and *administrative values*, such as efficiency, effectiveness, and performance.[5] Although the theories of these and other "founding fathers" shaped discourse for most of the last century, all had significant weaknesses: Frederick Winslow Taylor assumed that there was only "one best way" to complete a task, without considering external politics or internal organizational dynamics; Max Weber failed to recognize that bureaucracies could be inefficient and misdirected; and Woodrow

contracting out

practice under which private-sector contractors provide designated goods or services to governments, or to individual agencies, for an agreed-on fee; an example both of a "twilight zone" between public and private sectors and of public-sector responses to growing fiscal stress; services contracted for include trash collection and fire protection; see also **privatization**.

Wilson naïvely believed that politics could be separated from administration (detailed in Chapter 1).[6] These flaws, among others, led to counter theories that encouraged greater citizen choice, participation, and partnerships with nongovernmental organizations (NGOs), private firms, community-service organizations, and faith-based and nonprofit agencies.[7]

As discussed previously, chronic fiscal pressures, changing policy priorities, and shifts in funding sources have forced many governments to draw greater shares of their operating revenues from proprietary services, designated trust funds, and user fees collected directly from recipients for specific purposes, such as airport operations, highway maintenance, water and sewer, trauma centers, or solid-waste disposal. This significant change has affected legislative proposals as well. For example, the 2001 Aviation Security Act authorized airlines to collect a "security fee" from all passengers to pay for new equipment and training for airport security officers. In many jurisdictions, parallel public *and* private providers offer the same services. Various service providers, such as airports, mosquito abatement districts, transportation systems, utilities, and waste management districts, use fees only for designated purposes. Restrictions on federal assistance programs, taxes, and other sources of *general revenue* increase the need to collect operating funds directly from recipients and also create opportunities for greater devolution and privatization. This trend has accelerated with proposals to cut federal and state spending in order to reduce budget deficits.

In many large state and local governments, the fee-based, proprietary, trust fund, and intergovernmental portions of annual operating budgets now equal or exceed the amount collected from general (tax-based) revenue sources, such as property and sales taxes. State and local governments operate closer to their local communities and must treat citizens as valued customers, especially when fines, license fees, service charges, and tolls are paid directly by service recipients and designated for specific self-supporting public purposes. This is especially true for educational, law enforcement, judicial, public safety, transportation, security, and regulatory compliance functions. The shifting revenue base of many states and local governments also favors the extended use of competitive, entrepreneurial, and market-based mechanisms such as user charges for allocating public resources. Regardless of the type of organization or service offered, training public employees to think differently about customers, managers, suppliers, and themselves is critical to any policy implementation effort.

All governments, especially those at the local level, recognize the connection between administration and the private-business market sector.[8] Consequently, many public agencies are applying various performance management theories designed to run public agencies more like competitive, customer-oriented, results-driven, and market-based private businesses (see Chapter 10). Advocates of the market-based public choice model ignore significant differences between the public and private sectors: among them, the definition of recipients as customers rather than citizens. Citizens do have certain rights and responsibilities and may also be "entitled" (if eligible) to receive services from various governmental agencies. These services may be funded indirectly from individual income, property, and sales taxes, or directly from fines, designated trust funds, service charges, or user fees. Private firms view customers as those who purchase a product or service from a provider at a competitive price. Businesses need customers to stay in business, whereas many citizens pay taxes whether or not they receive governmental services. Under means-tested and redistributive policy formulas common in all governments, some citizens receive more resources than they pay in taxes, whereas others share the costs of services that they never receive.

Competing goals of diverse interest groups force elected officials to reconcile multiple, vague, and often conflicting demands between those who pay more in taxes (or *think* they pay higher taxes) and those who receive more public benefits or services. Under such conditions, the temptation to distribute resources *broadly*, rather than to *target* high-priority problems, is always present. Governments are unique entities that serve broader social interests and are not obligated to "sell" their products or services at costs suited to prevailing markets. Concerns about equality, fairness, special interests, and redistribution of public resources may inhibit public agencies from applying market-based, entrepreneurial, or "for-profit" approaches such as deregulation, privatization, or contracting out to nonprofit or private firms. Thousands of communities worldwide are outsourcing a full range of services, from trash removal, utility billing, voter registration, and street lighting to ambulance services, prison operation, golf course maintenance, firefighting services, and street maintenance.[9] Given the fundamental importance of political decision making, legitimate concerns have been raised about just how much authority can and should be transferred from the public to the private sector. In theory, government services are outsourced to reduce the size of government and to create a competitive private-market environment. This, in turn, supposedly stimulates competition among companies seeking to obtain these contracts, thereby reducing costs and possibly increasing service quality. In practice, however, this is often a highly controversial decision for many government-funded programs—one that might contribute to the creation of monopolies, further exposing any administration's "cronyism" if not encouraging outright corruption.

Among the most controversial of these transferred duties, in recent years, is that of military operations. The wars in Afghanistan and Iraq have shown that the armed forces are no longer the sole protagonist in the military front of a war. The Pentagon spends nearly $450 billion annually on goods and services, and at least half of that amount is awarded through the controversial practice of **no-bid or limited-competition contracts**. Even from a technical acquisitions perspective, no-bid contracts are questionable and raise questions about accountability, performance, and the promise of more efficient service delivery. Members of Congress are increasingly concerned about the practice of

no-bid or limited-competition contracts

government goods and services contracts awarded to private companies with limited or no competition.

awarding contracts with little or no competition. These concerns go beyond the obvious moral and ethical ones; even from a theoretical perspective, the effects of these no-bid contracts could have devastating effects on public confidence in the fairness and the structure of public administration. This is especially true for recipients of contracts from the Department of Defense (DoD), Department of Energy, Department of Homeland Security, Federal Emergency Management Agency (FEMA), and Department of State.[10] From a bureaucratic perspective, the new role for these companies represents a dramatic change in the perceived mission of government and public administration.

The controversy over this policy issue lies not only in the rising costs of outsourcing services that have traditionally been provided by government, but also in the questionable manner in which companies have operated in bidding for contracts. Private defense contractors such as Bechtel, Halliburton, KBR (Kellogg Brown and Root), and security consulting firm Blackwater Worldwide (now known as Xe) have provided goods and services for the U.S. State Department and military forces in Afghanistan and Iraq. (According to Congressional Budget Office [CBO] estimates, these conflicts will eventually cost the nation many thousands of lives and as much as $3.6 *trillion* in total economic losses.) The controversy is stirred by the fact that the sole financial beneficiaries of these contracts are companies that have had historical connections with high-ranking members of the administration in power—former Vice President Dick Cheney was CEO of Halliburton, former Defense Secretary Donald Rumsfeld served on Bechtel's Board of Directors, and Blackwater CEO Eric Prince had strong ties with both Bush administrations. Changes in the military procurement systems to promote accountability and transparency are under review by Congress, and Xe's contracts with the Bush administrations, among many other questionable arrangements, came under scrutiny.[11]

Contracting out, or privatization, is a practice in which governments either join with, or yield responsibility outright to, private-sector enterprises to provide services previously managed and financed by public entities. Its advocates claim that this strategy reduces the size of government; increases productivity, efficiency, and competition; and promises to reduce cost. When such firms enjoy a no-bid advantage, the competitive factor that might help reduce costs and provide better-quality services disappears; any advantage to having private alternatives perform these services may therefore have been compromised.

The transfer or contracting out of government services to private companies is not particular to the current wars, or to just a single provider. Moreover, it would be naïve to assume that this peculiar form of cronyism is inherently a Republican or Democratic trait. There are abundant examples of politicians from all sides of the political spectrum who, if given the opportunity, reward their supporters with multimillion-dollar contracts (recall the discussions of clientele-centered politics in Chapter 2 and earmarking in Chapter 8). Federal no-bid contracting by FEMA for the Katrina recovery effort, and by the Department of State for security services, also has been widely criticized. Despite the risk that scarce resources will be misused, the new boundaries of public and private administrative relationships are being drawn on a case-by-case basis, involving a broader range of policy areas, and greater numbers of both governments and private-sector service providers.

The long-term trend has been toward more partnerships and "shared-government" policy making, with active participation by private, as well as public, stakeholders.[12] Note that contracting out and privatization are obvious examples of shared governance, which may well continue to grow within policy-making arenas partly in response to intensified fiscal stress at all levels of government.

In sum, the part played by administrative entities in a given policy area or process can depend to a considerable extent on the type of policy, its specific issue content, political constituencies, and its impact on subsystem support networks. Elected politicians, affected interests, contract firms, and agency officials increasingly share common policy-making responsibilities.

POINT/COUNTERPOINT

THE ISSUE Governments are unique entities that serve broader social interests and lack the opportunity or obligation to "sell" their products or services at costs suited to prevailing markets. Given the selective nature of political decision making, legitimate concerns have been raised about just how much authority can and should be transferred from the public to the private sector.

Should authority be transferred from the public sector to the private sector? If so, how much and under what circumstances?

Arguments *for* Authority Being Transferred

- Government needs more flexibility in operations and procurement practices, and transfer of authority would achieve this.
- Outsourcing government services reduces the size of agencies and creates a private-market environment.
- Transfer of power stimulates economic competition among companies seeking to obtain government contracts, thereby reducing costs and increasing quality of government services.

Arguments *against* Authority Being Transferred

- Transfer of authority allows political influences to corrupt administrative systems and processes.
- Transfer of authority can lead to private monopolies and corruption.
- Transfer of authority raises questions about accountability, liability, performance, and the promise of more efficient service delivery.

The Policy-Making Process

The policy-making process involves multiple demands, pressures, conflicts, negotiations, compromises, and formal and informal decisions that result in the adoption of particular objectives and strategies through actions (or inactions) of government. This is a broad definition, and deliberately so, for making policy is not the exclusive province of any one branch or level of government. Policy making often conflicts with commercial enterprises and directly affects economic and social functions, such as assuring the quality of the nation's food supply or protecting citizens from overexposure to radiation.

Various authors have noted the intricate and complex nature of policy-making and implementation processes.[13] It is characterized by a lack of centralized direction, a focus on interactions of foreign, national, state, and local governments, and involvement of private interests pressing government to respond to their specialized concerns. It is very loosely coordinated, highly competitive, fragmented and specialized (like budgeting), and largely incremental. Thus, the policy process is not a smoothly functioning, ongoing sequence with one phase predictably following another. Rather, it responds to pressures placed on it at many points along the way, so that policy usually reflects the influence of myriad economic and political forces.

Where administrative agencies play a central role in the policy process, policy making can be described as occurring in four stages.[14] The first is a *legislative* stage involving both Congress and the president (and often agency administrators), in which basic legislation is drawn up, considered, and approved as law. Nothing of substance would be achieved at the legislative stage without the advice of bureaucrats, whose expertise is often called upon to draft coherent bills. In addition, policy agendas often are forcefully advanced by government agencies. As holders of near-monopolistic control of information, agencies have considerable ability to shape public opinion and drive legislators to action. In the second and third stages, which are primarily administrative, the agency writes detailed regulations and rules governing application of the law; this is followed by actual implementation. Failure to consider coordination among agencies and interoperable linkages among related programs, together or horizontally, often leads to policy weakness or failures. The fourth is a *review* stage, by the courts or Congress or perhaps both, during which modifications of existing policy are possible for legal, substantive, or political reasons. These stages are part of continuous policy cycles, during which policies are defined and redefined, with incremental adjustments made to accommodate major interests, changing conditions, and so on (see Plan-Do-Study-Act cycle in Figure 9–1, p. 389).

The legislative stage normally centers on actions of the chief executive (the president, governors, or mayors) and of key legislators on Capitol Hill (and their counterparts in state and local governments). But the role of higher-level administrators (both political appointees and senior career officials) in formulating and proposing new policy options is also very important. For example, agency personnel—usually in responsible positions—may perceive a need to modify legislative authorizations and appropriations in order to smooth out implementation difficulties. They may wish to initiate a new activity to fulfill their own policy objectives. Or they may propose curtailing part of a program in order to concentrate attention, energies, and resources on matters of higher priority to them. Under-funding a program already in operation can also diminish its effectiveness. In all such cases, their proposals must wend their way through the usual legislative process, and administrators must call on legislative (and executive) allies to ensure a proper hearing for their ideas. The main point, however, is that administrators are regular participants at this stage of the policy cycle, not merely passive observers.

Administrative involvement in subsequent stages of the policy process can assume a variety of forms. These include rule making, adjudication, law enforcement, and program operations. *Rule making*, a quasi-legislative power delegated to agencies by Congress, represents authority to enact "an agency statement of general applicability and future effect that concerns the rights of private parties and has the force and effect of law."[15] Rules may serve different functions—elaborating on general statutory provisions, defining terms (such as aviation security, food safety, small business, discrimination, or safe speed, etc.), indicating probable agency behavior in particular matters. Agencies well known for their rule-making decisions include the Federal Trade Commission (FTC), the Food and Drug Administration (FDA), the Occupational Safety and Health Administration (OSHA), and the Department of Transportation (DOT). The FDA is a regulatory agency within the Department of Health and Human Services charged with assuring the quality of over $1 trillion worth of products, accounting for 25 cents of every dollar spent annually by American consumers. The FDA assures that food is safe and wholesome, that cosmetics will not be harmful, that medicines and medical devices are safe and effective, and that radiation-emitting products such as microwave ovens will not do harm. Feed and drugs for pets and farm animals also come under FDA scrutiny. The FDA ensures that all of these products are labeled truthfully (as a responsibility shared with the FTC) and that people have information they need to use them properly (see Chapter 11). Despite these responsibilities and the fact that its actions impact the lives of virtually every American every day, the FDA's budget has been cut, threatening its ability to implement policy and protect Americans. Recent cases of toxic residue contained in imported pet food are only the most visible of several life-threatening incidents involving the restricted ability of the FDA to perform its assigned mission.

Adjudication, unlike rule making, is a quasi-judicial function involving the application of current laws or regulations to particular situations by case-to-case decision making, such as the FDA's power to seek criminal penalties. The scope of such actions is much narrower than that of rule making but, collectively, they can have great impact on policy as a whole. Agencies that engage in adjudication include the **Securities and Exchange Commission (SEC)**, which has used the process in settling fraudulent stock and securities "insider trading" cases since its creation in 1934; the Social Security Administration (SSA), which became a separate clientele-based agency in 1995, in determining eligibility for

Securities and Exchange Commission (SEC)

federal regulatory agency responsible for regulation of stocks, securities, and investments.

Internal Revenue Service (IRS)

responsible for administration of federal tax policy, enforcement of tax codes, and collection of tax revenue from individuals and corporations.

benefits; and the **Internal Revenue Service (IRS)**. Adjudication is an adaptation of, and a substitute for, possible formal proceedings in a court of law—particularly in the cases brought by the SEC and the IRS.

Law enforcement refers to securing compliance with existing statutes and rules (and not necessarily to police functions) and, more specifically, to the enthusiasm an agency brings to the task of implementing legislative authorizations. By exercising administrative discretion, an agency may influence the policy process by countless kinds of action—or inaction. For example, in the early 1960s, a U.S. Justice Department task force on voting rights of black Southerners might have wanted to file suit on behalf of blacks denied an opportunity to register, but the 1957 and 1960 Civil Rights Acts did not confer that power on the Justice Department. A plaintiff had to shoulder the legal burden, particularly the costs, if a case was to reach the courts. Not until the passage of the 1964 Civil Rights Act did the Justice Department acquire the ability to act on behalf of aggrieved citizens claiming improper denial of voting rights (Justice Department attorneys themselves sought that authority at the legislative stage). Even then, another year passed before the Voting Rights Act broadened national authority to register voters directly in areas where fewer than half of those eligible were registered.

Program operations, including the actual administration of loans, grants, insurance, purchasing, services, or construction activities, constitute a large part of agencies' impacts on the policy process. Again, budgets, discretionary authority, and staff resources are vital to policy success; out of thousands of small-scale decisions come large-scale policies. Later in this chapter, we will look in more detail at program implementation and the politics involved in it.

One further aspect of policy making deserves mention: the extensive impact of intergovernmental relations on both policy development and policy implementation (see Chapter 3). Many facets of program funding and administration are closely tied either to intergovernmental collaboration or competition, or to parallel activities of some kind, as in the case of environmental policy and homeland security. This serves to complicate both policy making and any effort to trace the roots of a particular policy direction. Legislative and administrative mechanisms at each level of government are complex, affording many opportunities for interested parties to have some say in the policy-making process. Slight alterations in policy are possible each time influence is exerted, and their cumulative effects at the same level of government can be significant. It is not difficult to imagine how these patterns found at multiple levels of government can shape policy. Intergovernmental dimensions, then, constitute an important contributing factor in the overall policy process.[16] Private firms that bid to supply a government with a service or product, or contract with governments to provide direct services, are increasingly involved with intergovernmental policy making and operations.

In sum, the diffuse nature of policy making helps to account for the disjointed nature of most public policies. Multiple opportunities for exerting influence and an absence of centralized direction characterize many phases of policy making, producing policies that look (accurately) as though they were arrived at from many directions at once. It is not difficult for a chief executive, for example, to define a formal policy intention, but it is another matter altogether to put it into effect. On one occasion, John F. Kennedy signed a bill into law, then turned to his aides and remarked: "We have made the law. Now it remains to be seen whether we can get our government to do it."[17]

It is clear that the word "policy" refers to intentions and symbols as well as actual *results* of governmental activity. We must be careful, therefore, about the sense in which the term is used. Results, however, are normally sought and evaluated in the context of specific government programs rather than broad policy objectives. Programs, in turn, can be further divided into projects dependent for their completion on individual performance on the job. The linkages among *policies, programs, projects,* and individual *performance* are important. Policies are put into effect only to the degree that program objectives related to them are met; programs are, in turn, the sum totals of supporting projects; and each project represents the labors of individuals within the responsible agencies. Discussion of public policy, in a management sense, must focus, then, on programs and projects, the essential building blocks of what government does. Although there are some differences between the two in terms of organization and direction them, we will emphasize management concerns common to both: (1) planning and analysis, including problem definitions; (2) implementation, or carrying out policies and programs; (3) evaluation, studying the effects of policy and program changes; and (4) making recommendations for change based on results (see Chapter 10). These are linked conceptually; to the extent that they are linked in practice, they greatly enhance program management and effectiveness. Whether a program is accomplishing what it was designed to do is a key issue for managers. It also affects future planning of program efforts as the process is repeated in a continuous cycle of policy formulation and revision (see Figure 9–1).

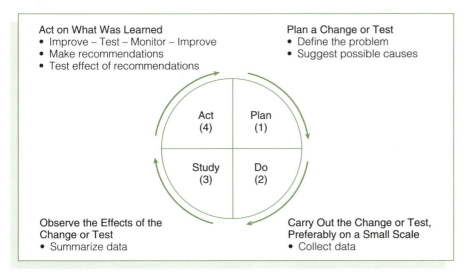

FIGURE 9-1

The Plan-Do-Study-Act Cycle

Act on What Was Learned
- Improve – Test – Monitor – Improve
- Make recommendations
- Test effect of recommendations

Plan a Change or Test
- Define the problem
- Suggest possible causes

Act (4)   Plan (1)

Study (3)   Do (2)

Observe the Effects of the Change or Test
- Summarize data

Carry Out the Change or Test, Preferably on a Small Scale
- Collect data

Source: Michael E. Milakovich, "Creating a Total Quality Healthcare Environment," *Healthcare Management Review,* 16 (Spring 1991): 16.

Planning and Analysis

Just as governmental and political goals need to be clearly defined, individual program or project goals do also. Ideally, goals at this level should be clearly operationalized—that is, formulated in specific and tangible terms related to the general mission or purpose of the agency. **Planning and analysis**, even though they are carried out imperfectly much of the time, are essential elements of the goal definition process.

All organizations function according to some type of basic plans, but program administrators must both promote planning by others in their organizations and weave "various plans together into a common purpose pattern. In essence . . . administrative planning is purposeful action to develop purposefulness."[18] The keys to planning are to be found in accurate forecasts of future need, goal definition, means-ends linkages, and the kind of coordination and direction supplied by the organization's administrator. (Note the heavily rationalistic flavor of the first three "keys.")

Complicating the planning process is the fact that goals exist at different conceptual levels within any public agency or organization. Ideally, then, linkages should be forged among different types of goals. Also, the interrelationships among goals, plans, programs, and projects are important. For example, one official *goal* of the U.S. government is to increase the educational attainment level of American students. An **operational goal** is the achievement of a certain minimum reading level for every American. One *plan* for achieving this operational goal includes educational assistance to urban high-risk areas. A *program* consists of activities designed to strengthen technological capacities in inner-city schools. An example of a *project* was the proposal by the Clinton administration (unsuccessful as it turned out) to provide computers and wire every schoolroom in the United States to the Internet.

Administrators at all levels of bureaucracy must operate within this complex web of objectives and arrangements and, in particular, must successfully organize activities addressed to meeting the goals of the administrative unit (for example, processing unemployment checks, monitoring eligibility rolls, and serving related clientele needs). The recipients of job placement services, for example, are not likely to share the goal of limiting benefits or many of the program efficiency concerns of senior program administrators.

Public managers are encouraged to use **strategic planning** to determine a course of action, beginning with preliminary consideration of goals. Essential steps are identifying desired outcomes, assessing environmental constraints, determining the appropriate mix of public and private responsibility for program management, establishing performance expectations, and assessing probabilities of achieving desired outcomes.[19] Depending on the results of such deliberations, goals can be selected, and perhaps modified, by those involved. However, in one form or another, this must be done early in the life cycle of a project or program, and periodically throughout its existence, to make

planning and analysis

process of deliberately defining and choosing the operational goals of an organization, analyzing alternative choices for resource distribution, and choosing methods to achieve those goals over a specified time period; increasingly important tools for public management.

operational goal

specific and measurable goal for organizational attainment.

strategic planning

process used by organizations to formulate a mission statement; consider environmental opportunities, threats, strengths, and weaknesses; identify areas for strategic action; conduct cost–benefit analysis to evaluate and select actions; draw up implementation plans; and incorporate operational goals into annual budgets.

any sense out of varied support activities. For example, it would be considered careless policy making to spend public funds for "improving education" without a clear idea of specific project goals—remedial reading instruction, additional equipment and materials, more counseling services, or better testing methods and devices. These are demonstrably related to the broader program goal of "improving education," which, in turn, may be part of an urban policy designed to "improve the quality of urban life." At the federal executive agency level, such planning has been mandatory since the early 1990s and is now part of the budgeting and appropriations processes.

That these imperatives exist in an organization does not guarantee that planning will be undertaken or that it will serve its purpose if it is undertaken. Other factors may interfere with agency planning processes. These include "a threatening political environment, an unrecognized or unacknowledged intraorganizational conflict, a lack of trust or communication [among] planning participants, and conflicting perceptions of the goals, values, and norms of the organization."[20] An important task for public managers is to ensure that these potential obstacles to effective planning are recognized and dealt with in a timely way.

As noted in Chapters 5 and 6, goals are not simply "there" to start with. They must be arrived at in deliberate fashion and can reflect varying combinations of administrative and political judgments about the need to pursue them. More important in an operating sense, program and project managers are not ordinarily official goal setters. They may not even dominate the process, though they do usually contribute significantly to shaping formally adopted goals. Thus, goal definition for the middle-level manager is a shared process, one in which the most influential voices are often those outside the agency. Senior police officials must be sensitive to the needs of the community in deploying officers to prevent crime; a school superintendent must heed the wishes of the school board; the senior managers of a municipal airport must be sensitive to city council members' preferences. Yet a concerted effort to delineate goals must be made *inside* the agency as well.[21]

Approaches to Analysis

Planning leads directly to processes of analysis—of examining alternative options (however systematically) and attempting to identify and compare potential outcomes. To the extent that planning produces or represents consensus among key individuals regarding appropriate program directions, formal plans can serve as a guiding standard for subsequent analysis and choice. If, however, significant dissent from adopted plans persists (which often happens), that dissension can complicate analysis by extending political conflict into analytic processes themselves.

Agency performance frequently depends on the quality of prior analysis regarding projected impacts of activities on the problem at hand. Politically, the adage "Good government is good politics" has never been truer if good government is taken to mean better performance. For agencies with strong political backing, a solid foundation of objective program analysis adds substance to strength. For weak agencies, careful and thorough analysis of their options before selecting the most appropriate one(s) might make the difference between organizational vitality and decay.

The purpose of analysis is to facilitate sound decisions by establishing relevant facts about a situation before attempting to change it in some way and by determining, if possible, the respective consequences of different courses of action. The nature of a given problem is not always clear—for example, in education, poverty, crime control, or energy—and analysis can help sharpen the focus of decision makers as they consider various objectives and options. Analysis is also crucial to improving public management as a key aid to appropriate use of scarce resources and targeting of programs.

policy analysis

systematic investigation of alternative policy options and the assembly and integration of evidence for and against each; emphasizes explaining the nature of policy problems, and how public policies are put into effect.

Policy analysis is defined as "the systematic investigation of alternative policy options and the assembly and integration of the evidence for and against each option."[22] Activities suggested by such a definition have long been a part of the government process, but only in the past four decades has a distinct analysis function become formally associated with public decision making. A key emphasis is on explaining the nature of problems, and how policies addressing those problems are put into effect. An equally legitimate function, however, is to improve processes of policy making as well as policy content. In its broadest sense, policy analysis makes it possible to investigate policy outcomes in interrelated fields, to examine in depth the causes of societal and other problems, and to establish cause-and-effect relationships among problems, the contexts in which they occur, and potential solutions to them. Program or project managers generally concentrate on analyzing considerations most relevant to their immediate responsibilities.

Because problems vary widely in their scope and complexity, policy analysis needs to be flexible enough to permit selection of analytical approaches and techniques appropriate to the particular problem under study.[23] One proposal (among many others) for dealing with this dimension of policy analysis suggests four types of analysis suitable to four different sets of circumstances.[24] These are (1) *issue analysis*, when there is a relatively specific policy choice (for example, whether a particular group of businesses or industries should receive a tax reduction) and a highly politicized environment of decision making; (2) *program analysis*, involving both design and evaluation of a particular program (for example, a staff-training program); (3) *multiprogram analysis*, in which decisions must be made concerning resource allocation among programs dealing with the same problem (for instance, different staff-training programs); and (4) *strategic analysis*, when the policy problem is very large (for example, an economic development strategy for a depressed region).

At the programmatic level, the process and the analyses resulting from it should meet most of the following technical criteria.[25] First, clearly define issues and problems being addressed, including identifying clientele groups, specifying appropriate evaluation criteria, and providing estimates of future need. Second, present alternatives in a form specific enough to be evaluated. Third, in considering each alternative, accurate cost estimates should be provided. These should include direct and indirect costs (for example, employee benefits as well as salaries), costs incurred by other agencies (such as higher jail and court costs stemming from an increased police force), and documentation that demonstrates solid grounding for current and future costs. Fourth, carefully estimate program effectiveness by ensuring that evaluation criteria are themselves comprehensive, by using multiple measures of effectiveness, and by ensuring that data adequate to measure both present and future circumstances can be employed in assessing program results. Fifth, acknowledge any uncertainty in basic assumptions and program data—that is, the probability of inaccuracies and the likely consequences of error. Sixth, the time period of the program should be identified, with a clear statement of whether enough time is allowed to provide a fair comparison among alternatives. Finally, an analysis should contain recommendations based on substantive data rather than on unsubstantiated information, should discuss any anticipated difficulties in implementation, and should document all relevant assumptions. The following are the steps in the standard-form policy analysis.

1. Define the problem.
2. Establish criteria for problem resolution.
3. Propose alternatives.
4. Collect data relevant to the problem.
5. Analyze the likely consequences of each alternative.
6. Evaluate the trade-offs.
7. Select an alternative strategy.

Policy analysis faces some obstacles, however. For one thing, it is not always clear what kind of analysis can be done and what uses can (or should) be made of the results when negotiation and bargaining among competing political forces are the most common means of carving out policy. Another difficulty is limitations on the applicability of various analytical techniques used, depending on the kind of problem at hand.[26] That there are any limitations at all is unfortunate because the aim of analysis is essentially to facilitate the targeting, design, and operation of programs in the most effective and efficient ways possible. But even the most rigorous, sophisticated techniques are not always appropriate. For example, decision tools rooted in mathematics and economics are used to best effect when problem definition is straightforward, when there is "a convenient method of quantifying the problem (usually in terms of probability or monetary units), and when there is some function or set of functions (such as time, profit, payoff, or expected value) to be maximized or minimized."[27] In contrast, if a problem involves questions and issues not readily measurable in economic or quantitative terms, these decision tools are less appropriate.

Analytical Tools

Perhaps the broadest analytical approach is systems analysis. This approach is usable (in principle) for integrating how all elements of political, social, economic, or administrative systems might affect and be affected by a given project or program (see the discussion of systems theory in Chapter 4). Managers utilizing systems analysis need to understand the nature of interrelated systems, carefully measure objectives and performance, and analyze the external social environment, available resources, system components, and how processes internal to the system can be better managed. The overriding objective of systems analysis is to produce greater rationality in management decision making, and efficiency and effectiveness in actual program operations. In terms of the discussion of decision making in Chapter 5, systems analysis is devoted to the rational approach. The comments made there about seeking comprehensiveness, coping with information needs, and maximizing return on a given investment of resources also apply here.

Perhaps the greatest advantage of systems analysis is its potential for bringing some order in decision making out of the confusion and discord often prevalent in the policy process (as well as society at large). A companion strength is that it permits a broader view of constraints and consequences relating to an individual program. A weakness, besides those associated with rational decision making, is the possibility that trying to achieve rationality within a single system will cause decision makers to ignore other interdependent systems that might also be relevant. An example would be an effort to analyze political factors influencing grants-in-aid to states and localities without also analyzing the condition of the nation's economy, which provides the tax base for raising revenues. A greater weakness, from a practical standpoint, a greater weakness is that systems analysis can generate such a staggering workload that decision makers have little chance of coping with it while still reaching a decision.

Cost–benefit analysis is the most frequently used methodology for designing and measuring relative gains and losses resulting from alternative policy or program options. Usually implying quantitative measures and assuming objectivity, it can assist decision makers and program managers in determining the most beneficial path of action to follow. By assigning economic value to various options, a cost–benefit analysis seeks to identify the actions with the most desirable ratio of benefit to cost. Given adequate information, cost–benefit analysis can be useful in narrowing a range of choices to those most likely to yield the greatest desired gains for an affordable cost. An example of cost–benefit analysis might involve a decision to construct a reservoir in an uninhabited area. Benefits (new jobs, new business, reduced flooding) and costs (construction expenses, environmental damage, foreclosed options for other uses of the land) are calculated, as well as the ratio between them. The same technique can be used to measure alternative benefits from other uses of the same funds and the related effects of constructing the dam (for example, on residential and tourist patterns in adjoining areas). Such an analysis might be useful both in advance of the project and as an evaluative instrument after the fact.

Operations research (OR) actually represents a collection of specific decision-making techniques using systems theory, modeling, and quantitative methods to ascertain how best to utilize available resources. The greatest value of OR lies in solving problems of efficiency and logistics—such as scheduling bus stops, managing aircraft in a holding pattern, or processing military recruits—rather than in helping to select particular alternatives. After policy choices have been made, OR makes use of mathematical techniques such as linear programming for reaching the optimal solution. Where "routine" administrative problems repeat themselves, OR can be especially valuable.

In sum, analysis is a key managerial activity. As noted earlier, knowledge is power in administrative politics, and analysis greatly enhances a manager's ability to obtain, organize, and apply relevant information in the course of choosing desirable program options.

operations research (OR)

set of specific decision-making and analytical tools used in systems theory, modeling, and quantitative research to determine how best to utilize resources.

Program Implementation

In speaking of implementation, we adopt Charles O. Jones's definition of the term, as well as his elaboration of it:

> Let us say simply that implementation is that set of activities directed toward putting a program into effect. Three activities, in particular, are significant: (1) *organization*—the establishment or rearrangement of resources, units, and methods for putting a program into effect; (2) *interpretation*—the translation of program language (often contained in a statute) into acceptable and feasible plans and directives; and (3) *application*—the routine provision of services, payments, or other agreed-upon program objectives or instruments.[28]

By transforming legislative language into clear administrative guidelines, by developing necessary arrangements and routines, and by actually furnishing mandated services, programs are carried out and, ultimately, policies are implemented.

All of that sounds rather routine. Citizens expect program implementation to be relatively easy under normal conditions. We therefore seek to explain programmatic failures in terms of ideological conflict, extraordinary events, or unexpected circumstances that develop in the course of implementation. However, failure to implement programs in accordance with our expectations can often be attributed to less dramatic factors. For example, consider the difficulties that were encountered in putting into effect a much-heralded job training program of the U.S. Economic Development Administration (EDA) in Oakland, California, that was designed to provide permanent employment to minorities through economic development:

> The evils that afflicted the EDA program in Oakland were of a prosaic and everyday character. Agreements had to be maintained after they

were reached. Numerous approvals and clearances had to be obtained from a variety of participants. . . . These perfectly ordinary circumstances present serious obstacles to implementation. . . . If one is always looking for unusual circumstances and dramatic events, he cannot appreciate how difficult it is to make the ordinary happen.[29]

Thus, few things can be taken for granted in implementation, least of all that participants in a program will automatically fall into line in trying to make it work. Not that they harbor devious motives; it is simply a case of cooperation having to be induced on a routine basis rather than being assumed. Virtually everyone participating in program management has other responsibilities, causing some distractions among even the most conscientious individuals. In sum, a concerted effort is required to manage minimal aspects of **program implementation**. It is no wonder, then, that so many programs (and policies) are said to be only partially implemented—contrary to legislative mandates, executive orders, and public expectations. The essential point, however, is this: Failures in implementation are traceable far more often to these rather unexciting obstacles than to anything more dramatic.

Dynamics of Implementation

On occasion, it is necessary to create a separate organizational unit to implement a new program or to pursue a different policy direction. This can happen in several ways. One is creation of a totally new agency, such as the U.S. Department of Veterans Affairs in 1989. Another is merging, upgrading, or dividing existing agencies, which is what happened, amid considerable conflict, with the creation of the Department of Homeland Security in 2002. More often, programs are assigned to existing agencies, which must still interpret and apply the laws or regulations and develop appropriate implementation methods.[30] In most legislation, deadlines are imposed but Congress's intentions regarding program implementation are stated very broadly, such as to carry out a program in a "reasonable" manner or "in the public interest, convenience, and necessity."[31] Laws and regulations may be more or less specific in their details, goals, timelines, and intended results. Thus, the responsible agency has discretion in developing operating guidelines and substantive procedures. This can result in a key agency role in shaping legislated programs and possibly modifying congressional intent. Political pressure on agencies responsible for implementing congressional and presidential directives is both real and constant. If it is true that "programs often reflect an attainable consensus rather than a substantive conviction,"[32] it follows that, if the political consensus changes in the course of implementing a law, chances are good that its implementation will also be modified to accommodate the change.

Because legislative language is so often vague, interpreting legislative intent can present pitfalls for an agency. Legislators themselves frequently cannot comprehend all the implications of their enactments. Without clear

program implementation

general political and governmental process of carrying out programs in order to fulfill specified policy objectives; a responsibility chiefly of administrative agencies, under chief-executive and/or legislative guidance; also, the activities directed toward putting a policy into effect.

guidance, an agency may be left to fend for itself in the political arena and—worse—be caught up in disputes over just what the legislature meant in the first place. Not only is it difficult to make interpretations of initial legislative intent, it is also a tricky business to keep abreast of changing intent after passage of the original law (and in the absence of formal amendments to it). That can happen as committee membership changes, new interests surface, and the like. For example, during the months following the 2010 congressional elections, there was considerable confusion on Capitol Hill as all Democratic committee chairs in the House were replaced by incoming Republicans.

Many times, authorizing legislation represents the best available compromise among competing forces. Under those circumstances, it is nearly certain that conflicts avoided or diluted in the course of formulating a law will crop up in the processes of interpreting and implementing it. Such controversy is not likely to do the responsible agency any good in the political process. Thus, interpretation without legislative guidance, although necessary, has many potential pitfalls for the administrator.

Application of legislation follows from its interpretation by an agency and usually represents a further series of accommodations. Applying a law is complicated by the likelihood that other agencies also have an interest in the policy area and may well have programs of their own, by difficulties in determining optimum methods for carrying out legislative intent, and even by continuing uncertainty about the nature of a problem or program goals. Many programs are put into operation without full appreciation of a problem's dimensions; political need to "do something" can outweigh careful and thorough consideration of what is to be done. One example of this phenomenon was the federal funding made available to state and local law enforcement agencies through the U.S. Law Enforcement Assistance Administration (LEAA). Public concern about rising crime rates prompted Congress to allocate funds for more (and presumably better) crime-fighting hardware, police officer training, and so on. But in retrospect, although there have been some improvements in fighting crime, it is not clear that LEAA did what it was supposed to—partly because there is less than universal agreement on just what that was and partly because the problem of crime has many more facets to it than the ability of the police to control it.[33] Frustration over the failure of crime control policies led to an equally ambitious $30 billion crime bill, enacted in mid-1994. Similar obstacles have hampered application of other policies and programs designed to ensure accurate intelligence and homeland security as well.

It is necessary, then, for agencies to determine the limits to which they can go in enforcing a policy. Usually, informal understandings are reached between program managers and people or groups outside the agency about what will and will not be done. One danger here, of course, is *co-optation* (or capture) of the program by external forces (see Chapter 2). Depending on the balance of forces, programs may be more or less vigorously pursued; the more controversial a program, the more likely it is that there will be resistance to it.

Support for an individual program is also affected by other programs an agency is responsible for managing and the order of priority among them within the agency. Other factors affecting program application are the values and preferences of agency personnel concerning individual programs, as well as their own roles and functions. An example that illustrates these points is the response of the EDA, particularly its Seattle regional office serving the San Francisco–Oakland area, when the head of the agency formulated a program for promoting minority hiring in Oakland. An Oakland task force was also established, bypassing normal organizational channels. Many in EDA felt more comfortable working with its traditional concern, which was rural economic development. After the person who had set up the Oakland program and task force departed from EDA, the project was treated with far less urgency by EDA, a reflection of its reduced standing in the eyes of most EDA employees working with it.[34]

Approaches to Implementation

There are numerous program management approaches that might be used in carrying on agency activities. Until the mid-twentieth century, little attention was paid to this aspect of administration. It was apparently assumed that, once a program was in place, with adequate funding and political support, writing operating rules and regulations and actually administering the program followed routinely. However, specific management approaches that apply to tasks of program operation have evolved since World War II. We will examine two of the most important: the **program evaluation and review technique (PERT)**, which can include a related tool known as the **critical path method (CPM)**, and **management by objectives (MBO)**.

The analytical approach known as PERT is founded on the belief that it is necessary to map out a sequence of steps in carrying out a program, or a project within a program. The steps involved normally include (1) deciding to address a given problem, (2) choosing activities necessary to deal with all relevant aspects of the problem, and (3) drawing up estimates of the time and other resources required, including minimum, maximum, and most likely amounts.[35] These help the administrator determine what needs to be done and—more important—in what order, as well as time and other resource constraints for completion of various steps in a process. Ideally, a PERT chart should indicate how various processes are related to one another in terms of their respective timetables, sequence of execution, and relative resource consumption. The critical point of the PERT analysis is that at least some of these steps can logically be taken only *after* other steps have been completed. A clear implication of PERT is its potential for assisting program managers in their coordinative roles, discussed in Chapters 3 and 6.

A PERT chart also can be useful in calculating not only the time, funding, personnel, and materials that will be necessary, but also how much extra

program evaluation and review technique (PERT)

management technique of program implementation in which the sequence of steps for carrying out a project or program is mapped out in advance; involves choosing necessary activities and estimating time and other resources required.

critical path method (CPM)

management approach to program implementation (related to PERT) in which a manager attempts to assess the resource needs of different paths of action, and to identify the "critical path" with the smallest margin of extra resources needed to complete all assigned program activities.

management by objectives (MBO)

management technique designed to facilitate goal and priority setting, development of plans, resource allocation, monitoring progress toward goals, evaluating results, and generating and implementing improvements in performance.

of each the agency will have as a cushion against unforeseen difficulties. For this reason, PERT charts are often used to calculate probable resource requirements for alternative paths of action. Such charts enable a program manager to see which path of action represents the best choice in terms of having margins of safety, as well as helping to evaluate alternative paths. The path with the smallest margins of extra resources with which to complete all assigned program activities is the *critical* path because any breakdown in program management, for whatever reason, becomes critical in determining the program success or failure. Advance knowledge of such possibilities is clearly in the best interests of the manager, the program, and the agency. (For an expanded definition and an example of a PERT chart, see http://www.netmba.com/operations/project/pert/.)

Despite increasing sophistication in methods such as PERT and CPM, there remains a large component of human calculation in determining optimum paths of action. Activities are interdependent and must therefore be planned with an eye toward step-by-step execution, but there are no assurances that calculations will be accurate. "Best estimates" are often the most reliable data available in projecting into the future. These can be very educated guesses, but there are risks in placing too much stock in them. Even so, a best estimate is often all a program manager has to go on.

A second major approach to implementing a program or policy is MBO. First outlined explicitly almost sixty years ago,[36] MBO has been put into practice in national and state governments as a fairly flexible approach to defining long- and short-term agency objectives and to keeping a record of actual program results and (perhaps) effectiveness. It is another in a succession of efforts to improve governmental effectiveness and is related in some respects to performance budgeting, PPB, and other movements toward "better management." MBO is more effective when integrated into other management approaches than when used alone. Some important features of MBO include setting objectives, tracking progress, and evaluating results, along with the potential to make objectives explicit, to recognize the multiple-objective nature of administration, to identify conflicting objectives and deal with them, to provide opportunities for employee involvement in defining organization objectives, and to provide for feedback and measurement of organizational accomplishment.[37] Some have suggested that MBO makes it possible to pinpoint conflicting objectives before efforts are begun to pursue them.

Involvement of employees in participative management has been regarded by some as one of MBO's most important elements; this aspect has been described as fostering employee commitment to organizational objectives, as well as employee participation in determining objectives.[38] At the same time, there is evidence that MBO can shift power *upward* in an organization by forcing information upward (especially bad news about program performance).[39] Thus, an effective MBO system could alter somewhat the relationship between managers and their subordinates for two reasons: (1) it is harder for subordinates to shield from their superiors information that something is awry in program activities (for which the subordinates might be held accountable), and (2) early information about program difficulties is very useful to agency managers if they are to succeed in correcting the problems.

As with other approaches to improving management, there are obstacles to MBO's full realization (some of which we discussed earlier in reference to goals). Management authority Peter Drucker has noted that agencies often have ambiguous goals that are difficult to make operational.[40] Another dimension is that an organization's stated objectives may not be its real ones. Furthermore, there are "no commonly accepted standards for monitoring performance or measuring achievements of many public objectives."[41]

If, however, objectives can be defined in operational terms, MBO can be a useful management instrument. Although its application in the national government already appears to have waned somewhat, its residual effects seem destined to become part of the foundation for further management developments. For one thing, MBO may have value in helping decision makers choose which programs to delay or eliminate. In a time of great concern about priority setting and "less government," MBO may prove a harbinger of things to come. (For a contemporary example of goal setting, see discussion of the Government Performance and Results Act in Chapter 10, pp. 421–424.)

Problems and Politics of Implementation

Despite the availability of numerous approaches to implementation, problems common to many managerial situations persist. It is appropriate to treat briefly three of the most important ones.

First, management control is a continuing challenge. This has two dimensions: one relates to management's ability to secure subordinates' cooperation in program activities and one concerns the agency's ability to cope with specific situations and with the surrounding environment, which in some instances change continuously. The more pressing of the two, from a manager's standpoint, is the former. Control of staffing, allocation of fiscal resources, designation of work assignments, and delegating discretionary authority are potentially useful devices for enhancing managerial efficiency, resulting in program effectiveness. Even these, however, do not guarantee effective direction of internal activities.

Related to management control is the challenge of developing harmonious, productive, and beneficial working relationships within an agency. The lessons of the human relations school of organizational theory and of organizational humanism, and concerns about effective leadership (see Chapters 4 and 6, respectively), enter into the organizational life of both manager and employee in this regard. Of central importance are vertical (leader and fol-lower) and horizontal (teamwork and peer-group) relationships in all their forms. Meeting ego needs, regularizing on-the-job recognition for excellence, developing opportunities for employee empowerment or creativity, and facili-tating communication among employees represent possible ways of creating and maintaining the kinds of relationships sought. Managers must be alert to all the possibilities.

Any time an organization is called on to undertake a task, the potential for change is present. Pressures for change can be real and direct, prompt-ing employee reluctance to go along. The conserver in Anthony Downs's typology of bureaucrats may not be the only one within an agency to exhibit a degree of conservatism; others of every type and description may at times resist change and even the prospect of change. Overcoming such resistance is often a delicate managerial task. It is made more complicated by the fact that managers themselves may fear "upsetting the applecart" in their existing situa-tion. Much of the time (though not always), this is due to a survival instinct that can be difficult for outsiders to understand. Nonetheless, the problem is real. It can hamper development of new activities, adaptation of existing operations to new circumstances or challenges, and maintenance of sufficient flexibility to meet emergencies. Moreover, in the new resource-scarce budgetary environ-ment, more bureaucrats are expected at least to think like entrepreneurs, to raise rather than just spend revenue, and to economize wherever possible. Whatever the causes, costs of resisting change can be substantial, and constant effort is necessary to gain and maintain support for many kinds of change in administrative behavior.

In the midst of criticism concerning the failure of programs to live up to their promise, a little-noticed aspect of implementation deserves attention: the real possibility that agency implementation of a law may entail actually changing its purpose(s) in order to satisfy shifting political demands. If the legislative coalition that was strong enough to pass a law does not continue to support the agency in charge of implementation, it may turn out, on later examination, that effects of the law were different from those envisioned for it. It is not uncommon for those who failed to "win" the legislative struggle to recover some of their losses by applying pressure on administrative agen-cies, thus altering the nature of the program that the majority thought it was adopting. Sometimes administrators are willing allies in this effort, sometimes not. Either way, the outcome is the same: substantive modification of pro-grams or policies.

Consider the following case history of policy making in education. Title I of the Elementary and Secondary Education Act (ESEA) of 1965 greatly increased the national government's presence in many phases of education nationwide, most of all in funding local school districts and, to a lesser extent, state education agencies.[42] Title I of ESEA "dictated the use of massive [national] funds for the general purpose of upgrading the education of children who were culturally and economically disadvantaged," while leaving considerable discretion in the hands of local education agencies to develop local programs for achieving that goal.[43] "If there was a single theme characterizing the diverse elements of the 1965 . . . Act, it was that of reform. . . . ESEA was the first step toward a new face for American education."[44] The key emphasis of Title I was infusion of aid to school districts in which there were large numbers of poor children, with the idea that education could contribute to ending poverty for these students, at least in their adult years. The national government's prevailing political focus was on combating poverty, and educational aid allocated as special-purpose funding was viewed by many as essential to that effort.

There were, however, other purposes of Title I that, although they did not conflict with aid to disadvantaged students, made it more difficult for program administrators to determine what the central purpose of Title I really was. These included raising achievement levels, "pacifying" urban ghettos, promoting bilingual education, building bridges to private (sectarian) schools, and providing fiscal relief to school districts. Depending on which of these was to receive the greatest emphasis, it would be possible to draw varying conclusions about whether the purpose of Title I was being fulfilled.

The point, however, is that actual congressional intent—as distinguished from the legislation's stated purpose—changed during the first two decades of the law's operation (1965–1985), until the only form of aid to education that could gain majority support in Congress was general-purpose, not special-purpose, assistance. As the political scene changed in the late 1990s, support for Title I in its original, legislated form changed also. As a result, funding under Title I came increasingly to be general-purpose, matching long-standing preferences of bureaucrats in the Office of Education. But, more significantly, Congress itself broadened Title I aid categories to include general-purpose aid. What the most powerful education subsystems wanted, they got—and poverty-related education aid was not their highest priority. Redirecting implementation of a law also can occur when a new chief executive, such as George W. Bush and Barack Obama, regards it as sufficiently important to do so.

The passage of the controversial No Child Left Behind Act (NCLB) in 2002, at Bush's urging, reauthorized the ESEA and marked a major overhaul in federal educational policy. This reauthorization stressed a significantly greater federal role, high-stakes testing, accountability, teacher qualifications, and scientifically based instruction. The controversial act called for states to establish "academic proficiency standards" and to implement accountability measures holding schools responsible for students' success in meeting those standards. Assessment data provide indicators to federal, state, and local policy makers who allocate public funds on the basis of students' academic progress.

The NCLB applied national performance standards to state schools, generally without funding to pay for the required testing or correct the deficiencies after they were found. Not surprisingly, only a few districts initially met such strict standards. Several states opted out of this federal program because they were unable to raise to additional resources required the correct problems if they did not meet standards.[45]

In 2011, the Obama administration became more vocal about overhauling the NCLB by requesting Congress to revise the contentious education law. Schools have been given until 2014 to meet student proficiency standards, yet little has been done to ensure that deadline holds. Secretary of Education Arne Duncan has emphasized the statistic that 80 percent of U.S. schools will not meet proficiency standards and that the United States is falling behind in global education.

The goal of standardized testing—a key element of the 2002 statute—is to provide a uniform assessment of student achievement while attempting to control for environmental factors, such as school resources, demographics, and grade point averages, which might affect outcomes. The theory behind standardized testing is at least partially believable as a measure of skills requisite to advance to the next level within the educational system. Standardized testing has caused as much debate as any topic in public education at the K–12 level ever has. To receive a high school diploma, students in several states must pass a graduation qualifying exam. Not all public (and very few private) schools are required to meet the same standards. The implementation of standardized tests superimposed on our fragmented federal system is still a subject of considerable political controversy. Discrepancies between the results of the states' tests and federal standards have raised more questions about the accuracy and reliability of several state evaluation procedures.[46]

Opponents of **high-stakes testing** for all students express concerns about the equity of testing procedures, the frequency and costs of testing, and how reliance on standardized tests, tied to state standards, shapes curriculum decisions and determines school funding. Teachers often buckle under the pressure of the tests and find themselves preparing students mainly (or only) for the test rather than truly teaching them. In many states, the schools themselves are graded (A, B, C, D, and F) in accordance with student achievement. Schools that do not improve their "grade point average" may be shut down and their parents given vouchers for their children to attend private schools. Diverting public funds from "failing" public schools to private schools using vouchers was successfully challenged by opponents as unconstitutional in the Florida courts in 2006.[47]

President Obama visited the Columbia Heights Educational Campus, which includes Lincoln Multicultural Middle School and Bell Multicultural High School in Washington, D.C., in the spring of 2011 and stressed the importance of revising the rigid measurement tools used throughout

high-stakes testing

federal requirement that requires states (without compensation) to develop standardized testing in order to rank students and maintain federal funding.

standardized testing. Speaking to students in a town hall meeting, Obama stated that one thing he

> never want[s] to see happen is schools that are just teaching the test because then you're not learning about the world, you're not learning about different cultures, you're not learning about science, you're not learning about math. . . . All you're learning about is how to fill out a little bubble on an exam and little tricks that you need to do in order to take a test and that's not going to make education interesting.[48]

In addition to diluting the empowerment of teachers, rigid standardized testing requirements undermine other important facets of quality in education, opponents say. Critics argue that calls for more standardized tests come from politicians eager to prove they are serious about school reform in order to meet the "high skills" requirement of an internationally competitive workforce—a valid concern in today's global economy. According to opponents of standardized testing, however politicians use failure to meet testing standards as an excuse to use state funds to privatize schools or force the adoption of voucher plans.[49] They claim that proponents of standardized testing pay little or no attention to more important factors that actually affect quality in the classroom, and focus instead on standardized test results, which can only provide results of learning processes after the fact and without providing any real direction for improvement. Factors such as class size, teacher education, economic equality or inequality, and efficiency of resource utilization are among those that are more closely related to quality in education. If standardized testing continues in its prominence and issues like those previously mentioned are ignored, then results will be more than just a poor measure of quality: They could contribute to lowering overall quality in the nation's classrooms.

Furthermore, nationally imposed standardized testing requirements left to the states to administer under the NCLB could not possibly reflect the complex nature of education in each of more than 13,000 school districts in the United States. Using test results to "rank" schools and students often becomes an attempt to force schools to meet certain unrealistic standards. Focusing too heavily on standardized test preparation stresses facts over creative thoughts and rote memorization over reading and writing skills. By definition, standardized tests have one right answer. However, changes in educational goals stress teaching students that there is always a possibility of multiple correct answers as long as one has the verbal skills and writing ability to support one's answer. When that standard is not met, instantly a "blame game" of finger pointing ensues. Politicians and administrators blame teachers for poor student performance, and students are held back or not allowed to graduate based on one test score without any consideration of their past performance in school. But what is actually occurring is failure to eliminate all causes of variation among school districts (unequal funding, parental neglect, student dissatisfaction, teacher preparation, and so on) that also affect student learning. Because test results usually lead to questioning of individuals and not processes, using tests solely as a final measure of achievement cannot guarantee that individual districts are graduating competent, knowledgeable, and qualified students. For these and other reasons, parents pressured local school districts to offer greater choices of the types of schools their children could attend, including academies, magnet schools, and charter schools.

Charter schools parallel the market-based entrepreneurial movement and are designed to circumvent the power of public school lobbies. They are partially state-funded alternatives that students can choose to attend. According to proponents, exposing schools to "market forces" allows parents to select the type of school their children will attend, stimulates competition, increases efficiency and quality of schools, and forces low-performing schools to improve or close. When a charter school is full, attendance is open to low-income students on a lottery (random selection) basis.

According to President Obama, "It's not enough to leave no child behind. We need to help every child get ahead."[50] He has addressed educational reform with a **Race to the Top** program, which includes austere measures that enforce sanctions on the so-called nonperforming schools, including firing teachers and closing failing schools. Although federal government efforts affect only about 1 percent of all public schools, they are being reinforced at the local level by the downsizing of many underperforming districts, especially those in already vulnerable urban areas suffering from high drop-out rates.

charter schools

publicly funded, privately operated K–12 schools; public schools staffed without teachers' unions.

Race to the Top

the Obama administration's $4.35 billion U.S. Department of Education program designed to encourage reforms in state and local district K–12 education. Funded as part of the American Recovery and Reinvestment Act of 2009.

HOW WOULD YOU DECIDE?

Waiting for "Superman"

In *Waiting for "Superman,"* filmmaker Davis Guggenheim follows the stories of five promising young students within the American public education system. The Academy Award–nominated film seeks to emphasize that even with the best intentions and, at times, adequate financial resources, the public education system in the United States leaves much to be desired and is in dire need of reform and change. Reduced workforce size and declining manpower and financial resources (in many cases) present a real need to re-examine the public education system across the country. The film introduces several children waiting to be accepted into charter schools without a clear delineation of why these non-union schools are in most instances superior to public schools.

The film has been criticized for vilifying the American Federation of Teachers (AFT), a union created to protect teachers' rights. Guggenheim's message, however, is that unions need to be flexible and that Americans need to think more carefully about the ultimate purpose of a union such as the AFT—that is, teaching the children within the public school system. Attention needs to be given to how to fight for keeping the best teachers, how to assess all teachers, and how to handle teachers who are not performing at the level needed or desired.

Most state and local government agencies, including those in the education system, have reduced the size of their workforces. This declining manpower must deal with increasing workloads, often using antiquated technology and resources.

Should agency budgets be increased to compensate for this trend? What alternatives are there? Are these alternatives desirable? Why or why not?

Source: http://film.waitingforsuperman.com/, accessed March 31, 2011.

Program Evaluation

Program evaluation is a central concern to virtually all administrative policy makers, most political executives, legislators, and the public. Only since the early 1970s, however, has widespread interest developed among public managers in systematic rather than intuitive evaluation procedures. The latter have been in use for some time—by political superiors, clienteles, the mass media, and academics, among others. As used here, *evaluation* can be defined as systematic measures and comparisons to provide specific information on program results to senior officials for use in policy or management decisions.[51] This definition suggests that evaluation can be used in both policy-related and programmatic decision making to monitor, test, and ultimately improve policy making. In the former, evaluation can be a useful device for identifying, documenting, and clarifying the most important objectives of a project, program, or agency; it can also be used to develop measures for success that can be incorporated into management processes. At the programmatic level, evaluations can help managers continuously monitor resources spent, activities under way, and actual performance compared to performance standards. They may or may not assist in determining the ultimate results or effectiveness of a public policy.

program evaluation

systematic examination of government actions, policies, or programs to determine their success or failure; used to gain knowledge of program impacts, establish accountability, and influence continuation or termination of government activities.

Program evaluation can be used for three purposes: (1) to learn about a program's operations and effects, (2) to define accountability of those responsible for program implementation, and (3) to influence the responses of those in the program's external political environment. Most agency managers fail to take full advantage of these possibilities, however, by beginning their evaluation programs too late, assigning evaluation responsibilities to staff members who lack the requisite skills, or yielding to temptations to distort or suppress unfavorable evaluation findings. Thus, simply understanding the mechanics of conducting evaluations is not enough—managers must be aware of the potential pitfalls and take steps to avoid them.

Evaluation Procedures

Evaluation requires certain preconditions and a series of steps. The most important preconditions are, first, an understanding of the problem toward which a government program or policy was directed and, second, clarity of goals that the program or policy was designed to achieve. It makes no sense to evaluate in a vacuum—that is, without some conception of what was supposed to be accomplished. Evaluation deliberately related to program goals has grown out of recent linkages to the budgeting process, where cost-efficiency criteria alone revealed little about what an enterprise was actually doing. Performance budgeting, too, fell short in this regard, though not by as much. For example, a study of per capita expenditures in a governmental program might yield some information about political influence and governmental commitment but not much about the effects of money being spent. The process of evaluation is only as useful as the ability of evaluators to convincingly demonstrate program effectiveness or ineffectiveness.

Steps to be taken in an evaluation include at least the following.[52] First, there must be specification of what is to be evaluated, regardless of how narrow and precise or broad and diffuse the object of evaluation is. A nationwide program to immunize children against measles and one to reduce illiteracy among poor adults can both be specified for purposes of evaluation. The second step is measurement of the object of evaluation by collecting data that demonstrate the performance and effect of the program or policy. There are several possibilities, ranging from highly systematic, empirical data and methods to casual, on-the-scene observations by untrained observers. The third step is analysis, which can vary in the rigor with which it is carried out. How each of these steps is defined and executed affects the final evaluation product.

In order to make a coherent and rational evaluation of program or policy effectiveness, a clear cause-and-effect relationship has to be established between given actions by an agency and demonstrated impacts on a societal problem. For example, FBI crime data indicated that, during the coldest months of a recent winter, the number of crimes usually committed outdoors—muggings, assaults, and so on—dropped dramatically. Some might have argued that this was due to beefed-up police patrols or to larger law enforcement expenditures. Yet the bitter cold weather seems to have played a bigger part than either of these. The crux of the matter, however, is that, if police patrols *had* been beefed up or if expenditures *had* risen sharply, it might have been easy—and politically profitable—to conclude that these factors, not the weather, *caused* the drop in crime. That an intended result materializes is no guarantee that the relevant program caused it to occur. Certainly, there is a chance that a cause-and-effect relationship does exist, but it is useful to confirm that.

Program evaluation is a complex task involving several possible research designs. It is important to tailor a design to the particular program being evaluated so that the results can be relied on. Programs as diverse as garbage collection, school meals and nutrition, and downtown redevelopment require varied evaluation schemes appropriate to their respective objectives, modes of operation, and units of measurement. In all cases, however, the question that evaluators would ideally ask is: "What actually happened, compared to what would have happened had the program not existed and everything else had been exactly the same?" Four evaluation designs are commonly used (though there are others), each of which lends itself to specific techniques.

Before-versus-after studies compare program results at some appropriate time after implementation, compared with conditions as they were just before the program got under way. It is especially useful when time and

before-versus-after studies

evaluation and comparison of results before and after program implementation to determine what results, if any, were achieved.

personnel available to conduct the evaluation are in short supply and when the program is short-term and narrow in scope. One drawback is that it is difficult, using this method, to be sure that any improvements are, in fact, due to the program's operation (recall the example of fewer crimes in cold weather).

Time-trend projection of pre-program data-versus actual post-program data compares results with preprogram projections. This method can be used to measure various kinds of trends as they are affected by a program. An example might be a local volunteer-sponsored paper collection and recycling effort that gives way to a municipal recycling program. Data can be gathered on tons of paper collected over a period of years before municipal recycling, and projections made concerning the likely increase in tonnage without the program change. Later, comparisons of actual tonnage to those projections can shed light on actual program impact.

A somewhat related method is comparisons with jurisdictions or population segments not served by the program, which have the advantage of controlling for nonprogrammatic factors. That is, by comparison with other jurisdictions, or with parts of the internal population not served by the program, it is possible to determine whether any change was due to the program. An example is the state of Connecticut's strict highway speed enforcement program. One criterion for evaluating the program was its effectiveness in reducing the number of traffic fatalities per 100,000 population. Initial data indicated a decline in traffic deaths, starting at about the time the enforcement program went into effect. But could evaluators be sure that the decline was not due to other factors—safer cars, more advertising stressing careful driving, gas shortages? To answer that, Connecticut's highway death rate was compared to those in neighboring states in which no new enforcement program had gone into effect, and it was found that the fatality rate had indeed declined relative to the statistics for the other states. Thus, it was evident that some factor unique to Connecticut, a reasonable inference being the speed enforcement program, had accounted for reducing traffic deaths.

Many evaluation techniques compare planned versus actual performance and measure postprogram data against targets set in prior years, whether before or during program implementation. This is a more general device, one used by many state and local governments to compare performance of a program to implied rather than explicit targets. For example, one state found that its guaranteed student loans were being used by far more middle-income families than those with lower incomes. It was not that the former were ineligible, but simply that the general need for student aid was assumed to be greater among the latter. (Perhaps it was, but that apparently was not a determining factor in patterns of use.) Ideally, this method should be used to supplement one or more of the other techniques.

Controlled experimentation, one of the most complex and costly methods of evaluation, involves comparing preselected, similar groups of people,

time-trend projection

comparison of preprogram data with actual postprogram data.

controlled experimentation

involves comparisons of two groups of similar people, one served by the program and another (control group) not served, or served differently; the most expensive and least practiced form of evaluation.

some served by the program and some not (or served in different ways). Most important, here, is seeking to ensure that the two groups are as similar as possible, except for their participation (or nonparticipation) in the program. This can be accomplished either by deliberately matching individuals having similar characteristics and subsequently placing them in the different groups, or by random selection (randomization) of members in both groups. The experimental and control groups (for example, individuals involved and not involved in manpower training or alcohol abuse treatment programs) would be subjected to performance measures of their relevant behaviors before and after program implementation.[53] If the experimental group showed substantially greater improvement, this would provide strong evidence that the program was responsible. This method can be used in combination with time-trend projections and jurisdictional comparisons but much greater precision is required—principally by seeking close similarity between the two groups or populations being studied.

Problems and Politics of Evaluation

If the purpose of evaluation is to assess program performance and accomplishment objectively, it is evident that numerous difficulties are involved. Some concern problems of performance measurement, such as the nature of evaluation data, criteria of evaluation, and information quality. Others pertain to political factors that can be injected into an evaluation or measurement process, changing the nature or even the very purpose of a program evaluation. These difficulties often overlap, compounding the existing problems.

A central problem in evaluating public programs is considerable uncertainty about the reliability of performance indicators. Available indicators of accomplishment that have been used extensively are widely regarded as inadequate. It has been difficult to develop measures with enough objective precision to produce meaningful evaluative results. In part, this is a matter of deficiencies in obtaining necessary information although, in recent years, more sophisticated management information systems have been designed and put into operation. Improved information capability should enhance the total process of evaluation as an objective function of public administration.

Another dimension of the problem of performance indicators is the fact that the same data can often be manipulated and interpreted in different ways to produce different results. For example, educational information is quite confusing—few can be certain how well our educational systems function. Yet we have hundreds of studies of educational attainment, test scores, measures of test validity, and a great deal more. What does it all mean? A dozen different experts might give a dozen different answers, and our earlier discussion of various educational reforms illustrates this point all too clearly. Improving evaluation instruments remains very much on our agenda of unfinished public business.

A third factor is whether there are major disparities between a program's official goals and those of the program's key implementers. This seems to have occurred to some extent in the case of ESEA. One of the harshest evaluations of Title I implementation accused the Office of Education of not fulfilling the mandates of Title I—specifically, of not ensuring that money intended for educating poor schoolchildren was actually being spent by state and local school officials for that purpose. The problem, according to one observer, was that the reformers and implementers were different people and that the Office of Education staff did not regard itself as investigation-oriented and was not inclined to monitor state agencies in their expenditure of Title I funds.[54]

One other problem is the time frame in which programs operate and how much time is required before a meaningful appraisal of program results can be made. Because no program works perfectly, it is natural for those in charge to seek more time than others might want them to in order to correct shortcomings and produce positive results (another instance in which political considerations overlap). But, even in purely objective terms, required time frames of different programs vary. And reasonable time requirements have to be taken into account, assuming that "reasonable" can be satisfactorily defined.

The "politics of evaluation" raises different kinds of issues, although they are not unrelated to those already discussed. Evaluations are used in the most general sense to determine whether there is justification for continuing a program to the same extent, in the same manner, and for the same cost. But *justification* is a tricky term, and it raises a fundamental issue in the evaluation process. On the one hand, evaluation, in an ideal sense, is designed to be value free and objective; on the other, justification is value loaded because, in order to justify something, a context of values must be present. That is, nothing is ever simply justified; it is only justified in terms of something else. Thus, an evaluation to determine whether a program is justified necessarily becomes bound up with different sets of values about what constitutes adequate justification.

The usual pattern seems to be that evaluations by those in charge of a program or policy are more favorable to its continuation in substantially the same form than are evaluations carried out by independent third parties, especially those who are skeptical. It is not unduly cynical to suggest that an agency will almost always be kinder in judging its own data than will others who do not have the same stake in the agency's activities, that the agency will adopt the time frame most likely to produce the intended program effect, and that it will try to ignore other variables that could also have produced the desired effect(s).[55] Because program survival may depend on whether evaluations are positive or negative, a process that many see as value-free and therefore politically neutral is, like so many other things in public administration, weighted down with political implications. That is why internal evaluations so often point up program successes, whereas external evaluations tend to emphasize deficiencies and ways to improve program management.

Perhaps the mix of factors frustrating truly objective evaluations can best be summed up by the following description of Title I evaluation by the Office of Education (USOE):

> Since the beginning of the program, evaluation has been high on the list of rhetorical priorities, but low on the list of actual USOE priorities. The reasons for this are many. They include fear of upsetting the [national]-state balance, recognition of [the fact] that little expertise exists at the state and local levels to evaluate a broad-scale reform program, and fear of disclosing failure. No administrator is anxious to show that his [or her] program is not working.[56]

There is another important dimension to evaluation: the uses made of evaluation results. Even when evaluations produce entirely objective data (which, as noted earlier, is infrequent), there is no assurance that they will become the basis of efforts to bring about significant change, whether in program goals, in the way program activities are carried out, or in ultimate performance. Concentrated and effective political support for or against a given program can render evaluations of that program virtually irrelevant, whether those evaluations are favorable or unfavorable.

This point is illustrated by the national government's housing program (particularly public housing), which has consistently fallen far short of its projected goals, according to a number of separate evaluations. A national goal, established during the Truman administration in 1949, was construction of 810,000 housing units for low-income families over a period of six years; more than sixty years later, that number has still not been reached. Regardless of the many criticisms of these efforts, those who favor the housing program have not generated the necessary political support for reaching its goals. The interests served by building low-income public housing (the urban poor, primarily) are severely outweighed by the influence of other interests for whom public housing is a low priority—bankers, contractors, real estate brokers, and the majority of the population that is not low-income. Criticism of the program's alleged failures did not sway its opponents, and the program has continued as merely a shadow of what it was supposed to be.[57]

Several concluding observations about evaluation are in order. First, despite the aura of value neutrality that frequently is associated with evaluation, its true significance may lie in its having caused public managers and others to focus "on the fundamental value choices that are inherent in the decision to initiate or terminate a policy, or to increase or reduce funding for a program."[58] This would indicate both how important and how difficult it is to conduct evaluations with a high degree of impartiality. Second, as psychologist Donald Campbell suggested, one way to reduce the political "liability of honest evaluation" would be to "shift from . . . advocacy of a specific reform [program] to . . . advocacy of the *seriousness of the problem* [that the program is designed to address], and hence to the advocacy of persistence in alternative . . . efforts *should the first one fail*."[59]

Third, although government fiscal constraints make it more difficult to proceed in this manner, taking this approach might well mean that more dispassionate and sound evaluations would result. In recent years, the **Government Accountability Office (GAO)** has conducted an increasing number of systematic evaluations of national government programs. The GAO has established a reputation for professionalism, political neutrality, and conducting objective evaluations.[60]

Finally, "evaluation is likely to lead to better program performance only if the program design meets three key conditions: (1) program objectives are well defined, (2) program objectives are plausible, and (3) intended use of information is well defined."[61] That is, if we are to evaluate public programs properly, those programs must have had the capacity to be evaluated built into them from the outset. (This caveat brings us full circle—back to program planning and design as a key building block of all program operations and management.) In the final analysis, elected officials are the final arbiters and interpreters of the results of public policies. As evaluation continues to grow in significance, our sophistication in designing and conducting evaluations and interpreting results will have to keep pace.[62]

Government Accountability Office (GAO)

investigative arm of Congress that helps Congress oversee federal programs and operations to ensure accountability through a variety of activities including financial audits, program reviews, investigations, legal support, and policy/program analyses.

Summary

Public policy making is a highly diffuse series of interrelated processes, involving a multitude of actors inside and outside of government. Program management is expected to be of good quality, leading to the achievement of program and policy goals. The way in which policies and programs are managed affects virtually every facet of the administrative process. Policies differ in their rationales, broad impacts, and administrative components; major policy types have been described as distributive, redistributive, regulatory, self-regulatory, and privatization. The policy-making process is complex, loosely coordinated, highly competitive, disjointed, fragmented, specialized, and largely incremental, resulting in a great deal of inconsistency in the policies adopted and sometimes outright contradictions.

Policies, programs, projects, and performance measurement are systemically interrelated, all contributing to the results of government operations. Programs and projects are the building blocks of policy and, from a management standpoint, require particular attention: planning and analysis, implementation, and evaluation.

Discussion Questions

1. Discuss the importance of the dynamics of policy making in America to an understanding of American public administration.
2. What factors influence the roles that bureaucracy plays in the ultimate success or failure of government problem solving?
3. What features of the American political system promote fragmentation, lack of coordination, and inconsistencies in the policy-making process? In your view, how could this incremental system of policy making be changed?
4. Compare and contrast the major types of policies said to exist in the policy process, paying particular attention to the variable roles that different administrative entities play in each type of policy.
5. When administrative agencies play a central role in the policy process, policy making can be described as occurring in four stages. Identify and discuss each stage. Also, discuss the administrative activities involved in rule making, adjudication, law enforcement, and program operations.
6. From among the wide range of unresolved social problems, how and why are some problems redefined as public-policy issues, brought to the public agenda, and addressed by government agencies?
7. What major problems face an agency attempting to implement a program? How might these problems be solved, or at least dealt with adequately? In your judgment, what should our expectations be (both as managers and as citizens) about the extent to which programs will in fact be implemented? Explain.
8. What general procedures and specific methods exist for evaluating government programs? Discuss the factors that may affect evaluations, especially those that could yield misleading results. How can those factors be counteracted, if at all?
9. What are the principal criteria for devising program analyses? Are these criteria realistic? Are they comprehensive? Why or why not? Illustrate with examples.
10. Compare the NCLB program with Race to the Top. What are the principal lessons regarding implementation that can be learned from the experiences of both statutes and earlier acts? Choose one to research and discuss.

Key Terms and Concepts

Suggested Readings

Bardach, Eugene. *A Practical Guide for Policy Analysis: The Eightfold Path to More Effective Problem Solving.* 3rd ed. Washington, D.C.: CQ Press, 2008.

Barzelay, Michael. *Breaking through Bureaucracy: A New Vision for Managing in Government.* Berkeley: University of California Press, 1992.

Berman, Evan M., and Jack Rabin. *Encyclopedia of Public Administration and Public Policy.* 2nd ed. Boca Raton, Fla.: CRC Press, 2007.

Biggs, Selden, and Lelia B. Helms. *The Practice of American Public Policymaking.* New York: M.E. Sharpe, 2007.

CQ Researcher. *Issues for Debate in American Public Policy: Selections from CQ Researcher.* 11th ed. Washington, D.C.: CQ Press, 2010.

DiIulio, John J., Jr., Gerald Garvey, and Donald F. Kettl. *Improving Government Performance: An Owner's Manual.* Washington, D.C.: Brookings Institution Press, 1993.

Gerston, Larry N. *Public Policy Making: Process and Principles.* 3rd ed. Armonk, N.Y.: M.E. Sharpe, 2010.

Holzer, Marc, and K. Callahan. *Government at Work: Best Practices and Model Programs.* Thousand Oaks, Calif.: Sage, 1998.

Holzer, Marc, and Seok-Hwan Lee, eds. *Public Productivity Handbook.* 2nd ed. Boca Raton, Fla.: CRC Press, 2004.

Ingraham, Patricia W., Philip G. Joyce, and Amy Donahue. *Government Performance: Why Management Matters.* Baltimore: Johns Hopkins University Press, 2003.

Kamarck, Elaine C. *The End of Government . . . As We Know It: Making Public Policy Work.* Boulder, Colo.: Lynne Rienner Publishers, 2007.

Kettl, Donald F. *Government by Proxy: (Mis?)Managing Federal Programs.* Washington, D.C.: CQ Press, 1988.

Lee, Dalton S., and N. Joseph Cayer. *Supervision for Success in Government: A Practical Guide for First Line Managers.* San Francisco: Jossey-Bass, 1994.

Levin, Martin A., and Mary Bryna Sanger. *Making Government Work: How Entrepreneurial Executives Turn Bright Ideas into Real Results.* San Francisco: Jossey-Bass, 1994.

Light, Paul. *Government's Greatest Achievements: From Civil Rights to Homeland Security.* Washington, D.C.: Brookings Institution Press, 2002.

———. *A Government Ill Executed: The Decline of the Federal Service and How to Reverse It.* Cambridge, Mass.: Harvard University Press, 2008.

Meier, Kenneth J. *Politics and the Bureaucracy: Policymaking in the Fourth Branch of Government.* 3rd ed. Pacific Grove, Calif.: Brooks/Cole, 1993.

Meier, Kenneth J., and Jeffrey L. Brudney. *Applied Statistics for Public Administration.* 7th ed. Belmont, Calif.: Wadsworth, 2008.

Nathan, Richard. *Turning Promises into Performance: The Management Challenge of Implementing Workfare.* New York: Columbia University Press, 1993.

Neiman, Max. *Defending Government: Why Big Government Works.* Upper Saddle River, N.J.: Prentice Hall, 1999.

Newell, Charldean, ed. *The Effective Local Government Manager.* 3rd ed. Washington, D.C.: International City/County Management Association, 2005.

Peters, B. Guy. *American Public Policy: Promise and Performance.* 8th ed. Washington, D.C.: CQ Press, 2009.

Pressman, Jeffrey L., and Aaron Wildavsky. *Implementation.* 3rd ed. Berkeley: University of California Press, 1984.

Rainey, Hal G. *Understanding and Managing Public Organizations.* 4th ed. San Francisco: Jossey-Bass, 2009.

Riley, Dennis D., and Bryan E. Brophy-Baermann. *Bureaucracy and the Policy Process: Keeping the Promises.* Lanham, Md.: Rowman & Littlefield, 2005.

Rushefsky, Mark. *Public Policy in the United States: At the Dawn of the Twenty-First Century.* 4th ed. New York: M.E. Sharpe, 2007.

Schwarz, Roger M. *The Skilled Facilitator: Practical Wisdom for Developing Effective Groups.* New rev. ed. San Francisco: Jossey-Bass, 2002.

Spitzer, Robert J. *The Politics of Gun Control.* 4th ed. Washington, D.C.: CQ Press, 2008.

Sylvia, Ronald D., and Kathleen M. Sylvia. *Program Planning and Evaluation for the Public Manager*. 3rd ed. Long Grove, Ill.: Waveland Press, 2004.

Thompson, Frank J., ed. *Revitalizing the State and Local Public Service: Strengthening Performance, Accountability and Citizen Confidence*. San Francisco: Jossey-Bass, 1993.

Van Horn, Carl E., Donald D. Baumer, and William Gormley Jr. *Politics and Public Policy*. 3rd ed. Washington, D.C.: CQ Press, 2001.

Werner, Alan. *A Guide to Implementation Research*. Washington, D.C.: Urban Institute Press, 2004.

PART IV

Challenges and Prospects in a Turbulent Future: Results, Regulation, and Responsiveness

THIS CONCLUDING section covers two critical aspects of contemporary public administration and considers prospects for the future of the discipline and its practice: (1) results measurement and performance management; (2) the regulatory process; and (3) the future of public administration.

Chapter 10 describes the critical, and increasing, importance of productivity improvement and performance management at all levels of government. This function has always been important, but in recent decades, public managers have placed greater emphasis on particular managerial activities to improve administrative responsiveness. These activities emphasize objective measurement and include a "customer" focus, a "results" orientation, expanded use of electronic government, and citizen relationship management. Improving performance in the public sector is not a new concern, although new technologies are being used more frequently. What is new is that there are now more results-oriented initiatives—including a broader range of policy options—for achieving heightened levels of performance and providing citizens with information about improvements via Internet and smartphone-accessible websites.

As discussed in Chapter 11, the regulatory process is one of the most pervasive, complex, and controversial aspects of governmental activity. Government regulation is now carried on by a host of federal, state, and local agencies, with impacts on virtually every aspect of American economic and social life. Its depth and scope also have sparked intense pressures for deregulation, in and out of government. In a growing number of areas, such as airport security, consumer protection, employee retirement plans, health care, Internet pornography, ensuring government benefits, nuclear power plants, child protective services, and nursing home inspections, there have been calls for *increased* regulatory activity. A related field—administrative law—also remains an important and expanding area of public policy and administration.

Chapter 12 concludes our examination of this rapidly changing field and discusses how public administration copes with continuing risks and with uncertainties about the future. How public administrators react to domestic and international crises and respond to changing domestic social environments determines, to a great extent, the quality of life for millions of Americans, as well as increasing numbers of citizens in other countries. We will first consider the social and governmental environment, and the growing dissatisfaction with certain practices of governmental administration, and then review evolving issues and challenges in its study and teaching. We conclude by noting some continuing features—and questions—in the field. Throughout this discussion, several themes will be evident, including: (1) the presence of numerous paradoxes in public administration; (2) tensions existing among these paradoxes, and the challenge of dealing with them; (3) creative application of information communication technologies (ICTs); and (4) the accelerating pace of change in administrative theory and practice.

Performance Management in the Public Sector

Government should be results-oriented—guided not by process but guided by performance. There comes a time when every program must be judged either a success or a failure. Where we find success, we should repeat it, share it and make it the standard. And where we find failure we must call it by its name. Government action that fails in its purpose must be reformed or ended.

George W. Bush
Campaign Speech, 2000

In this chapter, we trace the evolution of recent attempts to improve productivity and measure results, as well as "reinvent" and "rethink" performance management in government. We look at the theoretical underpinnings of major approaches to better managing bureaucracy, consider the politics and consequences of making government more productive and **results-oriented**, describe legislation to achieve that goal, and directly compare performance management approaches of the Bush and Obama administrations. In addition, we discuss various strategies such as electronic government (e-gov), citizen relationship management (CzRM), and quality awards to improve responsiveness and citizen access to government. Public managers must pay particular attention to performance management strategies because failure to meet predetermined goals in the current political climate could result in significant program cutbacks, modification, or even termination.

Government Productivity and Measurement of Results

results-oriented

government programs that focus on performance in exchange for granting greater discretionary decision-making power to managers.

Within an economic and political framework of scarce resources and downsizing, making optimum use of public resources is a primary concern of all public managers; thus, the productivity of government programs has taken on increasing importance in the last thirty years. Links between productivity and other aspects of management—such as budgeting, efficiency, information communication technology (ICT), goal setting, and strategic planning—also have been stressed. A brief look at key elements of productivity will indicate where scholarly observers and others have placed the most emphasis.[1]

Productivity and efforts to achieve it are lineal descendants of concern for scientific management and efficiency in government, yet they encompass a broader range of concerns and goals.

Productivity focuses on both efficient use of governmental resources and actual impacts of what government does—that is, on efficiency (of programs) and effectiveness (of program results). It springs also from efforts to identify specific program objectives and to measure progress toward achieving them. The task is made more difficult by the fact that measures available to public managers for effectively monitoring programs are often less precise and can be continuously subjected to ideological reinterpretation. In addition, measures of public productivity are not as simple as those employed in the private sector. There is no equivalent "bottom-line," profit-and-loss measure of results for most public agencies. Much of what government tries to do involves *preventing* various social, economic and physical threats—aircraft accidents, crimes, diseases, school dropouts, mortgage frauds, teen pregnancies, terrorist attacks, and destruction of lives and property. How does one measure the "productivity" of such functions? There is no easy answer. Yet it is possible to develop some useful measures for assessing the productivity of individual programs in conjunction with other emphases on program analysis and evaluation.

The first approach deals with programs in which output is more easily measurable or quantifiable—for example, tons of refuse collected per sanitation truck shift, where the goal is reducing the total unit cost while improving responsiveness and reducing costs. Routine urban functions such as upkeep of park facilities, repair of potholes, and maintenance of sanitation vehicles lend themselves more readily to unit-cost measurement of productivity.

The second approach concerns programs or functions in which output is harder to measure—for example, academic achievement, provision of police or fire protection, or administration of federal unemployment and public assistance programs. Here the intent is to improve deployment of resources by assessing probable needs to ensure that resources will be available when and where they are needed most. This approach also can be usefully employed in emergency management, sanitation departments, snow removal, rescue services, and homeland security services. State governments can and do use productivity measures to assess the impact of programs in a wide range of policy areas such as corrections, education, health care, and transportation.

Efforts to improve productivity, however measured, may encounter a variety of obstacles. Table 10–1 lists common problems at the local government level, with possible ways to overcome them. Two general approaches to solving productivity problems have been used. One approach stresses improving organizational and processing procedures, particularly through imaginative use of information communication technology (ICT) and management information systems. Government agencies extensively involved in provision of social services, with attendant record-keeping needs, find technology

productivity

measurable relationship between results produced and the resources required for production; quantitative measure of the efficiency of the organization.

TABLE 10-1 Some Common Problems of Low Productivity in Local Government and Suggestions for Corrective Action

Problem	Possible Corrective Action	Illustrative Examples
Sufficient work not available or workloads unbalanced	Reallocate manpower Change work schedules Reduce crew size	Housing complaint bureau schedules revised and temporary help employed during peak winter season Mechanics rescheduled to second shift when equipment is not in use Collection crew size reduced from 4 to 3 people
Lack of equipment or materials	Improve inventory control system Improve distribution system Improve equipment maintenance Reevaluate equipment requirements	Inventory reorder points revised to reduce stock-out occurrences Asphalt deliveries expedited to eliminate paving crew delays Preventive maintenance program instituted Obsolete collection trucks replaced
Self-imposed idle time or slow work pace	Train supervisors Use performance standards Schedule more work	Road maintenance supervisors trained in work scheduling, dispatching, and quality-control techniques "Flat rate" manual standards adopted to measure auto mechanics' performance Park maintenance crews mobilized and work scheduling system installed
Too much time spent on nonproductive activities	Reduce excessive travel time	Permit expiration dates changed to reduce travel time of health inspectors
Excessive manual effort required	Reevaluate job description and task assignments Mechanize repetitive tasks	Building inspectors trained to handle multiple inspections Automatic change and toll collection machines installed and toll collector staffing reduced
Response or processing slow	Combine tasks or functions Automate process Improve dispatching procedures Revise deployment practices Adopt project management techniques	Voucher processing and account posting combined to speed vendor payments Computerized birth record storage and retrieval system installed Fire alarm patterns analyzed and equipment response policies revised Police patrol zones redefined to improve response time Project control system installed to reduce construction cycle

Source: From So, *Mr. Mayor, You Want to Improve Productivity. . . .*, National Commission on Productivity and Work Quality (Washington, D.C.: 1974).

especially beneficial for increasing cost efficiency in a wide variety of programs. For instance, federal public assistance, tax refunds, and Social Security benefits are deposited directly into recipients' bank accounts. Electronic delivery and direct deposit of monthly checks now cover nearly all 52 million Social Security recipients, reducing fraud and saving nearly $500 million annually. Internal Revenue Service (IRS) forms are available only to taxpayers online; e-filing is recommended for taxpayers and will soon be mandated for all professional taxpayers. Complicated citizen-government interactions—such as applying for unemployment compensation or a business license, and renewing a driver's license or a passport—are now transacted online or via the U.S. Postal Service with increased efficiency at lower costs. **Geographic Information Systems (GIS)** are being used to encourage citizen participation in a wider range of state and local government services.[2] Newer, more innovative, applications include the expanded use of **social media** such as Facebook, Twitter, MySpace, and YouTube to inform citizens and seek feedback on program success.[3]

Computer and software applications can make a noticeable difference in areas such as educational systems, unemployment compensation and retraining, welfare-to-work programs, monitoring of capital construction programs, electronic procurement of goods or services, and online payments to those who provide goods or services to a government or to an individual agency. Development and application of new technological devices and software result in both more effective management practices and more efficient use of human resources. For example, the Transportation Security Administration (TSA) has deployed complex security equipment, together with better-trained personnel, at the nation's airports. It must be emphasized, however, that many government managers still view computerization and technology as capital investments rather than as techniques for productivity improvement. Other productivity-enhancing techniques are human resource training, upgrading of methods (or software), and computer and information-processing training.

Measurement of performance, productivity, and results have been persistent concerns for all executive agencies at all levels of government. The ability to measure performance at the federal level was enhanced by the **Government Performance and Results Act (GPRA)** of 1993, a major step taken by the federal government that shifted the focus of government officials from program "inputs" to program execution and measurement of results. To bring about this shift in focus, the Results Act (as it is known) sets out requirements for defining long-term general goals, setting specific annual performance targets derived from general policy goals, and annual reporting of actual performance compared to the targets. (Notice the similarity between these standards and those of management by objectives, described in Chapter 9.) As federal managers are held more accountable for achieving measurable results, they are also given more discretion in how to manage programs for optimum outcomes (see Chapter 1). The legislation established

Geographic Information Systems (GIS)

technological software tools that diagram spatial information visually.

social media

tools and technologies that connect individuals by one or more specific types of interdependency, such as common interest, friendship, kinship, financial exchange, likes and dislikes, sexual preferences, or relationships of beliefs, knowledge or prestige. *Facebook, MySpace, Twitter,* and *YouTube* are among the leading examples.

Government Performance and Results Act (GPRA)

commonly called the Results Act, this 1993 statute requires federal managers to plan and measure performance in new ways.

1. Defining an agency's mission and setting general goals and objectives are inherently viewed as budget and policy issues that involve broad groups of agency, congressional, and public stakeholders.

2. Annual performance goals should correspond to requests for program resources and be linked to budget requests.

3. There should be emphasis on agencies' identification of performance measures, so that performance goals can be properly set and evaluated.

4. With implementation ultimately an executive agency responsibility, administrators must take a leadership and coordinative role during the pilot phase, in preparation for full-scale implementation.

5. Agencies will have substantial discretion in defining annual goals and performance measures.

6. Prescriptive directives or guidance, such as "how-to" instructions from the Office of Management and Budget, will be limited.

7. Implementation should be limited to existing agency resources as much as possible and should apply existing systems and processes.

8. Use the pilot phase (1994–1996) as a "lessons learned" opportunity to identify and resolve problems.

Source: © 2013 Cengage Learning.

various performance and budgeting concepts, and called for implementation of performance measurement in all federal agencies. Full-scale government-wide implementation of strategic planning, annual program goal setting, and annual program reporting of performance began for all federal agencies in 1997 and was completed by 2008. The legislation is characterized by the policy-making principles noted in Table 10–2.

With the full implementation of GPRA, there has been a much greater emphasis on the execution of results measurement programs (outcomes, outputs, and results) than on traditional policy analysis. This has led to "demonstration" projects in state and local governments, as well as more effective use of expenditures because ineffective programs will be either improved or terminated. Much of GPRA's success depends on the skill of senior managers in implementing management and evaluation systems. Without such support, GPRA (like ZBB, PERT/CPM, and MBO before it), with its "detached" mechanistic approaches to decision making and results measurement, may "misinform as much as … inform, if users are unaware of the subtle limitations of measurement systems."[4]

Efforts to improve **performance management (PM)** have not been immune from partisan politics, as both political parties view with suspicion legislation to improve performance; many have regarded such proposals as a political tool for winning elections as much as a management reform.[5] The Results Act directed most federal agencies to develop performance measures ultimately aimed at delivering better services with fewer resources. This led to

**performance
management (PM)**

results-driven decision making
that attempts to link goal
achievement with budgetary
allocations.

numerous pilot projects in federal agencies, as well as in some state and local governments, to increase the potential for more effective (or perhaps selective) use of expenditures to improve or terminate ineffective (or politically unpopular) programs. The act's sponsors argued that government performance should not be judged on the basis of amounts of money spent or activities conducted, but rather on whether ideas and approaches produce real, tangible results for the taxpayer's dollar. But definition of terms such as "real" and "tangible" are still subject to political authority and partisan interpretation.[6]

As the GPRA moved to its implementation stages in the late 1990s, partisan battles erupted as agencies began submitting departmental management plans to Congress. As a result of Republican electoral victories in 1994, President Clinton was no longer working with a Democratic House and Senate. Many feared that the GPRA evaluations would become partisan exercises, with the Republicans grading unpopular agencies rigorously on criteria unrelated to the requirements of the law. Although both national political parties differ on policy goals, they present themselves to the electorate as supporters of more efficient government, lower taxes, and results-driven PM. Republicans sought to cut what they defined as "excess" expenditures and portray Democrats as supporters of unnecessary and wasteful spending. Although President Clinton was opposed to congressional oversight and there were no legislative requirements to do so, various committees reviewed the first performance plans.[7] Low grades enabled Republicans to gain political support and further criticize the "bloated" federal bureaucracy for wasteful spending and "big government" programs. By 2006, under a Republican-led Congress, a total of 72 percent of all programs had been rated "effective," "moderately effective," or "adequate"; by contrast, during the first year of GPRA evaluations, only 45 percent of the programs received such scores.[8]

Productivity and results measurement concerns will continue to grow in importance, if for no other reason than public awareness of the increasingly limited resources available to implement public policies. Fourteen years after the passage of the Results Act, in November 2007, President Bush signed an executive order directing all federal agencies to designate chief performance officers as a central point of accountability. In addition, a government-wide system was created to track and report performance and results. The order embedded into the machinery of government the performance improvement reforms started under both Presidents Clinton and Bush, such as strategic planning, regular program assessments, and the evaluation of employees based on the performance of their agencies' programs.[9] Congress later passed, and President Obama signed, an extension of the **Government Performance and Results Modernization Act of 2010**. The new legislation creates a more precise performance framework by defining a governance structure and by better connecting plans, programs, and performance information. The new law requires more frequent reporting and reviews (quarterly instead of annually) that are intended to increase the use of performance information in program decision-making.

Government Performance and Results Modernization Act of 2010

extension of the 1993 legislation.

So long as future presidents maintain the structure created by GPRA, administrations will inherit a network of skilled senior career executives capable of improving performance and making results of agency programs publicly accessible. This will not eliminate partisan political conflicts over the substance of future policy, but it would be more difficult for future administrations not committed to performance improvement, results-driven management, or transparency of results to take decisive actions to change course.

Reinvention, Standards, and Quality Awards

In the early 1990s, a set of issues surfaced around the widespread public perception that government was failing to fulfill even its own goals, much less those of its citizens; many small problems within bureaucracy had combined and multiplied into larger ones. In particular, calls for **reinventing government** were heard, suggesting that government should give its utmost attention to "serving its customers well," and try to instill an "entrepreneurial spirit" into as many of its operations as possible. Journalist David Osborne attracted a considerable following with facile prescriptions for *Reinventing Government* (coauthored with former city manager Ted Gaebler) and *Banishing Bureaucracy*, as well as with his "operations manual," *The Reinventor's Fieldbook: Tools for Transforming Your Government* (the latter two coauthored with Peter Plastrick).[10] The content of these advocacy books was endorsed publicly by many influential people at all levels, both inside and outside of government. There is no question that these authors caught the imagination of many in this country who were anxious to see significant changes in government operations. The reinvention movement was a controversial mix of theory, ideology, and practice that emphasized competitive, customer-driven, and market-based solutions to perceived inefficiencies in the delivery of government services.

The Clinton administration expended considerable resources at the beginning of its first term on a national commission to study and recommend strategies for reinventing government—that is, to drastically alter the ways in which the federal government conducted its affairs and interacted with the "customers" (citizens) it serves. The final report of the **National Performance Review (NPR)** incorporated reinventing government principles and exhorted federal agencies to downsize, eliminate unnecessary regulation, focus on results, and offer customer service equal to or better than "the best in business."[11] The NPR criticized the limited range of management options available to government and public managers, and recommended a greater number of choices, such as competition, coproduction of services, community ownership, entrepreneurism, and diversion of public resources to the market-driven private sector.[12] One of its explicit goals was to give public administrators incentives and tools to manage their agencies more like the private sector. Although the NPR emphasized competition, privatization, and market-driven

---

reinventing government

the Clinton–Gore administration initiative based on the best-selling 1992 book *Reinventing Government: How the Entrepreneurial Spirit Is Transforming the Public Sector*, by David Osborne and Ted Gaebler. The book documents successful public-sector efforts to apply market-based, quality, and customer-service principles to government. See also **National Partnership for Reinventing Government (NPRG),** formerly the National Performance Review.

National Performance Review (NPR)

the Clinton–Gore administration's effort (1993–2001) to reform the federal government; the name of this effort was changed in 1997 to the National Partnership for Reinventing Government.

solutions, theoretical foundations rested on empowering public employees and restructuring, rather than replacing, public workers or agencies.[13]

In 1997, the name of the NPR was changed to the **National Partnership for Reinventing Government (NPRG)** and the effort was given a new slogan, "America@Its Best" (which intentionally read like an e-mail address), to emphasize the commitment to greater public access through the expanded use of ICTs such as e-gov and social media, and the Internet. Reform efforts focused on partnerships with twenty-nine "high-impact" federal agencies to achieve measurable goals of customer service. These "reinvention impact centers" consisted of federal agencies that employ 1.1 million of the 2.4 million civilian employees and have the most contact with the public and businesses, including the IRS, Environmental Protection Agency (EPA), Federal Aviation Administration (FAA), Food and Drug Administration (FDA), Federal Emergency Management Agency (FEMA), Occupational Safety and Health Administration (OSHA), and Social Security Administration (SSA). New technology was used to gather public comments on goals, to communicate directly with citizens, and to distribute reports from high-impact agencies on their progress toward reaching goals. The reinvention movement lasted from 1993 until 2001 and eliminated 250 outdated government programs and 16,000 pages of regulations; cut more than 640,000 pages of internal rules; reduced the federal budget by more than $137 billion; gave out more than 1,200 Hammer Awards to teams of federal employees responsible for $37 billion in cost savings; and created more than 350 "reinvention laboratories" to stimulate innovation, improve performance, and eliminate unnecessary regulations. The federal civilian workforce was reduced by 13 percent—nearly 317,000 employees. These reforms resulted in the lowest government employment totals, as a percentage of the national population, since the 1950s.

The NPR, like its modern predecessors (the Ash, Hoover, Packard, and Grace Commissions), targeted opportunities for waste reduction and offered hundreds of specific recommendations for managerial and technological improvements. High-level initiatives avoided extreme politicization and received generally positive evaluations for achieving most major goals. Reinvention, responsiveness, and restoring faith and trust in government also figured prominently in other broad-scope-reform initiatives.[14] Reform proposals were drawn from the best practices of private manufacturing successes in Japan and the United States during the previous decade and selectively converted to the public sector. Many ideas originated in countries such as Australia, Chile, Canada, New Zealand, and the United Kingdom, where national governments exercise significantly greater centralized federal control over budgets than governments in the United States.[15]

Policy initiatives such as the NPR were part of a broader government reform trend in American public administration and its European counterpart, **New Public Management (NPM)**. When this trend surfaced in the 1990s, it significantly influenced the Clinton administration's market-based, customer-focused,

National Partnership for Reinventing Government (NPRG)

reform effort formerly known as the **National Performance Review**. See also **reinventing government**.

New Public Management (NPM)

trend that surfaced in Europe, Australia, and New Zealand during the 1990s that had significant influence on the Clinton administration's market-based, customer-focused, quality-driven reinvention effort.

quality-driven reinvention effort.[16] One of the key components of NPM was acknowledging the role of citizens as customers. The case for this strategy rested upon the fact that as budgets were constrained, more local government services were becoming fee-for-service based, and that citizens in general are demanding a level of service quality equivalent to that provided by the private sector. Who would not welcome 24/7 accessibility to government or receiving timely, businesslike, and quality service when accessing government information centers or websites? But the fact that the reinvention movement was based on a specific set of values originating from the private sector led some to argue that these strategies did not apply equally well to the public sector. Adopting the "entrepreneurial" paradigm in favor of the "administrative management" approach that had prevailed in the public sector since the late 1800s might have resulted in unknown long-term consequences, including a lack of political accountability among those private companies that assume governmental responsibilities (see Chapter 9).

Critics called for refocusing on long-standing concepts such as *democracy*, *citizenship*, and *pride* when talking about government and governmental actions, instead of emphasizing buzzwords such as *market-driven*, *competitive*, and *customer-focused*. A contemporary criticism of the entrepreneurial paradigm is: "Public servants do not deliver customer service; they deliver democracy."[17] **New Public Service (NPS)** is based on the view that democratic theory and definitions of the public interest should result from a dialogue and deliberation about common interests and shared values. NPS assumes public servants are motivated by a desire to contribute to society and to respect law, constitutional principles, community values, political norms, professional standards, and citizen interests. By contrast, reinvention presumed that all public servants were motivated by an "entrepreneurial spirit" and a desire to reduce the size of government. It assumed the basic notion of citizens as self-interested consumers with egocentric goals. The public interest, on the other hand, is seen as an aggregation of individual citizen interests, rather than customers in the private market yearning to be "satisfied" and choosing services on the basis of lowest costs and narrow individual interests. Advocates of NPS argue that there is, or should be, a distinction between customers and citizens. The former chooses among products in the marketplace, whereas the latter decides which functions are so vital that government must perform them at public expense. NPS advocates stress that:

> Citizens are described as bearers of rights and duties within the context of a wider community. Customers are different in that they do not share common purposes but rather seek to optimize their own individual benefits.[18]

Thus, citizens are viewed as an integral part of the governmental system, not just as recipients of government services. In their roles as customers, citizens are not required to think about the broader interests of others or society.

New Public Service (NPS)

government service based upon the view that democratic theory and definitions of the public interest should result from a dialogue and deliberation about shared values. Public servants are motivated by a desire to contribute to society and to respect law, community values, political norms, professional standards, and citizen interests.

Thus, when citizens are transformed into customers, the public interest may be diluted, with damaging effects on democratic governance and public administration. We are reminded that one of the fundamental reasons for there even *being* a public sector was to correct imperfections in private markets. The NPS perspective emphasizes that, if citizens are merely transformed into customers with individual egoistic interests, there are consequences for values within public administration. NPS is especially concerned about reducing the roles of citizens to customers of government services, because governmental institutions should respond not only to individual interests, but to the shared public interest as well. Some mix of these two theories has combined to create the present-day operational realities of public administrators.

Establishing Customer Service Standards

Among the NPR's key achievements was establishing standards for improved customer service in most federal agencies. After an intense review by the NPR staff, President Clinton issued Executive Order 12862 in September 1993,[19] mandating that all federal agencies identify their customers, find out what those customers want, and develop **customer-service standards** and means to achieve them. The order emphasized that the quality of government services should equal or exceed the best service available in the private sector, and in order to reach that goal, it described actions which needed to be taken by the agencies. Eventually, the NPR established nearly 4,000 customer-service standards in 570 federal organizations. Each agency was required to identify its customers, find out the customers' wants and current level of satisfaction with services, post service standards, and measure achieved results against them; these results would then be benchmarked against the best in business.

customer-service standards

explicit standards of service quality published by federal agencies and part of the reinventing government initiative.

Federal executive agencies published more detailed customer-service standards, and individual agencies have since established specific performance indicators. Standards were derived from customer surveys, evaluations, feedback, data analysis, and employee input. Customer attitudes and opinions must be carefully measured and compared to improve performance and productivity.[20] Standards were published so both customers and suppliers would be aware of mutual expectations. This approach generated visible baseline data on relative agency performance; this effort continues today in nearly all federal agencies.

What differentiates current customer-service quality efforts from past attempts to achieve results? Past public-sector efforts stressed *externally* imposed methods of goal setting, decision making, individual performance appraisal, inspection, and program evaluation to achieve public priorities. Although methodologically sophisticated, these efforts used techniques such as ranking employees for pay purposes, merit increases, and bonuses to increase output from individuals, which motivated some employees, but neglected customer service, teamwork, and measurement of results. Applications of such techniques have not eliminated complaints of inefficient or ineffective services, wasted resources, or lack of responsiveness from public employees.

Achieving customer-service quality without increasing costs (higher taxes or user fees) in the long term is difficult (but not impossible) in the public sector, for two reasons. One is the role played by elected politicians as the final decision makers; the other is the complex relationships among elected officials and the appointed public administrators who actually implement decisions. As we have learned in previous chapters, the two groups often live in separate (but often overlapping) worlds of public accountability, leadership, special interests, and policy making. They must collaborate to achieve customer-driven service quality improvement (which is easier said than done).

Since September 1994, more than 200 federal agencies have been asking their customers what they wanted and how they judged good service. These surveys, focus groups, and opinions have been used to establish customer-service standards, such as the following, for all federal agencies:

- Identify customers who are, or should be, served by the agency.
- Survey customers to determine the kind and quality of service they want and their level of satisfaction with existing services.
- Post service standards and measure results against them.
- Benchmark customer-service standards against the "best in business."
- Survey frontline employees on barriers to, and ideas for, matching the best in business.
- Provide customers with choices in both the sources of service and the means of delivery.
- Make information, services, and complaint systems easily accessible.
- Provide means to address customer complaints.

All agencies have compiled customer profiles to establish standards, and the specifics of these standards are being worked out on an agency-by-agency basis. More importantly, the precedent has been set that *customers matter*, and some agencies have already achieved the goal of providing service that "meets or exceeds" the best in business.

Rewarding Employee Participation and Quality Improvement

Application of quality improvement techniques by state and local agencies responds to citizen demands for better service quality, improves government's ability to effectively solve public problems, and provides a promising model for employee participation and "customer-responsive" public management practices. Although too numerous to describe in detail, many other public agencies, universities, nonprofit organizations, and service organizations are involved as well. Forty-five states have established state quality awards patterned after the federal government's **Malcolm Baldrige National Quality Awards (BNQA),** and many localities have launched service quality improvement efforts. This award program led to the creation of a new public–private partnership; principal support for the program comes from the Foundation for the Malcolm Baldrige National Quality Awards, established in 1988. Although administered by the National Institute of Standards and Technology (NIST), the program is funded by application fees from organizations applying for the award.

The BNQA was originally proposed to answer the challenge of global economic competition by improving the quality of American manufactured goods. Public recognition of improvements and achievements provided examples for others to emulate. Winners are required to publicly share information about quality strategies at a national conference to assist other organizations and to encourage them to become part of the national quality improvement effort. This requirement is important because learning from the experience of others can stimulate organizations to become part of the quality process and find more effective ways to manage performance. Many state and local organizations also have their own awards and encourage recipients to share their success formulas. Three-quarters of the states also require winners to showcase their procedures with potential applicants in an effort to disseminate best practices.

The Obama administration developed a **Strategy for American Innovation** calling for federal agencies to create more transparent, participatory, and collaborative government using prizes and challenges. Federal agencies are encouraged to use awards, certificates, charters, and prizes to motivate and reward employees and as internal self-assessment tools for refining and updating service quality initiatives.[21]

Reflecting our federal system of diverse, decentralized, and divided authority, specific projects and strategies to implement total quality management (TQM) and productivity improvement differ substantially from locality to locality. Considerable progress has been made toward standardization, however, since the late 1980s. The federal government has implemented TQM, with over two-thirds of all agencies participating; state initiatives date from the early 1990s, with over one-half involved;[22] and about one-fourth of local governments (cities with a population of more than 25,000) report enhanced customer service, quality improvement, or employee empowerment in at least one function.[23] Local initiatives have been established to promote better customer service in such diverse areas as Hampton, Virginia; Coral Springs, Florida (one of the 2007 Baldrige Award winners); Lauderhill, Florida; Jackson, Michigan; Maricopa County, Arizona; Erie, Pennsylvania; the Port Authority of New York and New Jersey (affecting Kennedy, La Guardia, and Newark Airports, together with numerous ground-transportation systems); San Carlos, California; Salt Lake City, Utah; and Sunnyvale, California. Local governments are adopting a process approach to improving common functions such as personnel

Malcolm Baldrige National Quality Awards (BNQA)

created by Public Law 100–107, and signed into law on August 20, 1987; the award program led to the creation of a new public–private partnership. Principal support for the program comes from the Foundation for the Malcolm Baldrige National Quality Awards.

Strategy for American Innovation

Obama administration's initiative for sustainable growth and job creation. For details, see http://www.whitehouse.gov/administration/eop/nec/StrategyforAmericanInnovation/

benchmarking

quality and productivity improvement methodology that examines those organizations that are best at performing a certain process or set of processes (for example, employee relations) and then transplanting the methods into one's own organization.

administration, record keeping, vehicle maintenance, and community development. Cities and counties are **benchmarking** the best practices of leaders in various processes.[24] In this way, management improvements are being made, and standards set, on the basis of experience in other, similar jurisdictions.

Public agencies are learning from each other how best to respond to the needs of all those they serve.[25] It is becoming more widely accepted in government and elsewhere that administrators have to "make do" with what they have. The promise of greater productivity lies in the fact that ICTs such as e-gov and social media have not yet been fully applied to this area, and there is a growing track record of successes that should encourage similar efforts elsewhere.[26]

Responding to demands for improved service from citizens, clients, constituents, or taxpayers—all the "customers" of government—is a continuing challenge facing all public organizations. Implementing policies that meet standards for customer-driven service quality requires changes in existing organizational structures, closer customer–supplier relationships, an empowered and self-directed workforce, and better measurement of results. All public services, but especially those receiving a substantial share of revenues directly from user fees, tolls, or service charges, must provide the training, leadership, and resources necessary to initiate customer-driven total quality service (TQS).[27] Above all else, responsiveness to a wide range of customers necessitates an attitudinal change. Senior public officials are increasingly aware that traditional productivity enhancement efforts alone will not improve customer satisfaction.

The challenge for public managers is to motivate employees toward higher levels of performance while continually lowering costs and improving areas defined by customers as needing improvement. Not unlike the concept of TQM applied to private industry, TQS is a theory-based strategic option that allows public managers to reward truly exceptional individual performance, yet increase the capacity for organization-wide cooperation and continuous process improvement.

Despite persistent calls for reform, few governments have thus far succeeded in simultaneously improving service quality, increasing productivity, and reducing costs. In recent years, more and more emphasis has been placed on productivity improvement strategies variously known as TQM, continuous quality improvement (CQI), and customer relationship management (CRM), to achieve closer customer–taxpayer–provider–supplier relationships. All generally incorporate the following five principles:

1. Commitment to meeting customer-driven quality standards
2. Employee participation, or empowerment, to make decisions at the point closest to the customer
3. Actions based on data, facts, outcome measures, results, and statistical analysis
4. Commitment to process improvement and CQI
5. Organizational changes and teamwork to encourage implementation of the above-mentioned elements.

To sustain long-term public-service quality and productivity improvement initiatives, these basic changes are needed, coupled with new attitudes and management practices. Three blue-ribbon national commissions recommended similar reforms focusing on leadership at the local, state, and federal government levels, and numerous other studies reinforce the importance of PM.[28]

The Politics of Performance Management

The apparent failure of traditional budgetary processes, policy analysis, evaluation, and productivity improvement approaches may have prompted many fiscal conservatives, early in 2011, to recommend radical cuts in spending or shifting public responsibilities to the private sector (see Chapters 8 and 9). Although always an option—simply divesting public-sector functions, via downsizing, privatization, or contracting out, without structural changes to assure accountability and equality, is unlikely to achieve the broader goals of economy, equity, and customer-service quality improvement. Competitive (and often partisan) political forces constantly push elected representatives to focus on immediate political decisions, rather than on long-term professional-administrative values such as efficient use of resources and increased productivity (recall the discussion of conflicting administrative and political values in Chapter 2). There are always some exceptions to this generalization, but annual budget cycles, scarce resources, and continuing crisis-driven management tend to reinforce a short-term perspective in most governments. Instead of responding with innovative solutions, many elected officials often claim to be frustrated by bureaucratic resistance. At the same time, some politicians avoid political accountability for results by blaming public employees or previous administrations for failure to improve conditions. This **claim-and-blame strategy** has become a vicious circle, with no winners and too many losers, especially taxpayers and clienteles of wasteful and inefficiently-managed government programs. The results have been frustrating for both politicians and administrators, causing further loss of public confidence in the ability of government to deal with basic societal issues, and prompting some to call for abolishing government programs altogether.

Appointed public managers have typically operated in a noncompetitive, "monopolistic" environment with far less control than their private-sector counterparts in staffing, defining missions, and controlling markets. Most are not required to run for reelection or raise revenue and have largely been protected from being fired by civil service rules. One of the conditions of becoming more results-oriented is to allow individual public managers more discretionary authority in removing employees who do not perform well. Still, many bureaucrats are aware of the limitations of current public management practices, but claim to be powerless to change them without political approval.

Despite apparent differences in their respective environments, elected officials and public administrators share common goals: regardless of their rank or position, empowered public employees, managers, and elected officials must provide the best services to all those served at the least cost. This axiom has never been truer than in today's harsh political environment.

In the second decade of the twenty-first century, neither side has been willing to examine internal organizational structures and take the actions necessary to reform existing public management processes and strategies. The issue has too often been framed in ideological terms rather than addressing how best to resolve a specific set of problems. Some (including former President George W. Bush) argued that, if given a choice, most citizens would prefer private alternatives or smaller, more expensive, local governments. This debate has evolved into a larger, hotly-contested issue over federal spending for entitlements. Whether governmental institutions can be improved or should be dismantled and replaced by private institutions is part of this debate. Most advocates of privatization typically ignore the loss of accountability, benefits to special interests, the need for closer monitoring, and the corruption that accompanies many such efforts. Maintaining some degree of government efficiency, overlapping functions, and checks and balances reminds us that "the responsibility for providing

claim-and-blame strategy

situation in which politicians "blame" bureaucrats and bureaucrats "claim" not to have the authority to act.

services—determining their scope, level, and the conditions under which they are delivered—should remain in the hands of government officials committed to the public interest."[29]

The budget reforms, deficit agreements, and new management and performance improvement systems initiated nearly twenty years ago succeeded in downsizing the federal bureaucracy to its lowest level, in both total size and ratio of employees to population, since the 1950s (see Chapter 7). Congressional legislation further required federal executive agencies to publish customer-service standards, identify performance goals, specify measures, and submit results to executive and legislative oversight agencies such as the Office of Management and Budget, the Congressional Budget Office, and the Government Accountability Office. Federal agencies must also comply with stringent laws, such as the Chief Financial Officers Act of 1990 (P.L. 101-576), the Federal Workforce Restructuring Act of 1994 (P.L. 103-226), and the Government Performance and Results Act of 1993 (P.L. 103-62, 107 Stat. 285).[30]

Although the Clinton administration's capacity-building efforts initially received tacit support from Congress, management reforms became highly politicized and limited in scope.[31] Nonetheless, the NPR did help prepare many federal agencies for the unimaginable challenges to public management and homeland security that they faced during the first years of the twenty-first century. Despite being caught in a political struggle for power, the reinvention movement contributed important lessons for public managers, many of whom were previously reluctant to consider, much less initiate, results-oriented management systems. Federal managers enhanced their PM skills, but these reforms had little impact on public opinion or electoral results for the incumbent administration.

The NPR played an insignificant role in the 2000 presidential campaign, with nearly 60 percent of voters mistakenly believing that, under Clinton, the number of federal employees had actually increased; worse yet, only a little more than half the electorate had even heard of reinvention.[32] Even though the size of government was smaller than when Clinton took office, performance data, which should have been neutral, became part of an ideological power struggle within Congress. The 2000 presidential election defeat of Democratic candidate Al Gore, a strong supporter of the NPR, showed just how difficult it is to define efficient management, overcome stereotypes, and translate improved performance into political gains. Clinton and Gore failed to demonstrate how they decreased government's size and improved its efficiency, and what difference it made to the average voter; Republicans successfully advocated legislation to cut "wasteful" programs and reduce taxes by exposing program failures. Candidate Bush was able to capitalize on voter distrust of "big government" and continue the Republican tradition of bureaucracy bashing, painting a picture of Washington as full of incompetent bureaucrats, inefficiencies, unmanageable programs, and wasteful spending.

The Bush administration shelved many of the NPR initiatives in early 2001 and the momentum for institutional reforms stalled in the 108th Congress.

The use of performance data to make budgetary and programmatic decisions became the foundation of Bush's **President's Management Agenda (PMA)**, the ideological blueprint for improving management performance during his administration. Among the leading advocates of the market-driven model, President Bush and Vice President Cheney espoused competition and privatization as the best option to overcome bureaucratic resistance. Indeed, under the PMA, federal agencies were *required* to show how public programs achieve results more efficiently than other methods, such as faith-based, private, or nonprofit alternatives. Even before Bush's reelection in 2004, the administration had shifted the burden of proof to bureaucracy to show why private alternatives are less effective and less cost-efficient.

During his 2008 presidential campaign, Barack Obama pledged to use ICT tools—including social media—to make government less beholden to special interest groups and to promote greater citizen involvement in decision-making. Part of this high-tech approach included the development of the Technology, Innovation, and Government Reform (TIGR) working groups, a team of more than thirty tech-industry professionals whose mission was to create a twenty-first century government that is more open and effective, leverage technology to grow the economy, create jobs, and solve pressing national problems. Each working group is organized into four teams: (1) Innovation and Government, (2) Innovation and National Priorities, (3) Innovation and Sciences, and (4) Innovation and Civil Society. The focus of the working groups was to develop the highest-priority policy proposals and plans for action during the Obama–Biden administration in the following: economy; education, energy, and environment; health care; immigration; national security; and technology innovation and reform.[33] In addition, federal agencies were encouraged to respect the integrity of and renew the historic commitment to science and technology to catalyze active citizenship and partnerships in shared governance with civic institutions. The Obama administration proved far less effective in communicating administrative changes via new forms of technology during its first two years. Nonetheless, ICTs—including social media—have become a permanent part of American political processes offering greater numbers of citizens the option to exercise new forms of civic participation.

When compared with management processes in the private sector, where competition, standardization, and markets dominate, many governments have had problems initiating management reforms. In the past, when governments have succeeded in becoming more efficient, elected legislatures have tended to reduce their budgets (see Chapter 8). Federal agencies were encouraged to become more results-oriented, as opposed to inputs-oriented. Program

President's Management Agenda (PMA)

the Bush administration's effort to better manage federal agencies managers who achieve measurable targets would be allowed to keep a portion of the "profits" and distribute them to their staff, like bonuses in the private sector, by way of a predetermined formula. Although there are now more "incentives" to become customer-focused and results-oriented, there is still no equivalent to the "bottom-line" profit motive for determining whether customer-service or productivity standards are being met in the public sector. Nonetheless, public managers now have a broader range of choices among various PM strategies from which to select; most were unavailable or nonexistent a only few years ago.

Despite the bureaucracy bashing and harsh political campaign rhetoric often accompanying calls for private, nonprofit, or faith-based alternatives to government services, most citizens strongly support renewed efforts to improve the administrative efficiency of existing public agencies. Rather than replacing government with private-sector alternatives, most Americans want government services that respond to their needs and "deliver more for less cost." This preference was reinforced by the results of the 2004 presidential elections and 2006 congressional elections. Public opinion about the quality and equality of government services has varied, and prior to September 11, 2001, higher levels of support for private-sector alternatives reflected pervasive citizen dissatisfaction with many public services. Public agencies at all levels of government are experimenting with various performance measurement and management techniques to respond to the needs of citizens as customers in a timely and efficient manner. However, there are major differences between a competitive, market-based service environment, on the one hand, and a regulated, nonmarket environment, on the other. For instance, if customer-service expectations remain unfulfilled in a competitive market, there is nearly always an option to select another provider. Citizens dissatisfied with public services typically have no recourse other than to purchase services (if available) from a private provider, an option that raises serious equity issues as it is unavailable to all but the wealthiest citizens.[34]

Comparing Alternative Performance Management Strategies

Different PM strategies are intrinsically linked to the political environment in which public policy making occurs. Many governments are reexamining how to simultaneously reduce costs, strengthen performance, and achieve results. Public agencies are experimenting with performance measurement and management systems designed to meet public policy goals and respond to citizen demands. Various reform models have been proposed, and public administrators now expend considerable time, effort, and resources exchanging "best practices," finding "best value," and "rethinking" government operations. This section compares the PM initiatives of the Bush administration known as the President's Management Agenda (PMA) with more recent actions of the Obama administration.

Although equally important, less effort has been devoted to PM strategies within increasingly complex, ideologically charged, and politicized decision-making environments. The dilemma for public administrators is to determine which of many approaches best "fits" the varied and often contradictory systems for delivering public services in a decentralized and locally influenced governance system. Government agencies continuously struggle to find the best strategies to implement politically mandated reforms within traditional rules-driven bureaucracies. Strategic needs, as well as the organizational dynamics of diverse cultural, social, and political environments, determine which theoretical models, if any, can be successfully applied. Various alternatives should receive careful scrutiny, especially with regard to accountability and oversight, implications for citizenship, competition, needs of recipients, and equity of services provided to citizens.[35] Different reform models have been implemented within existing organizational structures; less effort has been devoted to determining how to improve performance within the kinds of decision-making environments that presently exist.

During the past decade, the federal government initiated comprehensive and controversial legislation supporting downsizing, e-gov, and results-oriented management encouraging agencies to establish standards, enforce regulations, monitor results, and post key performance measures. For several years, all U.S. cabinet-level federal agencies have had chief operating officers (COOs) and chief financial officers (CFOs) to provide comprehensive performance measures and detailed financial statements to congressional committees, the OMB, and the president. In addition, nearly all agencies now have **chief information officers (CIOs)** to coordinate and direct improved ICT and e-gov initiatives. Public management capacity has been strengthened as these positions did not even exist in most agencies a decade ago.

Despite diligent efforts to promote PM strategies, public agencies still face difficult dilemmas: Should they deploy the bottom-up, incremental, mixed, participatory "reinvention" models proposed by New Public Management (NPM) theorists; or implement the "pure" top-down, corporate, private-market-based PM approach; or perhaps find a middle ground or "hybrid" approach more consistent with NPS, such as cooperative public–private–nonprofit partnerships with a mix of public, private, and nongovernment participants; or just do nothing at all and wait for the next round of reforms? The rationales for each of these strategies are as varied as the political ideologies and theories supporting them.[36]

Privatization and outsourcing are politically attractive productivity improvement and cost-saving measures that also raise serious questions about

chief information officers (CIOs)

high-level corporate or governmental officials responsible for the maintenance of communications and information technology systems in public or private organizations.

accountability, competition, democracy, equity, and management oversight.[37] As quasi-monopolistic service providers, most governments are isolated from the competitive pressures of private markets and reluctant to accept customer-focused and market-driven changes. Unlike profit-driven private companies, most public agencies, nonprofits, and so-called nongovernmental organizations (NGOs) depend on multiple sources of revenue, ranging from private donations to public funds, for much of their operating revenues. Except in rare circumstances, public agencies are prohibited from generating profits or increasing market share, and rely instead on personal income, property, sales taxes or user fees for operating revenue. To ensure accountability, public budgetary and fiscal policy decisions have heretofore focused on inputs, rather than on outputs, outcomes, or results. Consequently, public managers have fewer incentives to treat citizens as customers, reward exemplary performance by empowered employees, or implement results-driven PM processes. According to popular (and largely unexamined) stereotypes, incrementalism and "status quo" thinking, rather than entrepreneurism and innovation, prevail in many public agencies.

Rather than suggesting ways to more efficiently deliver services to citizens, improve policy content, or respond to recipient needs, ardent supporters of outsourcing were reluctant to acknowledge the profound changes in performance and structure that occurred during the NPR reinvention era (1993–2001). During that period, the Clinton administration and the U.S. Congress passed major executive-branch reforms to promote market-driven and results-oriented systems for allocating public resources.[38] As a result, more agencies decentralized decision-making authority, empowered employees, and began to treat citizens as valued customers. As satisfaction with services improved, citizen expectations about the level and quality of services also increased.

Performance Management Agendas: Rethinking Public Bureaucracy

The 2000 presidential election resulted in a partisan change in the U.S. presidency, which was reinforced in 2004 with George W. Bush winning a second four-year term. A focus on improved management practices was vigorously maintained throughout both of his terms. President Bush focused on five government-wide initiatives. The goals of the PMA were surprisingly similar to those of the NPR: focus government on the needs of citizens, not bureaucracy; integrate performance with budgeting; and become "results-oriented" and "market-based," ultimately creating greater trust between the citizen and the government. Rather than offering hundreds of specific guidelines, the PMA included just five government-wide recommendations (Table 10–3). The fifth government-wide

Bush's PMA (2001–2009)	Obama's Six Themes
1. Strategic Management of Human Capital	1. Put performance first
2. Competitive sourcing— privatization	2. Ensure responsible spending of the American Recovery and Reinvestment Act (ARRA)
3. Improved financial performance	3. Transform the federal workforce
4. Expand electronic government	4. Manage across sectors by partnering with the private sector and collaborating across levels of government
5. Budget and performance integration	5. Reform federal contracting and acquisition
	6. Install transparency, technology, and participatory democracy

Source: © 2013 Cengage Learning.

initiative contained a specific promise to provide the American people with an overview of how government programs are performing and also a tool to compare performance and cost across programs. It reinforced and strengthened the Government Performance and Results Act (GPRA) and addressed the problem that managers believed their agencies were losing ground in building organizational cultures that support a focus on results.[39] In addition, there were nine agency-specific reforms that included faith-based and community initiatives to "correct" the situation in which the "federal government too often ignores or impedes the efforts of faith-based and community groups to address social problems by imposing an unnecessarily and improperly restrictive view of their appropriate role."[40] The precise language, specific focus, and strong leadership commitment from President Bush distinguished the PMA from previous reform agendas.

The PM strategies of the Obama administration show continuity in the long-term efforts to reform federal agencies. Obama's six themes for improving performance are similar to the goals of previous administrations, but place less emphasis on "competitive sourcing" and privatization. The new administration's economic stimulus plan under the American Recovery and Reinvestment Act (ARRA) of 2009 reinforced the importance of performance by appointing new officials to the OMB; sought to transform the federal workforce; encouraged cross-functional management by collaborating with the private sector and forming partnerships; reformed the way federal agencies procure goods and services; and connected government with citizens by expanded use of technology to increase participation and open government (Table 10–3).

The Bush administration distinguished the PMA from the earlier NPR by infusing the report with political rhetoric and an overall lack of specifics. During the 2000 election campaign, Bush mocked the reinvention movement, and insisted instead that federal agencies "rethink government" and focus on results when spending citizens' tax dollars. Then–Texas Governor Bush clearly stated his intention, if elected, to eliminate waste and inefficiency by making government more results-driven. During the campaign, he avoided acknowledging that the federal workforce had been reduced, doing so only after the election. Foreshadowing massive deficit-driven cuts in the domestic portion of the federal budget, Bush criticized the previous administration's successful efforts to downsize the workforce, using across-the-board reductions without considering the needs of individual agencies. He was also skeptical about Clinton's e-gov initiatives to expand the use of information technology (IT). Technology was a major aspect of the NPR, resulting in greater numbers of citizens having increased access to government through the Internet. Bush later rethought this strategy and adopted this idea with *his* e-gov initiative.

The reform principles announced in the PMA government-wide initiative on expanded e-gov were followed by legislative action, when the E-Government Act of 2002 was signed into law on December 17, 2002. This legislation included an effort to expand the use of Internet resources to deliver government services and to make government citizen-centered, results-oriented, and market-based. The stated purposes of the act are to: (1) provide effective leadership for federal IT projects, (2) require the use of Internet-based IT initiatives to reduce costs and increase opportunities for citizen participation in government, (3) transform agency operations, promoting interagency collaboration for e-gov processes, and (4) to make the federal government more transparent and accountable.

The overall goals of the e-gov initiatives are to provide high-quality customer service regardless of whether the citizen contacts the agency by phone, in person, or on the Web; cut government operating costs; provide citizens with easy access to government services; and make government more transparent and accountable. Building upon the Clinger-Cohen Act of 1996, the E-Government Act served as the primary legislative vehicle to guide evolving federal IT strategies and promote initiatives to make government information and services available online. The seventy-two-page law was divided into five titles and incorporated the language from at least four other bills that were introduced separately in Congress. It also amended different parts of the *United States Code* in the areas of federal information policy and information security.

Office of Electronic Government

established by the Bush administration in 2002 to administer provisions of the Electronic Government Act (http://www.egov.gov/).

Title I established the **Office of Electronic Government** in OMB, headed by an administrator appointed by the president. The administrator assists the deputy director of OMB and the OMB director of management in coordinating the efforts of the administrator of the Office of Information and Regulatory Affairs, another OMB unit, to carry out relevant responsibilities for prescribing guidelines and regulations for agency implementation of the Privacy Act, the Clinger-Cohen Act, IT acquisition pilot programs, and the Government Paperwork Elimination Act. Title I also required the General Services Administration (GSA) to consult with the administrator of the Office of Electronic Government on any efforts by GSA to promote e-gov. It established the Chief Information Officers Council (CIO Council) by law, with the OMB deputy director of management as chair, and detailed its organizational structure and mandate; it also established an e-gov fund for integrity IT projects.

Title II focused on enhancing a variety of e-gov services, establishing performance measures, and clarifying OMB's role as the leader and coordinator of federal e-gov services. It required agencies to participate in the CIO Council and to submit annual agency e-gov status reports; required executive agencies to adopt electronic signature methods; directed the federal courts and regulatory agencies to establish websites containing information useful to citizens; and outlined responsibilities of the OMB director for maintaining accessibility and usability, and for preservation of government information. It also required that privacy requirements regarding agency use of personally identifiable information and privacy guidelines be established for federal websites, and created a public–private exchange program for mid-level IT workers, for the exchange of information between government agencies and private-sector organizations. Finally, Title II amended a chapter of the *United States Code* by adding a new section facilitating incentives and procedures to encourage agencies to use and share in savings for procurement techniques; amending a section the *Code* by allowing state or local governments to use federal supply procurement procedures for IT purchases; and mandating the development of common protocols for GIS.

Federal Information Security Management Act (FISMA)

provides general authority to the OMB director and individual agencies to develop and maintain federal information security policies and practices; requires agencies to conduct annual independent evaluations of their information security programs and practices.

Title III, known as the **Federal Information Security Management Act (FISMA)** of 2002, superseded similar language in the Homeland Security Reform Act. It also amended a subchapter of the *United States Code* by stipulating the general authority, functions, and responsibilities of the OMB director and individual agencies relating to developing and maintaining federal information security policies and practices, and required agencies to conduct annual independent evaluations of their information security programs and practices. Agencies operating or controlling national security systems are also responsible for maintaining the appropriate level of information security protection for these systems. FISMA amended the Clinger–Cohen Act by requiring the U.S. Secretary of Commerce, on the basis of proposals developed by the NIST, to promulgate information security standards for federal information systems.

It also amended the NIST Act by affirming the role of NIST to develop standards, guidelines, and minimum requirements for information systems used by federal agencies or by contractors on behalf of the agency, as well as replacing the existing Computer System Security and Privacy Advisory Board with the new Information Security and Privacy Advisory Board.

Title IV authorized appropriations for the bill through 2007, and Title V is the Confidential Information Protection and Statistical Efficiency Act of 2002. It designated the OMB director as being responsible for coordinating and overseeing the confidentiality and disclosure policies, establishing limitations on the use and disclosure of data and information by government agencies. It also identified the Bureau of the Census, the Bureau of Economic Analysis, and the Bureau of Labor Statistics each as a "designated statistical agency" and outlined their responsibilities regarding the use, handling, and sharing of data.[41]

Beginning in the FY 2003 budget cycle, the Bush administration attempted to introduce rigorous results-based management reforms. In addition to expanding e-gov and integrating budgetary with performance indicators through the GPRA, other long-term goals included creating a "flatter and more responsive" bureaucracy, tax simplification, partial privatization of Social Security, and competitive outsourcing. The PMA recommended expanded competition to replace as many as 850,000 federal workers with private contractors, the creation of an Office of Electronic Government to promote e-gov initiatives, partnerships with faith-based and nonprofit providers, and the opening of federal contracts to faith-based organizations and private businesses to (in Bush's words) "promote rather than stifle" innovation through competition.[42]

Unlike President Clinton, President Bush had the full support of a Republican Congress until January 2007, and enjoyed public backing for additional expenditures, especially for homeland security, fighting terrorism, and improving the economy. Consequently, he introduced several bills to further reinforce his initiatives. The Managerial Flexibility Act of 2001 gave federal managers additional tools and authority to create a "motivated" workforce. The Freedom to Manage Act of 2001 similarly reduced statutory impediments and established fast-track authority to move legislation quickly through Congress. Both of these bills would have given federal managers greater authority to achieve government-wide management reform. Despite the Republican majorities in both houses of Congress, however, many members of both parties viewed these pre-September 11, 2001, initiatives as "executive branch power grabs," and neither bill survived congressional consideration.

The Obama Administration and New Media Technology

Several laws have been enacted to accelerate the digitization of government documents, integrate websites, and expand ICTs. Legislation and regulation have improved the management and promotion of e-gov services and processes. This provides a framework for performance measures using ICTs to improve citizen access to government information and services, as well as for other purposes.[43]

After assuming office in 2009, one of President Obama's first administrative actions was to appoint a federal CIO. In March 2009, President Obama appointed Vivek Kundra as CIO, responsible for coordinating IT policy and operations across federal agencies. He was assigned the difficult task of saving federal government resources while helping to institute the president's vision for a Web 2.0 government.[44] The CIO reports directly to the White House, and is not only expected to economize with Web-based approaches but also potentially to encourage entirely new waves of economic development. Elevating the position to White House level helps ensure that the public will have access to information, and to rethink how citizens interact with government in an information-based economy. Kundra's office launched Data.gov, an innovative open-source website that publishes vast arrays of government data and employs new technologies for public dissemination. The integration of open-source coding with government holds the potential to fundamentally change the political economy. Besides making data available for citizens, the federal government also hosts space online where citizens can turn to each other for solutions to social problems, much as they do now on social networking sites.

In April 2009, President Obama appointed Aneesh Chopra, formerly Virginia's Secretary of Technology, as the nation's first **chief technology officer (CTO)**. Chopra and Kundra met nearly a decade ago as entrepreneurs in Northern Virginia's Indian-American business community. They worked together in former Virginia Governor Timothy M. Kaine's administration, and then as technology and innovation advisers on President Obama's TIGR transition team. The CTO focuses on overall technology policy and innovation strategies across departments, while the CIO oversees day-to-day IT spending and operations within agencies. Chopra is in the Office of Science and Technology Policy and Kundra in OMB. Both have established impressive track records for taking innovative approaches to using technology in government. Kundra's efforts helped spur the development of Recovery.gov, a website designed to track federal stimulus funding. Their jobs include modifying budgets, organizing federal employees and contractors, and reworking technology systems, all while stimulus money is being distributed to create jobs and support new projects.

President Obama named a Washington-based entrepreneur and management consultant, Jeffrey Zients, as the federal government's first **chief performance officer (CPO)**. He also serves as deputy director for management at the Office of Management and Budget. Anything but an outsider, Zients is a multimillionaire who made his fortune as a management consultant running Portfolio Logic, a consulting firm that invests in business services and health care companies. Zients was a connected Washington insider

---

chief technology officer (CTO)

focuses on overall technology policy and innovation strategies across federal agencies and departments. President Obama appointed the first CTO in April 2009.

---

chief performance officer (CPO)

a position in the Office of Management and Budget (within the Executive Office of the President of the United States) first announced on January 7, 2009, by President-elect Barack Obama. The new post concentrates on the federal budget and government reform.

who served as chief executive officer and chairman of the Washington-based Advisory Board Company and as head of the Corporate Executive Board. The job requires a broad set of skills including both knowledge of technology and the ability to connect with the IT industry while operating within the confines of government.

Assessing Performance and Results: Political Hype or Managerial Reform?

As broad statements of general purpose, the PMA and ICT approaches are similar in many respects, especially considering the ideological differences between Bush and Obama and the divisiveness of recent presidential campaigns.[45] Both presidents emphasized downsizing and sought to make government more efficient, emphasizing results and "doing more with less." The real distinction between the two strategies is not whether performance indicators are used to achieve better results, but *how* the results are used. The PMA focuses on results-driven privatization as the primary basis for budgetary decisions (sharply contrasting with Obama's focus on linking government to citizen) and motivates federal employees to perform better despite fewer resources. This distinction in the use of PM reforms mirrors long-standing partisan differences in political battles surrounding passage and implementation of the GPRA as well as other PM initiatives. Instead of relying solely on incentives, as had occurred in the past, Bush claimed that under his administration there would be consequences (that is, punishment) for failure. Such a policy, where funds are given to programs that work while others are reduced or eliminated, has had far-reaching implications for Washington, as well as for intergovernmental relationships between the federal government and the states. It also was aligned with the neo-conservative 2000 Republican platform that emphasized the federal government's role as setting high standards and expectations, then allowing states to operate programs to achieve policy goals as they best know how (see Chapters 2 and 3).

President Bush's emphasis on PM was obvious throughout the PMA and incorporated in each of the five government-wide initiatives (see Table 10–3). Government officials as well as the American people are now able to follow closely how well the different departments and agencies are doing on implementing those initiatives by using an executive-branch management scorecard. A simple color-coded scorecard, the **Performance Assessment Rating Tool (PART)**, which identified how well each department or agency is doing in each of the five initiatives by using the very familiar and basic principle of a traffic light, determines a program's ranking by giving three scores: red for failing, yellow for progress, and green for success. The pilot effort began in FY 2003 with scores given after 20 percent of the agencies filled out yes/no questionnaires composed of twenty-five questions in seven different formats related to (1) program purpose and design, (2) strategic planning, (3) program

Performance Assessment Rating Tool (PART)

management "scorecard" used to rate the performance of federal executive agencies.

management, and (4) program results. Twice a year, scorecards are distributed, one for management and the other for general program performance. These are separate because, even if agencies are efficiently managed, the PART ranking may no longer be relevant if agencies' missions have been achieved or changed.[46] The simple scorecard reflects a grading system used in businesses, which President Bush wanted to apply to the public sector to give him greater "leverage over the federal government's vast empire of programs, agencies, and bureaucrats."[47] Updated performance ratings of individual agencies can be found on an archived OMB website.[48]

Although Bush's PM initiatives did not prove to be long-lasting, organizations involved in improving governmental systems agreed that the Bush agenda was "deserving of thoughtful consideration" and gave PART positive reviews.[49] However, under PART, of the 234 programs evaluated prior to the release of the 2004 federal budget, only 6 percent were judged effective and about 50 percent received a rating of "results not demonstrated" because of lack of data.[50] Although the scorecard can be viewed as a "work in progress" and an oversimplified tool that may ignore important details, it also "serv[es] the key purpose of getting agency attention and focus on improvement" by motivating administrators to improve and by subjecting them to pressure from peers and constituent groups.[51] Despite some methodological reservations, General Accountability Office (GAO) has been generally supportive of GPRA, PART, and OMB evaluations.

Continuity and Change in Performance Management

Federal assistance programs are difficult to assess because they consist mainly of so-called mandatory entitlement transfers for health care, retirement, and social-insurance payments to individuals, and for medical services or research grants to institutions; *very few federal agencies perform direct domestic customer-service functions.* Critics believed that the Bush administration focused too heavily on whether a department was contracting out enough, emphasizing that higher rates were superior. In response, many federal employees insisted that after working in the government for several years, they should not be subjected to rigorous competition to determine whether private contractors would do a better job. As a result, managers were placed in a very difficult position, because they had to accommodate policies of the Bush administration while continuing to effectively motivate their workers. Many of the PM initiatives of the Obama administration have become subjugated to the attempts by both parties to reduce billions of dollars in current year and future federal government expenditures.

There also is a pressing need to improve performance at the state and local levels, where citizens *are* the direct recipients of education, law enforcement, disaster assistance, health care, and a variety of other services from public administrators. In many states, far less concern exists about who delivers services than about how to meet current service demands and employee payrolls. Nearly one-half of the states faced 10 to 35 percent deficits in FY 2012 budget projections and were being forced to cut employee benefits, increase public school class sizes, raise user fees, reduce social services, and release prisoners before the end of their sentences. How these issues are resolved not only has obvious financial implications for public budgeting but also directly affects personnel management, labor relations, and the push for greater public productivity.

Despite the expanded use of e-gov, privatization, service standards, and a results orientation in the national government, it is still too early to determine the *level* of commitment or the long-term impact of PM strategies on intergovernmental relations. The focus of domestic policy during George W. Bush's second term shifted from managing performance to "lean" budgeting, with executive budget recommendations to eliminate or reduce 151 "wasteful and inefficient" domestic social programs in FY 2009, including proposals for big cuts in Medicare and Medicaid. Proposed cuts in these entitlements are likely to be even greater for future years. Although unlikely to pass Congress, changes in these programs would affect millions of individuals, all states, and many local governments. Consistent with President Bush's budgetary cuts and challenge to public agencies, there is a need for more empirical research to determine whether PMA reforms lead to fundamental shifts in the administrative values of public officials.

There are numerous practical administrative and political challenges in implementing PART and PMA. Some agencies resisted the development of "objective" performance measures and reductions in manager-to-employee ratios that repeat the mistakes that occurred under Presidents Clinton and Reagan. Despite ambiguous promises to engage in "strategic management of human capital," Bush provided no additional funding for investments in the workforce, such as training and employee development. To the contrary, departments were challenged to find resources for retention and recruitment bonuses by cutting what they spend on training and technology. Program evaluations raise two further concerns. First, even if a policy is failing, it is sometimes politically impossible to cut funding for popular, congressionally-mandated programs. On the other hand, PART may be used to validate cutting budgets and programs with marginal scores, instead of improving management. In 2002, the Department of Education released a study of the Clinton administration's "21st Century Schools" program, demonstrating there was little evidence that after-school services offered by the program improved education. As a result of performance data contained in the study, the Bush administration cut DoE spending rather than make improvements without cuts.[52]

Second, there also were fears that PART would be used as a "political gimmick," with many more politically acceptable agencies such as Homeland Security and Department of Defense receiving "greens," whether warranted or not.[53] During 2004, OMB awarded "clean opinions" to twenty-one of twenty-four agencies for their internal audits, up from eighteen in the previous fiscal year. The White House insisted that agencies make greater use of the GPRA to determine whether programs were effective and well managed. Bush officials emphasized the need to conduct more research and impose consequences for failure, but were reluctant to fund such studies.

Although the final impact of the PMA and PART cannot yet be fully determined, implementation has shown progress in accomplishing four mutually compatible, yet difficult to achieve, public-policy goals: (1) improving the productivity of bureaucracy with fewer resources, (2) downsizing domestic government, (3) becoming more politically accountable, and (4) restoring public faith and trust in government. Citizen demands for lower taxes and political campaign rhetoric calling for leaner, more efficient government encourage federal executive agencies to achieve PM goals by changing the way they define performance, measure productivity, and improve results. Congress passed administrative reforms mandating budget deficit reductions, personnel caps, and the use of results-oriented systems to achieve these goals.

Policy makers must carefully analyze various models using explicit criteria that will not transfer elements that might further alienate citizens already distrustful of government actions and motives. As illustrated by the passage of the Medicare Prescription Drug Improvement and Modernization Act in December 2005 (now Part D of the Medicare program), advocates of market-driven private health care plans clearly dominated the direction of public-policy making during the Bush administration. Not only did initial cost estimates (less than $400 billion) balloon to over $450 billion during FY 2004, but that amount doubled to over $725 billion in FY 2005, amid sharp questions about how estimates were arrived at and whether the Bush administration withheld higher estimates to facilitate passage of the legislation. Implementation has been slow as Congress has reexamined cost estimates, and as seniors assess the impact of these changes on their own budgets. Drug companies clearly profit from the program and, with nearly sixty plans to choose from, many seniors who might otherwise be eligible for added coverage are confused about alternatives. Audits indicate that tens of thousands of Medicare recipients have been victimized by deceptive sales practices or have had claims improperly denied by private insurers that now dominate the system.

Many administrators still question the long-term wisdom of Bush's competitive outsourcing policies, both inside and outside government, because they undercut many previously documented successes and increased the federal budget deficit at a time when more resources were being diverted to military programs. Despite the attempts at high-level organizational reforms, many fiscal-policy conflicts—such as battles over judicial appointments and over additional funding for the war in Iraq—delayed many of President Bush's plans for administrative reform. Nonetheless, Bush asked his officials for more detailed studies of how their organizations were performing, reflecting a dogged commitment to improved PM. In mid-November 2007, Bush issued an executive order "imposing accountability for how each federal agency sets targets for improving the performance of its programs and tracks progress. The order required agency heads to set goals, develop ways to measure progress, use performance data in budget requests and set up Web sites that describe 'the successes, shortfalls and challenges of each program' and efforts to improve them."[54] Despite such last-ditch efforts to cajole agencies into compliance, in the end it is elected policy makers, not public managers, who interpret the numbers and are accountable to the electorate for the success or failure of reform alternatives.

Assessing Alternative PM Strategies

Advocates of market-based reforms such as those proposed in the PMA minimize the distinction between public and private functions and argue that government productivity will improve merely with the application of competition and business processes. To others, "running government like a business" is a code word for neo-conservative ideologies that emphasize efficiency and downsizing over citizenship and political accountability. According to critics, "private marketers" view the public disparagingly as "customers" in a commercial transaction, rather than as citizens who govern themselves through active participation in democratic electoral (and other) processes.[55] Those who espouse greater privatization distrust "the public" and rely instead on powerful, well-funded private-interest groups, such as health maintenance organizations (HMOs), insurance companies, and pharmaceutical firms, to identify and implement self-serving policy alternatives.

Past successes such as welfare-to-work reforms suggest that alternative models to achieve public accountability and PM are not necessarily incompatible. Public managers generally understand the technical details of various alternatives, and some are even beginning to apply more advanced approaches, such as European ISO 9000 standards, knowledge management, TQM, and Six Sigma systems, often as a result of political pressures for expanded e-gov initiatives.[56] Still, public administrators are cross-pressured by conflicting ideological demands and face difficult decisions selecting among various alternatives for improving performance.[57] Subtle differences among various management strategies, combined with the lack of consensus on which theoretical alternatives consistently work best within specific public-policy arenas, add to the difficulty of selecting successful reform models.

The business market model emphasizes results-oriented customer-service quality to increase market share and retain both customers and employees. Businesses must provide the highest level of service or lose customers to other competitive providers who offer the same product or service at a lower price. Successful businesses focus on creating an atmosphere of creative rewards and continuous organizational learning to equip employees with the knowledge to provide value-added service (without additional costs) to greater numbers of customers. Individuals within an organization must develop a shared sense of common purpose by respecting the rights of customers and making their satisfaction a primary goal. Providing more responsive service by educating public employees to implement results-based systems—within constitutional limits set by policy makers—is one promising strategy that is being implemented by several public agencies.[58] In addition, recognizing employees as valuable *internal* customers and responding to their needs may help to alleviate the so-called "quiet crisis" of retiring senior executives now threatening to undercut many of the productivity gains made by U.S. federal agencies in the past several years.[59]

Administrative procedures that uncritically favor private- over public-sector solutions may actually discourage the development of objective outcome measures. The "demonstration effect" of federal management reforms on states and local governments may be compromised as well because subnational agencies are under severe budgetary pressures, geographically isolated from Washington, and more vulnerable to interest group pressures. In contrast to federal agencies, state and local governments provide a far greater range of services directly to citizens and devote a greater share of their budgets to employee benefits and salaries. Consequently, more nonfederal employees fear losing their jobs from budget cuts and privatization initiatives; thus, resistance to market-driven reinvention and performance measurement is generally more intense at the state and local level.[60] Changes in attitudes are more difficult to integrate with governmental operations in a noncentralized and fragmented system of federalism (see Chapter 3). Although there is a generally agreed-on need to base decisions on objective performance models and results, the challenge for public administrators is finding ways to reinvent as well as to restructure existing management systems to integrate the strongest features of both models. But despite measurable increases in productivity, determining the feasibility of private market-based alternatives in specific policy areas is a challenging task.

During the last several decades, many administrative practices have been established, altered, revised again, and then perhaps made routine or even discarded. Such changes are relatively easy to identify and describe. However, it is far more difficult to say with certainty when value shifts occur and, when they do occur, if they are going to be temporary or permanent. This is particularly true in times of national crises, war, and economic recession or during periods of profound cynicism and distrust about all government actions. The ultimate measure of success for such efforts, however, is a change in public attitudes about the ability of government agencies to cope with basic social expectations and deliver on promises of increased efficiency and service quality. The data generated from evaluations of past successes (or failures) can help to assist public managers in determining which private-sector models (if any) are better suited for application by government. The public managers can then attempt to integrate systems responsive to citizens with information technologies to better link individuals with specific government agencies.

Citizen Relationship Management and Electronic Government

Customer relationship management (CRM) is an established, profit-driven business strategy which helps companies to better serve customers and improve their understanding of customers' wants and needs.[61] In the private sector, an evolution and a transformation of customer relationships took place during the 1980s, when customers were no longer regarded as passive buyers with predetermined consumption habits. Customers are now viewed as active participants, partners, cocreators of business value, collaborators, and coproducers of personalized experiences.[62] This perception has radically changed how all organizations provide information, deliver services, and interact with current and future customers. From the CRM perspective, the customer is seen as an individual with a unique set of interests and needs; he or she has the right to customized, quick, and convenient service.[63] Self-service technologies give today's customers the ability to have their needs met whenever they want by using (for example) online banking, electronic account statements, and e-commerce. As customers experience an increase in access, reduced costs, and involvement in private-sector transactions, they are more likely to demand the same from the public sector.[64]

At the same time, governments are pressured by population growth and demographic changes, technological and knowledge "explosions," and increased citizen expectations combined with reluctance to increase taxes. As a result, governments are beginning to adopt CRM practices in order to respond to the demands of citizens, and referring to it as **citizen relationship management (CzRM)**. The core of CzRM focuses on providing citizens timely, consistent, responsive access to government information and services using the channel that the citizen prefers. CzRM is about strengthening the links and cooperation between government and its citizens, realizing operational and financial efficiencies, and building an environment that encourages innovation within government. Accordingly, CzRM strategies should be multi-channel, developed from a "360-degree view" of the citizen, and oriented *first* around the citizen's needs, not those of the organization.

The combination of CzRM and e-gov promises higher service quality at lower costs through multi-channel interactions with government agencies organized around the needs of the citizen. Changes in citizens' perceptions and expectations about government are driven more by fundamental and complex changes in American society. The implementation of CzRM practices in the United States is visible through several different policy initiatives, discussed earlier. Although some initiatives do not refer to the specific term CzRM, they include its perspectives and require implementation of its practices.

E-gov is also a growth industry, not just in Europe and the United States but worldwide. In 2001, an Internet search on the term "electronic government" found 44,979 *html* documents.[65] By 2004, a similar Google search

citizen relationship management (CzRM)

strategy focusing on providing citizens timely, consistent, responsive access to government information and services using Internet links; fosters cooperation between government and its citizens, seeks operational and financial efficiencies, and builds an environment that encourages innovation within government.

yielded 12 million "hits"; in 2009, the same search yielded *53 million* results. Another Google search, on the term "digital government" in late 2010, yielded 107 million hits—an enormous exponential increase reflecting the global growth in government-to-citizen Internet links. Electronic government differs from traditional "in office" public service delivery in the following ways: (1) it is digital and becoming mobile and wireless, rather than paper-based and wired; (2) it is available to citizens/customers twenty-four hours a day, seven days a week; and (3) it provides information and service delivery of various types and degrees of complexity not found in other mass media.[66] E-gov influences relationships between citizens and governments, and provides a tool for enhanced information transfer and more efficient delivery of public services. According to one observer, e-gov needs to be paired with CzRM to be truly of service to the citizens, because the core of CzRM is government for the people in the sense that it provides much more effective, efficient, and simplified public services.[67] As e-gov experiences have increased in popularity and usage, the concept can be examined from a CzRM perspective to determine the possible gains or problems related to this approach as a performance enhancement strategy.

E-government differs from traditional public service delivery in that it provides information and access to service in various ways and degrees of complexity.[68] These definitions are compatible in the sense that they emphasize an important aspect of e-gov: the use of the World Wide Web and other electronic systems to provide citizens directly with information and services. They also converge because the latter definition also includes exchanges between agencies and other units, and also explicitly mentions e-gov as a way to improve efficiency, effectiveness, and transformation. Thus, e-gov can be divided between an internal government-to-government (G2G) perspective as well as external government-to-citizen (G2C) and government-to-business (G2B) perspectives. Internal operations refer to the use of IT for automation, cooperation, and integration among agencies and as an information-gathering and decision-making tool; in this sense, e-gov has existed for several decades. The external use of Internet technology to provide information and deliver G2C e-gov needs to be paired with CzRM to truly be of service to the citizens. Availability of services to citizens via the Internet is less than two decades old and offers the potential for significant changes in the way government services are delivered.

Under ideal circumstances, government should predict all possible services needed by the citizen, and provide the needed service in an integrated solution, for example, website, call center, or "one-stop shop." Governments are recognizing the advantages of having a single website as a **portal**, where citizens can find information about all government services, contact information on public offices, e-mail questions, and so forth. A call center could provide a single telephone access number to contact public offices, thus making it easier for the citizen to know to how to get in contact with government entities. Governmental one-stop shops provide the citizen with a single place to

portal

single entry site for access to, and information about, a specific topic containing numerous links to other related websites.

meet with public servants when they have to do ordinary things such as moving, paying taxes, or applying for a passport or Social Security number.

Implementing CzRM and e-gov within government organizations requires a shift in culture and a reorientation by public administrators. Services provided by the public sector should be focused toward citizens' needs, not merely to meet requirements of administrative and bureaucratic processes. CzRM facilitates government becoming **citizen-centric**. To become truly citizen-centric, government should provide several different channels of access to information and services. This multi-channel integrated service network further increases the possibility of self-service by citizens, which both reduces cost and improves the level of public service. If a citizen can fill out a form online, then that transaction does not take up time of a public servant, who is available to serve others. According to the Deputy Associate Administrator of the GSA Office of Citizen Services and Communications, the cost and quality of service are not proportional. The multi-channel service within CzRM provides a higher quality of service at a lower cost.[69] Thus, adoption of the CzRM approach within the public sector enables citizens to receive a higher level of service at a lower cost. Overall, the best and most inexpensive service quality is provided by a combination of face-to-face, telephone, fax, website self-service, e-mail, and interactive voice response systems. This relationship is illustrated in Figure 10–1.

citizen-centric

an attribute of public-policy decision making focused on meeting the needs of citizens.

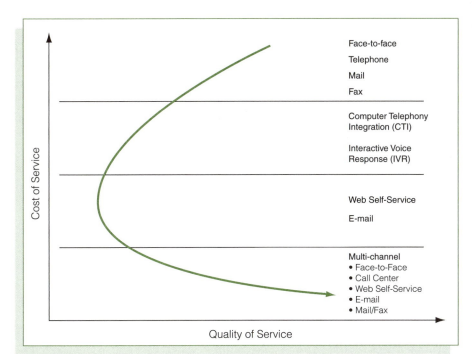

FIGURE 10-1

Relationship Among Cost, Quality, and Type of Service

Source: C. Coleman, "Citizen Relationship Management," *U.S. General Services Administration Newsletter,* Issue 14 (January 2004), p.7.

A multi-channel contact center gives citizens the ability to access government services and information any time they want. In the past, it could be time-consuming to get information about government benefits, and even more difficult to actually apply for them for citizens working from 9 A.M. to 5 P.M. The CzRM perspective within government makes it easier for citizens to receive information about government services and apply for government benefits. In addition to the use of Internet transactions, CzRM also opens the possibility of cost savings from self-service. When specific service costs were assessed, service delivery over the Internet was found to be less expensive than service delivered by persons or manually.[70] In the case of ServiceArizona—a website where citizens can, among other things, renew their vehicle registrations—each transaction made over the Internet costs the government $1.60 whereas the manual transaction cost was $6.60.[71] These and other studies demonstrate the case for self-service government and show the potential for huge government savings on service delivery. At the same time, it is critical to remember that CzRM is not without expenditures to implement, and demands investment in computers, communication infrastructure, software, web design, expert staff, and training of employees. Reduced costs cannot be achieved overnight, and the benefits of the reduced service costs may occur in a different fiscal year from the year the investment was made. For citizens, the overall benefit of a CzRM strategy is better-quality services at lower costs.

Among the concerns about direct government-to-citizen linkages are the following: (1) the NPS assertion that transformation of "citizens" into "customers" could damage democratic governance and public administration; (2) the existence of so-called "digital divides," suggesting that unequal citizen access to education and computer technology may result in unequal distribution of improved public services; and (3) persistent questions about accountability and the expanded role of consultants as intermediaries.

Citizen-Focused Government: Overcoming Digital Divides

The tremendous increase in use of the Internet and social media for government services and information amplifies the risk that government services will be available to some and not others, based on (and corresponding to) other existing inequalities in society.[72] Therefore, another related concern when examining the implementation of e-gov in the public sector is the existence of the **digital divide**. Because they lack the skills and equipment necessary to access the Internet, undereducated, many elderly, and some other citizens do not have the same opportunity to benefit from improved service via the World Wide Web. According to a report by the Kaiser Family Foundation, 75 percent of children from families with median incomes above $75,000 reported having Internet access, compared to only 37 percent of children whose family

digital divide

differential knowledge about available technology caused by inequalities in education, income, and access to computers and the Internet.

incomes were under $20,000.[73] This disparity has been amplified by school failures that increase drop-out rates among low-income and minority students in rural and urban school districts.[74] New and less expensive ICTs such as tablet computers and smart phones are expanding at a faster rate than laptop and desktop computers, and have the potential to close the digital divide.

Comprehensive and well-organized web portal access provides information and extensive links to all branches and levels of government for citizens, businesses, and public officials. E-gov initiatives could thereby result in a type of "negative redistribution," especially if the new forms such as CzRM become fee based, as many citizens would like them to be. Citizens would have to either "pay to go online," or "get in line." Under the NPM perspective, making government more Internet or smart-phone-based, 24/7 accessible, and convenient to all citizens should be combined with a concern for ensuring skills, abilities, and possibilities for all citizens to go online.

Ensuring Accountability with the Use of Intermediaries

Another core value of public administration, as noted in earlier discussions, is accountability. This is a complex concept, and in its narrowest sense, it means holding elected officials accountable for their actions by some kind of external control—that is, political accountability. Reinventing government and the NPS represent two different views of accountability within public administration—different aspects are emphasized. Reinventing government emphasizes empowering administrative leaders and executives, giving them the discretion to be creative and innovative in carrying out government policies. Accountability becomes a matter of satisfying the preferences of individual customers of governmental services. The NPS pays more attention to process and policy, and agencies and officials have to be accountable to citizens, not customers. Differing perceptions of accountability originate from the complex relationship between the values of political and administrative systems (see Chapter 2).

By imposing the entrepreneurial and technical paradigm on public administrative practices, both reinventing government and CzRM tend to emphasize administrative values and a clear distinction between the political and administrative system. The NPS, on the other hand, represents a view suggesting that the "political" and "administrative" should not be regarded as two separate systems with completely distinct values:

> Ultimately, those in government must recognize that public service is not an economic construct, but a political one. That means that issues of service improvement need to be attentive to not only the demands of "customers" but also to the distribution of power in society. Ultimately, in the New Public Service, providing quality service is a first step in the direction of widening public involvement and extending democratic citizenship.[75]

Public service is seen as a continuation of the political system, and therefore representative of the same basic values. Thus, the entrepreneurial paradigm in public administration can have consequences for how we define the basic political values of citizenship, participation, accountability, responsiveness, and democracy in the United States. The perception of whether citizens can be regarded as customers and the idea that public servants should serve their individual interests originate from a different understanding of the relationship between political and the administrative systems, their values, and the issue of accountability.

Thousands of private consultants have developed expertise related to CRM. Whereas the private sector today is influenced by CRM practices, a whole new market, quite a large one, is developing for consulting companies when CzRM is disseminated to the public sector. Consultants have the specialized knowledge that government entities now find useful in order to deal with present challenges. Consultant companies are experts in CRM, not CzRM. Private-sector consultant companies are familiar with implementing a CRM strategy to enhance commercial "drivers," not government drivers. Commercial drivers are bolstering the top line by increasing revenue and sales, increasing

POINT/COUNTERPOINT

THE ISSUE As a widely-implemented strategy for managing a company's interactions with clients, CzRM is used throughout companies and corporations. With the E-government Act of 2002, legislative support was given to the implementation of CzRM practices.

Is CzRM feasible in the public sector?

Arguments *supporting* CzRM in the Public Sector:

- CzRM, ideally, provides much more effective and improved service quality for citizens at lower cost by integrating nonemergency service requests through centralized 311 call systems.

- Government operations are organized according to the needs of citizens and thereby enhance government access for all citizens.

- CzRM practices within the public sector provide opportunity to improve both the level of customer service and accessibility to government services at lower costs to taxpayers.

Arguments *against* CzRM in the Public Sector:

- Implementation tends to be fragmented and disjointed, thereby making it difficult to create a united front.

- CzRM stimulates cooperation with private-sector companies, but at the same time forces public officials to become more aware of different drivers present in the private and public sectors.

- CzRM responds to structural changes taking place in American society in recent years and reinforces the business-oriented model of governance.

the bottom line by reducing the cost of sales and service, and improving customer satisfaction in an effort to increase customer retention. In contrast, government drivers are meeting performance and service goals at the lowest cost to taxpayers, improving quality of service within shrinking budgets, and increasing citizen satisfaction at the lowest cost.

Will Performance Management Lead to Improved Results?

Despite earnest attempts of Presidents Bush and Obama to downsize government and infuse the public sector with the spirit of competition and entrepreneurship, the unique environment of public-policy making cannot be ignored. Political reforms, often recycled from the past, can contribute to positive results, but they may also isolate some groups of citizens and pressure public administrators to respond defensively. Campaign rhetoric always seems to stress the aim of better government. After being elected, however, chief executives attempt to push through their own political agendas. Although elected on promises, politicians are ultimately judged by the electorate on results; the success of administrative policies is inextricably linked to the politics that surround them. Whatever the directions of future developments, there is a continuous need for a discussion of government's role, and more specifically, the role of public administration, in securing both the *quality* and *equity* of government services.

Progress and innovation in democracy result from good policies imposed through power struggles to develop something with a lasting effect. Circumstances and priorities shift, however, reflecting the unpredictable nature of politics that ultimately governs the course of administrative reforms. Management decisions in government are not simply choices to better utilize resources; they are rarely motivated by economic determinants alone, but by political forces as well. Both the Bush and Obama management reform agendas outlined a vision to achieve important procedural goals of their administrations. The ongoing challenge for public administrators is to remain as neutral and detached as possible from the politics of administration and to better understand the results of policy decisions.

Just as President Bill Clinton could not escape the political situation surrounding and eventually enveloping his administration, the environment had a significant impact on the outcome of the PMA. When George W. Bush ran for office in 2000, almost no one foresaw the dramatic events of September 11, 2001, or how he would choose to react to them. His consequent actions, especially the decision to aggressively pursue the war on terrorism on Iraqi soil, overshadowed much of the overall Bush reform agenda. Management decisions come into play with the creation of government agencies with new 24/7 missions, such as the Department of Homeland Security and the Office of the Director of National Intelligence (DNI). Issues of particular importance involved agency reorganization, contracting out, congressional oversight, and personnel reallocations. Barack Obama admits to suffering a clear loss to Tea Party Republicans in the 2010 midterm elections. How this opposition will impact his remaining time in office, his efforts to further strengthen administrative performance, and his 2012 re-election bid remains to be seen.

The proving ground for PM reforms has dramatically changed; the performance of many U.S. public agencies is now measured in practical terms by assisting citizens whose lives have been disrupted by floods, hurricanes, fires, tornados, and snow storms, as well as protecting domestic security and fighting the war against terrorism. Despite campaign rhetoric about smaller government and more efficient management, controversy over the best strategies for managing performance reflects the century-old debate about the "proper" relationships among politics, policy, and private management of public-sector functions. Public administrators are responsible for analyzing options and recommending policies to elected political leaders who, in turn, decide which alternatives to adopt. Rather than assuming the ideological superiority of one model over another, public managers need to be more informed about fact-based strategic options that best achieve the goals of specific public-policy areas. For example, which model, or combination of approaches, best achieves airline transportation security while overseeing day-to-day airport operations and also maintaining responsibility for public expenditures? Is the customer-centered entrepreneurial approach applicable to all sectors of public management? And if it is not, how do public managers choose where (and when) to apply it?

Senior public administrators are cross-pressured by conflicting ideological demands and must understand the theoretical as well as practical foundations of alternative PM strategies. Compared to the early 1990s, greater numbers of managers now possess the authority, as well as the knowledge and "tools," to improve performance. Without objective, research-based data, political forces nearly always restrict decision-making options and trump management reforms. Administrators and policy makers need objective data to decide whether to support the incremental public-oriented reforms of the last decade, encourage the greater use of private-market-driven options (such as charter schools, contracting out, privatization, or vouchers), or form cooperative partnerships with NGOs. Such decisions require solid theory-based research findings to bolster support for recommended policy changes and to provide advice to elected officials. Ultimately, citizens exercising democratic freedoms and responsibilities at the ballot box will be the final judges of the success or failure of such efforts.

Summary

During the past two decades, the federal government has initiated comprehensive and controversial efforts supporting downsizing, e-gov, reinvention, and results-oriented management. The reinvention movement attempted to improve performance by promoting competitive, customer-driven, and market-based solutions to perceived inefficiencies in the delivery of government services. The NPR committed resources to study and recommend strategies for reinventing government and drastically altering the ways in which the federal government conducts its affairs and interacts with its "customers" (citizens). Various strategies and tactics have been devised for conscientious managers who want to improve their administrative operations and their responsiveness to customers. Customer service is becoming an important productivity improvement strategy in many governments.

Concern for government productivity and alternative sources of delivering services is on the rise. Productivity of government programs has taken on increasing political, economic, and social significance within an economic framework of scarce resources and downsizing. Links between productivity and other aspects of management, such as efficiency, goal setting, and strategic planning, have also been stressed. Under conditions of limited resources (of all kinds), productivity in government and elsewhere will continue to be important.

Citizen demands for lower taxes and political campaign rhetoric calling for leaner, more efficient government encourage federal executive agencies to achieve these goals by changing the way they define performance, measure productivity, and improve results. Congress passed administrative reforms mandating budget deficit reductions, personnel caps, and the use of results-oriented systems to achieve these goals. President Obama has emphasized ICTs, including social media, to better inform citizens and encourage participation.

In many states, far less concern exists about who delivers service than about how to meet current service demands and employee payrolls. Many states and some local governments are facing severe deficits in current budget projections because of declines in income and sales tax revenues, and because of lower property tax collections due to falling real estate prices; many are being forced to increase public school class sizes, raise user fees, reduce social services, and release prisoners.

Discussion Questions

1. Which units of government have developed the true capacity to measure performance? By what means do they achieve this goal? What new systems, tools, or techniques are required to measure performance effectively?

2. What approaches exist to improve government productivity? What problems exist in this endeavor? In your view, how important is it that we improve productivity of government programs? Why?

3. Have reform efforts such as the NPR or PMA made any difference in public opinion about the productivity and effectiveness of government programs?

4. What incentives can public administrators use to sustain these reforms after refocusing their mission and implementing PM systems and techniques?

5. How will the customer-service approach to government impact bureaucratic processes and relations with elected officials?

6. How do administrators (public and private) manage across unclear lines of demarcation or "fuzzy boundaries" between government agencies and other entities?

7. What can be learned from state and local contracting and public–private partnerships for the design and construction of public facilities that have led to innovative practices, shared efficiencies and risks, and improved delivery of services?

8. Does the market model eliminate participatory democracy from public-sector management? How will performance be measured on this dimension, and who will interpret the results?

9. If public administrators withdraw from direct contact with citizens by outsourcing or privatization, who is accountable to whom and for what results?

10. What difficulties might a public manager face when trying to implement new management techniques borrowed from the private sector?

Key Terms and Concepts

results-oriented, *418*

productivity, *419*

Geographic Information Systems (GIS), *421*

social media, *421*

Government Performance and Results Act (GPRA), *421*

performance management (PM), *422*

Government Performance and Results Modernization Act of 2010, *423*

reinventing government, *424*

National Performance Review (NPR), *424*

National Partnership for Reinventing Government (NPRG), *425*

New Public Management (NPM), *425*

New Public Service (NPS), *426*

customer-service standards, *427*

Malcolm Baldrige National Quality Awards, *429*

Strategy for American Innovation, *429*

benchmarking, *430*

claim-and-blame strategy, *432*

President's Management Agenda (PMA), *434*

chief information officers (CIOs), *436*

Office of Electronic Government, *440*

Federal Information Security Management Act (FISMA), *440*

chief technology officer (CTO), *442*

chief performance officer (CPO), *442*

Performance Assessment Rating Tool (PART), *443*

citizen relationship management (CzRM), *449*

portal, *450*

citizen-centric, *451*

digital divide, *452*

Suggested Readings

Barzelay, Michael, with Babak Armajani. *Breaking through Bureaucracy: A New Vision for Managing in Government.* Berkeley, Calif.: University of California Press, 1992.

Beam, George. *Quality Public Management: What It Is and How It Can Be Improved and Advanced.* Chicago, Ill.: Rowman & Littlefield, 2001.

Behn, Robert. *Rethinking Democratic Accountability.* Washington, D.C.: Brookings Institution Press, 2000.

Bhatnagar, Subhash. *E-Government: From Vision to Implementation—A Practical Guide with Case Studies.* Thousand Oaks, Calif.: Sage, 2004.

Boyne, George A., Kenneth J. Meier, Laurence O'Toole, and Richard M. Walker. *Public Service Performance: Perspectives on Measurement and Management.* New York: Cambridge University Press, 2006.

Callehan, Kathe. *Elements of Effective Government: Measurement, Accountability, and Participation.* Boca Raton, Fla.: CRC Press, 2007.

Chadwick, Andrew and Phillip Howard. *The Routledge Handbook for Internet Politics.* London and New York: Routledge, 2009.

Denhardt, Janet V. and Robert B. Denhardt. *The New Public Service: Serving, not Steering.* Armonk, New York: M.E. Sharpe, 2011.

Enos, Darryl D. *Performance Improvement: Making It Happen.* 2nd ed. Boca Raton, Fla.: CRC Press, 2007.

Fountain, Jane. *Building the Virtual State.* Washington, D.C.: Brookings Institution Press, 2001.

Gormley, William T., Jr., and Steven J. Balla. *Bureaucracy and Democracy: Performance and Accountability.* Washington, D.C.: CQ Press, 2007.

Greene, J. *Cities and Privatization: Prospects for the New Century.* Upper Saddle River, N.J.: Prentice Hall, 2009.

Gronland, Ake. *Electronic Government: Design, Applications and Management.* Hershey, Penn.: Idea Group Publishing, 2002.

Heeks, Richard. *Reinventing Government in the Information Age.* London: Routledge, 2001.

Hodge, Graeme A. *Privatization: An International Review of Performance.* Boulder, Colo.: Westview Press, 2000.

Homberg, Vincent. *Understanding E-Government: Information Systems in Public Administration.* London: Routledge Taylor and Francis Group, 2008.

Ingraham, Patricia W., and Laurence E. Lynn, Jr., eds. *The Art of Governance: Analyzing Management and Administration.* Washington, D.C.: Georgetown University Press, 2004.

Ingraham, Patricia W., James R. Thompson, and Ronald Sanders, eds. *Transforming Government: Lessons from the Reinvention Laboratories.* San Francisco, Calif.: Jossey-Bass, 1997.

Kamensky, John M., and Albert Morales, eds. *Managing for Results 2005.* Lanham, Md.: Rowman & Littlefield, 2004.

Kettl, Donald F., and John J. DiIulio, eds. *Inside the Reinvention Machine.* Washington, D.C.: Brookings Institution Press, 1995.

Klitgaard, Robert, and Paul C. Light. *High-Performance Government: Structure, Leadership, Incentives.* Santa Monica, Calif.: Rand Corporation. 2005.

Klofstad, Casey.A. *Civic Talk: Peers, Politics, and the Future of Democracy.* Philadelphia, Penn.: Temple University Press, 2011.

Light, Paul C. *Monitoring Government.* Washington, D.C.: Brookings Institution Press, 1993.

Mayer-Schonberger, Victor and David Lazer. *Governance and Information Technology: From Electronic Government to Information Government.* Cambridge, Mass.: The MIT Press, 2007.

Milakovich, Michael E. *Digital Governance: New Technologies for Improvement Public Service.* New York and London: Routledge, 2012.

Norris, Donald. *Current Issues and Trends in E-Government Research.* Hershey, Penn.: Idea Publishing Group, 2007.

Noveck, Beth Simone. *Wiki Government: How Technology Can Make Government Better, Democracy Stronger and Citizens More Powerful.* Washington, D.C.: Brookings Institution Press, 2009.

Radin, Beryl. *Challenging the Performance Management Movement: Accountability, Complexity, and Democratic Values.* Washington, D.C.: Georgetown University Press, 2006.

Rosenau, P. V. *Public-Private Policy Partnerships.* Cambridge, Mass.: MIT Press, 2000.

Stanton, Thomas H., and Benjamin Ginsberg, eds. *Making Government Manageable: Executive Organization and Management in the Twenty-First Century.* Baltimore: Johns Hopkins University Press, 2004.

White, Jay. *Managing Information in the Public Sector.* New York: M.E. Sharpe, 2007.

Government Regulation and Administrative Law

We're also going to have to look at how it is that we shredded so many regulations. We did not set up a twenty-first century regulatory framework to deal with these [economic] problems. And that, in part, has to do with the economic philosophy that says that regulation is always bad.

Barack Obama
October 2008

Good or bad, regulating various aspects of business and society is a long-standing and often controversial aspect of government, especially at the national level. Much of what the national government does (or fails to do) has an impact on individual citizens, private corporations and other business enterprises, agricultural producers and marketers, foreign governments, labor unions, and state and local governments. But, as discussed in Chapter 9, some functions are explicitly regulative in nature, setting and enforcing the rules for many private—especially economic—activities.

As we shall see in this chapter, the first national regulatory efforts in the late 1800s were aimed at punishment for, and then prevention of, abuses in the marketplace—antitrust violations and price gouging, for example. During the twentieth century, government regulation became even more extensive, focusing not only on *preventing* certain kinds of practices but also on *requiring* that certain operating standards can and should be met. For example, before they are marketed, new products must meet industry safety standards for their intended purposes. Examples of operating standards are accuracy in information supplied to consumers—the truth-in-labeling, truth-in-packaging, or truth-in-lending requirements, enacted mainly in the 1970s. Contradictory policies have contributed to greater regulation in some areas, such as airport transportation security, automobile fuel economy, financial services, health insurance companies, and mortgage loan practices—and far less regulation in other domestic public policy areas, such as banking, equal employment opportunity, and public housing.

In the past fifty years, more than a dozen new regulatory agencies have been created at the national and state government levels, following the passage of scores of new regulatory statutes. Regulatory actions touch virtually every part of our lives—our transportation safety (air bags, airport security procedures, seat belts, aircraft maintenance and safety standards, freight rates), the food we eat, what can or cannot go into our beverages (health warnings for products containing saccharin and aspartame), medications that may be used to treat disease, air and water quality standards, consumer health care, safety, and working conditions. In addition, a number of recent regulations have been of a different type from the previous ones. There are significant differences between "traditional" regulations, which emphasize competition in the economic marketplace, price controls, and service enhancement, and "new" regulations which are designed to prevent harm from a process, a product, or their side effects.[1] New regulations incorporate social as well as economic goals into the regulatory process, and they have been much farther-reaching in their effects.

Some government actions that are seemingly unrelated to regulating private lives, in fact, do so. These include local building codes and zoning laws; government housing loan programs with minimum income requirements, effectively cutting off many poorer citizens from a chance to buy homes; immigration and national security applications limiting (especially) graduate students from other nations; school desegregation guidelines; equal opportunity requirements in employment, housing, and education; nursing home inspections; minimum-wage laws; hygiene, handicapped access, and safety requirements in the workplace; and tax policies at all levels of government. National and state energy policies touch most areas of our lives; including air and automobile travel the cost and availability of energy resources such as gasoline, natural gas, and home-heating fuel; gasoline consumption and mileage requirements; home insulation; nuclear power; and so on. Regulatory processes now attempt to deal with global problems such as those related to energy consumption and pollution, including mileage requirements that will encourage the U.S. auto industry to produce more fuel-efficient cars by 2020. In addition, state and local regulation of banks, insurance companies, real estate, and public utilities directly affects consumers' pocketbooks.

The whole subject of government regulation in a "free-enterprise" capitalist economy can be highly complicated and is always controversial. Some contend that the most effective regulator is **free-market competition** among those seeking to attract the buying public. They argue that **government regulation**, by interfering with the marketplace, works to the disadvantage of both consumers and producers. Advocates of government regulation, however, see greater need to monitor and guide the course of competition; they believe that a completely unrestrained market will inevitably lead to **monopolistic practices**, higher costs, underserved segments of society, and lower-quality goods and services. In the twentieth century, the national government tried increasingly to strike a balance between regulating producers and permitting, indeed encouraging, competition in the marketplace, supporting both the right of consumers to purchase products that meet certain quality and safety standards and the right of producers to make a reasonable profit.

free-market competition

basis of U.S. and other free-enterprise economic systems in which the means of production and distribution of goods and services are owned by private corporations or individuals, and the government's role in the economy is minimal.

government regulation

government activity designed to monitor and guide private economic competition; specific actions (characterized as *economic regulation*) have included placing limits on producers' prices and practices, and promoting commerce through grants or subsidies; other actions emerging more recently (termed *social regulation*) have included regulating conditions under which goods and services are produced and attempting to minimize product hazards and risks to consumers.

monopolistic practices

situation in which a certain company or group of companies controls the production and distribution system of a market to exclude all other competitors.

independent regulatory boards and commissions (IRCs)

entities which are delegated authority by Congress to enforce both executive and judicial authority in the application of government regulations.

Regulatory activities are conducted by a wide variety of government entities. The earliest regulatory bodies—the **independent regulatory boards and commissions** (usually referred to as IRCs) of the national government—first appeared in the late nineteenth century and subsequently expanded their numbers and activities. Independent regulatory bodies are similar to other administrative entities (such as cabinet departments) in operating under delegated legislative authority, exhibiting functional overlap, and being influenced by political considerations. They differ in the kind of work for which they are legally responsible and in structural design. Regulation has been an increasing responsibility of administrative bodies housed within cabinet departments or standing independent of any other administrative "home." This chapter discusses their origins, both societal and political; analyzes the formal and political settings in which they operate, and with what consequences; and discusses some of the most volatile issues concerning government regulation during the past fifty years.

administrative law

important body of U.S. law pertaining to the legal authority of public administrative entities to perform their duties, and to the limits necessary to control those agencies; administrative law has been created both by judicial decisions (especially in the national government courts) and by statute (principally in the form of Administrative Procedure Acts, enacted by both national and state governments).

We will also discuss a related, and increasingly important, area of public administration: **administrative law**. All public administrators are governed in their operations by this body of law, as well as by legislative and chief-executive enforcement directives. Administrative law is particularly significant in the regulatory process because these written pronouncements bear directly on private rights and obligations. Rulings are also subject to judicial review and can be challenged in court. Viewing the relationship between regulation and administrative law another way, we might say that regulation involves certain kinds of constraints that government places on private citizens, groups, and institutions, whereas administrative law is concerned with the constraints government places on itself. After discussing government regulation, we will take up administrative law and attempt to place the relationship between the two in its proper perspective.

It is especially important to understand the terminology used in this chapter because of the number and variety of government entities currently engaged in some form of regulation. The term *regulatory agency* will be used to refer to a regulatory body headed by a single individual (most commonly a director or an administrator); a *regulatory commission* is headed by a group of commissioners (or, sometimes, board members); the term **regulatory body** will refer to both kinds of structures. These terms are consistent with the formal titles of such entities. [2] For example, the Environmental Protection Agency (EPA) is headed by a single administrator, unlike the Federal Communications Commission (FCC). These usages will help us understand some of the differences among different types of regulators, in their operations as well as their formal structures.

regulatory body

refers to all types of dependent and independent regulatory boards, commissions, and executive entities with regulatory authority.

The Rise (and Fall?) of Government Regulation

Historically, government regulatory activities have taken one of two forms: (1) putting certain limits on prices and practices of those who produce commercial goods and services, and (2) promoting commerce through incentives, grants, or subsidies, on the theory that such payments are a public investment that will yield greater returns for the consuming public in the form of better goods and services. Prime examples are subsidies for rail transportation, farmers, and oil companies. The second of these overall forms of regulatory activity has a longer history than the first.

Regulation of interstate commerce under Congress's direction was a constitutional power of the national government (Article I, Section 8) right from the start. Yet, for virtually all of our first century as a nation, responsibility fell to the states to carry on most of whatever regulation existed—for example, transportation tolls on and across rivers, prices farmers had to pay to grist mills and cotton gins, water rates, and railroad fares. In the post–Civil War period of industrialization, the national government gradually assumed more responsibility for both controlling and promoting commerce, although the states still played an important role in developing and testing ways of controlling prices and commercial practices. As the emerging national economy grew and flourished, however, pressure began to mount for the national government to enter more extensively into the regulatory arena. This pressure stemmed from strong demands that the abusive practices of the railroad industry, in particular, be brought under control. State regulatory agencies, some of which were quite active, lacked jurisdiction to deal with enterprises that crossed state lines (such as oil companies and railroads). Beginning with the New Deal (1932–1939), the national government came to exercise primary responsibility for both controlling and promoting economic activity. Although the states are still primary regulators of many industries, such as health care, insurance, and real estate and secondary regulators of industries such as banking, Washington is now the center of regulatory activity.

Making government regulatory policy has been regarded as a legislative power under the Constitution. Yet Congress and most state and local legislatures have found it difficult to write all the varied and detailed provisions that are a necessary part of governing a dynamic and complex society. There are two dimensions of the problem for a legislative body. First, most legislatures lack the time and technical expertise required to establish detailed rules and regulations on such complex subjects as air safety; nuclear energy; monetary policy; or offshore deep-water oil drilling and exploration for, and marketing of, natural gas. As these and other areas of policy became more important, especially in crisis situations, it became increasingly necessary to create regulatory bodies able to deal with them. Second, even if legislatures had the time and skills, a large, collective decision-making body lacks the flexibility needed to adjust existing rules and regulations to changing conditions, again justifying creation of other specialized entities to concentrate on each area.

Thus, even in the limited national government of the nineteenth century, it was apparent that it would be necessary to delegate authority to administrative agencies, with Congress monitoring their operations and adjusting their authority but doing little actual regulation. This pattern was followed throughout the twentieth century as well, and continues today at all levels of government. In a very real sense, then, regulation emerges as the outcome of legislative delegation of authority (see Chapter 2). Thus, any strengths or weaknesses of regulatory agencies and processes can be attributed, in the first instance, to actions of local, state, and national legislatures.

The first major institutional development in the national government was the creation in 1887 of the Interstate Commerce Commission (ICC) in response to public disenchantment with the railroads, especially in the Mississippi Valley and the West. Unlike the eastern portion of the country, where numerous rail lines were engaged in vigorous competition, the nation's midsection and expanding West were served by a small number of railroads that engaged in monopolistic practices. Establishment of the now-defunct ICC signaled a clear change from the prevailing notion of governmental action taken to punish unlawful acts after they had occurred. This was the first step in preventing such acts from occurring and doing so by laying down rules that applied to a class of industries and actions, relieving government of the need to proceed on the previous case-by-case basis in the courts.

Public pressure for controlling industry became stronger in the late 1800s and early 1900s, led by men such as James Weaver of the Greenback Party in the 1880 presidential election and, especially, populist Democrat (and three-time presidential candidate) William Jennings Bryan. The "great trustbuster," Theodore Roosevelt, was later followed in the White House by Woodrow Wilson; both men favored government measures to maintain economic competition and fair trade practices. In response to the stock market crash of 1929 and the other economic woes of the Great Depression, Franklin Roosevelt opened the way for even more stringent and far-reaching regulation. These individuals and their allies, and the policies they promoted, led to significant increases in the scope of national government regulation.

The **Sherman Antitrust Act** of 1890 made it illegal to conspire to fix fares, rates, and prices or to monopolize an industry. Although enforcement mechanisms were not provided for in the original act, in 1903 the Antitrust Division of the U.S. **Justice Department** (which is not an independent regulatory agency) was created to directly enforce the Sherman Act. This proved difficult because of unclear language in the law and lack of authority delegated to the division. The result was increasing reliance on the courts to interpret legislative language and, some maintained, an inappropriate and perhaps excessive involvement of the courts in direct policy making. With delegation of authority to the ICC as a precedent, Congress attempted to solve the problem by creating another independent regulatory agency modeled after the ICC. In 1914, the **Federal Trade Commission (FTC)** was established to assist in antitrust enforcement, principally by interpreting and enforcing provisions of the **Clayton Act**, which had been passed the same year and which prohibited price discrimination if the purpose or effect of such discrimination was to

Sherman Antitrust Act

first major antitrust legislation, passed in 1890, which made it illegal to fix prices or to monopolize an industry.

Justice Department

cabinet-level executive agency responsible for the enforcement of federal law.

Federal Trade Commission (FTC)

independent regulatory commission charged with enforcing antitrust acts, including the Sherman and Clayton Acts, to protect customers against unfair trade practices.

Clayton Act

1914 law that prohibits price discrimination to eliminate competition or create a monopoly.

lessen competition or to create a monopoly.[3] The FTC's involvement eased the burden on the courts, although it did not remove it entirely; the commission has been active continually over the years in settling antitrust questions. The FTC was also given responsibility for controlling deceptive trade practices, but until 1938, this was not a primary function.

Subsequently, other entities were also established, modeled after the ICC and FTC. The Federal Power Commission (FPC) was created in 1920 to regulate interstate sale of wholesale electric energy and the transportation and sale, along with rates, of natural gas; in 1977, the FPC was reorganized as the **Federal Energy Regulatory Commission (FERC)** and made part of the newly created Department of Energy. The FCC, established in 1934, regulates civilian radio and television communication (except for rates), as well as interstate and international communications by wire, cable, and radio (including rates). The FCC assigns frequencies and licenses operators of radio and television stations and has become increasingly involved in issues concerning cable television franchises and pay television. The Securities and Exchange Commission (SEC), also founded in 1934, was one means used by the government to try to prevent a repetition of the 1929 stock market crash. The Civil Aeronautics Board (CAB) was created in 1938 to regulate airline passenger fares and freight rates, promote and subsidize air transportation, and award passenger service routes to commercial airlines. The CAB was disestablished on January 1, 1985—the first major regulatory agency to close its doors permanently—and its functional responsibilities were divided among the Federal Aviation Administration (FAA), the Department of Transportation (DOT), and the National Transportation Safety Board (NTSB).

There are other, similarly organized commissions. Also, as government activity generally has increased, regulative functions have come to be exercised by other types of agencies as well. It is possible to play "Washington alphabet soup" with the EPA, FAA, FERC, OSHA (Occupational Safety and Health Administration), and FDA (Food and Drug Administration), to name only a few (see Table 11–1). Important areas of regulatory responsibility are under these entities' jurisdictions.

Mention also should be made of state regulatory agencies, many of which are patterned after those at the national level, and local regulatory activities that have an impact on certain local economic enterprises.[4] As noted previously, states have primary responsibility for regulating insurance companies and are involved secondarily in the regulation of banks. States also examine and license physicians, insurance agents, funeral homes, mortgage brokers, and real estate agents, and certify those qualified to practice medicine and law. In highly technical and professional fields, such as medicine and law, the respective professional associations have key roles in setting state standards for entry into the professions. Indeed, in some instances, formal state decisions amount merely to ratifying standard-setting actions taken by professional associations (the *self-regulatory* category of public policy noted in Chapter 9).

Federal Energy Regulatory Commission (FERC)

regulates and oversees energy industries in the economic, environmental, and safety interests of the American public.

| **TABLE 11–1** | Selected Major U.S. Regulatory Bodies* |

Consumer Product Safety Commission (CPSC) www.cpsc.gov
Founded in 1972. Develops and enforces uniform safety standards for consumer products, and can recall hazardous products.
Budget: $105 million   Personnel: 530

Equal Employment Opportunity Commission (EEOC) www.eeoc.gov
Founded in 1964. Investigates and rules on charges of racial and other arbitrary discrimination by employers and unions, in all aspects of employment. Updates current legal issues and regulations on employment discrimination and labor unions.
Budget: $367 million   Personnel: 2,385

Environmental Protection Agency (EPA) www.epa.gov
Founded in 1970. The mission of the EPA is to protect human health and to safeguard the natural environment—air, water, and land—on which life depends. Issues and enforces pollution control standards regarding air, water, solid waste, pesticides, radiation, and toxic substances.
Budget: $10.2 billion   Personnel: 17,278

Federal Communications Commission (FCC) www.fcc.gov
Founded in 1934. Regulates interstate and international radio, television, cable television, telephone, telegraph, and satellite communications; licenses U.S. radio and television stations; offers information on legislation, technological advancements, and media systems.
Budget: $335 million   Personnel: 1,924

Federal Energy Regulatory Commission (FERC) www.ferc.gov
Founded in 1977, FERC regulates interstate transmission of electricity, natural gas, and oil; reviews proposals to build liquefied natural gas (LNG) terminals and interstate natural-gas pipelines, and licenses hydropower projects. The **Energy Policy Act of 2005** gave FERC additional responsibilities.
Budget: $298 million   Personnel: 1,528

Federal Trade Commission (FTC) www.ftc.gov
Founded in 1914. Regulates business competition, including some antitrust enforcement, and acts to prevent unfair and deceptive trade practices.
Budget: $287 million   Personnel: 1,495

Food and Drug Administration (FDA) www.fda.gov
Founded in 1930. Located in the Department of Health and Human Services; conducts testing and evaluation programs—and sets standards of safety/efficacy—for foods, food additives and colorings, over-the-counter drugs, and medical devices; certifies some products for marketing; and conducts research in other areas such as radiological health, veterinary medicine, and the effects of toxic chemical substances.
Budget: $3.2 billion   Personnel: 9,416

U.S. International Trade Commission (ITC) www.usitc.gov
Founded in 1916. Renamed in 1974. Advises the president as to the potential economic effect on domestic industry and consumers of modifications to trade barriers. Investigates the impact of increased imports on domestic industries, unfair practice, and imports of agricultural products that interfere with U.S. Department of Agriculture programs.
Budget: $83 million   Personnel: 425

Energy Policy Act of 2005

a comprehensive "pork-barrel" law that also attempts to meet growing energy needs by providing tax incentives and loan guarantees for energy production of various types; before Hurricane Katrina, it was estimated to cost the U.S Treasury $12.3 billion in tax expenditures and lost revenue through 2015.

(continued)

TABLE 11-1   Selected Major U.S. Regulatory Bodies (continued)

National Labor Relations Board (NLRB) www.nlrb.gov
Founded in 1935. Conducts elections to determine labor union representation; prevents and remedies unfair labor practices.
Budget: $283 million   Personnel: 1,632

Nuclear Regulatory Commission (NRC) www.nrc.gov
Founded in 1975. Issues licenses for nuclear power plant construction and operation, and monitors safety aspects of plant operations; provides information on nuclear power plant safety, regulations, operations, and construction.
Budget: $1.07723 billion   Personnel: 3,750

Occupational Safety and Health Administration (OSHA) www.osha.gov
Founded in 1970. Located in the Department of Labor; develops safety and health standards for private business and industry; monitors compliance and proposes penalties for noncompliance.
Budget: $486 million   Personnel: 2,150

Securities and Exchange Commission (SEC) www.sec.gov
Founded in 1934. Regulates issuance and exchanges of stocks and securities; also regulates investment and holding companies. Under the **Sarbanes–Oxley Act of 2002**, the SEC was reauthorized to aggressively investigate and prosecute CEOs and corporate boards who defraud investors.
Budget: $1.026 billion   Personnel: 3,932

Sarbanes–Oxley Act of 2002

created to protect investors by improving the accuracy and reliability of corporate disclosures. The act establishes a corporate accounting oversight board, and requires auditor independence, corporate responsibility, and enhanced financial disclosure.

*Budget figures shown represent net budget authority; personnel figures represent full-time equivalent employees (2010 estimated).

Source: *Budget of the United States Government, 2010, 2011, 2012 Appendix.* (Washington, D.C.: U.S. Government Printing Office, 2010). http://www.whitehouse.gov/omb/budget/fy2010/pdf/appendix/lab.pdf.

Other state entities also have regulative impact. As noted earlier, public utility commissions have a great deal to do with setting intrastate retail rates for electricity and natural gas. Some also have the authority to investigate whether gasoline stations are "gouging" customers during periods of rapidly increasing fuel costs. State commerce commissions regulate commercial activity occurring entirely within state boundaries and can have a substantial influence on shipping rates and other shipping practices. Liquor control boards (in some states, there are state-run "package stores" or liquor outlets), recreation departments, and environmental protection agencies are further examples of state entities that affect private economic enterprise. These can all act on their own authority and initiative without being subject to decisions made at the national level. In some areas of regulation, however, state and national agencies have collaborated on standard setting, accounting systems, and the like, contributing to the patterns of specialized intergovernmental contacts discussed in Chapter 3. Examples include cooperation prior to the mid-1960s between the ICC, FDA, FCC, and FTC and their respective state counterparts, and more recently, between state and national homeland security, counterterrorism, and law enforcement agencies.[5]

At the local level, regulation of business activities most often involves granting licenses for operating taxis and establishments such as hotels, restaurants, and taverns. Other kinds of local regulative activities, however, can be very significant, such as housing and building codes, zoning ordinances, and interagency transportation planning. There has been little research on local government regulatory impacts, which may be an unfair reflection on their scope and importance.

The New Social Regulation

The distinction between economic (old) and social (new) regulation (Table 11–2) merits further examination. While "the old-style economic regulation typically focuses on markets, rates, and the obligation to serve, the new-style social regulation affects the conditions under which goods and services are produced, and the physical characteristics of products that are manufactured."[6]

TABLE 11–2   Selected Regulatory Bodies Engaging in "Old" and "New" Regulation*

Old
Civil Aeronautics Board (1938–1985)
Federal Communications Commission
Federal Power Commission (until 1977)
Securities and Exchange Commission (until 2002)
Federal Trade Commission

New
Consumer Financial Protection Bureau
Consumer Product Safety Commission
Equal Employment Opportunity Commission
Environmental Protection Agency
Federal Communications Commission
Financial Stability Oversight Council
Federal Energy Regulatory Commission (since 1977)
Food and Drug Administration
International Trade Commission
National Labor Relations Board
Nuclear Regulatory Commission
Occupational Safety and Health Administration
Securities and Exchange Commission (after 2002)

*Many of the agencies listed here also appear in Table 11–1, classified according to their size and principal responsibilities.

Source: From Lawrence S. White, Reforming Regulations and Problems © 1981, pp. 32–33, 36–39. Adapted by permission of Pearson Education Inc., Upper Saddle River, NJ.

As of the early 1960s, the national government had significant economic regulatory responsibilities in just four areas: antitrust, financial institutions, transportation, and communications. In each of these areas, the policy objective was to prevent or mitigate the economic damage associated with provision of goods or services, typically within a single industry. Thus, while regulatory agencies might possess broad-ranging discretionary authority to influence actions within a specific economic sector, their standards and guidelines generally did not affect the economy as a whole.[7]

How can we account for so drastic a shift in both the substance and the processes of government regulation? One explanation is that, in the late 1950s, there was increased public concern about perceived threats to human life, such as carcinogens (cancer-causing agents such as air pollution and asbestos), and about how pollutants affected ecosystems. This resulted in a series of social regulatory initiatives that thrust government into new areas of health, consumer affairs, environmental protection, and many aspects of safety regulation (for example, food, transportation, and in the workplace). These initiatives were backed by the growing environmental and consumer movements, as well as "the activities of other specialized interest groups mobilized at least in part by heightened awareness of risks."[8] Thus, social regulation (unlike economic regulation) centrally addresses minimizing, or at least reducing, "public involuntary and occasionally even voluntary exposure to risk."[9] Congressional response to these public and scientific pressures has taken several forms: delegation of broad discretionary powers to regulatory agencies (as with the Clean Air and Clean Water Acts); defining and dealing with problems in narrower terms (for example, regulation of potentially hazardous chemicals); and enlarging Congress's own "role in determining how the goals of regulation will be attained."[10] (Note again the importance of the role of Congress, and the significance of legislative delegation of authority as the basis for regulatory activity.) Although the total number of "regulators" has declined slightly during the past twenty years, almost 75 percent are employed by federal social regulatory agencies. Some of these initiatives contributed to the emergence of intergovernmental regulation, discussed in Chapter 3.

Dealing with the problem of risk reduction, however, has not been easy. A fundamental difficulty has been how to determine the degree of risk involved in use of, or exposure to, a product or substance (such as alcohol, firearms, saccharin, caffeine, or tobacco), and at what point a level of product risk becomes unacceptable (as a general standard). Compounding the problem are the high economic stakes involved in risk assessment; a finding of risk has come to carry with it the real possibility of a product being banned or otherwise restricted in the marketplace. Furthermore, the need for technical expertise, and for agreed-on criteria, in defining risk was joined to the issues mentioned earlier. Because of the economic stakes involved, however, little agreement has been reached on risk criteria. Finally, with expert opinion looming ever larger in disputes over just how much risk a given product or substance entails, the

social regulatory initiatives

government actions in the late 1960s and early 1970s to regulate new social areas involving individual health, environmental protection, and public safety; resulted in the creation of several regulatory bodies.

spectacle of "dueling experts" (in public debates, legislative testimony, agency reports, and the like) has become more frequent. Thus, the stature of experts and of their knowledge became a sub-issue within the larger context of regulatory politics. Numerous issues have emerged in connection with regulating products that many of us voluntarily use. The question of involuntary exposure to products such as hazardous chemicals, secondhand smoke from tobacco, automotive exhaust, or toxic wastes only compounded the matter, especially with regard to the potential urgency of making new regulations and rules for risk reduction. In sum, as even the most casual observer of recent American politics can testify, considerable tension has characterized the regulatory arena, most of it centering on the new focus—and style—of regulating private economic activity.

Why Government Regulation Has Developed: Other Perspectives

The extent of regulatory activity prompts us to ask what other factors account for its development. One way to explain it is a scenario of deliberate decisions by bureaucrats and their political allies to expand their sphere of influence over private-sector activities. This explanation is often heard from conservatives to criticize regulations which they oppose. Although this scenario may have occurred in some instances, it is not a generally applicable explanation. More important is the growth of "red tape" as government has responded to pressures for dealing with a broader range of societal problems or meeting specific social objectives.[11] The average citizen, confronted with nuisances (such as noise pollution) and outright menaces (such as toxic wastes), reacts by saying, "There ought to be a law. . . ." If enough organized opinion exists, pressure can be brought to bear on government to enact such laws. Regulations have become more widespread in just this way, focused particularly on two noteworthy social purposes—demonstrating compassion for the individual and ensuring representativeness and fairness in governing processes.

Motives of compassion have led to rules and regulations aimed at protecting people from each other—governing relations between buyers and sellers, employers and employees, universities and students, tenants and landlords, or lenders and borrowers. Government has also been asked to alleviate various kinds of human distress—through Supplemental Security Income (SSI) payments; aid to the disabled, the handicapped, and the elderly; aid to the poor; disaster relief; toxic-waste cleanup; and unemployment compensation. In all such cases, rules and regulations accompany basic legislation to make it possible to administer such programs fairly and equitably. The national government, in particular, has acted to prevent major disruptions in national (and international) economic and political systems—stepping in to mediate labor-management disputes in vital industries, attempting to bring inflation under control, protecting supplies of vital natural resources, or resolving international conflicts that menace the peace. It is, of course, expedient politically for leaders to respond to pleas for governmental assistance, but that may only increase the proliferation of rules and regulations accompanying government action.

The broader use of regulations also stems from efforts to increase public representativeness in government decision-making processes as one way to maintain popular control and equitable treatment. Provisions of the **Administrative Procedure Act of 1946** require procedural fairness in administrative agency operations (including detailed guidelines for advance notice and public participation in many aspects of administrative decision making). A maze of rules is designed to minimize dishonesty and corruption in public affairs. Also, American tax laws reflect a desire that citizens receive a "fair shake" from their government. Yet all such protections involve lengthy and complex elaboration in substantive and procedural rules, which add still further to the tangle of red tape.

It would seem, in short, that regulation has been fostered by a willingness to have government protect individuals, groups, and society at large from many ills and evils. In virtually all cases, no *intent* to create red tape has existed, but it has inevitably accompanied each effort. The rise of **protective regulation** might well be explained, in sum, in the words of an old cartoon character, Pogo the Possum, who said, "We have met the enemy, and he is us!"

Past administrations streamlined many aspects of the national government's regulatory activity and placed a high priority on reducing "regulatory overkill." Although a large part of this focus on regulatory restructuring was directed toward cutting internal agency regulations (that is, regulations that national government administrators must follow), past administrations have been concerned about regulations that affect private citizens and organizations. The National Performance Review (NPR) emphasized an awareness of the content, administrative burdens, and costs involved, and signaled a clear intent to cut back "unnecessary" regulation, in all respects.[12] The Bush administration continued to selectively apply a deregulatory strategy on a case-by-case and agency-by-agency basis, leaving most regulatory entities weaker and a few others stronger. President Obama entered office with an aggressive regulatory agenda, but struggled to sustain momentum following the 2010 congressional elections.

Administrative Procedure Act of 1946

law on which all federal administrative procedures are based.

protective regulation

advantages certain groups or individuals by granting special access or licenses; used with professionals.

Structures and Procedures of Regulatory Bodies

The national government's regulatory bodies have certain features in common with other administrative entities, but differ in important respects. One similarity (already noted) is that all administrative entities operate under authority delegated by Congress, and they must therefore be aware of congressional sentiment about their operations. On occasion, Congress as a whole has been persuaded to restrict regulatory activities in some way, as was the case with the FTC more than once in the past thirty years. A second similarity is that there can be functional overlap among regulatory bodies, just as with other entities. For example, during the controversy over cigarette smoking and public health in the mid-1960s, one question was whether allegedly deceptive radio and television advertising of cigarettes was properly under the jurisdiction of the FTC, which is responsible for controlling deceptive trade practices, or the FCC, which generally regulates radio and television advertising.[13] A third similarity is that political influence is sometimes as important in the regulatory process as in other aspects of public administration—at times, more important. Although the design of government regulation seems to assume some separation between regulation and "politics," in truth, interested groups and individuals expend considerable effort to influence regulatory activity. Close ties usually link clientele groups and so-called **dependent regulatory agencies (DRAs)**—agencies charged with regulating economic activity but housed within an existing cabinet department or other executive structure. Examples are the National Highway Traffic Safety Administration (NHTSA) in the DOT, the Agricultural Marketing Service in the Department of Agriculture, and the FDA in the Department of Health and Human Services (HHS). But, regardless of organizational form, regulatory politics is a very real phenomenon.

dependent regulatory agencies (DRAs)

regulatory units or subdivisions of executive agencies.

Regulatory Structures

Regulation was initially to be a function conducted by administrative boards and commissions with greater independence—in particular, independence from control by the president. That being the case, the structuring of those entities was a matter of some importance. As regulatory activities spread more widely through the executive branch, however, those activities did not have the effect of altering the structure of existing entities (most of which were, and are, agencies with a single head). Thus, questions of organizational structure are now less significant than they once were. The scope of regulation that is undertaken, the types of regulations issued and enforced, and the impacts of those regulations are often at least as great for other regulators as for the older, independent regulatory boards and commissions.

There are some structural differences between DRAs and their more autonomous counterparts, the IRCs. In general, IRCs have plural, not individual, leadership; a collective decision-making process exists from the start. Board members or commissioners do not serve "at the pleasure of the president" as do cabinet secretaries and other political appointees, and presidential powers to remove them are sharply curtailed. Their terms of office are fixed and are often quite long—for example, the fourteen-year terms of Federal Reserve Board members. Also, terms of office are staggered—that is, every year or every other year, only one member's term expires. Thus, no president is able to bring about drastic shifts in policy by appointing several board members at once, nor is policy within the agency likely to change abruptly because of membership turnover. Each commission or board has an odd number of members, ranging from five to eleven, and decisions are reached by a majority vote. Members may issue dissents on issues with which they disagree. Finally, there must be a nearly even partisan balance among the members—a five-member board must be three to two Republican or Democratic, a seven-member commission must be four to three one way or the other, and so on.

The combined effect of these provisions is, or was intended to be, that these entities were better insulated from political influence and manipulation than others in the executive branch. In particular, it was deemed centrally important to prevent presidential interference with regulatory processes and to make the regulators answerable to Congress. The effectiveness of political insulation can be questioned, however. Decisions clearly favoring some interests over others are not uncommon, although most decisions have substantive legal as well as political roots. The larger purpose behind organizing the boards and commissions in this manner is to protect the public interest in preference, and sometimes in opposition, to private economic interests. But where and how to draw the line between them is frequently decided through the political process rather than as a result of clearly defined boundaries.

Does regulatory structure make any real difference in the operations of regulatory bodies? Surprisingly, existing opinion on that question consists mainly of impressions and conventional wisdom; it is not based on careful research, of which there is very little. When comparing DRAs with IRCs, there is no hard evidence that structure affects regulatory policy making. However, a study of twenty-three regulatory bodies (divided about equally between DRAs and IRCs) indicated that DRAs (1) have political environments much more supportive of regulation than do IRCs; (2) are usually designed to regulate in the interests of those regulated (which might explain the degree of support for regulation); (3) usually have other, nonregulatory functions that lead to their having larger workforces, larger budgets, and greater geographic decentralization; and (4) operate with more discretion and can make greater use of their rule-making powers.[14] It is perhaps significant that DRAs, such as the FDA and the NHTSA, generated political controversy since the 1980s, as have IRCs, such as the FTC and the Consumer Product Safety Commission (CPSC). Some DRAs, in other words, may be less inclined now than in the past to regulate only in the interests of those regulated.

It should be noted, too, that regulatory structure seems not to matter on those occasions when either Congress or the president (or the courts, for that matter) attempts to impose restraints on regulatory bodies that may have acted unacceptably or illegally. As we shall see later in this chapter, different regulatory bodies are subject to the same sorts of constraints, regardless of structure. In much the same way, the procedures followed by diverse entities have become increasingly uniform. To these we now turn.

Regulatory Procedures

Procedures used by regulatory bodies fall into two broad categories: **rule making** and **adjudication** proceedings. Regulators are empowered under the 1946 Administrative Procedure Act to engage in rule making, a quasi-legislative action involving the issuance of formal rules that cover a general class of activities. It has about the same effect as a law passed by Congress or another legislature. For example, a rule issued by the DOT might limit the width of tractor-trailers on interstate highways or require lower shipping rates for products made from raw materials than for those made from recycled material (as in the case of many paper products). Rules apply to all individual operators, shippers, and others who come under their provisions. Rule making is more formal than adjudication, rules apply uniformly, and all cases within a given category are affected.

The rule-making process calls for regulators to issue notices of proposed rules relevant to administration of any given statute, with a period of public comment lasting at least thirty days (and often longer).[15] The notice of proposed rule making is published in the *Federal Register*, the government's official medium for disseminating information to the public concerning implementation of a statute. Written comments can be submitted by interested parties, and, if deemed appropriate, oral presentations also can be made. Although legislation can specify a deadline for publishing proposed rules and regulations, these deadlines are not always met. Considerable time can elapse between the effective date of a law and proposed rules and, again, between public comment and issuance of a final rule published in the **Code of Federal Regulations**—sometimes as long as seven years.

Several important points should be made about this process. It is almost always the organized public—clientele groups and other interest groups—that responds to opportunities for public comment; very few average citizens pay close attention to proposed rules (or anything else) in the *Federal Register*. Thus, the version of public opinion rendered in public comments is not likely to truly represent general popular sentiment. Regulators vary in their responsiveness to public comment. The right to comment does not by itself confer influence over ultimate action, and more powerful groups can expect to have their views heeded more closely than those of others. Perhaps most important, however, that the general public can become involved in rule-making processes means that regulators must be mindful of public feeling and must try to anticipate public reactions.

In adjudicatory proceedings, rulings are made on a case-by-case basis, and procedural requirements somewhat resemble those observed in a court of law. In a majority of cases, there is no formal proceeding before the decision. The regulators routinely settle such questions as whether to renew FCC radio station licenses. In such instances, a regulator is likely to follow informal precedents set in earlier rulings involving similar circumstances, although regulatory precedents do not carry the same legal force as court precedents do in judicial decision making.

rule making

quasi-legislative power delegated to agencies by Congress; a rule issued under this authority represents an agency statement of general applicability and future effect that concerns the rights of private parties, and has the force and effect of law.

adjudication

quasi-judicial power delegated to agencies by Congress, under which agencies apply existing laws or rules to particular situations, in case-by-case decision making; related term: *adjudicatory proceeding.*

Federal Register

complete listing of all proposed and active federal regulations, available online at http://www.gpoaccess. gov/fr/.

Code of Federal Regulations

record of all rules that authorize regulatory agency actions.

Sometimes, however, adjudicatory proceedings are quite formalized. This usually occurs during a class action, when major interests are affected involving thousands of people or millions of dollars, when a case is contested, or when there is no applicable precedent. Under such circumstances, the rules followed represent an adaptation of courtroom procedures and congressional hearing requirements, including formal rules governing attorneys, evidence, testimony, and witnesses. Some groups make use of a public counsel, much like a public defender, who argues the consumer's point of view at public hearings. A much more common figure in adjudicatory proceedings is the **administrative law judge**, formerly known as the hearing examiner, who acts for commissioners or board members in conducting public hearings, taking testimony, and then writing a preliminary recommendation, which is the basic factual summary presented to the regulatory body. This procedure is designed to keep cases from going to court and greatly reduces the time it takes to reach a decision.

Administrative law judges, now numbering well over 1,500 in thirty different agencies, are among the most highly specialized national government employees. They are career employees assigned to regulatory bodies who occupy a unique niche in the public service, yet they are independent of their nominal superiors and have a degree of job security unusual even among merit employees. The nature of adjudication requires that they are expected to avoid being arbitrary and unfair while exercising sufficient freedom to write recommendations on the basis of information received and interpretation of those data.[16] Although their recommendations do not carry final authority and can be appealed to the regulatory entity, administrative law judges enjoy considerable prestige, and their recommendations are commonly accepted.[17]

Apart from rule making and adjudicatory procedures, regulators frequently attempt to resolve disputes or disagreements by encouraging informal, voluntary compliance with regulatory requirements. The FTC, for example, employs three principal devices to secure voluntary cooperation. The first is issuance of an **advisory opinion**, indicating clearly how the FTC would decide a particular question if it were to formally come before the commission. Regulatory bodies, unlike courts, are permitted to issue such opinions on questions that might, but have not yet, come before them. The second is convening of a trade practices conference, to which all or most members of an industry are invited for a general airing of their regulatory problems and, it is hoped, for promoting better understanding on all sides of the problems discussed. The third is a **consent order**, representing an agreement voluntarily reached between the FTC and an industry before, or possibly during, an adjudicatory proceeding. (Consent orders are sometimes described as promises made by an industry to stop doing something it hasn't admitted doing in the first place.) Without devices such as these, regulatory bodies would have an even more difficult time keeping up with their caseloads than they do now.

administrative law judge

member of the executive branch who performs quasi-judicial functions.

advisory opinion

one means used by some U.S. regulatory entities to secure voluntary compliance with regulatory requirements; involves issuance of a memorandum indicating how the entity (for example, the FTC) would decide an issue if it were presented formally.

consent order

one means used by some U.S. regulatory entities to secure voluntary compliance with regulatory requirements; involves a formal agreement between the entity and an industry or industries in which the latter agree to cease a practice in return for the regulatory entity's dropping punitive actions aimed at the practice.

The Politics of Regulation

Regulatory politics is only rarely the partisan politics of Democrats and Republicans. Rather, it is the politics of privilege, in terms of those with a stake in regulatory policies gaining preferred access to decision makers, and to a lesser extent, of *patronage*, in the appointment of commissioners, board members, legal counsels, and staff personnel.[18] This is especially true of IRCs but (in the case of patronage) much less true of DRAs. It is also a many-sided game played by the regulators themselves, who are sensitive to pressures placed on them and who are aware that reappointment may depend on political forces; by executives and legislators because businesses, industries, and labor unions subject to regulation are important constituents; and by those regulated, who cannot afford not to play. Fifty years ago, the only ones who seemed to be excluded were consumers, although that has changed decisively; now consumers play the game hard, and well.

Regulatory politics for both IRCs and DRAs is also characterized by issues of distribution, quality, and price. An excellent example is the cable television industry. Communications regulators have had to answer a host of questions as cable television expanded into more and more markets. Among the most important questions are the following: Which communities will be granted cable TV or satellite service to begin with? What criteria will be used in evaluating franchise applications, and how will those criteria be determined? What requirements (if any) will be imposed concerning service quality provided and type of service available? How many channels will the system offer, and which ones? What prices will be charged, and how many price packages will be offered? Although this is one of the most complex regulatory areas, similar issues arise in almost every other regulatory sphere.

The politics of regulation in the national government merits further discussion. A leading study of the FCC suggests that in addition to Congress, there are five major institutional influences on broadcast regulatory policy: the FCC itself, the broadcasting industry, citizens' groups, the courts, and the White House.[19] It is another indication of the nature of regulatory politics, however, that in the study cited, the focal point of the discussion was Congress. The relative strength of these participants in broadcast regulation, their respective abilities to make Congress act, and the rules Congress writes for the FCC and the courts (regarding access to judicial review of FCC decisions) all play a part in shaping broadcast policy. Regulatory policies in other areas result from similar configurations of institutions and power.

The political environment of regulation includes many of the same features that apply to all other administrative agencies: legislative oversight by committees of Congress; expenditure concerns centering on the appropriations committees, the Office of Management and Budget (OMB), and the budget committees; an increasing focus on potential effects of budget cuts and deficit reduction; and attention to a political clientele—which, for a regulatory body, is frequently the very industry or industries it is responsible for regulating. One example of this kind of relationship involves the FDA and the pharmaceuticals industry. In addition, business and corporate interests generally have their own partisan leanings. It follows that there might well be partisan undercurrents in regulatory politics, depending in part on which party holds the White House.

Furthermore, the degree of independence possessed by an agency may fall short of that apparently conferred on it. As already noted, the president, Congress, and powerful economic interests frequently interact with a regulatory agency, thereby affecting what it does. Critics of regulatory agencies have charged that they often are more effective in protecting the industries they are supposed to regulate than they are in regulating them—a charge not without some foundation. At the same time, however, another set of criticisms has begun to be heard, accusing some regulatory bodies of going too far in the exercise of their discretionary authority. Thus, regulatory agencies are increasingly caught in a squeeze.

Independence from the President

Regulatory agencies operate in much the same relationship to the president or governor that other agencies do: political appointees head the overall organization, but career employees direct the work of the regulatory entity itself. On the other hand, regulatory boards and commissions are designed to answer to Congress's direction and to be shielded from presidential influence. Commissioners cannot be fired by the president; staggered terms inhibit presidential ability to "sweep out the old and bring in the new"; and partisanship in the agencies' makeup is limited by law. At the same time, a president such as George W. Bush who served two full terms—or even part of a second term, as in the case of Richard Nixon—can have a powerful impact on agency composition and, therefore, policy directions. Former President Nixon, during five and a half years in the White House, appointed or reappointed the *full* membership of eight regulatory entities, including the FCC, CAB, FPC, and SEC, and most of the members of all other regulatory bodies.

Jimmy Carter sought to bring regulatory bodies under tighter control and direction. In March 1978, Carter issued Executive Order 12044, designed to improve regulations in a number of ways: simplicity and clarity of the rules themselves, improved public access during rule making, and more publicity about "significant regulations under development or review." The executive order also sought more control by regulatory entity heads, some of whom were directly accountable to Carter.[20] Ronald Reagan went much further in an effort to slow regulatory growth by suspending, postponing, or canceling numerous rules and regulations while they were still in the proposal stage. As public concern about overregulation has increased, recent presidents—and Congress, too, as we will see—have moved against individual regulators with some success.

One other aspect of presidential influence, in the realm of appointing and reappointing board or commission members, deserves mention. The most common practice is for presidents to avoid, if possible, any appointment that will generate controversy. The most convenient method is to allow leaders of regulated industries an informal voice in the selection process. Not all presidents give equal weight to these informal recommendations, but rare indeed is the president who goes ahead with an appointment that is publicly and vigorously opposed by a regulated industry.

There are two reasons for this presidential deference to industries. First, all presidents, regardless of political party, count on significant support from business and industrial leaders, and it is common courtesy to listen to supporters who touch base on a matter of considerable interest to them. Second, a president runs the risk of shaking business confidence and, in the long run, continued economic vitality by setting himself in perpetual opposition to Wall Street and to the nation's business and financial communities. As a result, most presidents take care to keep their fences mended with business and industry. What effect that has on a process of regulation designed to be objective and detached is another matter, but the president's political needs may account for some of the gap between promise and performance of regulatory bodies.

Under the Reagan administration, another tool of presidential control was used to strengthen the president's ability to direct the general emphasis of regulatory activity, if not specific rules themselves. The OMB was authorized, in a series of executive orders, to review proposed regulatory rules and to influence their content substantively if OMB deemed it appropriate to do so. In one such case, OMB was accused of blocking parts of a so-called workers' right-to-know regulation that had been issued by the Occupational Safety and Health Administration (OHSA). In the ensuing controversy, OMB was also accused of singling out health and safety regulations for more drastic paperwork reduction, compared to some other regulations, under provisions of the Paperwork Reduction Act of 1980.[21] The Clinton administration took another approach to reducing the scope of regulation by proposing frequent consultation and negotiation involving OMB and agencies of the national government regarding the regulatory process. This was far different from the pattern followed during the Reagan presidency, which emphasized a more centralized mode of operation, with OMB "directing traffic" in a much more systematic way. This was also consistent with the broader approach followed by President Clinton in his efforts to bring about far-reaching change in governmental activities. One of the first actions of the Bush administration was to undo most of the regulatory reforms passed by the Clinton administration. Under the Bush administration and (until 2007) a Congress supportive of the president, there were few comprehensive regulatory reform initiatives. President Obama initiated regulatory reforms in a number of areas, including consumer protection, energy consumption, financial transactions, food and drug safety, health care, and workplace safety.

Sicko

The 2007 documentary *Sicko* analyzes health care in the United States, with close attention paid to health insurance and pharmaceutical industries. The director, Michael Moore, uses the film as a platform to compare the U.S. health care system with those of countries in which universal health care is provided.

The documentary addresses the history of the health care debate within the United States, centering on past presidential administrations and the failed reform. Moore visits Canada, the United Kingdom, and France, interviewing physicians with each stop. There are no out-of-pocket payments for treatments in the United Kingdom, and prescriptions are free. The French government provides social services for its citizens, including health care. In the United States, Moore finds that September 11, 2001 rescue volunteers have been denied government funds for physical and psychological ailments that they suffer from as a result of the attack. People who thought they had coverage have been denied care time and time again.

The film's underlying argument is that people should be taking care of one another and looking out for one another. Moore (and others) believes that much needs to be done in the policy-making process to change the American health care system.

The recent health care reform proposals by the Obama administration and the legislation passed by Congress sought to change the American health care system. The legislation has been met with disapproval from some and questions from many. It remains to be seen just how great the change can, and will, be.

Should government-funded health care be provided for every American citizen?

Source: http://sickothemovie.com/index.html, accessed April 26, 2011.

Independence from Congress

From the standpoint of Congress as a whole, regulatory bodies have a great deal of independence. After an entity is established and the processes of regulation are initiated, the main contact that members of Congress have collectively with the entity is in considering its annual appropriations. Congress does exercise considerable influence, however, through committee oversight of regulatory bodies, especially if complaints have been received about the activities of a given regulator. Because the regulators operate under delegated legislative authority, it is the prerogative of Congress to review and possibly modify the authority that was granted, and regulatory entities are cautious about offending powerful interests in Congress that could trigger committee action "to rein them in." This does not happen often, but the possibility does exist.

At times, Congress's interaction with, and influence over, a regulator is direct and forceful. In the 1960s, at the beginning of the continuing controversy over the health hazards involved in smoking cigarettes (a conflict that foreshadowed more recent lawsuits by states against tobacco companies over the health risks associated with smoking and the medical costs to treat victims of smoke-related diseases), several regulatory entities including the FTC tried, with limited success, to counter tobacco advertising that depicted smoking in a very favorable light. Current controversies, however, over the health hazards posed by secondhand smoke, restrictions on cigarette advertising, and treatment of nicotine as an addictive drug indicate that public pressure on the tobacco industry has intensified, and Congress appears to be responding to that pressure in more decisive terms than it did fifty years ago.

With the cigarette advertising conflict in mind, are regulatory bodies truly independent of Congress? The answer is no, but a word of caution is in order. Although regulatory bodies were never designed to be completely independent, they can gain some measure of independence if their political support is strong enough—including congressional support. An "essential characteristic of independent regulatory commissions [and DRAs] is their need of political support and leadership for successful regulation in the public interest."[22] An entity that is truly an "independent operator" is the exception rather than the rule because neither Congress nor industry is likely to consent willingly to such autonomy. Regulators that try to act independently find themselves reined in by congressional committees or Congress as a whole far more often than they are turned loose. It is the nature of the game, depending on the balance of political forces at work. But there is almost always a balance of some kind, and regulators have to adapt to this, ensuring (if possible) that their support is always stronger than their opposition.

The question of independence from the president and from Congress has no final answer. William Cary, onetime chair of the SEC, once described regulatory entities as "stepchildren whose custody is contested by both Congress and the Executive, but without very much affection from either one."[23] That sounds as though regulatory bodies are caught in a crossfire between the White House and Capitol Hill, and in fact, that is often the case. If neither the president nor Congress regularly lends support and if support is still needed, a dilemma develops from which one escape seems most promising. Regulators can try to reach acceptable operating understandings with the industries they regulate, in exchange for their support—which poses a whole new set of problems for regulators' independence.

Independence from Those Regulated

Among the most intense criticisms of regulatory bodies has been the charge that they are "owned," unduly influenced, or have been co-opted by the industries they are supposed to regulate. The most devastating critiques probably were those of "Nader's Raiders," a group associated with consumer advocate and three-time presidential candidate Ralph Nader, aimed at such venerable agencies as the ICC and (ironically) the FTC. Charges of lack of experience on the part of regulators, unfamiliarity with problems of particular industries, political cronyism in appointments, and lack of initiative and vigor in pursuing violators of regulatory requirements were the most common criticisms. A companion theme has been that regulatory commissioners often were first actively involved in affairs of industry, then came to serve in regulatory entities, and subsequently returned to those same industries. The central theme underlying such allegations was that regulatory bodies do more to protect and promote "their" industries than to regulate industry in the public interest.

The fact remains, however, that those serving on regulatory bodies can never be expected to isolate themselves personally from those with whom they deal. On the contrary, some interaction is considered necessary in order that those working for the regulatory body understand fully the workings of the regulated industry. How to maintain that interaction and still keep an acceptable degree of detachment and objectivity is the central question.

Regulators have all kinds of direct social and professional involvement with individuals in the industries they regulate. Frequently, contact occurs in private, informal rule-making and adjudicatory proceedings, where problems can be addressed without all the trappings of a formal regulatory action. Just what comes out of such meetings in terms of protection of the public interest is not easy to determine (assuming the public interest itself can be defined), and the private nature of the conferences is one irritant to observers such as Nader and the nonprofit public-interest lobbying group **Common Cause**.

Regulators also routinely attend industry conferences, where they are frequently the main speakers, and friendly conversation during the social hour is not at all out of place under such congenial circumstances. Then there are private chats in offices, out-of-town visits to companies by regulatory officials, and luncheons and dinners at which regulators and industry representatives are part of a larger social gathering.

Three aspects of these relationships should be emphasized. First, these social and professional contacts are routine occurrences not inconsistent with the job of regulation. Second, private industries have a legitimate economic self-interest to uphold, and industry executives fear that, if they do nothing to present their cases to government regulators, their competitors will. Third, out-and-out industry pressure on a regulator is rare—bribery appears to be almost nonexistent, as are blatant attempts to intimidate or otherwise pressure regulatory officials. Direct exchanges of views, combined with the indirect pressure that can be placed on an entity through the president and Congress, are usually enough to ensure industries a fair hearing.

That regulatory bodies and their members are expected to be expert as well as detached raises yet another question: How does one become knowledgeable about an industry without also coming to share that industry's values and outlooks? Appointees to regulatory positions often come from industry backgrounds, a natural training ground for acquiring relevant expertise but also a likely place to adopt perspectives favorable to industry interests. Also, as noted earlier, a revolving-door pattern has emerged—regulators can often expect to go to work, or go back to work, for a regulated industry when their terms expire. Other appointees have backgrounds that hardly equip them to deal with the industries—some are named as political favors, others simply because they are noncontroversial appointees (or sometimes for both

Common Cause

a nonpartisan, nonprofit advocacy organization, founded in 1970 by civic activist John Gardner, through which citizens make their voices heard in the political process and try to hold their elected leaders accountable to the public interest.

reasons). In either instance, the industry has an advantage; individual regulators are likely to be sympathetic to—or else largely ignorant of—the industry's problems and are consequently reluctant to intervene in industry affairs.

Sometimes, an industry maverick is named to a regulatory body, someone who does not share the predominant economic or social outlook of the industry even though he or she has been a part of it. But such appointments are exceptions to the rule. The pattern of appointing people with industry backgrounds is so well entrenched that it is considered news when someone is rejected by the Senate for that reason. Thus, the need for both expertise and detachment in regulatory entities clearly presents a dilemma that is not easily solved.

Consumers, Consumerism, and Regulation

The consumer movement has had significant impact on government regulatory activity. Before the rise of consumerism, almost all major economic interest groups represented manufacturers or producers—those involved in the assembly, growing, processing, shipping, and selling of products in the marketplace. These groups naturally sought to shape market regulation in favor of producer needs and preferences. Customers or consumers were largely unrepresented in any organized fashion. Major conflicts, however, over cigarettes and public health, safety of children's toys and prescription drugs, climate change, and automotive safety and fuel economy have changed that situation.

Leaders of the budding consumer movement looked to regulatory entities and other administrative bodies to promote and protect consumer interests. They apparently placed little faith in Congress, reasoning that legislators would be far more likely to respond to producers' wishes than to contrary pressures applied by consumer groups. Rightly or wrongly, they chose to make use of administrative weapons in fighting their political battles, which of course brought them into conflict with both producers and Congress. In addition, advocates of change, such as the Nader spin-off organizations, saw a need to reform administrative regulation in order to maximize consumer gains. Not all consumer groups agreed with that view, but they generally supported efforts for reform.

There is little question that consumerism changed the face of government regulation, both because of new political pressures applied and because of primary reliance on regulatory agencies. Several studies of consumer protection have noted that administrative processes were key targets in the growth of consumer protection policy and that "consumer measures [such as tobacco warning labels] depended heavily on the power of administrative agencies to make public policy."[24] Pressure was placed on Congress, with some success, not only to respond directly to consumer demands but also to increase access to regulators and to the courts for redress of consumer grievances. Congress's record in these respects is mixed, but even that represents an improvement over the past, when consumer groups were much weaker and less organized and could point to only a handful of gains over long periods of time.

The Nader phenomenon and the rise of consumerism are not unrelated. There is informed opinion that without the expertise, full-time commitment, and vigorous criticism by the Nader organizations of both corporate power and regulatory efforts, the consumer movement would not have enjoyed the influence it has. By awakening consciousness of consumer interests among the general public, Nader and others strengthened, or perhaps even created, a constituency with sufficient political power to contest the influence of long-established producer groups. Consumer pressure clearly accounted for much of the increase in government regulation during the past fifty years, as well as for increased political conflict over regulation.

In more recent years, however, the pendulum has swung the other way; there seems to be more resentment of, rather than sustained support for, distinctly consumer-oriented regulation. Congress and Presidents Reagan and the elder Bush seemed more sympathetic to producers than their predecessors had been. President Clinton's position on the general question of government regulation appeared to differ in important respects from the positions of Reagan and the first Bush, but the Clinton administration clearly moved cautiously in undertaking new regulatory initiatives, focusing efforts on eliminating regulations or simplifying existing "necessary" ones. More important, perhaps, is the fact that public opinion is shifting on the question of what constitutes appropriate government regulation. Illustrative of the interplay between regulators and public sentiment and of the difficulties confronting conscientious regulators is the case of the FDA. This agency has acted frequently to ban various products and substances said to endanger human health because they were unsafe, ineffective, or both. FDA officials said, more than once, that the agency, under existing legislation, had no choice but to remove a product from the market when its potential disease-causing properties were demonstrated under controlled laboratory conditions. This was an especially important position politically in the controversy over the FDA's proposal to ban saccharin, which had been linked to cancer, first in laboratory rats and then in human males in a number of Canadian tests.

The FDA's stand caused a powerful coalition to question the basic law requiring FDA action against carcinogens (substances linked to cancer). Key elements in that coalition were food companies, manufacturers of soft drinks, and, perhaps most important, an aroused group of citizens (such as diabetics) who, for various reasons, needed or wanted sugar-free beverages available. Pressure was applied on both sides of the issue, with some arguing that suspected carcinogens should be banned as required by law, regardless of public outcry, and others arguing that it was time to update the 1958 legislation requiring FDA action and permit the FDA to examine potential benefits in relation to the cancer risk.[25] Any time that an agency receives 70,000 letters over a single issue, there is reason to reconsider its decision, which the FDA did. Its course of action was affected, however, more by congressional pressure for a delay in banning saccharin than by either direct industry or public pressure.

The latter has to be translated into congressional action to be truly effective. The proposed saccharin ban and public reaction to it were not the only episodes in which the general public has been critical of regulatory action.

Another controversy involved the regulations mandating both driver- and passenger-side air bags on all new automobiles, ostensibly as a safety measure. Air bags increased the costs of cars by as much as $500 and were never intended to be used without seat belts. It was known for some time that improperly installed child restraint seats (also required by some states) could severely injure or kill infants when air bags inflate, even in relatively minor accidents. Many consumers, however, were unaware of the dangers that rapidly inflating air bags could pose to children or to small adults.[26]

Still another issue highlighting public frustration and disenchantment with regulation was the controversy over Laetrile, some years ago, as a treatment for cancer patients. Laetrile, a substance extracted from apricot pits and said by some to be effective as a cancer treatment, was not approved by the FDA. Yet, during the late 1970s, demands became more insistent that those who wanted to be treated with Laetrile should have the chance, FDA approval or not, with some arguing that this was an issue of freedom versus government control. The respective points of view have been summed up as follows:

> Freedom is the issue. The American people should be allowed to make their own decisions. They shouldn't have the bureaucrats in Washington, D.C., trying to decide for them what's good and what's bad—as long as it's safe. The FDA is typical of what you get in regulatory agencies—a very protective mentality in bureaucrats who want to protect their own jobs and their own positions. It's easier for them to say "No" to a product—Laetrile or anything else—than it is to say "Yes."… The simple fact is that stringent drug regulation for society as a whole limits therapeutic choice by the individual physician who is better able to judge the risks and benefits for the individual patient. I think the whole argument centers on FDA's intervention on the basis of a product's efficacy…. I agree that no one should be allowed to defraud the public, but you don't need to rely on the FDA. The real question is: Should the government be protecting you from yourself?[27]

And, on the other side of the Laetrile/FDA question:

> I believe in a society that protects the consumer from the unscrupulous vendor. There was a time in America when we gave free rein to the philosophy of *caveat emptor:* let the buyer beware. We abandoned that a couple of generations ago, and now we have all kinds of consumer protections built into our society.[28]
>
> Instead of freedom of choice, it could be freedom of the industry to defraud the consumer. With the tremendous number of drugs available, it is not possible for the physician and the consumer to really have

the information necessary upon which to base an informed judgment in regard to the safety and effectiveness [of a drug].[29]

Even though such disputes continue to be with us, government regulators continue to follow the statutory directives of Congress, as the following actions, paraphrased from newspaper accounts, indicate.

- *Item:* In August 1987, the Labor Department extended "right-to-know" regulations, requiring companies to tell workers about hazardous chemicals and other toxic substances present in the workplace, to 18 million workers at more than 3.5 million work sites. OSHA officials estimated at the time that the regulations would reduce the number of chemical-related injuries, illnesses, and deaths by 20 percent in nonmanufacturing industries.[30]
- *Item:* The SEC decided, in mid-1989, to offer cash rewards to individuals who provide information that leads to the conviction of so-called "inside traders" on securities (stocks and bonds) markets.[31]
- *Item:* In 1990, the Secretary of Labor, in announcing mandatory safety belt use for all private-industry employees who drive or ride in motor vehicles on the job, estimated that the rules would save almost 700 lives and prevent as many as 32,000 lost-time injuries on the job each year. The secretary also estimated that the original safety belt rule issued in 1984 had saved more than 20,000 lives between 1984 and mid-1990.[32]
- *Item:* In late 1993, the Agriculture Department proposed (for the second time) new rules requiring information on safe handling, thawing, cooking, and storing of raw meat and poultry. The department did so in the midst of pressure from three directions: from Congress for not moving quickly enough to improve inspections, from the meat and poultry industry for reissuing rules that had previously been struck down by a federal judge, and from Vice President Gore's reinventing government team, which sought to transfer meat and poultry inspection from the department to the FDA. These actions were sparked by the deaths of three children and the hospitalization of forty other people in the state of Washington in January 1993 after they ate undercooked hamburger meat at a fast-food restaurant.[33]
- *Item:* One intended purpose of the 1990 Americans with Disabilities Act (ADA) was to provide jobs and eliminate architectural impediments for the disabled. Regulations require employers to make reasonable accommodation for otherwise qualified persons who are physically challenged or in wheelchairs. However, studies show that the proportion of people with disabilities in the workplace has actually *declined* since the ADA was passed, despite the regulations and benefit programs available to disabled persons.[34] One important organization working to reverse that trend is the Disability Rights Education and Defense Fund (DREDF). Founded in 1979 by people with disabilities and parents of children

with disabilities, the DREDF is a national law and policy center dedicated to protecting and advancing the civil rights of people with disabilities through legislation, litigation, advocacy, and technical assistance (http://www.dredf.org/).

• *Item:* Despite the evidence of increased use of drugs by teenagers, the voters of California and Arizona approved statewide initiatives in November 1996 to legalize the medical use of marijuana for treatment of glaucoma. In effect, the voters of these states increased the potential availability of marijuana without waiting for the FDA, or any other regulatory body, to approve its expanded use for treatment of eye disease. For many, the issue was not protection from harmful effects of drugs but rather the freedom to use an otherwise controlled substance for personal medical reasons. In the fall of 2010, Californians voted again, this time on whether to legalize the recreational use of marijuana, but the amendment failed. Several other states are considering similar changes as a result of the pressing need to meet severe budget deficits, because if marijuana is legalized, states (and local governments) could impose sales or user taxes on it.

• *Item:* The Department of Agriculture, which sets industry standards for American, Cheddar, Colby, Monterey Jack, and Swiss cheese, proposed allowing producers of Swiss cheese to make their product with holes smaller than the three-eighths of an inch required by federal regulation. Producers hoped the changes would satisfy buyers who complained that cheese with larger holes would "gum up" their cheese slicers. In 2001, Wisconsin cheese manufacturers pushed for the smaller holes, arguing that U.S. manufacturers are at a competitive disadvantage with European producers because eye-size requirements are out of step with changing consumer tastes and marketing trends. There was no public comment from cheese inspectors.[35]

Whether such activity is regarded by most as being in our best interest, or unnecessary bureaucratic meddling, seems to be at the core of current controversies surrounding government regulation. Clearly, not all consumers share the values and objectives of consumer groups; these conflicting views contribute to the squeeze on regulatory agencies and others, such as the Department of Homeland Security, FDA, and NTSB, which are increasingly active in regulation. It has been well known for some time that many people do not use their seat belts, despite impressive statistical evidence that seat belt use can greatly reduce risk to life and limb. Although the proportion of seat belt users is increasing, many people resent having to pay for safety and for mandatory pollution-control devices on their automobiles. An auto ignition–seat belt interlock system, which would have forced all drivers to "buckle up" before starting their cars, was defeated rather handily in Congress once the public's negative sentiments became evident. That could happen again—with regard to auto safety, the effectiveness of medicines, the safety of food products, and other areas.

Given the abstract choice between clean and polluted air, pure and impure food and drugs, safe and unsafe cars, and so on, most of us would clearly select the former in each instance. But how to ensure and maintain such conditions without imposing excessive compliance costs or changes in personal lifestyles is what most controversies are all about. And what may be happening is simply a shift in prevailing political views about what constitutes appropriate regulation of particular products. Perhaps the best way to view such controversies is as cyclical processes, with the tide of public opinion ebbing and flowing on behalf of vigorous government regulation.

In addition to promulgating new regulations, the Obama administration has been particularly active in the creation of new regulatory agencies. The 2007–2010 financial crisis resulted in a massive public outcry against Wall Street, unscrupulous financial practices, and businesses that were seemingly "too big to fail," or whose insolvency could destroy the economy. In response, President Obama proposed, and Congress enacted, new legislation designed to both prevent such financial disasters and protect consumers from the unprincipled financial practices of banks, investment firms, mortgage brokers, savings and loans, and other financial entities. The legislation resulted in the passage of the **Dodd-Frank Wall Street Reform and Consumer Protection Act** (P.L. 111-203), creating three new regulatory agencies as well as greatly augmenting the strength of existing ones. These three agencies—the Consumer Financial Protection Bureau, the **Financial Stability Oversight Council (FSOC)**, and the **Office of Financial Research (OFR)**—did not become fully functional until the summer of 2011, yet they have already faced considerable opposition when they have attempted to act on issues involving consumer protection and regulation. Will these new agencies have the ability to carry out the President's financial and protection policy goals? How effective will they be in doing so? Will opposition from Congress, banks, retailers, Wall Street, and other fiscal actors slow their pace of rulemaking? In addition, the downgrading of the credit rating of the United States in late summer 2011 (by Standard & Poor's) sparked a dramatic downturn in the securities markets, thereby creating a new set of very serious and interrelated challenges to President Obama's fiscal, monetary, and international finance policies. How the Obama administration responds to these challenges, and how these regulatory agencies attempt to answer these questions, will have a substantial impact in the next few years on the well-being of the U.S. economy—and very possibly on the global economy as well.

Dodd-Frank Wall Street Reform and Consumer Protection Act

legislation proposed by President Obama and passed by Congress, aimed at changing the American financial regulatory environment and affecting all federal financial regulatory agencies and nearly every aspect of the nation's financial services industry.

Financial Stability Oversight Council (FSOC)

established under the Dodd-Frank Act, the FSOC provides for comprehensive monitoring to ensure the stability of our nation's financial system. The council identifies threats to the financial stability of the United States, promotes market discipline, and responds to emerging risks to the U.S. financial system.

Office of Financial Research (OFR)

an agency established by the Dodd-Frank Act within the Treasury Department to improve the quality of financial data available to policymakers and to facilitate more sophisticated analyses of the financial system.

Government Regulation of Tobacco Products

The use of tobacco products is one of the most controversial issues in public policy today. The debate centers on how to regulate a product that is unhealthy when used as intended, but remains legal for people over the age of eighteen. The policy debate is about when, how, and under what circumstances the government can regulate personal choice, and it relates to several other questions: Under what circumstances can government limit individual freedoms to protect citizens from their personal lifestyle? What is the role of the federal, state, and local governments in regulating the use of tobacco? What is the relationship between government intervention to protect public health and a person's individual liberties?

Federal activity to regulate smoking has had a mixed history. Antismoking legislation was first enacted in the late nineteenth century in response to concerns about fire hazards and the morality of smoking. Opposition to smoking on moral grounds was swept aside because of the economic benefits in the form of cigarette taxes to the states associated with tobacco production and consumption.[36] By 1927, all states had repealed such statutes; political action did not begin again until the 1960s and did not gain momentum until the 1980s. Most of the legislative debate in the 1970s and 1980s at the state level centered around personal-freedom issues. The tobacco industry emphasized individual rights as its defense; however, as scientific evidence of harmful effects of tobacco grew, legislative activity also grew on state and federal levels. Along with providing tobacco farmers with subsidies, Congress has limited federal regulation of tobacco products because of industry lobbying pressure.[37] At the same time, the surgeon general spoke out against smoking as a health hazard. In response to the historic 1964 *Surgeon General's Report* on smoking, Congress enacted the Cigarette Labeling and Advertising Act in 1965, which required health warnings on all cigarette packages. In 1967, the FCC ruled that the fairness doctrine be applied to cigarette commercials. As a result, all broadcasters who carried cigarette advertising were required to provide equal time to warn the public about cigarettes. In 1969, all cigarette ads were banned from TV and radio with the passage of the Public Health Cigarette Smoking Act. Between 1972 and 1986, many laws were passed that required warnings to be placed on packages of cigarettes and smokeless tobacco products, and in 1989, Congress voted to ban cigarettes on airplane flights of less than six hours.

In the 1990s, the debate shifted toward the effects of smoking on children. Antismoking forces embraced this as an effective strategy because of its political attractiveness to legislators and because it is difficult for the tobacco industry to publicly oppose restrictions on youth access to tobacco products. In 1992, the federal government enacted the Alcohol, Drug, and Mental Health Agency Reorganization Act, known as the Synar Amendment, requiring states to enact and enforce laws against the sale and distribution of tobacco products to individuals under the age of eighteen. All states have now enacted youth access restrictions to comply with the Synar Amendment (note the federalism-related implications of this action). In 1994, Congress passed the Pro Children Act, which prohibited smoking in indoor facilities that are routinely used for the delivery of certain services to children, including schools, libraries, day care, health care, and early childhood development centers.[38] On February 25, 1994, the FDA announced that it was considering regulating tobacco products under the authority of the federal Food, Drug, and Cosmetic Act. To receive this authority, the FDA would have to find that "tobacco products were drug-delivery devices for nicotine and determine whether the products were intended to affect the structure or function of the body."[39] The FDA investigated this, as well as the effects of advertising and marketing by the tobacco industry on children and adolescents. On August 10, 1995, President Clinton announced that the agency's evidence and analysis supported a finding that the nicotine in cigarettes and smokeless tobacco products is a drug and that cigarettes are a drug-delivery device under the terms of the act. Citing evidence that smoking begins in childhood as a "pediatric disease," the FDA proposed a regulatory program that would reduce the use of cigarettes and smokeless tobacco by young people by limiting its advertising and sale.

In April 1997, the tobacco industry appealed the decision to the U.S. District Court in Greensboro, North Carolina, but it was upheld. The court ruled that the FDA does have jurisdiction under the Food, Drug, and Cosmetic Act to regulate nicotine-containing cigarettes and smokeless tobacco. It also upheld the restrictions that prohibited the sale of these products to people under the age of eighteen, and required that retailers check for proof of age for people under the age of twenty-seven. However, the ruling invalidated the restrictions that the FDA put on advertising and promotion of cigarettes, finding that the agency had exceeded its statutory authority. Both sides appealed this ruling. In August 1998, a three-judge panel of the U.S. Court of Appeals in Richmond, Virginia, ruled that the FDA lacks the jurisdiction to regulate tobacco products. Its decision was based on evidence that Congress did not intend the Food, Drug, and Cosmetic Act to be applied to tobacco products. This resulted in the repeal of the provisions that restricted the sale and distribution of cigarettes to children and adolescents.

Much has changed in the tobacco industry since April 14, 1994, when representatives from seven of the leading tobacco companies stood before Congress and swore that nicotine was not an addictive substance. The tobacco industry has since admitted that tobacco is an addictive and dangerous substance that was marketed aggressively to minors.[40] As a result, the tobacco industry agreed to a settlement of $246 billion with forty-six states in November of 1998. This deal settled all state lawsuits pending against the industry. The settlement poured billions into state treasuries and provided about $1.5 billion for research and for advertising against underage tobacco use. Another positive outcome of the settlement was the acceptance of the FDA's limited power to regulate the tobacco industry. Most power of regulation will be at the state and local levels. As a result, the number of ordinances restricting smoking has increased. New York City even prohibits smoking outdoors as well as indoors, and in all public places. Over 500 counties and cities have enacted antismoking ordinances, most of which have targeted teenagers. At least thirty cities have outlawed the use of cigarette-vending machines, and others require the machines to be placed in view of an employee working in that location. In addition to federal advertising regulations, several localities have restricted advertising for tobacco products. This includes banning ads on mass-transit systems and on publicly visible billboards. The settlement also calls for tobacco companies to open a website that includes all documents produced in state and other smoking and health-related lawsuits.

Since July 1999, the distribution and sale of apparel and merchandise with tobacco logos is banned. The settlement also bans payment to promote tobacco products in movies, television shows, theater productions, live or recorded music performances, videos, and video games. For events with a significant youth audience or where the participants are under age, brand-name sponsorship is also prohibited. To ensure the enforcement of the settlement's terms, the courts have jurisdiction for implementation. If the tobacco industry violates any of the agreements, the courts may order monetary, civil contempt, or criminal sanctions to enforce compliance. State attorneys general have access to company documents, records, and personnel to enforce the agreement.

There have been numerous debates on how different states will spend the money from the tobacco settlement. Governors and lawmakers say that they are skeptical about pouring millions into untried programs designed to cut smoking rates. Some say that because of a nationwide antismoking campaign, the programs are not needed. Others say that the money should be spent like any other state funds used for a wide variety of purposes. The National Conference of State Legislatures said that more than 400 bills have been introduced around the country proposing how the money should be spent. Only four states have pledged to fund tobacco control programs beyond a minimum level. There have been many federal proposals mandating that an arbitrary percentage of the settlement go to programs aimed at reducing smoking. The states feel that they should not be required to spend a significant portion of the settlement on smoking reduction and prevention. The reason is that many states have already committed funds to these types of programs, and mandating spending on certain types of programs will limit the state's ability to fund other critical programs, such as expanding health care benefits to low-income children. Unfortunately, in light of major revenue shortfalls in many states, governors and legislators often have used tobacco money to plug growing budget "gaps"—some in the tens of billions of dollars.

Despite many of the positive outcomes, the tobacco settlement is under attack from many health groups which say that it is a disaster. The tobacco industry has fought back by spending millions of dollars lobbying, making substantial contributions to the Republican Party, and launching a $40 million advertising campaign.[41] Because of the tobacco industry's power through lobbying and campaign contributions, the settlement also prohibits the industry from opposing proposed state or local laws that are intended to limit youth access and consumption of tobacco products. The industry must require its lobbyists to certify in writing that they have reviewed and will fully comply with settlement terms, including disclosure of financial contributions regarding lobbyists' activities and new corporate-culture principles.

Tobacco control advocates, the state attorneys general, the FDA and FCC, and individual cases have brought a wide range of forces down upon the tobacco industry. For over thirty years, the tobacco industry went unchecked in its marketing abuses and indifference toward public health concerns. Because of these actions by the tobacco industry, there has been an emerging movement by the public and mass media to expose the industry's wrongdoing. This led Congress to hold hearings before the House Subcommittee on Nicotine and Product Regulation, and publish a report by former FDA head David Kessler focusing on regulation of tobacco products. Some of the policy recommendations included the following: (1) Congress should repeal the federal law that precludes state and local governments from regulating tobacco advertisements occurring entirely within a state's borders; (2) communities should work toward smoke-free environments and receive assistance from state and local public health agencies to develop ordinances and implementation strategies; (3) the National Cancer Institute should be active in designing, promoting, and evaluating tobacco control strategies; (4) the Centers for Disease Control and Prevention should provide sufficient funds to ensure statewide, community-based tobacco use prevention and control programs; and (5) the industry should be subject to penalties if youth tobacco use fails to drop 15 percent in two years, 30 percent in five years, 50 percent in seven years, and 60 percent in ten years.[42]

The subcommittee applauded the work of the anti-tobacco groups and the coverage of the mass media to expose the tobacco industry's fraud, deceit, and conspiracy. The media's effect can be seen in opinion polls that show dramatic increases in public recognition of tobacco as an addictive drug, public belief that tobacco companies deliberately target youth in their ads, and public support for criminal prosecution of tobacco executives for lying to Congress. Graphic television commercials and cigarette labels support antismoking campaigns, and are targeted largely at teens and young adults to prevent them from smoking. Antismoking ads are aired on channels such as MTV and Comedy Central, and are easily found on YouTube as well.

No matter how successful the antismoking campaign is in lowering cigarette consumption and putting the tobacco industry on the defensive, the industry remained a strong and relentless opponent. In March 2000, the U.S. Supreme Court ruled against the Clinton administration's policies to control how cigarettes are marketed. In a 5–4 decision, the Court ruled that under federal law, the FDA lacks the power to regulate the tobacco industry. In recent years, several states have taken the lead in raising taxes on tobacco products to, among other things, provide for children's health care programs. Most states have raised cigarette taxes, which on average are now double the federal tax rate. The federal tobacco excise tax was 39 cents a pack and has not been increased since 1997. In 2007, Congress proposed increasing cigarette taxes by 61 cents a pack, to $1.00. With the backing of the tobacco industry, President Bush twice vetoed the bill. The additional $35 billion raised by this tax also would have been used to support a children's health care insurance program. In 2009, President Obama kept his campaign promise and signed a law expanding health care benefits for 3.5 million uninsured children. The expansion is being paid for by raising the federal tax on cigarettes, cigars, and

POINT/COUNTERPOINT

Should persons with preventable diseases such as alcoholism, drug addiction, and cigar- and cigarette-related conditions resulting from misuse of harmful substances be entitled to government health care benefits?

THE ISSUE Several state legislatures have considered bills to deny benefits to those who engage in behaviors that are known to cause long-term damage, such as smoking. Should those who knowingly consume or use harmful substances be afforded the same health care benefits as those who do not?

Arguments *for* Denial of Benefits:

- Cost savings achieved from denying benefits can be redirected toward medical research to find cures for these conditions.
- Private insurance companies already charge higher premiums for smokers; if patients are eligible for Medicaid or Medicare, government agencies are paying extra for their care without being compensated.
- Denial of benefits encourages personal responsibility and preventive health care.

Arguments *against* Denial of Benefits:

- Denying benefits to a category of citizens uniformly punishes those with genetic predispositions toward certain diseases.
- It would be illegal and unfair to deny benefits because everyone is forced to contribute the same amount to federal programs such as Medicare.
- Denial of benefits would be difficult to implement, as some diseases are difficult to diagnose in the first place, making it difficult to determine who qualifies as having a condition stemming from misuse of harmful substances.

other tobacco products to $1.01 a pack. Not only will this raise more revenue for children's health programs, but it is thought that higher prices for tobacco products will discourage smoking.

The issue of the relationship between the right of the government to protect public health and the equally powerful right of a person to decide to live life without government interference, regardless of the social consequences, is still in debate. Nonetheless, antismoking advocates have come a long way in reducing the public's exposure to cigarettes and the harmful effects of tobacco.

Administrative Law

As discussed in previous chapters (especially Chapters 1 and 3), the regulatory function of public administration developed on an ever-larger scale beginning over a hundred years ago. In many ways, that growth was traceable to the need "to get a certain kind of twentieth-century job done: the regulation of huge, complex, rapidly changing [industrial] enterprises."[43] The doctrine of separation of powers, so central to our governmental scheme, seemed in this context to be something of a barrier to meeting contemporary needs. That doctrine, in the past as in the present, is designed not to promote efficiency but rather to promote liberty. Although certain kinds of liberty are served by separation of powers, speed and efficiency are not; it is precisely speed, efficiency, and reliability that are required for the governance in the twenty-first century. The loss of large-scale manufacturing jobs resulting from globalization and the shift in the U.S. economy to smaller, less centralized small businesses, high-tech firms, and service industries have contributed to the reversal of public attitudes about regulation, in a less favorable direction. Business leaders and many politicians reinforce people's fears about future job losses by stressing the need to compete with other countries, reduce regulation, and lower labor costs. The recent instability of global and U.S. stick markets only heightens fears of further job losses and a prolonged economic recession. Inevitably, calls for deregulation conflict with existing programs designed to ensure job security, maintain benefits, and provide public welfare.

As a perceived need for greater governmental efficiency grew, the administrative apparatus of all government grew with it. As an offshoot of that growth, concern rose for establishing safeguards in the administrative system for the rights and liberties of those touched by the system—meaning virtually all of us, but especially those in direct contact (or conflict) with regulators.

The Nature of Administrative Law

As noted earlier, administrative law pertains to the legal authority of public administrative agencies to perform their duties and also to "the limits necessary to control [those agencies]."[44] It should be noted, however, that administrative law is not clearly or neatly separated from other areas of the law. Rather, there is a distinctive focus to this legal area that sets it apart conceptually from other areas. The principal foci of administrative law, giving it a separate identity as an emergent field, are (1) the rules and regulations set out by administrative agencies and (2) the law concerning the powers and procedures of those agencies across a whole host of administrative operations.[45]

We have already considered some aspects of administrative activity that involve administrative law—for example, the discussion of red tape earlier in this chapter; the various types of policy implementation operations in which agencies can engage (Chapter 9); and certain aspects of public employee protections (Chapter 7). Many criticisms of regulations that are designed to achieve fairness in administrative operations are direct references to the growth of administrative law; various approaches to achieving fairness (which we will consider shortly) are themselves examples of how law, administration, and politics come together in a multitude of circumstances in support of **procedural fairness** or, more accurately, **procedural due process**.

Administrative law expert Kenneth Warren has suggested a number of "vital administrative law questions" that he contends shed light on the scope and nature of the subject. Among these are the following:

1. How much power should be delegated to administrative agencies?
2. How much administrative discretion is too much?
3. What constitutes arbitrary and capricious agency decisions?

procedural fairness

ensures fairness in the adjudication process.

procedural due process

legal term that refers to the legal rules governing a specific case.

4. What are the components of a fair hearing?
5. How much official immunity should be extended to governmental administrators?
6. How can administrative abuses be effectively checked?
7. What role should the courts play in the review of agency decisions?
8. What should be done to control the regulators?[46]

Several different challenges complicate how such questions can be answered. The precise meaning of an individual protection or procedural guarantee may vary from situation to situation. Answers to any one of these questions—even if they are definitive—may help to shape (or be shaped by) responses to other questions. Courts and judges have made a significant contribution to the incremental rise of administrative law in that they have been asked, via judicial decisions, to define precisely how due process requirements can be applied to administrative procedure. This is not to say that legislatures have stood idly by as this body of law has evolved. Indeed, administrative procedure acts (both state and national) have given added meaning to due process, as have the everyday actions of thousands of public administrators. Out of all these steps in the evolution of administrative law have come a number of distinct and identifiable patterns of protection for the individual who comes into contact with the public administrative system. We shall consider key provisions governing the general rule-making process, provisions governing the process of administrative adjudication, authority for (and restrictions on) administrative discretion, and some of the most important court decisions which constitute significant guideposts in administrative law.

Rule Making and Administrative Law

As noted in Chapter 9, rule making involves administrative issuance of statements and other guidelines that have general applicability—they set out enforceable standards that affect a category or classification of enterprises or activities. Rule making, especially if it occurs informally, is constrained by far fewer procedural restrictions than is administrative adjudication, whether these restrictions arise from statutes or from judicial decisions.[47] There are requirements that apply to rule making. First, public participation is considered essential. In order to make that possible, public notice of proposed rule making is required almost universally. Administrative procedure acts that may be largely silent on rule making nevertheless include this provision. (There are some circumstances in which prior notice may not be required.[48]) Another provision relating to public participation concerns the opportunity to present views—that is, access to the process for interested outside parties who wish to enter their view into the record (however formally or informally that record may be kept). Presentation can take the form of filing petitions, consulting informally, or becoming involved in several varieties of hearings. A second requirement designed to promote procedural fairness in rule making is postponing effective dates of newly issued rules while publicizing the content of what has been decided; a third requirement (not always found) is judicial review of proposed or actual rules.

Administrative entities are authorized to make three kinds of rules: substantive, procedural, and interpretive.[49] *Substantive rules* apply to, or direct, law or policy—for example, Nuclear Regulatory Commission rules that set safety regulations for nuclear power plants, or FTC rules governing TV advertising directed at children. *Procedural rules* embody requirements for an agency's organization, procedures, or practices. These may be imposed by an administrative procedure act but may also be issued—or perhaps supplemented—by agencies themselves (in the latter case, agencies are bound to honor their own rules in the same way they follow those set by statute). *Interpretive rules* are an agency's views of the meanings of its regulations or of the statutes it administers. Interpretive rules are analogous to advisory opinions that might be issued by a regulatory (or other) entity; that is, they give some indication of how an administrator perceives or understands existing law. One familiar example of an interpretive rule is the advice that taxpayers might receive from the Internal Revenue Service (IRS) about permissible deductions in the course of preparing their tax returns. Occasionally, a dispute may arise over whether a particular rule is substantive, procedural, or interpretive. Such disputes are normally resolved by the courts, with both the government agency and the affected individuals bound by the results.

Administrative Adjudication and Administrative Law

When administrative agencies engage in adjudication, they act in the manner of a court—that is, settling "controversies among named parties, and [determining] legal rights and obligations of the parties on the points in dispute."[50] Courts have historically gone to greater lengths to ensure procedural fairness to individuals than to the public at large; this is one of the main reasons why administrative adjudication is the focus of so much administrative law. Adjudication may occur either formally or informally. Formal procedures entail at least three essential due process guarantees born in constitutional law and embodied (at the national level) in the Administrative Procedure Act of 1946: fair notice, an opportunity to be heard, and a decision rendered by an impartial decision maker.[51] Other due process requirements that must usually be met include the individual's right to counsel, the right to present evidence, and the right to cross-examine. Informal adjudication (the more common of the two) may be conducted on the basis of mutual consent of the parties; thus, it can take many forms, and it generally operates within looser constraints, as noted earlier.

A wide range of issues has been disputed and resolved by the courts regarding adjudication (especially the formal variety). In particular, the nature of the hearing itself is often at issue. Potential questions abound: (1) Is a hearing required and, if so, at what point in an administrative action? (2) What kind of hearing is required? (3) What sorts of evidence can be presented? (4) How will the presiding officer (usually an administrative law judge) evaluate the evidence presented, and how will he or she weigh the evidence in determining the outcome? The way such questions are answered is central to procedural due process, which, in turn, is at the heart of administrative adjudication and all its attendant rules.

Administrative Discretion and Administrative Law

Much has already been said in this book about *administrative discretion*—the reasons for it, some disputes about it (see Chapters 1 and 2), and some of its consequences, direct and indirect. Factors that have contributed to increased discretion already discussed are legislative delegations of authority to administrative entities, professional expertise of administrators, and political support from organized groups. In this context, however, the central question pertaining to administrative discretion is how to balance what have been called *administrative imperatives*, such as expertise, flexibility, and efficiency, and *judicial imperatives*, such as due process, equal protection, and substantive justice.[52] Many conflicts manifested in administrative law have revolved around concerns that administrative arbitrariness might result from the flexibility enjoyed by administrators acting in pursuit of efficiency. Consistent with this line of reasoning, those mindful of the judicial imperatives look to responsible administrators, executive and legislative oversight of bureaucracy, and judicial remedies as safeguards of the life, liberty, and property of individuals affected by administrative actions. In the next section, we examine several cases that simultaneously illustrate some of the most difficult problems addressed in administrative law and indicate why judicial review—as a check on administrative discretion—can be of major significance.

Selected Cases and Rulings in Administrative Law[53]

Before passage of the Administrative Procedure Act in 1946, the U.S. Supreme Court handed down several major rulings dealing with substantive and procedural fairness in administrative actions. Among the best known of these early cases was *Morgan v. United States* (304 U.S. 1 [1938]), one of a series of cases in which the Court "conveyed the clear message [that] public agencies needed to improve their hearing procedures to make them more consistent with constitutional due process standards."[54] Morgan, a stockyard operator, argued that the Secretary of Agriculture had violated his (Morgan's) due process rights by setting the maximum rate Morgan could charge in his business without a hearing.[55] Congress, in legislation enacted in 1921, had delegated considerable discretion to the secretary for setting maximum and reasonable rates for meatpackers and stockyards. However, it also had required a "full hearing" for stockyard operators—a hearing that Morgan claimed had never been held. The Court ruled in Morgan's favor and, in its opinion, elaborated on what constituted, in its judgment, a "fair hearing." The ruling in this case served as a prototype for many of the provisions regarding fair hearings that were included in the Administrative Procedure Act enacted eight years later.

Another landmark decision came in the case of *Goldberg v. Kelly* (397 U.S. 254 [1970]). Goldberg, as director of the New York State Department of Social Services, was sued by Kelly and other Aid to Families with Dependent Children (AFDC) recipients after the department had terminated their welfare payments. The department maintained that the recipients' due process rights were protected by the combination of a pretermination review and a fair hearing after termination; Kelly and the others argued that a hearing before benefits were terminated was an essential element of due process in these circumstances. One central issue, then, was whether a pretermination hearing was necessary for the state to meet recipients' due process requirements. Another issue, not as obvious, was whether the welfare benefits in question were rights (and as such procedurally protected by constitutional standards) or privileges (and thus not afforded the same protections, such as a fair hearing). In the *Goldberg* case, the Court actually tried to establish a somewhat different basis for deciding whether a hearing was needed, arguing that the right to a hearing should depend "on the extent to which a person might be expected to suffer a 'grievous loss,'"[56] not on whether a right or a privilege had been protected or denied. The Court ruled in favor of Kelly, holding that the recipients must have timely and adequate notice of the termination of benefits and that the decision to terminate must be based entirely on rules and evidence introduced at the pretermination hearing.

Numerous other cases, covering a wide variety of issues, circumstances, and procedural questions, have come before the Supreme Court. A sampling of cases suggests just how broad the range of concerns has been. In *Bi-Metallic Investment Company v. State Board of Equalization of Colorado* (239 U.S. 441 [1915]), the Court ruled that it does not violate the due process clause of the Fourteenth Amendment for a governmental body to take a general rule-making action (in this case, raising the property tax in the city of Denver) without giving each individual an opportunity to dispute the action. In *Energy Reserves Group, Inc. v. U.S. Department of Energy* (589 F.2d 1082 [Temp. Emer. Ct. App., 1978]), the Court held that it is not necessary for an agency to use the notice-and-comment provisions of the Administrative Procedure Act before it publishes a proposed rule as long as that rule only interprets existing law rather than formulating new law. The case of *Federal Crop Insurance Corporation v. Merrill* (332 U.S. 380 [1947]) illustrates how the principle known as estoppel can be applied in administrative law. *Estoppel* is the act of being stopped from proving or presenting something in court because the party involved did something previously that contradicts that party's present position. In this case Merrill, a farmer, had asked an agent of the Federal Crop Insurance Corporation (FCIC) if spring wheat planted on land that had grown winter wheat was insurable under the Federal Crop Insurance Act. After the agent assured him that it was, Merrill planted spring wheat, which was then destroyed by drought. When Merrill applied for payment, the FCIC refused on the grounds that its regulations prohibited the insuring of reseeded crops. Merrill, claiming that he had been misled by the government, filed suit. The issue before the court was this: Is a governmental agency prohibited (estopped) from relying on written regulations as a defense when a claimant relies on a verbal statement that turns out to be incorrect? In this case, the Court held that when terms and conditions for creating governmental liability are defined in explicit language in a statute, there is no liability for which a claimant may collect damages—even if both the claimant and the FCIC were ignorant of such a restriction. The Court, in effect, put its weight behind the explicit (written) nature of the regulation as the guiding standard to be followed—and to be used in case of legal challenge.

Administrative Law and Government Regulation

The field of administrative law encompasses considerably more than government regulation, narrowly defined. Agencies of all kinds and at all levels of government are subject to rulings of the courts and to provisions of administrative procedure acts regarding many aspects of their operations. Nevertheless, it is government's regulatory activities that are at the heart of administrative law precisely because regulation sits at the crossroads between government power and private behavior. It should be no surprise that administrative law grew initially because of the expansion of government regulation. Ironically, however, even if regulation does not continue to expand, administrative law is likely to become more extensive in its scope and reach. The same forces that would urge reforms in, if not a slowdown of, government regulation would also be likely to support *expanding* an area of American law that places at least procedural, and sometimes substantive, restraints on the actions government agencies can take relative to our nation's citizens.[57]

The Future of Government Regulation

Regulatory reform has been a recurring theme over the years, with every president since John F. Kennedy paying at least some public attention to the subject. Studies undertaken at presidential request, as well as other proposals, have become part of the reform literature.[58] Presidents Ford, Carter, Reagan, and Clinton made regulatory reform a high-priority matter, and the issue took on greater urgency in and out of government.

Complicating regulatory reform, however, is the wide variety of motives, assumptions, and policy objectives that have given rise to reform efforts.

More effective (and more cost-effective) regulation of the private sector is one potential goal. Another is enhancing regulatory accountability to the president; a third is increasing accountability to Congress.[59] Yet another is ending existing fragmentation in substantive areas of regulatory responsibility (for example, transportation); still another is separating responsibilities that can conflict, for example, regulation of an industry versus promotion of that industry's products. During the past forty years, various reform proposals have been put forward that embodied one or more of these emphases.[60]

Finally, of course, there is the policy option of pursuing deregulation— of reducing the national government's overall regulatory presence. Though this last goal was most clearly identified with the Reagan administration, it was not Ronald Reagan's only regulation-related objective. Nor was he the first president to seek deregulation. Under Jimmy Carter, major steps were taken (especially in trucking, rail and air transportation) to reduce regulatory activity and power.[61]

deregulation

strategy to reduce or remove government regulations.

Ronald Reagan came to office ideologically committed to "regulatory relief" for American business. In the context of the values and objectives noted earlier, his program was founded on a combination of deregulation and increased presidential control, with apparent attention to more cost-effective regulation as well. Although here, as elsewhere, the president did not achieve all he sought, the impacts of his actions continue to be felt.

That is especially true with regard to budget and personnel reductions affecting regulatory bodies. These merit brief attention because of the impacts these reductions had, and continue to have, on the capacity of regulators to carry out their statutory responsibilities.[62] With the exception of a few regulatory bodies, the 1990s and 2000s saw deep reductions (in both dollars and personnel) in regulatory budgets. Bill Clinton targeted some regulatory bodies for further cuts while boosting the budgets and responsibilities of others, particularly the OSHA and CPSC. Others came in for particularly severe cuts. Examples are the ICC's 50 percent workforce reduction (followed by disestablishment in 1995) and the FTC's 30 percent personnel cut. More specifically, fewer than half of the twelve regulatory bodies included in Table 11–1 received additional funding or personnel increases; additional funding was provided to commissions whose responsibilities were enhanced by new legislation: the FCC, FERC, Nuclear Regulatory Commission (NRC), and SEC. It should be remembered, however, that the figures used as the basis for this assessment are in current dollars; measured in constant dollars (that is, controlling for inflation), most regulators continue to lag behind 1980s funding levels. In short, the harsh treatment of some regulators under Ronald Reagan (especially) in his first term did not improve under the first President Bush, Bill Clinton, or George W. Bush. Efforts under the Obama administration to reregulate have met with stiff resistance from many business executives and opposition political leaders.

As always, however, all may not be what it seems in the debate over necessary and unnecessary regulation. For one thing, it is not uncommon to find some businesses that regard regulation as advantageous to their interests and, therefore, wish to remain regulated. Two examples are various segments of the trucking industry, including the Teamsters Union (even though the ICC no longer exists and a deregulation bill is now law), and the communications industry, particularly with reference to regulation of new video technologies.[63] Another unexpected twist involves a regulatory commission attempting to ease the regulatory burden, while being willing to go much further than the Congress—witness the FCC, which decides the future course of those same video technologies over which many broadcasters want the agency to retain a measure of control. The communications revolution poses serious questions regarding regulation of this aspect of American life, especially the emergence of satellite radio systems, high-speed broadband cable for faster access to the Internet, and links for creating interactive communication for homes, schools, and businesses.

Predictably, strong movement toward deregulation opened up new issues concerning its impacts. It is impossible to generalize about the impacts, simply because so many fields of economic activity (air, rail, and highway transport; communications; securities trading; and savings and loans institutions, to name only a few) have been affected by deregulation and, in some cases, in markedly different ways. Taking airline transportation as just one example, there are indications that deregulation, regardless of the benefits claimed for it, has been a mixed blessing. Some claim that because of deregulation, air fares have come down, while others disagree; some claim that competition among air transport companies has improved while other argue otherwise; and there are real concerns about air safety in the wake of deregulation based on cutbacks in air traffic control, safety inspections, and the like. It is not surprising if an observer comes away from a review of such commentaries a bit bewildered. Expert observers of just this one area of economic activity disagree as to the effects of deregulation.

reregulation

decision by Congress or an administrative agency to strengthen or reestablish government regulatory requirements.

Under the Obama administration, momentum in the direction of **reregulation** has increased, attempting to reverse the direction set by past Republican administrations. Here, again, a key focus is on homeland security and airlines, with various government efforts addressing concerns about the prevention of further terrorist attacks; safety of start-up airlines; provision of air service to smaller communities; lack of FAA inspections; transportation of hazardous materials in commercial passenger aircraft; and frequency of passenger complaints about lost luggage. Congress showed a willingness to respond to consumer pressures when, in 1992, it overrode George H. W. Bush's veto of a cable TV regulatory measure; in mid-1993, it enacted legislation regulating the charges that cable companies can levy for cable service. As previously indicated, in 1994, the FDA signaled its clear intention to bring cigarettes under direct federal regulation if it could be proved that the tobacco industry had deliberately manipulated cigarette nicotine levels, knowing that at certain levels, nicotine can become addictive. Other regulatory debates have also surfaced—for example, the possibility that lack of sufficient staff to enforce FAA regulations may have contributed to commercial aviation disasters, and the possible expansion of the FDA's role in food inspection, given the well-publicized fatalities that were due to *E. coli* bacteria poisoning and the animal fecal material allegedly found in some beef products. Reregulation has already been proposed in several other areas as well (notably concerning airport security, border control, emergency management coordination, various products imported from some other countries, and immigration).

In early 2007, President George W. Bush issued an executive order (EO 13422) amending an earlier policy statement regarding the procedures for executive agencies, issuance of "significant" and "economically significant" regulations. The order required each agency to establish a **Regulatory Policy Office (RPO)** headed by a political appointee to oversee the development of rules and regulations covering regulated industries.[64] Although the White House described the order as a necessary reform, various consumer, labor, and environmental groups opposed it as giving too much control of regulatory policies to big business groups supporting Republican interests.

Plainly, ongoing and ever more intense debates over government regulation are inevitable in the years ahead. With regulatory activity strongly supported by some as a means of ensuring fairness and equity in the marketplace, as well as safety and good product quality, while opposed with equal vigor by others on the grounds that it constitutes unwarranted interference and a potential threat to individual economic and social freedoms, any conflict is bound to be intense. Regulation continues to be at a crossroads. Much more is at stake than a rule here or a regulation there—the nature of our economy and government's relation to it are also at issue.

Regulatory Policy Office (RPO)

established in each executive agency under OMB direction as a result of Bush Executive Order 13422 (amending EO 12866), issued on January 18, 2007.

Summary

Government regulatory activity dates back to the late 1800s. IRCs as well as other government entities engage in regulation that in recent decades has become broader in scope and more controversial. Regulation is a mix of two principal approaches: regulating producers and encouraging competition in the marketplace. The focal point of regulatory activity has shifted steadily over time from the states to the national government. Both Congress and state legislatures have increasingly delegated legislative authority for regulation to entities created specifically as regulatory bodies.

In addition to regulating insurance and banking, state agencies examine and license physicians, lawyers, insurance agents, real estate agents, and so on. Other examples are state commerce commissions, liquor control boards, and recreation departments. Local regulation consists primarily of licensing certain businesses, and setting and enforcing various regulative codes.

Government regulations have developed in large part as a result of decisions designed to protect individuals and to maintain representativeness and fairness in governing. A by-product of the growth of the regulatory bureaucracy has been a mounting tangle of red tape. Regulatory procedures fall into the categories of rule making and adjudication. Rule-making procedures involve publication of proposed changes in rules, a period of public comment, issuance of final rules, and codification in the Code of Federal Regulations. The increase in regulatory decisions, particularly in adjudication, has meant a substantial increase in the importance of administrative law judges. The growth of administrative law itself has been a major phenomenon of the regulatory process.

The independence of regulatory bodies from the president is far from absolute, though structural features do shield members from some presidential influence. Presidential appointment power, with Senate consent, is substantial, and other forms of White House intervention are not unknown. Independence from Congress is limited, although regulators have more to do with individual committees than with Congress as a whole. However, they occasionally become more involved with the whole Congress, and with committees, if there is adverse public or industry reaction to proposed actions. Regulators are in frequent contact with industry leaders, both professionally and socially. Industries have a legitimate self-interest to uphold, but direct pressure on regulators is the exception, not the rule. Another problem is that individuals having the kind of expertise needed and sought by regulatory bodies often received their training and experience in the regulated industries themselves, thus bringing with them a natural "industry slant" on problems and needs. Administrative law has expanded in response to a growing governmental administrative apparatus.

Administrative law pertains to the authority needed by administrative entities to perform their duties and to the limits necessary to control their activities. This field focuses on the rules and regulations issued by administrative entities and on administrative powers and procedures, and brings law, administration, and politics together. National and state administrative procedure acts have given meaning to procedural due process.

Rule making is governed by requirements of public participation (including prior notice and opportunity for the public to present its views), publication of rules, and judicial review of proposed or actual rules. Rules themselves can be substantive, procedural, or interpretive. Adjudication involves settling controversies between contending parties and determining legal rights and obligations. Formal adjudication entails fair notice, opportunity to be heard, and a decision rendered by an impartial arbiter. Informal adjudication is far more common, often occurring on the basis of mutual consent within looser constraints. Legal issues surrounding the exercise of administrative discretion center on how to balance administrative and judicial imperatives; a central concern is bureaucratic arbitrariness.

Regulatory reform can be addressed to a variety of objectives that are not necessarily consistent with one another. Under recent presidents, deregulation has assumed greater importance. Regulatory relief involves reviews of existing rules, a slowdown in issuing major new regulations, relaxing enforcement of existing rules, and making significant reductions in regulatory budgets and personnel. Ironically perhaps, not all industries wish to be deregulated, and not all regulators have sought to retain their authority. Debates over government regulation are likely to continue well into the future.

Discussion Questions

1. In your judgment, what should the role of government regulators be? How much regulation should there be, in the abstract and in specific instances? What types of regulation should there be? What economic activities should be most carefully regulated?

2. Discuss social ("new") regulation, and the factors that seem to have led to its emergence. Compare and contrast social regulation with economic ("old") regulation.

3. Does the structure of regulatory agencies make any real difference in the operations of regulatory bodies? Why or why not?

4. Discuss the nature of regulatory politics—the issues that most frequently arise, the regular participants in political conflict, and how (if at all) regulatory politics differs from other kinds of administrative politics.

5. What lessons can regulatory bodies learn from the experience of the FTC in the cigarette-package-labeling controversy and in its conflicts with Congress? What lessons can be learned by advocates of change in any regulatory policies? What can advocates of the status quo learn?

6. Assess the steps taken toward the direction of deregulation of various enterprises. In your judgment, are these appropriate steps? Should regulators be "reined in" by the national government in other instances? By what standards should decisions be made—and by whom?

7. Is cost-benefit analysis appropriate as a basis for regulatory policy decisions? (In your answer, deal with the values underlying both the cost-benefit approach and your own view of its appropriateness.)

8. What values other than strictly monetary costs and benefits might be employed as a basis for establishing and evaluating regulatory policy?

9. Discuss the role of the courts in effectively monitoring the activities of administrative agencies. How have judicial interpretations changed the basic concept of bureaucratic autonomy and discretionary authority?

10. Do you believe that overall government regulation serves useful purposes? Why or why not? If yes, what purposes does it serve? Discuss.

Key Terms and Concepts

free-market competition, *461*

government regulation, *461*

monopolistic practices, *461*

independent regulatory boards and commissions (IRCs), *462*

administrative law, *462*

regulatory body, *462*

Sherman Antitrust Act, *464*

Justice Department, *464*

Federal Trade Commission (FTC), *464*

Clayton Act, *464*

Federal Energy Regulatory Commission (FERC), *465*

Energy Policy Act of 2005, *466*

Sarbanes–Oxley Act of 2002, *467*

social regulatory initiatives, *469*

Administrative Procedure Act of 1946, *471*

protective regulation, *471*

dependent regulatory agencies (DRAs), *472*

rule making, *474*

adjudication, *474*

Federal Register, *474*

Code of Federal Regulations, *474*

administrative law judge, *475*

advisory opinion, *475*

consent order, *475*

Common Cause, *481*

Dodd-Frank Wall Street Reform and Consumer Protection Act, *487*

Financial Stability Oversight Council (FSOC), *487*

Office of Financial Research (OFR), *487*

procedural fairness, *493*

procedural due process, *493*

deregulation, *499*

reregulation, *500*

Regulatory Policy Office (RPO), *501*

Suggested Readings

Barry, Donald D., and Howard R. Whitcomb. *The Legal Foundations of Public Administration*. 3rd ed. Lanham, Md.: Rowman & Littlefield, 2005.

Cann, Steven J. *Administrative Law*. 4th ed. Thousand Oaks, Calif.: Sage, 2006.

Cherni, Judith A. *Economic Growth versus the Environment: The Politics of Wealth, Health, and Air Pollution*. New York: Palgrave, 2002.

Cooper, Phillip J. *Public Law and Public Administration*. 4th ed. Itasca, Ill.: Wadsworth, 2006.

Derthick, Martha A. *Up in Smoke: From Legislation to Litigation in Tobacco Politics*. 3rd ed. Washington, D.C.: CQ Press, 2011.

Eisner, Marc. *Regulatory Politics in Transition*. 2nd ed. Baltimore: Johns Hopkins University Press, 2000.

Fritschler, A. Lee, and Catherine E. Rudder. *Smoking and Politics: Bureaucracy Centered Policy Making*. 6th ed. New York: Longman, 2007.

Hall, Daniel E. *Administrative Law: Bureaucracy in a Democracy*. 5th ed. Upper Saddle River, N.J.: Prentice-Hall, 2012.

Hamilton, Michael S., ed. *Regulatory Federalism, Natural Resources and Environmental Management*. Washington, D.C.: American Society for Public Administration, 1990.

Harris, Richard A., and Sidney M. Milkis. *The Politics of Regulatory Change: A Tale of Two Agencies*. 2nd ed. New York: Oxford University Press, 1996.

John, DeWitt. *Civic Environmentalism: Alternatives to Regulation in States and Communities*. Washington, D.C.: Congressional Quarterly Press, 1993.

Kerwin, Cornelius M. *Rulemaking: How Government Agencies Write Law and Make Policy*. 3rd ed. Washington, D.C.: CQ Press, 2003.

Kettl, Donald F. *Leadership at the Fed*. New Haven, Conn.: Yale University Press, 1988.

_____. *The Politics of the Administrative Process*. Washington, D.C.: Congressional Quarterly Press, 2011.

Landy, Marc K., Marc J. Roberts, and Stephen R. Thomas. *The Environmental Protection Agency: Asking the Wrong Questions from Nixon to Clinton*. Expanded ed. New York: Oxford University Press, 1994.

Rosenbloom, David H., and Richard D. Schwartz, eds. *Handbook of Regulation and Administrative Law*. New York: Marcel Dekker, 1994.

Scheberle, Denise. *Federalism and Environmental Policy: Trust and the Politics of Implementation*, 2nd ed. Washington, D.C.: Georgetown University Press, 2004.

Schlosberg, David. *Environmental Justice and the New Pluralism*. New York: Oxford University Press, 2002.

Skrzycki, Cindy. *The Regulators: Anonymous Power Brokers in American Politics*. Lanham, Md.: Rowman & Littlefield, 2003.

Strauss, Peter L., Todd Rakoff, W. A. Gellhorn, and Cynthia Farina, eds. 10th ed. *Gellhorn and Byse's Administrative Law: Cases and Comments*. Westbury, N.Y.: Foundation Press, 2003.

Teske, Paul. *Regulation in the States*. Washington, D.C.: Brookings Institution Press, 2004.

Tolchin, Susan J., and Martin Tolchin. *Dismantling America: The Rush to Deregulate*. Boston: Houghton Mifflin, 1983.

Warren, Kenneth. *Administrative Law in the Political System*. 4th ed. Boulder , Colo.: Westview Press, 2004.

Conclusion:
Public Administration in a Time
of Conflict and Social Change

Our examination of public administration in the United States is now complete. From treatment of topics in the text, several impressions should have emerged clearly. The current state of public administration is characterized by considerable unrest caused by fiscal stress and intense political conflict due to excessive borrowing, lower property values, and natural and man-made disasters. In addition, U.S. involvement in three costly foreign conflicts, concern with global financial stability, and dramatic developments in and out of the field are affecting its likely future shape. Advocates of competing political points of view argue forcefully for *their* vision of the appropriate future role for government and public administration in America, as Barack Obama and John McCain did so vigorously during the 2008 presidential campaign. Since the first edition of this book was published more than a generation ago, we have been led by six different presidents (three Democrats and three Republicans), each with vastly different ideologies and visions of the nation's needs, and each with sharply divergent policy priorities.

Yet another reality is that although it may be desirable to maintain various features of governmental and administrative practice—such as accountability, efficiency, participation, performance standards, and strong leadership—it is difficult to achieve all or even most of them simultaneously. Political conservatives (such as Sarah Palin, Senator Mitch McConnell, House Republican leader John Boehner, and former Minnesota Governor Tim Pawlenty) seek less government, more private-sector alternatives and

The best way to begin genuine bipartisanship to make America stronger is to work together on the real crises facing our country, not to manufacture an artificial crisis to serve a special interest agenda out of touch with the needs of Americans.

Senator John Kerry (D-Mass.)

greater consumer choice, and lower taxes. Such objectives often conflict directly with social goals of more liberal politicians (such as President Barack Obama, Vice President Joe Biden, Senate Democratic Leader Harry Reid, Senator John Kerry, and Secretary of State Hillary Clinton), on issues such as providing a minimum "safety net" for those members of society least able to fend for themselves, assuring access to quality public education and affordable health care, promoting diversity in the workforce, providing equal employment opportunity, redistributing resources, and expanding citizen participation. This poses difficult questions for us. On which feature(s) do we place greatest value? Which are we willing to sacrifice in order to achieve others? Who benefits and who is harmed by choosing one over another? In short, intricate and perplexing questions abound—questions for which there are no easy answers.

In this concluding chapter, we will discuss how public administration interacts within the context of citizen demands and frustrations, and of continuing risk and uncertainty about the future. How public administrators react to domestic and global crises and how they cope with changing domestic economic and social environments determines, to a great extent, the quality of life for large numbers of citizens in the United States, and increasingly those in other countries seeking the same economic and political freedoms we enjoy. First we will consider the social and governmental environment, and then the growing dissatisfaction with certain practices of governmental administration, review evolving issues and challenges in its study and teaching, and conclude by noting some continuing features and questions, in the field. Throughout this discussion several themes will be evident: (1) the presence of numerous paradoxes in public administration, (2) tensions existing among these paradoxes and the challenge of dealing with them, and (3) the accelerating pace of change in administrative theory and practice.

The Social and Governmental Environment

For the past sixty years, social and political struggles have taken new forms in the United States, imposing continuous pressures on our values and institutions. Rising global tensions and value conflicts stem from our resolve to pursue objectives such as political freedom and social diversity while maintaining economic freedom and independence. Societal relations are directly affected by political interests and global economic competition. If those relations are tense and combative, as they have been since the early 1970s, that will be reflected in political values and procedures, including those in public administration. The national government "has become a microcosm of the conflicts and differences that pervade society . . . As government [at all levels] becomes coextensive with society in composition and function, it experiences the disorganization . . . of society itself."[1]

There is much more to the social and governmental environment, however, than simply promoting economic freedom and social diversity. Recent turbulence surrounding public administration has resulted from a host of changes, paradoxes, and conflicts. Chief among them is rapid social change, not only in population growth, immigration patterns (for example, increasing numbers of Asian, Caribbean, Latino, and Middle Eastern immigrants escaping repressive political regimes and seeking new economic opportunities), but also in rapidly changing governmental roles, and a multitude of technological innovations. Our capacity for economic growth is seriously hampered by a weaker U.S. dollar and dependence on imported goods and raw materials, chiefly petroleum, but also finished products and metals from other countries, as well as limits resulting from depletion of our natural resources. As the world's largest debtor nation, the United States buys more from foreign providers than it sells on global markets. This weakens our **balance of trade** with other nations, and results in income and job losses from our products and services being less competitive on world markets. The imbalance of trade has become somewhat more favorable to U.S. economic interests with the weakness of the U.S. dollar against other major foreign currencies, making some of our export products less expensive vis-à-vis foreign competitors. Our economy, however, has become more vulnerable to changes in the larger global economy. And politically, as a nation, the United States continues to search for greater consensus regarding the direction in which we should try to move.

Another factor affecting our economic viability is the **knowledge explosion**, including the spread of technology, growing use (and possible misuse) of information communication technologies (ICTs), and the expansion of electronic government (e-gov) and **social networking**, which carries with it increasing potential for very different kinds of human interactions—both positive and negative. Growth of knowledge, science, and **technological change** are closely linked with changes in the nature of society and in human capabilities, values, and behavior. As examples, scientific explanations about the origins of the universe and of life on this planet may profoundly affect traditional religious beliefs; new high-speed wireless communications linkages permit direct citizen-to-citizen contacts across international borders. Such unfiltered contacts also increasingly make it possible to foment revolutionary uprisings in repressive political regimes, and access to previously restricted databases promises to revolutionize knowledge management in many different organizational settings.

Such developments have an ironic twist. We have had faith for decades that expanding our knowledge would make our world both safer and more predictable, and that science would help us answer age-old questions with much more precision and certainty. Yet we have found just the opposite: the more we learn, the less certain everything seems. Many people are disturbed by all this uncertainty, and it is possible that expanded knowledge contributes to social instability, with many seeking to return (in effect) to "the good old

balance of trade

the difference between the value of a nation's exports and the value of its imports over a period of time (usually one year), adjusted for currency valuations.

knowledge explosion

the social phenomenon, creating Internet-enhanced information communication technologies and vast new areas of research; examples are biogenetic engineering, cloud computing, unmanned space exploration, mass communications, open-sourcing, nuclear technology, and energy research.

social networking

Internet linkages between and among individuals (or organizations) connected by one or more specific types of interdependency, such as common interest, friendship, kinship, financial exchange, likes and dislikes, sexual relationships, or relationships of beliefs, knowledge, or prestige. *Facebook, MySpace, Twitter,* and *YouTube* are among the leading examples.

technological change

rapidly emerging patterns of change (related in part to the knowledge explosion) in communication, medical, and transportation technologies, among others, with significant implications both for the societal challenges confronting government and for the means and resources increasingly available to government for conducting public affairs.

fundamentalism

practice of certain religious
groups that adhere to
strict beliefs and literal
interpretation of a set of basic
religious principles.

days" that many remember as a less unnerving past. One indication of this is the phenomenon of religious revivalism, or **fundamentalism**, among growing numbers of Christians, Jews, and Muslims in many countries of the world (including our own).

The present unstable social and political environment in the United States threatens long-standing safety nets for many millions of low-income, disadvantaged, unemployed, physically challenged, and elderly Americans. Debates over the future of Medicare, Medicaid, Social Security, welfare, and universal health care reflect, among many citizens, a new "fend-for-yourself" attitude in coping with the social and economic problems that many of us face. At the same time that social programs for low-income Americans are being cut, compensation for presidents and chief executive officers of major corporations have risen to a point where the *average* CEO now earns nearly $12 million in salary and bonuses per year—over 350 times the salary of the average worker. Real wages for full-time and part-time workers (that is, adjusted for inflation) have not risen for thirty years, and only one in three employers provides health care benefits. Of the nearly 50 million Americans who lack access to health insurance, *80 percent are employed*. Moreover, the IRS reports that the wealthiest 1 percent of Americans earned 24 percent of all adjusted gross income in 2010, up from 19 percent in 2004. This is the largest share of income held by the rich since before the Great Depression of the 1930s.

Despite the economic recession, wealth continues to accumulate among fewer and fewer Americans. Many are asking if this "survival of the fittest" approach to capitalism, and its consequences for governance, has now exceeded our capacity to absorb massive social and economic shocks brought about by natural and man-made disasters such as the Wall Street collapse in August 2011, Hurricane Katrina, extensive flooding in the Midwest, the *Deepwater Horizon* oil spill in the Gulf of Mexico, the catastrophic tornadoes across much of the South during the spring of 2011, and the escalating costs of gasoline, health care, higher education and foreign wars.

There is a direct link between these new grim realities and public administration, because governments are involved with virtually every major challenge and opportunity we face. These range from the **war on terror** and disaster relief to controlling crime; from providing health care not only to the poor and elderly, but also to working middle-income Americans; creating new jobs for the unemployed and protecting meager retirement savings for elderly Americans; and from combating discrimination based on disability, race, gender, national origin, or sexual orientation to debating and adopting fair taxing and spending policies. Other challenges include providing student grants and loans; protecting individual retirement plans; strengthening anti-terrorism and emergency preparedness planning; prosecuting corrupt chief executives and other elected officials; and rescuing bankrupt savings and loan companies, some of which may have engaged in fraudulent business practices. These expectations continue to grow despite the fact that many problems cannot be fully resolved,

war on terror

the U.S. government's response
to political violence directed at
U.S. citizens and institutions here
and abroad.

but only temporarily coped with until the next crisis erupts. In some cases, demands on the bureaucracy to truly *solve* problems may be unrealistic.

The high cost of entitlements is creating "intergenerational conflict" among younger workers, baby boomers, and older retirees. When Social Security was enacted in 1935, there were forty workers for every one retiree. That ratio is now only 3-to-1, and political movements are gaining strength to "redistribute" more government programs from the elderly to younger workers, students, and parents of young children. Yet, George W. Bush's forceful lobbying efforts to reform Social Security and allow younger workers to create private retirement accounts, similar to Individual Retirement Accounts (IRAs), fell largely on deaf ears. No one, it seems, wants to threaten his or her own retirement benefits by making radical changes in the current system. These attitudes are becoming more prevalent, especially as larger numbers of private corporations and public agencies "downsize" by outsourcing jobs and eliminating employee health care and retirement benefits. Barack Obama's 2012 budget plan called for the beginning of long-term adjustments and changes for Social Security, but worry still exists as the baby boomer generation continues to age. Such concerns manifested themselves during the summer of 2011 as Congress and the president grappled with the pressing need to raise the national debt limit as well as the continuing recession. Congress and the White House responded by authorizing a "supercommittee" composed of 6 Democrats and 6 Republicans (3 each from the U.S. House and Senate, appointed by its leaders) to propose $1.2 trillion in budget cuts for FY 2012. If the supercommittee fails to act by the end of 2011, proportional reductions will be made in both defense and domestic spending.

Nevertheless, there is an imbalance between public and private sectors in dealing with society's deeply rooted social problems. The public (governmental) side of the scale still carries most of the overall responsibility—but this may not always be the case. For example, the housing and financial crises have heavily impacted the U.S. economy, convincing a growing number of Americans that government should do more to regulate soaring energy costs, control corrupt banking and real estate practices, protect homeowners from foreclosures, and assist failing businesses. President Obama received substantial support from Americans in his call to regulate these industries more closely. However, the increasing complexity of public problems makes it less likely that elected representatives can cope with more than a few significant issues at a time. This has made it more difficult for many public officials to address the full scope of changes required to meet various public needs. At the same time, more Americans appear reluctant to use nongovernmental alternatives such as private retirement accounts, nonprofit organizations, faith-based groups, school vouchers, and privatization to deliver traditional public services. In many policy areas, evidence of fraud, waste, and corruption has created further mistrust between citizens and those advocating alternative forms of providing public services. More than ever, public administrators must acquire and demonstrate the technical skills necessary to advise elected officials and citizens about which of the much more numerous courses of action are most likely to successfully implement public policies. Thus, the role of expert administrators to whom discretionary authority and responsibility for program management are delegated becomes ever larger (although not unlimited).

One other persistent and significant aspect of the immediate social and governmental environment of public administration, with enormous implications for the future conduct of government generally, is **chronic fiscal stress**. As corporate downsizing, declining real estate values, and global outsourcing combine with decreasing tax revenues and declining productivity to slow economic growth in the private sector, the revenue bases of all governments are shrinking. Consequently, administrative agencies and governmental units, by the hundreds, must absorb deep cutbacks in funding, personnel, and the levels of services they can provide. Deficit increases and conflicts over spending priorities between Barack Obama and the House of Representatives nearly brought the federal government to a standstill in the summer of 2011. Crises were averted, however, with last minute deals, requiring additional compromise between Democrats and Republicans. The unwillingness of taxpayers to assume additional tax burdens has only compounded the problem for government officials.

Numerous state governments are facing large deficits in current budget projections and are being forced to increase public school class sizes, reduce social services (and, as in the case of Minnesota in the summer of 2011, reduce—or shut down entirely—all manner of other services as well), and release prisoners before they serve their full sentences.[2] As another example (also in the summer of 2011), the Democratic governor of Illinois announced his intention to cancel pay raises for approximately 30,000 unionized state employees, including prison guards and public health workers. The governor maintained that the FY (fiscal year) 2012 budget adopted by the state legislature did not include sufficient funds to cover the costs of the raises. The American Federation of State, County, and Municipal Employees (AFSCME) filed suit in federal court; it also sought a ruling from an independent mediator, as well as asking the legislature to act. Similar budget-related actions were taken in a number of other states during 2009, 2010, and 2011. Such decisions have obvious financial implications for public budgeting. They also directly affect personnel management, labor relations, and the push for greater equity, efficiency, effectiveness, service quality, productivity, and accountability in public management.

The central difficulty, however, is the need to adjust our assumptions about economic growth as the foundation for continued governmental growth. Agencies, their administrators, and their clienteles, accustomed to successive increases in operating budgets and the programmatic benefits they could provide, have been rudely jolted by new economic and political realities. Explicit and increasing attention is now being paid at all levels of government to the need for "doing more with less," even though there is mounting evidence that in many places, doing *less* with less is the emerging reality. The present environment in this respect has bred increasing hostility toward "big government"—out of economic necessity, if not always due to direct public animosity. The long-term

---

chronic fiscal stress

condition confronting increasing numbers of governments and public agencies, resulting from a combination of economic inflation, declining productivity, slower economic growth, and taxpayer resistance to a larger tax burden.

consequences of this change may prove to be both permanent and fundamental in their impact on government, and on administrative operations in particular.

All this is occurring in the context of more fundamental value changes in society. A wide range of beliefs and institutions is under attack from new and competing ideologies. Central to change at this basic level is decline in respect for authority; traditional sources and centers of authority, including parents, teachers, religious leaders, politicians, and judges exert diminishing influence on greater numbers of young (and some older) people. Decline of authority suggests evolving institutional patterns. One of the many negative consequences of this decline is an increasing failure rate among high school students, as high as 30 to 50 percent in many urban and rural districts, referred to in the most negative terms as "dropout factories."[3] Declining math, reading, and science scores of American students are serious social issues with global economic consequences. Young males in particular have been negatively affected by loss of well-paying jobs in this country and elsewhere. Economists have noted that unemployment rates of 20 to 30 percent among young males are not uncommon in Arab countries. The ability of government to govern may well be compromised by these institutional failures, to say nothing of how other institutions, such as businesses, religions, universities, and the military, will be affected.

Current (and growing) opposition to repressive central governments in many parts of the world has led to severe consequences for millions of individuals. Distrust of the Russian government in Moscow, accompanied by the rise of organized crime within the newly independent republics of the former Soviet Union, illustrates the decline of other democratic institutions, such as a free press and a multiparty system, within that crumbling centralized system. In reaction, authoritarian measures have been re-imposed and are apparently being accepted (albeit reluctantly) by a substantial majority of the Russian population.[4] Despite some promising changes in Egypt, Saudi Arabia, Tunisia, and Yemen, the same pattern of brutal repression has been repeated, and continues, in Bahrain, Iran, Libya, and Syria. Other societies where wealth and political power are concentrated in the hands of a narrow elite sector are experiencing the emergence of similar pro-democracy movements clashing with repressive political authorities.

Social and Governmental Paradoxes

Public administration is affected by a series of other paradoxical developments, some within this country alone and others worldwide in their scope. For one, there has been a blurring of distinctions between public and private sectors in the United States, contrary to the popular belief that they are separate and distinct. Every important program to raise revenue, maintain employment and economic productivity, improve educational performance, relieve social distress, correct abuses, guarantee health care and Social Security, and protect citizen rights has "entailed the creation of new and complex arrangements in which the distinction between [nonprofit], public, and private has become more blurred."[5] Examples are numerous: Amtrak, the Corporation for Public Broadcasting (a frequent target of conservative lawmakers in both parties), the National Aeronautics and Space Administration (NASA), and the U.S. Postal Service at the national level; charter schools, community-action agencies, health systems agencies, and Planned Parenthood at the local level (all bridging nonprofit, public–private, and intergovernmental boundaries); and quasi-public organizations such as the Red Cross and United Way, established to work with government in public programs such as disaster relief, Medicare, Medicaid, and community development. The influence of these public and private partnerships has grown considerably, and may continue to do so in an entrepreneurial, market-based, and results-driven environment.

revolution of rising expectations

social phenomenon of the period since World War II, affecting many nations, in which people who have been relatively poor have sought to increase their level of prosperity both as individuals and as groups; related in part to faith in technological and social advances.

We also are experiencing a pervasive global **revolution of rising expectations**, which still dominates politics in developing nations and many portions of our own population. At the same time, some others have voiced an appeal for a *lowering* of our expectations. Both refer to expectations about political freedom, personal consumption, income and economic development, higher productivity, more leisure time, acquisition of material possessions, and increased standards of living. In this country, rising expectations and some governmental responses in the past sixty years have centered on recent immigrant, poor, and middle-income Americans, who have by no means given up their aspirations to the "good life." Countertrends toward breaking the dependence on government and on so-called "lesser expectations" reflect an economic realism about the decline in workers' wages resulting in loss of real income over the past thirty years, concern for environmental quality, finite resources, population stabilization rather than continuous growth, and "quality of life" as opposed to "standard of living." Ideological and political controversies over climate change, the energy crisis, "economy versus ecology," job retraining, and the uncertain future of entitlements such as Social Security, Medicare, and Medicaid, among others, illustrate this paradox.

postindustrialism

social and economic phenomenon emerging in many previously industrialized nations; characterized by a relative decline in the importance of production, labor, and durable goods, and an increase in the importance of knowledge, new technologies, the provision of services, and leisure time.

Another paradox exists between continuing emphasis on industrialization (closely linked to economic development and rising expectations) and the emergence of what has been called the "postindustrial society." **Postindustrialism** refers to a socioeconomic order in which there is a relative decline in importance of production, land, and labor as economic forces, and a relative upsurge in importance of knowledge, information, new technologies, rendering of services (as opposed to production of goods), and available leisure time. Implications for government and public administration are immense: changes in revenue patterns, educational and service needs, information technologies and capabilities, political demands, and so on. Elements of postindustrial society have become an integral part of the fabric of social and economic life, and therefore of the complex forces pressing on business, industry, and government. This paradox is complicated further by an emerging emphasis on global trade and reindustrialization—that is, upgrading and modernizing of our aging physical plant and production capacity to avoid falling further behind other more competitive nations such as, Brazil, China, India, South Korea, and Russia. Furthermore, forces of nationalism still run deep and strong in many parts of the world, though conflicting currents of so-called **globalization** have arisen and are gaining strength. Globalization has been defined as an acceleration of transcontinental flows of capital, ideas, American culture, and goods and services across national boundaries via the Internet in a networked society.[6] Jagdish Bhagwati, one the leading proponents of global trade, defines globalization as "the integration of national economies into the international economy through trade, direct foreign investment by [various international financial institutions], short-term capital flows, and international flows of technology."[7] In some of the older nation-states, nationalism (identity with a national unit of government, patriotism, observance of duties of citizenship, and pride in one's country) seems to be in decline.

Globalization has eroded the importance of national sovereignty and increased the influence of overlapping networks of integrated technology and the power of **multinational corporations (MNCs)**. Postnational cynicism toward patriotism and political symbols such as anthems and flags, and growing alienation from government institutions, all mark this decline. At the same time, economic globalization requires that governments develop policies that address various disaffected groups, such as "outsourced" factory workers in developed nations (including the United States), who are being displaced by this new economic order. Postnationalism combined with increasing globalization could mean one of two things. It could mean an awakening of feeling for a larger "community," for organizing economic and political arrangements that would eliminate trade barriers and strengthen international bonds of cooperation and respect, such as the **European Union (EU)** and the North American Free Trade Agreement (NAFTA).

Postnationalism, however, also could spawn a countertrend toward emphasizing individual group identities *within* nations at the expense of established political entities. Tribalism in many African nations, the reemergence of National Socialism in Germany, the Quebec separatist movement, language rivalries in Belgium, and ethnic tensions in Iraq, Serbia, Lebanon, Spain, and the former Soviet Union are examples of the latter. A third possibility, perhaps ironically, is a *reawakening* of nationalism, as a reaction against globalizing forces. And, *transcending* the forces of nationalism, we have seen the emergence of a global pro-democracy movement among citizens in countries that have long suppressed basic political and economic freedoms. One explanation for this sudden resurgence of protest movements is the spread of Internet communications. Whether ICTs have become a significant force in world politics weakening government's power to control and censor information or an instrument for further repression is being closely monitored.[8]

The uprising that began in Egypt in late January of 2011 is instructive regarding the impacts of **social media**. This revolt was inspired by the relatively

globalization

an acceleration of transcontinental flows of capital, ideas, culture, and goods and services across national boundaries via the Internet in a networked global society leading to an integration of national economies into the international economy through trade, direct foreign investment (by multinational corporations), short-term capital flows, and international flows of technology.

multinational corporations (MNCs)

large American, European, and Asian corporations that exert significant influence on economic policies of many countries while working outside the legal or regulatory systems of any particular nation.

European Union (EU)

trading bloc of twenty-seven European countries, twelve of which have converted to a common currency, the euro, to eliminate trade barriers among those nation-states.

social media

various communication tools and technologies that connect individuals by one or more specific types of interdependencies, relationships, or beliefs. *Facebook, MySpace, Twitter, and YouTube* are among the leading examples.

bloodless ousting of the government in Tunisia months earlier. Citizens took to the streets to protest high unemployment, corruption, and the thirty-year military rule of pro-American President Hosni Mubarak. The protests were the largest since the 1970s, with Egyptians coming together via the expanded use of social networking. The government responded by attempting to block *Twitter*, which not only enraged citizens, but brought increased international attention to the uprising. Egypt attempted to block *Facebook* while riot police took to the streets, arresting and injuring hundreds. When the government learned about a big protest planned in Tahrir Square, it took further action, shutting down the Internet completely.

As the protests continued, the United States and other countries intensified their criticism of Mubarak. President Obama even contacted the Egyptian president and asked him to prepare for a transition of power. Despite brutal repression, there was no indication that protests were abating, leading to the March 31, 2011, resignation of President Mubarak and the announcement that there would be a countrywide referendum held to draft a new constitution. Celebrations erupted in Cairo's Tahrir Square, now renamed Liberation Square.[9]

In Iran and Syria, the governments employed brutal crackdowns in an attempt to repress the demonstrations. Why did repressive tactics fail in Egypt and succeed in other countries? One major difference is that Egypt relies on the United States for substantial amounts of foreign aid, and relations between the countries were strained as the American media broadcast images of Mubarak's violent crackdowns. Iran has no diplomatic relations with the United States and is thus immune from such pressure. Egypt enjoyed more civil freedoms under Mubarak than Iran does under President Mahmoud Ahmadinejad, which may have limited the amount of violence that the Egyptian administration and U.S. government were comfortable condoning. While further protests also were met with severe crackdowns in Libya and Syria, the protests gave supporters a new sense of hope, even though these movements are still far from bringing about the kind of fundamental changes that have occurred in Egypt and Tunisia.

There is evidence to suggest that new media technology may win out in the long run in the fight to overthrow repressive regimes. Conservative media commentator George Will argues that technological coordination will outpace government repression. "All modern tyrannies have depended on intellectual autarky being able to seal off the consciousness of its people from the outside world . . . it can't be done anymore."[10] The wave of revolutions in 2011 may yet validate Will's statement. As individuals communicate directly with protesters in other countries via social media, they have sparked protests in their own countries.[11]

A related paradox involves tendencies toward violence (including those defined as terrorist acts) and nonviolence. Violence is no stranger to world affairs or to our own domestic scene. Huge stockpiles of nuclear weapons in the United States and former Soviet Union, with other countries such as Iran, Israel, North Korea, India, and Pakistan joining the "nuclear club," create the potential for worldwide holocaust. Non-nuclear conflicts exist between or within nations—such as those in the Middle East and some republics of the former Soviet Union—reminding us of how far we are from a world order characterized by the peaceful rule of law. The 1998 attacks on the U.S. embassies in Kenya and Tanzania; the September 11, 2001, attacks on the World Trade Center and the Pentagon; the Madrid train bombings in March 2004; the London Underground and bus bombings of July 7, 2005; and insurgent violence targeting U.S. troops in Afghanistan and Iraq reflect a higher level of violence in the resolution of international conflicts. The assassination of former Pakistani Prime Minister and opposition leader Benazir Bhutto, in late December 2007, created considerable chaos in a nuclear-armed nation, which the Western world depends upon to help oppose the spread of terrorist violence. Rising sentiment, however, also exists for nonviolent resolution of disputes, accompanied by considerable organizational sophistication in some instances, with the United Nations and its complex of organizations as the best-known example. Martin Luther King, Jr. patterned his nonviolent civil rights movement after the example of Mohandas Gandhi, leader of India's independence movement against Britain in the 1940s. The antiwar movement that tried to stop U.S. involvement in Vietnam during the late 1960s and early 1970s was generally (although not entirely) nonviolent. Growing opposition to nuclear weapons, which first surfaced in the 1980s, has been largely nonviolent. Another irony exists in that some revolutionary movements use violence as a means to promote "peaceful" aims. Bombings by revolutionary and separatist groups have occurred in Great Britain, Iraq, the Philippines, India, Israel, Spain, Germany, Pakistan, Russia, Japan, and France, despite countermeasures to secure public places such as airports, buses, railroads, and subway stations.

The values of limited government and deregulation of private activity continue to exert a firm hold on our thinking in this country, yet many political agendas, government programs, and regulatory activities seem to conflict with it. The need for greater domestic security in order to prevent future terrorist attacks, as well as further government regulation to protect consumers, are prime examples. To the extent that we look to government to protect us from corporate fraud, natural disasters, market abuses, terrorist attacks, and medical malpractice, we create the potential for government to regulate more than just economic behavior. How limited we want our government to be will continue to be an issue in politics and administration for the foreseeable future. The re-emergence of neo-conservatism, and Republican victories in recent congressional elections, further reinforce the popularity of this restrictive view of government. On the other hand, Bill Clinton's defeat of Republicans George H. W. Bush in 1992 and Bob Dole in 1996, Republican losses in congressional races in 1998 followed by House Speaker (and later, Republican

Electoral College

a mechanism established under the Constitution to choose the president and the vice president of the United States. Each state has as many electoral votes as members in Congress and its delegates, called electors, can be selected by any method. Candidates who win the popular vote in each state receive all of that state's electoral votes (except in Maine and Nebraska). Under this system, a presidential candidate can lead in the nationwide popular vote and can still fail to win the required majority in the Electoral College: for example, Bush versus Gore in 2000.

campaign finance reform

efforts by reform groups and some candidates to limit the influence of money in political campaigns. In 2002, the McCain–Feingold Act (sponsored by the presidential candidate and former Senator John McCain [R-AZ] and Senator Russ Feingold [D-WI]) was signed into law, limiting "soft money" spent by political parties on behalf of candidates through issue advertising and get-out-the-vote drives.

Citizens United vs. Federal Election Commission

a controversial Supreme Court decision that declared that corporate funding of independent political broadcasts in candidate elections cannot be limited under the U.S. Constitution.

presidential hopeful) Newt Gingrich's resignation, Clinton's survival of the Republican impeachment attempt in 1999, the Bush–Gore **Electoral College** debacle in 2000, Democratic gains in U.S. House and Senate races in 2006, and voter reactions in 2010 to the first two years of the Obama presidency, make it difficult to predict how voters will respond in the future. Conservative members of the Republican Party are troubled by what they see as blatant disregard of long-standing constitutional and fiscal principles. According to Patrick J. Buchanan, former Nixon press secretary, presidential candidate, and national media commentator, "with [September 11], we got a wake-up call. With Katrina, the smoke alarm went off. America today needs an authentic conservatism that will end our Asian wars, shed this empire, bring the budgets back into balance, no matter the political cost, and make demands on us all for sacrifices."[12] Indeed, during the George W. Bush administration (2001–2009), the discretionary share of the federal budget, primarily military and homeland security expenses, increased at a faster rate than at any time since World War II. These sentiments were reflected in the anti-Bush and anti-Republican votes in 2006 and 2008 that led to Democrats winning substantial majorities in both the U.S. House and Senate. Democrats also regained control of several state legislatures and many state governorships. By 2010, however, the pendulum had swung back to a more conservative anti-Washington, anti-incumbent mood, resulting in Republicans taking control of the House of Representatives. The issue of "how much government is too much government?" will continue to drive public debates and political choices.

In spite of our expressed reverence for democratic representative institutions, there is increasing concern with electoral processes that some see as antiquated, especially our system of statewide caucuses and winner-take-all presidential primaries as key elements in the presidential nomination process, and continuing to use the Electoral College (technically) for choosing the president and vice president of the United States. Also, access and influence are unevenly distributed throughout the population, and both major political parties advocate **campaign finance reform** (albeit with protections for their own loyal contributors). In fact, most contributors give money to candidates and political parties for the express purpose of gaining access to those in office after electoral decisions are made. Similarly, influence in the political process (partly dependent on access) is clearly enjoyed by some more than others. Influencing the outcome of elections became far easier with the Supreme Court's 2010 decision in the case of ***Citizens United vs. Federal Election Commission*** (130 S. Ct. 876). Besides money, which can now flow more freely from large lobbying groups, a key factor is organization. Well-organized groups have long been acknowledged as having the advantage in exercising political influence. Reform of electoral processes and campaign financing is difficult because of the dominance of organized over unorganized interests. Large institutions, such as corporations, government agencies, colleges and universities, farm organizations, and labor unions, will always place their institutional interests over the interests of individuals. This makes it impossible to sustain a claim of comparable influence among different groups in a system in which organization, wealth, and political power go hand in hand.[13]

Complicating matters further is the fact that, in many cases, clear public preferences on policy questions simply do not exist. Contrary to popular belief, voters usually do not confer policy mandates (clear statements of policy preference) when they go to the polls. Barack Obama's victory over John McCain in 2008, George W. Bush's over John Kerry in 2004, Bill Clinton's over Bob Dole in 1996, Ronald Reagan's over Walter Mondale in 1984, and Richard Nixon's over George McGovern in 1972, were all substantial, but many of those who voted for the winners clearly did not agree with their every policy position. Rather, in many instances, they voted *against* the candidate of the opposition party. Narrower electoral victories, such as Bush over Gore in 2000, and Bill Clinton over George H. W. Bush in 1992, said even less about voters' policy preferences. In 2000, a few hundred votes in Florida (less than one vote per precinct) determined the outcome of the closest election in American history. George W. Bush received fewer votes nationally than did his opponent, Al Gore, but he prevailed in enough individual states (which as always chose their respective members in the venerable, but often-criticized, U.S. institution, the Electoral College) to win the presidency.

HOW WOULD YOU DECIDE?

Recount

The 2008 made-for-TV HBO film about the 2000 presidential election follows the unfolding drama centered on the presidential contest between Texas Governor George W. Bush and Vice President Al Gore. The election occurred on November 7, 2000 and concluded with a Supreme Court ruling made in December that stopped any additional voting recounts in the state of Florida.

Florida, a swing state, faced divisive results due to ballot irregularities. The placement of candidate names within the "butterfly ballots" used throughout the state gained a great number of votes for Reform Party candidate Pat Buchanan. Incompletely punched holes in ballots resulted in the now-infamous "hanging chad" controversy, where an indentation appeared to have been made by a voter but the chad had not been completely punched out, thus making it difficult to tell who was to receive the vote. The Gore campaign's demand for hand recounts of the ballots across Florida and pressure on Florida's Secretary of State, Katherine Harris, led to a statewide recount of votes in December 2000. An appeal to the U.S. Supreme Court by the Bush campaign overruled that decision and the presidency was eventually awarded to George W. Bush. The 2008 Outstanding Made-For-Television Movie and Emmy-Award-winning film garnered national attention with a cast including Kevin Spacey, Laura Dern, and Denis Leary, bringing back to the spotlight the topic of the Electoral College and bureaucracy within America.

After a situation such as the 2000 election, how should state and local government election-related bureaucracies make operational adjustments to best confront the challenges that have the potential to arise within elections and electoral policy?

Source: http://www.hbo.com/movies/recount/index.html accessed May 2, 2011.

A further paradox exists in the tendencies of many people to regard government and, more specifically, bureaucracy with hostility while also wanting public agencies to satisfy their demands. Parallel to the emerging "fend-for-yourself" view of government programs, a prevailing attitude appears to be one of "I want mine" from government, while not respecting or trusting government institutions very much. This may explain the reluctance of many, including younger citizens, to adopt a semi-privatized Social Security system or market-driven privatized health care. More generally, many have come to demand less government in the abstract, while still looking to government officials for protection from dangers that are all too tangible. It takes *more* government and bureaucracy, not less, to protect the public against natural and man-made disasters such as floods, hurricanes, terrorist attacks, toxic-waste dumps, wildfires, nuclear accidents, or potentially unsafe modes of transportation. Another aspect of this "hostile dependence" is criticism of, and calls for restraining, bureaucratic program growth by individuals who refer to programs that benefit others, and rarely to those programs that benefit *them*. The less government there is, the more we like it—that is, until natural disasters such as Hurricane Katrina and widespread tornado outbreaks, or a man-made disaster such as the *Deepwater Horizon* oil spill in the Gulf of Mexico overwhelm us and we ask: Where is Uncle Sam when I need help?

Finally, multiple meanings of "representation" pose an important paradox. Throughout our discussion, we have referred to the calls for representativeness as calls to include in decision-making processes those whose interests are affected by decisions made, especially those previously excluded. An older, more traditional meaning of representation refers to **"overhead democracy"**—a representative process.[14] Old and new meanings of representation have collided in theory and practice during the past four decades, and no slackening of the conflict between them is in sight. Ultimately, it is a conflict between concepts stressing, respectively, majoritarian and minoritarian political representation—generalized majority rule versus systematic inclusion of diverse social, political, and economic minorities.

"overhead democracy"

majority control through political representatives who supervise administrative officers responsible and loyal to their superiors for carrying out the will of elected representatives.

These paradoxes have a number of aspects in common. Where our values change (for example, from nationalism to postnationalism), it is impossible to pinpoint just when the emphasis shifts from one to the other or, for that matter, just how far it has moved. Also, divergent tendencies present in all the paradoxes are related to one another in some instances. For example, this phenomenon is evident in antipoverty programs where rising expectations, public–private overlap, and postnationalism come together; in farm subsidies that artificially inflate the costs of basic commodities such as corn or sugar; in the highway program, where many people still prefer few limits on fuel economy but worry about air pollution, the cost of gasoline, climate change, offshore oil drilling, and vehicle emissions and, most of all, do not want highways built through their neighborhoods; and in the escalating costs of, and quest for, access to quality health care, which everyone wants, but no one wants to pay for. The net effect of this paradox is to exclude or "ghettoize" millions of Americans from the benefits of a democratic, free-market economy, thus increasing so-cial-service costs and very likely creating future public debt for all citizens. Key groups that often experience this are the poor, the dependent elderly, and those unable to afford health care insurance for their families.

Most important, these paradoxes have crucial implications for public ad-ministration as a whole. Administration is the machinery that government uses to deal with general social problems; consequently, it is located in or between the paradoxes that exist in the surrounding society. Whatever social or economic forces and turbulence exist within a society will influence government attempts to act, and to restrain or change policy direction. Because of public expecta-tions that government will act, administrative agencies and personnel must do so, even when choices are unclear, consequences are only dimly perceived, and political pressures arising from these paradoxes are troublesome and unyield-ing. Globalization, inflation, and increasing social diversity are facts of life, and they present problems politically in America. The next generation of pub-lic administrators clearly will face tough choices in a more turbulent economic and social environment.

In sum, the existing environment, with the turbulence and paradoxes al-ready present, poses many challenges to public administration. Because the outlook is for even more global and societal complexity in the future, the prognosis for public administration is that it will experience continued pres-sures—for more efficient and economical service delivery, adaptation to new needs and challenges, and political responsiveness to varied (and often con-flicting) interests.

Ferment and Change in Public Administration: Concepts and Practices

This discussion of public administration will cover some of the same ground explored in earlier chapters. However, it is appropriate here to re-examine the contours of change in the context of what it may portend for the future.

The "architecture" of bureaucracy has changed considerably in the past half-century. The command- and control-oriented Weberian bureaucratic hierarchy, with its emphasis on formal structure, secrecy, routinization, and efficiency in its narrow sense, is rapidly becoming obsolete. It is especially inadequate for networked and open-systems organizations (public, private, and nonprofit) operating within a swiftly changing global environment, facing increasing complexity in their programs, and staffed heavily with highly pro-fessional or specialized personnel. In order to maintain the needed flexibility, creativity, and innovativeness, new public organizations must be structured around projects or problems to be solved rather than as permanent hierar-chies. A core staff will remain for various administrative purposes, such as

POINT/COUNTERPOINT

Can social media be used to expand access to individual freedom and democratic values?

THE ISSUE: Social media can vastly expand the ability of ordinary citizens, in individual countries and around the globe, to communicate instantly with one another. Because tight control over information is a hallmark of repressive government regimes, social media represent a potential threat to their maintaining power over their citizens.

Arguments *for* social media expanding access to individual freedom and democratic values:

- Social media create possibilities for citizen interactions totally independent of government constraints.
- The ability of individuals to communicate freely with one another is essential to an open, free society, and is often severely restricted under repressive leaders.
- The unhampered exchange of information among politically involved and active citizens is always a potential threat—and can become a *direct* threat—to rulers who want to dominate the flow information within their countries. Such rulers seek to control information as *part of their effort* to control many other aspects of the lives of their citizens.

Arguments *against* social media expanding access to individual freedom and democratic values:

- Social media, by themselves, merely *make possible* some of the conditions that can lead to greater individual freedom and political democracy. There are no guarantees that those will actually happen.
- Social media can be used by supporters of repressive regimes to monitor the communications of regime opponents, creating the possibility that using social media can place those opponents at risk of their lives, health, and safety.
- Even if social media help to undermine repressive regimes, any alternative regime may or may not expand democratic practices or increase individual freedoms. And a repressive regime may be able to find creative ways to use social media to *tighten*, rather than loosen, its grip on the lives of its citizens.

record keeping, financial auditing, and performance evaluation, and for fixing final responsibility, but work processes are being organized around flexible fast-response teams. Decisions will be made collegially through the pooling of the perspectives and techniques of various specialists. Leadership will become increasingly stimulative and collaborative rather than directive. This assessment is in keeping with the discussion of alternative, so-called "network" forms of organization in Chapter 4.

A dramatic change in Weberian practices as well as structures has already occurred as a result of changing organizational structures and improved Internet technology. Among Webster-style bureaucracy's most basic functions were orderliness, predictability, and control, each of which has been profoundly affected by contemporary turbulence in and around public administration. Stable bureaucracy often overcame economic and social disruption caused by weak political leadership and fundamental political changes. Another irony is evident: many people longing for bureaucratic predictability are among the harshest critics of **"overhead bureaucracy,"** which highly values increased citizen participation and greater sensitivity to bureaucracy's "customers." The control function has been redefined a number of ways (including a shift in emphasis toward greater accountability for results rather than simply more control). Much more complex and dynamic leader–follower relations have been prescribed by the human relations school, organizational humanists, scholars of leadership, and advocates of organization development, who emphasize democratic leadership and employee participation. Also, the control function is disrupted by subsystem politics, as noted in Chapter 2, wherein administrators develop foundations of power outside traditional vertical bureaucratic channels of command and responsibility.

> **"overhead bureaucracy"**
> refers to increased costs of administering government programs imposed by mandates to include those affected by policymaking decisions; program efficiency tends to decrease as participation increases.

Finally, official secrecy, which Weber saw as a protection for bureaucrats, has been diminished considerably by technology that has increased public access to records and decision processes. Such functions have expanded significantly in the past four decades. The National Performance Review estimated that as many as one-third of all federal employees serve as inspectors, checking the work of the other two-thirds. The seemingly permanent movement away from Weberian formalism toward much less structured, decentralized, and more diversified and networked organizational forms also indicates that Weber's influence lingers, but decreasingly. Finally, although transparency of information is a valued aspect of democratic governance, it can lead to unforeseen negative consequences for public administrators.

Other major changes are also occurring. First is a far wider range of impacts—on government generally and on administrative activities in particular— being felt from using social media. In these pages we have referred to the increasing use of *Facebook, Twitter, MySpace,* and *YouTube* to inform citizens about government activities, and to solicit citizen feedback. Over two-thirds of all Americans belong to one or more of these social networks, and nearly half say they would use the Internet to communicate with family and friends in the event of an emergency. Along the same lines, since the late 1990s the national government has mounted an effort to utilize "America@Its Best," involving the use of the same social media to facilitate direct citizen contact with "high impact" federal agencies, such as the IRS, EPA, FDA, FEMA, and the Social Security Administration (see Chapter 10). Another purpose of the "America@ Its Best" effort was—and is—to identify *measurable* goals of customer service. Furthermore, the expanded use of e-gov with all forms of social media is being explored as a means of increasing workforce productivity; in a time of ever tighter government fiscal resources, the potential of these instruments holds real promise. (In the face of all this, how likely is it that official secrecy, mentioned earlier, can be maintained very easily?)

The 2008 Obama campaign used social media in unprecedented ways and was particularly effective in generating campaign donations and activating literally millions of new voters. Similarly, using blogs—and now "vlogs" (video blogs)—as means of direct political communication has skyrocketed in recent years, with no likely end in sight. (We will discuss the 2008 Obama campaign in more detail, later.)

Finally, in Chapter 11 we referred to an episode involving the FDA, which issued a ban on the use of saccharin, an artificial sweetener. The responsible administrator within the FDA subsequently received 70,000 letters from irate supporters of saccharin, prompting the agency to reconsider its decision. A relevant point, here, is that this occurred in *1977*—some thirty-five years ago. One can only imagine the number of e-mails, *Facebook* postings, tweets, and so on that we would find today, in response to a similar administrative action taken by a federal agency (the number surely would far exceed 70,000!).

Another major change concerns the efforts to expand public participation, as well as demands for new forms of interacting with government (including access via e-gov, social media, and the Internet). From what is usually known as the liberal side of the political spectrum has come a call for greater internal participation, or **empowerment**, in decision making by agency employees as well as external participation by affected clienteles. In the 1990s, however, both of these themes were taken up by others whose politics are decidedly not liberal, including President Clinton. But participation has two other dimensions as well. One is devolution (transfer) of federal programs to states and local governments, advocated by many political conservatives and also espoused by former high-level Clinton administration appointees. As described in Chapter 3, federal block grants began a major effort to shift responsibility for important social programs to state governments. The potential long-term significance of this shift is immense, politically and administratively. Persistent demands for greater participation and for devolution reflect a basic distrust of "bigness," and represent an attempt to gain control of decisions affecting clienteles and interest groups. The other dimension of participation is structural in nature but reflects the same impulse for greater popular control over government. Regional associations of governments, special-purpose districts, economic development commissions, and community-action organizations have sprung up, partly at the behest of national planners but also in response to local involvement, such as that which characterized the early professional career of then-Senator Barack Obama. Elements of participation and devolution combined with expanded use of ICTs, as well as specific administrative and economic considerations, have played a significant part in developing such organizations.

Since 2004, existing preferences for access, devolution and participation have been incorporated into American virtual organizational reality via computers and smart phones. During the 2008 presidential campaign, President Obama created a **virtual campaign** office where supporters could sign on together and collaborate on different tasks, such as advance planning, canvassing, and retreats. But he knew that supporters would participate only if they

empowerment

approach to citizen participation or management that stresses extended customer satisfaction, examines relationships among existing management processes, seeks to improve internal agency communications, and responds to valid customer demands; in exchange for the authority to make decisions at the point of customer contact, all "empowered" employees must be thoroughly trained, and the results must be carefully monitored.

virtual campaign

deliberate use of Internet communication technology to communicate with potential voters and manage political campaigns.

believed he was actively managing the effort. Rather than delegating the task to his staffers, Obama himself sent out e-mails to supporters asking if they would reach out to their friends and family on his behalf. The e-mail was written in a conversational but personal tone reading: "[t]he most extraordinary things happen at the personal level when you make that personal connection to a voter and discover that you share a common vision of what ought to be. Make a call and make that connection today."[15] Obama's personalized e-mail presented the delegation of campaign efforts as a heartfelt request from the candidate, rather than as a faceless intrusion.

President Obama successfully used a variety of new media technologies to help raise $600 million and recruit 10 million supporters online. His strategies demonstrated that ICTs could be used to connect to voters in new ways and allow them to more easily and effectively participate in the campaign. They also demonstrated that new media could be used to better administer elections by providing low-cost, instantaneous, and personalized communication. The Obama campaign fundamentally altered how many political campaigns will be conducted in the future.

Another significant change has been further development of information technology and management science techniques that have contributed to more sophisticated and systematic administration. One dimension involves the growing use of e-government, Enterprise Resource Planning (ERP) systems, quantitative methods, and computers—in short, management science applied to operations of government. Others include project management, a package of techniques designed to move individual projects along paths set out for them; business process reengineering and citizen relationship management, techniques emphasizing parallel rather than sequential processing, the wide availability of procedural information, rapid paperless transfer and automation, and the sometimes questionable practices of outsourcing and contracting out, under which private contractors or independent consultants provide designated goods or services to government agencies for an agreed-on fee. (Note, also, that trends toward more community participation and more systematic management methods may conflict—but that has not prevented many governments from pursuing both.)

A quite divisive development is the widespread effort to eliminate—or at least to weaken—public-employee unionization and collective bargaining. Some have warned that the new alternative pay systems were merely an excuse to return to the "good old days" of political patronage, when civil service employees were hired, and received raises and promotions, based on whom they knew rather than on their competence and job-related skills.[16] Underlying this development is an ideological stance strongly opposing public-sector unions, thus creating value conflicts over legitimate concerns for job security, coupled with the rise of a service-oriented economy with a larger proportion of "knowledge workers" engaged in public employment. Also, general social and economic pressures have contributed to relaxation of laws and regulations covering public-sector unionization. These developments directly impact public personnel management, but also have an impact on government's role in economic and social affairs and the status and nature of government itself as an employer. As noted earlier, these may be changing again, this time in different directions. Public employee union members outnumber private sector union members by a ratio of 6 to 1. Public-sector union membership has stabilized at about 36 percent, whereas the percentage of union members in private service and manufacturing firms has declined to just 6.5 percent of the workforce. This huge and growing disparity between the percentages of nonunionized workers in the private and public sectors is creating political conflicts over collective bargaining, job security, pay for performance, and privatization. Many congressional supporters of the government workforce have been engaged in a protracted conflict over the implications of these changes. In these and in other respects, there is much about which to be concerned in contemporary personnel management.

The growing pressures on government spending, at all levels, also is of concern, with many serious budgetary constraints such as increasing public debt, extensive reductions in public funding, deep cuts in personnel and in services rendered, substantial boosts in pay-as-you-go self-financing for programs that remain in operation, and so on. There is substantial public frustration evident regarding the proper role and desirability of government expenditures across a wide range of program areas at all levels of government—not to mention continued taxpayer resistance to proposed increases in government revenues or the elimination of tax expenditures (loopholes). State and local governments, especially, have been hard-pressed to raise new revenues because of declining real estate values and the prolonged economic recession. Moreover, in many government jurisdictions, election outcomes have been heavily influenced by which of the candidates was able to strike more of an antitax pose before the electorate. With the national (and global) economies more difficult to manage and predict, issues concerning government revenue have, if anything, become more complex and challenging than in the decades immediately past.

We should note other developments as well. Continuing specialization and professionalization raise the challenge of bridging gaps among specialists within different professions and at different levels of government. More states permit their governors to submit reorganization package proposals to their legislatures, and Presidents Carter, Reagan, Clinton, and George W. Bush (all former governors) stressed reorganization as a policy instrument. Executive reorganization may be reexamined in the years ahead in light of recent developments. The Bush administration undertook massive reorganizations of federal intelligence, homeland security, and emergency management bureaucracies without strengthening coordination among professionals in the over thirty-seven federal and the hundreds of state and local agencies potentially involved in policy making. The apparent failure to respond to Hurricane Katrina has forced a closer look at some parts of these reorganizations, which may have "unintentionally create[d] new sources of vulnerability and fail[ed] to take the steps necessary to plug the system's holes."[17] Substantial fiscal resources will be required to repair the damage caused by the system's failure to respond to its own emergency management plans. On another front, continuing unrest—and potentially major change—in fiscal federalism are affecting state and local administration in thousands of program areas. Finally, public administration has been affected by efforts to **debureaucratize** organizational life in the public service. This refers, among other things, to downsizing agency staffs, deemphasizing credentials of public servants, broadening decision making, decreasing rigidities, and increasing lateral communication within bureaucracies—especially to the extent that recommendations of the various national initiatives were accepted by Congress and put into practice in the federal bureaucracy.

debureaucratize

strategy to decentralize and deregulate the public sector by reductions-in-force, promoting greater flexibility in personnel decisions, and increasing results-oriented incentives to reduce "overhead" costs.

Paradoxes in Concept and Practice

Just as there are paradoxes in the environment surrounding public administration, there are paradoxes in its concepts and practices. One broad paradox revolves around impacts of participation in administrative decision making by divergent, and frequently conflicting, groups. These include program clienteles, members of public-employee unions, and agency personnel seeking to participate in internal management consistent with their own organizational values. All three kinds of participation offer potential opposition to the values of rationality, professionalism, leadership, and accountability.

Participation can conflict with rationality because the former is based on political inclusion of new and varied interests, whereas the latter presumes to objectively identify the most advantageous courses of action without regard to particular political interests or impact on them. Furthermore, participation can conflict with professionalism because, as noted earlier, its advocates seek to have decisions framed in terms of impact on those affected rather than on the basis of what professionals think is best for the people. One way out of this dilemma is negotiation and political mediation by a respected third party not clearly identified with either side of the issue. Participation, however, also can conflict with traditional forms of leadership by acting as a constraint on leaders' ability to set the direction of organizations or political systems. Participation is a potential counterweight to what leaders desire, although it also can be a source of leadership support. It comes down to a question of what views and interests are added to the decision-making process by expanding participation.

Finally, participation can conflict with accountability. Considering that the former is specifically designed to promote the latter, how is this statement justified? By increasing participation in decision making, it becomes more difficult to pinpoint just who was responsible for initiating and enforcing a decision, and therefore to hold those persons accountable for their actions. A skillful leader may be able to guide a participatory decision-making system along lines he or she prefers, with none the wiser; such a technique camouflages where responsibility for a given decision really lies. Thus, although intended to promote accountability, broader participation has the potential for doing precisely the opposite.

Recalling the discussion of scientific management in Chapter 4, emphasis on participation reflects a strong faith in process leading to "correct" results. Americans have a reputation for being pragmatic people with concern for not only *what* is done, but also *how* it is done. Yet this discussion of participation brings up an important lesson, both in and out of public administration. Programs that are managed *efficiently* are not always *effective*. Casually assuming a relationship between "doing it the right way" and getting the desired results can be risky. It may be necessary to examine precisely what is produced via particular steps to determine whether that is the way participants or clienteles wish to continue operating. Concern with consequences, as opposed to simply "perfecting the machinery," is growing, though it is hoped that we will not end up ignoring means and concentrating only on results in participative management terms, or in any other respect.

A second paradox involves contradictory tendencies toward centralization and decentralization, with the latter preferred by many Americans. Moving away from centralization has looked increasingly attractive (at least in the abstract) to millions of citizens, and appeals to this popular preference have become more common as a basis for government action. Yet many factors in the social and economic environment still illustrate the need for well-coordinated (centralized) responses to shared problems—for example, whether one state's driver's licensing requirements will permit positive identification has implications for other states in preventing terrorism; education standards in one state might impact the emerging workforce elsewhere in the country; and economic development policies in individual states or localities might impact national economic growth. In short, geographic interdependence within this nation and between our country and others has increased in recent decades, and such global interdependence requires some degree of centralization in public (as well as private) policy. With public support for greater decentralization, the challenge for officials confronted by policy problems stemming from global interdependence has been to move in both directions at the same time—no easy task! Another dimension of global interdependence involves what the West may learn from developing countries, in the process of implementing a more truly global agenda.[18] Such an agenda could focus, among other things, on how we might reduce political and economic corruption; how we might increase citizen participation around the world; how governments can employ scarce resources to deliver basic services;, and what the global, ethical, and social responsibilities of multinational corporations in developed nations are regarding developing nations.[19]

Interestingly, this centralization-versus-decentralization paradox has sparked renewed attention to federalist-style arrangements in both public and private organizations, in which some functions are delegated to a general unit or level, whereas others are assigned to smaller (often neighborhood, community, or citizen) organizations. The European Union (EU) is struggling to form a federalist system composed of twenty-seven countries with nearly 500 million inhabitants. Ratification of the proposed new constitution has been delayed by negative votes in Ireland, France, and Holland, and there are rumblings of discontent about too much central government and difficulties in balancing powers among branches of government and the member states. The European debt crisis has delayed further political integration among potential EU members. Another contemporary example of this attention to federalist possibilities were the efforts of the U.S.-backed Iraqi government to incorporate principles of federalism into the proposed Iraqi constitution.

Another paradox is the need for better communication among diverse professionals in the face of continued emphasis on electronic government and professional specialization. It is not merely a matter of teams of professionals assembling to work on specific projects. Rather, problems in today's society are so complex and have so many dimensions that professionals from different fields must learn to work together to alleviate them. Growing professional interoperability will characterize public administration in the future much more so than in the past. This is perhaps due, in part, to pressures for cutting back on the numbers of government employees, as well as the increasing complexity and interrelatedness of many policy challenges such as crime control, health care reform, combating terrorism, and environmental protection.

Another dimension of diversity, of course, is demographic, ethnic, and racial diversity in the workforce itself. This involves both the challenge of attracting a more diverse cross-section of the population to government service, and harnessing their energies in a common effort to strengthen service provision and program management.

Finally, there is a fundamental paradox in the overall perspectives that exist on strengthening public bureaucracy, performance management, and the like. As noted in Chapter 1, a number of observers have suggested that our public administrative apparatus, at all levels, demonstrates a level of performance that is already strong, vital, and reliable. Of course there are mistakes, misjudgments, and imperfections; no human enterprise, of any kind, operates without them. And of course the number of such errors, simply by the sheer scope and magnitude of bureaucratic activity, is bound to be high. But public administration in this country fares quite well, when it comes to its overall efficiency and effectiveness—in proportion to overall bureaucratic performance in government agencies, in comparison to performance in large private-sector organizations, and in comparison to that in public bureaucracies in many other nations.

Those who advocate greater competition, entrepreneurism, outsourcing, and market orientation in organizational life see emphasis on careerism in the public service as an impediment to those goals. This view is based on the assumption that careerism limits one's options for doing innovative work or otherwise taking risks because of real or imagined potential for harming one's career aspirations. A related implication is conflict between individual talents such as creativity, initiative, innovation, and experimentation on the one hand, and efficient, coordinated (often controlling and incremental) organizational leadership on the other. Obviously, that would depend on situational factors, primarily on whether the tasks and leadership of an organization are conducive to allowing or encouraging innovation by group members. There is little question, however, that leaders often regard themselves as custodians of their organization's mission, thus discouraging their subordinates' participation and creativity. In many cases, the pattern appears to be one of conflict between central, control-oriented, incremental, and directive leadership and flexible, creative, innovative, and participative "followership" in organizational operations.

Administrative discretion has become an issue and is likely to remain one for some time. Plainly, discretionary actions by administrative professionals may not promote representational qualities; at the same time, discretion does not necessarily interfere with achieving accountability. We might legitimately try to achieve one or both, but they must be understood properly as separate and distinct features of administrative politics in order to pursue either of them sensibly.

It would appear that as a nation we are uncertain about how to achieve accountability. The design of our political system stresses accountability to the people through a complex, interrelated web of institutional channels. However, current efforts seem to focus on making all of government accountable to all of the people, all of the time. It is difficult to see how that can be done. Direct accountability to the people is an appealing idea, but it may also be said that if officials are accountable to everybody, they are accountable to nobody. It requires careful structuring of mechanisms of accountability to maximize the chances of attaining it. Can we, then, rely on a single mechanism? Probably not; that would result in too much power in too few hands. The next best thing would seem to be a variety of mechanisms, each acting as a channel for public control but also held to account for what it does. There is a label for such a complex mechanism of multiple accountability: checks and balances.

We may simply need to gain better control over them, again, in order to ensure accountability to public preferences and interests.

Ferment and Change in Public Administration as a Field of Study

Given the wide-ranging changes in concepts and practices of public administration, it is not surprising that the academic field of study known by the same name is subject to considerable turbulence as well. Some of these areas were discussed previously, particularly in Chapter 1, but we will deal with them as interrelated factors helping to shape the future of the discipline.

First, movement away from political science—its ancestral home, so to speak—has characterized much of public administration and its academic professionals. Developments in both fields after World War II led to increasingly divergent emphases, with political science stressing behavioral research of a type that many in public administration found uncongenial to their work. The latter was often treated as an academic "second-class citizen," giving rise to pressure for separation in the form of interdisciplinary programs in public administration and growing numbers of independent programs and departments. Yet post–behavioral changes in political science raise the possibility that the two may be able to draw somewhat closer together. The emergence of "public policy" as a distinct and legitimate field of study has helped to bridge the methodological gap between the two disciplines.

Second, some schools of management and business administration have inaugurated distinct public-sector management portions of their course offerings, recognizing both the growing importance of education in public-sector-related fields for business graduates and the intentions of larger numbers of their students to work in the public sector upon graduation. Public administration, however, has never been—nor will ever be—merely a branch of business administration. Efforts to develop joint business and public-policy degrees based on the "best practices" of both public and private management hold promise for preparing future careerists.

Third, schools, programs, and institutes of public administration have proliferated in the past sixty years, with a number of distinctive features. They are generally separate from political science departments, as already implied. They tend to be graduate-level rather than undergraduate programs, building on a base of a good general education. And they clearly reflect a flexible, heterogeneous approach to the subject matter taught. Labels such as "public administration," "public policy," "public affairs," "management," and "management science" abound.

Also, organizational humanism and organizational development have continued to exert an influence in public administration. Organizational humanism, stressing increased self-realization and greater organizational democracy, has found some response within public administration, especially in organizations with less structured tasks permitting greater creativity and initiative. Organizational development has evolved from early emphasis on hardware and systems, with less concern for interpersonal relations, to a more widely supported focus on human components of the organization and concern for normative organizational goals and values (what *should* be done). Although both approaches have had only limited impact in the great majority of public (and private) organizations, their influence seems to be on the rise.

The rise in the study and application of quality and productivity improvement systems, such as Total Quality Management, has similarly had a substantial impact on public administration as a field of study. The scholarly community has been paying much greater attention in the past twenty-five years to computer applications, information technology, team building, customer service quality, the roles of leadership, and so on—and it seems likely that this attention will continue. Along the same lines, there can be little doubt that themes such as New Public Management, reinventing government, empowerment, and simplifying both regulations and procedures have made their way into the classroom and into relevant academic literature. The recommendations of various commissions examining government operations—such as the Grace Commission, the National Performance Review, the Robb–Silberman Commission, the 9/11 Commission, Iraq Study Group, the Winter Commission (which focused on state and local management), and the Bipartisan Commission on Fiscal Responsibility (which has made recommendations regarding tax reform and reducing the national debt)—have become a part of the field of study, as have numerous reactions to those recommendations, reflecting myriad perspectives.[20] This model provided the framework for the bipartisan Congressional supercommittee entrusted with the responsibility of determining future spending cuts (hopefully) Leading to a balanced federal budget.

Furthermore, teaching administrative ethics has assumed a more prominent place in the study of public administration.[21] Government administrators have both the need and the opportunity to make value choices affecting the lives of others in the course of discharging their responsibilities. Moral and ethical questions abound. There has been, therefore, a resurgence of interest in ethics in public administration curricula. Part of the vitality of this area lies in the growing recognition among academics of both the complexity of the subject and the diversity of possible approaches to it (see Chapter 5). Attention to ethical issues, to maintaining ethical standards, and to ethics education and training is certain to continue in the future.

Finally, the very nature of the academic field, and of the subject matter that it comprises, remains an unsettled question. One observer, discussing constitutional separation of powers and administrative theory, has noted three separate approaches to public administration: a "managerial" approach most closely associated with the chief executive, a "political" approach geared to legislative concerns, and a "legal" approach associated with the judiciary.[22] Public administration scholars will probably never agree on the proper blend of elements in their discipline. In light of these divergent tendencies, it appears unlikely that any "*single* school or philosophy, academic discipline, or type of methodology—or combination of these—would . . . persuade public administration to march under its banner."[23] This may not be altogether a bad thing. A complex, swiftly changing global environment may be better addressed by a curriculum that contains many facets, perspectives, interests, and methodologies: one that is eclectic, experimental, and open-ended.

A number of other observations merit inclusion here in assessing the academic field of public administration. One of its most important functions has been professional training, in programs that offer a Master of Public Administration (or, sometimes, Public Affairs) (MPA) degree, of those who go on to take administrative positions at all three levels of government. Some observers are concerned about the kind of training available, stressing particularly that programs should not turn out narrowly specialized individuals who "can't see past the end of their noses." The late Frederick Mosher advocated well-trained professionals "who also have perspective on themselves and their work, and on social and political contexts in which they will find themselves working." Further, he noted that universities are "equipped to open the students' minds to the broader value questions of the society and of their professions' roles in that society."[24] Mosher and others have argued for a generalist preparation, rather than narrow professional specialization which limits the level of knowledge about the society and the culture in which public administrators live and apply their skills.

The academic discipline of public administration, then, appears to be in flux. There is a need to teach courses with an applied focus with less emphasis on pure theory. If rapid change, diversity, and uncertainty characterize the discipline now, they will be ever more characteristic of it in the years ahead. Of course, that is true of the practical side of the field as well.

Further Thoughts and Observations

In this closing section, we will take the opportunity to add a few comments that seem important in the overall scheme of things in public administration. They are intended to supplement what has been said earlier in this chapter and to point out other significant areas in the field.

First, we must reinforce the increasing importance of *effectively managing* public programs. More to the point, those of us not engaged in managerial activities in the public sector should recognize how crucial it is that we appreciate the complexities *unique to* public-sector management. It is easy enough to criticize what is done or not done by public administrators; we would find, however, that things look very different from the manager's perspective.

Bureaucratic ways of doing things may not be entirely understandable to the outside observer, but (as noted in Chapter 5) they may be politically justifiable in terms of bureaucracy's ongoing needs and responsibilities. This is not to excuse shortcomings, or worse, in administrative behavior—it is only to suggest that we should not be too quick in passing judgment or too harsh in our assessments regarding bureaucratic actions. Public administrators are indeed engaged in honorable work.

The challenge is to reinvigorate the profession by persuading aspiring students as well as mid-careerists that there is value to the public service, that it is not all negative. Equally important is reinspiring all citizens with an appreciation of the bureaucracy as an organic whole that is capable of responding to its environment, and convincing students and mid-careerists that they can change the things that need changing.

At the same time, we must pay more attention than we have recently to controlling bureaucratic waste, fraud, and mismanagement. Recently, these concerns have become more of a political issue, frequently (though far from exclusively) involving defense spending. Both the Office of Management and Budget (OMB) and the Government Accountability Office (GAO) have taken numerous steps to combat waste, fraud, and abuse. These have included investigations of allegedly lax accounting procedures; reports on government waste in areas such as Pentagon procurement contracts, Medicaid and Medicare fraud, and spare-parts disposal practices; and establishing a 24-hour toll-free hotline to report incidents of possible waste and mismanagement. The rapidly increasing availability of smart phones, GIS (Geographic Information Systems), and other "apps" has the potential to sharply reduce costs and improve service. One potentially significant development in this area is that increasing attention is being paid to the use of GIS systems and social media as a means of combating waste, mismanagement, and fraud.[25] Courses in these subjects are finding their way into MPA curricula.

Two cautionary words are in order here. First, we should not put too much faith in sophisticated management techniques as remedies for these problems, because such techniques can be used to commit wasteful or fraudulent acts as well as to control them. We may instead need to rediscover and revitalize traditional practices such as financial auditing if we are to move effectively against these challenges. Second, we should be discriminating in our judgments, in the best sense of the phrase, about bureaucrats' behavior—taking care not to condemn the many because of the actions of a few. Nonetheless, renewed concern over these matters is entirely appropriate, especially at the state and local government levels, where opportunities still exist for politically inspired graft and corruption.

In a larger sense, we should not dwell so much on problems and weaknesses of bureaucracy as a form of organization that we overlook its strengths.[26] One is bureaucracy's very orderliness (at least potentially), which is so often denounced as inflexibility; if the alternative is patronage, nepotism, capricious judgment, or chaos (which it often was in Max Weber's time), that is a plus. During times of national crisis, this distinction often becomes clearer and more important to many Americans. Another strength is the system of legal guarantees against arbitrariness that governs so much administrative activity; still another is the "commitment of bureaucracy to democratic decision making—and the processes of consultation, negotiation, and accommodation" where it is clear that "broad and complex tasks require broad and complex organizations"[27]— a recognition of bureaucracy's appropriateness to many organizational activities. Furthermore, if the rise of bureaucracy was originally tied to the increasing complexity of society, the outlook in these complex times is at least for survival of this form of organization, if not its further expansion.

There are other areas of concern. For example, it is likely that there will be continued pervasive ambiguity concerning goals in politics and administration. Efforts to define our goals will probably continue, but goals in our pluralist democratic society will also continue to be only partially agreed on (at best). With goals vaguely defined or even in conflict, measuring performance against common goals is, of course, impossible. Nevertheless, developing improved performance indicators within specific programs and projects will yield some benefits incrementally in the form of improved planning and direction of those programs.

Also, the role and scope of government regulation continue to be in flux. This has several aspects. One is the movement toward deregulation, though how fast, how far, and in how many areas of economic and social activity are questions still to be answered. (The possibility of *re*regulation has also emerged from this policy debate, but it is uncertain at this writing whether the next president—Barack Obama or someone else—will be inclined to implement new policies and regulations.) Another aspect is the concern about bureaucratic red tape discussed previously; demands for protection and risk reduction in our daily lives account for a large part of regulatory growth. A serious issue here is how far we as a nation should go, and wish to go, in reducing risks and ensuring public health and safety. Most agree that it is unrealistic to strive for a "no-risk" society, and that such an endeavor is not only futile but may also be detrimental to other functions in society (such as private-sector productivity).

There is precedent for pursuing at least one alternative approach: using government agency performance as a basis for comparison with (a "yardstick" against which to measure) private-sector performance. A memorable case in point was (and is) the Tennessee Valley Authority (TVA), which for nearly eighty years has marketed electric power in seven mid-South states at rates noticeably lower than those charged by private power companies elsewhere (this is still true, despite substantial TVA rate increases since the 1970s). Another issue concerns the calls for use of cost-benefit analysis in evaluating proposed (and operative) regulations. The question here is whether such analysis can be truly neutral. If so, it could add a useful dimension to processes of drafting and enforcing regulations. If not, however, it is likely that insisting on its use would continue to generate substantial controversy among contending forces in government regulation, because of disagreements over whether dollar costs should be regarded as the sole—or even the primary—consideration in evaluating the effectiveness of regulations. Such controversies could thus make it much more difficult to sensibly reform government regulation while maintaining regulatory effectiveness.[28]

There is one final regulatory issue. It is clear that sentiment has been growing for wholesale reduction of government regulations of all kinds. At the same time, perhaps not enough attention has been paid to the consequences of that course of action.[29] There even appears to be some feeling that almost anything government does is "regulation." That perception is not accurate, of course, but in a democracy, what the citizens believe to be the case may be more important in some instances than the objective reality. This, then, also will influence the future course of government regulation.

Managing public personnel is another area of significant change and challenge. At least three issues are central in this regard. One is the question of maintaining the partisan and policy neutrality of the civil service versus enhancing the political responsiveness (if not outright loyalty) to the chief executive that exists among administrative personnel. This has been a recurring issue in our political history, and it surfaced again in the George W. Bush presidency. Since then, the Office of Personnel Management (OPM) has taken various actions to change policies and eliminate unnecessary regulations. A second basic personnel concern is related to what motivates public servants. Specifically, even though financial bonuses and merit pay have been established in the national civil service (with parallel systems in about half of the states), there is some question as to whether monetary incentives—so crucial to many reform initiatives of the past thirty-five years—are in fact the most effective motivators of senior career executives (recall Chapter 4, and the discussion of motivation in the organizational humanism school of organization theory). These theoretical formulations have recently been given support; evidence has come from several sources that interesting work, job satisfaction, personal and group recognition, and a sense of group identity are at least as important as modest financial incentives. To the extent that is so, it suggests that bonuses and pay-for-performance may have been misdirected. It may also help explain why these financial incentive plans (at least for a time) failed to slow the exodus of veteran senior executives from the national civil service (they could even have accelerated that trend).[30]

Closely related to the preceding concerns (as we saw in Chapter 7) is a growing morale and recruitment problem, especially in the national civil and military services. After many years of various politicians and the public "taking potshots" at public servants, these individuals have now experienced even more severe buffeting about, which introduced more uncertainty into the national civil service than existed for about a century.[31] The Clinton administration itself sent conflicting signals to the bureaucracy, thus adding to the uncertainty. The National Performance Review called for streamlined procedures and other steps designed to increase empowerment of federal civil servants. But on the other hand, Bill Clinton made it clear that more personnel cutbacks were necessary to "reform" bureaucratic operations. George W. Bush heightened the anti-bureaucracy rhetoric by enforcing the President's Management Agenda (PMA) and proposing to eliminate organized labor-management collective bargaining and civil service pay scales, and privatize up to one-third of the federal workforce. (None of these proposals was implemented in full.)

There also is growing interest in administrative discretion. The literature on public administration has tended to reflect the position that perhaps discretion should not be hemmed in—that we should attempt instead to legitimize, in Woodrow Wilson's words, "the exercise of large and unhampered" administrative discretion, with the expectation that public servants will act in the public interest. This may be a fleeting hope; one observer has suggested, for example, that "there are numerous ways to check agency power at the national government level . . . [and] bureaucrats typically face many of these checks simultaneously; the degree of freedom to make policy enjoyed by an agency is always limited to one degree or another. Autonomy may ebb and flow with time, but it is rarely if ever absolute."[32] The public's view of administrative discretion would obviously be more favorable if it were perceived that civil servants acted most often in the broad public interest.

Something else to be borne in mind—as we refine our theories of organization, leadership, and management control—is that there are limits on how widely such theories can be applied. The nature of work, workers, and organizations affect applicability of theories (such as organizational humanism), leadership styles, and methods of management control (see Chapters 4, 6, and 10, respectively). These limitations must be respected to avoid problems resulting from wholesale acceptance of any one theory or combination of theories.

Also, there is some irony in the current pursuit of greater efficiency, rationality, and productivity—three major elements in Frederick Taylor's theory of scientific management. This is not to say we have returned to his concepts with nothing else changed. We may find these norms more attractive now, however, due to growing constraints on our resources, financial and otherwise. It should be noted that the appeal of these values has also permeated the study of public administration. The public management approach has accurately been described as having a strong philosophical link with the scientific management tradition.

Furthermore, some favorite terms and concepts we apply to public administration may require rethinking. We tend to speak of a leader, whereas we should be concerned instead with the relationship of leaders to their respective organization units—in terms of that which is led. In the same way, we may need to speak of politicians and administrators who are accountable *to*, not just accountable; responsive *to*, not simply responsive; bureaucracies efficient *at*, not merely efficient; and organizations productive *in terms of*, not just productive. We must bear in mind that these values are most important as means of achieving other, higher ends and not as ends in themselves. Yet all too often we treat them as the latter. For example, *why* is it important to be efficient? Is it always desirable? The norm of efficiency is not a truly neutral standard; one cannot always be efficient at doing something challenging, and values are almost always involved. Further, is efficiency (or anything else) to be pursued in all cases, even at the expense of other desired ends? It can even be necessary to choose between competing focal points for being efficient. For example, an automobile driver may have to think about maximizing miles per hour (thus using more fuel) or maximizing miles per gallon (which usually requires traveling at slower speeds). Which version of efficiency will one use? The answer in a particular situation depends upon the needs of the driver and/or passengers in the vehicle *in that situation*. These are troubling considerations, and they should serve as reminders that we need to think clearly about our own assumptions. Clear thinking is especially necessary in turbulent times.

The political environment of public administration also has changed dramatically, as discussed previously. But certain contemporary elements of that change deserve mention as we close. Emphasis on both effectiveness and accountability of administrative agencies has led to numerous adjustments in their relationships to other institutions in the political system, and companion emphases on privatization, customer service standards, employee empowerment, and measurement of results have only reinforced this trend. Among the areas affected by these changes are the politics of structure, bureaucratic neutrality versus advocacy, elimination of collective bargaining agreements, the significance of "overhead" control of administration, altered budget procedures involving Congress and the president, "fend-for-yourself" federalism and "devolved" intergovernmental relations, and new initiatives to improve homeland security.

Such conflicts spawned related debates over the very nature of the changes being proposed in the early twenty-first century. Accepting without question the underlying assumptions of new public management, for example, means willingly adopting the "entrepreneurial" paradigm as a substitute for the "administrative management" paradigm that has been in use for more than a century—with consequences that are difficult to predict. One other salient point that has been raised is simply that presidential efforts to reform the bureaucracy often seem to overlook the "joint custody" nature of American public agencies—a custodial responsibility that is shared between the chief executive and the legislature. Thus, unilateral efforts to impose new systems and procedures often run afoul of legislative prerogatives—not to mention legislative preferences.[33]

Furthermore, there is now less tension between the concept of the individual recipient of public services as "customer" of government agencies/services on the one hand and as "citizen" of the republic on the other. The former clearly implies that service provision is a primary concern of government, and serving the "customer" must necessarily be a high priority for all those involved in that endeavor—including legislators and chief executives as well as administrators themselves. The latter, by contrast, suggests a very different relationship between the individual and his or her government, one in which the citizen is an integral part of a larger governmental system, and not only a consumer of government services. But clearly, citizens (as well as others residing in the United States) are "consumers," if not outright "customers," seeking services from national, state, and local governments.

Although a great deal of progress has been made since the reinvention era began in the early 1990s, many governments still need to be encouraged to respond to multiple citizen-customer demands. Private-sector, market-based methods and techniques may be used, albeit selectively, as they are not easily applied to decentralized, locally controlled, and fragmented "cottage industries" of the public sector. There is simply no "one best way" to implement public policy, and most citizens are staunch supporters of diversity, local government, and pluralism. At the same time, citizens, appointed administrators, elected officials, suppliers, and recipients of public services are demanding to be treated as *both* citizens and customers.

Though acknowledging the importance of citizenship, civic governance, and partisanship to maintain accountability, democratic values, equity, and pluralist democracy,[34] appointed and elected officials must respect citizens' rights to receive full value for their tax dollars. Public managers cannot excuse unacceptable employee behavior, failure to meet service standards, or poor customer service because some citizens fail to participate as actively as others in the partisan aspects of government. Public services (even law enforcement, immigration, emergency management, homeland security, and regulatory compliance actions) can respect customer service standards set by accrediting associations, other governments, or the private sector. If this means drawing from successful cases, methods, or techniques of other governments or private providers, then governments should welcome the challenge as well as the opportunity to show how they, too, can meet citizen demands for improved service quality.[35]

A related concern also exists, namely, the contrast between "public-oriented" versus "private-oriented" conceptions of government. If government, acting in an entrepreneurial manner, simply serves "customers," then what is its unique role as distinct from the activities—and purposes—of private-sector businesses? Few, if any, of those advocating higher quality in the provision of public services would quarrel for a moment with the conceptions of citizenship that are at the foundation of the republic, nor would they hesitate to defend the basic political relationships that are defined in the Constitution and our subsequent governmental history. But the point is this: What we choose to emphasize about our governmental processes reflects what we think is important, at the moment, about government, and it may influence our thinking in the years ahead as well. In other words, we could end up moving in a direction that causes us, intentionally or not, to redefine what sort of broader governmental system we will have. In short, if we focus so heavily on budget cuts, productivity improvement, results, or empowerment that we lose sight of some of the basic assumptions and concepts underlying the political system, we may have made some useful short-term gains, but in the process we might trade off (or trade in) more fundamental notions of who we are as a polity.

Put somewhat differently, citizens have both rights *and* responsibilities; customers, on the other hand, because they are purchasing a good or service on the open market, have few if any of the latter. Perhaps the rise of the customer is a sign of the times in this nation, where more attention has been paid to *individual* rights and liability issues in recent decades. Some say that this has occurred at the expense of proper attention to *collective* responsibilities. But another implication of this is that only as we exercise responsible citizenship will we be in a position to improve the quality of government services available to customers (us). Nonetheless, persistent calls for more contracting out, privatization, and deregulation of the public sector continue to be heard, and (as noted in Chapters 9 and 10) the results of various efforts in this regard have been mixed and uneven. Numerous factors will affect whether that trend continues. Many have questioned the degree to which government should privatize, deregulate, or form partnerships with nongovernmental entities, rather than on whether we should do so at all.

One other aspect of the tension between citizen and customer concepts is that it seems to parallel some of the existing tension between concepts reflecting political science and public administration approaches to government. For there can be no doubt that providing highest-quality and lowest-cost services to those who want and need them is a major responsibility of government today. Not even the most avid "political" observer of modern American government can afford to overlook the complexity of both public demand and public services, as these affect what government does and what it is asked to do. Nevertheless, the larger point here is that we would do well to keep all relevant conceptions of government in mind, especially as we make whatever efforts we choose to make to strengthen government performance in ways that are both meaningful and enduring.

Another key dimension of the political environment is the presidency and the executive branch, especially the extent of recent presidential efforts to change the direction of government. A significant legacy of the Clinton years (with continuing impact on the national executive branch) was the ongoing effort to reduce the sheer size of the public sector—in personnel, budgets, regulatory authority, and general scope. The Clinton administration placed considerable emphasis on budget deficit reduction and, with the success of these efforts, came the short-lived dilemma (from 1998 until 2002) of deciding how to best spend the budget surplus projected for the early twenty-first century. However, the weakened economy; the war on terrorism; the advent of floods, hurricanes, and tornadoes; and the military conflicts in Afghanistan, Iraq, and Libya, erased the surplus and created huge deficits that now threaten social entitlement programs for the elderly, handicapped, poor, and retired segments of our population. The Obama administration also undertook several new costly initiatives (the 2009 stimulus package and healthcare reform, to name two of the largest in scope), the results of which—fiscally and in terms of the size of the federal workforce—may not be entirely clear for some time to come.

Several other political dimensions also stand out. For example, the federal courts are now deeply involved in many substantive aspects of public administration. Most important, perhaps, are federalism and intergovernmental relations, affirmative action, labor relations, and government regulation; but in case after case, across the board, court decisions shape both the environment and the content of administrative decision making. Public administration is not alone in that, but the impacts on its future will be substantial.

In a turbulent and tense political atmosphere, many sincere (and often impatient) citizens might do well to distinguish between the individuals with whom they disagree and agencies themselves. There is another implication as well: Such attacks foster an atmosphere of **public cynicism and distrust**, making it far more difficult for administrative agencies to retain the capacity to respond when we do call upon them! And we surely will continue to do so, to deal both with large-scale public problems such as wars and with occasional crises such as earthquakes, civil disorders, hurricanes, floods, or public health emergencies. Adding to the already full agendas of many public agencies are the new and unprecedented challenges to protect homeland security, prevent further acts of terrorism, secure our borders, and maintain a U.S. leadership role in world peace and nuclear disarmament—all while maintaining public confidence in such efforts.

Another point worth bearing in mind pertains to that same impatience about governmental action (or inaction) in the context of our basic and limited governmental system. Those who framed our Constitution sought generally to place limits on what government is able to do, without diluting its essential ability to govern. The Founders did not want government to be too efficient or adventurous. "Overall, the government was designed to be responsive slowly to relatively long-term demands and to require the development of relatively broad agreement among the electorate prior to taking action."[36] In other words, for government agencies to operate *not* under pressure would require time and broad popular support—both of which often seem to be lacking in controversial policy areas such as gun control, police–minority relations, and sex education in public schools. Our impatience with government action seems to be directly related to the extent and the depth of policy disagreements dividing the nation. Public administration is squarely in the middle of popular discontent, reflecting the disorganization and policy differences present in society itself.

There are three other matters to consider. For over forty years, we have been experiencing a crisis of confidence—indeed, a **"crisis of legitimacy"**—regarding

public cynicism and distrust

negative public opinion about politics and government reflected in opinion polls and low voter turnouts.

"crisis of legitimacy"

political condition in which government officials are perceived to lack the legal authority and right to make binding decisions for the people.

government and its actions.[37] More recently, certain new assumptions or premises appear to be gaining currency in shaping (and perhaps reflecting) popular perceptions of government. These have been expressed as follows: (1) public programs are counterproductive to the social and economic well-being of the country; (2) the public no longer expects public programs to work, and is increasingly unwilling to spend additional funds on them; (3) public programs are better administered at the state and local level; further, many functions should be taken over by private organizations and voluntary community efforts; (4) national government program managers are becoming less important, with fewer needed; and (5) public managers are already overpaid, and any system of reward or penalties in the public sector will be abused.[38] Such thinking may be fashionable, but it can also be highly dysfunctional, not to mention inaccurate. Diminished public trust does not bode well for maintenance of either democratic processes or effective government. Many individuals of all political persuasions have fallen prey to this crisis of confidence.[39]

One symptom (perhaps a result) of this crisis of confidence has been public pressure to enact sunshine and sunset laws, discussed in Chapter 2. These apply more to legislative than to administrative entities, but they affect the latter as well. Yet one of the unintended impacts of the "open government" laws may have been to make compromise and accommodation harder to achieve, among contending forces. In the words of one observer:

> Representative democracy rests upon our ability to create a consensus. This requires that the system be open to compromise (a dirty word in America) and bargaining. Without these, we either reach no decision or we impose a decision. The former leads to deadlock, the latter to authoritarianism. What has been lost by "opening the doors" [meetings] is the decision makers' ability to make concessions, and to reach an accommodation, with dignity and decency. Now that the interest groups are all watching, no one can afford to make "public" policy; rather, they must yield to the pressures that are sometimes very narrow.[40]

Ironically, this dark mood of mistrust is, if anything, *unwarranted*. Scholarly studies of public opinion, both of recent vintage and earlier, have indicated that the public's voice is heard by those in government, including those in bureaucracy, if that voice is clear in what it is saying and forceful in its expression. The "voice of the people" is really many voices, saying many things—about particular policies, the effectiveness of government activities generally, public ethics, and much more. Yet it has been demonstrated that when public opinion is generally united on a position and feelings run strong on the matter, government's response is nearly always in the direction desired by the majority. Thus, perhaps we can afford a somewhat more optimistic view of governmental responsiveness to majority preferences than many seem to hold at this point.

One final matter remains, related in part to the level of public confidence in what government does. In this era of rampant downsizing and deregulation, how might we judge the value of government expenditures? James Joseph, a retired undersecretary of the Interior Department, offered five criteria (standards) derived from an appropriate source: the preamble to the United States Constitution. The criteria are, simply, the degree to which a government project contributes to the sense of equity, community, utility, security, and quality of life in America.[41] It should be noted, as we even think about these criteria, that they alone do not capture the full dimensions of all that public servants do, nor the dedication that most public servants bring to their tasks.

Clearly, we have been forced in recent years to consider ever larger and more difficult questions about the role and activities of government—and not only concerns about how high government expenditures will be. For example, how much bureaucracy is necessary to maintain domestic and international security? In light of that, these sorts of criteria might well be useful as we continue to sort out what kind of government we expect, and the qualities of individuals that will be needed to manage these changes in the years ahead. An integral part of that debate will be the role of public administration in securing the quality and equality of community life for the society we want to create in the future.

What, then, is the prognosis for the future of public administration? Without question it will continue to be a focal point of concern in our system of governance, with controversy encompassing virtually every major policy area and every political interest with a stake in administrative operations. In the words of the late political scientist Carl Friedrich, public administration is "the core of modern government." Clearly, then, public administration "is and will be a focal area for change and transformation in society generally."[42] The only certainty in all this is the uncertain directions public administration will take in the future.

Discussion Questions

1. What kinds of criteria are, or should be, used to determine the role of government and the goals and objectives of public administration and to evaluate the productivity and performance of programs and individuals?

2. What may be predicted about the future impact of ICTs on citizen participation in governance, based especially on the example of the Obama election campaign in 2008?

3. Describe the forces promoting centralization and those promoting decentralization. What solutions exist to resolve this conflict? Why are solutions necessary?

4. What are the "crisis of confidence" and "crisis of legitimacy" in government? Is there any way to resolve these crises? If so, how? If not, what are the implications for the future of democratic government?

5. Is the field of study known as "public administration" merely a restatement of principles from the fields of management, politics, social psychology, economics, and law? Or are there other principles, distinct to public administration, that should be taught to those who intend to work in public service? If so, what are they? Explain your choices. If not, defend your answer.

6. Participation in government by conflicting internal and external individuals and groups is inconsistent with accountability, professionalism, rationality, and strong leadership. Describe the

tensions between participation and each of these conflicting values.

7. Modern public administration is expected to simultaneously optimize accountability, efficiency, public participation and representativeness, rapidity, and strong leadership. How does one reconcile internal and external participation with the modern meaning of public administration?

8. Are Weber's ideas still applicable to modern public administration? Why or why not? Should government agencies be more or less Weberian than they are today? Defend your answer.

9. What are the major social and governmental paradoxes in the environment in which public administration operates, and how do these paradoxes affect public administration? Specifically, what paradoxes exist in the electoral process, and how have public policy decisions and implementation been affected?

10. What are the most important components of rapid social change in the past half-century? Explain why you chose the components that you did.

Key Terms and Concepts

balance of trade, *507*

knowledge explosion, *507*

social networking, *507*

technological change, *507*

fundamentalism, *508*

war on terror, *508*

chronic fiscal stress, *510*

revolution of rising expectations, *512*

postindustrialism, *512*

globalization, *513*

multinational corporations (MNCs), *513*

European Union (EU), *513*

social media, *513*

Electoral College, *516*

campaign finance reform, *516*

Citizens United vs. Federal Elections Commission, 516

"overhead democracy", *518*

"overhead bureaucracy", *521*

empowerment, *522*

virtual campaign, *522*

debureaucratize, *525*

public cynicism and distrust, *539*

"crisis of legitimacy", *539*

Suggested Readings

Beneveniste, Guy. *The Twenty-First Century Organization: Analyzing Current Trends—Imagining the Future.* San Francisco: Jossey-Bass, 1994.

Box, Richard C. (ed) *Democracy and Public Administration.* New York: M.E. Sharpe, 2007.

Box, Richard C. *Public Administration and Society: Critical Issues in American Governance.* 2nd ed. Armonk, N.Y.: M. E. Sharpe, 2009.

Bozeman, Barry. *All Organizations Are Public.* San Francisco: Jossey-Bass, 1987.

DiIulio, John J., Jr., ed. *Deregulating the Public Service: Can Government Be Improved?* Washington, D.C.: Brookings Institution Press, 1994.

Etzioni, Amitai. *Public Policy in a New Key.* New Brunswick, N.J.: Transaction, 1993.

Fry, Brian R and Jos C.N. Raadschelders. *Mastering Public Administration: From Max Weber to Dwight Waldo.* 2nd ed. Washington, D.C.: CQ Press, 2008.

Heady, Ferrel. *Public Administration: A Comparative Perspective.* 6th ed. Boca Raton, Fla.: CRC Press, 2001.

Hummel, Ralph. *The Bureaucratic Experience: The Post-Modern Challenge.* New York: M.E. Sharpe, 2007.

Jones, Larry R., and Frank Thompson, eds. *Public Management: Institutional Renewal for the Twenty-First Century, Vol. 10.* Amsterdam: Elsevier Science, 2000.

Jreisat, Jamil. *Comparative Public Administration and Policy.* Boulder, Colo.: Westview Press, 2002.

Kettl, Donald F. *The Transformation of Governance: Public Administration for Twenty-First Century America.* Baltimore: Johns Hopkins University Press, 2002.

_____. *The Global Public Management Revolution: A Report on the Transformation of Governance.* 2nd ed. Washington, D.C: Brookings Institution Press, 2005.

_____. *System Under Stress: Homeland Security and American Politics*. 2nd ed. Washington, D.C.: CQ Press, 2007.

Lane, Jan-Erik. *The Public Sector: Concepts, Models, and Approaches*. 3rd ed. Newbury Park, Calif.: Sage, 2000.

Lynn, Naomi B., and Aaron Wildavsky, eds. *Public Administration: The State of the Discipline*. Chatham, N.J.: Chatham House, 1990.

Fischer, Michael. *Terrorism and Homeland Security*. Belmont, Calif.: Wadsworth Cengage Learning, 2010.

Martin, Daniel W. *The Guide to the Foundations of Public Administration*. New York: Marcel Dekker, 1989.

O'Leary, Rosemary. *The Ethics of Dissent: Managing Guerilla Government*. Washington, D.C.: CQ Press, 2006.

Ostrom, Vincent. *The Intellectual Crisis in American Public Administration*. 3rd ed. Tuscaloosa: University of Alabama Press, 2008.

Peters, Guy. *The Future of Governing*. 2nd ed. Lawrence: University Press of Kansas, 2001.

Thai, Khi V., with Dianne Rahm and Jerrell D. Coggburn, eds. *Handbook of Globalization and the Environment*. Boca Raton, Fla.: CRC Press, 2007.

Thompson, Frank J., and William Winter, eds. *Revitalizing the State and Local Public Service: Strengthening Performance, Accountability and Citizen Confidence*. San Francisco: Jossey-Bass, 1993.

Waldo, Dwight. *The Administrative State*. New edition. Piscataway, N.J.: Transaction, 2006.

Wamsley, Gary L., et al. *Refounding Public Administration*. Newbury Park, Calif.: Sage, 1990.

White, Jonathan R. *Terrorism and Homeland Security*. 6th ed. Belmont, Calif.: Wadsworth, 2008.

APPENDIX

Professional Associations for Information and Job Opportunities and Public Administration Journals for Research

Professional Organizations and Internet Job-Search Links

Like all other professions, public administration has a number of affiliated and specialized groups concerned with technical areas within the discipline. These range from civil engineering to law enforcement, to housing, state government, and welfare administration. Most of these groups have websites, publish journals or newsletters, and advertise for jobs. They can be a rich resource for students seeking initial job appointments or for midcareerists seeking new jobs. The names, addresses, and websites (when available) of selected academic, professional, and public interest organizations, as well as selected job-search links, are listed alphabetically.

Academy for State and Local
Government
444 N. Capitol St. NW, Ste. 349
Washington, DC 20001

American Association of School
Administrators
801 N. Quincy St., Ste. 700
Arlington, VA 22203
http://www.aasa.org

American Correctional Association
206 N. Washington St.
Alexandria, VA 22314
http://www.aca.org/

American Enterprise Institute for Public
Policy Research
1150 Seventeenth St. NW
Washington, DC 20036
http://www.aei.org/

American Management Association
Centers in Arlington, VA, Atlanta,
Chicago, New York, and
San Francisco
http://www.amanet.org/

American Planning Association
122 S. Michigan Ave., Ste. 1600
Chicago, IL 60603
1776 Massachusetts Ave. NW
Washington, DC 20036-1904
http://www.planning.org

American Political Science Association
1527 New Hampshire Ave. NW
Washington, DC 20036-1206
http://www.apsanet.org

American Productivity and Quality Center
123 N. Post Oak Lane
Houston, TX 77024
http://www.apqc.org

American Public Human Services
Association
810 First St. NE, Ste. 500
Washington, DC 20002-4267
http://www.aphsa.org

American Public Transportation
Association
1666 K St. NW
Washington, DC 20006
http://www.apta.com

American Public Works Association
2345 Grand Blvd., Ste. 700
Kansas City, MO 64108
1401 K St. NW, 11th Floor
Washington, DC 20005
http://www.apwa.net/

American Society for Public
Administration
1301 Pennsylvania Ave. NW, Ste. 700
Washington, DC 20004
http://www.aspanet.org/scriptcontent/index.
cfm

Association of Government Accountants
2208 Mt. Vernon Ave.
Alexandria, VA 22301
http://www.agacgfm.org

Brookings Institution
1775 Massachusetts Ave. NW
Washington, DC 20036
http://www.brookings.edu/

Canadian Association of Programs in
Public Administration
http://www.cappa.ca/

Carter Center
One Copenhill
453 Freedom Pkwy.
Atlanta, GA 30307
http://www.cartercenter.org/

Cato Institute
1000 Massachusetts Ave. NW
Washington, DC 20001-5403
http://www.cato.org/

Center for Community Change
1536 U St. NW
Washington, DC 20009
http://www.communitychange.org

Center on Budget and Policy Priorities
820 First St. NE, Ste. 510
Washington, DC 20002
http://www.cbpp.org

Committee for Economic Development
2000 L St. NW, Ste. 700
Washington, DC 20036
http://www.ced.org

Common Cause
1133 19th St. NW, 9th Floor
Washington, DC 20036
http://www.commoncause.org

Commonwealth Institute
P.O. Box 398105, Inman Square Post
Office
Cambridge, MA 02139
http://www.comw.org/

Conference Board
845 Third Ave.
New York, NY 10022
http://www.conference-board.org/

Conference of Minority Public
Administrators (COMPA)
P.O. Box 1552
Norfolk, VA 23501-2741
http://www.compahr.org

Congressional Quarterly Service
1255 22nd St. NW
Washington, DC 20037
http://www.cq.com/

Council for Excellence in
Government
1301 K St. NW, Ste. 450
Washington, DC 20005
http://www.excelgov.org/

Council of State Community
Development Agencies
1825 K St., Ste. 515
Washington, DC 20006
http://www.coscda.org

Council of State Governments
2760 Research Park Dr.
P.O. Box 11910
Lexington, KY 40578-1910

Freedom of Information Center
133 Neff Annex
University of Missouri
Columbia, MO 65211
http://www.nfoic.org/foi-center/

Government Finance Officers
Association (formerly the Municipal
Finance Officers Association)
1301 Pennsylvania Ave. NW, Ste. 309
Washington, DC 20004
203 N LaSalle St., Ste. 2700
Chicago, IL 60601
http://www.gfoa.org

Government Management Information
Sciences Headquarters
8315 SW 183rd Terrace
Palmetto Bay, FL 33157
http://www.gmis.org

Governmental Research Association
Room 219 Brooks Hall, Samford
University
P.O. Box 292300
Birmingham, AL 35229
http://www.graonline.org/

Heritage Foundation
214 Massachusetts Ave. NE
Washington, DC 20002-4999
http://www.heritage.org/

Hoover Institution
434 Galvez Mall, Stanford
University
Stanford, CA 94305-6010
http://www.hoover.org/

Inter-Governmental Network
7910 Woodmont Ave., Ste. 1430
Bethesda, MD 20814

International Association of Chiefs
of Police
515 N. Washington St.
Alexandria, VA 22314
http://www.tiacp.org

International Association of Fire Chiefs
4025 Fair Ridge Dr.
Fairfax, VA 22033
http://www.iafc.org/

International City/County Management
Association
777 North Capitol St. NE, Ste. 500
Washington, DC 20002-4201
http://icma.org/main/sc.asp

International Institute of Municipal Clerks
8331 Utica Ave., Ste. 200
Rancho Cucamonga, CA 91730
http://www.iimc.com

International Public Management
Association
1617 Duke St.
Alexandria, VA 22314
http://www.ipma-hr.org

Internet Job-Hunting Sites—Public
Policy and Administration
http://www.uww.edu/career/

Jobs in Government
http://jobsingovernment.com

Local Government Institute
1231 Farallone Ave.
Tacoma, WA 98466
http://www.lgi.org/

National Academy of Public Administration
900 7th St. NW, Ste. 600
Washington, DC 20001
http://www.napawash.org/

National Assembly of State Arts Agencies
1029 Vermont Ave. NW, 2nd Floor
Washington, DC 20005
http://www.nasaa-arts.org

National Association for the Advancement
of Colored People (NAACP)
4805 Mt. Hope Dr.
Baltimore, MD 21215
http://www.naacp.org

National Association of Counties
25 Massachusetts Ave. NW
Washington, DC 20001
http://www.naco.org/

National Association of Housing and
Redevelopment Officials
630 I St. NW
Washington, DC 20001-3736
http://www.nahro.org/

National Association of Regional
Councils
1666 Connecticut Ave. NW
Washington, DC 20009
http://narc.org

National Association of Schools
of Public Affairs and Administration
(NASPAA)
1029 Vermont Avenue, NW,
Suite 1100
Washington, DC 20005
http://www.naspaa.org

National Association of State Chief
Information Officers
201 East Main St., Ste. 1405
Lexington, KY 40507
https://www.nascio.org/

National Association of Towns and
Townships
1130 Connecticut Ave. NW, Ste. 300
Washington, DC 20036
http://www.natat.org

National Center for Public
Productivity
360 Dr. Martin Luther King Blvd.
Hill Hall 701, Rutgers
Newark, NJ 07102
http://www.ncpp.us/

National Civic League
1640 Logan St.
Denver, CO 80203
http://www.ncl.org/

National Conference of State
Legislatures
7700 East First Place
Denver, CO 80230
444 North Capitol St. NW, Ste. 515
Washington, DC 20001
http://www.ncsl.org/

National Electronic Commerce
Coordinating Council (NECCC)
444 N. Capitol St. NW, Ste. 234
Washington, DC 20001
http://ec3.org/

National Governors Association
Hall of the States
444 N. Capitol St., Ste. 267
Washington, DC 20001
http://www.nga.org/

National Institute of Governmental
Purchasing
319 Congress Ave., Ste. 200
Austin, TX 78701
http://www.nigp.com/

National League of Cities
1301 Pennsylvania Ave. NW
Washington, DC 20004
http://www.nlc.org

National Public Employer Labor
Relations Association
NPELRA Administrative Office
1012 South Coast Highway,
Ste. M
Oceanside, CA 92054
NPELRA Legislative Office
815 Connecticut Ave. NW, Ste. 500
Washington, DC 20006-4004
http://www.npelra.org

National Recreation and Park
Association
22377 Belmont Ridge Rd.
Ashburn, VA 20148
http://www.nrpa.org/

National Society for Experiential
Education
Talley Management Group, Inc.
19 Mantua Rd.
Mt. Royal, NJ 08061
http://www.nsee.org/home.htm

National States Geographic Information
Council
2105 Laurel Bush Rd., Ste. 200
Bel Air, MD 21015
http://www.nsgic.org

Opportunities in Public Affairs
http://www.opajobs.com/

Policy Studies Organization
1527 New Hampshire Ave. NW
Washington, DC 20036
http://www.ipsonet.org

Public Service Research
Foundation
320 D Maple Ave.
East Vienna, VA 22180
http://www.psrf.org/

Public Technology, Inc.
1301 Pennsylvania Ave. NW,
Ste. 830
Washington, DC 20004
http://www.pti.org/

Rand Corporation
1776 Main St.
Santa Monica, CA 90401-3208
http://www.rand.org/

Society of Government Meeting
Professionals (SGMP)
908 King St., Lower Level
Alexandria, VA 22314
http://www.sgmp.org

Society for Human Resource Management
(formerly the American Society for
Personnel Administration)
1800 Duke St.
Alexandria, VA 22314
http://www.shrm.org/

Tax Foundation
2001 L St. NW, Ste. 1050
Washington, DC 20036
http://www.taxfoundation.org

United States Conference of Mayors
1620 I St. NW, 4th Floor
Washington, DC 20006
http://www.usmayors.org/

Urban Institute
2100 M St. NW, 4th Floor
Washington, DC 20037
http://www.urban.org/

USA Jobs
http://www.usajobs.opm.gov

Women Executives in State Government
1225 New York Ave. NW, Ste. 350
Washington, DC
http://www.expertclick.com/ProfilePage/
default.cfm?GroupID=5447&SearchCriteria
=Government&Serial=Y-64212

Journals for Research

The following list identifies selected journals that are relevant to various
subfields of public administration. They cover a broad spectrum of specialized areas in the core areas of the discipline such as budget and financial
administration, personnel, public policy, and regulations as well as other
adjacent fields of study. They are listed alphabetically, with addresses and

websites when available. When searching for a specific article or journal, be sure to enter the name of the journal on your browser to see if it has been added to the Internet or if the web address has changed since this printing.

Academy of Management Review
P.O. Box 3020
Briarcliff Manor, NY 10510-8020
http://www.aomonline.org/
Scholarly journal for the organizational sciences publishes academically rigorous, conceptual papers that advance the science and practice of management.

Administration and Society
Virginia Polytechnic Institute and State University
Center for Public Administration and Policy
Blacksburg, VA 24060
http://aas.sagepub.com/
This journal strives to advance understanding of public and human service organizations, their administrative processes, and their effects on society.

Administrative Science Quarterly
Cornell University
Johnson Graduate School of Management
130 East Seneca St., Ste. 400
Ithaca, NY 14850
http://www.johnson.cornell.edu/publications/asq/
Top-rated journal for research in administrative and organization theory.

American Journal of Public Health
800 I Street, NW
Washington, DC 20001-3710
http://www.ajph.org/
Monthly publication of articles in both general and specialized areas of the science, art, and practice of public health.

American Political Science Review
4289 Bunche Hall, Box 951472
Los Angeles, CA 90095-1472
http://www.apsanet.org/section327.cfm
Leading journal in political science, with occasional articles on public-policy making and public organizations.

American Politics Quarterly
P.O. Box 413
Milwaukee, WI 53201
http://www.uwm.edu/Org/APQ/
Articles examine and explore topics in every area of government, from local and state to regional and national.

American Review of Public Administration
University of Missouri—St. Louis
One University Blvd, 406 Tower
St. Louis, MO 63121-4400
http://www.umsl.edu/divisions/graduate/ppa/arpa.html
One of the leading journals in its field, dedicated to the study of public affairs and public administration; features articles that address rapidly emerging issues in the field.

Annals of the American Academy of Political and Social Science
The American Academy of Political and Social Science
3814 Walnut St.
Philadelphia, PA 19104
http://www.aapss.org/
Published bimonthly, the *Annals* is a collection of single-theme issues exploring topics of current concern.

Australian Journal of Public Administration
University of Queensland
Royal Institute of Public Administration
Department of Government
http://www.blackwellpublishing.com/journal.asp?ref=0313-6647
For those interested in Australian public administration and comparative analysis.

California Management Review
University of California, Berkeley
F501 Haas School of Business #1900
Berkeley, CA 94720-1900
http://cmr.berkeley.edu/
This high-quality journal publishes articles that are both research-based and address issues of current concern to managers.

Colloqui: Cornell Journal of Planning and Urban Issues
Cornell University
Department of City and Regional Planning
212 West Sibley Hall
Ithaca, NY 14853
Founded in 1985 as a forum for practitioners, faculty, and students in planning and related fields, *Colloqui* strives to present planning issues from a wide range of social, political, economic, geographic, and historical perspectives.

The Electronic Hallway Journal
Daniel J. Evans School of Public Affairs
109 Parrington Hall, Box 353055
University of Washington
Seattle, WA 98195-3055
https://hallway.org/
Case journal for public policy and administration.

Evaluation Review
http://erx.sagepub.com/
Offers the latest applied evaluation methods used in a wide range of disciplines and provides up-to-date articles on the latest quantitative and qualitative methodological developments, as well as commentaries on related applied-research issues.

The Executive
Newsletter version of the American Management Association journal.

Foreign Affairs
http://www.foreignaffairs.org/
Dedicated to promoting improved understanding of international affairs.

Foreign Policy
Carnegie Endowment for International Peace
1179 Massachusetts Ave.
Washington, DC 20036
http://www.foreignpolicy.com/
Launched in 1970 to encourage fresh and more vigorous debate on the vital issues confronting U.S. foreign policy.

GAO Journal
U.S. Government Accountability Office
Office of Public Affairs
411 G St. NW
Washington, DC 20548
http://www.gao.gov/
Published by the U.S. Government Accountability Office; focuses on accountability, integrity, and reliability involving fiscal issues in government.

Governance
http://www.blackwellpublishing.com/journal.asp?ref=0952-1895&site=1
International journal providing a forum for the theoretical and practical discussion of executive politics, public policy, administration, and the organization of the state.

Governing
Congressional Quarterly, Inc.
1100 Connecticut Ave. NW, #1300
Washington, DC 20036
http://www.governing.com
Popular journal with emphasis on the political and administrative management of state and local governments.

Government Executive
National Journal Group, Inc.
http://www.govexec.com
Government's business magazine,
    focusing on management issues and
    agencies at the federal level.

Government Technology
http://www.govtech.com/
Monthly journal detailing technological
    solutions to problems of state and local
    governments.

Government Union Review
320 D Maple Avenue
East Vienna, VA 22180
http://www.psrf.org/gur/index.jsp
Journal that traces labor-management
    relations at the federal, state, and local
    levels.

Harvard Business Review
Harvard Business School Publishing
60 Harvard Way
Boston, MA 02163
http://harvardbusinessonline.hbsp.harvard.
edu/hbsp/hbr/index.jsp?_requestid=70573
Major journal that publishes a variety of
    administrative articles by top experts
    in the field.

Human Relations
The Tavistock Institute
30 Tabernacle Street
London EC2A 4UE
http://hum.sagepub.com/
International interdisciplinary forum for
    the publication of high-quality original
    papers across a wide range of the social
    sciences.

Human Resource Management
http://www.blackwellpublishing.com/journal.
asp?ref=0954-5395&site=1
Themes related to personnel
    administration with no distinction
    between the public and private
    sectors.

Industrial and Labor Relations Review
520 Ives Hall
Cornell University
Ithaca, NY 14853-3901
http://www.ilr.cornell.edu/ilrreview/
Journal devoted to public and private
    sectors in industrial relations.

*The Institute of Public Administration in
Canada*
1075 Bay St., Ste. 401
Toronto, Ontario, Canada M5S2B1
http://www.ipaciapc.ca
For those interested in Canadian public
    administration and comparative
    analysis.

*International Journal of Public
Administration*
4 Park Square
Milton Park
Abingdon
Oxfordshire
OX14 4RN, UK
http://www.tandf.co.uk/journals/
titles/01900692.asp
Public administration journal with
    a comparative and international
    emphasis.

Journal of Accounting and Public Policy
The Boulevard
Langford Lane
Kidlington Oxford
OX5 1GB, UK
http://www.elsevier.com/wps/find/
journaldescription.cws_home/505721/
description#description
Discusses the interaction of accounting
    and public policy in both the private
    and public sectors.

*Journal of the American Planning
Association*
97774 Eagle Way
Chicago, IL 60678-9770
http://www.planning.org/japa/
Covers land-use planning in the public
    sector.

Journal of Collective Negotiations (formerly *Journal of Collective Negotiations in the Public Sector*)
http://www.baywood.com/journals/PreviewJournals.asp?Id=0047-2301
Presents clear discussions of the problems involved in negotiating contracts; resolving impasses, strikes, and grievances; and administering contracts in the various areas of public employment.

Journal of Criminal Justice
http://www.elsevier.com/wps/find/journaldescription.cws_home/366/description#description
Focuses on issues of importance to crime research and the criminal justice system.

Journal of Criminal Law and Criminology
Northwestern University School of Law
357 East Chicago Avenue
Chicago, IL 60611-3069
http://www.law.northwestern.edu/jclc/
Top-ranked journal publishes articles on policy and administration of law enforcement.

Journal of Organizational Behavior
111 River Street
Hoboken, NJ 07030
http://www3.interscience.wiley.com/journal/4691/home
http://www.jstor.org/journals/08943796.html
Aims to report and review the growing research in the industrial/organizational psychology and organizational behavior fields around the world.

Journal of Organizational Behavior Management
Western Michigan University
Department of Psychology
Kalamazoo, MI 49008
https://www.haworthpress.com/store/product.asp?sid=XPGUGEC212KP8H7FJS8-WN1K6JADL48BA&sku=J075
Publishes research and review articles, case studies, discussions, and book reviews on topics that are critical to today's organizational development practitioners.

Journal of Policy Analysis and Management
111 River Street
Hoboken, NJ 07030
http://www.jstor.org/journals/02768739.html
Outlet for graduate and undergraduate public-policy programs, research institutions, and individuals in the public-policy and management fields.

Journal of Political Economy
The University of Chicago Press
Journals Division
1427 E. 60th Street
Chicago, IL 60637-2954
http://www.jstor.org/journals/00223808.html
JPE has been presenting significant research and scholarship in economic theory and practice since its inception in 1892. Publishing analytical, interpretive, and empirical studies, the journal presents work in traditional areas as well as in such interdisciplinary fields as the history of economic thought and social economics.

Journal of Politics
Vanderbilt University
VU Station B #351817
Nashville, TN 37235-1817
http://www.vanderbilt.edu/jop/
Important regional political science journal.

Journal of Public Administration Research and Theory
Oxford University Press
2001 Evans Road
Cary, NC 27513
http://jpart.oxfordjournals.org/
International interdisciplinary quarterly devoted to building the body of knowledge of public administration.

Journal of Public Affairs Education
1029 Vermont Ave., NW, Suite 1100
Washington, DC 20005
http://www.naspaa.org/initiatives/jpae/jpae.asp
This journal is dedicated to advancing teaching and learning in public affairs, including the fields of policy analysis, public administration, public management, and public policy.

Journal of Public Policy
Cambridge University Press
100 Brook Hill Drive
West Nyack, NY 10994-2133
http://journals.cambridge.org/action/displayJournal?jid=PUP
British journal covering a wide range of policy issues.

Journal of State Government
http://www.enotes.com/spectrum-journal-state-government-journals
Current articles on issues of importance to state government.

Journal of Urban Affairs
Urban Affairs Association
298 Graham Hall
University of Delaware
Newark, Delaware 19716
http://www.blackwellpublishing.com/journal.asp?ref=0735-2166&site=1
Official journal of the Urban Affairs Association, the only international professional organization for urban scholars and practitioners.

Monthly Digest of Tax Articles
http://www.amazon.com/Monthly-Digest-of-Tax-Articles/dp/B00006KOGS
A publication that addresses recent tax issues.

National Civic Review
National Civic League
1640 Logan St.
Denver, CO 80203
http://www.ncl.org/publications/ncr/
Publishes brief articles on a wide variety of urban public-policy issues.

National Journal
The National Journal Group
The Watergate 600 New Hampshire Ave, NW
Washington, DC 20037
http://www.nationaljournal.com/njmagazine/
A weekly publication designed as a monitor of all federal actions, but especially in the executive agencies.

National Tax Journal
Management and Strategy Department
Kellogg School of Management
Northwestern University
2001 Sheridan Road
Evanston, IL 60208
http://ntj.tax.org/
A periodical on issues of government finance and taxation.

Nonprofit Management and Leadership
Jossey-Bass
Journals Customer Service
989 Market Street
San Francisco, CA 94103
http://www3.interscience.wiley.com/journal/104049461/home
Focuses on managing and leading nongovernment not-for-profit organizations.

Organizational Behavior and Human Decision Processes
The Boulevard
Langford Lane
Kidlington Oxford
OX5 1GB, UK
http://www.elsevier.com/wps/find/
journaldescription.cws_home/622929/
description#description
Features articles that describe original empirical research and theoretical developments in all areas of human decision processes.

Philippine Journal of Public Administration
http://worldcat.org/wcpa/top3mset/1762245
For those interested in Southeast Asian administration and comparative analysis.

Policy Sciences
http://www.springerlink.com/
content/102982/
With an interdisciplinary and international focus, this journal encourages different perspectives and especially welcomes conceptual and empirical innovation.

Policy Studies Journal
1527 New Hampshire Avenue, NW
Washington, DC 20036
http://www.ipsonet.org/web/page/395/
sectionid/374/pagelevel/2/interior.asp
Addresses a wide range of public-policy issues at all levels of government.

Policy Studies Review
Policy Studies Organization
1527 New Hampshire Avenue, NW
Washington, DC 20036
http://vnweb.hwwilsonweb.
com/hww/Journals/getIssues.
jhtml?sid=HWW:OMNIS&issn=0278-4416

Public Administration
RIPA International (formerly the Royal Institute of Public Administration)
http://www.ripainternational.co.uk/
For those interested in British administration and comparative analysis; also lists recent British government publications.

Public Administration Quarterly
http://www.spaef.com/PAQ_PUB/index.html
Journal with a broad orientation on public administration; also contains job listings.

Public Administration Review
American Society for Public Administration
1301 Pennsylvania Ave. NW, Ste. 700
Washington, DC 20004
http://www.aspanet.org/scriptcontent/
index_par.cfm
Most significant American journal concerned with public administration.

Public Administration Times
American Society for Public Administration
1301 Pennsylvania Ave. NW, Ste. 700
Washington, DC 20004
http://www.aspanet.org/scriptcontent/
index_patimes.cfm
Newsletter of the American Society for Public Administration; contains job announcements.

Public Budgeting and Finance
Association for Budgeting and Financial Management
Arizona State University
School of Public Affairs
411 North Central Avenue—Suite 400
Phoenix, AZ 85004-0950
http://www.blackwellpublishing.com/journal.
asp?ref=0275-1100&site=1

Public Finance Review
University of New Orleans
http://pfr.sagepub.com/
Professional forum devoted to U.S. policy-oriented economic research and theory.

Public Management
International City/County Management Association
777 North Capitol Street, NE
Suite 500
Washington, DC 20002-4201
http://icma.org/pm/9002/
Devoted to the profession of local government management with concise, timely articles on specific topics, editorial commentary, and selected departments.

The Public Manager
2000 Corporate Ridge
McLean, VA 22102
http://www.thepublicmanager.org/
Short articles with a federal emphasis.

Public Performance and Management Review
National Center for Public Performance
Rutgers School of Public Affairs and
Administration
360 Dr. Martin Luther King Blvd.
Hill Hall 701
Newark, NJ 07102
http://andromeda.rutgers.edu/~ncpp/
publications/ppmr.html
Focuses on the need for greater
    understanding of issues in public
    productivity and public management.

Public Personnel Management
International Public Management
Association for Human Resources
1617 Duke St.
Alexandria, VA 22314
http://www.ipma-hr.org/content.
cfm?pageid=87
Features groundbreaking articles on
    labor relations, assessment issues,
    comparative personnel policies,
    government reform, and more.

Public Productivity Review
M.E. Sharpe. Inc.
80 Business Park Drive
Armonk, NY 10504
http://classic.jstor.org/journals/03616681.html

Publius
http://publius.oxfordjournals.org/
Devoted to intergovernmental relations
    and federalism.

Review of Public Personnel Administration
http://rop.sagepub.com/
Devoted to all aspects of the field,
    particularly at the state and local levels
    of government.

Society
Applies social science research to
contemporary social- and public-policy
problems.

Spectrum: The Journal of State Government
http://www.csg.org/pubs/pubs_spectrum.
aspx
Features leading-edge public-policy
    information from think tanks,
    government agencies, and other
    research agencies.

State and Local Government Review
University of Georgia
Carl Vinson Institute of
Government
Athens, GA 30602-4582
http://www.cviog.uga.edu/slgr/

State News (formerly *State
Government News*)
2760 Research Park Drive
Lexington, KY 40578
http://www.csg.org/pubs/statenews.aspx
Provides nonpartisan information
    on state government trends,
    political protocol, and leaders
    in state government making a
    difference.

Urban Affairs Review
http://uar.sagepub.com/
Leading scholarly journal on urban issues
    and themes.

Washington Monthly
1319 F Street, N.W. Suite 810
Washington, DC 20004
http://www.washingtonmonthly.com/
Lively and entertaining liberal
    journalistic publication with
    provocative articles on politics
    and public bureaucracy, as well as
    on policy issues; has book review
    section.

GLOSSARY

A

American Recovery and Reinvestment Act (ARRA) an economic stimulus package proposed by President Obama and enacted by the 111th U.S. Congress in February 2009. The stimulus bill was intended to create jobs and promote investment and consumer spending to help recover from recession. (see p. 99).

accountability a political principle according to which agencies or organizations, such as those in government, are subject to some form of external control, causing them to give a general accounting of, and for, their actions; an essential concept in democratic public administration (see p. 59).

achievement-oriented criteria standards for making personnel judgments based on an individual's demonstrated, job-related competence (see p. 290).

adjudication quasi-judicial power delegated to agencies by Congress, under which agencies apply existing laws or rules to particular situations in case-by-case decision making; related term: *adjudicatory proceeding* (see p. 474).

administrative efficiency a normative model of administrative activity characterized by concentration of power (especially in the hands of chief executives), centralization of governmental policy making, exercise of power by experts and professional bureaucrats, separation of politics and administration, and emphasis on technical or scientific rationality (arrived at by detached expert analysis); the principal alternative to the **pluralist democracy** model (see p. 58).

administrative law important body of U.S. law pertaining to the legal authority of public administrative entities to perform their duties, and to the limits necessary to control those agencies; administrative law has been created both by judicial decisions (especially in the national government courts) and by statute (principally in the form of Administrative Procedure Acts, enacted by both national and state governments) (see p. 462).

administrative law judge member of the executive branch who performs quasi-judicial functions (see p. 475).

Administrative Procedure Act of 1946 law on which all federal administrative procedures are based (see p. 471).

advisory opinion one means used by some U.S. regulatory entities to secure voluntary compliance with regulatory requirements; involves issuance of a memorandum indicating how the entity (for example, the Federal Trade Commission) would decide an issue if it were presented formally (see p. 475).

affirmative action in the context of public personnel administration, a policy or program designed to bring into public service greater numbers of citizens who were largely excluded from public employment in previous years; also, the use of goals and timetables for hiring and promoting women, blacks, and other minorities as part of an equal employment opportunity program (see p. 51).

American Society for Public Administration (ASPA) Code of Ethics effort by the nation's leading professional association of public administrators to draw up and enforce a set of standards for official conduct (see p. 216).

ascriptive criteria standards for making personnel judgments that are based on attributes or characteristics other than skills or knowledge (see p. 290).

B

backdoor financing practice of eliminating discretionary decision-making control from the appropriations stage of the budgetary process (see p. 349).

balance of trade the difference between the value of a nation's exports and the value of its imports over a period of time (usually one year), adjusted for currency valuations (see p. 507).

bargaining or conflict model communication model that assumes the presence in an organization of considerable sustained conflict, strong tendencies toward secrecy, and motives of expediency on the part of most individuals (see p. 174).

before-versus-after studies evaluation and comparison of results before and after program implementation to determine what results, if any, were achieved (see p. 407).

benchmarking   quality and productivity improvement methodology that examines those organizations that are best at performing a certain process or set of processes (for example, employee relations) and then transplanting the methods into one's own organization (see p. 430).

bilateral bargaining   collective bargaining negotiations in which only management and labor are represented (see p. 301).

Bipartisan Commission on Fiscal Responsibility   See National Commission on Fiscal Responsibility (see p. 339).

block grants   form of grant-in-aid in which the purposes to be served by the funding are defined very broadly by the grantor, leaving considerable discretion and flexibility in the hands of the recipient (see p. 124).

blogosphere   is the portions of the Internet consisting of blogs and their interconnections. (see p. 35).

bonded indebtedness   revenue-raising tool for governments to issue notes or promises to pay a certain amount (principal) at a certain time (maturity date) at a particular rate of interest (see p. 338).

bounded rationality   the notion that there are prescribed boundaries, controls, or upper and lower limits on the decision-making abilities of individuals within organizations (see p. 209).

brainstorming   free-form and creative technique for collecting and discussing ideas from all participants without criticism or judgment (see p. 265).

broadbanding   the consolidation of existing job classifications into fewer and broader categories, reducing complexity and specialization in job classifications (see p. 293).

Brownlow Report   recommendations for reform of the federal bureaucracy from a 1937 committee, appointed by President Franklin Roosevelt and chaired by Louis Brownlow, that included respected scholars and practitioners in the emerging discipline of public administration (see p. 287).

budget deficit   the difference between the amount of revenue raised by taxes and the amount of federal government spending in a fiscal year. See also **deficit** (see p. 338).

Budget Enforcement Acts of 1990, 1997, and 2002   informal title of the Omnibus Budget Reconciliation Act, signed into law on November 5, 1990, and August 1997; an extension of the Gramm–Rudman–Hollings Act requiring that all new spending be offset by either new taxes or reductions in expenditures; provided for a special five-year process for deficit reduction, made permanent changes in the congressional budget process, changed the treatment of Social Security revenues in the U.S. federal budget, and established limits on federal discretionary spending (see p. 345).

budget obligations   orders placed, contracts awarded, services rendered, or other commitments made by government agencies during a given fiscal period that require expenditure of public funds during the same or some future period (see p. 346).

budget outlays   agency expenditures during a given fiscal period, fulfilling budget obligations incurred during the same or a previous period (see p. 346).

budget surpluses   occur when government brings in more revenue than it spends (p. 341).

Bureau of Consumer Protection (BCP)   federal superagency created in 2011 to protect consumers and buyers from unfair, deceptive, and fraudulent business practices (see p. 64).

bureaucracy   (1) a formal organizational arrangement characterized by division of labor, job specialization with no functional overlap, exercise of authority through a vertical hierarchy (chain of command), and a system of internal rules, regulations, and record keeping; (2) in common usage, the administrative branch of government (national, state, or local) in the United States; also, individual administrative agencies of those governments (see p. 6).

bureaucratic accountability   principles of political accountability applied in an effort to control bureaucratic power (see p. 89).

bureaucratic imperialism   the tendency of agencies to try to expand their program responsibilities (see p. 76).

bureaucratic neutrality   a central feature of bureaucracy whereby it carries out directives of other institutions of government (such as a chief executive or a legislature) in a politically neutral way, without acting as a political force in its own right; a traditional notion concerning bureaucratic behavior in Western governments; also called *political neutrality* (see p. 30).

bureaucratic resistance   feature of administrative agencies that emphasizes gradualism, and political caution when dealing with newly selected political leadership in the executive branch (see p. 243).

C

campaign finance reform   efforts by reform groups and some candidates to limit the influence of money in political campaigns. In 2002, the McCain–Feingold Act (sponsored by the presidential candidate and former Senator John McCain [R-AZ] and Senator Russ Feingold [D-WI]) was signed into law, limiting "soft money" spent by political parties on behalf of candidates through issue advertising and get-out-the-vote drives (see p. 516).

capitalist system   an economic system in which the means of production are owned by private citizens (see p. 50).

casework   refers to services performed by legislators and their staff on behalf of constituents (see p. 91).

categorical grants   a form of grant-in-aid with purposes narrowly defined by the grantor, leaving the recipient relatively little choice as to how the grant funding is to be used, substantively or procedurally (see p. 115).

central clearance   key role played by the Office of Management and Budget (OMB) regarding review of agency proposals for legislation to be submitted to Congress, with OMB approval required for the proposals to move forward. A similar role or pattern exists in many state governments and some local governments, in the relationship among chief executives, administrative agencies, and legislatures. Central clearance also is practiced with regard to submission of budget proposals from executive-branch agencies to legislatures, during the budget-making process (see p. 238).

centralization   an organizational pattern focusing on concentrating power at the top of an organization (see p. 179).

charter schools   publicly funded, privately operated K–12 schools; public schools staffed without teachers' unions (see p. 405).

checks and balances   a governing principle, following from separation of powers, that creates overlapping and interlocking functions among the executive, legislative, and judicial branches of government. These include the president's power to veto an act of Congress (and Congress's power to override a presidential veto by a two-thirds majority), the Senate's power to confirm or reject

presidential appointments to executive and judicial positions, and the power of the courts to determine the constitutionality of the actions of other branches (see p. 28).

chief information officers (CIOs)   high-level corporate or governmental officials responsible for the maintenance of communications and information technology systems in public or private organizations (see p. 436).

chief performance officer (CPO)   a position in the Office of Management and Budget (within the Executive Office of the President of the United States) first announced on January 7, 2009, by President-elect Barack Obama. The new post concentrates on the federal budget and government reform (see p. 442).

chief technology officer (CTO)   focuses on overall technology policy and innovation strategies across federal agencies and departments. President Obama appointed the first CTO in April 2009 (see p. 442).

chronic fiscal stress   condition confronting increasing numbers of governments and public agencies, resulting from a combination of economic inflation, declining productivity, slower economic growth, and taxpayer resistance to a larger tax burden (see p. 510).

citizen relationship management (CzRM)   strategy focusing on providing citizens timely, consistent, responsive access to government information and services using Internet links; fosters cooperation between government and its citizens, seeks operational and financial efficiencies, and builds an environment that encourages innovation within government (see p. 449).

citizen-centric   an attribute of public-policy decision making focused on meeting the needs of citizens (see p. 451).

Citizens United vs. Federal Election Commission   a controversial Supreme Court decision that declared that corporate funding of independent political broadcasts in candidate elections cannot be limited under the U.S. Constitution. The 5–4 decision resulted from a dispute over whether the lobbying group could air a film critical of Hillary Clinton, and whether it could advertise the film in broadcast ads featuring Clinton's image, in apparent violation of the 2002 Bipartisan Campaign Reform Act, commonly known as the McCain–Feingold Act (see p. 516).

1964 Civil Rights Act landmark legislation prohibiting discrimination by the private sector in both employment and housing (see p. 314).

Civil Service (Pendleton) Act a law formally known as the Civil Service Act of 1883 (sponsored by Ohio Senator George Pendleton), establishing job-related competence as the primary basis for filling national government jobs; created the U.S. Civil Service Commission to oversee the new "merit" system (see p. 287).

Civil Service Reform Act of 1978 law designed to reinforce merit principles, protect whistle-blowers, delegate personnel authority to agencies, reward employees for measurable performance, and make it easier to discharge incompetent workers; created the Federal Labor Relations Authority (FLRA), Office of Personnel Management (OPM), Senior Executive Service (SES), and the Merit Systems Protection Board (MSPB) (see p. 304).

claim-and-blame strategy situation in which politicians "blame" bureaucrats and bureaucrats "claim" not to have the authority to act (see p. 432).

Clayton Act 1914 law that prohibits price discrimination to eliminate competition or create a monopoly (see p. 464).

clientelism a phenomenon whereby patterns of regularized relationships develop and are maintained in the political process between individual government agencies and particular economic groupings; for example, departments of agriculture, labor, and commerce, working with farm groups, labor groups, and business organizations, respectively (see p. 31).

closed systems organizations that, in systems theory, have very few internal variables and relationships among those variables, and little or no vulnerability to forces in the external environment (see p. 163).

Code of Federal Regulations record of all rules that authorize regulatory agency actions (see p. 474).

collective bargaining formalized process of negotiation between management and labor; involves specified steps, in a specified sequence, aimed at reaching an agreement (usually stipulated in contractual form) on terms and conditions of employment, covering an agreed-on period of time; a cycle that is repeated on expiration of each labor–management contract or other agreement (see p. 300).

Commission on Economy and Efficiency established in 1909 by President William Howard Taft (1909–1913); recommended that a national budgetary process be instituted under direction of the president (see p. 358).

Common Cause a nonpartisan, nonprofit advocacy organization founded in 1970 by civic activist John Gardner, through which citizens make their voices heard in the political process and try to hold their elected leaders accountable to the public interest. (see p. 481).

communication vital formal and informal processes of interacting within and between individuals and units within an organization, and between organizations (see p. 170).

community control legal requirements that groups affected by political decisions must be represented on decision-making boards and commissions (see p. 67).

comparable worth extended the "equal pay for equal work" principle to develop criteria for compensation based on the intellectual and physical demands of the job, not market determination of its worth (see p. 314).

competitive sourcing one of Bush administration's five performance management improvements designed to outsource more federal jobs to private contractors. See also **outsourcing** (see p. 320).

Congressional Budget and Impoundment Control Act of 1974 changed the congressional budget process and revised timetables for consideration of spending bills; created the **Congressional Budget Office** (see p. 350).

Congressional Budget Office (CBO) created in 1974; the budget and financial planning division of the U.S. Congress; see **Congressional Budget and Impoundment Control Act of 1974** (see p. 333).

consensual or consensus-building model communication model that assumes that by cooperation instead of power struggles and political trade-offs, administrators may seek to reach agreement with potential adversaries as a means of furthering mutual aims (see p. 175).

consent order one means used by some U.S. regulatory entities to secure voluntary compliance with regulatory requirements; involves a formal agreement between the entity and an industry or industries in which the latter agree to cease a practice in return for the regulatory entity's dropping punitive actions aimed at the practice (see p. 475).

constituency any group or organization interested in the work and actions of a given official, agency, or organization, and a potential source of support for it; also, the interests (and sometimes geographic area) served by an elected or appointed public official (see p. 84).

continuing resolution a type of appropriation used by Congress to fund agencies when a formal appropriations bill has not been passed (see p. 353)

contracting out practice under which private-sector contractors provide designated goods or services to governments, or to individual agencies, for an agreed-on fee; an example both of a "twilight zone" between public and private sectors and of public-sector responses to growing fiscal stress; services contracted for include trash collection and fire protection; see also **privatization** (see p. 381).

controlled experimentation involves comparisons of two groups of similar people, one served by the program and another (control group) not served, or served differently; the most expensive and least practiced form of evaluation (see p. 408).

co-optation a process in organizational relations whereby one group or organization acquires the ability to influence activities of another, usually for a considerable period of time (see p. 68).

coordination the process of bringing together divided labor; efforts to achieve coordination often involve emphasis on common or compatible objectives, harmonious working relationships, and the like; linked to issues involving communication, centralization/decentralization, federalism, and leadership (see p. 170).

cost–benefit analysis technique designed to measure relative gains and losses resulting from alternative policy or program options; emphasizes identification of the most desirable cost–benefit ratio, in quantitative or other terms (see p. 197).

cost–benefit ratios the proportional relationship between expenditure of a given quantity of resources and the benefits derived therefrom; a guideline for choosing among alternatives, of greatest relevance to the rational model of decision making (see p. 197).

Council of Economic Advisers (CEA) U.S. president's chief advisory and research source for economic advice. The council consists of three economists (one appointed as chair) and assists the White House in preparing various economic reports (see p. 340).

"crisis of legitimacy" political condition in which government officials fail to receive a vote of confidence and are perceived to lack the legal authority and right to make binding decisions for the majority of the population (see p. 539).

critical path method (CPM) management approach to program implementation (related to PERT) in which a manager attempts to assess the resource needs of different paths of action, and to identify the "critical path" with the smallest margin of extra resources needed to complete all assigned program activities (see p. 398).

customer-service standards explicit standards of service quality published by federal agencies and part of the reinventing government initiative (see p. 427).

cybernetics emphasizes organizational feedback that triggers appropriate adaptive responses throughout an organization; a thermostat operates on the same principle (see p. 165).

D

debt ceiling the statutory limit on the federal debt; periodically raised by Congress (see p. 334).

debureaucratize strategy to decentralize and deregulate the public sector by reductions-in-force, promoting greater flexibility in personnel decisions, and increasing results-oriented incentives to reduce "overhead" costs (see p. 525).

decentralization an organizational pattern focused on distributing power broadly within an organization (see p. 179).

decision analysis the use of formal mathematical and statistical tools and techniques, especially computers and sophisticated computer models and simulations, to improve decision making (see p. 205).

decision making a process in which choices are made to change (or leave unchanged) an existing condition and to select a course of action most appropriate to achieving a desired objective (however formalized or informal the objective may be), while minimizing risk and uncertainty to the extent deemed possible; the process may be characterized by widely varying degrees of self-conscious "rationality" or by willingness of the decision maker to decide incrementally, without insisting on assessment of all possible alternatives, or by some combinations of approaches (see p. 194).

deficit   amount by which governmental outlays exceed governmental receipts in a fiscal year (see p. 333).

Department of Homeland Security (DHS)   a U.S. federal "mega-agency" created in 2002 by merging twenty-two existing agencies. Its mission is to respond to natural and man-made disasters, secure our borders, and prevent domestic terrorism and violence (see p. 13).

dependent regulatory agencies (DRAs)   regulatory units or subdivisions of executive agencies (see p. 472).

deregulation   strategy to reduce or remove government regulations (see p. 499).

devolution   a process of transferring of power or functions from a higher to a lower level of government in the U.S. federal system (see p. 137).

digital divide   differential knowledge about available technology caused by inequalities in education, income, and access to computers and the Internet (see p. 452).

discretionary authority   power defined according to a legal and institutional framework and vested in a formal structure (a nation, an organization, a profession, or the like); power exercised through recognized, legitimate channels. The ability of individual administrators in a bureaucracy to make significant choices affecting management and operation of programs for which they are responsible; particularly evident in systems with separation of powers.

discretionary spending   category of budget authority that comprises budgetary resources (except those provided to fund direct-spending programs) in appropriations acts (see p. 332).

distributive policies   policy actions such as subsidies or tax deductions that deliver widespread benefits to individuals or groups who often do not bear the costs directly (see p. 379).

diversity   reflects the goal of many affirmative action programs to diversify the workforce to reflect the population demographics (makeup) in the affected jurisdiction (see p. 278).

Dodd-Frank Wall Street Reform and Consumer Protection Act   legislation proposed by President Obama and passed by Congress, aimed at changing the American financial regulatory environment and affecting all federal financial regulatory agencies and nearly every aspect of the nation's financial services industry (see p. 487).

downsizing   current fiscal pressures on public organizations have spawned the need for downsizing in many places, forcing leaders to use a variety of new tactics. At the same time, they must strive to maintain organization morale and performance levels, while holding to a minimum the negative effects of organizational decline. See also **reductions-in-force (RIFs)** (see p. 267).

due process of law   emphasizes procedural guarantees provided by the judicial system to protect individuals from unfair or unconstitutional actions by private organizations and government agencies (see p. 53).

E

earmarking   revenues are "earmarked" for designated purposes (such as elementary, secondary, and higher education; road construction and maintenance; or operating game preserves), leaving the bureaucracy without discretion to change them (see p. 365).

egalitarianism   philosophical concept stressing individual equality in political, social, economic, and other relations; in the context of public personnel administration, the conceptual basis for "government by the common person" (see p. 287).

Electoral College   a mechanism established under the Constitution to choose the president and the vice president of the United States. Each state has as many electoral votes as members in Congress and its delegates, called electors, can be selected by any method. Candidates who win the popular vote in each state receive all of that state's electoral votes (except in Maine and Nebraska). Under this system, a presidential candidate can lead in the nationwide popular vote and can still fail to win the required majority in the Electoral College: for example, Bush versus Gore in 2000 (see p. 516).

electronic government (e-gov)   takes the information technology concept further by integrating disparate information sources into one-stop web "portals" for improving access to information about government; for example, http://www.usa.gov (see p. 31).

eminent domain power of governments to take private property for a legitimate public purpose without the owner's consent (although governments are required to pay an owner "just compensation" [a fair price]) (see p. 108).

empowerment approach to citizen participation or management that stresses extended customer satisfaction, examines relationships among existing management processes, seeks to improve internal agency communications, and responds to valid customer demands; in exchange for the authority to make decisions at the point of customer contact, all "empowered" employees must be thoroughly trained, and the results must be carefully monitored (see p. 69).

Energy Policy Act of 2005 a comprehensive "pork-barrel" law that also attempts to meet growing energy needs by providing tax incentives and loan guarantees for energy production of various types; before Hurricane Katrina, it was estimated to cost the U.S. Treasury $12.3 billion in tax expenditures and lost revenue through 2015 (see p. 466).

entitlements government programs (mainly for individuals) created under legislation that defines eligibility standards but places no limit on total budget authority; the level of outlays is determined solely by the number of eligible persons who apply for authorized benefits, under existing law (see p. 331).

entrepreneurial government emphasizes productivity management, measurable performance, privatization, and change (see p. 10).

1972 Equal Employment Opportunity Act amended Title VII, the Civil Rights Act of 1964; designed to strengthen the authority of the Equal Employment Opportunity Commission (EEOC) to enforce antidiscrimination laws in state and local governments as well as in private organizations with fifteen or more employees (see p. 314).

Equal Employment Opportunity Commission (EEOC) investigates and rules on charges of racial and other arbitrary discrimination by employers and unions, in all aspects of employment (http://www.eeoc.gov) (see p. 314).

Equity Pay Act of 1963 prohibited gender-based (or other) discrimination in pay for those engaged in the same type of work (see p. 314).

European Union (EU) trading bloc of twenty-five European countries, twelve of which have converted to a common currency, the euro, to eliminate trade barriers among those nation-states (see p. 513).

exception principle assumption in traditional administrative thinking that chief executives do not have to be involved in administrative activities unless some problem or disruption of routine activity occurs—that is, when there is an exception to routine operations (see p. 251).

executive budgets budgets prepared by chief executives and their central budget offices for submission to the legislature for analysis, consideration, review, change, and enactment (see pp. 239).

Executive Order (EO) 10925 issued by President Kennedy in 1961, this EO required for the first time that "affirmative action" guidelines be used to prohibit discrimination in employment by federal agencies and contractors (see p. 314).

Executive Order (EO) 10988 issued by President Kennedy in 1962, this order extended the right to organize and bargain collectively to all national government employees (see p. 303).

executive privilege the claim, largely unsupported by the federal courts, made by presidents that confidential information exchanged between themselves and their advisers cannot be released without the president's approval (see p. 252).

Executive Schedule compensation schedule for the federal Senior Executive Service (see p. 291).

external (legal-institutional) checks codes of conduct, laws, rules, and statutes that serve as safeguards to ensure that individual administrative actions are ethical (see p. 217).

externalities the economic consequences or impacts of federal grants-in-aid at the regional and local levels (see p. 115).

F

Federal Information Security Management Act (FISMA) specifies the general authority of the OMB director and individual agencies relating to developing and maintaining federal information security policies and practices; requires agencies to conduct annual independent evaluations of their information security programs and practices (see p. 440).

Federal Energy Regulatory Commission (FERC)   regulates and oversees energy industries in the economic, environmental, and safety interests of the American Public (see p. 465).

Federal Labor Relations Authority (FLRA)   replaced the Federal Labor Relations Council and increased the strength of the bipartisan, three-member panel to supervise the creation of bargaining units and union elections, and deal with labor–management relations in federal agencies (see p. 304).

Federal Mediation and Conciliation Service (FMCS)   created by Congress in 1947 as an independent agency to promote sound and stable labor–management relations (see p. 303).

Federal Register   complete listing of all proposed and active federal regulations, available online at http://www.gpoaccess.gov/fr/ (see p. 474).

Federal Reserve System   independent board that serves as the central bank of the United States. "The Fed" administers banking, credit, and monetary policies and controls the supply of money available to member banks (see p. 339).

Federal Trade Commission (FTC)   independent regulatory commission charged with enforcing antitrust acts, including the Sherman and Clayton Acts, to protect consumers against unfair trade practices (see p. 464).

federalism   a constitutional division of governmental power between a central or national government and regional governmental units (such as states), with each having some independent authority over its citizens (see p. 100).

Financial Stability Oversight Council (FSOC)   established under the Dodd–Frank Act, the FSOC provides for comprehensive monitoring to ensure the stability of our nation's financial system. The council identifies threats to the financial stability of the United States, promotes market discipline, and responds to emerging risks to the U.S. financial system (see p. 487).

First Hoover Commission   (1947–1949) chaired by former president Herbert Hoover, this group tried to reduce the number of federal agencies created during World War II; recommended an expansion of executive budgetary powers (see p. 359).

fiscal federalism   the complex of financial transactions, transfers of funds, and accompanying rules and regulations that increasingly characterizes national-state, national-local, and state-local relations (see p. 110).

fiscal mismatch   differences in the capacity of various governments to raise revenues, in relation to those governments' respective abilities to pay for public services that they are responsible for delivering (see p. 111).

fiscal policy   refers to government actions aimed at development and stabilization of the private economy, including taxation and tax policy, expenditures, and management of the national debt; monetary and credit controls are also related to fiscal policy (see p. 334).

formal communication   official written documentation within an organization, including electronic mail, memoranda, minutes of meetings, and records; forms the framework for organizational intent and activity (see p. 170).

formal theory of organization   stresses formal, structural arrangements within organizations, and "correct" or "scientific" methods to be followed in order to achieve the highest degree of organizational efficiency; examples include Weber's theory of bureaucracy and Taylor's scientific management approach (see p. 147).

formula grants   type of national government grant-in-aid available to states and local governments for purposes that are ongoing and common to many government jurisdictions; distributed according to a set formula that treats all applicants uniformly, at least in principle; have the effect of reducing grantors' administrative discretion. Examples are aid to the blind and aid to the elderly (see p. 115).

Freedom of Information Act (FOIA)   passed by Congress and some state legislatures establishing procedures through which private citizens may gain access to a wide variety of records and files from government agencies; a principal instrument for breaking down bureaucratic secrecy in American public administration (see p. 62).

free-market competition   basis of U.S. and other free-enterprise economic systems in which the means of production and distribution of goods and services are owned by private corporations or individuals, and the government's role in the economy is minimal (see p. 461).

full-time equivalent (FTE) employees actual number of full-time government personnel plus the number of full-time people who would have been needed to work the hours put in by part-time employees (see p. 281).

functional overlap a phenomenon of contemporary American bureaucracy whereby functions performed by one bureaucratic entity may also be performed by another; conflicts with Weber's notions of division of labor and specialization (see p. 148).

fundamentalism practice of certain religious groups that adhere to strict beliefs and literal interpretation of a set of basic religious principles (see p. 508).

G

game theory a modern theory viewing organizational behavior in terms of competition among members for resources; based on distinctly mathematical assumptions and employing statistical data collection methods (see p. 165).

Geographic Information Systems (GIS) technological software tools that diagram spatial information visually. Citizens are using geospatial platforms to report the locations of crimes in progress, potholes, water leaks, accidents, lost animals, and other events that cities should potentially address (see p. 421).

General Schedule (GS) pay scale for federal employees, based on grades and steps (see p. 291).

globalization an acceleration of transcontinental flows of capital, ideas, culture, and goods and services across national boundaries via the Internet in a networked society leading to an integration of national economies into the international economy through trade, direct foreign investment (by **multinational corporations**), short-term capital flows, and international flows of technology (see p. 513).

goal articulation process of defining and clearly expressing goals generally held by those in an organization or a group; usually regarded as a function of organization or group leaders; a key step in developing support for official goals (see p. 214).

goal congruence agreement on fundamental goals; refers to the extent of agreement among leaders and followers in an organization on central objectives; in practice, its absence in many instances creates internal tensions and difficulties in goal definition (see p. 215).

gobbledygook misleading jargon or meaningless technical terms often used purposely to obscure communications within organizations (see p. 173).

Government Accountability Office (GAO) investigative arm of Congress that helps Congress oversee federal programs and operations to ensure accountability through a variety of activities including financial audits, program reviews, investigations, legal support, and policy/program analyses (see p. 412).

Government Performance and Results Act (GPRA) commonly called the Results Act, this 1993 statute requires federal managers to plan and measure performance in new ways (see p. 421).

Government Performance and Results Modernization Act of 2010 extension of the 1993 legislation (see p. 423).

government regulation government activity designed to monitor and guide private economic competition; specific actions (characterized as *economic regulation*) have included placing limits on producers' prices and practices, and promoting commerce through grants or subsidies; other actions emerging more recently (termed *social regulation*) have included regulating conditions under which goods and services are produced and attempting to minimize product hazards and risks to consumers (see p. 461).

grants-in-aid money payments furnished to a lower level of government to be used for specified purposes and subject to conditions spelled out in law or administrative regulation (see p. 112).

GRH Act informal title of the Balanced Budget and Emergency Deficit Control Act of 1985, which mandated steadily decreasing national government annual budget deficits through fiscal year 1991. (see p. 353)

gridlock derived from term referring to traffic that is so congested that cars cannot move; government is so divided that no consistent policy direction can be established (see p. 87).

gross domestic product (GDP) sum of goods and services produced by the economy, including personal consumption, private investments, and government spending (see p. 337).

gross national product (GNP)   the sum of goods and services produced by *all Americans*, wherever they may be located around the world, during a given period of time, typically one year (see p. 341).

groupthink   a mode of thinking that people engage in when they are deeply involved in a cohesive in-group, when members striving for unanimity override their motivation to realistically appraise alternative courses of action; facilitated by insulation of the decision group from others in the organization and by the group's leader promoting one preferred solution or course of action (see p. 207).

gubernatorial   a term that refers to anything concerning the office of a state governor—for example, gubernatorial authority or gubernatorial influence (see p. 118).

H

Hawthorne or "halo" effect   tendency of those being observed to change their behavior to meet the expectations of researchers; named after a factory in Cicero, Illinois, where studies took place in the late 1920s and early 1930s (see p. 153).

Health Care and Education Reconciliation Act   compromise legislation signed into law by President Obama on March 23, 2010, with the **Patient Protection and Affordable Care Act of 2010 (PPACA)** addressing comprehensive healthcare and student loan reform (see p. 74).

hierarchy   a characteristic of formal bureaucratic organizations; a clear vertical chain of command in which each unit is subordinate to the one above it and superior to the one below it; one of the most common features of governmental and other bureaucratic organizations (see p. 146).

hierarchy of needs   psychological concept formulated by Abraham Maslow holding that workers have different kinds of needs that must be satisfied in sequence—basic survival needs, job security, social needs, ego needs, and personal fulfillment in the job (see p. 159).

high-stakes testing   federal requirement that requires states (without compensation) to develop standardized testing in order to rank students and maintain federal funding (see p. 403).

homeostasis   describes organizations in a state of equilibrium, by balancing pressures and responses, demands and resources, and worker incentives and contributions with external environmental factors (see p. 165).

House Ways and Means Committee   primary committee in Congress concerned with taxation and fiscal policy (see p. 342).

human relations   theories of organization that stress workers' noneconomic needs and motivations on the job, seeking to identify these needs and how to satisfy them, and focusing on working conditions and social interactions among workers (see p. 152).

human resources development (HRD)   training and staff development of public employees designed to improve job performance (see p. 279).

I

impasse procedures   in the context of labor–management relations and collective bargaining, procedures that can be called into play when collective negotiations do not lead to agreement at the bargaining table; these include mediation, fact finding, arbitration, and referendum (in some combination, or following one another should one procedure fail to resolve the impasse) (see p. 309).

impoundment   in the context of the budgetary process, the practice by a chief executive of withholding final spending approval of funds appropriated by the legislature, in a bill already signed into law; may take the form of deferrals or rescissions; presidential authority to impound limited by Congress since 1974 (see p. 350).

incrementalism   a model of decision making that stresses making decisions through limited, successive comparisons, in contrast to the rational model; also focuses on simplifying choices rather than aspiring to complete problem analyses, on the status quo rather than abstract goals as a key point of reference, on "satisficing" rather than "maximizing," and on remedying ills rather than seeking positive goals (see p. 199).

independent regulatory boards and commissions (IRCs)   entities which are delegated authority by Congress to enforce both executive and judicial authority in the application of government regulations (see p. 462).

individualism   a philosophical belief in the worth and dignity of the individual, particularly as part of a political order; holds that government and politics should regard the well-being and aspirations of individuals as more important than those of the government (see p. 52).

informal communication all forms of communication, other than official written documentation, among members of an organization; supplements official communications within an organization (see p. 170).

information communication technologies (ICTs) various forms of New Media technology connecting Internet users with service providers and websites. ICT methods include communication protocols, transmission techniques, and communications equipment as well as systems for computer storage and information retrieval (see p. 12)

information theory modern theory of organization that views organizations as requiring constant input of information in order to continue functioning systematically and productively; assumes that a lack of information will lead to chaos or randomness in organizational operations (see p. 165).

innovation the introduction of something new into an organization (see p. 266).

instruments, or tools, of leadership various mechanisms such as legislative support, policy initiatives, and emergency decision-making powers available to chief executives to help direct bureaucratic behavior (see p. 234).

interest groups private organizations representing a portion (usually small) of the general adult population; they exist in order to pursue particular public policy objectives and seek to influence government activity so as to achieve their objectives (see p. 77).

intergovernmental relations (IGR) all the activities and interactions occurring between or among governmental units of all types and levels within the U.S. federal system (see p. 100).

internal (personal) checks personal values of, and actions taken by, individuals who are concerned with behaving in an ethical and moral manner (see p. 217).

Internal Revenue Service (IRS) responsible for administration of federal tax policy, enforcement of tax codes, and collection of tax revenue from individuals and corporations (see p. 388).

interoperability the capacity of governmental organizations to share and integrate information using common standards to use the full power of existing technologies to achieve higher levels of two-way interactions with businesses, citizens, or other governments (see p. 286).

iron triangle see **subsystem** (see p. 86).

issue networks in the context of American politics (especially at the national level), open and fluid groupings of various political actors (in and out of government) attempting to influence policy; "shared knowledge" groups having to do with some aspect or problem of public policy; lacking in the degree of permanence, commonality of interests, and internal cohesion characteristic of subsystems (see p. 87).

item veto (or line-item veto) constitutional power available to more than forty of America's governors, under which they may disapprove some provisions of a bill while approving the others (see p. 240).

J

job action any action taken by employees (usually unionized) as a protest against an aspect of their work or working conditions; includes, but is not limited to, strikes or work slowdowns (see p. 310).

judicial review the constitutional power of the courts to review the actions of executive agencies, legislatures, or decisions of lower courts to determine whether judges, legislators, or administrators acted appropriately (see p. 51).

jurisdiction in bureaucratic politics, the area of programmatic responsibility assigned to an agency by the legislature or chief executive; also a term used to describe the territory within the boundaries of a government entity such as "a local jurisdiction" (see p. 16).

Justice Department cabinet-level executive agency responsible for the enforcement of federal law (see p. 464).

K

knowledge explosion the social phenomenon, creating new Internet-enhanced information communication technologies and vast new areas of research; examples are biogenetic engineering, cloud computing, unmanned space exploration, mass communications, open-sourcing nuclear technology, and energy research (see p. 507).

knowledge revolution a global shift, particularly in Western industrial nations, from post-industrial to information-based economies and societies creating new technological linkages and value-added products and services (p. 34).

L

labor–management relations formal setting in which negotiations over pay, working conditions, and benefits take place (see p. 300).

lateral or cross-functional communication patterns of oral and written communication within organizational networks that are interdisciplinary and typically cut across vertical layers of hierarchy. See also, interoperability (see p. 171).

leader as catalyst (and innovator) formalized conception of the "spark plug" role in a group setting. As part of the catalyst role, a leader is also expected to introduce innovations into an organization (see p. 265).

leader as coordinator (and integrator) involves bringing some order to the multitude of functions within a complex organization (see p. 264).

leader as crisis manager involves coping with both immediate and long-term difficulties, more serious than routine managerial challenges (see p. 267).

leader as director refers to the challenge of bringing some unity of purpose to an organization's members (see p. 264).

leader as gladiator leadership role in which the leader seeks to promote the work of an organization, often in an effort to secure additional resources, as well as defending the organization in the external environment (see p. 266).

leader as motivator key task centering on devices such as tangible benefits, positive social interaction, work interest, encouragement by job supervisors, and leadership that is self-confident, persuasive, fair, and supportive (see p. 264).

learning organizations concept of organizations that emphasizes the importance of encouraging new patterns of thinking and interaction within organizations to foster continuous learning and personal development; see http://www.brint.com, a commercial business technology and knowledge management site for information about knowledge management and learning organizations, and http://www.learningorg.com to find out more about learning organizations (see p. 169).

legislative intent the goals, purposes, and objectives of a legislative body, given concrete form in its enactments (though actual intent may change over time); bureaucracies are assumed to follow legislative intent in implementing laws (see p. 30).

legislative oversight the process by which a legislative body supervises or oversees the work of the bureaucracy in order to ensure its conformity with legislative intent (see p. 30).

legitimacy the acceptance of an institution or individual such as a government, family member, or state governor as having the legal and publicly recognized right to make and enforce binding decisions (see p. 211).

liberal democracy a fundamental form of political arrangement founded on the concepts of popular sovereignty and limited government (see p. 50).

limited government refers to devices built into the Constitution that effectively limit the power of government over individual citizens (see p. 50).

line functions substantive activities of an organization, related to programs or policies for which the organization is formally responsible, and usually having direct impact on outside clienteles; the work of an organization directed toward fulfilling its formal mission(s) (see p. 178).

line-item budgeting earliest approach to modern executive budget making, emphasizing control of expenditures through careful accounting for all money spent in public programs; facilitated central control of purchasing and hiring, along with completeness and honesty in fiscal accounting (see p. 358).

line-item veto a constitutional power available to more than forty of America's governors with which they may disapprove a specific expenditure item within an appropriations bill instead of having to accept or reject the entire bill (see p. 90).

locality pay adjustments to federal pay scales that make allowances for higher- or lower-cost areas where employees live (see p. 299).

M

Malcolm Baldrige National Quality Awards created by Public Law 100–107, and signed into law on August 20, 1987; the award program led to the creation of a new public–private partnership. Principal support for the program comes from the

Foundation for the Malcolm Baldrige National Quality Awards (see p. 429).

management by objectives (MBO) management technique designed to facilitate goal and priority setting, development of plans, resource allocation, monitoring progress toward goals, evaluating results, and generating and implementing improvements in performance (see p. 398).

mandatory or direct spending category of outlays from budget authority provided in laws other than appropriations acts for entitlements and budget authority for food stamps (p. 332).

Medicaid federal health care program operated by the states to assist the poor (see p. 116).

Medicare Prescription Drug Act passed by Congress in December 2005 and provides supplemental (Part D) prescription drug coverage for seniors eligible for Medicare (see p. 130).

merit pay approach to compensation in personnel management founded on the concept of equal pay for equal contribution (rather than for equal activity); related to, and dependent on, properly designed and implemented performance appraisal systems; applied to managers and supervisors in grades GS-13 through GS-15 in the national executive branch, under provisions of the Civil Service Reform Act of 1978 (see p. 291).

merit system a system of selection (and, ideally, evaluation) of administrative officials on the basis of job-related competence, as measured by examinations and professional qualifications (see p. 148).

mixed scanning a model of decision making that combines the rational-comprehensive model's emphasis on fundamental choices and long-term consequences with the incrementalists' emphasis on changing only what needs to be changed in the immediate situation (see p. 200).

modern organization theory body of theory emphasizing empirical examination of organizational behavior, interdisciplinary research employing varied approaches, and attempts to arrive at generalizations applicable to many different kinds of organizations (see p. 162).

money supply amount of money available to individuals and institutions in society (see p. 339).

monopolistic practices situation in which a certain company or group of companies controls the production and distribution system of a market to exclude all other competitors (see p. 461).

multilateral bargaining public-sector collective bargaining negotiations that include the broadest number of affected public-employee and other groups (see p. 301).

multinational corporations (MNCs) large American, European, and Asian corporations that exert significant influence on economic policies of many countries while working outside the legal or regulatory systems of any particular nation (see p. 513).

multiple referral a legislative tactic that has strengthened the power of Congress over policy subsystems (see p. 86).

N

National Commission on Fiscal Responsibility and Reform (known as the Fiscal Responsibility Commission or the Simpson–Bowles Commission after the names of its cochairs) established in 2010 by President Obama to identify areas to improve the U.S. fiscal policies and achieve long-term sustainability. The commission first met on April 27, 2010, and released its final report December 1, 2010. A supermajority of fourteen votes were needed to formally endorse the blueprint, but only eleven members voted to support its recommendations (see p. 339).

national debt the cumulative sum of borrowing necessary over time to pay the difference between the amount raised and spent in the annual federal budget. For current estimate, see the National Debt Clock at: http://www.brillig.com/debt_clock (see p. 338).

National Labor Management Association (NLMA) national membership organization devoted to helping management and labor work together for constructive change (see p. 304).

National Labor Relations Board (NLRB) independent federal agency created in 1935 to enforce the National Labor Relations Act; conducts secret-ballot elections to determine whether employees want union representation, and investigates and remedies unfair labor practices by employers and unions (see p. 303).

National Partnership for Reinventing Government (NPRG) (formerly known as the National

Performance Review). For details, see **reinventing government** (see p. 425).

National Performance Review (NPR) the Clinton–Gore administration's effort (1993–2001) to reform the federal government; the name of this effort was changed in 1997 to the **National Partnership for Reinventing Government** (see p. 424).

nepotism a form of favoritism based on hiring family members or relatives (see p. 287).

Neo-Conservatives those who subscribe to the philosophical-ideological basis for the George W. Bush administration's policy decisions favoring preemptive military action, privatization, lower taxes, and cutbacks in domestic social programs (see p. 72).

New Public Management (NPM) trend that surfaced in Europe, Australia and New Zealand during the 1990s that had significant influence on the Clinton administration's market-based, customer-focused, quality-driven reinvention effort (see p. 425).

New Public Service (NPS) government service based on the view that democratic theory and definitions of the public interest should result from a dialogue and deliberation about shared values. Public servants are motivated by a desire to contribute to society and to respect law, community values, political norms, professional standards, and citizen interests (see p. 426).

no-bid or limited-competition contracts government goods and services contracts awarded to private firms with limited or no competition (see p. 383).

No Child Left Behind Act (NCLB) a controversial statute that reauthorized Elementary and Secondary Education Act in 2002 and established national assessment standards for annual testing of students and yearly accountability reports on progress toward meeting objectives for individual schools (see p. 104).

o

Office of Electronic Government established by the Bush administration in 2002 to administer provisions of the Electronic Government Act (http://www.egov.gov/) (see p. 440).

Office of Financial Research (OFR) an agency established by the Dodd–Frank Act within the Treasury Department to improve the quality of financial data available to policymakers and to facilitate more sophisticated analyses of the financial system (see p. 487).

Office of Management and Budget (OMB) an important entity in the Executive Office of the President that assists the president in assembling executive-branch budget requests, coordinating programs, developing executive talent, and supervising program management processes in national government agencies (see p. 19).

Office of Personnel Management (OPM) key administrative unit in the national government operating under presidential direction; responsible for managing the national government personnel system, consistent with presidential personnel policy (see p. 291).

Office of the Director of National Intelligence (DNI) federal office created in 2005 by restructuring fifteen intelligence agencies to coordinate national intelligence-gathering and analysis efforts (see p. 24).

Omnibus Budget Reconciliation Act (OBRA) of 1993 extended the provisions of earlier legislation through 1998 and established stricter limits on discretionary spending (see p. 355).

open-systems theory a theory that views organizations not as simple, "closed" bureaucratic structures, separate from their surroundings, but as highly complex entities, facing considerable uncertainty in their operations, and constantly interacting with their environment; assumes that organizational components will seek an equilibrium among the forces pressing on them and their own responses to those forces (see p. 164).

operational goal specific and measurable goal for organizational attainment (see p. 390).

operations research (OR) set of specific decision-making and analytical tools used in systems theory, modeling, and quantitative research to determine how best to utilize resources (see p. 395).

organizational humanism a set of organization theories stressing that work holds intrinsic interest for the worker, that workers seek satisfaction in their work, that they want to work rather than avoid it, and that they can be motivated through systems of positive incentives, such as participation in decision making and public recognition for work well done (see p. 157).

organized anarchies organizations in which goals are unclear, technologies are imperfectly understood, histories are difficult to interpret, and participants wander in and out; decision making in such organizations is characterized by pervasive ambiguity, with so much uncertainty in the decision-making process that traditional theories about coping with uncertainty do not apply (see p. 226).

outsourcing reallocation of jobs to more favorable economic environments (that is, lower wages, less taxes, less regulation, and so on), typically seen as movement of jobs from developed countries to less developed ones. See also, **contracting out** and **competitive sourcing** (see p. 341).

"overhead bureaucracy" refers to increased costs of administering government programs imposed by mandates to include those affected by policy-making decisions; program efficiency tends to decrease as participation increases (see p. 521).

"overhead democracy" majority control through political representatives who supervise administrative officers responsible and loyal to their superiors for carrying out the will of elected representatives (see p. 518).

P

parliamentary form of government a form of government practiced in most democratic nations, including France, Germany, the United Kingdom, and Japan, in which the chief executive and top-level ministers are themselves members of the legislature (see p. 28).

participatory democracy a political and philosophical belief in direct involvement by affected citizens in the processes of governmental decision making; believed by some to be essential to the existence of democratic government. Related term: *citizen participation* (see p. 53).

partisanship political-party pressures on elected members of Congress, state legislature, or local boards and commissions (see p. 87).

partnerships government-funded programs involving a wider range of participants, including private and nonprofit organizations, faith-based groups, and corporations (see p. 380).

Patient Protection and Affordable Care Act of 2010 (PPACA) health care reform law signed by President Obama on March 23, 2010, along with the **Health Care and Education Reconciliation Act of 2010** (see p. 74).

patronage selection of public officials on the basis of political loyalty rather than merit, objective examination, or professional competence (see p. 147).

pay-as-you-go (PAYGO) procedure requiring that spending increases be offset by other decreases in annual appropriations so as not to increase the deficit; Congress failed to reauthorize in 2002 (see p. 355).

pay for performance pay system proposed to replace the existing General Schedule, giving managers more power to award merit pay and weakening the power of unions (see p. 305).

pay gap the difference between public and private salaries for comparable positions (see p. 298).

performance appraisal formal process used to document and evaluate an employee's job performance; typically used to reinforce management's assessment of the quality of an individual's work, punish workers who are "below standard," and reward others with bonuses, higher salaries, and promotions (see p. 305).

Performance Assessment Rating Tool (PART) management "scorecard" used to rate the performance of federal executive agencies (see p. 443).

performance budgeting approach to modern executive-budget making that gained currency in the 1930s and then again in the 1950s, emphasizing not only resources acquired by an agency but also what it did with them; geared to promoting effective management of government programs in a time of growing programmatic complexity (see p. 358).

performance management (PM) results-driven decision making that attempts to link goal achievement with budgetary allocations (see p. 422).

pervasive ambiguity a situation of long-term uncertainty that pervades the decision-making environment of an organization (see p. 226).

picket-fence federalism a term describing a key dimension of U.S. federalism—intergovernmental administrative relationships among bureaucratic specialists and their clientele group, in the same substantive areas; suggests that allied bureaucrats at different levels of government exercise considerable power over intergovernmental programs. See also **vertical functional autocracies** (see p. 119).

planning and analysis process of deliberately defining and choosing the operational goals of an organization, analyzing alternative choices for resource distribution, and choosing methods to achieve those goals over a specified time period;

increasingly important tools for public management (see p. 390).

pluralism   a social and political concept stressing the appropriateness of group organization, and diversity of groups and their activities, as a means of protecting broad group interests in society; assumes that groups are good and that bargaining and competition among them will benefit the public interest (see p. 52).

pluralist democracy   a normative model of administrative activity characterized by dispersion of power and suspicion of any concentration of power, by exercise of power on the part of politicians, interest groups, and citizens, by political bargaining and accommodation, and by an emphasis on individuals' and political actors' own determination of interests as the basis for policy making; the principal alternative to the **administrative efficiency** model (see p. 57).

policy analysis   systematic investigation of alternative policy options and the assembly and integration of evidence for and against each; emphasizes explaining the nature of policy problems and how public policies are put into effect (see p. 392).

policy development   general political and governmental process of formulating relatively concrete goals and directions for government activity and proposing an overall framework of programs related to them; usually but not always regarded as a chief executive's task (see p. 233).

policy implementation   general political and governmental process of carrying out programs to fulfill specified policy objectives; a responsibility chiefly of administrative agencies, under chief-executive and/or legislative guidance; also, the activities directed toward putting a policy into effect (see p. 233).

political corruption   all forms of bribery, favoritism, kickbacks, and legal as well as illegal rewards; commonly associated with reward systems in which partisan patronage is in use; more generally, patterns of behavior in government associated with providing access, tangible benefits, and so on, to some more than others, on an "insider" basis (see p. 219).

political persuasion or "jawboning"   power of chief executives to convince legislators, administrators, and the general public that their policies should be adopted; jawboning is quite literally the primary tactic, that is, talking, used by presidents, governors, or mayors to achieve this goal (see p. 232).

political rationality   a concept advanced by Aaron Wildavsky suggesting that behavior of decision makers may be entirely rational when judged by criteria of political costs, benefits, and consequences, even if irrational according to economic criteria; emphasizes that political criteria for "rationality" have validity (see p. 223).

politically neutral competence   idea that appointments to civil service positions should be made on the basis of demonstrated job competence, and not based on age, ethnicity, gender, politics, or race (see p. 279).

politics–administration dichotomy   originally proposed by Woodrow Wilson in the 1880s, divides politics and policy making from policy implementation and public administration (see p. 39).

popular sovereignty   government by the ultimate consent of the governed, which implies some degree of popular participation in voting and other political actions; does not necessarily mean mass or universal political involvement (see p. 50).

portal   single entry site for access to, and information about a specific topics containing numerous links to other related websites (see p. 450).

POSDCORB   acronym standing for the professional watchwords of administration: **P**lanning, **O**rganizing, **S**taffing, **D**irecting, **CO**ordinating, **R**eporting, **B**udgeting (see p. 40).

position classification   formal task of American public personnel administration intended to classify together jobs in different agencies that have essentially the same types of functions and responsibilities, based on written descriptions of duties and responsibilities (see p. 292).

Posse Comitatus Act of 1878   common law term (Latin for "the power of the county") referring to the authority of the sheriff to conscript able-bodied males over age fifteen to assist him or her in keeping the peace; also the name of federal statute forbidding the use of U.S. military personnel for domestic law enforcement purposes (see p. 248).

postindustrialism   social and economic phenomenon emerging in many previously industrialized nations; characterized by a relative decline in the importance of production, labor, and durable goods, and an increase in the importance of knowledge, new technologies, the provision of services, and leisure time (see p. 512).

power vacuum   where power to govern is splintered, there will inevitably be attempts by some to exercise that power that is not clearly defined and is, therefore, "up for grabs" (see p. 29).

preemptions   the assumption of state or local program authority by the federal government (see p. 108).

President's Management Agenda (PMA)   the Bush administration's effort to better manage federal agencies (see p. 434).

privatization   a practice in which governments either join with or yield responsibility outright to private-sector enterprises to provide services previously managed and financed by public entities; a pattern especially evident in local government service provision, though with growing appeal at other levels of government. See also **contracting out** (see p. 39).

procedural due process   legal term that refers to the legal rules governing a specific case (see p. 493).

procedural fairness   ensures fairness in the adjudication process (see p. 493).

productivity   measurable relationship between the results produced and the resources required for production; quantitative measure of the efficiency of the organization (see p. 419).

productivity bargaining   labor–management negotiations that link productivity improvements to employee wage increases as an alternative to reductions-in-force (see p. 310).

program evaluation   systematic examination of government actions, policies, or programs to determine their success or failure; used to gain knowledge of program impacts, establish accountability, and influence continuation or termination of government activities (see p. 406).

program evaluation and review technique (PERT)   management technique of program implementation in which the sequence of steps for carrying out a project or program is mapped out in advance; involves choosing necessary activities and estimating time and other resources required (see p. 398).

program implementation   general political and governmental process of carrying out programs in order to fulfill specified policy objectives; a responsibility chiefly of administrative agencies, under chief executive and/or legislative guidance; also, the activities directed toward putting a policy into effect (see p. 396).

project grants   form of grant-in-aid, available by application, to states and localities for an individual project; more numerous than formula grants but with less overall funding by the federal government (see p. 115).

protective regulation   advantages certain groups or individuals by granting special access or licenses; used with professionals (see p. 471).

public administration   (1) all processes, organizations, and individuals acting in official positions associated with carrying out laws and other rules adopted or issued by legislatures, executives, and courts (many activities are also concerned with formulation of these rules); (2) a field of academic study and professional training leading to public-service careers at all levels of government (see p. 11).

public cynicism and distrust   negative public opinion about politics and government reflected in opinion polls and low voter turnouts (see p. 539).

public interest groups (PIGs)   organized lobbying groups that represent primarily noneconomic interests in influencing public policy. Examples are Common Cause and Greenpeace (see p. 67).

public management   a field of practice and study central to public administration that emphasizes internal operations of public agencies and focuses on managerial concerns related to control and direction, such as planning, organizational maintenance, information systems, budgeting, personnel management, performance evaluation, and productivity improvement (see p. 12).

public personnel administration (PPA)   policies, processes, and procedures designed to recruit, train, and promote people who manage government agencies (see p. 279).

public policy   (1) organizing framework of purposes and rationales for government programs that deal with specified societal problems; (2) complex of programs enacted and implemented by government (see p. 375).

R

Race to the Top   the Obama administration's $4.35 billion U.S. Department of Education program designed to encourage reforms in state and local district K–12 education. Funded as part of the American Recovery and Reinvestment Act of 2009 (see p. 131).

rational approach   an approach to decision making that is derived from economic theories of how to make the "best" decisions; involves efforts to move toward consciously held goals in a way that requires the smallest input of scarce resources; assumes the ability to separate ends from means, rank all alternatives, gather all possible data, and objectively weigh alternatives; stresses rationality in the process of reaching decisions (see p. 196).

reconciliation process   important step in congressional budgeting, when Congress makes adjustments in existing laws to achieve conformity with annual spending targets adopted in each year's concurrent resolution; these adjustments can take the form of spending reductions, revenue increases, or both (see p. 354).

redistributive policies   deliberate efforts by governments to shift the allocation of valued goods in society from one group to another; highly controversial and often accompanied by bitter political conflicts (see p. 379).

reductions-in-force (RIFs)   systematic reductions or downsizing in the number of personnel positions allocated to a government agency or agencies; usually the result of higher-level personnel management policy decisions related to other policy objectives, including budget cuts and executive reorganizations (see p. 245).

regulatory body   refers to all types of dependent and independent regulatory boards, commissions, and executive entities with regulatory authority (see p. 462).

regulatory federalism   an approach to intergovernmental relations under which federal agencies use regulations as opposed to grants to influence state and local governments (see p. 135).

regulatory policies   establish restrictions on the behavior of those subject to the regulations, aim to protect certain groups, range broadly in scope, and are often enforced against businesses (see p. 379).

Regulatory Policy Office (RPO)   established in each executive agency under OMB direction as a result of Bush Executive Order 13422 (amending EO 12866), issued on January 18, 2007 (see p. 501).

reinventing government   the Clinton–Gore administration initiative based on the best-selling 1992 book *Reinventing Government: How the Entrepreneurial Spirit Is Transforming the Public Sector*, by David Osborne and Ted Gaebler. The book documents successful public-sector efforts to apply market-based, quality, and customer-service principles to government. See also **National Partnership for Reinventing Government (NPRG)**, formerly National Performance Review (see p. 424).

relational leadership   leaders must not only be competent at traditional skills such as goal setting, conflict management, and motivation, but also be able to acquire information from group members and adapt their leadership styles to fit the needs of followers (see p. 262).

reorganization   authority delegated by the legislature to the chief executive to add or reduce staff positions, or to restructure organizational arrangements, to achieve policy goals as well as increased economy, efficiency, and effectiveness of bureaucratic agencies (see p. 247).

representation   a principle of legislative selection based on the number of inhabitants or amount of territory in a legislative district; adequate, fair, and equal representation has become a major objective of many who feel they were denied it in the past and now seek greater influence, particularly in administrative decision making (see p. 51).

representative democracy   representatives are nominated and elected from individual districts. They comprise a legislature that makes binding decisions for its society (see p. 53).

representativeness   groups that have been relatively powerless should be represented in government positions in proportion to their numbers in the population (see p. 51).

reregulation   decision by Congress or an administrative agency to strengthen or reestablish government regulatory requirements (see p. 500).

results-oriented   government programs that focus on performance in exchange for granting greater discretionary decision-making power to managers; see also **performance management** (see p. 418).

reverse discrimination   unfavorable actions against white males to achieve affirmative action goals to hire and promote more women and minorities (see p. 315).

reverse pyramid   a conception of organizational structure, especially in service organizations, whereby managerial duties focus on providing necessary support to frontline employees (particularly those whose work centers around information and information technology) who deal directly with individuals seeking the organization's services (see p. 12).

revolution of rising expectations   social phenomenon of the period since World War II, affecting many nations, in which people who have been relatively poor have sought to increase their level of prosperity both as individuals and as groups; related in part to faith in technological and social advances (see p. 512).

rule making   quasi-legislative power delegated to agencies by Congress; a rule issued under this authority represents an agency statement of general applicability and future effect that concerns the rights of private parties, and has the force and effect of law (see p. 474).

S

Sarbanes–Oxley Act of 2002   created to protect investors by improving the accuracy and reliability of corporate disclosures. The act establishes a corporate accounting oversight board, and requires auditor independence, corporate responsibility, and enhanced financial disclosure (see p. 467).

scientific management   formal theory of organization developed by Frederick Winslow Taylor in the early 1900s; concerned with achieving efficiency in production, rational work procedures, maximum productivity, and profit; focused on management's responsibilities and on "scientifically" developed work procedures, based on time-and-motion studies (see p. 149).

Second Hoover Commission   1955 blue-ribbon commission appointed by President Eisenhower and chaired by former President Hoover to study higher-level positions in the civil service (see p. 287).

Securities and Exchange Commission (SEC)   federal regulatory agency responsible for regulation of stocks, securities, and investments (see p. 387).

self-regulatory policies   protective regulations that either advantage certain professions or classes or remove from the government the power to regulate (see p. 380).

Senate Finance Committee   principal Senate committee concerned with revenue generation, taxation, and the operations of the Internal Revenue Service (IRS) (see p. 342).

Senior Executive Service (SES)   established in the national Civil Service Reform Act of 1978; designed to foster professional growth, mobility, and versatility among career officials (and some "political" appointees); incorporated into national government personnel management an emphasis on performance appraisal and merit pay concepts as part of both the SES and the broader merit system reform; see **Civil Service Reform Act of 1978** (see p. 288).

sequestration   withholding of budgetary resources provided by discretionary or direct spending legislation, following various procedures under the Gramm–Rudman–Hollings Act of 1985 and the Budget Enforcement Acts of 1990 and 1997; the withholding of budget authority, according to an established formula, up to the dollar amount that must be cut in order to meet the deficit-reduction target (see p. 354).

shared vision   foundation of core values within which leaders, managers, and employees interact and on which everything else in the organization is based (see p. 268).

Sherman Antitrust Act   first major antitrust legislation, passed in 1890, which made it illegal to fix prices or to monopolize an industry (see p. 464).

single-issue groups   ideologically oriented groups that focus on a single issue, such as a woman's right to terminate a pregnancy or abortion rights, to the exclusion of all others. Elected officials who do not support groups on the issue are targeted for defeat (see p. 375).

single state agency requirement   a requirement contained in federal grants designating only one state agency to administer national grants, and to establish direct relationships with its counterpart in the national government bureaucracy (see p. 118).

situational approach   method of analyzing leadership in a group or an organization that emphasizes factors in the particular leadership situation, such as leader–follower interactions, group values, and the work being done (see p. 260).

social media   tools and technologies that connect individuals by one or more specific types of interdependencies, relationships, or beliefs. *Facebook*, *MySpace*, *Twitter*, and *YouTube* are among the leading examples (p. 421).

social networking   Internet linkages between individuals (or organizations) connected by one or more specific types of interdependency, such as common interest, friendship, kinship, financial exchange, likes and dislikes, sexual relationships, or relationships of beliefs, knowledge, or prestige.

Facebook, MySpace, twitter, and *YouTube* are among the leading examples (see. p. 507).

social regulatory initiatives   government actions in the late 1960s and early 1970s to regulate new social areas involving individual health, environmental protection, and public safety; resulted in the creation of several regulatory bodies (see p. 469).

social-demographic changes   shifts in the population and economies of various regions that impact the delivery of public services (see p. 33).

span of control   the number of people an individual supervises within a subunit of the organization. Each supervisor should have only a limited number of subordinates to oversee; this expands the chain of command to produce the needed ratio of supervisors to subordinates at each level, in the interest of overall coordination (see p. 183).

specialized language   technical vocabulary used by bureaucratic agencies, one effect of which is to restrict access and outside influence (see p. 79).

staff functions   originally defined to include all of an organization's support and advisory activities that facilitated the carrying out of "line" responsibilities and functions; more recently, redefined by some to focus on planning, research, and advisory activities, thus excluding budgeting, personnel, purchasing, and other functions once grouped under the "staff" heading (see p. 178).

stakeholders   bureaucrats, elected officials, groups of citizens, and organized and unorganized interests affected by the decisions of federal, state, and local governments; those having a stake in the outcome of public policies; see also **interest groups, issue networks, subsystem** (see p. 11).

statistical process control (SPC)   the use of statistics to control critical processes within organizations; frequently used with **TQM** and **Theory Z** Japanese management techniques (see p. 167).

Strategy for American Innovation   Obama administration's initiative for sustainable growth and job creation. For details, see http://www.whitehouse.gov/administration/eop/nec/StrategyforAmerican-Innovation/ (see p. 429).

strategic planning   process used by organizations to formulate a mission statement; consider environmental opportunities, threats, strengths, and weaknesses; identify areas for strategic action; conduct cost–benefit analysis to evaluate and select actions; draw up implementation plans; and incorporate operational goals into annual budgets (see p. 390).

substantive goals   an organizational goal focusing on the accomplishment of tangible programmatic objectives (see p. 211).

subsystem   in the context of American politics (especially at the national level), any political alliance uniting some members of an administrative agency, a legislative committee or subcommittee, and an interest group according to shared values and preferences in the same substantive area of policy making; sometimes called an **iron triangle** (see p. 84).

summitry   in national government budget making, the practice of initiating negotiations among leaders of Congress and the White House, involving top Democrats meeting with top Republicans (usually away from public view), in efforts to confront more effectively the seemingly intractable budget (and budget deficit) challenges (see p. 369).

sunk costs   in the context of organizational resources committed to a given decision, any cost involved in the decision that is irrecoverable; resources of the organization are lessened by that amount if it later reverses its decision (see p. 208).

sunset laws   provisions in laws that government agencies and programs have a specific termination date (see p. 61).

sunshine laws   acts passed by Congress and by some states and localities requiring that various legislative proceedings (especially those of committees and subcommittees) and various administrative proceedings be held in public rather than behind closed doors; one device for increasing openness and accountability (see p. 61).

symbolic actions   proposals for policy changes that serve some limited political purpose, but do not threaten the current situation (see p. 378).

symbolic goals   organizational objectives reflecting broad, popular political purposes, frequently unattainable (see p. 212).

systems analysis   analytical technique designed to permit comprehensive investigation of the impacts within a given system of changing one or more elements of that system; in the context of analyzing policies, emphasizes overall objectives, surrounding environments, available resources, and system components (see p. 167).

systems theory a theory of social organizations holding that organizations—like biological organisms—may behave according to inputs from their environment, outputs resulting from organizational activity, and feedback leading to further inputs; also, that change in any one part of a group or organizational system affects all other parts (see p. 162).

T

task forces temporary cross-functional teams responsible for achieving a particular goal, often drawn from several departments within a larger agency; typically disbanded after the goal is accomplished (see p. 250).

tax expenditure financing revenue losses from provisions in the federal, state, or local tax codes that allow a special exclusion, exemption, or deduction from gross income or that provide a special tax credit, a preferential rate of tax, or a deferral of tax liability (see p. 339).

taxation primary means by which governments raise revenues for public services; taxes can be collected from individuals and corporations on income (earned and unearned), profits, property value, sales, and services (see p. 335).

technological change rapidly emerging patterns of change (related in part to the knowledge explosion) in communication, medical, and transportation technologies, among others, with significant implications both for the societal challenges confronting government and for the means and resources increasingly available to government for conducting public affairs (see p. 34).

Theory X model of behavior within organizations that assumes that workers need to be motivated by extrinsic (external) rewards or sanctions (punishments) (see p. 158).

Theory Y model of organizational behavior that stresses self-motivation, participation, and intrinsic (internal) job rewards (see p. 158).

Theory Z Japanese management system that stresses deliberative, "bottom-up" collective accountability and decision making, long-term planning, and closer relationships among managers and workers (see p. 165).

time-trend projection comparison of preprogram data with actual postprogram data (see p. 408).

total quality management (TQM) management approach that encourages organization-wide commitment, teamwork, and better quality of results by providing incentives to increase the success of the whole enterprise. Elements of TQM include commitment to meeting customer-driven quality standards; employee participation or empowerment to make decisions at the point closest to the customer; actions based on data, facts, outcome measures, results, and statistical analysis; commitment to process and continuous quality improvements; and organizational changes and teamwork to encourage implementation of the above elements (see p. 167).

traits approach traditional method (now used less widely by scholars) of analyzing leadership in a group or an organization; assumes that certain personality characteristics such as intelligence, ambition, tact, and diplomacy distinguish leaders from others in the group (see p. 259).

tunnel vision results from a fear of mistakes, missed deadlines, and focus on a narrow work environment, which limits the ability to see an organization's activities as a whole (see p. 265).

U

unfunded mandates federal (or state) laws or regulations that impose requirements on other governments, often involving expenditures by affected governments, without providing funds for implementation (see p. 101).

USA PATRIOT Act short title of the controversial post–9/11 antiterrorist legislation (P.L. 107–56) "**U**niting and **S**trengthening **A**merica by **P**roviding **A**ppropriate **T**ools **R**equired to **I**ntercept and **O**bstruct **T**errorism" that increased central government powers to investigate, detain, and wiretap persons suspected of engaging in terrorist activity (see p. 73).

V

veterans' preference special consideration given to whose who served on active duty in the U.S. Armed Forces and were separated under honorable conditions may be eligible; does not apply to positions in the Senior Executive Service or to internal agency actions such as a reassignment or promotion (see p. 297).

vertical functional autocracies   informal associations of federal, state, and local professional administrators who manage intergovernmental programs also referred to as **picket-fence federalism** (see p. 119).

veto power   constitutional power of an elected chief executive to overrule an appropriation, a bill, or a decision by the legislature. At the national government level, requires a two-thirds majority of both houses of Congress to override (see p. 240).

virtual campaign   deliberate use of Internet communication technology to communicate with potential voters and manage political campaigns (see p. 522).

W

war on terror   the U.S. government's response to political violence directed at U.S. citizens and institutions here and abroad (see p. 508).

whistle-blowers   those who make any disclosure of legal violations, mismanagement, gross waste of funds, abuse of authority, or dangers to public health or safety, whether the disclosure is made within or outside the formal chain of command (see p. 221).

WikiLeaks   website founded in 2006 with access to several million leaked diplomatic and military documents. WikiLeaks has released thousands of leaked documents about the war in Afghanistan not previously available for public review. In 2010, this set off a firestorm of protests from the Obama administration that such sensitive records may jeopardize the lives of U.S. and coalition soldiers serving in the region (see p. 64).

Z

zone of acceptance   the extent to which a follower is willing to be led and to obey the leader's commands or directives; concept originally proposed by Chester Barnard, who wrote about leadership in 1930s (see p. 154).

NOTES

Chapter 1: Approaching the Study of Public Administration

1. An NBC News/*Wall Street Journal* poll conducted by Peter Hart (D) and Bill McInturff (R) in January 2008 found that 67 percent of Americans disapproved of George W. Bush's handling of the war in Iraq (N=1,008 adults nationwide). Accessed Feb. 28, 2008, at http://www.pollingreport.com/iraq.htm.

2. For a review of the accomplishments and biographies of several representatives of this age group, see Tom Brokaw, *The Greatest Generation* (New York: Random House, 1998).

3. Remarks of President Bill Clinton, February 17, 1993 (emphasis added).

4. Charles T. Goodsell, *The Case for Bureaucracy: A Public Administration Polemic*, 4th ed. (Washington, D.C.: CQ Press, 2004), especially chap. 2. See also, H. George Frederickson, *The Spirit of Public Administration* (San Francisco: Jossey-Bass, 1997); Max Neiman, *Defending Government: Why Big Government Works* (Upper Saddle River, N.J.: Prentice Hall, 2000); and Paul Light, *Government's Greatest Achievements: From Civil Rights to Homeland Security* (Washington, D.C.: Brookings Institution Press, 2002).

5. Goodsell, p. xi (emphasis added). Possible consequences of this intense criticism of bureaucracy and bureaucrats are discussed in Bernard Rosen, "Effective Continuity of U.S. Government Operations in Jeopardy," *Public Administration Review*, 43 (September/October 1983): 383–92, especially 383–86; H. Brinton Milward and Hal G. Rainey, "Don't Blame the Bureaucracy!" *Journal of Public Policy*, 3 (May 1983): 149–68; and Bruce Adams, "The Frustrations of Government Service," *Public Administration Review*, 44 (January/February 1984): 5–13.

6. The University of Michigan Business School conducts customer satisfaction surveys, and federal agencies are included in the comparative rankings. For full results, see website at http://www.bus.umich.edu/research/nqrc/government.html. For an expansion of this theme, see Goodsell, *The Case for Bureaucracy*; Kenneth Cooper, "Customer Ratings Up for Federal Agencies," *Washington Post*, December 22, 2000, p. A31, retrieved at: http://www.washingtonpost.com/ac2/wp-dyn/A39386-2000Dec21; Richard J. Stillman II, *The American Bureaucracy: The Core of Modern Government*, 3rd ed. (Belmont, Calif.: Thomson/Wadsworth, 2004); and "Americans Happier with Federal Government than with Private Sector," *PA Times*, 29(1) (January 2006): 1–2.

7. Dwight Waldo, "Introduction: Trends and Issues in Education for Public Administration," in Guthrie S. Birkhead and James D. Carroll, eds., *Education for Public Service 1979* (Syracuse: Maxwell School of Citizenship and Public Affairs, Syracuse University, 1979), pp. 13–26, at pp. 25–26.

8. See, for example, Kenneth J. Meier, *Politics and the Bureaucracy: Policy Making in the Fourth Branch of Government*, 5th ed. (Belmont, Calif.: 2006); B. Guy Peters, *The Politics of Bureaucracy: A Comparative Perspective*, 6th ed. (London: Routledge, 2009); Carl E. Van Horn, Donald Baumer, and William T. Gormley, Jr., *Politics and Public Policy*, 3rd ed. (Washington, D.C.: CQ Press, 2001); and B. Guy Peters, *American Public Policy: Promise and Performance*, 8th ed. (Washington, D.C.: CQ Press, 2009).

9. For a full discussion of administrative failures in the aftermath of Hurricane Katrina, see special supplementary issue of *Public Administration* Review, 67 (November/December, 2007).

10. Richard Heeks, *Reinventing Government in the Information Age* (London: Routledge, 1999); C. Richard Neu, Robert Anderson, and Tora K. Bikson, *Sending Your Government a Message: E-mail Communication between Citizens and Government* (Santa Monica, Calif.: Rand Corporation, 1999); Jane Fountain, *Building the Virtual State* (Washington, D.C.: Brookings Institution Press, 2001); Ake Gronland, *Electronic Government: Design, Applications, and Management* (Hershey, Pa.: Idea Group Publishing, 2002); David Garson, *Public Information Technology and E-Governance: Managing the Virtual State* (Sudbury, Mass.: Jones and Bartlett, 2006); and Jay D. White, *Managing Information in the Public Sector* (New York: M. E. Sharpe, 2008). For discussion of the changing expectations of managers and leaders, see Warren H. Schmidt and Jerome P. Finnigan, *The Race without a Finish Line* (San Francisco: Jossey-Bass, 1992),

chaps. 5–11. For details on managerial leadership in the new global economy, see Michael E. Milakovich, *Improving Service Quality in the Global Economy* (Boca Raton, Fla.: Auerbach Publications, 2006).

11. Perhaps the best sources detailing the nature of the Iran–Contra scandal are *President's Special Review Board: The Tower Commission Report* (New York: Bantam Books and Times Books, 1987); and Lawrence Walsh, *Final Report of the Independent Counsel for Iran/Contra Matters* (Washington, D.C.: U.S. Court of Appeals for the D.C. Circuit, 1993). See also P. A. Kowert, "Leadership and Learning in Political Groups: The Management and Advice in the Iran–Contra Affair," *Governance: An International Journal of Policy and Administration*, 14(2) (2001): 201–33.

12. President's Commission to Strengthen Social Security, *Final Report* (Washington, D.C., 2005).

13. There are 9 committees and 26 subcommittees in the House of Representatives that claim some jurisdiction over various aspects of homeland security, and this list does not include the oversight responsibilities of the House Armed Services Committee, the International Relations Committee, or the House Appropriations Committee. In the Senate, there are at least 10 committees and 22 subcommittees that have some role in homeland security, without including the Senate Foreign Relations Committee and the Senate Appropriations Committee. This increases congressional involvement to at least 19 committees and 48 subcommittees. Cited by Michael L. Koempel, CRS Report for Congress, *Homeland Security: Compendium of Recommendations Relevant to House Committee Organization and Analysis of Considerations for the House, and the 109th and 110th Congress Epilogue*, Congressional Research Service, March 2, 2007.

14. National Commission on Terrorist Attacks upon the United States (also known as the 9/11 Commission), July 22, 2004, retrieved at: http://www.9-11commission.gov/commission.gov/; and the Commission on the Intelligence Capabilities of the United States Regarding Weapons of Mass Destruction (also known as Silverman–Robb Commission) issued its final report on May 27, 2005, at: http://www.wmd.gov/report/index.html.

15. Richard A. Best, Jr., "The Director of National Intelligence and Intelligence Analysis," *Congressional Research Service, Library of Congress*, February 11, 2005.

16. James Q. Wilson, "The Rise of the Bureaucratic State," *The Public Interest*, 41 (Fall 1975): 77–103, at 88. See also Stephen Skowronek, *Building a New American State: The Expansion of National Administrative Capacities, 1877–1920* (New York: Cambridge University Press, 1982); and Louis Galambos, ed., *The New American State: Bureaucracies and Policies since World War II* (Baltimore: Johns Hopkins University Press, 1987).

17. After each decennial (ten-year) census, the U.S. Bureau of the Census makes available many volumes of data that illuminate the changes in American society. This section relies on summary treatments of census data found in Theodore H. White's *The Making of the President 1960* (New York: Atheneum, 1961), chap. 8, and *The Making of the President 1972* (New York: Atheneum, 1973), chap. 6; President's Commission for a National Agenda for the Eighties, *A National Agenda for the Eighties* (New York: New American Library, 1981), chap. 2; and various reports published by the U.S. Bureau of the Census, Department of Commerce.

18. The 2010 census revealed the internal migration within the United States was the least in 60 years, since end of Great Depression in 1940. For an analysis of these trends, see: Raven Molloy, Christopher L. Smith, and Abigail Wozniak, "Internal Migration in the United States," *Journal of Economic Perspectives*, 25 (2) Spring, 2011: 1–42.

19. Statistics retrieved at: http://www.census.gov/prod/cen2010/briefs/c2010br-02.pdf.

20. For examples, see Barry Bozeman and Dianne Rahm, "The Explosion of Technology," in James L. Perry, ed., *Handbook of Public Administration* (San Francisco: Jossey-Bass, 1989), pp. 54–67; Richard R. Davis, *The Web of Politics: The Internet's Impact on the American Political System* (New York: Oxford University Press, 1999); Kevin A. Hill and John E. Hughes, *Cyberpolitics: Citizen Activism in the Age of the Internet* (Lanham, Md.: Rowman & Littlefield, 1998); Wayne Rash, Jr., *Politics on the Net: Wiring the Political Process* (New York: Freeman, 1997); and David E. McNabb, *Knowledge Management in the Public Sector: A Blueprint for Innovation in Government* (New York: M. E. Sharpe, 2006).

21. See Alvin Toffler, *Power Shift: Knowledge, Wealth, and Violence at the Edge of the Twenty-First Century* (New York: Bantam, 1991); Phillip J. Cooper, Linda P. Brady, Olivia Hidalgo-Hardeman, et. al., *Public Administration for the Twenty-First Century*

(Fort Worth, Tex.: Harcourt Brace Publishers, 1998); and Donald F. Kettl, *The Transformation of Governance: Public Administration in the Twenty-First Century* (Baltimore, Md.: Johns Hopkins University Press, 2002).

22. See, for elaboration, Albert S. Gore, *Earth in the Balance: Ecology and the Human Spirit* (New York: Rodale, 2006); and Gore, *The Assault on Reason* (New York: The Penguin Group, 2007).

23. Barry Bozeman, "Dimensions of 'Publicness': An Approach to Public Organization Theory," in Barry Bozeman and Jeffrey Straussman, eds., *New Directions in Public Administration* (Pacific Grove, Calif.: Brooks/Cole, 1984), pp. 46–62; Michael Lipsky and Steven Rathgeb Smith, "Nonprofit Organizations, Government, and the Welfare State," in Frederick S. Lane, ed., *Current Issues in Public Administration*, 5th ed. (New York: St. Martin's Press, 1994), pp. 414–36; Hal G. Rainey, *Understanding and Managing Public Organizations* (San Francisco: Jossey-Bass, 1996); Jeffrey Brudney, ed., *Advancing Public Management, New Developments in Theory, Methods, and Practice* (Washington, D.C.: Georgetown University Press, 2000); Ali Farazmand, ed., *Privatization or Public Enterprise Reform? International Case Studies with Implications for Public Management* (Westport, Conn.: Greenwood Press, 2000); Bernard Ross and Clare Segal, *Breakthrough Thinking for Nonprofit Organizations* (Hoboken, N.J.: Wiley, 2003); Patricia Ingraham, *Government Performance: Why Management Matters* (Baltimore: Johns Hopkins University Press, 2003); and James L. Perry and Kenneth L. Kraemer, eds., *Public Management: Public and Private Perspectives* (San Francisco: Jossey-Bass, 2003).

24. This discussion draws especially on Joseph L. Bower, "Effective Public Management: It Isn't the Same as Effective Business Management," *Harvard Business Review* 55(2) (1977): 131–40. See also Gordon Chase and Betsy Reveal, *How to Manage in the Public Sector* (Reading, Mass.: Addison-Wesley, 1983); and Steven S. Goldsmith, "Can Business Really Do Business with Government?" *Harvard Business Review*, 75(3) (1997): 110–21.

25. Richard C. Box, "Running Government Like a Business: Implications for Public Administration Theory and Practice," *American Review of Public Administration*, 29(1) (1999): 19–43. For a useful discussion of distinctly *public* management, see Barry Bozeman and Jeffrey D. Straussman, *Public Management Strategies: Guidelines for Managerial Effectiveness* (San Francisco: Jossey-Bass, 1990). Another perspective on public versus private management can be found in Barry Bozeman, *All Organizations Are Public* (San Francisco: Jossey-Bass, 1987). See also Lloyd A. Blanchard, Charles Hinnant, and Wilson Wong, "Market-Based Reforms in Government," *Administration and Society*, 30(5) (1998): 483–513; Julia Beckett, "The 'Government Should Be Run Like a Business' Mantra," *American Review of Public Administration*, 30(2) (2000): 185–204; Rebecca Blank, "When Can Public Policy Makers Rely on Private Markets? The Effective Provision of Social Services," *Economic Journal*, 110(462) (March 2000): C34–C49; Bozeman, "Public-Value Failure: When Efficient Markets May Not Do," *Public Administration Review*, 62(2) (2001): 137–45; John Forrer, "Private Finance Initiative: A Better Public-Private Partnership," *Public Manager*, 31(2) (2002): 36–43; and A. Hefetz and M. Warner, "The Uneven Distribution of Market Solutions for Public Goods," *Journal of Urban Affairs*, 24(4) (2002): 445–59.

26. This section relies especially on Alan A. Altshuler, "The Study of American Public Administration," in Alan A. Altshuler and Norman C. Thomas, eds., *The Politics of the Federal Bureaucracy*, 2nd ed. (New York: Harper & Row, 1977). See also, among others, Frederick C. Mosher, ed., *American Public Administration: Past, Present, Future* (Tuscaloosa: University of Alabama Press, 1975); Dwight Waldo, *The Study of Public Administration* (New York: Random House, 1955); Dwight Waldo, *The Enterprise of Public Administration* (Novato, Calif.: Chandler & Sharp, 1980); and Nicholas Henry, *Public Administration and Public Affairs*, 11th ed. (Englewood Cliffs, N.J.: Prentice Hall, 2010).

27. Quoted by Altshuler, "The Study of American Public Administration," p. 2.

28. See Jameson Doig, "'If I See a Murderous Fellow Sharpening a Knife Cleverly': The Wilsonian Dichotomy and the Public Authority Tradition," *Public Administration Review*, 43 (July/August 1983): 292–304, especially pp. 292–94; and James H. Svara, "Complementarity of Politics and Administration as a Legitimate Alternative to the Dichotomy Model," *Administration and Society*, 30(6) (1999): 676–705.

29. Altshuler, "The Study of American Public Administration," p. 3; Henry, *Public Administration and Public Affairs*, pp. 24–25. See also Luther Gulick and Lyndall Urwick, eds., *Papers on the Science of Administration* (New York: Institute of Public Administration, 1937).

30. Rowland Egger, "The Period of Crisis: 1933 to 1945," in Frederick C. Mosher, ed., *American*

Public Administration: Past, Present, Future (Tuscaloosa: University of Alabama Press, 1975), pp. 49–96, at p. 55.

31. Ibid., pp. 91–92.
32. Altshuler, "The Study of American Public Administration," p. 3.
33. See James W. Fesler, "Public Administration and the Social Sciences: 1946 to 1960," in Mosher, ed., *American Public Administration*, pp. 97–141.
34. Altshuler, "The Study of American Public Administration," p. 5.
35. Herbert A. Simon, "The Proverbs of Administration," *Public Administration Review*, 6 (1946): 53–67.
36. Altshuler, "The Study of American Public Administration," pp. 10–11.
37. Ibid., p. 13.
38. See, among others, Jerald Hage and Michael Aiken, *Social Change in Complex Organizations* (New York: Random House, 1970).
39. See Larry Kirkhart and Neely Gardner, eds., "Symposium on Organization Development," *Public Administration Review*, 34 (March/April 1974): 97–140; Paul R. Lawrence and Jay W. Lorsch, *Developing Organizations: Diagnosis and Action* (Reading, Mass.: Addison-Wesley, 1969); and Gerald Zaltman, Robert Duncan, and Jonny Holbeck, *Innovations and Organizations* (New York: Wiley, 1973).
40. The academic field of public administration is treated also by Brack Brown and Richard J. Stillman II, *A Search for Public Administration* (College Station: Texas A&M University Press, 1986); Naomi Lynn and Aaron Wildavsky, eds., *Public Administration: The State of the Discipline* (New York: McGraw-Hill, 1990); Kenneth Meier and Laurence O'Toole, Jr., *Bureaucracy in a Democratic State: A Governance Perspective* (Baltimore: Johns Hopkins Press, 2006); Jay M. Shafritz, E. W. Russell, and Christopher Borick, *Introducing Public Administration*, 6th ed. (New York: Addison-Wesley Longman, 2008); David H. Rosenbloom, Deborah Rosenbloom, and Robert Kravchuk, *Public Administration: Understanding Management, Politics, and Law in the Public Sector*, 5th ed. (New York: McGraw-Hill, 2008); Donald R. Kettl and James W. Fesler, *The Politics of the Administrative Process*, 4th ed. (Washington, D.C.: CQ Press, 2008); Robert B. Denhardt, *Public Administration, An Action Orientation*, 6th ed. (Belmont, Calif.: Wadsworth, 2009); Richard J. Stillman II, *Public Administration: Concepts and Cases*, 9th ed. (Belmont, Calif.: Cengage, 2010); and Nicholas Henry, *Public Administration and Public Affairs*, 11th ed. (Englewood Cliffs, N.J.: Prentice Hall, 2010).

Chapter 2: Public Administration, Democracy, and Bureaucratic Power

1. As early as 2003, the vast majority of Americans (92%) informed pollsters they would vote for an African-American as president. "Can You Trust What Polls Say about Obama's Electoral Prospects? Two Important Trends Suggest Americans May Now Be Ready to Elect an African-American President" by Scott Keeter and Nilanthi Samaranayake, February 7, 2007, Pew Research Center for People and the Press. Accessed January 8, 2008, at http://www.pewresearch.org/pubs/408/can-you-trust-what-polls-say-about-obamas-electoral-prospects.
2. Our discussion of this subject is based on the excellent treatment by Richard S. Page in "The Ideological-Philosophical Setting of American Public Administration," in Dwight Waldo, ed., *Public Administration in a Time of Turbulence* (Scranton, Pa.: Chandler, 1971), pp. 59–73. See also Douglas Yates, *Bureaucratic Democracy: The Search for Democracy and Efficiency in American Government* (Cambridge, Mass.: Harvard University Press, 1982; paperback edition, 1987), pp. 10–13. There are other ways, however, to view the public interest; see, for example, Glendon Schubert, *The Public Interest* (Glencoe, Ill.: Free Press, 1960; reprinted, 1982).
3. Herbert Kaufman, "Administrative Decentralization and Political Power," *Public Administration Review*, 29 (January/February 1969): 3–15, at 5 (emphasis added).
4. "Justices Are Long on Words but Short on Guidance" by Adam Liptak, *New York Times*, November 17, 2010. Retrieved at: http://www.nytimes.com/2010/11/18/us/18rulings.html?adxnnl=1&ref=supremecourt&adxnnlx=1299866110-I14LFFcI-H0BpC5tWtfMmrw. See also, Linda Harriman and Jeffrey D. Straussman, "Do Judges Determine Budget Decisions? Federal Court Decisions in Prison Reform and State Spending for Corrections," *Public Administration Review*, 43 (March/April 1983): 343–51; Donald L. Horowitz, "The Courts as Guardians of the Public Interest," *Public Administration Review*, 37 (March/April 1977): 148–54; David H. Rosenbloom, "Public Administration and the Judiciary: The New Partnership," *Public Administration Review*, 47 (January/February 1987): 75–83; Jeffrey D. Straussman, "Courts and Public Purse Strings: Have Portraits of Budgeting Missed Something?" *Public Administration Review*, 46 (July/August 1986): 345–51.

5. Horowitz, "The Courts as Guardians of the Public Interest," p. 150.

6. For more information, see: www.supremecourtus.gov/ and www.findlaw.com/casecode/supreme.html)

7. Though given renewed emphasis in recent decades, the idea of direct participation dates back to the founding of the Republic. Douglas Yates cites historian Andrew Hacker, an expert on the political thought of James Madison. Hacker suggests that Madison recognized the need for government to "regulate the activities of groups in society," but that Madison also "wanted groups to have a positive role in making governmental policy." See Yates, *Bureaucratic Democracy*, pp. 10–11.

8. This discussion draws on a commentary written by public administration scholar Dwight Waldo and cited by Page in "The Ideological-Philosophical Setting," p. 62. Waldo's *The Administrative State: A Study of the Political Theory of American Public Administration*, 2nd ed. (New York: Holmes & Meier, 1984) is a valuable examination of the evolution of American thinking regarding public administration.

9. Page, "The Ideological-Philosophical Setting," p. 63.

10. This balanced view of power held by the Framers finds an analogy in the writings a century later of Woodrow Wilson, one of the foremost administrative reformers. In his famous essay, "The Study of Administration" (1887), Wilson advanced the "politics–administration dichotomy" and the notion of bureaucratic neutrality. What is not as well remembered is that Wilson also argued that administrators should exercise "large powers and unhampered discretion." The principal emphasis of Wilson's essay may be reinterpreted by giving more weight to his prescription for what Jameson Doig has called "administrative energy and administrative discretion." See Doig, "If I See a Murderous Fellow Sharpening a Knife Cleverly': The Wilsonian Dichotomy and the Public Authority Tradition," *Public Administration Review*, 43 (July/August 1983): 292–304, especially 292–94. The quote cited is from p. 294.

11. See Martin Landau, "Redundancy, Rationality, and the Problem of Duplication and Overlap," *Public Administration Review*, 29 (July/August 1969): 346–58; and Kenneth Meier and Laurence J. O'Toole, "Political Control vs. Bureaucratic Values: Reframing the Debate," *Public Administration Review*, 66 (March/April, 2006): 177–192.

12. Yates, *Bureaucratic Democracy*, pp. 31–33.

13. In *Bureaucratic Democracy*, Douglas Yates offers a thoughtful and carefully crafted approach to how these values can, in fact, be reconciled. See also John Rohr, *To Run a Constitution: The Legitimacy of the Administrative State* (Lawrence: University Press of Kansas, 1986); Laurence J. O'Toole, Jr., "Doctrines and Developments: Separation of Powers, the Politics-Administration Dichotomy, and the Rise of the Administrative State," *Public Administration Review*, 47 (January/February 1987): 17–25; John P. Burke, "Reconciling Public Administration and Democracy: The Role of the Responsible Administrator," *Public Administration Review*, 49 (March/April 1989): 180–85; and John A. Rohr, "The Constitutional Case for Public Administration," in Gary L. Wamsley, et al., *Refounding Public Administration* (Newbury Park, Calif.: Sage, 1990).

14. Emmette S. Redford, *Democracy in the Administrative State* (New York: Oxford University Press, 1969), pp. 19–22.

15. Useful and insightful discussions of accountability—and of the related concern for bureaucratic responsibility discussed elsewhere in this chapter—can be found in John P. Burke, *Bureaucratic Responsibility* (Baltimore, Md.: Johns Hopkins University Press, 1986); Barbara S. Romzek and Melvin J. Dubnick, "Accountability in the Public Sector: Lessons from the Challenger Tragedy," *Public Administration Review*, 47 (May/June 1987): 227–38; Yates, *Bureaucratic Democracy*, especially chap. 6; Ronald C. Moe and Thomas H. Stanton, "Government-Sponsored Enterprises as Federal Instrumentalities: Reconciling Private Management with Public Accountability," *Public Administration Review*, 49 (July/August 1989): 321–29; Barbara S. Romzek and Melvin J. Dubnick, "Issues of Accountability in Flexible Personnel Systems," in Patricia W. Ingraham, Barbara Romzek, and associates, eds., *New Paradigms for Government: Issues for the Changing Public Service* (San Francisco: Jossey-Bass, 1994); Regina Herzlinger, "Can Public Trust in Non-Profits and Government Be Restored?" *Harvard Business Review*, 74 (1996): 97–108; and Bernard Rosen, *Holding Government Bureaucracies Accountable*, 3rd ed. (Westport, Conn.: Greenwood Press, 1998).

16. William B. Eimicke, *Public Administration in a Democratic Context: Theory and Practice* (Beverly Hills, Calif.: Sage, 1974), p. 17. On a related theme, see Gregory Streib, "Professional Skill and Support for Democratic Principles: The Case of Local Government Department Heads in Northern Illinois," *Administration & Society*, 24 (May 1992): 22–40.

17. In most instances, agency accountability has been greatly enhanced because information has become available on the internet or brought to light by the

mass media or interest groups. See also Harold C. Relyea, "Introduction," in Harold C. Relyea, ed., "Symposium on the Freedom of Information Act," *Public Administration Review*, 39 (July/August 1979): 310–32, at 310.

18. The FOIA Act was amended in 1986 to make it easier for businesses to block the release of trade secrets. See *Congressional Quarterly Weekly Report*, 44 (September 27, 1986): 2325. See also Lotte E. Feinberg and Harold C. Relyea, eds., "Symposium: Toward a Government Information Policy—FOIA at 20," *Public Administration Review*, 46 (November/December 1986): 603–39; U. Lynn Jones, "See No Evil, Hear No Evil, Speak No Evil: The Information Control Policy of the Reagan Administration," *Policy Studies Journal*, 17 (Winter 1988–1989): 243–60; and William H. Abrashkin and Ernest Winsor, *Freedom of Information in Massachusetts* (Westport, Conn.: Auburn House, 1989). For a discussion of how the FOIA was used to expose overzealous FBI data collection, see Eric Lichtblau, "FBI Data Mining Reached Beyond Initial Targets," *New York Times*, September 9, 2007.

19. The following discussion relies on Tess Chichioco, "Making It Hard to Get Records; Government Agencies Are Using Computers to Hinder Disclosure under the Freedom of Information Act," *Editor & Publisher*, 123 (March 31, 1990): 16; Jane E. Kirtley, "Electronic Roadblocks to Freedom of Information: A Press Perspective," *Bulletin of the American Society for Information Science*, 17 (August/September 1991): 10–11; Kate Doyle, "Hiding Space: NASA's Tips for Avoiding Scrutiny," *Columbia Journalism Review*, 31 (July/August 1992): 18–19; Terry Anderson, "My Paper Prison," *New York Times Magazine*, April 4, 1993, 34; Margo Nash, "The Anderson File," *The Nation*, 256 (April 19, 1993): 509; Mark Fitzgerald, "Losing Access to Public Records," *Editor & Publisher*, 126 (May 15, 1993): 9; Debra Gersh, "New FOIA Directives Issued," *Editor & Publisher*, 126 (October 9, 1993): 18–19; Michael K. Frisby, "Clinton Lawyer Secured U.S. Subpoena to Prevent Release of Whitewater Files," *Wall Street Journal*, January 6, 1994, p. A14; and "Reno Seeks to Speed Up Release of Some Documents," *Wall Street Journal*, February 4, 1994, p. A12. See also Edward Greer, "There Goes FOIA," *The Progressive*, 54 (September 1990): 16–17; Debra Gersh, "Secrecy as Usual," *Editor & Publisher*, 125 (April 11, 1992): 12–15; and "FOIA Act Weakened by California Supreme Court," *Editor & Publisher*, 126 (July 3, 1993): 26.

20. See among others, Michael Hoefges, Martin Halstuk, and Bill F. Chamberlin, "Privacy Rights Versus FOIA Disclosure Policy: The 'Uses and Effects' Double Standard in Access to Personally-Identifiable Government Records," *William & Mary Bill of Rights Journal*, 12 (1), 2003; 1–65; Gary H. Anthes, "Federal Groups Urge Openness," *Computer-world*, 24 (July 30, 1990): 89; Seth Shulman, "Freedom of Information in the Computer Era," *Technology Review*, 93 (July 1990): 14–15; and M. L. Stein, "Computers and the FOIA," *Editor & Publisher*, 123 (June 9, 1990): 16–17.

21. Albert S. Gore, *The Assault on Reason* (New York: The Penguin Group, 2007), pp. 119–20.

22. Former George W. Bush Attorney General Alberto Gonzalez's "loose" interpretation of due process and judicial review requirements for electronic surveillance and wiretaps proved embarrassing for the Bush Administration and was a factor leading to his resignation in 2007. See also, Bill Kizorek, "Information Access: Is There a Balance?" *Security Management*, 35 (December 1991): 98–99; and Evan I. Schwartz, "Americans Fear Data Raiders Are Snatching Their Privacy," *Business Week* (December 21, 1992): 860.

23. See Gordon P. Whitaker, "Coproduction: Citizen Participation in Service Delivery," *Public Administration Review*, 40 (May/June 1980): 240–46. See also Jeffrey L. Brudney and Robert E. England, "Toward a Definition of the Coproduction Concept," *Public Administration Review*, 43 (January/February 1983): 59–65; and Charles Levine, "Citizenship and Service Delivery: The Promise of Coproduction," in H. George Frederickson and Ralph Clark Chandler, eds., "Citizenship and Public Administration: Proceedings of the National Conference on Citizenship and Public Service," *Public Administration Review*, 44 (March 1984): 178–87.

24. Specific purposes of participation can also include some or all of the following: (1) providing information to citizens; (2) receiving information from or about citizens; (3) improving public decision processes, programs, projects, and services; (4) enhancing public acceptance of governmental activities; (5) altering patterns of political power and allocations of public resources; (6) protecting individual and minority-group rights and interests; and (7) delaying or avoiding difficult public-policy decisions.

25. Organized anti-government movements, such as the Ruby Ridge, Idaho and Waco, Texas, incidents in August, 1992 and April, 1993, and the bombing of the Alfred R. Murrah Federal Building in Oklahoma

City in April, 1995, illustrate the extremes to which some groups have gone to protest actions of government agencies. For a broad-ranging assessment of organized citizen activity, see Harry C. Boyte, *The Backyard Revolution: Understanding the New Citizen Movement* (Philadelphia: Temple University Press, 1980). See also Neil S. Mayer, *Neighborhood Organizations and Community Development: Making Revitalization Work* (Washington, D.C.: Urban Institute Press, 1984); Harry C. Boyte, Heather Booth, and Steve Max, eds., *Citizen Action and the New Populism* (Philadelphia: Temple University Press, 1986); Sarah F. Liebschutz, "Neighborhood Revitalization in the United States: The Decentralization Dynamic," *Public Administration Quarterly*, 14 (Spring 1990): 86–107; Frances Moore Lappe and Paul Martin Du Bois, *The Quickening of America: Rebuilding Our Nation, Remaking Our Lives* (San Francisco: Jossey-Bass, 1994); Lucy Brewer, *Public Works Administration: Current Public Policy Perspectives* (Thousand Oaks, Calif.: Sage, 1997); John J. Kirlin and Mary K. Kirlin, "Strengthening Effective Government-Citizen Connections through Greater Civic Engagement," *Public Administration Review*, 62 (September 2002): 80–86; and, for insights on presidential candidate Barack Obama's early career and frustrations as a community organizer, see: *Dreams from My Father: A Story of Race and Inheritance* (New York: Random House, 2004). See also, Casey A. Klofstad, *Civic Talk: Peers, Politics, and the Future of Democracy* (Philadelphia: Temple University Press, 2011).

26. Walter A. Rosenbaum, "The Paradoxes of Public Participation," *Administration & Society*, 8 (November 1976): 355–383, at p. 373.

27. The description comes from a speech by U.S. Senator Daniel Patrick Moynihan (D-NY), delivered at Syracuse University, May 8, 1969; cited in Harold Seidman and Robert Gilmour, *Politics, Position, and Power: From the Positive to the Regulatory States*, 4th ed. (New York: Oxford University Press, 1986), pp. 207–8.

28. This discussion relies in part on Eimicke, *Public Administration in a Democratic Context*, pp. 33–44.

29. Redford, *Democracy in the Administrative State*, p. 44.

30. Thompson, "Bureaucracy in a Democratic Society," 207 (emphasis added).

31. See, among others, Brian J. Cook, "The Representative Function of Bureaucracy: Public Administration in Constitutive Perspective," *Administration & Society*, 23 (February 1992): 403–29; and Fred W. Riggs, "Bureaucracy and the Constitution," *Public Administration Review*, 54 (January/February 1994): 65–72.

32. Joel D. Aberbach and Bert A. Rockman, "From Nixon's Problem to Reagan's Achievement: The Federal Executive Reexamined," in Larry Berman, *Looking Back on the Reagan Presidency* (Baltimore, Md.: Johns Hopkins University Press, 1990), pp. 175–94, at p. 192.

33. For an interesting account of the crafting of the Uniting and Strengthening America by Providing Appropriate Tools Required to Intercept and Obstruct Terrorism Act, known as the USA PATRIOT Act, or the Patriot Act, see Robert O'Harrow, Jr., "A Proper Balance: The Patriot Act Allows Government Snooping, But at What Cost to Privacy?" *Washington Post Weekly National Edition*, 20 (November 4–10, 2002): 6–9. See also Sarah Sun Beale, James E. Felman, and Charles Lowndes, "The Consequences of Enlisting Federal Grand Juries in the War on Terrorism: Assessing the USA Patriot Act's Changes to Grand Jury Secrecy," *Harvard Journal of Law and Public Policy*, 25(2) (Spring 2002): 699–721; Michael W. Spicer, "The War on Terrorism and the Administration of the American State," *Public Administration Review*, 62 (September 2002): 63–69; Jon B. Gould, "Playing with Fire: The Civil Liberties Implications of September 11th," *Public Administration Review*, 62 (September 2002): 74–80; and Carol W. Lewis, "The Clash between Security and Liberty in the U.S. Response to Terror," *Public Administration Review*, 65 (January/February 2005), 18–30.

34. Challenges to the constitutionality of the Patient Protection and Affordable Care Act by residents of New Jersey were dismissed by a federal court judge in April, 2011. Lawsuits in other states are pending and the issue of whether the federal government can mandate health care coverage became a topic of intense debate during the 2012 presidential campaign.

35. See Allan W. Lerner and John Wanat, "Fuzziness and Bureaucracy," *Public Administration Review*, 43 (November/December 1983): 500–9. This "fuzziness" and its consequences (among other factors) prompt administrators to nurture favorable ties with legislatures as institutions and with individual legislators.

36. Norton E. Long, "Power and Administration," *Public Administration Review*, 9 (Autumn 1949): 257–64, at 258.

37. Ibid., pp. 258–59.

38. Ibid., p. 259.

39. Lerner and Wanat, "Fuzziness and Bureaucracy," p. 502.

40. For a variety of reasons, chief executives (presidents, governors, mayors) may seek to avoid a leading role in giving detailed direction to administrative implementation of public policy. For administrators, there are both advantages and disadvantages to this course of action: On the one hand, administrators are not bound to follow every executive dictate exactly; on the other hand, they are not able to rely routinely on presidential, gubernatorial, or mayoral power or prestige for political support.

41. Matthew Holden, "Imperialism in Bureaucracy," *American Political Science Review*, 60 (December 1966): 943–51, at 951 (emphasis added).

42. Francis E. Rourke, *Bureaucracy, Politics, and Public Policy*, 3rd ed. (Boston: Little, Brown, 1984).

43. See Anthony Downs, *Inside Bureaucracy* (1967; reprint, Prospect Heights, Ill.: Waveland Press, 1994), chap. 10, especially pp. 118–27; and Martin Landau, "Redundancy, Rationality, and the Problem of Duplication and Overlap," *Public Administration Review*, 29 (July/August 1969): 346–58.

44. For an introduction to the theoretical roles and political activities of interest groups in American politics, see V. O. Key, Jr., *Politics, Parties, and Pressure Groups*, 5th ed. (New York: Crowell, 1964), especially chaps. 2–6; and Lester W. Milbrath, *The Washington Lobbyists* (Chicago: Rand McNally, 1963). Interactions between agencies and interest groups are examined (with other topics) by Glenn Abney in "Lobbying by the Insiders: Parallels of State Agencies and Interest Groups," *Public Administration Review*, 48 (September/October 1988): 911–17; Jeanne Nienaber Clarke and Daniel McCool, *Staking Out the Terrain: Power Differentials among Natural Resource Management Agencies* (Albany: State University of New York Press, 1985); Martha Derthick, *Agency under Stress: The Social Security Administration in American Government* (Washington, D.C.: Brookings Institution Press, 1990); Todd Kunioka and Lawrence S. Rothenberg, "The Politics of Bureaucratic Competition: The Case of Natural Resource Policy," *Journal of Policy Analysis and Management*, 12 (Fall 1993): 700–25; Jeffrey M. Berry and Clyde Wilcox, *The Interest Group Society*, 4th ed. (New York: Longman, 2006); and Allan J. Cigler and Burdett A. Loomis, *Interest Group Politics*, 7th ed. (Washington, D.C.: CQ Press, 2006).

45. Agency-clientele group relationships exist, among many others, between the Pentagon and defense contractors, the Social Security Administration and senior-citizen groups, the Department of Agriculture and the tobacco industry, the Maritime Administration and the shipping industry, state commerce commissions and private business associations, and both state and national departments of labor and the labor unions.

46. For example, the Illinois Agricultural Association, the state component of the American Farm Bureau Federation, is a vital source of political strength for the state Department of Agriculture; in California, farm organizations help sustain both the Department of Agriculture and the Department of Water Resources. In return, these agencies are expected to advocate and defend the interests of their supporters, such as irrigation for California's farmers. These relationships often become at least semipermanent.

47. The literature on subsystem politics includes Emmette S. Redford, *Democracy in the Administrative State* (New York: Oxford University Press, 1969), especially chap. 4; A. Lee Fritschler and James M. Hoefler, *Smoking and Politics: Policy Making and the Federal Bureaucracy*, 5th ed. (Upper Saddle River, N.J.: Prentice Hall, 1995); Roger H. Davidson, Walter Oleszek and Francis E. Lee, *Congress and Its Members*, 12th ed. (Washington, D.C.: CQ Press, 2009), esp. chap. 12; and Martha Derthick, *Up in Smoke: From Legislation to Litigation in Tobacco Politics*, 3rd. ed. (Washington, D.C.: CQ Press, 2011).

48. The American Association of Retired Persons (www.aarp.org/) is a nonprofit, nonpartisan association dedicated to serving aging members of population. Founded in 1958, AARP is the nation's largest organization of midlife and older people, with more than 30 million members. The American Hospital Association (www.hospitalconnect.com) is an interest group representing hospitals and health care organizations; the American Medical Association (www.ama-assn.org) represents doctors.

49. This discussion relies on "Members' Health Concerns Now Center on Turf Wars," *Congressional Quarterly Weekly Report*, 51 (October 9, 1993): 2734–35, and Davidson and Oleszek, *Congress and Its Members*, pp. 218–19. See also Barbara Sinclair, *Unorthodox Lawmaking: New Legislative Processes in the U.S. Congress*, 2nd ed. (Washington, D.C.: CQ Press, 2000), pp. 89–92.

50. See Hugh Heclo, "Issue Networks and the Executive Establishment," in Anthony King, ed., *The*

New American Political System (Washington, D.C.: American Enterprise Institute for Public Policy Research, 1978), at p. 103.

51. This was especially true of AIDS research policy under President Reagan and the policy on gays in the military under Presidents Clinton and Obama. It is not surprising that none of these policies was clearly defined until the Obama administration convinced Congress in late 2010 that the "don't ask, don't tell" policy was unfair and unworkable.

52. *Bloomington (Ill.) Pantagraph*, July 2, 1980, p. A4 (emphasis added).

53. See, among others, Joseph P. Harris, *Congressional Control of Administration* (Washington, D.C.: Brookings Institution Press, 1964); and Allen Schick, "Politics through Law: Congressional Limitations on Executive Discretion," in Anthony King, ed., *Both Ends of the Avenue: The Presidency, the Executive Branch, and Congress in the 1980s* (Washington, D.C.: American Enterprise Institute for Public Policy Research, 1983), pp. 154–84, especially pp. 170–79.

54. Lawrence C. Dodd and Richard L. Schott, *Congress and the Administrative State* (New York: Wiley, 1979), p. 183; this book (especially chaps. 5 and 6) is one of the best studies of change within Congress and its relationship to changes in legislative oversight. In this regard, see also Morris P. Fiorina, *Congress: Keystone of the Washington Establishment*, 2nd ed. (New Haven, Conn.: Yale University Press, 1989), especially chaps. 5 and 7. The development of the constituent-service emphasis is examined in John R. Johannes, *To Serve the People: Congress and Constituency Service* (Lincoln, Neb.: University of Nebraska Press, 1984). More generally, see Douglas Arnold, *Congress and the Bureaucracy* (New Haven, Conn.: Yale University Press, 1980); Randall B. Ripley and Grace A. Franklin, *Congress, the Bureaucracy, and Public Policy*, 5th ed. (Monterey, Calif.: Brooks/Cole, 1991); Berry and Wilcox, *The Interest Group Society*; William P. Browne, *Groups, Interests, and Public Policy* (Washington, D.C.: Georgetown University Press, 1998); John R. Wright, *Interest Groups and Congress: Lobbying Contributions and Influence*, Longman Classics Edition (New York: Longman. 2002); and David Mayhew, *Congress: The Electoral Connection*, 2nd ed. (New Haven, Conn.: Yale University Press, 2004).

55. Congress lost one oversight instrument that it had employed for over fifty years—the legislative veto—when the Supreme Court declared the single-chamber legislative veto unconstitutional by a 7-2 ruling in *Immigration and Naturalization Service v. Chadha*, 103 S. Ct. 2764 (1983). The legislative veto was included in more than 200 statutes enacted between 1932 and 1983. This veto required the executive branch to inform Congress of the actions that the executive branch planned to take in implementing a new law and to receive approval from Congress of the actions before actually carrying them out. Within a fixed time period, usually sixty to ninety days, one or both chambers of Congress had the option to vote down, by simple majority, a proposed administrative action. But the veto was increasingly criticized, mainly on the grounds that it unconstitutionally intruded on the president's authority to direct executive-branch agencies. Critics of the veto assumed that only the president should have authority to direct activities of the executive branch. This assumption, however, contradicts both established legal tradition within the framework of separation of powers and a variety of congressional practices, such as GAO audits and studies and committee hearings and investigations, designed to promote Congress's influence over administration of the laws. The 1983 ruling articulated a legal doctrine of near-total separation of powers, which had not existed before *Chadha* and has not operated since *Chadha*. In the first year after the Court's ruling, Congress enacted thirty provisions allowing legislative vetoes of agency decisions (most in the form of committee review of proposed agency actions). *Congressional Quarterly Weekly Report*, 42 (July 21, 1984): 1, 797. For details, see Louis Fisher, "The Administrative World of *Chadha* and *Bowsher*," *Public Administration Review*, 47 (May/June 1987): 213–19.

56. See Joel D. Aberbach, *Keeping a Watchful Eye: The Politics of Congressional Oversight* (Washington, D.C.: Brookings Institution Press, 1990).

57. Fiorina, *Congress: Keystone of the Washington Establishment*, p. 80. See also James Q. Wilson, "The Rise of the Bureaucratic State," *The Public Interest*, 41 (Fall 1975): 77–103, at 103. For a study of legislative influence on the activities of public administrators in two state governments, see Richard C. Elling, "State Legislative Influence in the Administrative Process: Consequences and Constraints," *Public Administration Quarterly*, 7 (Winter 1984): 457–81.

58. For insightful discussion of the relationships between government officials and the press, see, among others, Stephen Hess, *The Government-Press Connection* (Washington, D.C.: Brookings Institution Press, 1984); and Charles Press and Kenneth VerBurg,

American Politicians and Journalists (Glenview, Ill.: Scott, Foresman, 1988). A selection from Press and VerBurg's book appears as "Bureaucrats and Journalists," in Frederick S. Lane, ed., *Current Issues in Public Administration*, 4th ed. (New York: St. Martin's Press, 1990), pp. 225–34.

59. See, among others, Richard C. Elling, "Bureaucratic Accountability: Problems and Paradoxes; Panaceas and (Occasionally) Palliatives," *Public Administration Review*, 43 (January/February 1983): 82–89; John P. Burke, *Bureaucratic Responsibility* (Baltimore: Johns Hopkins University Press, 1986); William M. Pearson and Van A. Wigginton, "Effectiveness of Administrative Controls: Some Perceptions of State Legislators," *Public Administration Review*, 46 (July/August 1986): 328–31; Dan B. Wood and Richard W. Waterman, *Bureaucratic Dynamics* (Boulder, Colo.: Westview Press, 1994); David N. Ammons, "Overcoming the Inadequacies of Performance Measurement in Local Government: The Case of Libraries and Leisure Services," *Public Administration Review*, 55 (January/February 1995): 37–47; Bernard Rosen, *Holding Government Bureaucracies Accountable*, 3rd ed. (Westport, Conn.: Greenwood Press, 1998); William T. Gormley Jr., "Accountability Battles in State Administration," in Frederick S. Lane, *Current Issues in Public Administration*, 6th ed. (Boston: Bedford/St. Martin's, 1999), pp. 123–40; Robert Behn, "The New Public Management Paradigm and the Search for Democratic Accountability," *International Public Management Review*, 1(2) (1999): 131–65; Robert Behn, *Rethinking Democratic Accountability* (Washington, D.C.: Brookings Institution Press, 2001); and Kaifeng Yang and Jun Yi Hsieh, "Managerial Effectiveness of Government Performance Measurement: Testing a Middle-Range Model," *Public Administration Review*, 67 (September/October, 2007): 861–79.

Chapter 3: Federalism and Intergovernmental Relations

1. Albert Gore, *Common Sense Government: Works Better and Costs Less* (New York: Random House, 1995), p. 18.
2. William Anderson, *Intergovernmental Relations in Review* (Minneapolis: University of Minnesota Press, 1960), p. 3, cited by Deil S. Wright, *Understanding Intergovernmental Relations*, 3rd ed. (Monterey, Calif.: Brooks/Cole, 1988), p. 14.
3. Wright, *Understanding Intergovernmental Relations*, p. 15.
4. Richard H. Leach, *American Federalism* (New York: Norton, 1970), pp. 59–63; see also chaps. 2 and 10.
5. Russell L. Hanson, "The Intergovernmental Setting of State Politics," in Virginia Gray, Herbert Jacob, and Kenneth N. Vines, eds., *Politics in the American States: A Comparative Analysis*, 4th ed. (Boston: Little, Brown, 1983), p. 28 (emphasis added). See also Michael J. Rich, "The Intergovernmental Environment," in John J. Pelissero, ed., *Cities, Politics, and Policy: A Comparative Analysis* (Washington, D.C.: CQ Press, 2003), pp. 35–67.
6. Cornell W. Clayton and J. Mitchell Pickerill, "Guess What Happened on the Way to Revolution? Precursors to the Supreme Court's Federalism Revolution," *Publius: The Journal of Federalism*, 34 (Summer 2004): 85–114, at p. 85. The cases involved were *Gregory v. Ashcroft*, 501 U.S. 452 (1991); *United States v. Lopez*, 514 U.S. 549 (1995); and *United States v. Morrison*, 529 U.S. 598 (2000).
7. Ibid. The cases involved were *City of Boerne v. Flores*, 521 U.S. 507 (1997); *Adarana Constructors v. Pena*, 515 U.S. 200 (1995); *Kimel v. Florida Board of Regents*, 528 U.S. 62 (2000); and *United States v. Morrison*, 529 U.S. 598 (2000).
8. Dale Krane, "The State of American Federalism, 2003–2004: Polarized Politics and Federalist Principles," *Publius: The Journal of Federalism*, 34 (Summer 2004): 1–53, at p. 8.
9. Ibid.
10. This account is taken from an Associated Press report appearing in the *Bloomington (Ill.) Pantagraph*, January 22, 2004, p. A8. The case was *Alaska Department of Environmental Conservation v. U.S. Environmental Protection Agency* (02-658).
11. See, among others, Joseph F. Zimmerman, *Federal Preemption: The Silent Revolution* (Ames: Iowa State University Press, 1991); and Timothy J. Conlan, Robert L. Dudley, Paul L. Posner, Paul Teske, and Joseph F. Zimmerman, "The Nature and Political Significance of Preemption," *PS: Political Science and Politics*, 38 (July 2005): 359–78.
12. Associated Press report, as it appeared on CNN.com, June 24, 2005. See also Elaine B. Sharp and Donald Haider-Markel, "At the Invitation of the Court: Eminent Domain Reform in State Legislatures in the Wake of the *Kelo* Decision," *Publius: The Journal of Federalism*, 38 (Summer 2008): 556–75.
13. Associated Press report, as it appeared on CNN.com, June 24, 2005.

14. John Dinan, "The Rehnquist Court's Federalism Decisions," *Publius: The Journal of Federalism*, 41 (Winter 2011): 158–67, at p. 159.

15. For a comprehensive overview of national government aid to cities prior to the 1960s, see Roscoe C. Martin, *The Cities and the Federal System* (New York: Atherton, 1965).

16. Michael D. Reagan and John G. Sanzone, *The New Federalism*, 2nd ed. (New York: Oxford University Press, 1981), p. 33.

17. In this connection, see Donald F. Kettl, *Government by Proxy: (Mis?)Managing Federal Programs* (Washington, D.C.: CQ Press, 1988).

18. Reagan and Sanzone, *The New Federalism*, pp. 37–43. See also Parris N. Glendening and Mavis Mann Reeves, *Pragmatic Federalism: An Intergovernmental View of American Government*, 2nd ed. (Pacific Palisades, Calif.: Palisades Publishers, 1984), pp. 253–56; and Carol E. Cohen, "State Fiscal Capacity and Effort: An Update," *Intergovernmental Perspective*, 15 (Spring 1989): 15–20.

19. The following description relies on Reagan and Sanzone, *The New Federalism*, chap. 3. See also George E. Hale and Marian Lief Palley, *The Politics of Federal Grants* (Washington, D.C.: CQ Press, 1981), pp. 18–21.

20. This discussion relies on Arnold M. Howitt, *Managing Federalism: Studies in Intergovernmental Relations* (Washington, D.C.: CQ Press, 1984), pp. 27–28.

21. Ibid., p. 28.

22. Reagan and Sanzone, *The New Federalism*, pp. 125–26.

23. See Daniel J. Elazar, *American Federalism: A View from the States*, 3rd ed. (New York: Harper & Row, 1984), pp. 85–91. Ironically, it was under Eisenhower—a Republican president—that a systematic effort was made to define broad national goals in the late 1950s. See President's Commission on National Goals, *Goals for Americans* (Englewood Cliffs, N.J.: Prentice Hall, 1960).

24. See James L. Sundquist, with the collaboration of David W. Davis, *Making Federalism Work: A Study of Program Coordination at the Community Level* (Washington, D.C.: Brookings Institution Press, 1969), pp. 3–6. For a more recent examination of the Johnson years, see David M. Welborn and Jesse Burkhead, *Intergovernmental Relations in the American Administrative State: The Johnson Presidency* (Austin: University of Texas Press, 1989).

25. See Ann O'M. Bowman, "American Federalism on the Horizon," *Publius: The Journal of Federalism*, 32 (Spring 2002): U.S. Office of Management and Budget, *Analytical Perspectives, Budget of the United States Government, Fiscal Year 2008*, Crosscutting Programs, Part 8—Aid to State and Local Governments, Table 8–3. Trends in Federal Grants to State and Local Governments, p. 107.

26. Harold Seidman and Robert Gilmour, *Politics, Position, and Power: From the Positive to the Regulatory State*, 4th ed. (New York: Oxford University Press, 1986), p. 197.

27. U.S. Advisory Commission on Intergovernmental Relations, *Urban America and the Federal System* (Washington, D.C.: U.S. Advisory Commission on Intergovernmental Relations, 1969), p. 5.

28. Terry Sanford, *Storm over the States* (New York: McGraw-Hill, 1967), p. 80.

29. David B. Walker, "Federal Aid Administrators and the Federal System," *Intergovernmental Perspective*, 3 (Fall 1977): 10–17, at p. 17 (emphasis added). See also, by Walker, *The Rebirth of Federalism: Slouching Toward Washington*, 2nd ed. (New York: Chatham House, 2000), especially pp. 136–40.

30. See Hale and Palley, *The Politics of Federal Grants*. See also Lawrence D. Brown, James W. Fossett, and Kenneth T. Palmer, *The Changing Politics of Federal Grants* (Washington, D.C.: Brookings Institution Press, 1984).

31. Juliet F. Gainsborough, "Bridging the City-Suburb Divide: States and the Politics of Regional Cooperation," *Journal of Urban Affairs*, 23(5) (2001): 497–512.

32. One illustration of this involved a decision in North Kansas City, Missouri, to build a senior citizens' center with GRS funds, whereas nearby Kansas City incorporated the dollars into its annual budget. When GRS stopped, North Kansas City needed only to find funding for maintenance and upkeep of the center; Kansas City, on the other hand, had to eliminate $24 million from its operating budget—and took most of it out of street lighting, an essential service that most central cities must provide to their citizens. Our thanks to an anonymous reviewer for providing this example.

33. This portion of the block grants discussion rests on the treatment of Reagan and Sanzone, *The New Federalism*, chap. 5, and Wright, *Understanding Intergovernmental Relations*, chap. 6. See also Reagan and Sanzone, *The New Federalism*, pp. 131–46, and Hale and Palley, *The Politics of Federal Grants*, pp. 107–11. For treatment of the CDBG program, see, among others, Ruth Ross, ed., "The Community Development Block Grant Program," *Publius: The*

Journal of Federalism, 13 (Summer 1983): 1–95, and Eric B. Herzik and John P. Pelissero, "Decentralization, Redistribution, and Community Development: A Reassessment of the Small Cities CDBG Program," *Public Administration Review*, 46 (January/February 1986): 31–36.

34. Wright, *Understanding Intergovernmental Relations*, pp. 212–13.

35. U.S. Advisory Commission on Intergovernmental Relations, *Block Grants: A Comparative Analysis* (Washington, D.C.: ACIR, 1979), p. 39.

36. U.S. Advisory Commission on Intergovernmental Relations, *A Catalog of Federal Grant-in-Aid Programs to State and Local Governments Funded, FY 1984*, Report M–139 (Washington, D.C.: U.S. Government Printing Office, 1984), p. 2.

37. Among other sources on GRS, see Richard P. Nathan, Allen D. Manvel, Susannah E. Calkins, and associates, *Monitoring Revenue Sharing* (Washington, D.C.: Brookings Institution Press, 1975); Richard P. Nathan, Charles F. Adams Jr., and associates, *Revenue Sharing: The Second Round* (Washington, D.C.: Brookings Institution Press, 1977); and David A. Caputo and Richard L. Cole, "City Officials and General Revenue Sharing," *Publius: The Journal of Federalism*, 13 (Winter 1983): 41–54.

38. For further information on block grants, see, among others, Timothy J. Conlan, *New Federalism: Intergovernmental Reform from Nixon to Reagan* (Washington, D.C.: Brookings Institution Press, 1988); and, also by Conlan, *From New Federalism to Devolution: Twenty-five Years of Intergovernmental Reform* (Washington, D.C.: Brookings Institution Press, 1998).

39. Michael A. Fletcher, "Two Fronts in the War on Poverty," *Washington Post National Weekly Edition*, May 23–29, 2005, pp. 29–30, at p. 29. See also J. Edwin Benton, "George W. Bush's Federal Aid Legacy," *Publius: The Journal of Federalism*, 37 (Summer 2007): 371–89.

40. David S. Broder, "The Heat Is on the GOP," *Washington Post National Weekly Edition*, April 11–17, 2005, p. 4.

41. Isaiah J. Poole, "Grant Program's Fight for Life," *CQ Weekly*, 63 (April 11, 2005): 872–74, at p. 872.

42. U.S. Office of Management and Budget, *Special Analyses: Budget of the United States Government, Fiscal Year 1990* (Washington, D.C.: U.S. Government Printing Office, 1989), p. H26.

43. One indication of the growing stature of state governments is the increasing interest devoted to them by scholarly observers. See, among others,

David C. Nice, *Policy Innovation in State Government* (Ames: Iowa State University Press, 1994); Laurence J. O'Toole, Jr., ed., *American Intergovernmental Relations*, 4th ed. (Washington, D.C.: CQ Press, 2006); Carl E. Van Horn, ed., *The State of the States*, 4th ed. (Washington, D.C.: CQ Press, 2006); and Virginia Gray and Russell L. Hanson, eds., *Politics in the American States: A Comparative Analysis*, 9th ed. (Washington, D.C.: CQ Press, 2007).

44. Jim VandeHei, "So Much for 'Limited Government,' " *Washington Post National Weekly Edition*, February 14–20, 2005, p. 11. See also Paul Posner, "The Politics of Coercive Federalism in the Bush Era," *Publius: The Journal of Federalism*, 37 (Summer 2007): 390–412.

45. VandeHei, "So Much for 'Limited Government.' " See also Christopher Banks and John Blakeman, "Chief Justice Roberts, Justice Alito, and New Federalism Jurisprudence," *Publius: The Journal of Federalism*, 38 (Summer 2008): 576–600.

46. VandeHei, "So Much for 'Limited Government.' "

47. See John Shannon, "The Return of Fend-for-Yourself Federalism: The Reagan Marks," *Intergovernmental Perspective*, ACIR 13 (Summer–Fall 1987): 34–37; cited in Walker, *The Rebirth of Federalism*, p. 30.

48. This section draws upon Thomas L. Gais, "Federalism During the Obama Administration," presented at the 27th Annual Conference of the National Federation of Municipal Analysts, May 7, 2010. Gais' presentation can be found at http://www.rockinst.org/pdf/federalism/2010-05-07-federalism_during_obama_administration.pdf

49. Ibid., p. 15.

50. Ibid., p. 16.

51. Ibid., p. 17.

52. Ibid., p. 18.

53. Ibid.

54. Ibid., p. 19. See also Timothy J. Conlan and Paul L. Posner, "Inflection Point? Federalism and the Obama Administration," paper delivered at the annual meetings of the American Political Science Association, Washington, DC, September 2, 2010.

55. Adapted from Brian Skoloff, "Cities Enticing Residents to Go Green," Associated Press online story, December 27, 2007.

56. "States' Probe May Force Reform," Associated Press wire-service story appearing in the *Bloomington (Ill.) Pantagraph*, October 14, 2010, p. C1.

57. "Calif[ornia] Rejects Legal Pot, But Cities Embrace It," Associated Press wire-service story appearing in the *Bloomington (Ill.) Pantagraph*, November 14, 2010, p. A6.

58. See John Buntin, "Cap and Fade," Governing, December 26–31, 2010.

59. See "States Take Aim to Block Healthcare Plan," online Reuters News Service story, March 21, 2010; "States Joined in Suit Against Healthcare Reform," online Reuters News Service story, May 14, 2010; "EPA Takes Over Permits in Texas," Associated Press wire-service story appearing in the *Bloomington (Ill.) Pantagraph*, December 24, 2010, p. A7; "Number of Illegal Immigrants on Decline," Associated Press wire-service story appearing in the *Bloomington (Ill.) Pantagraph*, September 2, 2010, p. A1; "Utah Governor Signs Arizona-like Immigration Law," online Reuters News Service story, March 16, 2011; and, among other sources, "Conservatives Push Amendment," Associated Press wire-service story appearing in the *Bloomington (Ill.) Pantagraph*, December 1, 2010, p. A7.

60. "States Put Own Spin on Obama Healthcare Law," online posting on Newsmax.com, March 16, 2011.

61. Ibid.

62. See, among others, David Osborne, *Laboratories of Democracy* (Boston: Harvard Business School Press, 1988); Elazar, *American Federalism: A View from the States*; Dale Krane, "The Middle Tier in American Federalism: State Government Policy Activism During the Bush Presidency," *Publius: The Journal of Federalism*, 37 (Summer 2007): 453–77; John Dinan, "The State of American Federalism 2007–2008: Resurgent State Influence in the National Policy Process and Continued State Policy Innovation," *Publius: The Journal of Federalism*, 38 (Summer 2008): 381–415; and Bryan Shelly, "Rebels and Their Causes: State Resistance to No Child Left Behind," *Publius: The Journal of Federalism*, 38 (Summer 2008): 444–68.

63. See, among others, Paul Posner, *The Politics of Unfunded Mandates: Whither Federalism?* (Washington, D.C.: Georgetown University Press, 1998); and William T. Gormley, Jr., "Money and Mandates: The Politics of Intergovernmental Conflict," *Publius: The Journal of Federalism*, 36 (2006): 523–40.

64. Donald F. Kettl, *The Regulation of American Federalism* (Baton Rouge: Louisiana State University Press, 1983); paperback text edition (Baltimore: John Hopkins University Press, 1987), pp. 3–4.

65. Ibid., p. 4.

66. Ibid., pp. 5–6. For details of implementation problems with the ADA, see Jay W. Spechler, *Reasonable Accommodation: Profitable Compliance with the Americans with Disabilities Act* (Delray Beach, Fla.: St. Lucie Press, 1996).

67. John Kincaid, "The Devolution Tortoise and the Centralization Hare," *New England Economic Review* (May/June 1998): 13; cited in Bowman, "American Federalism on the Horizon," p. 10.

68. Bowman, "American Federalism on the Horizon," p. 12.

69. Ibid.

70. Ibid.

71. For further information about the evolution (and devolution) of federalism, contact the American Council on Intergovernmental Relations, a nonprofit organization established in 1996 by former staff members of the U.S. Advisory Commission on Intergovernmental Relations as a successor to that agency, a clearinghouse on federalism, and nonpartisan policy and research forum with links to European Union federalism projects (http://www.library.unt.edu/amcouncil/). The Urban Institute's state-by-state multiyear research project, Assessing the New Federalism, at http://www.newfederalism.urban.org/ provides public access to over 5,000 indicators of policies to analyze the devolution of responsibility for social programs from the federal government to the states, focusing primarily on health care, income security, job training, and social services. The Center for the Study of Federalism (Temple University) is an interdisciplinary research and educational institute committed to the study of federal principles, institutions, and processes as practical ways to organize political power (http://www.temple.edu/federalism). The Council of State Governments (CSG) at http://www.csg.org/ presents extensive links to state and local government websites. There are also links to databases, regional offices of the CSG, and information about policy areas. See also Charles R. Wise and Rania Nader, "Organizing the Federal System for Homeland Security: Problems, Issues, and Dilemmas," *Public Administration Review*, 62 (September 2002): 44–57; and Patrick S. Roberts, "Dispersed Federalism as a New Regional Governance for Homeland Security," *Publius: The Journal of Federalism*, 38 (Summer 2008): 416–43.

Chapter 4: Organizational Theory

1. H. H. Gerth and C. Wright Mills, *From Max Weber: Essays in Sociology* (New York: Oxford University Press, 1946), pp. 196–203. This ideal model of professionalism is changing in practice as more governments seek ways to reduce the costs of employee benefits and pensions.

2. Julien Freund, *The Sociology of Max Weber* (New York: Vintage Books, 1969), pp. 142–48.

3. Frederick W. Taylor, *The Principles of Scientific Management* (New York: Norton, 1967); first published in 1911.

4. For a humorous, first-person account of life with two other time-and-motion experts, see Frank B. Gilbreth and Ernestine Gilbreth Carey, *Cheaper by the Dozen*, rev. ed. (New York: Crowell, 1963).

5. Hindy Lauer Schachter, *Frederick Taylor and the Public Administration Community: A Reevaluation* (Albany: State University of New York Press, 1989); Robert Kanigel, *One Best Way: Frederick Winslow Taylor and the Enigma of Efficiency* (New York: Viking Press, 1997); and Schachter, "Does Frederick Taylor's Ghost Still Haunt the Halls of Government? A Look at the Concept of Government Efficiency in Our Time," *Public Administration Review*, 67 (September/October 2007): 800–10. See also Anne M. Blake and James L. Moseley, "One Hundred Years after *The Principles of Scientific Management* Frederick Taylor's Life and Impact on the Field of Human Performance Technology," *Performance Improvement*, 49 (April 2010): 27–34.

6. For a website dedicated to the writings of Frederick Winslow Taylor, see, among others, http://www.fordham.edu/halsall/mod/1911taylor.html.

7. See Luther Gulick and Lyndall Urwick, eds., *Papers on the Science of Administration* (New York: Institute of Public Administration, 1937).

8. Ibid., pp. 1–46. A contemporary analysis of the foundations of these and other principles can be found in Robert E. Goodin and Peter Wilenski, "Beyond Efficiency: The Logical Underpinnings of Administrative Principles," *Public Administration Review*, 44 (November/December 1984): 512–17.

9. The best source on the Hawthorne experiments is F. J. Roethlisberger and William J. Dickson, *Management and the Worker* (Cambridge, Mass.: Harvard University Press, 1939). See also Elton Mayo, *The Human Problems of an Industrial Civilization* (Boston: Harvard Business School, 1933), for a statement of Mayo's general approach to his research.

10. See the summary of findings in Amitai Etzioni, *Modern Organizations* (Englewood Cliffs, N.J.: Prentice Hall, 1964), pp. 34–35.

11. See Chester Barnard, *The Functions of the Executive* (Cambridge, Mass.: Harvard University Press, 1938), especially pp. 92–94. See also William G. Scott, "Barnard on the Nature of Elitist Responsibility," *Public Administration Review*, 42 (May/June 1982): 197–201; and William G. Scott and Terence R. Mitchell, "The Universal Barnard: His Meta-Concepts of Leadership in the Administrative State," *Public Administration Quarterly*, 13 (Fall 1989): 295–320.

12. Warren G. Bennis, "Organizational Developments and the Fate of Bureaucracy," in Fred A. Kramer, ed., *Perspectives on Public Bureaucracy*, 3rd ed. (Cambridge, Mass.: Winthrop, 1981), pp. 5–25, at pp. 11–12. See also James G. March and Herbert A. Simon, *Organizations* (New York: Wiley, 1958), pp. 83–88.

13. The following is taken from Ralph White and Ronald Lippitt, "Leader Behavior and Member Reaction in Three 'Social Climates,' " in Dorwin Cartwright and Alvin Zander, eds., *Group Dynamics, Research and Theory*, 3rd ed. (New York: Harper & Row, 1968), pp. 527–53. Other studies of leadership include Fred E. Fiedler, *A Theory of Leadership Effectiveness* (New York: McGraw-Hill, 1967); Fred E. Fiedler and Martin Chemers, *Leadership and Effective Management* (Glenview, Ill.: Scott, Foresman, 1974); Philip Selznick, *Leadership in Administration: A Sociological Interpretation* (Berkeley: University of California Press, 1984); Robert H. Guest, Paul Hersey, and Kenneth H. Blanchard, *Organizational Change through Effective Leadership*, 2nd ed. (Englewood Cliffs, N.J.: Prentice Hall, 1986); and Paul Aitken and Malcolm Higgs, *Developing Change Leaders* (Oxford, U.K.: Butterworth-Heinemann, 2009). See also Chapter 6 of this book.

14. See, for example, Etzioni, *Modern Organizations*, p. 44.

15. Robert Blauner, *Alienation and Freedom: The Factory Worker and His Industry* (Chicago: University of Chicago Press, 1964).

16. Douglas McGregor, *The Professional Manager* (New York: McGraw-Hill, 1967) and *The Human Side of Enterprise: Twenty-fifth Anniversary Printing* (New York: McGraw-Hill, 1985).

17. Chris Argyris, *Personality and Organization* (New York: Harper & Row, 1957), *Integrating the Individual and the Organization* (New Brunswick, N.J.: Transaction Publishers, 1990), and *Organizational Traps: Leadership, Culture, Organizational Design* (New York: Oxford University Press, 2010).

18. Frederick Herzberg, Bernard Mausner, and Barbara Synderman, *The Motivation to Work* (New York: Wiley, 1959); Herzberg, *Work and the Nature of Man* (Cleveland, Ohio: World, 1966); and Rensis Likert, *New Patterns of Management* (New York: McGraw-Hill, 1961).

19. See Abraham H. Maslow, Robert Frager, and James Fadiman, *Motivation and Personality*, 3rd ed. (New York: Harper Collins, 1987), pp. 35–58.

20. Robert Dubin, "Industrial Worker Worlds: A Study of the 'Central Life Interests' of Industrial Workers," *Social Problems*, 4 (May 1956): 136–40. See also Dubin's "Persons and Organization," in Robert Dubin, ed., *Human Relations in Administration, with Readings*, 4th ed. (Englewood Cliffs, N.J.: Prentice Hall, 1974).

21. H. Roy Kaplan and Curt Tausky, "Humanism in Organizations: A Critical Appraisal," *Public Administration Review*, 37 (March/April 1977): 171–80.

22. John M. Pfiffner and Frank P. Sherwood, *Administrative Organization* (Englewood Cliffs, N.J.: Prentice Hall, 1960).

23. Jay M. Shafritz and Philip H. Whitbeck, eds., *Classics of Organization Theory* (Oak Park, Ill.: Moore Publishing, 1978), Introduction to Part III, "The Systems Perspective," p. 119. See also Steven J. Ott, Sandra J. Parkes, and Richard B. Simpson, *Classic Readings in Organizational Behavior*, 3rd ed. (Belmont, Calif.: Wadsworth, 2003).

24. A basic source applying systems theory to the political process is David Easton, *A Framework for Political Analysis* (Chicago: University of Chicago Press, 1979); for a more recent description of general systems theory, see Jeffrey L. Whitten and Lonnie D. Bentley, *Systems Analysis and Design Methods*, 7th ed. (Boston, Mass.: McGraw-Hill Irwin, 2007).

25. This discussion draws on James D. Thompson, *Organizations in Action* (New York: McGraw-Hill, 1967), pp. 3–24.

26. Ibid.

27. Ibid., pp. 6–7.

28. Two other excellent sources in this area are Walter Buckley, *Sociology and Modern Systems Theory* (Englewood Cliffs, N.J.: Prentice Hall, 1967); and Daniel Katz and Robert L. Kahn, *The Social Psychology of Organizations*, 2nd ed. (New York: Wiley, 1978). See also Robert M. O'Brien, Michael Clarke, and Sheldon Kamieniecki, "Open and Closed Systems of Decision Making: The Case of Toxic Waste Management," *Public Administration Review*, 44 (July/August 1984): 334–40.

29. Donald F. Kettl, "Managing Boundaries in American Administration: The Collaboration Challenge," *Public Administration Review*, Special Issue, 66 (November/December 2006): 10–19.

30. See Stafford Beer, *Cybernetics and Management* (New York: Wiley, 1959); Karl Deutsch, *The Nerves of Government* (New York: Free Press, 1963); and Katz and Kahn, *The Social Psychology of Organizations*.

31. William G. Ouchi, *Theory Z—How American Business Can Meet the Japanese Challenge* (New York: Avon Books, 1982).

32. For example, see Ronald Contino and Robert M. Lorusso, "The Theory Z Turnaround of a Public Agency," *Public Administration Review*, 42 (January/February 1982): 66–72; David Carr and Ian Littman, *Excellence in Government: Total Quality Management in the 1990s* (Arlington, Va.: Coopers and Lybrand, 1990); Michael E. Milakovich, "Enhancing the Quality and Productivity of State and Local Government," *National Civic Review*, 79 (May/June 1990): 266–77; Milakovich, "Total Quality Management for Public Sector Productivity Improvement," *Public Productivity and Management Review*, 14 (Fall 1990): 19–32; Milakovich, "Total Quality Management in the Public Sector," *National Productivity Review*, 10 (Spring 1991): 195–215; Ronald J. Stupak, "Driving Forces for Quality Improvement in the 1990s," *The Public Manager: The New Bureaucrat*, 22 (Spring 1993): 32; Milakovich, "Leadership for Public Service Quality Management," *The Public Manager*, 22 (Fall 1993): 49–52; James Bowman, "At Last, an Alternative to Performance Appraisal: Total Quality Management," *Public Administration Review*, 54 (March/April 1994): 129–36; Richard J. Hackman and Ruth Wegman, "Total Quality Management: Empirical, Conceptual, and Practical Issues," *Administrative Science Quarterly*, 40/2 (1995): 420–34; J. W. Koehler and J. M. Pankowski, *Quality Government: Designing, Developing, and Implementing TQM* (Delray Beach, Fla.: St. Lucie Press, 1996); Russell Hellein and James Bowman, "The Process of Quality Management Implementation," *Public Performance and Management Review*, 26 (September 2002): 75–93; Michael E. Milakovich, *Improving Service Quality in the Global Economy* (Boca Raton, Fla.: Auerbach Publishers, 2006); and James R. Evans and William M. Lindsay, *Managing for Quality and Performance Excellence* (Mason, Ohio: Southwestern Cengage Learning, 2010).

33. James E. Swiss, "Adapting Total Quality Management (TQM) to Government," *Public Administration Review*, 52 (July/August 1992): 356–62.

34. Robert L. Dilworth, "Institutionalizing Learning Organizations in the Public Sector," *Public Productivity and Management Review*, 19 (June 1996): 407–21; Ake Gronlund, *Electronic Government: Design, Applications, and Management* (Hershey, Pa.: Idea Publishing Group, 2002); and John Renesch and

Sarita Chawla, *Learning Organizations: Developing Cultures for Tomorrow's Workplace* (New York: Productivity Press, 2006).

35. Peter M. Senge, *The Fifth Discipline: The Art and Practice of the Learning Organization* (New York: Doubleday, 2006); Peter M. Senge, Charlotte Roberts, Richard Ross, Bryan Smith, and Art Kleiner, *The Fifth Discipline Fieldbook* (New York: Currency Doubleday, 1994); and Peter Senge, Bryan Smith, Nina Kruschwitz Joe Laur, and Sara Schley, *The Necessary Revolution: Working Together to Create a Sustainable World* (New York: Crown Business, 2010).

36. Communication in small groups is treated in John F. Cragan and David W. Wright, *Communication in Small Group Discussion: An Integrative Approach*, 3rd ed. (St. Paul, Minn.: West, 1991). Sources on communication theory include David K. Berlo, *The Process of Communication* (New York: Holt, Rinehart & Winston, 1960); and Katz and Kahn, *The Social Psychology of Organizations*. Sources on communication in organizations include Gerald M. Goldhaber, *Organizational Communication*, 5th ed. (Dubuque, Iowa: Brown, 1990); and H. Wayland Cummings, Larry W. Long, and Michael L. Lewis, *Managing Communication in Organizations: An Introduction*, 2nd ed. (Dubuque, Iowa: Gorsuch Scarisbrick, 1987).

37. Among his other works, see Marshall McLuhan, *Understanding Media: The Extensions of Man* (New York: McGraw-Hill, 1964).

38. For further treatment of communication in administrative contexts, see James L. Garnett, *Communicating for Results in Government: A Strategic Approach for Public Managers* (San Francisco: Jossey-Bass, 1992); Herbert A. Simon, *Administrative Behavior: A Study of Decision-Making Processes in Administrative Organizations*, 4th ed. (New York: Free Press, 1997), chap. 8; and Sanjay K. Pandey and James L. Garnett, "Exploring Public Sector Communication Performance: Testing a Model and Drawing Conclusions," *Public Administration Review*, 66 (January–February 2006): 37–51.

39. For example, see Harold Seidman and Robert Gilmour, *Politics, Position, and Power: From the Positive to the Regulatory State*, 4th ed. (New York: Oxford University Press, 1986), chap. 10, especially p. 223; and J. D. Williams, *Public Administration: The People's Business* (Boston: Little, Brown, 1980), p. 226.

40. Seidman and Gilmour, *Politics, Position, and Power*, p. 223.

41. Williams, *Public Administration: The People's Business*, chap. 10, develops these themes more fully.

42. Bob Graham (with Jeff Nussbaum), *Intelligence Matters: The CIA, the FBI, Saudi Arabia, and the Failure of America's War on Terror* (New York: Random House, 2004); Richard A. Posner, *Preventing Surprise Attacks: Intelligence Reform in the Wake of 9/11* (Lanham, Md.: Rowman and Littlefield, in cooperation with the Hoover Institution, Stanford, Calif., 2005); and Mark Mazzetti, "C.I.A. Lays Out Errors It Made Before Sept. 11," *New York Times*, August 22, 2007.

43. See James L. Sundquist with the collaboration of David W. Davis, *Making Federalism Work: A Study of Program Coordination at the Community Level* (Washington, D.C.: Brookings Institution Press, 1969), p. 17. The original categorization was suggested by Charles Lindblom. See also Herbert Kaufman, "Organization Theory and Political Theory," *American Political Science Review*, 58 (March 1964): 5–14, at p. 7.

44. Sundquist, *Making Federalism Work*, p. 18.

45. For other perspectives on this topic, see Allen Schick, "The Coordination Option," in Peter Szanton, ed., *Federal Reorganization: What Have We Learned?* (Chatham, N.J.: Chatham House, 1981), pp. 85–113.

46. Leonard D. White, *Introduction to the Study of Public Administration*, 3rd ed. (New York: Macmillan, 1948), p. 30.

47. Allen W. Imershein, Larry Polivka, Sharon Gordon-Girvin, Richard Chackeriam, and Patricia Martin, "Service Networks in Florida: An Analysis of Administrative Decentralization and Its Effects on Service Delivery," *Public Administration Review*, 46 (March/April 1986): 161–69.

48. Paul Appleby, *Big Democracy* (New York: Knopf, 1945), p. 104.

49. For implications of these changes in the global economy, see Thomas Friedman, *The World Is Flat: A Brief History of the Twentieth Century* (New York: Farrar, Straus, and Giroux, 2005).

50. See Frederick C. Thayer, *An End to Hierarchy and Competition: Administration in the Post-Affluent World*, 2nd ed. (New York: Franklin Watts/New Viewpoints, 1980).

51. Warren G. Bennis and Philip E. Slater, *The Temporary Society* (New York: Harper & Row, 1998), p. 56.

52. Ibid.

53. Michael E. Milakovich, *Improving Service Quality in the Global Economy: Achieving High Performance*

in the Public and Private Sectors (Boca Raton, Fla.: Auerbach Publishers, 2006); Victor Mayer-Schonberger and David Lazer, *Governance and Information Technology: From Electronic Government to Information Government* (Cambridge, Mass.: MIT Press, 2007); and Vincent Homberg, *Understanding E-Government: Information Systems in Public Administration* (London: Routledge Taylor and Francis Group, 2008).

54. Thompson, *Organizations in Action*, pp. 8–9; March and Simon, *Organizations*; Richard M. Cyert and James G. March, *A Behavioral Theory of the Firm* (Englewood Cliffs, N.J.: Prentice Hall, 1963); and Simon, *Administrative Behavior*.

55. See, among others, Brian R. Fry and Jos C. N. Raadschelders, *Mastering Public Administration: From Max Weber to Dwight Waldo*, 2nd ed. (Washington, D.C.: CQ Press, 2008). For an insightful analysis of problems with bureaucratic responsiveness, see Donald F. Kettl, *System Under Stress: Homeland Security and American Politics*, 2nd ed. (Washington, D.C.: CQ Press, 2007), especially chap. 3.

Chapter 5: Decision Making in Administration

1. Herbert A. Simon, "Administrative Decision Making," *Public Administration Review*, 25 (March 1965): 31–37, at pp. 35–36.

2. An extensive literature has grown up in the area of decision making, including William J. Gore, *Administrative Decision Making: A Heuristic Model* (New York: Wiley, 1964); William J. Gore and J. W. Dyson, *The Making of Decisions* (New York: Free Press, 1964); Charles E. Lindblom, "The Science of 'Muddling Through,' " *Public Administration Review*, 19 (Spring 1959): 79–88; David Braybrooke and Charles E. Lindblom, *A Strategy of Decision*, New Ed ed. (New York: Free Press, 1970); Allan W. Lerner, *The Politics of Decision Making: Strategy, Cooperation and Conflict* (Beverly Hills, Calif.: Sage, 1976); Stephen Worchel, Wendy Wood, and Jeffry A. Simpson, eds., *Group Process and Productivity* (Newbury Park, Calif.: Sage, 1991); Herbert A. Simon, Robin L. Marris, and Massimo Egidi, *Economics, Bounded Rationality, and the Cognitive Revolution* (Brookfield, Vt.: Elgar Publishing, 1992); Young B. Choi, *Paradigms and Conventions: Uncertainty, Decision Making, and Entrepreneurship* (Ann Arbor: University of Michigan Press, 1993); Herbert A. Simon, *Administrative Behavior: A Study of Decision-Making Processes in Administrative Organizations*, 4th ed. (New York: Free Press, 1997); and Jacqueline

Vaughn and Eric Otenyo, *Managerial Discretion in Government Decision Making* (Boston: Jones and Bartlett, 2007).

3. Anthony Downs, *An Economic Theory of Democracy* (New York: Harper & Row, 1957), p. 4.

4. Ibid., pp. 4–5 (emphasis and parentheses added).

5. Lindblom, "The Science of 'Muddling Through,' " p. 81.

6. This discussion relies on Lindblom, "The Science of 'Muddling Through' "; Anthony Downs, *Inside Bureaucracy* (Boston: Little, Brown, 1967; reprint ed., Prospect Heights, Ill.: Waveland Press, 1994); and Aaron Wildavsky, *The Politics of the Budgetary Process*, 4th ed. (Boston: Little, Brown, 1984). See also Robert A. Heineman, William T. Bluhm, Steven A. Peterson, and Edward N. Kearny, *The World of the Policy Analyst: Rationality, Values and Politics*, 3rd ed. (Chatham, N.J.: Chatham House, 2002), esp. chap. 2.

7. The reference is to "The Science of 'Muddling Through.' " See also Lindblom's *The Intelligence of Democracy* (New York: Free Press, 1965), *The Policy-Making Process* (Englewood Cliffs, N.J.: Prentice Hall, 1968), *Politics and Markets* (New York: Basic Books, 1977), and "Still Muddling, Not Yet Through," *Public Administration Review*, 39 (November/December 1979): 517–26.

8. Simon, "Administrative Decision Making," p. 33.

9. Yehezkel Dror, "Muddling Through—'Science' or Inertia," in "Governmental Decision Making" (a symposium), *Public Administration Review*, 24 (September 1964): 153–57.

10. Amitai Etzioni, "Mixed Scanning: A 'Third' Approach to Decision Making," *Public Administration Review*, 27 (December 1967): 385–92.

11. Ibid., pp. 389–90 (emphasis added).

12. Lindblom, "Still Muddling, Not Yet Through," p. 517 (emphasis added).

13. For a thoughtful statement in defense of incrementalism in the planning process, see Sam Pearsall, "Multi-Agency Planning for Natural Areas in Tennessee," *Public Administration Review*, 44 (January/February 1984): 43–48. Etzioni has called for a reassessment of classical/economic rationality itself in his penetrating work *The Moral Dimension: Toward a New Economics* (New York: Free Press, 1990). See also Mary Zey, ed., *Decision Making: Alternatives to Rational Choice Models* (Newbury Park, Calif.: Sage, 1992).

14. Simon, "Administrative Decision Making," p. 31.

15. The work of Herbert A. Simon, including his research on economics and management, is accessible

at http://www.psy.cmu.edu/psy/faculty/hsimon/hsimon.html.

16. James Risen, *State of War: The Secret History of the CIA and the Bush Administration* (New York: Simon and Schuster, 2006); James Thurber, *Rivals for Power: Presidential-Congressional Relations* (Lanham, Md.: Rowman and Littlefield, 2006); and Scott McClellan, *What Happened: Inside the Bush White House and the Culture of Deception* (New York: Public Affairs Books, 2008).

17. For example, see James N. Danzinger, William H. Dutton, Rob Kling, and Kenneth L. Kraemer, *Computers and Politics: High Technology in American Local Governments* (New York: Columbia University Press, 1982); Kenneth L. Kraemer and James N. Danzinger, "Computers and Control in the Work Environment," *Public Administration Review*, 44 (January/February 1984): 32–42; and Stuart S. Nagel, *Decision-Aiding Software: Skills, Obstacles, and Applications* (New York: St. Martin's Press, 1991).

18. An outstanding analysis of the problem of obtaining reliability in organizational communications can be found in Martin Landau's "Redundancy, Rationality, and the Problem of Duplication and Overlap," *Public Administration Review*, 29 (July/August 1969): 346–58. The argument that multiple channels of communication can increase the accuracy of messages going to the same receiver has been made by Downs, *Inside Bureaucracy*, chap. 10. Arthur Schlesinger and Richard Neustadt have described persuasively how various American presidents have made use of multiple channels. See Schlesinger's "Roosevelt as Chief Administrator," in Francis E. Rourke, ed., *Bureaucratic Power in National Politics*, 3rd ed. (Boston: Little, Brown, 1978), pp. 257–69, especially pp. 259–63; and Neustadt's *Presidential Power and the Modern Presidents* (New York: Free Press, 1991), chap. 7.

19. Irving L. Janis, *Groupthink*, 2nd ed. (Boston: Houghton Mifflin, 1982), pp. 9, 257. In grappling with similar problems of "in-group" advice, public managers at all levels frequently solicit the opinions of outside advisors. Although this course of action is often useful, it has its own pitfalls. See Howell S. Baum, "The Advisor as Invited Intruder," *Public Administration Review*, 42 (November/December 1982): 546–52.

20. See Downs, *Inside Bureaucracy*, chap. 14.

21. See Simon, *Administrative Behavior*, chaps. 2, 5, and 11; James D. Thompson, *Organizations in Action* (New York: McGraw-Hill, 1967), p. 9; John Forester, "Bounded Rationality and the Politics of

Muddling Through," *Public Administration Review*, 44 (January/February 1984): 23–31.

22. Lawrence B. Mohr, "The Concept of Organizational Goal," *American Political Science Review*, 67 (June 1973): 470–81, at p. 474.

23. See Arnold Meltsner, *Policy Analysts in the Bureaucracy* (Berkeley: University of California Press, 1976).

24. See Downs, *Inside Bureaucracy*, chap. 8.

25. Ibid., p. 88.

26. Meltsner, *Policy Analysts in the Bureaucracy*.

27. F. J. Roethlisberger and William J. Dickson, *Management and the Worker* (Cambridge, Mass.: Harvard University Press, 1939); and John M. Pfiffner and Frank P. Sherwood, *Administrative Organization* (Englewood Cliffs, N.J.: Prentice Hall, 1960).

28. For example, see Alexander George, "The Case for Multiple Advocacy in Making Foreign Policy," *American Political Science Review*, 66 (December 1972): 751–95.

29. Stephen K. Bailey, "Ethics and the Public Service," in Roscoe C. Martin, ed., *Public Administration and Democracy* (Syracuse, N.Y.: Syracuse University Press, 1965), p. 293.

30. See Carl J. Friedrich, "Public Policy and the Nature of Administrative Responsibility," *Public Policy*, 1 (1940): 3–24; and Herman Finer, "Administrative Responsibility and Democratic Government," *Public Administration Review*, 1 (Summer 1941): 335–50.

31. Finer, "Administrative Responsibility and Democratic Government," p. 335 (emphasis added).

32. Ibid., p. 337.

33. DeWitt C. Armstrong III and George A. Graham, "Ethical Preparation for the Public Service," *The Bureaucrat*, 4 (April 1975): 6–23, at p. 6 (emphasis added).

34. Cited by Joseph A. Califano Jr., "Richard Nixon: The Resignation Option," *The Bureaucrat*, 2 (Summer 1973): 222–31, at p. 225.

35. Ibid., p. 226 (emphasis added).

36. Sources on administrative corruption include *Fraud in Government Programs: How Extensive Is It? Can It Be Controlled? A Report to the Congress of the United States by the Comptroller General*, General Accounting Office Report No. AFMD-82-3 (Washington, D.C.: U.S. Government Printing Office, November 6, 1981); Simcha B. Werner, "New Directions in the Study of Administrative Corruption," *Public Administration Review*, 43 (March/April 1983): 146–54; James S. Larson, "Fraud in Government Programs: A Secondary Analysis," *Public Administration Quarterly*, 7 (Fall 1983): 274–93; and

Michael Johnston, *Civil Society and Corruption: Mobilizing for Reform* (Lanham, Md.: University Press of America, 2005).

37. For further discussion of ethics in public administration, see Joel L. Fleishman, Lance Liebman, and Mark H. Moore, eds., *Public Duties: The Moral Obligations of Government Officials* (Cambridge, Mass.: Harvard University Press, 1981); Ralph Clark Chandler, "The Problem of Moral Reasoning in American Public Administration: The Case for a Code of Ethics," *Public Administration Review*, 43 (January/February 1983): 32–39; Louis C. Gawthrop, *Public Sector Management, Systems, and Ethics* (Bloomington: Indiana University Press, 1984); York Willbern, "Types and Levels of Public Morality," *Public Administration Review*, 44 (March/April 1984): 102–8; Dennis F. Thompson, "The Possibility of Administrative Ethics," *Public Administration Review*, 45 (September/October 1985): 555–61; John A. Rohr, *Ethics for Bureaucrats: An Essay on Law and Values*, 2nd ed., revised and expanded (London: Routledge, 1989); Mark Moore and Malcolm Sparrow, *Ethics in Government: The Moral Challenge of Public Leadership* (Englewood Cliffs, N.J.: Prentice Hall, 1990); Sheldon S. Steinberg and David T. Austern, *Government, Ethics, and Managers: A Guide to Solving Ethical Dilemmas in the Public Sector* (Westport, Conn.: Praeger, 1990); William M. Timmins, *A Casebook of Public Ethics and Issues* (Monterey, Calif.: Brooks/Cole, 1990); Harold F. Gortner, *Ethics for Public Managers* (Westport, Conn.: Praeger, 1991); W. J. Michael Cody and Richardson R. Lynn, *Honest Government: An Ethics Guide for Public Service* (Westport, Conn.: Praeger, 1992); Jonathan P. West, Evan Berman, and Anita Cava, "Ethics in the Municipal Workplace," in *Municipal Yearbook 1994* (Washington, D.C.: International City/County Management Association, 1994), pp. 3–16; Evan M. Berman and Jonathan P. West, "Values Management in Local Government: A Survey of Progress and Future Directions," *Review of Public Personnel Administration*, 14 (Winter 1994): 6–23; James S. Bowman, ed., *Ethical Frontiers in Public Management: Seeking New Strategies for Resolving Ethical Dilemmas* (San Francisco: Jossey-Bass, 1994); Terry L. Cooper, *The Responsible Administrator: An Approach to Ethics for the Administrative Role*, 4th ed. (San Francisco: Jossey-Bass, 1998); Melvin J. Dubnick, "Accountability and Ethics: Reconsidering the Relationships," in *Encyclopedia of Public Administration and Policy* (Milwaukee, Wis.: Marcel Dekker, 2003); Donald C. Menzel, *Ethics Management for Public Administrators: Building Organizations of Integrity* (New York: M.E. Sharpe, 2007); and Raymond W. Cox III, *Ethics and Integrity in Public Administration* (New York: M.E. Sharpe, 2009).

38. Many professional organizations such as the American Political Science Association (APSA) (http://www.apsanet.org/), the world's largest organization devoted to the study of politics; the Center for the Advancement of Applied Ethics at Carnegie Mellon University (http://www.caae.phil.cmu.edu/caae/); the Center for Public Integrity (http://www.publicintegrity.org/), a nonpartisan, nonprofit organization based in Washington, D.C.; and the Center for the Study of Ethics in the Professions (http://www.iit.edu/departments/csep/) at the Illinois Institute of Technology are among the many professional, research and development organizations that examine public service and ethics-related issues and focus on teaching people practical methods for analyzing and responding to real ethical problems.

39. This discussion relies primarily on Jonathan P. West, Evan Berman, and Anita Cava, "Ethics in the Municipal Workplace," in *The Municipal Yearbook 1993* (Washington, D.C.: International City/County Management Association, 1993), pp. 3–16; Berman and West, "Values Management in Local Government"; Steinberg and Austern, *Government, Ethics and Managers*; Gortner, *Ethics for Public Managers*; and Cody and Lynn, *Honest Government*. See also James H. Svara, *The Ethics Primer for Public Administrators in Government and Non-Profit Organizations* (Boston: Jones and Bartlett, 2006).

40. The responsibility for enforcing ethics is shared by all public agencies and overseen by the U.S. Office of Government Ethics (OGE), an executive agency responsible for directing policies to prevent conflicts of interest on the part of the federal executive branch officers and employees. (More details at http://www.osoge.gov/home.html.)

41. Aaron Wildavsky, *The Politics of the Budgetary Process*, 2nd ed. (Boston: Little, Brown, 1974), pp. 189–94, outlined concisely the nature of political rationality.

42. Ibid., p. 192 (emphasis added).

43. Wildavsky (ibid., p. 190) made a similar point with regard to advocates of budgetary reform in the national government.

44. Landau, "Redundancy, Rationality, and the Problem of Duplication and Overlap," especially pp. 350–53.

45. Ibid., pp. 349–50. For an appraisal of the potential benefits of redundancy in public organizations, see Jonathan B. Bendor, *Parallel Systems: Redundancy in Government* (Berkeley: University of California Press, 1985).

46. See Michael D. Cohen, James G. March, and Johan P. Olsen, "People, Problems, Solutions, and the Ambiguity of Relevance," in James G. March and Johan P. Olsen, eds., *Ambiguity and Choice in Organizations* (Bergen, Norway: Universitetsforlaget, 1976), pp. 24–37. The passage cited appears in the preface to the volume, at p. 8.

Chapter 6: Chief Executives and the Challenges of Administrative Leadership

1. See, among others, Dennis D. Riley, *Controlling the Federal Bureaucracy* (Philadelphia, Pa.: Temple University Press, 1987); Edward Paul Fuchs, *Presidents, Management, and Regulation* (Englewood Cliffs, N.J.: Prentice Hall, 1988); Donald F. Kettl, *Government by Proxy: (Mis?)Managing Federal Programs* (Washington, D.C.: CQ Press, 1988); John J. DiIulio, Gerald Garvey, and Donald F. Kettl, *Improving Government Performance: An Owner's Manual* (Washington, D.C.: Brookings Institution Press, 1993); Bernard Rosen, *Holding Government Bureaucracies Accountable*, 3rd ed. (Westport, Conn.: Greenwood Press, 1998); Louis Fisher, *The Politics of Shared Power: Congress and the Executive*, 4th ed. (College Station: Texas A&M University Press, 1998); Robert Behn, *Rethinking Democratic Accountability* (Washington, D.C.: Brookings Institution Press, 2001); Donald R. Kettl, *The Next Government of the United States: Why Our Institutions Fail Us and How to Fix Them* (New York: W. W. Norton, 2008); and Craig E. Johnson, *Meeting the Ethical Challenges of Leadership: Casting Light or Shadow* (Thousand Oaks, Calif.: Sage, 2008).

2. For an enlightening study of the Long years, see T. Harry Williams, *Huey Long* (New York: Knopf, 1969). Five useful, and contrasting, studies of Chicago's Mayor Daley are Mike Royko, *Boss: Richard J. Daley of Chicago* (New York: Dutton, 1971); Len O'Connor, *Clout: Mayor Daley and His City* (Chicago: Henry Regnery, 1975); Milton Rakove, *Don't Make No Waves … Don't Back No Losers: An Insider's Analysis of the Daley Machine* (Bloomington: Indiana University Press, 1975); Milton Rakove, *We Don't Want Nobody Nobody Sent* (Bloomington: Indiana University Press, 1979); and Adam Cohen, *American Pharaoh* (Boston: Little, Brown, 2001). Political developments in Chicago after Daley's death in 1976 are examined in Samuel K. Gove and Louis H. Masotti, eds., *After Daley: Chicago Politics in Transition* (Urbana: University of Illinois Press, 1982).

3. See Thad L. Beyle and J. Oliver Williams, eds., *The American Governor in Behavioral Perspective* (New York: Harper & Row, 1972); Larry Sabato, *Goodbye to Good-Time Charlie: The American Governorship Transformed*, 2nd ed. (Washington, D.C.: CQ Press, 1983); Thad L. Beyle, ed., *Governors and Hard Times* (Washington, D.C.: CQ Press, 1992); Thad L. Beyle, *State and Local Government: 2003–2004* (Washington, D.C.: CQ Press, 2003); Thad L. Beyle, "The Governors," in Virginia Gray and Russell L. Hanson, eds., *Politics in the American States: A Comparative Analysis*, 8th ed. (Washington, D.C.: CQ Press, 2004), pp. 194–231; and David L. Leal, *Electing America's Governors: The Politics of Executive Elections* (London, UK: Palgrave Macmillian, 2006).

4. See Richard E. Neustadt, *Presidential Power and the Modern Presidents* (New York: Free Press, 1991).

5. Douglas Fox, *The Politics of City and State Bureaucracy* (Pacific Palisades, Calif.: Goodyear Publishing, 1974), p. 25.

6. See, among others, Peggy Heilig and Roger J. Mundt, *Your Voice at City Hall: Politics, Procedures, and Policies of District Representation* (Albany: State University of New York Press, 1984); Glenn Abney and Thomas Lauth, *The Politics of State and City Administration* (Albany: State University of New York Press, 1986); Robert W. Kweit and Mary Grisez Kweit, *People and Politics in Urban America* (Pacific Grove, Calif.: Brooks/Cole, 1990); Kim Hill and Kenneth Mladenka, *Democratic Governance in American States and Cities* (Pacific Grove, Calif.: Brooks/Cole, 1992); John J. Harrigan and Ronald K. Vogel, *Political Change in the Metropolis*, 6th ed. (New York: Addison Wesley Longman, 2000); Dennis R. Judd and Todd Swanstrom, *City Politics: The Political Economy of Urban America*, 7th ed. (New York: Pearson Longman, 2009); Ann O'M. Bowman and Richard C. Kearney, *State and Local Government*, 8th ed. (Boston: Wadsworth: Cengage Learning, 2010); and Kevin B. Smith, *State and Local Government, 2010–2011* (Washington, D.C.: CQ Press, 2010). An interesting perspective on foundations of power for urban mayors is found in J. Phillip Thompson, "Seeking Effective Power: Why Mayors Need Community Organizations," *Perspectives on Politics*, 3 (June 2005): 301–8.

7. Studies of presidential leadership, in particular, that deal with the interrelationships among these

and other arenas include Thomas E. Cronin, *The State of the Presidency* (New York: Scott, Foresman and Co., 1980); Frank Kessler, *The Dilemmas of Presidential Leadership: Of Caretakers and Kings* (Englewood Cliffs, N.J.: Prentice Hall, 1982); Bert A. Rockman and Richard W. Waterman, eds., *Presidential Leadership: The Vortex of Power* (New York: Oxford University Press, 2008); Thomas E. Cronin and Michael A. Genovese, *The Paradoxes of the Modern Presidency* (New York: Oxford University Press, 2009); George Edwards III and Stephen J. Wayne, *Presidential Leadership: Politics and Policy Making*, 8th ed. (Belmont, Calif.: Wadsworth, 2009); and Nick Ragone, *Presidential Leadership: 15 Decisions That Shaped the Nation* (New York: Prometheus Books, 2011).

8. For example, see Glenn Abney and Thomas P. Lauth, "The Governor as Chief Administrator," *Public Administration Review*, 43 (January/February 1983): 40–49. For an overview of one management strategy used by many governors, see Alan Greenblatt, "A Rage to Reorganize," *Governing*, 18 (March 2005): 30–35.

9. William Langewiesche, "American Ground: Unbuilding the World Trade Center," in Richard J. Stillman II, ed., *Public Administration: Concepts and Cases*, 9th ed. (Boston: Houghton Mifflin, 2010), pp. 168–78.

10. For agency-specific details, see articles in "Special Issue on Administrative Failure in the Wake of Hurricane Katrina," *Public Administration* Review, 67 (November/December 2007). (For more information on the reorganized FEMA, see http://www.fema.gov.)

11. For details on government response to disasters, see Saundra K. Schneider, "Government Response to Disaster: The Conflict between Bureaucratic Procedures and Emergent Norms," *Public Administration Review*, 53 (March/April 1992): 135–45; Steven Cohen, William Eimicke, and Jessica Horan, "Catastrophe and the Public Sector: A Case Study of the Government Response to the Destruction of the World Trade Center," *Public Administration Review*, 62 (September 2002): 33–44; Saundra K. Schneider, "Administrative Breakdowns in the Governmental Response to Hurricane Katrina," *Public Administration Review*, 65 (September/October 2005): 515–16; Jonathan Walters and Donald Kettl, "The Katrina Breakdown: Coordination and Communication Problems between Levels of Government Must Be Addressed before the Next Disaster Strikes," *Governing*, 19 (December 2005):

20–25; and Christopher Swope and Zach Patton, "In Disaster's Wake," *Governing*, 19 (December 2005): 48–58. For a commentary on some of the difficulties faced by emergency officials (written *before* Hurricanes Katrina and Rita struck the Gulf Coast), see Ellen Perlman, "Hurricane Hubris: Evacuating Residents from the Path of a Storm Is Often a Frustrating Task for Emergency Officials," *Governing*, 18 (June 2005): 68; and *Deep Water: The Gulf Oil Disaster and the Future of Offshore Drilling* (Washington, D.C.: Report of the National Commission on the BP Deepwater Horizon Oil Spill and Offshore Drilling, 2011).

12. See Fisher, *The Politics of Shared Power*, especially chap. 6; Donald Axelrod, *Budgeting for Modern Government*, 2nd ed. (New York: St. Martin's Press, 1995); John Cranford, *Budgeting for America*, 2nd ed. (Washington, D.C.: CQ Press, 1989); Howard E. Shuman, *Politics and the Budget: The Struggle between the President and the Congress*, 3rd ed. (Englewood Cliffs, N.J.: Prentice Hall, 1992); Aaron Wildavsky and Naomi Caiden, *New Politics of the Budgetary Process*, 5th ed. (New York: Longman, 2004), chap. 10; Irene S. Rubin, *The Politics of Public Budgeting: Getting and Spending, Borrowing and Balancing* (Washington, D.C.: CQ Press, 2009); and James J. Gosling, *Budgetary Politics in American Governments* (New York: Routledge, 2009).

13. See the discussion of this office in Fuchs, *Presidents, Management, and Regulation*, chap. 4.

14. Carl W. Stenberg, "States under the Spotlight: An Intergovernmental View," *Public Administration Review*, 45 (March/April 1985): 319–26, at p. 321.

15. See, among others, Duane Lockard, ed., "A Mini-Symposium: The Strong Governorship: Status and Problems," *Public Administration Review*, 36 (January/February 1976): 90–98, at p. 96; Coleman Ransone, *The American Governorship* (Westport, Conn.: Greenwood Press, 1982); Beyle, "The Governors"; and Beyle, *Governors and Hard Times*.

16. Terry Sanford, *Storm over the States* (New York: McGraw-Hill, 1967), p. 30.

17. Some question has been raised as to whether the item veto effectively enables a governor to restrain the growth of state budgetary expenditures. See David C. Nice, "The Item Veto and Expenditure Restraint," *Journal of Politics*, 50 (May 1988): 487–99. See also Fisher, *The Politics of Shared Power*, pp. 209–14; "A Bush Line-Item Veto?" *Congressional Quarterly Weekly Report*, 47 (October 28, 1989): 2848; and Glenn Abney and Thomas P. Lauth, "Gubernatorial Use of the Item Veto for Narrative

Deletion," *Public Administration Review*, 62 (July/August 2002): 492–503.

18. There is an extensive literature on the decision-making powers of mayors and city managers. See David N. Ammons and Charldean Newell, *City Executives: Leadership Roles, Work Characteristics, and Time Management* (Albany: State University of New York Press, 1989); H. George Frederickson, *Ideal and Practice* (Washington, D.C.: International City and County Management Press, 1989); Richard J. Stillman II, *Preface to Public Administration: A Search for Themes and Direction* (New York: St. Martin's Press, 1991); and James H. Svara and Douglas J. Watson, *More Than Mayor or Manager: Campaigns to Change Form of Government in America's Large Cities* (Washington, D.C.: Georgetown University Press, 2010).

19. Harold Seidman and Robert Gilmour, *Politics, Position, and Power: From the Positive to the Regulatory State*, 4th ed. (New York: Oxford University Press, 1986), p. 104.

20. Ibid., p. 86 (emphasis added). See also p. 228.

21. See Hugh Heclo, *A Government of Strangers: Executive Politics in Washington* (Washington, D.C.: Brookings Institution Press, 1977). See also Robert Maranto, *Beyond a Government of Strangers: How Career Executives and Political Appointees Can Turn Conflict into Cooperation* (Lanham, Md.: Lexington Books, 2005).

22. This generalization held true for the period 1960–1972; see Heclo, *A Government of Strangers*, pp. 103–4.

23. Ibid.

24. Ibid., pp. 144, 148 (emphasis added).

25. See Cronin, *The State of the Presidency*, chap. 7.

26. This treatment of the Reagan management strategy is taken from Richard P. Nathan, *The Administrative Presidency* (New York: Wiley, 1983), chaps 6 and 7.

27. Ibid., p. 69 (emphasis added).

28. See President's Special Review Board, *Tower Commission Report* (New York: Bantam Books and Times Books, 1987).

29. Other policy "ailments" that have been the subject of reorganizational "cures" are noted in Seidman and Gilmour, *Politics, Position, and Power*, p. 4.

30. Herbert Kaufman, "Reflections on Administrative Reorganization," in Joseph A. Pechman, ed., *Setting National Priorities: The 1978 Budget* (Washington, D.C.: Brookings Institution Press, 1977), pp. 391–418, at p. 392. This discussion relies extensively on Kaufman's treatment.

31. Ibid., pp. 392–94.

32. Ibid., p. 402. For further discussion of executive reorganization, see Peter Szanton, ed., *Federal Reorganization: What Have We Learned?* (Chatham, N.J.: Chatham House, 1981), especially Lester M. Salamon, "The Question of Goals," pp. 58–84; I. M. Destler, "Reorganization: When and How?" pp. 114–30; and Destler, "Implementing Reorganization," pp. 155–70; Walter F. Baber, "Reform for Principle and Profit," *The Bureaucrat*, 13 (Summer 1984): 33–37; and William W. Newman, "Reorganizing for National Security and Homeland Security," *Public Administration Review*, 62 (September 2002): 126–38.

33. Remarks by the President in the 2011 State of the Union Address, retrieved at http://www.whitehouse.gov/the-press-office/2011/01/25/remarks-president-state-union-address.

34. John C. Donovan, *The Policy Makers* (New York: Pegasus, 1970), p. 48; Margaret Jane Wyszomirski, "The De-Institutionalization of Presidential Staff Agencies," *Public Administration Review*, 42 (September/October 1982): 448–58; and John Hart, *The Presidential Branch* (Elmsford, N.Y.: Pergamon Press, 1987).

35. Arthur Schlesinger Jr., *The Coming of the New Deal* (Boston: Houghton Mifflin, 1958), especially pp. 521–29, 533–37.

36. Despite the compromises and continuing controversy, an Associated Press (AP) poll on May 23, 2011, found that 54% of all Americans approved of Obama's handing of health care issues. Fully 60% also felt that neither Medicare nor Social Security should be cut to balance the federal budget. Retrieved at http://www.cbsnews.com/stories/2011/05/23/ap/congress/main20065404.shtml. For recent health care information from the Obama administration, see http://www.whitehouse.gov/healthreform.

37. See Anthony Downs, *Inside Bureaucracy* (Boston: Little, Brown, 1967; reprint ed., Prospect Heights, Ill.: Waveland Press, 1994), pp. 116–18.

38. Ibid., pp. 118–26.

39. Graham Allison, *Essence of Decision: Explaining the Cuban Missile Crisis* (Boston: Little, Brown, 1971), pp. 122–23; Richard M. Pious, "The Cuban Missile Crisis and the Limits of Crisis Management," *Political Science Quarterly*, 106, pp. 81–106; and D. A. Welch, "Crisis Decision Making Reconsidered," *Journal of Conflict Resolution*, 33(3) (1989): 430–45.

40. James Risen, *State of War: The Secret History of the CIA and the Bush Administration* (New York:

Simon and Schuster, 2006), pp. 142–43. See also Richard C. Clarke, *Against All Enemies: Inside America's War on Terror—What Really Happened* (New York: Free Press, 2004); Scott McClellan, *What Happened: Inside the Bush White House and the Culture of Deception* (New York: Public Affairs Books, 2008); and two U.S. Senate Intelligence Committee Reports on the accuracy of pre- and post-Iraq war intelligence findings, released June 5, 2008, and accessible at http://intelligence. senate.gov/.

41. These include the Academy of Management, a professional society primarily composed of professors who teach and research management (http://www. aomonline.org); the Association for Quality and Participation (AQP), an international nonprofit membership association dedicated to improving workplaces through quality and participation practices (http://www.aqp.org); the Center for Creative Leadership, located in Greensboro, North Carolina, one of the largest institutions in the world focusing solely on leadership (http://www.ccl. org/); the Center for Management Development at Wichita State University, which offers more than a hundred public seminars on topics ranging from leadership, quality improvement, team building, and communications to human resources and financial management (http://www.cmd.wichita. edu/); and the Council for Excellence in Government, located in Washington, D.C. (http://www. excelgov.org/).

42. See Fred E. Fiedler, *Leader Attitudes and Group Effectiveness* (Urbana: University of Illinois Press, 1958; reprint ed., Westport, Conn.: Greenwood Press, 1981); Fred E. Fiedler, *A Theory of Leadership Effectiveness* (New York: McGraw-Hill, 1967); Fred E. Fiedler and Martin Chemers, *Leadership and Effective Management* (Glenview, Ill.: Scott, Foresman, 1974); Stogdill, *Handbook of Leadership*; Robert C. Tucker, *Politics as Leadership* (Columbia and London: University of Missouri Press, 1981); Philip Selznick, *Leadership in Administration: A Sociological Interpretation* (Berkeley: University of California Press, 1984); Robert H. Guest, Paul Hersey, and Kenneth H. Blanchard, *Organizational Change through Effective Leadership*, 2nd ed. (Englewood Cliffs, N.J.: Prentice Hall, 1986); Peter B. Smith and Mark F. Peterson, *Leadership, Organizations, and Culture* (Newbury Park, Calif.: Sage, 1988); William G. Scott and Terence R. Mitchell, "The Universal Barnard: His Meta-Concepts of Leadership in the Administrative State," *Public Administration Quarterly*,

13 (Fall 1989): 295–320; Warren Bennis, *Why Leaders Can't Lead: The Unconscious Conspiracy Continues* (San Francisco: Jossey-Bass, 1989); Francis E. Rourke, "Responsiveness and Neutral Competence in American Bureaucracy," *Public Administration Review*, 52 (November/December 1992): 539–46; Peter Block, *Stewardship: Choosing Service over Self-Interest* (San Francisco: Berrett-Koehler, 1993); Owen B. Rounds, *Giuliani and Leadership: Executive Lessons from America's Mayor* (New York: Crown Publishing, 2003); James MacGregor Burns, *Transforming Leadership: The Pursuit of Happiness* (New York: Grove/Atlantic, 2003); James M. Kouzes and Barry Z. Posner, *The Leadership Challenge*, 4th ed. (New York: Jossey-Bass, 2008); Warren Bennis, *On Becoming a Leader*, 4th ed. (New York: Basic Books, 2009); and James M. Kouzes and Barry Z. Posner, *The Truth about Leadership Challenge: How to Get Extraordinary Things Done in Organizations*, 3rd ed. (New York: Jossey-Bass, 2010).

43. Fiedler discusses varieties of work situations as they relate to leadership in *A Theory of Leadership Effectiveness*; see especially chap. 7.

44. James D. Thompson, *Organizations in Action* (New York: McGraw-Hill, 1967), p. 10. This discussion relies on Thompson's treatment of the Parsons formulation; see also Talcott Parsons, *Structure and Process in Modern Societies* (New York: Free Press, 1960).

45. Ibid.

46. Ibid. (emphasis added).

47. Mary Parker Follett, "The Giving of Orders," in Jay M. Shafritz and Albert C. Hyde, eds., *Classics of Public Administration*, 3rd ed. (Pacific Grove, Calif.: Brooks/Cole, 1992), pp. 66–74; reprinted from Henry C. Metcalf, ed., *Scientific Foundations of Business Administration* (Baltimore: Williams & Wilkins, 1926).

48. Ibid., p. 67.

49. Fred E. Fiedler, "Style or Circumstance: The Leadership Enigma," *Psychology Today*, 2 (March 1969): 39–43.

50. Wilfred H. Drath, "Changing Our Minds about Leadership," *Issues & Observations*, 16(1) (1996): 1–4.

51. For example, see Harry Levinson, "Criteria for Choosing Chief Executives," *Harvard Business Review*, 58 (July/August 1980): 113.

52. For example, see Stogdill, *Handbook of Leadership*, and the discussion of authoritarian leadership style in the Iowa experiment, in Ralph White and Ronald Lippitt, "Leader Behavior and Member Reaction in Three 'Social Climates,'" in Dorwin

Cartwright and Alvin Zander, eds., *Group Dynamics: Research and Theory*, 3rd ed. (New York: Harper & Row, 1968), pp. 527–53.

53. The Society for the Advancement of Management (http://www.cob.tamucc.edu/sam/) sought to discover what workers in private companies felt was the single most positive feature in the behavior of their immediate supervisors. The most common response was that the supervisor had *encouraged* the employee in work performance. Because there is other evidence suggesting that the interaction between employees and their first-line supervisors is vital to group performance, morale, and individual job satisfaction, a positive, supportive attitude toward employees on the part of the supervisor takes on added importance.

54. For a case study of the importance of bureaucratic routines, see Allison, *Essence of Decision*. Consideration is given to problems of innovation in, among others, Warren G. Bennis, ed., *American Bureaucracy* (New Brunswick, N.J.: Transaction Books, 1970), pp. 111–87, especially pp. 135–64; and Guest et al., *Organizational Change through Effective Leadership*. It should be noted that leadership can just as easily resist innovation desired by members as the other way around. Under the circumstance of leaders resisting innovation sought by followers, the task of "leader as director" will be considerably frustrated as leadership and followership goals grow further apart.

55. See, among others, Peter F. Drucker, *Management: Tasks, Responsibilities, Practices* (New York: Harper & Row, 1974), chap. 38.

56. See Stogdill, *Handbook of Leadership*, pp. 365–70.

57. For more on leadership effectiveness, see Paul Hersey and John E. Stinson, eds., *Perspectives in Effectiveness* (Athens: Center for Leadership Studies, Ohio University, and Ohio University Press, 1980); and Harry Levinson, *Executive* (Cambridge, Mass.: Harvard University Press, 1981).

58. Victor A. Thompson, "How Scientific Management Thwarts Innovation," in Bennis, ed., *American Bureaucracy*, pp. 121–33, especially pp. 123–24. See also James D. Thompson, *Bureaucracy and Innovation* (Tuscaloosa: University of Alabama Press, 1969).

Chapter 7: Public Personnel Administration and Human Resources Development

1. Herbert Kaufman, "Administrative Decentralization and Political Power," *Public Administration Review*, 29 (January/February 1969): 3–15. See also Chapter 2 of this book.

2. N. Joseph Cayer, *Public Personnel Administration in the United States*, 4th ed. (Belmont, Calif.: Wadsworth, 2003), pp. 6–11; Norma Riccucci and Katherine C. Naff, *Personnel Management in Government: Politics and Process*, 6th ed. (New York: CRC Press, 2007); Steven W. Hayes, Richard C. Kearney, and Jerrell D. Coggburn, *Public Human Resource Management: Problems and Prospects*, 5th ed. (Upper Saddle River, N.J.: Prentice Hall, 2008); and Donald E. Klingner, John Nalbanian, and Jared E. Llorens, *Public Personnel Management*, 6th ed. (Englewood Cliffs, N.J.: Prentice-Hall, 2009).

3. The Clinton administration's National Performance Review (NPR) revealed 850 pages of detailed rules covering personnel law, supplemented by another 1,300 pages of regulations on how to apply that law. Additionally, 10,000 pages of guidelines for the federal executive branch were found to frequently hamper the 54,000 civil servants who work in personnel administration positions in the federal government. Albert Gore, *From Red Tape to Results: Creating a Government That Works Better and Costs Less: Report of the National Performance Review* (Washington, D.C.: U.S. Government Printing Office, 1993).

4. Seymour Martin Lipset and William Schneider, *The Confidence Gap: Business, Labor, and Government in the Public Mind*, rev. ed. (Baltimore: Johns Hopkins University Press, 1987), p. 81.

5. For instance, the U.S. Army needed 1,400 additional procurement officers to adequately oversee billions of dollars in civilian contract work in Afghanistan and Iraq. Dana Hedgpeth, "Army Needs 1400 Contract Officers: Independent Panel Says Shortfall in Expertise Contributes to Waste, Fraud, and Abuse," *Washington Post*, November 2, 2007, p. D03.

6. See Frederick C. Mosher, "The Changing Responsibilities and Tactics of the Federal Government," *Public Administration Review*, 40 (November/December 1980): 541–48, at p. 543. See also Paul Light, *Thickening Government: Federal Hierarchy and the Diffusion of Accountability* (Washington, D.C.: Brookings Institution Press, 1995). For data on the subcategories or federal, state, and local jobs, see U.S. Bureau of the Census, *Public Employment in 2007* (Washington, D.C.: U.S. Government Printing Office, 2008).

7. U.S. Bureau of Census, *Public Employment in 2010* (Washington, D.C.: U.S. Government Printing Office, 2011). The primary source of local government revenue is property taxes that have declined sharply as a result of lower housing values.

8. Frederick C. Mosher, *Democracy and the Public Service*, 2nd ed. (New York: Oxford University Press, 1982), chaps. 3 and 4; Nicholas Henry, *Public Administration and Public Affairs*, 10th ed. (Upper Saddle River, N.J.: Prentice Hall, 2006). Our thanks to an anonymous reviewer for suggesting this last category. For additional information on the impact of technology on political processes, see Andrew Chadwick, *Internet Politics: States, Citizens, and New Communication Technologies* (New York: Oxford University Press, 2006); Casey A. Klofstad, *Civic Talk: Peers, Politics, and the Future of Democracy* (Philadelphia: Temple University Press, 2011); and Michael E. Milakovich, *Digital Governance: New Technologies for Improving Public Service and Participation* (London and New York: Routledge Publishers, 2012).

9. Frederick C. Mosher, "Professions in Public Service," *Public Administration Review*, 38 (March/April 1978): 144–50, at pp. 145–46.

10. N. Joseph Cayer, *Managing Human Resources: An Introduction to Public Personnel Administration* (New York: St. Martin's Press, 1980), p. 35. Bank failures, health care reform, investment fraud, and the mortgage meltdown have prompted calls for more regulation, inevitably accompanied by more regulators.

11. It is also true, however, that managers must find ways to deal with the pressures generated by these conflicting personnel approaches. One way to address this problem is suggested in Debra W. Stewart, "Managing Competing Claims: An Ethical Framework for Human Resource Decision Making," *Public Administration Review*, 44 (January/February 1984): 14–22. See also Colleen A. Woodard, "Merit by Any Other Name—Reframing the Civil Service First Principle," *Public Administration Review*, 65 (January/February 2005): 109–16.

12. See Anne Freedman, *Patronage: An American Tradition* (Chicago: Nelson-Hall, 1993).

13. See William Winter, Chair, National Commission on the State and Local Public Service, *Hard Truths/Tough Choices: An Agenda for State and Local Reform* (Albany: Nelson Rockefeller Institute of Government, State University of New York–Albany, 1993), pp. 28–29.

14. Stephen Barr, "DHS Personnel Officer Resigns as Department Tackles Crucial Workplace Issues," *Washington Post*, May 30, 2006, p. D04.

15. Partnership for Public Service, "Making the Difference: A Blueprint for Matching University Students with Federal Opportunities," October 2007, accessed January 8, 2008, at http://www.docuticker.com/?p=17447.

16. Carolyn Ban and Patricia W. Ingraham, "Retaining Quality Federal Employees: Life after PACE," *Public Administration Review*, 48 (May/June 1988): 708–18, at p. 713.

17. Ban and Ingraham point out that the "pendulum swing" from central (OPM) to decentralized (agency) examination processes is typical of historical cycles of reform in national government personnel management. See their concluding remarks in ibid., p. 716.

18. The quote is taken from David Broder's column about Campbell, published not long after he became Civil Service Commission head. The column appeared under the headline "New Look in Civil Service," in the *Bloomington (Ill.) Pantagraph*, May 25, 1977, p. A4.

19. Brittany R. Ballenstedt, "Federal Salary Council Finds Widening Pay Gap," *Federal Executive.com*, October 3, 2007, accessed November 14, 2007, at http://www.govexec.com/story_page.cfm?articleid=38212&ref=rellink.

20. *Report and Recommendations of the National Commission on the Public Service to the Committee on Post Office and Civil Service, U.S. House of Representatives* (Washington, D.C.: U.S. Government Printing Office, 1989), p. 35.

21. Associated Press, "Bush Signs Order Allowing Pay Hikes," *Memphis* (Tenn.) *Commercial-Appeal*, December 27, 1989, p. A2.

22. In October 2007, the Federal Salary Council, an independent body of salary experts, employee representatives, and federal officials that usually makes recommendations on the allocation of locality pay, chose to leave it up to the president. In late 2007, President Bush recommended a 3 percent pay raise for federal civilian and military workers for fiscal year 2008. Karen Rutzick, "President Bush Changes Locality Pay Formula," *GovernmentExecutive.com*, November 30, 2006, accessed July 17, 2007, at http://www.govexec.com/dailyfed/1106/113006r1.htm.

23. Public-sector pension systems are collectively underfunded by as estimated $1 trillion, forcing many state governors and legislatures to cut health care and retirement benefits that were promised to public employees as a condition of employment. See "State Budgets: The Day of Reckoning," *CBS* "60 Minutes," December 10, 2010, accessed at http://www.cbsnews.com/stories/2010/12/60minutes/main7166220_page4.shtml.

24. This discussion is drawn from Cayer, *Managing Human Resources*, pp. 176–77; Lee C. Shaw and

R. Theodore Clark Jr., "The Practical Differences between Public and Private Sector Collective Bargaining," *UCLA Law Review*, 19 (1972): 867–86; and Harry H. Wellington and Ralph K. Winter Jr., "The Limits of Collective Bargaining in Public Employment," in Wellington and Winter, eds., *The Unions and the Cities* (Washington, D.C.: Brookings Institution Press, 1971), pp. 12–32.

25. For details, see http://www.nea.org/index.html and http://www.aft.org/. See also Cayer, *Managing Human Resources*, p. 182. See also Richard C. Kearney, *Labor Relations in the Public Sector*, 2nd ed. (New York: Marcel Dekker, 1992), p. 39.

26. The total number of employees in exclusive units increased nearly sixfold between 1963 and 1971 (from 180,000 to just over 1 million), with the rate of increase slowing after that date. Also, both the number and the percentage of all employees covered by formal agreements increased significantly, from some 110,000 in 1964 to over 1.1 million in 2009—a tenfold jump.

27. This discussion is taken from Kearney, *Labor Relations in the Public Sector*, pp. 57–63.

28. For a discussion of developments in the 1980s, see Douglas M. McCabe, "The Federal-Sector Mediation and Labor-Management Relations Process: The Federal-Sector Management Experience," *Public Personnel Management*, 19 (Spring 1990): 103–22.

29. Cayer, *Managing Human Resources*, p. 172.

30. The Federal Labor Relations Authority is an independent agency responsible for administration of labor–management relations programs for 1.9 million federal employees worldwide; the FLRA also strives to promote stable and constructive labor–management relations that contribute to efficient government (http://www.flra.gov/index.html). For details, see David Rosenbloom, "The Federal Labor Relations Authority," in David Rosenbloom and Patricia Ingraham, eds., "Symposium: The Federal Civil Service Reform Act of 1978," *Policy Studies Journal*, 17 (Winter 1988–1989): 311–447.

31. The National Performance Review (1993–2001) further signaled an intention to take matters to an even higher level of cooperation. It recommended that forming a partnership be made an explicit objective of labor–management negotiations, noting in the process that such informal partnerships already existed in a number of national government agencies and that management processes were enhanced by that development. For details, see Al Gore, *Creating a Government That Works Better and Costs Less* (New York: Random House, 1995), pp. 134–37.

32. The following overview of the CSRA is adapted from James S. Bowman, "Introduction," in James S. Bowman, ed., "Symposium on Civil Service Reform," *Review of Public Personnel Administration*, 2 (Summer 1982): 1–3, at p. 1; and Lawrence S. Buck, "Executive Evaluation: Assessing the Probability for Success in the Job," in Nicholas P. Lovrich, Jr., ed., "Performance Appraisal Reforms in the Public Sector: The Promise and Pitfalls of Employee Evaluation: A Symposium," *Review of Public Personnel Administration*, 3 (Summer 1983): 63–72, at p. 63. See also Charlotte Hurley, "Civil Service Reform: An Annotated Bibliography," *Review of Public Personnel Administration*, 2 (Summer 1982): 59–90; Patricia W. Ingraham and Carolyn Ban, eds., *Legislating Bureaucratic Change: The Civil Service Reform Act of 1978* (Albany: State University of New York Press, 1984); *The Senior Executive Service*, Hearings before the Subcommittee on Civil Service, Committee on Post Office and Civil Service, U.S. House of Representatives, 98th Congress, 2nd Session (Washington, D.C.: U.S. Government Printing Office, 1984); and Rosenbloom and Ingraham, eds., "Symposium: The Federal Civil Service Reform Act of 1978." For discussion of contemporary pressures within the SES, see Gerald Barkdoll and Nina Mocniak, "Strategically Managing the SES Crisis of 1994," *The Public Manager: The New Bureaucrat*, 22 (Spring 1993): 27–30.

33. Testimony of Alan K. Campbell, *The Senior Executive Service*, p. 314.

34. Whether protections for whistle-blowers have, in fact, operated as projected is open to question. See, among others, James S. Bowman, "Whistle Blowing: Literature and Resource Materials," *Public Administration Review*, 43 (May/June 1983): 271–76; "Whistleblowers," *Congressional Quarterly Weekly Report*, 47 (August 12, 1989): 2103; Philip H. Jos, Mark E. Tompkins, and Steven W. Hays, "In Praise of Difficult People: A Portrait of the Committed Whistleblower," *Public Administration Review*, 49 (November/December 1989): 552–61; and Jack Anderson and Dale Van Atta, "Whistle-Blower Hot Lines Lack Trust," *Washington Post*, July 23, 1990, p. D8.

35. Testimony of Rep. Patricia Schroeder, *The Senior Executive Service*, p. 373. See also *Political Appointees in Federal Agencies*, testimony before the Congress of the United States by Bernard L. Ungar, Director of Federal Human Resource Management

Issues, GAO, October 26, 1989; General Accounting Office Report GAO/T-GGD-90-4 (Washington, D.C.: U.S. Government Printing Office, 1989).

36. Panel discussion on civil service reform, held at a conference honoring Alan K. Campbell, Syracuse, New York, June 19, 1993.

37. The federal government ceased collecting detailed data on union membership in the mid-1990s.

38. Bureau of Labor Statistics, "Union Members Survey" (Washington, D.C.: U.S. Department of Labor, 2008), accessed January 28, 2008, at http://www.bls.gov/news.release/union2.nr0.htm.

39. Other organizations with sizable, powerful, and stable or growing memberships include the American Federation of State, County, and Municipal Employees (AFSCME), with 1.1 million members; the American Federation of Teachers (AFT), which brings together 780,000; and the International Association of Fire Fighters (IAFF), which registers 142,000 members. AFSCME is one the largest and most influential public-employee unions (http://www.afscme.org). See also Alan Edward Bent and T. Zane Reeves, *Collective Bargaining in the Public Sector* (Menlo Park, Calif.: Benjamin/Cummings Publishing, 1979), p. 21.

40. Cayer, *Managing Human Resources*, p. 174. In November 2005, California voters rejected all the initiatives endorsed by Governor Arnold Schwarzenegger to amend the state's constitution and weaken the power of state and local public-employee unions. The results were generally viewed as a victory for public labor organizations at the state and local level.

41. Kearney, *Labor Relations in the Public Sector*, p. 67.

42. As reported in *Governing*, 7 (January 1994), 15.

43. Marvin J. Levine and Eugene C. Hagburg, *Public Sector Labor Relations* (St. Paul, Minn.: West Publishing, 1979), p. 65 (emphasis added).

44. The following discussion relies on ibid., pp. 78–85 and 93–95; Cayer, *Managing Human Resources*, pp. 178–89; Bent and Reeves, *Collective Bargaining in the Public Sector*, chap. 2; and Kearney, *Labor Relations in the Public Sector*, chap. 3. See also Donald Klingner, "Public Sector Collective Bargaining: Is the Glass Half Full, Half Empty, or Broken?" *Review of Public Personnel Administration*, 13 (Summer 1993): 19–28; and Donald Klingner and John Nalbandian, *Public Personnel Management*, 5th ed. (Englewood Cliffs, N.J.: Prentice Hall, 2002).

45. Levine and Hagburg, *Public Sector Labor Relations*, p. 79.

46. Cayer, *Managing Human Resources*, p. 189. These comments draw on Cayer, pp. 189–91.

47. For a critique of the view that merit and collective bargaining necessarily are in conflict, see David Lewin and Raymond D. Horton, "The Impact of Collective Bargaining on the Merit System in Government," *Arbitration Journal*, 30 (September 1975): 199–211. An answer to that critique can be found in Joel M. Douglas, "State Civil Service and Collective Bargaining: Systems in Conflict," *Public Administration Review*, 52 (March/April 1992): 162–71.

48. Updates on current legal issues and regulations regarding employment discrimination and labor unions can be found at http://www.eeoc.gov.

49. The National Commission on Pay Equity (NCPE), founded in 1979, has been a major advocate in support of the comparable-worth principle. It is a national membership coalition of over 180 organizations including labor unions; women's and civil rights organizations; religious, professional, educational, and legal associations; commissions on women; state and local pay equity coalitions; and individual women and men working to eliminate sex- and race-based wage discrimination and to achieve pay equity (http://www.feminist.com/fairpay/).

50. The New Haven firefighters case was in *Ricci v. DeStefano*, 129 S. Ct. 2658, 2671, 174 L. Ed. 2d 490 (2009).

51. U.S. Census Bureau, *Statistical Abstracts of the United States, 2011: Table 498—Federal Employees—Summary Characteristics: 1990 to 2007*, p. 327. See also U.S. Office of Personnel Management, "Affirmative Employment Statistics" (Washington, D.C.: U.S. Government Printing Office, 1990); cited in Christopher Cornwell and J. Edward Kellough, "Women and Minorities in Federal Government Agencies: Examining New Evidence from Panel Data," *Public Administration Review*, 54 (May/June 1994): 265–70, at p. 265.

52. See Gregory B. Lewis, "Men and Women toward the Top: Backgrounds, Careers, and Potential of Federal Middle Managers," paper presented at the annual meeting of the American Society for Public Administration, April 1990, Los Angeles, Calif.; cited in Meredith Newman, "Gender and Lowi's Thesis: Implications for Career Advancement," *Public Administration Review*, 54 (May/June 1994): 277–84, at p. 277. Data for 1974 and 1984 were taken from *Distribution of Male and Female Employees in Four Federal Classification Systems, A Report to the Congress of the United States by the*

Comptroller General, General Accounting Office Report GAO/GGD-85-20 (Washington, D.C.: U.S. Government Printing Office, November 27, 1984), Table 1.

53. Continuing attention has been paid to these concerns, most notably by the U.S. Commission on Civil Rights (USCCR), an independent, bipartisan fact-finding agency of the executive branch, first established under the Civil Rights Act of 1957 to investigate allegations of discrimination (http://www.usccr.gov). On November 30, 1983, a new commission—devoted to monitoring these same policy areas—was established under the Civil Rights Act of 1983 (Public Law 98-183). U.S. Merit Systems Protection Board, *A Question of Equity: Women and the Glass Ceiling in the Federal Government* (Washington, D.C.: U.S. Government Printing Office, October 1992); as cited in Gore, *Creating a Government That Works Better and Costs Less*, p. 213.

54. Women and minorities have fared much better in the public sector overall than in the private sector. See, among others, Gregory B. Lewis, "Progress toward Racial and Sexual Equality in the Federal Civil Service?" *Public Administration Review*, 48 (May/June 1988): 700–7; John Nalbandian, "The U.S. Supreme Court's 'Consensus' on Affirmative Action," *Public Administration Review*, 49 (January/February 1989): 38–45; William G. Lewis, "Toward Representative Bureaucracy: Blacks in City Police Organizations, 1975–1985," *Public Administration Review*, 49 (May/June 1989): 257–68; Mary E. Guy, ed., *Women and Men of the States: Public Administrators at the State Level* (Armonk, N.Y.: M.E. Sharpe, 1992); Stephen B. Knouse, Paul Rosenfeld, and Amy Culbertson, eds., *Hispanics in the Workplace* (Newbury Park, Calif.: Sage, 1992); and Albert Mills and Peta Tancred, eds., *Gendering Organizational Analysis* (Newbury Park, Calif.: Sage, 1992). For treatment of another dimension of public-sector diversity, see Pan Suk Kim and Gregory B. Lewis, "Asian Americans in the Public Service: Success, Diversity, and Discrimination," *Public Administration Review*, 54 (May/June 1994): 285–90.

55. In November 1996, the voters of California passed this referendum by a 54–46 percent margin, abolishing preferential hiring based on gender or race in public hiring, contracting, or education, including admission to state universities.

56. See David H. Rosenbloom, "The Declining Salience of Affirmative Action in Federal Personnel Management," *Review of Public Personnel Administration*, 4 (Summer 1984): 31–40. Rosenbloom argues, however, that progress toward a socially representative public workforce can still be maintained even if his prediction proves correct.

57. President Bush's 2007 budget request of $323 million was $4 million less than the EEOC received the previous year. The agency's full-time staff has been cut by more than 19 percent since 2001, and a partial hiring freeze has kept the agency from filling many openings. As a result, the EEOC had a backlog of 47,516 charges of employment discrimination in 2007, up from an estimated 39,061 in 2006 and 33,562 in 2005. The agency logged 75,428 complaints in 2005 and more than 79,000 in 2004. See Christopher Lee, "EEOC Is Hobbled, Groups Contend Case Backlog Grows as Its Staff Is Slashed, Critics Say," *Washington Post*, June 14, 2006, p. A21.

58. U.S. Supreme Court, 2003, *Gratz et. al. v. Bollinger et. al.* (539 U.S. 244); *Grutter v. Bollinger, et. al.* (288 F.3d. 732).

59. Major cases relevant to this point include *Elrod v. Burns*, 427 U.S. 347 (1976), in which the U.S. Supreme Court ruled that lower-level government workers cannot be fired for partisan reasons; *Hollifield v. McMahan*, 438 F. Supp. 591 (1977), in which a U.S. District Court judge in Tennessee applied the principle to a dismissal of a deputy sheriff after the deputy had openly and actively supported his superior's opponent in an election campaign; *Shakman v. The Democratic Organization of Cook County*, 481 F. Supp. 1315 (1979), in which another district judge in Illinois extended that ruling to include promotions and demotions; *Branti v. Finkel*, 100 Sup. Ct. 1287 (1980), in which the U.S. Supreme Court held that two assistant public defenders in Rockland County, New York, could not be dismissed by their new Democratic boss solely because they were Republicans (thus extending the principle to higher-level officials); and *Rutan v. Republican Party of Illinois*, 110 Sup. Ct. 2729 (1990), in which the U.S. Supreme Court ruled by a 5–4 margin that it is a violation of public employees' First Amendment rights to hire, promote, or transfer most public employees based on party affiliation. See also Anne Freedman, "Doing Battle with the Patronage Army: Politics, Courts, and Personnel Administration in Chicago," *Public Administration Review*, 48 (September/October 1988): 847–59, and, also by Freedman, *Patronage: An American Tradition*.

60. Bernard Rosen, "Effective Continuity of U.S. Government Operations in Jeopardy," *Public*

Administration Review, 43 (September/October 1983): 383–92, at pp. 383–86.

61. This discussion relies on Gore, *Creating a Government That Works Better and Costs Less*.

62. Paul Light, "An Update on the Bush Administration's Competitive Sourcing Initiative," Testimony before the U.S. Senate Subcommittee on Oversight of Government Management, the Federal Workforce and the District of Columbia (New York University and the Brookings Institution, 2003). Accessed at http://www.govtaff.senate.gov/_files/072403light.pdf.

63. U.S. Government Accountability Office, "Competitive Sourcing: Greater Emphasis Needed on Increasing Efficiency and Improving Performance," Report to Congressional Requestors, February 2004; and Christopher Lee, "Bush's 'Competitive Sourcing' Worries Disabled Workers: Initiative May Put Employees with Special Needs at a Decided Disadvantage, Their Advocates Say," *Washington Post*, April 18, 2005, p. A15.

64. See Paul Volcker, Chair, *Leadership for America: Rebuilding the Public Service: The Report of the National Commission on the Public Service and the Task Force Reports to the National Commission on the Public Service* (Lexington, Mass.: Lexington Books, 1990).

65. Christopher Lee, "Civil Service System on the Way Out at DHS," *Washington Post*, January 27, 2005, p. 3, accessed at http://www.washingtonpost.con/ac2/wp-dyn/A39934-2995Jan26?language=printer.

66. Accessed at http://www.washingtontimes.com/news/2009/may/18/causey-obama-puts-spirit-back-in-civil-service/?page=1.

67. In this regard, see Paul Volcker, *Public Service: The Quiet Crisis* (Washington, D.C.: American Enterprise Institute, 1988).

Chapter 8: Government Budgeting

1. Robert D. Lee Jr., Ronald W. Johnson, and Philip G. Joyce, *Public Budgeting Systems*, 8th ed. (Boston, Mass.: Jones and Bartlett, 2008), pp. 42–44.

2. Charles L. Schultze, *The Politics and Economics of Public Spending* (Washington, D.C.: Brookings Institution Press, 1968), p. 8. Schultze notes that when Alexander Hamilton was George Washington's treasury secretary, he established a central executive budget that gave broad discretion to the executive and "contained the potential for development of a centrally planned budget and a deliberate allocation of resources among competing agencies" (pp. 7–8). Jefferson, however, ended that practice, opposing Hamilton's preferences for a strong central government and a strong executive within it. See also Naomi Caiden, "Paradox, Ambiguity, and Enigma: The Strange Case of the Executive Budget and the United States Constitution," *Public Administration Review*, 47 (January/February 1987): 84–92.

3. Aaron Wildavsky and Naomi Caiden, *The New Politics of the Budgetary Process*, 5th ed. (New York: Longman, 2004), pp. 7–8.

4. See also, among others, Jeffrey D. Straussman, "A Typology of Budgetary Environments: Notes on the Prospects for Reform," *Administration and Society*, 11 (August 1979): 216–26.

5. Wildavsky and Caiden, *The New Politics of the Budgetary Process*, Preface to the first edition, p. xxvii. They examine the rise of budgetary dissensus in chaps. 4–5.

6. Jesse Burkhead, *Government Budgeting* (New York: Wiley, 1956), pp. 59–60. See also Howard E. Shuman, *Politics and the Budget: The Struggle between the President and the Congress*, 3rd ed. (Englewood Cliffs, N.J.: Prentice Hall, 1992), chap. 5; C. Eugene Steuerle, *Contemporary U.S. Tax Policy*, 2nd ed. (Washington, D.C.: Urban Institute Press, 2008); Allen Schick, *The Federal Budget: Politics, Policy, Process*, 3rd ed. (Washington, D.C.: The Brookings Institution Press, 2007); and James Saturno, Bill Heniff, and TheCapitol.Net, *The Federal Budget Process: A Description of the Federal and Congressional Budget Processes, including Timelines* (Washington, D.C.: TheCapitol.Net, 2009).

7. Burkhead, *Government Budgeting*, p. 63.

8. For the current National Debt Clock, see http://www.brillig.com/debt_clock/.

9. The availability of pension benefits are much higher in the public sector (90 percent) than in the private sector (less than 50 percent). Many state retirement systems are also underfunded, creating concerns about a bond market collapse. See also Marilyn Cohen and Christopher R. Malburg, *Surviving the Bond Bear Market: Bondland's Nuclear Winter* (New York: Wiley, 2011).

10. The final report of the Commission is accessible online at http://www.fiscalcommission.gov/sites/fiscalcommission.gov/files/documents/TheMomentofTruth12_1_2010.pdf.

11. For policy and regulatory information regarding the Federal Reserve System, including monetary, credit, and banking regulations, see http://www.federalreserve.gov/. For an insightful study of the Federal Reserve Board, see Donald F. Kettl,

Leadership at the Fed (New Haven, Conn.: Yale University Press, 1986).

12. One of the most significant steps in this respect during the last forty years was enactment of the Economic Stabilization Act of 1970, the statutory basis for Richard Nixon's move in August 1971 to impose a ninety-day freeze on prices, rents, wages, and salaries. Under this intricate and comprehensive program, the national government attempted to directly control the economy, as distinguished from the more indirect methods utilized previously in fiscal and monetary policy.

13. See, among others, J. Richard Aronson and John L. Hilley, *Financing State and Local Governments*, 4th ed. (Washington, D.C.: Brookings Institution Press, 1986); Glenn Abney and Thomas P. Lauth, *The Politics of State and City Administration* (Albany: State University of New York Press, 1986); and Irene Rubin, "The Great Unraveling: Federal Budgeting, 1998–2006," *Public Administration Review*, 67 (July/August 2007): 608–23.

14. This discussion relies extensively on Lee, Johnson, and Joyce, *Public Budgeting Systems*, chaps. 8 and 9.

15. Lance T. LeLoup, *Budgetary Politics*, 4th ed. (Brunswick, Ohio: King's Court, 1988), p. 302.

16. As the chief financial advisers to our nation's governors, NASBO members are active participants in public-policy discussions at the state level. The NASBO website (http://www.nasbo.org) has excellent links to other substantive policy areas in state government.

17. Lee, Johnson, and Joyce, *Public Budgeting Systems*, pp. 294–97. In addition to the formal responsibilities discharged during the authorization and appropriations stages, there are opportunities for Congress to attempt to assert greater general control over executive agencies. Examples include adding "limitation amendments" to appropriations bills and enacting temporary authorizations. See Allen Schick, "Politics through Law: Congressional Limitations on Executive Discretion," in Anthony King, ed., *Both Ends of the Avenue: The Presidency, the Executive Branch, and Congress in the 1980s* (Washington, D.C.: American Enterprise Institute for Public Policy Research, 1983), pp. 154–84, at pp. 170–75.

18. The 1994 Bipartisan Commission on Entitlement and Tax Reform predicted that, unless major changes were made, entitlement expenditures, such as Social Security, Medicare, and interest on the national debt, would consume the *entire* federal budget by the year 2012. Bipartisan Commission on Entitlement and Tax Reform, *Interim Report to the President* (Washington, D.C.: The Commission, 1994), p. 6.

19. During tense budget negotiations between House Republicans and the White House in the spring of 2011, President Obama offered more support for the Simpson–Bowles recommendations. Lori Montgomery, "House GOP Group Proposes Deep Spending Cuts over Next Decade," *Washington Post*, January 21, 2011; and Lori Montgomery and Zachary A. Goldfarb, "Obama Turns to His Bipartisan Deficit Commissions Blueprint for Reducing Debt," *Washington Post*, April 11, 2011.

20. Ernest C. Betts Jr. and Richard E. Miller, "More about the Impact of the Congressional Budget and Impoundment Control Act," *The Bureaucrat*, 6 (Spring 1977): 112–20, at p. 114.

21. See, among others, Allen Schick, *Congress and Money: Budgeting, Spending, and Taxing* (Washington, D.C.: Urban Institute Press, 1980); Donald Axelrod, *Budgeting for Modern Government*, 2nd ed (New York: St. Martin's Press, 1995), chap. 8; and Shuman, *Politics and the Budget*, chap. 7.

22. See Walter J. Oleszek, *Congressional Procedures and the Policy Process*, 3rd ed. (Washington, D.C.: CQ Press, 1988), pp. 67–68.

23. Axelrod, *Budgeting for Modern Government*, p. 201. This overview of the GRH process draws substantially on Axelrod's discussion.

24. Craig Rimmerman, "Deficit Politics, Gramm–Rudman–Hollings, and the Deadlock of Democracy," paper presented at the annual meeting of the American Political Science Association, Washington, D.C., September 1988, p. 14.

25. Axelrod, *Budgeting for Modern Government*, pp. 201–2.

26. Quoted in Rimmerman, "Deficit Politics, Gramm–Rudman–Hollings, and the Deadlock of Democracy," p. 13.

27. For a detailed summary of revised deficit targets, discretionary spending limits, and timetables of sequestration, see Edward Davis and Robert Keith, *Budget Enforcement Act of 1990: A Brief Summary*, CRS Report for Congress (Washington, D.C.: Congressional Research Service, Library of Congress, November 1990), pp. 1–11; see also Axelrod, *Budgeting for Modern Government*, pp. 203–9.

28. Wildavsky and Caiden, *The New Politics of the Budgetary Process*, pp. 75, 90, 112–13.

29. See Albert Gore, *Creating a Government That Works Better and Costs Less: The Report of the National*

Performance Review (New York: Times Books, Random House, 1993), pp. 13–14.

30. Lee, Johnson, and Joyce, *Public Budgeting Systems*, p. 11. This description of early local government reform efforts relies on their treatment found on pp. 10–13.

31. Ibid. State governments have continued to be active in budgetary reforms of various kinds and with varying degrees of effectiveness. See, for example, Stanley B. Botner, "The Use of Budgeting/Management Tools by State Governments," *Public Administration Review*, 45 (September/October 1985): 616–20; and Robert B. Albritton and Ellen M. Dran, "Balanced Budgets and State Surpluses: The Politics of Budgeting in Illinois," *Public Administration Review*, 47 (March/April 1987): 143–52. Another perspective on state budgeting can be found in Joel A. Thompson and Arthur A. Felts, "Politicians and Professionals: The Influence of State Agency Heads in Budgetary Success," *Western Political Quarterly*, 45 (March 1992): 153–68.

32. Lee, Johnson, and Joyce, *Public Budgeting Systems*, p. 149.

33. Allen Schick, *Budget Innovation in the States* (Washington, D.C.: Brookings Institution Press, 1971), p. 7.

34. Allen Schick, "A Death in the Bureaucracy: The Demise of Federal PPB," *Public Administration Review*, 33 (March/April 1973): 146.

35. Zero-base budgeting got its start at Texas Instruments, Inc., under the guidance of Peter Pyhrr, who later helped implement it in Georgia during the administration of Governor Jimmy Carter (1971–1975). It is from this base that ZBB was launched in about a dozen other states, numerous industries, some local governments, and the national government. This discussion of ZBB relies on the following sources: Peter A. Pyhrr, "The Zero-Base Approach to Government Budgeting," *Public Administration Review*, 37 (January/February 1977): 1–8; and Frank D. Draper and Bernard T. Pitsvada, "ZBB—Looking Back after Ten Years," *Public Administration Review*, 41 (January/February 1981): 76–83.

36. Regarding proposed budget cuts in intergovernmental aid, see, among others, "Cities, States Say Cuts in Aid Will Create an Unfair Burden," *Congressional Quarterly Weekly Report*, 43 (February 16, 1985): 291–94. See also Ryan Holeywell, "How Bad Is It?" *Governing*, 24 (May 2011): 26–30; and John E. Petersen, "The Debt Demon: Have States

and Localities Borrowed Too Much?" *Governing*, 24 (May 2011): 62. See also Chapter 3 of this book.

37. Two-thirds of discretionary funding goes for military spending. For the relative distribution of other discretionary expenditures, see National Priorities Project at http://nationalpriorities.org/en/resources/federal-budget-101/budget-briefs/federal-discretionary-and-mandatory-spending/.

38. See the *New York Times*, February 8, 1994, pp. A1, A12, and A13, for an overview of the Clinton FY 95 budget proposals. See also *Congressional Quarterly Weekly Report*, 52 (February 14–21, 1994), for an extended discussion of the Clinton budget, and *Budget of the United States Government, Fiscal Year 1995* (Washington, D.C.: U.S. Government Printing Office, 1994).

39. For details, see Bob Graham with Jeff Nussbaum, *Intelligence Matters: The CIA, the FBI, Saudi Arabia, and the Failure of America's War on Terror* (New York: Random House, 2004); and Paul O'Neil, *The Price of Loyalty* (New York: Simon & Schuster, 2004).

40. President Obama's 2012 budget would also reduce federal expenditures from the current 25.3 percent of GDP to the 22 percent range for much of the next decade. In ten years, spending would be back at 23 percent; revenues are currently at a low 14.4 percent, but are projected to increase to 19 percent by 2015 and then to 20 percent in 2021, depending on the so-called revenue enhancements passed by Congress. The lower federal spending could be used to reduce the national debt.

41. See, among others, Jerry McCaffery, ed., "Special Issue: The Impact of Resource Scarcity on Urban Public Finance," *Public Administration Review*, 41 (January 1981); Robert W. Burchell and David Listokin, eds., *Cities under Stress: The Fiscal Crises of Urban America* (New Brunswick, N.J.: Rutgers University, Center for Urban Policy Research, 1982); Elaine B. Sharp and David Elkins, "The Impact of Fiscal Limitation: A Tale of Seven Cities," *Public Administration Review*, 47 (September/October 1987): 385–92; Helen F. Ladd and John Yinger, *America's Ailing Cities: Fiscal Health and the Design of Urban Policy* (Baltimore: Johns Hopkins University Press, 1989); and Thomas Swartz and Frank Bonello, *Urban Finance under Siege* (Armonk, N.Y.: M.E. Sharpe, 1993).

42. Former House Budget Committee Chairman James Jones (D-OK) once observed: "It's not the [congressional] budget process that's irritating people. It's that dividing scarcer resources is not as

easy as dividing growing resources." See Oleszek, *Congressional Procedures and the Policy Process*, p. 68.

43. Allen Schick, "The Road from ZBB," *Public Administration Review* (March/April 1978): 180.

44. Donald Kettl, "Myths, Trends, and Traditions in the Budgetary Process," paper presented at annual meeting of the American Political Science Association, Washington, D.C., September 1988, p. 4.

45. This observation was made in Hedrick Smith, *The Power Game* (New York: Random House, 1988), pp. 658–59; cited in Rimmerman, "Deficit Politics, Gramm–Rudman–Hollings, and the Deadlock of Democracy," p. 12.

46. Wildavsky and Caiden, *The New Politics of the Budgetary Process*, p. xx.

47. The Republican alternative to the 2012 Obama budget is "The Path to Prosperity: Restoring America's Promise," accessible at http://budget.house.gov/fy2012budget/.

48. See Alan Schick, "Incremental Budgeting in a Decremental Age," *Policy Sciences*, 16 (September 1983): 24.

Chapter 9: Public Policy and Program Implementation

1. See Murray Edelman, *The Symbolic Uses of Politics* (Urbana: University of Illinois Press, 1985). See also Donald F. Kettl, *Government by Proxy: (Mis) Managing Federal Programs?* (Washington, D.C.: CQ Press, 1988); Carl E. Van Horn, Donald Baumer, and William T. Gormley Jr., *Politics and Public Policy*, 3rd ed. (Washington, D.C.: CQ Press, 2001); and B. Guy Peters, *American Public Policy: Promise and Performance*, 8th ed. (Washington, D.C.: CQ Press, 2010).

2. Theodore Lowi, "American Business, Public Policy Case-Studies, and Political Theory," *World Politics*, 16 (July 1964): 677–715; Randall B. Ripley and Grace A. Franklin, *Congress, the Bureaucracy, and Public Policy*, 5th ed. (Pacific Grove, Calif.: Brooks/Cole, 1991); and James E. Anderson, *Public Policy Making*, 6th ed. (Boston: Houghton-Mifflin, 2006).

3. This discussion is taken from Anderson, *Public Policy Making*, pp. 14–15.

4. Richard J. Stillman, *Public Administration: Cases and Concepts*, 9th ed. (Boston: Houghton-Mifflin, 2010), pp. 2–4.

5. Frederick W. Taylor, *The Principles of Scientific Management* (New York: Norton, 1967); Douglas Yates, *Bureaucratic Democracy: The Search for Democracy and Efficiency in American Government* (Cambridge, Mass.: Harvard University Press, 1982; paperback edition, 1987); James Q. Wilson, *Bureaucracy: What Government Agencies Do and Why They Do It* (New York: Basic Books, 1989); Herbert Simon, *Administrative Behavior*, 4th ed. (New York: Free Press, 1997); and James H. Svara, "Complementarity of Politics and Administration as a Legitimate Alternative to the Dichotomy Model," *Administration and Society*, 30(6) (1999): 676–705.

6. Robert Behn, *Rethinking Democratic Accountability* (Washington, D.C.: Brookings Institution Press, 2001); and Janet V. Denhardt and Robert B. Denhardt, *The New Public Service: Serving, Not Steering*, 3rd ed. (Armonk, New York: M.E. Sharpe, 2011).

7. Richard C. Box, "Running Government Like a Business: Implications for Public Administration Theory and Practice," *American Review of Public Administration*, 29(1) (1999): 19–43; Mark Carl Rom, "From Welfare State to Opportunity, Inc.: Public–Private Partnerships in Welfare Reform," *American Behavioral Scientist*, 43(1) (September 1999): 155–76; E. S. Savas, *Privatization and Public-Private Partnerships* (Chatham, N.J.: Chatham House, 2000); and Graeme A. Hodge, *Privatization and Market Development: Global Movements in Public Policy Ideas* (Northampton, Mass.: Edward Elgar, 2006).

8. Richard C. Box, *Citizen Governance: Leading American Communities into the 21st Century* (Thousand Oaks, Calif.: Sage, 1998); W. L. Megginson and J. Netter, "From State to Market: A Survey of Empirical Studies on Privatization," *Journal of Economic Literature*, 39(2) (2001): 321–89; and Jeffrey D. Greene, *Cities and Privatization: Prospects for the New Century* (Upper Saddle River, N.J.: Prentice Hall, 2002).

9. See, among many others, James Ferris and Elizabeth Graddy, "Contracting Out: For What? With Whom?" *Public Administration Review*, 46 (July/August 1986): 332–44; Ted Kolderie, "The Two Differing Concepts of Privatization," *Public Administration Review*, 46 (July/August 1986): 285–91; Harold J. Sullivan, "Privatization of Public Services: A Growing Threat to Constitutional Rights," *Public Administration Review*, 47 (November/December 1987): 461–67; Ronald C. Moe, "Exploring the Limits of Privatization," *Public Administration Review*, 47 (November/December 1987): 453–60; Lyle C. Fitch, "The Rocky Road to Privatization," *American Journal of Economics and Sociology*, 47 (January 1988): 1–14; David R. Morgan and Robert E. England, "The Two Faces of Privatization," *Public*

Administration Review, 48 (November/December 1988): 979–87; Ronald C. Moe and Thomas H. Stanton, "Government-Sponsored Enterprises as Federal Instrumentalities: Reconciling Private Management with Public Accountability," *Public Administration Review*, 49 (July/August 1989): 321–29; John A. Rehfuss, *Contracting Out in Government: A Guide to Working with Outside Contractors to Supply Public Services* (San Francisco: Jossey-Bass, 1989); John G. Heilman and Gerald W. Johnson, *The Politics and Economics of Privatization: The Case of Wastewater Treatment* (Tuscaloosa: University of Alabama Press, 1992); H. Brinton Milward, "Implications of Contracting Out: New Roles for the Hollow State," in Patricia W. Ingraham, Barbara Romzek, and associates, eds., *New Paradigms for Government: Issues for the Changing Public Service* (San Francisco: Jossey-Bass, 1994); Graeme Hodge, *Privatization: An International Review of Performance* (Boulder, Colo.: Westview Press, 2000); E. S. Savas, *The Privatization of Public-Private Partnerships* (Chatham, N.J.: Chatham House, 2000); and Greene, *Cities and Privatization*. For case-specific discussion of privatization, see Leisha DeHart-Davis and Gordon Kingsley, "Managerial Perceptions of Privatization: Evidence from a State Department of Transportation," *State and Local Government Review*, 37(3) (2005): 228–41; Marilyn K. Dantico, "Reworking Relationships in the Face of Privatization: The Case of the Phoenix Water Services Department," *State and Local Government Review*, 37(3) (2005): 242–49; and Anna Ya Ni and Stuart Bretschneider, "The Decision to Contract Out: A Study of Contracting for E-Government Services in State Governments," *Public Administration Review*, 67(3) (May/June 2007): 531–44.

10. T. C. Miller, *Blood Money: Wasted Billions, Lost Lives, and Corporate Greed in Iraq* (New York: Little, Brown, 2006).

11. For details, see Jeremy Scahill, *Blackwater: The Rise of the World's Most Powerful Mercenary Army* (New York: Nations Books, 2007). In April 2011, a federal appeals court re-opened the case against four Blackwater Worldwide guards involved in a 2007 shooting in a Baghdad public square that killed seventeen Iraqi citizens. "Appeals Court Says Judge Erred in Dismissing Prosecution of Blackwater Guards in Iraq Shooting," Associated Press, April 22, 2011.

12. Donald F. Kettl, *Sharing Power: Public Governance and Private Markets* (Washington, D.C.: Brookings Institution Press, 1993); for an update on the same

subject, see Graeme A. Hodge and Carsten Greve, "Public-Private Partnerships: An International Performance Review," *Public Administration Review*, 67 (May/June 2007): 545–58.

13. See, for example, Lynton K. Caldwell, *Science and the National Environmental Policy Act: Redirecting Policy through Procedural Reform* (Tuscaloosa: University of Alabama Press, 1982); Amitai Etzioni, *Public Policy in a New Key* (New Brunswick, N.J.: Transaction Publishers, 1992); Gerald Garvey, *Facing the Bureaucracy: Living and Dying in a Public Agency* (San Francisco: Jossey-Bass, 1993); Marc K. Landy, Marc J. Roberts, and Stephen R. Thomas, *The Environmental Protection Agency: Asking the Wrong Questions from Nixon to Clinton*, expanded ed. (New York: Oxford University Press, 1994); A. Lee Fritschler, and Catherine E. Rudder. *Smoking and Politics: Bureaucracy Centered Policy Making*. 6th ed. (New York: Longman, 2007); Charles O. Jones, *An Introduction to the Study of Public Policy*, 3rd ed. (Belmont, Calif.: Wadsworth, 1998), especially chap. 2; Juliet F. Gainsborough, *Fenced Off: The Suburbanization of American Politics* (Washington, D.C.: Georgetown University Press, 2001); and Martha Derthick, *Up in Smoke: From Legislation to Litigation in Tobacco Politics*, 3rd ed. (Washington, D.C.: CQ Press, 2011).

14. Fritschler and Rudder, *Smoking and Politics*, p. 49.

15. Anderson, *Public Policy Making*, pp. 223–24.

16. See, among others, Lewis G. Bender and James A. Stever, eds., *Administering the New Federalism* (Boulder, Colo.: Westview, 1986); Robert Jay Dilger, *National Intergovernmental Programs* (Englewood Cliffs, N.J.: Prentice Hall, 1989); Paul E. Peterson, Barry G. Rabe, and Kenneth K. Wong, *When Federalism Works* (Washington, D.C.: Brookings Institution Press, 1986); and David Walker, *The Rebirth of Federalism: Slouching Toward Washington*, 2nd ed. (New York: Chatham House, 2000).

17. Quoted in Peter H. Rossi and Sonia R. Wright, "Evaluation Research: An Assessment of Theory, Practice, and Politics," *Evaluation Quarterly*, 1 (February 1977): 5–52, at p. 23.

18. Bertram M. Gross, "Planning: Developing Purposefulness," in Frederick S. Lane, ed., *Managing State and Local Government: Cases and Readings* (New York: St. Martin's Press, 1980), pp. 243–50, at p. 243.

19. See Paul C. Nutt and Robert W. Backoff, *Strategic Management of Public and Third Sector Organizations: A Handbook for Leaders* (San Francisco: Jossey-Bass, 1992); Mark Moore, *Creating Public*

Value: Strategic Planning in Government (Cambridge, Mass.: Harvard University Press, 1995); Jack Koteen, *Strategy Management in Public and Non-Profit Organizations: Managing Public Concerns in an Era of Limits* (Westport, Conn.: Praeger, 1997); and Paul Joyce, *Strategic Management for the Public Services* (Buckingham, U.K.: Open University Press, 1999).

20. Gerald L. Barkdoll, "Concentering: A Useful Preplanning Activity," *Public Administration Review*, 43 (November/December 1983): 556–60, at p. 556.

21. For more information related to planning, see, among others, Leonard I. Ruchelman, *A Workbook in Program Design for Public Managers* (Albany: State University of New York Press, 1985); and Barton Wechsler and Robert W. Backoff, "Policy Making and Administration in State Agencies: Strategic Management Approaches," *Public Administration Review*, 46 (July/August 1986): 321–27.

22. Jacob B. Ukeles, "Policy Analysis: Myth or Reality?" in Norman Beckman, ed., "Symposium on Policy Analysis in Government: Alternatives to 'Muddling Through,' " *Public Administration Review*, 37 (May/June 1977): 223–28, at p. 23. See also Yvonna Lincoln and Egon Guba, "Research, Evaluation, and Policy Analysis: Heuristics for Disciplined Inquiry," *Policy Studies Review*, 5 (February 1986): 546–65; and E. S. Quade, *Analysis for Public Decisions*, 3rd ed. (New York: Elsevier, 1989).

23. See, among others, M. E. Hawkesworth, *Theoretical Issues in Policy Analysis* (Albany: State University of New York Press, 1988); Robert A. Heineman, William T. Bluhm, Steven A. Peterson, and Edward N. Kearny, *The World of the Policy Analyst* (Chatham, N.J.: Chatham House, 1990); Barry Bozeman and Jeffrey D. Straussman, *Public Management Strategies: Guidelines for Managerial Effectiveness* (San Francisco: Jossey-Bass, 1990); and Barry Bozeman, ed., *Public Management: The State of the Art* (San Francisco: Jossey-Bass, 1993).

24. Ukeles, "Policy Analysis: Myth or Reality?" pp. 26–27.

25. This discussion relies on Harry P. Hatry, Louis Blair, Donald Fisk, and Wayne Kimmell, "An Illustrative Checklist for Assessing Program Analyses," in Harry P. Hatry et al., *Program Analysis for State and Local Governments*, 2nd ed. (Washington, D.C.: Urban Institute Press, 1987).

26. This discussion relies on Barry Bozeman, *Public Management and Policy Analysis* (New York: St. Martin's Press, 1979), pp. 267–76.

27. Ibid., pp. 269–70.

28. Adapted from Jones, *An Introduction to the Study of Public Policy*, p. 166.

29. Jeffrey L. Pressman and Aaron Wildavsky, *Implementation*, 3rd ed. (Berkeley: University of California Press, 1984), p. xx

30. See Walter Williams et al., *Studying Implementation: Methodological and Administrative Issues* (Chatham, N.J.: Chatham House, 1982); Robert T. Golembiewski and Alan Kiepper, "Lessons from a Fast-Paced Public Project: Perspectives on Doing Better the Next Time Around," *Public Administration Review*, 43 (November/ December 1983): 547–56; Laurence J. O'Toole Jr. and Robert S. Montjoy, "Interorganizational Policy Implementation: A Theoretical Perspective," *Public Administration Review*, 44 (November/December 1984): 491–503; M. A. Levin and B. Ferman, *The Political Hand: Policy Implementation and Youth Employment Programs* (New York: Pergamon Press, 1985); Peter J. May and Walter Williams, *Disaster Policy Implementation: Managing Programs under Shared Governance* (New York: Plenum Press, 1986); Randall B. Ripley and Grace A. Franklin, *Bureaucracy and Policy Implementation* (Homewood, Ill.: Dorsey, 1986); Malcolm L. Goggin, *Policy Design and the Politics of Implementation: The Case of Child Health Care in the American States* (Knoxville: University of Tennessee Press, 1987); Richard Nathan, *Turning Promises into Performance: The Management Challenge of Implementing Workfare* (New York: Columbia University Press, 1993); Robert C. Myrtle and Kathleen H. Wilber, "Designing Service Delivery Systems: Lessons from the Development of Community-Based Systems of Care for the Elderly," *Public Administration Review*, 54 (May/June 1994): 245–52; Daniel A. Mazmanian, *Implementation and Public Policy* (Lanham, Maryland: University Press of America, 1989); and Michael Hill and Peter L. Hupe, *Implementing Public Policy: An Introduction to the Study of Operational Governance*, 2nd ed. (Thousand Oaks, Calif.: Sage Publications, 2009).

31. Fritschler and Rudder, *Smoking and Politics*, pp. 48–49.

32. Jones, *An Introduction to the Study of Public Policy*, p. 34.

33. Malcolm M. Feeley and Austin D. Sarat, *The Policy Dilemma: Federal Crime Policy and the Law Enforcement Assistance Administration* (Minneapolis: University of Minnesota Press, 1981). See also Thomas E. Cronin, Tania Z. Cronin, and Michael E. Milakovich, *U.S. v. Crime in the Streets* (Bloomington: Indiana University Press, 1981).

34. Pressman and Wildavsky, *Implementation*, pp. 99–100.

35. This discussion relies on Nicholas Henry, *Public Administration and Public Affairs*, 11th ed. (Upper Saddle River, N.J.: Prentice Hall, 2009), pp. 161–62.

36. Peter F. Drucker, *The Practice of Management* (New York: Harper & Row, 1954).

37. Bruce H. DeWoolfson Jr., "Public Sector MBO and PPB: Cross Fertilization in Management Systems," *Public Administration Review*, 35 (July/August 1975): 387–94; Michael L. Moore and K. Dow Scott, "Installing Management by Objectives in a Public Agency: A Comparison of Black and White Managers, Supervisors, and Professionals," *Public Administration Review*, 43 (March/April 1983): 121–26; and James E. Swiss, "Establishing a Management System: The Interaction of Power Shifts and Personality under Federal MBO," *Public Administration Review*, 43 (May/June 1983): 238–45.

38. Peter F. Drucker, "What Results Should You Expect? A Users' Guide to MBO," in Jong S. Jun, ed., "Symposium on Management by Objectives in the Public Sector," *Public Administration Review*, 36 (January/February 1976): 12–19, at p. 18.

39. See Swiss, "Establishing a Management System: The Interaction of Power Shifts and Personality under Federal MBO," p. 239.

40. Drucker, "What Results Should You Expect? A Users' Guide to MBO," p. 13.

41. Frank P. Sherwood and William J. Page Jr., "MBO and Public Management," in Jong S. Jun, ed., "Symposium on Management by Objectives in the Public Sector," *Public Administration Review*, 36 (January/February 1976): 5–12, at p. 9.

42. See, among others, Stephen K. Bailey and Edith K. Mosher, *ESEA: The Office of Education Administers a Law* (Syracuse, N.Y.: Syracuse University Press, 1968); Jerome T. Murphy, "Title I of ESEA: The Politics of Implementing Federal Education Reform," *Harvard Educational Review*, 41 (February 1971): 35–63; and Milbrey W. McLaughlin, *Evaluation and Reform: The Elementary and Secondary Education Act of 1965/Title I* (Cambridge, Mass.: Ballinger, 1975).

43. Bailey and Mosher, *ESEA*, p. 3.

44. Murphy, "Title I of ESEA," pp. 35–36.

45. See, among other critical studies, Task Force Report of the National Conference of State Legislatures, February 23, 2005, http://www.ncsl.org/programs/press/2005/pr050223.htm. For analysis of measurement problems associated with large federal programs, see Sean Nicholson-Crotty, Nick A. Theobald, and Jill Nicholson-Crotty, "Disparate Measures: Public Managers and Performance Measurement Strategies," *Public Administration Review*, 66 (January–February 2006): 101–13. For analysis of the external political environment and stakeholder participation in performance measurement, see Kaifeng Yang and Jun Yi Hsieh, "Managerial Effectiveness of Government Performance Measurement: Testing a Middle-Range Model," *Public Administration Review*, 67 (September/October 2007): 861–79.

46. Claudia Wallis and Sonja Steptoe, "How to Fix No Child Left Behind," *Time Magazine*, May 24, 2007; and Jeffery A. Raffel "Why Has Public Administration Ignored Education, and Does It Matter?" *Public Administration Review*, 67 (January/February 2007): 135–51.

47. Since 1999, Florida courts have ruled on four separate occasions that the voucher program violates various provisions of the Florida constitution. Although the program has been under constitutional attack, the courts allowed the state to continue to offer an "Opportunity Scholarship Program" to students at public schools that had been identified by the state as failing. The Florida Supreme Court heard oral arguments in *Holmes v. Bush*, a case involving private school vouchers in June 2005. In January 2006, the program was struck down as unconstitutional.

48. Accessed at http://www.eschoolnews.com/2011/03/29/obama-says-too-much-testing-makes-education-boring/.

49. Using a parliamentary maneuver, the Republican-dominated Florida Legislature placed a constitutional amendment on the fall, 2008 ballot to decide whether vouchers can be used to fund private schools. The amendments were again challenged by pro-public education groups as unconstitutional. See Marc Caputo, "Word Changes Up Chances for School Vouchers," *Miami Herald*, June 4, 2008; and Mary Ellen Klas, "School Groups Attack 2 Ballot Items," *Miami Herald*, June 14, 2008.

50. Accessed at http://www.whitehouse.gov.

51. Joseph S. Wholey, "The Role of Evaluation and the Evaluator in Improving Public Programs," *Public Administration Review*, 36 (November/December 1976): 679–83, at p. 680.

52. Jones, *An Introduction to the Study of Public Policy*, p. 199.

53. For example, see Donald T. Campbell and Julian C. Stanley, *Experimental and Quasi-Experimental Designs for Research*, 2nd ed. (Chicago: Rand McNally, 1966), especially pp. 23, 25; Kenneth J.

Meier and Jeffrey L. Brudney, *Applied Statistics for Public Administration*, 4th ed. (Fort Worth, Tex.: Harcourt Brace Jovanovich, 1997), pp. 143–54; and Brian P. Macfie and Phillip M. Nufrio, *Applied Statistics for Public Policy* (Armonk, N.Y.: M.E. Sharpe, 2005).

54. Murphy, "Title I of ESEA," pp. 41–43.

55. James Q. Wilson, "On Pettigrew and Armor," *Public Interest*, 31 (Spring 1973): 132–34.

56. Murphy, "Title I of ESEA," p. 43.

57. Jones, *An Introduction to the Study of Public Policy*, pp. 218–24. See also E. J. Meeham, *The Quality of Federal Public Housing: Programmed Failure in Public Housing* (Columbia: University of Missouri Press, 1979); Beverly A. Cigler and Michael L. Vasu, "Housing and Public Policy in America," *Public Administration Review*, 42 (January/February 1982): 90–96; and Dennis R. Judd and Todd Swanstrom, *City Politics: The Political Economy of Urban America*, 5th ed. (New York: Pearson Longman, 2006), especially chaps. 6 and 9.

58. Larry Polivka and Laurey T. Stryker, "Program Evaluation and the Policy Process in State Government: An Effective Linkage," *Public Administration Review*, 43 (May/June 1983): 255–59, at p. 258.

59. Donald T. Campbell, "Reforms as Experiments," *American Psychologist*, 24 (April 1969): 409–10 (emphasis added).

60. For GAO policy reports, see http://www.gao.gov. Numerous nonprofit organizations are concerned with policy analysis and evaluation, including among many others, the Association for Public Policy Analysis and Management (http://www.qsilver.queensu.ca/appam/); the American Enterprise Institute (http://www.aei.org/); and the Brookings Institution (http://www.brook.edu/).

61. Martin A. Strosberg and Joseph S. Wholey, "Evaluability Assessment: From Theory to Practice in the Department of Health and Human Services," *Public Administration Review*, 43 (January/February 1983): 66–71, at p. 66. See also Ruchelman, *A Workbook in Program Design for Public Managers.*

62. Other useful sources on program and policy evaluation include "Mini-Symposium on Program Evaluation—The Human Factor," *Public Administration Review*, 44 (November/December 1984): 525–38; Theodore H. Poister, "Linking Program Planning, Evaluation, and Management: Will It Ever Happen?" *Public Administration Review*, 46 (March/April 1986): 179–83; Dennis Palumbo, ed., *The Politics of Program Evaluation* (Newbury Park,

Calif.: Sage, 1987); and Michael E. Kraft and Scott R. Furlong, *Politics, Analysis and Alternatives*, 3rd ed. (Washington, D.C.: CQ Press, 2009).

Chapter 10: Performance Management in the Public Sector

1. Edward K. Hamilton, "Productivity: The New York City Approach," in Chester A. Newland, ed., "Symposium on Productivity in Government," *Public Administration Review*, 32 (November/December 1972): 739–850, at 784–95. See also John Matzer, Jr., ed., *Productivity Improvement Techniques: Creative Approaches for Local Government* (Washington, D.C.: International City Management Association, 1986); Robert O. Brinkerhoff and Dennis E. Dressler, *Productivity Measurement: A Guide for Managers and Evaluators* (Newbury Park, Calif.: Sage, 1989); Deborah Cutchin, "Municipal Executive Productivity: Lessons from New Jersey," *Public Productivity and Management Review*, 13 (Spring, 1990): 245–70; Stephen Worchel, Wendy Wood, and Jeffery A. Simpson, eds., *Group Process and Productivity* (Newbury Park, Calif.: Sage, 1991); Mary Ellen Guy, "Workplace Productivity and Gender Issues," *Public Administration Review*, 53 (May/June 1993): 279–82; P. M. Jackson, "Productivity and Performance of Public Sector Organizations," *International Journal of Technology Management*, 17 (1999): 753–70; Carl DeMaio, "Pioneering Performance," *Government Executive*, 34(9) (2002): 76; Marc Holzer and Seok Hwan-Lee, *Public Productivity Handbook*, 2nd ed., revised and expanded (New York, Marcel Dekker, 2004); and Colin Talbot, *Theories of Performance: Organizational and Service Improvement in the Public Domain* (New York: Oxford University Press, 2010).

2. For details, see J. Cassidy, *Enterprise GIS Strategies Strengthen Government Operations*, Government Technology Online. Available at: http://www.govtech.com/pcio/articles/265061, 2008; and Sukumar Ganapati, "Uses of Public Participation Geographic Information Systems Applications in E-Government," *Public Administration Review* 71 (3) (May–June 2011): 425–435.

3. Elaine C. Kamarck and J.S. Nye Jr. *Governance.com: Democracy in the Information Age.* (Washington, D.C.: Brookings Institution Press, 2002); H. Chen, L. Brandt, V. Gregg, R. Traunmueller, S. Dawes, E. Hovy, A. Macintosh, C. Larson, *Digital Government: E-Government Research, Case Studies, and Implementation* (New York: Springer Science and

Business Media, 2008); Andrew Chadwick. *Internet Politics: States, Citizens, and New Communication Technologies* (New York: Oxford University Press, 2006); Andrew Chadwick and Phillip Howard, *The Routledge Handbook for Internet Politics* (London and New York: Routledge, 2009); James Hendricks and R. E. Denton, *Communicator-in-Chief: How Barack Obama Used New Media Technology to Win the White House* (New York: Lexington Books, 2010); and Michael E. Milakovich, *Digital Governance: New Technologies for Improving Public Service and Participation.* (London and New York: Routledge, 2012).

4. Robert S. Kravchuk and Ronald W. Schack, "Designing Effective Performance Measurement under the Government Performance and Results Act of 1993," *Public Administration Review*, 56 (July/August, 1996): 348–59. See also Kathryn E. Newcomer and Aaron A. Otto, "Is GPRA Improving the Performance of the Federal Government?" *The Public Manager*, 28 (2000): 21–25; and Jonathan R. Bruel, "The Government Performance and Results Act—10 Years Later," *Journal of Government Financial Management*, 52(1) (2003): 58–64. For critical review of measurement initiatives, see David G. Frederickson and H. George Frederickson, *Measuring Performance in the Hollow State* (Washington, D.C.: Georgetown University Press, 2006).

5. T. Curristine, "Reforming the U.S. Department of Transportation: Challenges and Opportunities of the Government Performance and Results Act for Federal-State Relations," *Publius*, 32(1) (2002): 25–45; and B. White, *Performance-Informed Managing and Budgeting for Federal Agencies: An Update* (Washington, D.C.: Council for Excellence in Government, 2003).

6. For details, see http://www.conginst.org/resultsact. For a list of domestic programs identified by the Obama administration in the 2011 federal budget as candidates for termination or reduction, see http://www.gpoaccess.gov/usbudget/fy010/pdf/budget/tables.pdf, Tables S-2 and S-5.

7. Former Congressman Dick Armey (R-TX), one of the sponsors of the bill, graded the first plans in 1997 on their compliance with the GPRA, not on their actual content. The average grade was 42 out of 100 in the 1997 evaluation. See also, Bruel, "The Government Performance and Results Act," p. 60.

8. Jonathan D. Bruel, "Three Bush Administration Management Reform Initiatives: The President's Management Agenda, Freedom to Manage Legislative Proposals, and the Program Assessment Rating Tool," *Public Administration Review*, 67 (January/February, 2007): 21–27. For a list of current performance ratings for over 1,000 federal executive agencies, see http://www.ExpectMore.gov.

9. Executive Order: Improving Government Program Performance, November 13, 2007. Accessed at http://www.whitehouse.gov/news/releases/2007/11/20071113-9.html. Surprisingly, Bush's Executive Order did not embed the specifics of either the PMA or the OMB Program Assessment Review Tool (PART).

10. David Osborne and Ted Gaebler, *Reinventing Government: How the Entrepreneurial Spirit Is Transforming the Public Sector* (Reading, Mass.: Addison-Wesley, 1992); David Osborne and Peter Plastrik, *Banishing Bureaucracy: Five Stages for Reinventing Government* (Reading, Mass.: Addison-Wesley, 1997); David Osborne and Peter Plastrik, *The Reinventor's Fieldbook: Tools for Transforming Your Government* (San Francisco, Calif.: Jossey-Bass, 2000); and David Osborne and Peter Hutchinson, *The Price of Government: Getting the Results We Need in an Age of Permanent Fiscal Crisis* (New York: Basis Books, 2004).

11. S. L. Durst and C. Newell, "Better, Faster, Stronger: Government Reinvention in the 1990s," *The American Review of Public Administration*, 29(1) (1999): 61–76; P. Kim and L. Wolff, "Improving Government Performance: Public Management Reform and the National Performance Review," *Public Performance and Management Review*, 18(1) (1994): 73–87; and G. Russell and R. Waste, "The Limits of Reinventing Government," *American Review of Public Administration*, 28(4) (1998): 325–46.

12. Osborne and Gaebler, *Reinventing Government*, p. 31, Appendix A, and chap. 10, pp. 290–98. A state-level example of a more deliberate entrepreneurial approach to managing the bureaucracy (in the state of Iowa) can be found in "A State Shapes Up," *Governing*, 19 (December 2005), 60–61.

13. J. Beckett, "The 'Government Should Be Run Like a Business' Mantra," *American Review of Public Administration*, 30(2) (2000): 185–204; and Osborne and Plastrik, *Banishing Bureaucracy*. For information on the Clinton Administration's federal executive agency reinvention efforts (1993–2001), including numerous case studies and links to other related sites, see http://www.govinfo.library.unt.edu/npr/index.htm.

14. Albert Gore, *From Red Tape to Results: Creating a Government That Works Better and Costs Less: Report of the National Performance Review* (Washington, D.C.: U.S. Government Printing Office,

1993); Steven J. Goldsmith, "Can Business Really Do Business with Government?" *Harvard Business Review*, 75(3) (1999): 110–21; National Academy of Public Administration, *A Government to Trust and Respect: Rebuilding Citizen-Government Relations in the 21st Century* (Washington, D.C.: National Academy of Public Administration, 1999); and Graeme Hodge, *Privatization: An International Review of Performance* (Boulder, Colo.: Westview Press, 2000).

15. Paul E. Atkinson, "New Zealand's Radical Reforms" *OECD Observer*, 205 (1997): 43; A. Jordan, "Special Education in Ontario, Canada: A Case Study of Market-based Reforms," *Cambridge Journal of Education*, 31(3) (2001) 349–71; L. E. Armijo and P. Faucher, "We Have a Consensus: Explaining Political Support for Market Reforms in Latin America," *Latin American Politics and Society*, 44(2) (2002): 1–40; R. F. Durant and J. S. Legge, Jr., "Politics, Public Opinion, and Privatization in France: Assessing the Calculus of Consent for Market Reforms," *Public Administration Review*, 62(3) (2002): 307–23; J. Forrer, "Private Finance Initiative: A Better Public–Private Partnership?" *Public Manager*, 31(2) (2002): 43; and Donald P. Moynihan, "Managing for Results in State Government: Evaluating a Decade of Reform," *Public Administration Review*, 66 (January–February, 2006): 77–89.

16. For a discussion of the origins and impacts of NPM, see Richard Batley and George Larbi, *The Changing Role of Government: The Reform of Public Services in Developing Countries* (Basingstroke, UK: Palgrave Macmillan, 2004); Michael Poole, Roger Mansfield, and Julian Gould-Williams, "Public and Private Sector Managers Over 20 Years: A Test of the 'Convergence Thesis,'" *Public Administration*, 84(4) (2006): 1051–76; and Stephen E. Congrey and R. Paul Battaglio, Jr., "A Return to Spoils? Revisiting Radical Civil Service Reform in the United States," *Public Administration Review*, 67 (May/June 2007): 425–36.

17. Richard C. Box, Gary S. Marshall, B. J. Reed, and Christine Reed, "New Public Management and Substantive Democracy," *Public Administration Review*, 61(September/October 2001): 608–619; Paul C. Light, *The New Public Service* (Washington, D.C.: Brookings Institution Press, 1999); and Janet V. Denhardt and Robert B. Denhardt, *The New Public Service: Serving, not Steering*, 3rd ed. (New York: M. E. Sharpe, 2011), p. ix.

18. Denhardt and Denhardt, *The New Public Service*, p. 60.

19. The White House, "Executive Order 12862: Setting Customer Standards," Office of the Press Secretary, 1993. Accessed December 6, 2004, at http://govinfo.library.unt.edu/npr/library/direct/orders/2222.html.

20. T. H. Poister, "Citizen Ratings of Public and Private Service Quality: A Comparative Perspective," *Public Administration Review*, 54(2) 1994: 155–60; J. E. Benton and J. L. Daly, "Measuring Citizen Evaluations: The Question of Question Order Effects," *Public Administration Quarterly* 16(4) (1993): 492–508; James H. Svara, "Reforming or Dismantling Government?" *Public Administration Review*, 56 (July/August 1996): 400–6; Joseph Pegnato, "Is a Citizen a Customer?" *Public Performance and Management Review*, 20(4) (1997): 397–404; John Alford, "Why Do Public-Sector Clients CoProduce?" *Administration and Society*, 34 (March 2002): 32–56; R. A. Pride, "How Critical Events Rather Than Performance Trends Shape Public Evaluations of the Schools," *Urban Review* 34(2) (2002): 159–78; G. Van Ryzin, "Expectations, Performance, and Citizen Satisfaction with Urban Services," *Journal of Policy Analysis and Management* 23(3) (2004): 71–82; Trevor Brown, "Coercion versus Choice: Citizen Evaluations of Public Service Quality across Methods of Consumption," *Public Administration Review*, 67 (May/June 2007): 559–72; and T. H. Poister and C. E. Thomas, "The Wisdom of Crowds: Learning from Administrators' Predictions of Citizen Perceptions," *Public Administration Review*, 67 (March/April 2007): 279–89.

21. Executive Office of the President, 2010, accessed at: http://www.whitehouse.gov/administration/eop/nec/StrategyforAmericanInnovation/.

22. Jonathan P. West, Evan Berman, and Michael E. Milakovich, "Total Quality Management in Local Government," *Municipal Yearbook 1994* (Washington, D.C.: International City/County Management Association, 1994), pp. 14–26.

23. Robert S. Kravchuk and Robert Leighton, "Implementing Total Quality Management in the States," *Public Productivity and Management Review* 17 (Fall 1993): 71–82; and Evan Berman, Michael E. Milakovich, and Jonathan P. West, "Implementing TQM in the States," *Spectrum: The Journal of State Government*, 67 (Spring 1994): 6–13.

24. Robert Camp, *Benchmarking: The Search for Industry Best Practices That Lead to Superior Performance* (Milwaukee, Wis.: ASQC Press, 1989); Patricia Keehley, S. Medlin, S. MacBride, and L. Longmore, *Benchmarking for Best Practices in the Public*

Sector (San Francisco, Calif.: Jossey-Bass, 1997); William W. Coplin and Carol Dwyer, *Does Your Government Measure Up?: Better Tools for Local Officials and Citizens* (Syracuse, N.Y.: Syracuse University Community Benchmarks Program, 2000); David Ammons, "Benchmarking as a Performance Management Tool: Experience among Municipalities in North Carolina," *Journal of Public Budgeting, Accounting and Financial Management*, 12(1) (2000): 106–24; and David C. Ammons, C. Coe, and M. Lombardo, "Performance-Comparison Projects in Local Government: Participants' Perspectives," *Public Administration Review*, 61(1) (2001): 100–10.

25. The International Benchmarking Clearinghouse contains information about the best practices, networking opportunities, and benchmarking resources to discover, research, understand, and implement emerging and effective improvement methods (http://www.apqc.org). The American Society for Quality applies, promotes, and provides quality-related activities, education, and services to several types of organizations, including governments (http://www.asq.org/). The National Center for Public Performance is recognized as a research and public-service organization devoted to improving productivity in the public sector (http://www.ncpp.us).

26. See, among others, Michael Weir, "Efficiency Measurement in Government," *The Bureaucrat*, 13 (Summer 1984): 38–42; Thomas J. Cook, ed., "Symposium: Performance Measurement in Public Agencies," *Policy Studies Review*, 6 (August 1986): 61–170; George Downs and Patrick Larkey, *The Search for Government Efficiency: From Hubris to Helplessness* (New York: Random House, 1986); James E. Swiss, *Public Management Systems* (Englewood Cliffs, N.J.: Prentice Hall, 1991); and Robert D. Behn, "Why Measure Performance? Different Purposes Require Different Measures," *Public Administration Review*, 63 (May/June 2003): 585–56.

27. Stanley A. Brown, *Total Quality Service: How Organizations Use It to Create a Competitive Advantage* (Englewood Cliffs, N.J.: Prentice Hall, 1992); Ronald Gilbert, *The TQS Factor and You* (Boca Raton, Fla.: Business Performance Publications, 1992); George Beam, *Quality Public Management: What It Is and How It Can Be Improved and Advanced* (Chicago, Ill.: Burnham Publishers, 2001); and Michael E. Milakovich, *Improving Service Quality in the Global Economy* (Boca Raton, Fla.: Auerbach Publishers, 2006).

28. Paul Volcker, Chair, *Leadership for America: Rebuilding the Public Service: The Report of the National Commission on the Public Service and the Task Force Reports to the National Commission on the Public Service* (Lexington, Mass.: Lexington Books, 1990); William Winter, Chair, National Commission on the State and Local Public Service, *Hard Truths/ Tough Choices: An Agenda for State and Local Reform* (Albany, N.Y.: Nelson Rockefeller Institute of Government, State University of New York–Albany, 1993); and Albert Gore, *From Red Tape to Results*. Numerous other studies and reports have also focused on many of the same questions addressed by these commissions. See, for example, Patricia W. Ingraham and Donald F. Kettl, eds., *Issues for the American Public Service* (Chatham, N.J.: Chatham House, 1992); Donald F. Kettl, John J. DiIulio, Jr., and Gerald Garvey, *Improving Government Performance: An Owner's Manual* (Washington, D.C.: Brookings Institution Press, 1993); Frank J. Thompson, ed., *Revitalizing the State and Local Public Service: Strengthening Performance, Accountability and Citizen Confidence* (San Francisco, Calif.: Jossey-Bass, 1993); John J. DiIulio, Jr., ed., *Deregulating the Public Service: Can Government Be Improved?* (Washington, D.C.: Brookings Institution Press, 1994); Patricia W. Ingraham, Philip G. Joyce, and Amy Kneedler Donahue, *Government Performance: Why Management Matters* (Baltimore, Md.: The Johns Hopkins University Press, 2003); David Edwards and John Clayton Thomas, "Developing a Municipal Performance-Measurement System: Reflections on the Atlanta Dashboard," *Public Administration Review*, 65 (May/June 2005), 369–76; and Patricia Wallace Ingraham, "Performance: Promises to Keep and Miles to Go," *Public Administration Review*, 65 (July/August 2005): 390–95. For a commentary on the adequacy of performance measures relating specifically to new technologies in the workplace, see Thomas R. Davies, "Performance Anxiety," *Governing*, 18 (June 2005): 58.

29. For an elaboration of this debate, see James H. Svara, "Reforming or Dismantling Government?" *Public Administration Review*, 56 (July/August 1996): 400–6.

30. For details on implementing this legislation, see http://www.omb.gov; http://www.cbo.gov; http://www.gao.gov; and http://www.opm.gov/gpra/index.htm. For information about recent reforms, see http://www.usa.gov and http://www.planetgov.com.

31. Though informed opinions differ, there is considerable evidence that the reinvention initiatives were

not implemented as intended and did not work entirely as predicted in the national government. The NPR—as well as the concept of reinventing government—was subjected to some sharp criticism. See, among others, James D. Carroll, "The Rhetoric of Reform and Political Reality in the National Performance Review," *Public Administration Review*, 55(3) (1995): 302–12; Charles Goodsell, "Re-Invent Government, or Re-Discover It?" *Public Administration Review*, 53 (January/February 1993): 85–87; John J. Dilulio, Jr., "Reinventing the Dinosaur?" *Brookings Review*, 11 (Fall 1993): 5; Jon Meacham, "What Al Gore Might Learn the Hard Way," *Washington Monthly*, 25 (September 1993): 16–20; David Segal, "What's Wrong with the Gore Report," *Washington Monthly*, 25 (November 1993): 18–23; Ronald C. Moe, "The 'Reinventing Government' Exercise: Misinterpreting the Problem, Misjudging the Consequences," *Public Administration Review*, 54 (March/April 1994): 111–22; Rob Gurwitt, "Entrepreneurial Government: The Morning After," *Governing*, 7 (May 1994): 34–40; Donald F. Kettl, "Reinventing Government? Appraising the National Performance Review," *CTM Report* (August 1994): 94–102; Donald F. Kettl and John J. DiIulio, Jr., eds., *Inside the Reinvention Machine* (Washington, D.C.: Brookings Institution Press, 1995); and Michael Hamilton, "The Career Service and Presidential Transition: From Bush to Clinton and the National Performance Review," *Public Administration Quarterly*, 20(1) (Spring 1996): 52–70.

32. Donald R. Kettl, "Relentless Reinvention," *Government Executive*, 32(1) (2000): 25–28. The link between public trust and government performance is not always clear. For details, see Kaifeng Yang and Marc Holzer, "The Performance-Trust Link: Implications for Performance Measurement," *Public Administration Review*, 66 (January–February, 2006): 114–26.

33. For an inside look at how one of the TIGR groups sought to reform the U.S. Patent and Trademark Office, see Beth Simone Novack, *Wiki Government: How Technology Can Make Government Better, Democracy Stronger and Citizens More Powerful.* (Washington, D.C.: Brookings Institution Press, 2009).

34. This problem was manifested in the wake of the Southern California wildfires in the fall of 2007, when wealthy homeowners, who could afford to have their homes sprayed with fire retardant just before the wind-blown fires hit, were able to save their houses, but the equally deserving homeowners who could not afford the costly additional service were not.

35. Richard C. Box, *Citizen Governance: Leading American Communities into the 21st Century* (Thousand Oaks, Calif.: Sage, 1998); L. A. Blanchard, C. C. Hinnant, and W. Wong, "Market-Based Reforms in Government," *Administration and Society*, 30(3) (1998): 30–48; Robert Behn, "The New Public Management Paradigm and the Search for Democratic Accountability," *International Public Management Review*, 1(2) (1999): 131–65; Beckett, "The 'Government Should Be Run Like a Business' Mantra"; M. S. Haque, "Public Service: The Diminishing Publicness of Public Service under the Current Mode of Governance," *Public Administration Review*, 61(1) (2001): 65–82; J. Alford, "Defining the Client in the Public Sector: A Social-Exchange Perspective," *Public Administration Review*, 62(3) (2002): 337–46; William Gormley and Scott Balla, *Bureaucracy and Democracy: Accountability and Performance* (Washington, D.C.: CQ Press, 2004); Mary K Marvel and Howard P. Marvel, "Outsourcing Oversight: A Comparison of Monitoring for In-House and Contracted Services," *Public Administration Review*, 67 (May/June 2007): 521–30; and Jonas Prager, "Contract City Redux: Weston, Florida, as the Ultimate New Public Management Model City," *Public Administration Review*, 68 (January/February 2008): 167–80.

36. Partly in response to budgetary restraints, changing national priorities, deficit spending, and fiscal stress, George W. Bush favored the broader use of private alternatives such as *competitive outsourcing* as a PM measure. President Obama has placed greater scrutiny on private firms seeking government contracts and emphasized increased productivity *within* public agencies.

37. Beckett, "The 'Government Should Be Run Like a Business' Mantra"; Gormley and Balla, *Bureaucracy and Democracy;* Behn, "The New Public Management Paradigm and the Search for Democratic Accountability"; L. Deleon and P. Deleon, "The Democratic Ethos and Public Management," *Administration and Society*, 34(2) (2002): 229–51; and David H. Rosenbloom, "Reinventing Administrative Prescriptions: The Case for Democratic-Constitutional Impact Statements and Scorecards," *Public Administration Review*, 67 (January/February 2007): 28–39.

38. Gore, *From Red Tape to Results*; Donald R. Kettl, *Reinventing Government: A Fifth-Year Report Card* (Washington, D.C: Brookings Institution Press,

1998); D. R. Kettl, "Relentless Reinvention"; James Thompson, "Reinvention as Reform: Assessing the NPR," *Public Administration Review*, 60(6) (2000): 508–22.

39. U.S. Government Accountability Office, *Managing for Results: Opportunities for Continued Improvements in Agencies' Performance Plans* (Washington, D.C.: GAO, 1999); U.S. Government Accountability Office, *Managing for Results: Enhancing Agency Use of Performance Information for Management Decision Making* (Washington, D.C.: GAO, September 2005).

40. George W. Bush, "Improving Government Performance," *President's Management Agenda, Fiscal Year 2002*, accessed at: http://www.whitehouse.gov/omb/budintegration/pma_ index.html, pp. 24–25 (accessed December 6, 2004).

41. Jeffery W. Seifert, "E-Governance in the United States," in Peter Hernon, Rowena Cullen, and Harold C. Relyea (eds.), *Comparative Perspectives on E-Government* (Lanham, Md.: Scarecrow Press, 2006), pp. 25–54.

42. Executive Office of the President, Office of Management and Budget, Office of Procurement Policy, Washington, D.C., January 25, 2005, retrieved at: http://www.whitehouse.gov/ results/agenda/cs_2004_report_rev5a2_doc.pdf.

43. President Obama focused attention on government accountability and program efficiency early in his administration. He asked department heads, during their first cabinet meeting for specific proposals, to cut their budgets. Obama proposed the elimination of dozens of government programs shown to be wasteful or ineffective, adding that there will be "no sacred cows, and no pet projects."

44. William Eggers, *Government 2.0: Using Technology to Improve Education, Cut Red Tape, Reduce Gridlock, and Enhance Democracy*. (Lanham, Md.: Rowman & Littlefield Publishers, Inc., 2005). Vivek Kundra resigned from his position in August 2011.

45. This section draws with permission from Michael E. Milakovich, "Comparing Bush–Cheney and Clinton–Gore Performance Management Strategies: Are They More Alike Than Different?" *Public Administration*, 84 (2006): 461–78.

46. H. George Frederickson, "Getting to Green," *PA Times*, 25(7) (2002): 11. See also Rosenbloom, "Reinventing Administrative Prescriptions," p. 31, for criticism of the "scorecard" system.

47. Donald R. Kettl, *Team Bush: Leadership Lessons from the Bush White House* (New York: McGraw-Hill, 2003), p. 135.

48. For archived performance rankings of all executive branch agencies, see http://www.ExpectMore.gov.

49. H. George Frederickson, "Getting to Green"; and B. White, "On a Wing and a Prayer," *Government Executive*, 35(9) (2003): 80–81.

50. Steven Barr, "Bush Team Waxes Resolute on Management Reforms," *Washington Post*, February 2, 2003, p. C2.

51. White, "On a Wing and a Prayer."

52. Cited by White, "On a Wing and a Prayer."

53. Barr, "Bush Team Waxes Resolute."

54. Stephen Barr, "From Bush, an Order for Agencies to Track Progress," *Washington Post*, November 15, 2007, p. D4.

55. Box et al., "New Public Management and Substantive Democracy."

56. R. Heeks, *Reinventing Government in the Information Age* (London: Routledge, 1999); Jane Fountain, *Building the Virtual State* (Washington, D.C.: Brookings Institution Press, 2001); and Ake Grönlund, *Electronic Government: Design, Applications and Management* (London: Idea Group Publishing, 2002).

57. B. Guy Peters, *The Future of Governing: Four Emerging Models* (Lawrence, Kan.: University of Kansas Press, 1998).

58. Beam, *Quality Public Management*; Milakovich, *Improving Service Quality in the Global Economy*.

59. Barr, "Bush Team Waxes Resolute"; Paul Light, "An Update on the Bush Administration's Competitive Sourcing Initiative," Testimony before the U.S. Senate Subcommittee on Oversight of Government Management, the Federal Workforce and the District of Columbia (New York University and the Brookings Institution, 2003), senate.gov_ files/072403light.pdf.

60. Patricia de Lancer Julnes and Marc Holzer, "Promoting the Utilization of Performance Measures in Public Organizations: An Empirical Study of Factors Affecting Adoption and Implementation," *Public Administration Review*, 61(6) (2001): 693–708; and Ian Sanderson, "PM, Evaluation and Learning in 'Modern' Local Government," *Public Administration*, 79(2) (2001): 297–313.

61. This section is drawn with permission from Bettina Larsen and Michael E. Milakovich, "Citizen Relationship Management and E-Government," in Maria Wimmer, Roland Traunmuller, Ake Grönlund, and Kim V. Andersen, eds., *Electronic Government* (Berlin: Springer-Verlag, 2005), pp. 57–69. See also Donald F. Norris and M. Jae Moon, "Advancing E-Government at the Grassroots: Tortoise or Hare?"

Public Administration Review, 65 (January/February 2005): 64–75; Antoinette J. Pole, "E-mocracy: Information Technology and the New York and Vermont State Legislatures," *State and Local Government Review*, 37 (2005): 7–24; James K. Scott, "E-Services: Assessing the Quality of Municipal Government Web Sites," *State and Local Government Review*, 37 (2005): 151–65; and David G. Garson, *Public Information Technology and E-Governance: Managing the Virtual State* (Boston, Mass.: Jones and Bartlett, 2006).

62. Michael E. Milakovich, "Balancing Public Service Expectations with Political Accountability," *International Public Management Review*, 4(2) (2003): 61–82; Tanya Heikkla and Kimberly Roussin Isett, "Citizen Involvement and Performance Management in Special-Purpose Governments," *Public Administration Review*, 67 (March/April 2007): 238–48; and Tony Bovaird, "Beyond Engagement and Participation: User and Community Coproduction of Public Services," *Public Administration Review*, 67 (September/October 2007): 846–60.

63. Teresa Nasif, "Using Customer Relationship Management to Serve Citizens," *U.S. General Services Administration Newsletter*, 14 (January 2004): 1.

64. M. J. Xavier, "Citizen Relationship Management—Concepts, Tools and Research Opportunities" (paper presented at the 6th Research Conference on Relationship Management, Atlanta, Georgia, June 2002, p. 3).

65. Grönlund, *Electronic Government*, p. 1.

66. Cited by Milakovich, *Digital Governance*.

67. Ramon Barquin, "Citizen Relationship Management (CzRM)—The Challenge and the Promise," *U.S. General Services Administration Newsletter*, 14 (January 2004): 20, http://www.gsa.gov/gsa/cm_attachments/GSA_DOCUMENT/OISNEWS-LETTERJan2004_R20A3-e_0Z5RDZ-i34K-pR.pdf (accessed December 2004).

68. C. K. Prahalad and Venkatram Ramaswamy, "Co-opting Customer Competence," in C. K. Prahalad, et al., eds., *Harvard Business Review on Customer Relationship Management* (Boston: Harvard Business School Press, 2001), p. 4.

69. Casey Coleman, "Citizen Relationship Management," *U.S. General Services Administration Newsletter*, 14 (January 2004): 6.

70. Steven Cohen and William Eimicke, "The Use of Internet in Government Service Delivery" (The PricewaterhouseCoopers Endowment for the Business of Government, February 2001), p. 7. http://www.businessofgovernment.org/main/publications/ grant_reports/details/index.asp?GID=80 (accessed December 6, 2004).

71. Grönlund, *Electronic Government*, p. 31.

72. Ibid., p. 39.

73. "Children, the Digital Divide, and Federal Policy" (Report by Kaiser Family Foundation, Menlo Park, California, September, 2004). Accessed at http://www.kff.org/entmedia/loader.cfm?url=/common-spot/security/getfile.cfm&PageID=46360.

74. Robert Balfanz and Nettie Letters, "Which High Schools Produce the Nation's Drop-Outs? Where Are They Located? Who Attends Them?" Center for Social Organization of Schools (Baltimore, Md.: Johns Hopkins University, 2004). Accessed October 18, 2007, at http://www.csos.jhu.edu/tdhs/rsch/Locating_Dropouts.pdf.

75. Denhardt and Denhardt, *The New Public Service*, p. 62.

Chapter 11: Government Regulation and Administrative Law

1. Paul W. MacAvoy, *The Regulated Industries and the Economy* (New York: Norton, 1979), pp. 17–24. See also Louis M. Kohlmeier, Jr., *The Regulators: Watchdog Agencies and the Public Interest* (New York: Harper & Row, 1969), pp. 307–9; Eugene Bardach and Robert Kagan, eds., *Social Regulation* (San Francisco: Institute for Contemporary Studies, 1982); David P. McCaffrey, *OSHA and the Politics of Health Regulation* (New York: Plenum Press, 1982); Robert E. Litan and William D. Nordhaus, *Reforming Federal Regulation* (New Haven, Conn.: Yale University Press, 1983), pp. 43–44; Richard A. Harris and Sidney M. Milkis, *The Politics of Regulatory Change: A Tale of Two Agencies*, 2nd ed. (New York: Oxford University Press, 1996); A. Lee Fritschler and James M. Hoefler, *Smoking and Politics: Policy Making and the Federal Bureaucracy*, 5th ed. (Englewood Cliffs, N. J.: Prentice Hall, 1995); and Marc Eisner, *The American Political Economy: Institutional Evolution of Market and State.* (New York: Rutledge, 2011).

2. This terminology is consistent with the usage suggested by Kenneth J. Meier, "The Impact of Regulatory Organization Structure: IRCs or DRAs?" *Southern Review of Public Administration*, 3 (March 1980): 427–43. We are indebted to an anonymous reviewer for suggesting this clarification.

3. Fritschler and Hoefler, *Smoking and Politics*, pp. 54–55.

4. For further examination of state-level regulation, see, among others, Patty D. Renfrow and

David J. Houston, "A Comparative Analysis of Rule-making Provisions in State Administrative Procedure Acts," *Policy Studies Review*, 6 (May 1987): 657–65; Jeffrey E. Cohen, *The Politics of Telecommunications Regulation: The States and the Divestiture of AT&T* (Armonk, N.Y.: M. E. Sharpe, 1992); and Evan J. Ringquist, *Environmental Protection at the State Level: Politics and Progress in Controlling Pollution* (Armonk, N.Y.: M. E. Sharpe, 1993).

5. Morton Grodzins, *The American System: A New View of Government in the United States* (Chicago: Rand McNally, 1966), pp. 75–80.

6. William Lilley III and James C. Miller III, "The New 'Social Regulation,'" *The Public Interest*, 47 (Spring 1977): 49–61, at 52–53 (emphasis added).

7. James L. Regens, Thomas M. Dietz, and Robert W. Rycroft, "Risk Assessment in the Policy-Making Process: Environmental Health and Safety Protection," *Public Administration Review*, 43 (March/April 1983): 137–45, at 138.

8. Ibid.

9. Thomas Moss and Barry Lubin, "Risk Analysis: A Legislative Perspective," in Chester R. Richmond, Phillip J. Walsh, and Emily D. Copenhaver, eds., *Health Risk Analysis* (Philadelphia: Franklin Institute Press, 1981), p. 30; cited by Regens, Dietz, and Rycroft, "Risk Assessment in the Policy-Making Process," 138.

10. Regens, Dietz, and Rycroft, "Risk Assessment in the Policy-Making Process," 138. See also George C. Eads and Michael Fix, *Relief or Reform? Reagan's Regulatory Dilemma* (Washington, D.C.: Urban Institute Press, 1984), chap. 5; and Leonard A. Cole, *Element of Risk: The Politics of Radon* (Washington, D.C.: AAAS Press, 1993).

11. Herbert Kaufman, *Red Tape* (Washington, D.C.: Brookings Institution Press, 1977), chap. 2.

12. According to the National Performance Review (NPR), 55 percent of the existing 86,000 pages of federal regulations had either been eliminated (16,000 pages) or revised (31,000). Teams of "re-inventors" succeeded, to some extent, in clarifying and simplifying the remaining 39,000 pages of regulations. See Albert Gore, *Common Sense Government Works Better and Costs Less* (New York: Random House, 1995), p. 40.

13. Fritschler and Hoefler, *Smoking and Politics*, p. 108.

14. This discussion is based on Meier, "The Impact of Regulatory Organization Structure," especially pp. 440–42.

15. This description of the rule-making process is taken from *Federal Register: What It Is and How to Use It* (Washington, D.C.: Office of the Federal Register, National Archives and Records Service, General Services Administration, 1980). Available online at http://www.gpoaccess.gov/fr/.

16. Fritschler and Hoefler, *Smoking and Politics*, pp. 138–39.

17. For further information regarding new regulations and recent regulatory developments of particular importance to adjudication proceedings before administrative law judges, see Office of Administrative Law Judges at http://www.oalj.dol.gov.

18. For example, see Seymour Scher, "Regulatory Agency Control through Appointment: The Case of the Eisenhower Administration and the NLRB," *Journal of Politics*, 23, (November 1961): 667–688.

19. Erwin G. Krasnow, Lawrence D. Longley, and Herbert A. Terry, *The Politics of Broadcast Regulation*, 3rd ed. (New York: St. Martin's Press, 1982), especially chapters 2 and 3. For an interesting case study of regulatory politics involving the FCC, see James L. Baughman, *Television's Guardians: The FCC and the Politics of Programming, 1958–1967* (Knoxville: University of Tennessee Press, 1985).

20. *Federal Register: What It Is and How to Use It*, p. 2.

21. See *Government Executive*, 22 (January 1990), 10.

22. The quote is taken from the second edition (1978) of *The Politics of Broadcast Regulation*, p. 28.

23. William L. Cary, *Politics and the Regulatory Agencies* (New York: McGraw-Hill, 1967), p. 4.

24. Mark V. Nadel, *The Politics of Consumer Protection* (Indianapolis: Bobbs-Merrill, 1971), p. 29; quoted by Fritschler and Hoefler, *Smoking and Politics*, p. 12. See also William F. West, "The Growth of Internal Conflict in Administrative Regulation," *Public Administration Review*, 48 (July/August 1988): 773–82.

25. *U.S. News & World Report*, March 28, 1977, p. 49.

26. After over fifty people were killed in minor accidents, public response was so intense that, in November 1996, the NHTSA reversed its policy by allowing individual car owners to voluntarily disconnect the air bags, pending installation in 1999 of air bags with sensors that adjust to a person's height and weight. These episodes of forced regulation without exhaustive testing for the dangers of "safety" equipment, and subsequent reversals of policy a few years later, do little to inspire public confidence in regulatory processes.

27. Interview with Representative (later Senator) Steven D. Symms (R-ID), in *U.S. News & World Report*, June 13, 1977, pp. 51–52.

28. Interview with Dr. David T. Carr, in *U.S. News & World Report*, June 13, 1977, pp. 51–52.

29. Donald Dalrymple, assistant counsel to the House Interstate and Foreign Commerce Subcommittee on Health and the Environment, quoted in *Congressional Quarterly Weekly Report*, 35 (July 2, 1977): 1348.

30. "OSHA Toxic Regulations Expanded," Associated Press wire service story, appearing in the *Bloomington (Ill.) Pantagraph*, August 20, 1987, p. D1.

31. "Rewards for Insider Trapping Tips," Associated Press wire service story, appearing in the *Bloomington (Ill.) Pantagraph*, June 29, 1989, p. D1.

32. "Buckling Up for Work," an editorial appearing in the *Washington Post*, July 16, 1990, p. A10.

33. "New Meat Label Rules Anger Industry," Associated Press wire service story, appearing in the *Bloomington (Ill.) Pantagraph*, November 5, 1993, pp. D1, D2.

34. Steven A. Holmes, "In 4 Years, Disabilities Act Hasn't Improved Jobs Rate," *New York Times*, October 23, 1994.

35. Cited in Cindy Skrzycki, *The Regulators: Anonymous Power Brokers in American Politics* (Lanham, Md.: Rowman & Littlefield, 2003), pp. 8–9.

36. Peter Jacobsen, "Historical Overview of Tobacco Legislation and Regulation," *Journal of Social Issues*, 53 (1997): 75.

37. See Fritschler and Hoefler, *Smoking and Politics*.

38. See Jacobsen, "Historical Overview of Tobacco Legislation and Regulation," pp. 79–84.

39. David Kessler, "The Food and Drug Administration's Regulation of Tobacco Products," *New England Journal of Medicine*, 335(13) (1996): 988.

40. "The Tobacco Settlement," Policy.com, March 16, 1998. http://www.policy.com/ issuewk/98/0316/031698a.html.

41. "Statement of John R. Garrison, CEO, American Lung Association on Global Tobacco Bailout," *Corporate Watch On-line*, 1998. http://www.corpwatch.org/feature/ tobacco/lung.html.

42. "Action on Smoking and Health," appendices to the *Report of the Koop–Kessler Advisory Committee on Tobacco Policy and Public Health*, 1998. http://www.ash.org/ appendix.html.

43. Robert S. Lorch, *Democratic Process and Administrative Law*, rev. ed. (Detroit, Mich.: Wayne State University Press, 1980), p. 32.

44. Phillip J. Cooper, *Public Law and Public Administration*, 2nd ed. (Englewood Cliffs, N.J.: Prentice Hall, 1988), p. 6. See also Leif Carter and Christine Harrington, *Administrative Law and Politics* (New York:

HarperCollins, 1991); and Peter L. Strauss, Todd Rakoff, and Walter A. Gellhorn, eds., *Gellhorn and Byse's Administrative Law: Cases and Comments* (Westbury, N.Y.: Foundation Press, 1995).

45. Lorch, *Democratic Process and Administrative Law*, p. 61.

46. Kenneth Warren, *Administrative Law and the Political System*. 4th ed. (Boulder, Colorado: Westview Press, 2004).

47. The discussions of rule making and adjudication rely primarily on Lorch, *Democratic Process and Administrative Law*, chaps. 5 and 6; and Cooper, *Public Law and Public Administration*, chaps. 5 and 6 (respectively). See also Warren, *Administrative Law in the Political System*, chaps. 5 and 6.

48. See Lorch, *Democratic Process and Administrative Law*, pp. 102–5.

49. The following discussion relies on Cooper, *Public Law and Public Administration*, pp. 119–23.

50. Lorch, *Democratic Process and Administrative Law*, p. 115.

51. Cooper, *Public Law and Public Administration*, p. 114.

52. Ibid., pp. 233–39.

53. We are especially indebted to Marla Calhoon for her assistance in gathering case-related materials for this section, and to Professor Thomas Eimermann for his valuable suggestions along the way.

54. Warren, *Administrative Law in the Political System*, p. 271.

55. This account relies on Warren, *Administrative Law in the Political System*, pp. 230–31.

56. Ibid., p. 233.

57. See Lorch, *Democratic Process and Administrative Law*, especially chap. 1. For a comprehensive treatment of both regulatory policy and administrative law, see David H. Rosenbloom and Richard D. Schwartz, eds., *Handbook of Regulation and Administrative Law* (New York: Marcel Dekker, 1994).

58. See, among others, U.S. Supreme Court Associate Justice Stephen Breyer, *Regulation and Its Reform* (Cambridge, Mass.: Harvard University Press, 1982); and Litan and Nordhaus, *Reforming Federal Regulation*.

59. See Litan and Nordhaus, *Reforming Federal Regulation*, chap. 5, especially pp. 100–13. For an overview of presidential efforts to increase control of regulatory bodies, see Howard Ball, *Controlling Regulatory Sprawl: Presidential Strategies from Nixon to Reagan* (Westport, Conn.: Greenwood Press, 1984). See also Marc K. Landy, Marc J. Roberts, and Stephen R. Thomas, *The Environmental Protection Agency:*

From Nixon to Clinton, expanded ed. (New York: Oxford University Press, 1994).

60. For a case study of reform in a specific context, see James R. Temples, "The Nuclear Regulatory Commission and the Politics of Regulatory Reform: Since Three Mile Island," *Public Administration Review*, 42 (July/August 1982): 355–62. See also Lynton K. Caldwell, *Science and the National Environmental Policy Act: Redirecting Policy through Procedural Reform* (Tuscaloosa: University of Alabama Press, 1982); and DeWitt John, *Civic Environmentalism: Alternatives to Regulation in States and Communities* (Washington, D.C.: CQ Press, 1993). For an interesting discussion of how best to achieve regulatory compliance, see Peter J. May, "Regulation and Compliance Motivations: Examining Different Approaches," *Public Administration Review*, 65 (January/February 2005): 31–44.

61. Regarding airline deregulation and its impacts, see, among others, Steven Morrison and Clifford Winston, *The Economic Effects of Airline Deregulation* (Washington, D.C.: Brookings Institution Press, 1986); and Anthony Brown, *The Politics of Airline Deregulation* (Knoxville: University of Tennessee Press, 1987). A sharply critical assessment of airline deregulation can be found in Alex Marshall, "Bad Air Days," *Governing*, 18 (April 2005): 68. For an incisive analysis of airline deregulation, and that of the trucking and telecommunications industry, see Martha Derthick and Paul J. Quirk, *The Politics of Deregulation* (Washington, D.C.: Brookings Institution Press, 1985). An interesting examination of the early rise of trucking regulation is found in William R. Childs, *Trucking and the Public Interest: The Emergence of Federal Regulation, 1914–1940* (Knoxville: University of Tennessee Press, 1985).

62. This discussion relies on Litan and Nordhaus, *Reforming Federal Regulation*, pp. 127–31; Kenneth J. Meier, *Regulation: Politics, Bureaucracy, and Economics* (New York: St. Martin's Press, 1985), p. 3; and data drawn from *Budget of the United States Government, 1982—Appendix* (Washington, D.C.: U.S. Government Printing Office, 1981); *Budget of the United States Government, 1986—Appendix* (Washington, D.C.: U.S. Government Printing Office, 1985); *Budget of the United States Government, 1995—Appendix* (Washington, D.C.: U.S. Government Printing Office, 1994); and *Budget of the United States Government, 2006—Appendix* (Washington, D.C.: U.S. Government Printing Office, 2005).

63. Michael R. Gordon, "Will Reagan 'Turn Business Loose' If Business Wants to Stay Regulated?" *National Journal*, 13 (January 3, 1981): 10–13, at 10.

64. Susan E. Dudley, Administrator, Office of Information and Regulatory Affairs, *"Memorandum for Regulatory Policy Officers,"* Executive Office of the President, Office of Management and Budget, Washington, D.C., April 25, 2007.

Chapter 12: Conclusion: Public Administration in a Time of Conflict and Social Change

1. James D. Carroll, "Putting Government's House in Order," *Maxwell News and Notes*, 13 (Fall 1978): 2 (Syracuse, N.Y.: Maxwell School of Citizenship and Public Affairs, Syracuse University).

2. "States' Budget Outlooks Bleak for New Year" *Los Angeles Times*, December 29, 2002, pp. A1, A32; "State Budget Gaps Grew by 50 Percent, Report Says," *Miami Herald*, February 5, 2003, p. 8A; and "Prison System: State Must Decrease Crowding," *Vallejo (California) Times Herald*, May 25, 2011.

3. The term refers to nearly 2,000 U.S. high schools in which more than one-half of the students fail to graduate in four years. Most are in urban or rural areas with high concentrations of low-income and minority students and minimal job opportunities.

4. "Putin's Potemkin Election: Russia's Parliamentary Elections Will Essentially Return the Country to a One-Party State," *Christian Science Monitor*, November 27, 2007; "Russian Election: How It Was Rigged," *The Economist*, December 3, 2007.

5. These paradoxes were first noted by public administration scholar Dwight Waldo in 1972, and if anything are more noticeable now than then. Dwight Waldo, "Developments in Public Administration," *Annals of the American Academy of Political and Social Science*, 404 (November 1972): 217–45, at 219. For another perspective on many of the same issues, see Deborah Stone, *Policy Paradox: The Art of Political Decision Making*, rev. ed. (New York: W.W. Norton, 2002).

6. For details, see Jagdish Bhagwati, *In Defense of Globalization* (New York: Oxford University Press, 2004); David Held and Anthony McGrew, *Globalization/Anti-Globalization* (Cambridge, U.K.: Blackwell Publishing, Polity Press, 2002); Douglas Kellner, "Theorizing Globalization," *Sociological Theory*, 20(3) (November 2002): 285–305; Anne Slaughter, *A New World Order* (Princeton, N.J.: Princeton University Press, 2004); Sean Kay,

"Globalization, Power, and Security," *Security Dialogue*, 35(1) (March 2004); Joseph E. Stiglitz, *Making Globalization Work* (New York: W.W. Norton, 2006); and Thomas L. Friedman, *The World Is Flat: A Brief History of the Twenty-First Century* (New York: Farrar Stauss, Giraux 2007). For an alternative and more pessimistic view of globalization, see Benjamin Barber, *Jihad vs. McWorld: How Globalization and Tribalism Are Reshaping the World* (New York: Random House, 1995).

7. Bhagwati, *In Defense of Globalization*, p. 3.

8. For opposing views, see Tim Wu, *The Master Switch: The Rise and Fall of Information Empires* (New York: Knopf, 2011); and Evgeny Morozov, *The Net Delusion: The Dark Side of Internet Freedom.* (New York: Public Affairs, 2011). See also Mary Beth Sheridan, "Autocratic Regimes Fight Web-Savvy Opponents with the Own Tools," *Washington Post*, May 23, 2011.

9. "Celebrations in Tahrir Square," February 18, 2011, retrieved at: http://video.nytimes.com/video/2011/02/18/world/middleeast/100000000651167/tc-021811-egyptcelebrate.html.

10. ABC News with Christiane Amanpour, February 16, 2011, "Tweet Heard 'Round the World," retrieved at: http://www.focusonlinecommunities.com/blogs/pluggedin/2011/02/16/tweet-heard-round-the-world.

11. Our thanks to Mark Daniels for researching this topic.

12. David S. Broder, "So, Now Bigger Is Better? Despite His Campaign Rhetoric, George W. Bush Is Expanding the Federal Government," *Washington Post Weekly National Edition*, 20(13) (January 20–26, 2003): 21–22. Patrick J. Buchanan also referred to George W. Bush as "self-indulgent and overextended" in the quote from the *Miami Herald*, September 9, 2005.

13. See, among others, Theodore J. Lowi, *The End of Liberalism: The Second Republic of the United States*, 2nd ed. (New York: Norton, 1979).

14. Frederick C. Mosher, "The Public Service in the Temporary Society," *Public Administration Review*, 31 (January/February 1971): 47–62, at 51. The phrase *overhead democracy* was used originally by Emmette Redford in *Democracy in the Administrative State* (New York: Oxford University Press, 1969), p. 70.

15. M. Hirschorn, "Only Connect," *Atlantic Monthly*, May, 2008, quoted in Richard M. Barron, "Master of the Internet: How Barack Obama Harnessed New Tools and Old Lessons to Connect,

Communicate and Campaign His Way to the White House," paper presented at the University of North Carolina, Chapel Hill, School of Mass Communications and Journalism, 2008. Accessed at: http://web.cs.swarthmore.edu/~turnbull/cs91/f09/paper/barron08.pdf.

16. Representative Steny H. Hoyer (D-MD) quoted in Stephen Barr, "At Rally, Searing Rhetoric against Overhauling the Defense Personnel System," *Washington Post*, July 13, 2005, p. B2.

17. Donald F. Kettl, *System Under Stress: Homeland Security and American Politics*, 2nd ed. (Washington, D.C.: CQ Press, 2007), p. 139.

18. Ferrel Heady, *Public Administration: A Comparative Perspective*, 6th ed. (Boca Raton, Fla.: CRC Press, 2001); Jan-Erik Lane, *The Public Sector: Concepts, Models, and Approaches*, 3rd ed. (Newbury Park, Calif.: Sage, 2000); Donald Klingner, "ASPA and Globalization," personal correspondence, November 10, 2002; and Michael E. Milakovich, *Improving Service Quality in the Global Economy*, 2nd ed. (Boca Raton, Fla.: Auerbach Publishers, 2006).

19. Klingner, "ASPA and Globalization," p. 3. See also Anne T. Lawrence, James Weber, and James M. Post, *Business and Society: Stakeholders, Ethics, and Public Policy*, 11th ed. (New York: McGraw-Hill, 2005); George A. Steiner and John F. Steiner, *Business, Government and Society*, 11th ed. (New York: McGraw-Hill, 2006); and Stiglitz, *Making Globalization Work*.

20. For example, see Richard C. Elling, "The Line in Winter: An Academic Assessment of the First Report of the National Commission on the State and Local Public Service"; Raymond W. Cox III, "The Winter Commission Report: The Practitioner's Perspective"; Delmer D. Dunn, "Public Affairs, Administrative Faculty, and the Winter Commission Report," *Public Administration Review*, 54 (March/April 1994): 107–08, 108–09, and 109–10, respectively; National Commission on Terrorist Attacks upon the United States (also known as the 9/11 Commission), http://www.9-11commission.gov/commission.gov/; and the Commission on the Intelligence Capabilities of the United States Regarding Weapons of Mass Destruction (also known as Robb–Silberman Commission), (Washington, D.C., May 2005). See also James Baker III, Lee H. Hamilton, Lawrence S. Eagleburger, Vernon E. Jordan Jr., Edwin Meese III, Sandra Day O'Connor, Leon E. Panetta, William J. Perry, Charles S. Robb, and Alan K. Simpson, *The Iraq

Study Group Report: The Way Forward—A New Approach, December 6, 2006. Accessed July 9, 2007, at http://www.usip.org/isg/iraq_study_group_report/report/1206/iraq_study_group_report.pdf.

21. See, among others, James S. Bowman, "Teaching Ethics in Public Administration," in Richard Heimovics and Ann Marie Rizzo, eds., *Innovations in Teaching Public Affairs and Administration* (monograph published jointly by Florida International University, Miami, and the University of Missouri–Kansas City, 1981), pp. 79–90; and Dalton S. Lee, "The Challenge of Teaching Public Administration Ethics," *The Political Science Teacher*, 2 (Fall 1989): 1–3.

22. See David H. Rosenbloom, "Public Administrative Theory and the Separation of Powers," *Public Administration Review*, 43 (May/June 1983): 219–27.

23. Waldo, "Developments in Public Administration," p. 243 (emphasis added).

24. Mosher, "The Public Service in the Temporary Society," p. 60.

25. For an analysis of potential uses of Geographic Information Systems for decision making and greater citizen participation, see Sukumar Ganapati, "Uses of Public Participation Geographic Information Systems Applications in E-Government," *Public Administration Review* (71) 3, May–June, 2011, pp. 425–435.

26. See Michael J. Wriston, "In Defense of Bureaucracy," *Public Administration Review*, 40 (March/April 1980): 179–83, especially 180; Charles T. Goodsell, *The Case for Bureaucracy: A Public Administration Polemic*, 4th ed. (Washington, D.C., CQ Press, 2004); Max Neiman, *Defending Government: Why Big Government Works* (Upper Saddle River, N.J.: Prentice Hall, 2000); and Paul Light, *Government's Greatest Achievements: From Civil Rights to Homeland Security* (Washington, D.C.: Brookings Institution Press, 2002).

27. Wriston, "In Defense of Bureaucracy," p. 180.

28. See Robert E. Litan and William D. Nordhaus, *Reforming Federal Regulation* (New Haven, Conn.: Yale University Press, 1983), p. 132.

29. See, among others, Alan Stone, *Regulation and Its Alternatives* (Washington, D.C.: CQ Press, 1982); Susan J. Tolchin and Martin Tolchin, *Dismantling America: The Rush to Deregulate* (Boston: Houghton Mifflin, 1983); and Larry N. Gerston, Cynthia Fraleigh, and Robert Schwab, *The Deregulated Society* (Pacific Grove, Calif.: Brooks/Cole, 1988).

30. In this connection, see, among others, Patricia A. Wilson, "Power, Politics, and Other Reasons Why Senior Executives Leave the Federal Government," *Public Administration Review*, 54 (January/February 1994): 12–19.

31. See Thomas W. Kell, "Negative Views Undermine Public Enterprise," *The Public Manager: The New Bureaucrat*, 22 (Spring 1993): 51–54. A somewhat different viewpoint about presidential efforts to undermine the bureaucracy may be found in Neil Skene, "Assault on Bureaucracy Never Materialized," *Congressional Quarterly Weekly Report*, 50 (November 7, 1992): 3608. See also Report of the National Commission on the Public Service (the Volcker Commission), *Leadership for America: Rebuilding the Public Service* (Lexington, Mass.: Lexington Books, 1989).

32. A. Lee Fritschler and James M. Hoefler, *Smoking and Politics: Policy Making and the Federal Bureaucracy*, 5th ed. (Upper Saddle River, N.J.: Prentice Hall, 1995), p. 148 (emphasis added).

33. For example, see Francis Rourke, "The 1993 John Gaus Lecture: Whose Bureaucracy Is This, Anyway? Congress, the President and Public Administration," *PS: Political Science & Politics*, 26 (December 1993): 687–91.

34. Ronald C. Moe, "The 'Reinventing Government' Exercise: Misinterpreting the Problem, Misjudging the Consequences," *Public Administration Review*, 54 (March/April 1994): 111–22; Hindy Lauer Schachter, *Reinventing Government or Reinventing Ourselves: The Role of Citizen Owners in Making a Better Government* (Ithaca: State University of New York Press, 1996); H. George Fredrickson, *The Spirit of Public Administration* (San Francisco: Jossey-Bass, 1996); Richard C. Box, "Running Government Like a Business: Implications for Public Administration Theory and Practice," *The American Review of Public Administration*, 29(1) (1999): 19–43; and Linda DeLeon and Robert B. Denhardt, "The Political Theory of Reinvention," *Public Administration Review*, 60 (March/April 2000): 89–98.

35. Michael E. Milakovich, "Balancing Public Service Expectations with Political Accountability," *International Public Management Review*, 4(1) (2003): 61–79.

36. Rosenbloom, "Public Administrative Theory and the Separation of Powers," p. 225.

37. See, among others, James O. Freedman, *Crisis and Legitimacy* (New York: Cambridge University Press, 1978); cited by Rosenbloom, "Public Administrative Theory and the Separation of Powers," p. 225.

38. Mark A. Abramson and Sandra Baxter, "The Senior Executive Service: A Preliminary Assessment from One Department" (paper presented at a 1981 symposium on civil service reform). Reprinted in *The*

Senior Executive Service, Hearings before the Subcommittee on Civil Service, Committee on Post Office and Civil Service, U.S. House of Representatives, 98th Congress, 2nd session (Washington, D.C.: U.S. Government Printing Office, 1984), pp. 483–513; the premises referred to appear at p. 512.

39. Attitudes toward government and bureaucracy are discussed in Kaufman, "Fear of Bureaucracy: A Raging Pandemic," *Public Administration Review*, 41 (January/February 1981): 1–9; Richard L. McDowell, "Sources and Consequences of Citizen Attitudes toward Government," in H. George Frederickson and Ralph Clark Chandler, eds., "Citizenship and Public Administration: Proceedings of the National Conference on Citizenship and Public Service," *Public Administration Review*, 44 (March 1984): 152–56; and Seymour Martin Lipset and William Schneider, *The Confidence Gap: Business, Labor, and Government in the Public Mind*, rev. ed. (Baltimore: Johns Hopkins University Press, 1987).

40. Adapted from the written comments of an anonymous reviewer, to whom we owe a considerable debt for these very salient and perceptive observations.

41. David Broder, "Ethics in Government?" *Washington Post* syndicated column appearing in the *Bloomington (Ill.) Pantagraph*, April 12, 1981, p. A8.

42. Waldo, "Developments in Public Administration," p. 244. See also Waldo's *The Enterprise of Public Administration* (Novato, Calif.: Chandler & Sharp, 1980), and *The Administrative State*, 2nd ed. (New York: Holmes & Meier, 1984).

INDEX